THE GEOGRAPHIC LABOURERS OF AREWA

Remembering the

NORTHERN NIGERIAN SURVEY

Recollections of Land Surveying, Mapping and related activities
in the pre and post independence Northern Nigeria, concentrating on the work of
the Survey Department of Northern Nigeria (Northern Nigerian Survey)
during the 1950s and 1960s.

EDITED BY

MALCOLM ANDERSON

Published in 2004 by
M.F.Anderson
7 Baskerfield Grove, Woughton on the Green
Milton Keynes, MK6 3ES

ISBN 1 871315 84 0

Printed in 2004 by

Cranfield University Press
Building 33, Cranfield University
Bedfordshire MK43 0AL
01234 754077
www.cranfield.ac.uk/press

Written with a slate pencil on a stone on the side of the mountain of Black Comb

Stay, bold Adventurer; rest awhile thy limbs
On this commodious seat ! for much remains
Of hard ascent before thou reach the top
Of this huge Eminence, - from blackness named,
And, to far-travelled storms of sea and land,
A favourite spot of tournament and war !
But thee may no such boisterous visitants
Molest; may gentle breezes fan thy brow;
And neither cloud conceal, nor misty air
Bedim, the grand terraqueous spectacle,
From centre to circumference, unveiled !
Know, if thou grudge not to prolong thy rest,
That on the summit whither thou art bound,
*A **geographic Labourer** pitched his tent,*
With books supplied and instruments of art,
To measure height and distance; lonely task,
Week after week pursued ! - To him was given
Full many a glimpse (but sparingly bestowed
On timid men) of Nature's processes
Upon the exalted hills. He made report
That once, while there he plied his studious work
Within that canvass Dwelling colours, lines
And the whole surface of the out-spread map
Became invisible; for all around
Had darkness fallen - unthreatened, unproclaimed -
As if the golden day itself had been
Extinguished in a moment; total gloom,
In which he sate alone, with unclosed eyes,
Upon the blinded mountain's silent top !

William Wordsworth   1813

THE GEOGRAPHIC LABOURERS OF AREWA

CONTENTS

PART 4 (181 - 294)

THE GEOGRAPHIC LABOURERS

PART 5 (295 -299)

THE LAST OBSERVATION

....

APPENDICES

....

INTRODUCTION

THE GEOGRAPHIC LABOURERS OF AREWA

INTRODUCTION

Arewa

Saidu Hadejia was one of our very best chainmen. His enthusiasm was unbounded. In a leather case slung around his neck he carried a prismatic compass. A glance from me in the direction of a distant point was sufficient for him to spring into action and announce "Thirty-two degrees thirty minutes", whether I needed such information or not. I conferred upon him a surveying 'CBE' ('compass bearings expert'). He was happy that the needle always pointed to the north, *arewa*, his homeland, and he could so easily find *gabas*, east, the direction of Mecca. But he harboured a suspicion that the compass was a surreptitious aid to Europeans; to guide them north and homeward, should the need arise.

It was the early 1960s. Nigeria had just achieved independence, but already there were question marks over the future, and the departure of many expatriates was imminent.

To the British, who imposed and surveyed Nigeria's internal and external boundaries, *Nijeriya ta arewa*, the north of the country, was never more than a semi-autonomous political region. But to Saidu and, apparently, to most of his countrymen at the time, *Arewa* seemed distinct enough to be a nation in its own right, and a unique one at that, confined by the Sahara to the north, admitting no commonality with the people of the forested country below the big rivers to the south, and maintaining little communication with the similar but 'French' territories to the east and the west.

The concept of northern unity and autonomy did not, however, withstand the rigorous tests which followed Nigeria's independence. For a while, the first Premier of Northern Nigeria, Alhaji Sir Ahmadu Bello, and his followers, were said to have visions of a nation called *Arewa*, or perhaps the ancient name *Songhai,* with alternative southward links to the sea through Dahomey. Following his assassination in the first of the military coups in 1966, there were cries of "*Araba ! Araba !*" (Divide ! Divide !) from his supporters, who saw themselves as future members of a nation state quite separate from the rest of Nigeria. The roots of such sentiments lay deep in the early history of a land which had become predominantly Moslem, but conflicted with the complex ethnic and multi-cultural dream that was Nigeria. The Yorubas of Western Nigeria also talked of a homeland; the Ibos, of Eastern Nigeria, actually declared a *"Republic of Biafra"*; but Nigeria's ethnic diversity ensured that opinions were as divided inside these areas as they were outside and, to this day, an overall desire for unity seems to remain.

Reunions

During the 1950s and early 1960s, a remarkable *esprit de corps* was engendered amongst the land surveyors of the Northern Region by virtue of their common experiences, lifestyles, and professional ideals. This spirit was strengthened both by their mutual dependence when they worked together and by the support of colleagues in headquarters when they were alone in remote areas. Many expatriates left Nigeria over the short period leading up to, and immediately following, independence. One by one, they returned to the United Kingdom, to their home countries in continental Europe, or other parts of the world, but something of the *camaraderie* they had experienced stayed with them. Some retired, some moved into related professions, and some remained in the surveying world. A few stayed on in Nigeria, seeing the Northern Nigerian Survey through to its eventual dissolution and transformation into a training centre and assisting, for a further ten years and more, with the establishment of surveying departments in newly created States.

Scattered by the four winds and leading diverse lives, with only the occasional exchange of seasonal greetings between them, these people might never have crossed paths again, each carrying their memories into oblivion or, at best, committing them to individual private memoirs. But an event which has, in recent years, revived the accord of the past, is an annual weekend reunion of former surveyors, planners and their wives. The first of these gatherings came about in 1988 as the result of a chance meeting of surveyors at an earlier event; an annual meeting of former members of the expatriate mining community of the Jos Plateau.

The Jos Plateau is the best known physiographical feature of northern Nigeria. Its 2,000 square miles of beautiful, open, high grassland sitting on average about 3,300 feet above sea level, enjoys, by tropical African standards, a pleasant and relatively cool climate in which European expatriates can live very comfortably. Geologically, it consists mainly of massive granites which have been eroded and weathered to yield extensive alluvial deposits of tin ore and many valuable related minerals. These ores have been extensively exploited since the turn of the last century. Since then, land surveyors have been busy surveying mining areas and maintaining an official mining cadastre. The area long had a large resident expatriate community engaged in mining and related supporting services. Small groups or individuals, amounting to several hundreds of people, were widely scattered across the plateau and the surrounding areas. A few larger groups were employed by the major mining companies, with higher concentrations of people near the principal centres and the hill station of Jos itself. By and large it was a close-knit community with just a few social centres; a common lifestyle and occupation was evident and close relationships and lifetime friendships were established. Very few of these expatriates could ever regard Nigeria as a permanent home and gradually, with their offspring, they migrated away, many returning to the United Kingdom, some of them maintaining the personal friendships they had made while abroad.

Beatrice and the late Donald MacPhee were a well known couple within that community and were based at Bukuru near Jos. After distinguished service in the Royal Navy during the war, Donald had first arrived in Nigeria in 1946 to work as a government land surveyor, he later obtained a licence to practise privately, and spent many years surveying mining titles. He went on to establish his own mining company and was later recalled temporarily to administrative survey duties for the Benue-Plateau State Government during the period of acute staff shortage which followed the setting up of the new States which replaced the Northern Region in 1968. I met the MacPhees during my first posting to Jos in 1957 and, when I finally left Nigeria to return to England in 1977, they were still engaged in mining, but we kept in touch and met socially on their visits to England. With many of their friends from the plateau, they helped to organise the annual "Keep in Touch" reunion for former Jos Plateau residents and my wife Monica and I were invited to one of these meetings at the Connaught Rooms in Great Queen Street in London in June 1983. There we met one or two other surveyors with whom we had been in infrequent contact and naturally, as a group, huddled together and resolved to 'spread the word' about future gatherings. In the summer of 1985 the number of ex-Nigeria surveyors and their wives attending had risen to nine or ten, and even more by 1987. At these meetings, the surveyors discovered they had much more in common, and much more to talk about amongst themselves, than with the rest of the ex-plateau mining community and, after the meeting in 1988,

Janet and Clifford Rayner suggested a Northern Nigerian Survey weekend at their home at West Bridgford in Nottingham. Twelve of us gathered there for non-stop talk and reminiscence. Every October since then, a Northern Nigerian Survey reunion has been held, hosted in turn by different people, in different parts of England, and we have gradually increased our numbers until more than forty people have attended, some travelling from as far away as Denmark, the Netherlands, Canada, the USA and Australia. A list of these reunions is given at Appendix XV.

Memoirs

When I had the opportunity of taking early retirement in 1992, I began giving some thought to recording personal memories of my surveying career, which would include a substantial section to cover the 20 years I served in Northern Nigeria. I mentioned this in the course of conversation at one of our meetings, regretting there was no written account of the work of the Northern Nigerian Survey, to which I could refer for missing detail, to fill some of the gaps of those memorable years. Frank Waudby-Smith, who lives in Canada, was having similar thoughts and, at the reunion which Monica and I hosted in Milton Keynes in 1995, he and I publicly sowed the seeds of this work. We asked those present if they would like to collaborate and make a written contribution to an account of our unique experiences before it was too late and our memories faded even further, knowing that a story of the Northern Nigerian Survey could never emerge from the scattered, inaccessible, lost, or forgotten records we all left behind in departmental archives in Nigeria. Those seeds took a while to germinate, but I circulated a questionnaire in 1996, made proposals for the content of the work and possible authors, and in 1997 started some research on known UK-held records, and in 1998 the first significant contributions began arriving.

To most people in the outside world in the 1950s and the 1960s, Nigeria meant the teeming, noisy and colourful streets of Lagos and the eloquent English-speaking leaders of the south. Northern Nigeria was, to them, but a geographical name. Home-coming wanderers from this little known region were accustomed to polite indifference about their experiences from those who had never set foot in remote tropical places, no matter how dramatic or out-of-the-ordinary those experiences may have been. Having hit the headlines so often, for all the wrong reasons, there is now probably little of the Nigerian past, especially the past life of Europeans out there, that the public wish to read, so the recollections contained in this work are unlikely to attract much public interest or acclaim. They may however be welcomed by the expatriates who formed the nucleus of the little known and now almost forgotten public organisation, the Northern Nigerian Survey; recording for posterity something of their unrepeatable experiences and their cross-cultural encounters in a place still almost unknown to the modern cosseted tourist, and filling a small gap in both Nigerian and land surveying history.

Over the past thirty years or so, many memoirs have been written, often pitched at quite a high level, by inveterate writers, like those in administration and education. It is less common to come across written work by some of the other equally proud and dedicated professionals who spent their time with their feet very firmly on the ground. Surveying and mapping get little attention in the many books about life in Nigeria, but one thing senior officers from all departments always seemed to value on their office wall was a large coloured map of the territory for which they had responsibility. It is accepted that readily available accurate maps, the production of which was long given very low priority, were of considerable assistance to orderly land administration, to planning, to development and to education.

This record of the Northern Nigerian Survey has been provided by a group of professional people who collectively, and because of the nature of their duties, and their constant travelling, probably became more familiar with the territory in which they worked than most of their contemporaries. Land surveyors explored, measured, and mapped; their work took them, very often on foot, into the hearts of towns, villages and back-streets, and into remote country, wild rugged hills and mountains, distant from developed and settled areas, to places frequently unseen by anyone other than a few indigenous people. Few of them regret spending some of the best years of their lives in Nigeria; some were sorry that circumstances did not allow them to stay longer and that the 14 years of the Northern Nigerian Survey from 1954 to 1968, which marked the most progressive and active period of mapping that Nigeria had even seen, was much too short a term to achieve all there was to be done.

Churchill once said "*Anecdotes are a valuable source of historical truth*". Accounts and anecdotes drawn from personal experience, the sort of thing that does not look well in official files, can sometimes provide a more telling image of the past than bulky factual tomes in museums and libraries. Those included in this work have the merit of being composed by people who were actually there, and have not been degraded by the notions of those who did not take part. Some recollections are serious; some are more light-hearted and recall social life and leisure activities.

Unlike present-day surveying contractors, most surveyors did not simply pay a brief visit, carry out a quick job, then depart without giving the country and its people much afterthought. More often than not they stayed for years, and were dedicated to their vocation. Time has inevitably dimmed their memories, but some of their experiences have become deeply etched and, to a certain extent, have conditioned their principles and values ever since. Authentic as the contributions are, a warning sounded by Huessler has to be borne in mind:-

> "............one has to be conscious of the limitations of human memory, the risk of indulgence in mild forms of self-congratulation, or even misguided or ignorant concealment of the truth, of pride and that indefinable combination of nostalgia and time-cushioning that makes it hard for anyone to transport himself back to the spirit of former days. It is all too easy to give ourselves the second chance that real life denies us".

But, in the words of Anthony Thwaite:-

> Sometimes you want to tell everything -
> Not all in a rush, but plain and full and true,
> And all in good time: everything you knew
> And all you have always known, telling
> All, without qualification,
> Without explanation

Records

The climate of Northern Nigeria was not conducive to the keeping of meticulous personal diaries, especially by those involved in practical work who, at the time, saw nothing very remarkable in their activities and the people they met. By evening, most were relieved to sit back and replace some of the pints of liquid they had lost perspiring throughout the day. With the passage of time, some people lost the inclination to record what they did and were happy to leave Nigeria, put their experiences aside, and to escape a hard and uncompromising life as soon as the prospect of a better career at home appeared. Amongst those who returned to Nigeria time and again were very busy, active men, doers not writers, with little time or inclination to keep personal records or for written self-analysis. Also, they were hesitant to record the events of the difficult and traumatic times following the first of the military coups, in case their writings were lost or confiscated and subsequently wrongly interpreted. In times of great sensitivity, the northern Nigerian trust in those who remained to help was as remarkable as it was gratifying. Time cannot, however, erase the vivid memories of atrocities, loss, misjudgement and the events which led to the abrupt demise of the Northern Nigerian Survey which had achieved so much and promised so much more in the future.

It is extremely unlikely that a comprehensive official history of the Survey Department will ever be compiled or considered necessary. It would require dedicated academic effort backed by access to official records in Nigeria, if indeed such records still exist. Task reports, survey records, work diaries, annual reports and the maintenance of personnel files were all routine activities which at one time filled office shelves. Much of value could lie in those sources if they could be consulted today, but the dissolution of Northern Nigeria in 1968 led to the subdivision of many records and their despatch to the new States. Some were deemed redundant and discarded. Others were retained by Kaduna Polytechnic or passed to the Nigerian archive or, because the ubiquitous plastic bag had yet to establish its universal presence, lost to the ravages of the climate and vermin in unsatisfactory stores. For this work therefore there has been no access to Nigeria-held records, and little to the limited public records held in the UK.

The Story

Though few expatriates acknowledged it at the time, they did, in fact, enjoy the privilege of being paid for experiencing, living and working in a fascinating land. Conditions, and attendant risks, have changed so much over the past few decades that it is extremely unlikely that a traveller today could experience, or begin to understand, the conditions under which those officers worked, and what motivated them, and would be unable to rekindle the incredible accord and close relationships with the indigenous peoples which were enjoyed by those who lived there and spoke the local languages.

This work does not pretend to be a comprehensive history of the Northern Nigerian Survey, neither does it trace in full detail the surveying and mapping of the whole of Nigeria. Equally, it does not purport to present an authoritative description of the turbulent political, ethnic and economic events which led to the establishment and, ultimately, to the demise of the Survey. There are, no doubt, some omissions and some unintended inaccuracies, and for those I apologise and ask the forgiveness of those who know better. Rather, it is a first hand attempt to bring together some of the memories of a representative cross section of officers and their wives, working in a specialised field, pursuing their own personal career ambitions, who served in the Northern Region during the progressive decade and a half which spanned Nigeria's achievement of Independence. They remember a period of their lives in which they take some pride, about a country to which many of them became very attached, and where they developed an abiding affection for its peoples and their future. Time spent in Northern Nigeria forms an indelible memory for them. Through their commitment and curiosity they came to know more about the geography of the country than did many Nigerians, particularly the ordinary people, many of whom were very parochial indeed. The work is limited only by the clarity of their own memories, any memorabilia they may have kept, and their personal willingness to contribute. It tries to record their contribution toward the establishment of an accurate and efficient system of land record, planning, apportionment and administration, similar to systems being inaugurated in so many other developing parts of the world. As a result of their efforts, Northern Nigerians were provided with the opportunity to build upon a working model by modifying it to their own changing needs, or allow it to decay through apathy and misuse. The evidence seems to be that subsequent administrations have, with a few notable exceptions, deliberately or unavoidably chosen the latter.

This work will be, perhaps, one of the last accounts of times when 'old fashioned' methods of surveying and mapping were used; when politics, values and technology were all remarkably different from those of this computerised age of remote-sensing and electronic positioning. 'Traditional', as those techniques were, they were 'state of the art' at the time and were applied assiduously to assist the emergence and development of a newly independent State. The now outdated methods used, to produce an abundance of mapping on the off chance that it might someday be needed, are today no longer viable or necessary. Much effort was put into systematic ground control and field mapping; tedious and laborious age-old processes which are today not necessarily required for successful development and administration of the land. Manually operated optical instruments were rigorously employed for the collection of reliable and accurate data. Electronics did not make a real impact on the profession until the late 1960s when revolutionary new calculators and distance-measuring instruments appeared. The only way to chart the country was to get out on the ground and measure it using long-established methods of triangulation; field astronomy; distance measurement using steel bands; height determination using levels and aneroid barometers; and direct plotting using plane tables. The only aids to the formidable volume of mathematical work were well-thumbed books of logarithms and trigonometrical functions and hand-cranked calculating machines. Large matrix calculations for the least squares adjustment of control networks, which can nowadays be done almost in the blinking of an eye, were formidable chores involving many hours, even days, of concentrated mental and noisy physical effort. Modern electronic technology, involving remote sensing and positioning from GPS satellites, automatically positioned airborne video recording, radar and laser imaging and other techniques, is now available to provide the information required for development schemes in remote areas, often at very short notice and in an even shorter time-frame, and has largely done away with the need for difficult and prolonged fieldwork and arduous life in the bush.

Following the long period of World War II and post-war austerity, suitably qualified senior staff, modern equipment and improved surveying methods became more readily available. The professions no longer had to take second place to military service. The dedication, optimism and foresight of a few experienced surveyors who had been in service before the war led to the build-up of a progressive and committed surveying organisation to serve the needs of a vast underdeveloped region with its great, largely agricultural, potential. A policy of Regionalisation set up a department to serve the specific needs of a huge area of Nigeria which had always suffered, and was indeed in the future destined to continue suffering, a great paucity of local indigenous recruits to the profession of land surveying. Expatriates recruited to the service were generally well educated, technically skilled and practical people, with a good grounding of mathematics and specifically trained in photogrammetry and cartography. A military-like discipline was a hallmark of surveying practice and went hand in hand with the planning and conduct of control and mapping projects. For their efforts they were not exceptionally well paid, living conditions could be basic and career prospects rather limited, but rewards came with the responsibilities of the work and the opportunity to practise their skills in a challenging environment, believing they were making an important contribution to the development of the country in which they had chosen to work.

The story of the Northern Nigerian Survey cannot be told without reference to the events which preceded its formation, which influenced its operation, and which led to its demise. It must surely be the dream of any nation, particularly a newly independent one, to stumble upon almost unlimited reserves of oil and gas. The present situation in Nigeria demonstrates that this good fortune can confer mixed blessings. Before Independence, a system of surveying, mapping and planning was established to serve a country with a steadily growing agricultural, but increasingly industrialised, economy. As time went by, the services, infrastructure and administrative systems of the past became increasingly unable to cope with the radical changes in the attitudes, morals and ambitions of its peoples. The story therefore begins by setting the scene; gives a glimpse of the North, its history, its complex ethnic mix, its economy; the creation of a new nation; and some of the principal political events. It continues with an account of the development of Survey from the establishment of a central department based in Lagos through to regionalisation, leading to the formation of the Federal Survey Department and the Northern Nigerian Survey itself. It then looks at the tasks and responsibilities of these organisations; goes on to describe the life and work of the *Geographic Labourers* (a general term used here to include surveyors, town planners, cartographers in their various guises, lithographers and all the support staff without whom Survey could not have functioned); and, finally, draws some general conclusions.

The story does not claim to be other than an expatriate view of a small part of Nigeria's history. It makes no apologies for not being written by Nigerians. Surveying, mapping and planning was done for them, a great deal of it was done by them, but without doubt the motivation, the leadership, the professional example, the training and the technical innovation came largely from European, mainly British, sources. In *The Colonial Reckoning* (Reith Lectures 1961) Margery Perham said:-

"Few Africans are ready to rationalise about our record or their own, still less to appreciate the services of colonialism. Their present mood is to give up being grateful, or humble, or afraid, or ashamed, or even impressed. They have had so much of that".

Perhaps, after 40 years or more, this is still the case, so it cannot be expected that an account such as this would materialise from Nigerian sources.

Acknowledgements

Some words used may today not seem quite 'politically correct'. If this causes offence then I apologise and hasten to say that none was intended. In their time, words like 'native', 'pagan', 'tribe', 'boy', etc. were used innocently and correctly by Nigerians and Europeans alike and it is a mistake to reject them, for they reflect empathy with the times and the people to which they relate.

The compilation of this work has involved much personal time and effort, but I owe a debt of gratitude to those former colleagues, abiding friends and correspondents who responded to my call for contributions and information. Without their help it would have been a much more routine commentary, based entirely upon my own memories and research. Inevitably there has been some common ground between those who have taken the time and trouble to assist and I hope they will forgive me for any abbreviations, alterations and omissions I have made. Appendix I lists those who have assisted in this way and Appendix II gives an outline of their careers and their service in Nigeria. I am particularly indebted to **Clifford Burnside** for his major contribution on Topographic Mapping. I also wish to acknowledge, with gratitude, the task of reading and correcting my drafts, which was so willingly and painstakingly undertaken by **Trevor Brokenshire**.

The majority of the photographic illustrations, the selection of which has been governed by subject matter, quality and reproduction costs, are from my own collection, but my thanks are also due to those listed in Appendix X who have provided additional illustrative material.

Most of the cartographic illustrations, which are listed in Appendix XI, are based upon and reproduced from maps produced many years ago by and for the Survey Departments in Lagos and Kaduna. I wish to record my thanks to **Fuad Kassim**, the current Surveyor-General of Nigeria, who has welcomed this work, and has kindly arranged for permission to be granted for the use of these maps.

Readers wanting further information regarding the subject of this work or related matters are invited to consult the lists of archives and sources and the selected bibliography given in Appendices XII, XIII and XIV.

(Maps 1 - 10 cover the entire country as it was in 1972 with place names mentioned in the text highlighted in green)

Malcolm F. Anderson
Woughton on the Green
Milton Keynes
U.K.

August 2003

PART 1

LAND AND PEOPLE

PART 1

LAND AND PEOPLE

A broad outline of the historical events which preceded the creation of the Northern Nigerian Survey in 1954, the circumstances and environment in which the department operated and the political events which led to its demise in 1968.

....

OUTLINE CHRONOLOGY

1500s	European traders, explorers and adventurers active along the West African coast.
Late 1700s	Rivers of the south penetrated
Early 1800s	European overland travellers in the north
1861	Lagos taken over by the British
1885	Trading treaties negotiated with northern emirates
1889	First British mapping of the southern parts
1890	Agreement between France, Germany and Britain regarding trading areas in West Africa
1893	Construction of western line of railway from Lagos begun
1897	Trading in the southern parts of the north by the Royal Niger Company. First Survey Department established at Lagos
1900	Declaration of the Protectorates of Northern and Southern Nigeria. Founding of the Southern Nigeria Survey
1903	Lugard captured Kano and Sokoto. Valuable tin deposits were confirmed on the Bauchi Plateau
1906	Lagos Survey Department merged with the Southern Nigeria Survey
1906-08	Surveying and mapping for the Anglo-French boundary from the Niger to Lake Chad
1910	A beginning made on the establishment of a town at Jos
1913	Lugard selected a site for the northern capital.
1914	Colony and Protectorate of Nigeria formed by the amalgamation of Northern and Southern Nigeria, with Lugard as Governor-General
1915	Construction of the northern capital began at Kaduna
1916	Capital of the Northern Provinces moved from Zungeru to Kaduna
1918	German colony of Kamerun divided into northern and southern parts and administered by Britain and France
1923	Nigeria's first political party formed
1928	K.H.Hunter arrived in Nigeria on his first appointment with the Survey Department
1931	Financial stringency put a brake on progress
1937	Anglo-French Cameroons boundary survey carried out by the Survey Department
1946	A new constitution created regional councils for the Northern, Western and Eastern groups of Provinces

1948	Another constitutional change devolved power to the Regions
1949	A new House of Assembly for the Northern Region met in Kaduna
1950	The Nigeria Survey Department started reorganising to cater for regionalisation and decentralisation
1951	The MacPherson constitution devolved more authority to regional organisations
1952	A revised Survey Ordinance transferred powers to the Regions to make regulations on most Survey matters
1953	Surveying in the North was administered as part of the Ministry of Social Development and Surveys
1954	Nigeria was declared a Federation and the Regions became largely self-governing. Federal Surveys and the Northern Survey Department came into being with Hunter as the first Northern Director
1955	The Town Planning Section in the North was transferred from the Public Works Department to the Survey Department A policy of Northernisation was in force. Expansion of the Northern Survey Department was under way and new buildings were being constructed
1957	The Survey Department became a division of the Ministry of Land and Survey and the name *Northern Nigerian Survey* was formally adopted
1958	The start of the busiest eight years of Survey expansion and progress.
1959	Northern Nigeria achieved self-government. An exodus of expatriate staff commenced. Hunter left on final retirement
1960	Regional Survey Departments became fully independent of Federal Surveys The Federation of Nigeria achieved Independence
1963	The last British Governor left the North The Federal Republic of Nigeria was inaugurated with Dr Azikwe as President. R.O.Coker became the first Nigerian Director of Federal Surveys
1964	Inter-regional mistrust aggravated by rigged census results.
1966	January. The first military coup. The Prime Minister of the Federation, the Sardauna of Sokoto, the Premier of the West and many other senior political and military leaders were assassinated May. The announcement of the intended abolition of all political parties, the Regions and the Federation sparked off great civilian unrest July. The first military counter-coup September. Massive anti-Ibo civilian uprising in the North
1967	May. State of Emergency declared. An announcement of the intention to divide Nigeria into internal States. July. Eastern Region declared itself an independent nation "Biafra". Civil war commenced and the breakaway state was invaded
1968	The Regions ceased to exist. The Northern Region was divided into six new States. The Northern Nigerian Survey was divided into six State departments with a residual unit at Kaduna to serve their training and, temporarily, their mapping needs
1970	The civil war ended and Nigeria was reunited.
1970 onwards	The Federal Military Government enforced its rule through a series of coups and dictatorial administrations

....

Islamic Influence

Whilst the southern parts of Nigeria had adopted ways of thought introduced from their long association with Europeans, only a few, far sighted, people envisaged what a crucial, challenging and dominant role the north would play in the future of Nigeria.

'Northern Nigeria' was a political concept, devised by the British in 1900, which survived for only 8 years following Nigerian independence 60 years later. It was an uneasy alliance of a huge diversity of peoples and cultures, strongly influenced by Islam. The British had always said that, while they would stop the abhorrent practices of slaving, warring and extortion, and act as overseers for progress, development and well-being, they would in no way interfere with the Moslem religion and, by inference, the way the North was governed at local level.

The territory was not well known to many in Europe and, to the few who knew about it, it was an area which progress had by-passed, a feudal land governed by mysterious noble aristocrats still apparently living in the middle ages, not inclined to replace their age old ways with untrusted ideas from abroad. Seeing Kano, the largest northern settlement, for the first time was to feel transported back in time, to a place which appeared more North African or Middle Eastern than West African. Suddenly, in the name of progress, this ancient, bustling, ochre and terracotta-coloured city, which appeared to have thrived and changed so little over the centuries, with its mud buildings, narrow dusty alleys and defensive perimeter walls, its throngs of white robed people, its busy markets and its donkeys, goats and camels, apparently needed the attention of surveyors.

The People

Although there is little recorded authenticated history prior to the end of the 16th century, a thousand years ago the main part of what was to become Northern Nigeria is thought to have been inhabited by a self-sufficient people called the Habe, the original inhabitants of Hausaland. The most influential tribe of the north was the Fulani who probably originated in Upper Egypt and migrated westwards towards Senegal and also into Hausaland. The nomadic Fulani pastoralists, tall, tough handsome people called the Bororo, did not intermarry with the Habe and retained their spare, wiry frames and their pale olive or light bronze skin colour. A propensity to avoid contact with modern ways is common to this day. To them hard labour is demeaning, they disdain agriculture and will claim they arose from the same stock as the Europeans. They are people of the dry and harsh lands of the desert fringes, an environment which has engendered a resilience and toughness, giving them a warlike and aggressive temperament and a strong will to survive.

Arab invaders and traders from the desert brought Islam during the 13th and 14th centuries, but not all the Habe were converted. It is a common mistake to regard the Hausa as a tribe; rather they are a group of people speaking the Hausa language. Hausa is also the lingua franca, but not the mother tongue, of a mixed group of people living in a belt running roughly along the alignment of the rivers Benue and Niger, where Islam is present but only as a minority religion.

By the early years of the 19th century the Hausa state of Gobir had abandoned some of its religious principles and conflict arose when Islam underwent a revival under Othman Dan Fodio. He overcame the Hausa horsemen in battle, became their Shehu and was proclaimed Sarkin Musulmi, Commander of the Faithful, and the religious leader of the whole of the western Sudan. His jihad in 1804 resulted in the emergence of the powerful Fulani empire in and around what was later to become Northern Nigeria, but its eastern advance was halted by the people of Bornu. Othman died in 1817 and his son Muhammadu Bello succeeded him as Sultan, and founded Sokoto.

The Kanuris *(Photo. 1)*, a mixture of Hamitic, Arab and Negroid tribes, living in Bornu in the far north-eastern corner of the country, succeeded in resisting full Fulani invasion from the west, but the nomadic Fulanis moved their grazing herds throughout the Kanuri lands and surrounding areas and still do so today. The founders of the ancient empire of Kanem-Bornu were said to be Berber nomads from North Africa in about the 11th century and within 200 years, having adopted the teachings of Islam, had extended its influence from the Niger across to the Nile. Their connections with the east were strong and 750 years ago they had students in Egypt and had connections with Tunis. The power and influence of the empire had waxed and waned over the centuries and became centred on Bornu. Having largely resisted Othman's Fulanis they were overrun at the end of the 19th century by an army of slave traders, led by Rabeh, who were being pushed out of the Sudan. This force conquered Bornu and killed Shehu Kiari (the Kanuri equivalent of the Sultan of Sokoto). Rabeh was eventually killed near Lake Chad in 1900 by the French who, having been awarded control of eastern Bornu under the Anglo-French convention of 1898, restored the Kanemi dynasty to Dikwa. Bornu became divided by the incoming colonial powers; France, Germany and Britain. The Kanuris are a confident and colourful people, intensely proud of their history and ancestry but who have taken well to western technology and administration. They use Hausa with some reluctance and adhere strongly to the use of the Kanuri language but, like others in the North, speak English fluently as the lingua franca and the language of government. Many of them took senior positions in Regional, Federal and later Military administration.

The undisputed and often brutal Fulani power had something of a corrupting effect, the leaders assumed the status of emirs and the borders of their lands with 'pagan' areas continued to be the scene of slaving. The word 'pagan' is not used here, nor anywhere else in this work, in a derogatory sense, for in Nigeria it was universally used when talking of people described as neither Moslem nor Christian. Zazzau (Zaria), for example, was one of seven original states of Hausaland (the *Hausa Bakwai*) and, like most of the others, owed much of its prosperity to its traffic in slaves. This, in due course, brought them into contact with the British who had long resolved to stamp out this practice. For defensive purposes the pagans tended to live in the hills, sometimes at their very summits, safe from the marauding horsemen on the plains, and where animism, or worshipping of spirits dwelling in natural features, in hills, rocks, trees and unusual places was, and no doubt still is, commonplace.

The Nupe people, living mostly in what became Niger Province, who have cultural and ethnic origins similar to the Yorubas of the south-west, were also overrun by the Fulanis. Like many others in this part of Africa their distant origins probably lay in the Nile valley and they brought with them craftsmanship skills, and the area around Bida was well known for its pottery, brasswork, glass bead making and weaving.

The Tivs and the Idomas are an important, minority, largely non-Moslem, people living south of the Benue. The Gwaris, or Gbagyis as they prefer to be called, who live mostly in Niger and the southern parts of Zaria Provinces, and the Igalas, Igbirras and the 'Northern Yorubas' of Kabba and Ilorin Provinces were also partly converted to Islam. Offa, in Ilorin Province, was the first big town across the border from the Western Region and it marked the southernmost camp of the Fulani invasion which had swept with increasing difficulty through forested country towards the sea in the early 1800s.

The Kare Kare are the pagan people of the Emirate of Fika whose lands support a generous sprinkling of seasonal nomadic Fulani. Other pagans live in the rugged area of Biu, in the south of Bornu, in similar situations in Adamawa, Zaria *(Photo.3)* and Bauchi Provinces, and on the Jos Plateau.

The inhabitants of the Jos Plateau, the Birom people *(Photo.77)*, became familiar to expatriates working in tin mining and are mentioned later. The Plateau became a stronghold within the middle belt of Nigeria and was concerned about Moslem domination after independence. Local leaders resented the patronising attitude of the aristocratic Moslem areas to the north and, until they were equitably represented on the northern Executive Council, exemplified, as in so many other parts of the north, and by virtue of differences in language, culture and religion, the underlying fallacies of so-called 'Northern Unity'.

In the far north, right across the borderlands with the Niger Republic and with Chad, in the dry season, can be seen the Buzu people, the Tuaregs, similar to the nomadic Fulanis, moving south from the desert areas, and wearing the indigo head-dress so distinctive of this region. These almost secretive people had a reputation, perhaps not deserved, for their proud individuality and cool ruthlessness. The more settled of them were valued as very reliable guards and watchmen.

European Traders and Explorers

Records do not show early inland travel by Europeans, but from the end of the 15th century traders, explorers and adventurers had been active along the West African coast.

In the late 18th century Britain had declared that, when it took up the role of trustee, it would see that its dependent territories were in the fullness of time brought through to independent nationhood, retaining whatever was best of the local cultural heritage, enhanced by whatever was in the long term found to be suitable from the British way of life. From that time on there was, amongst an increasing number, a sense of sharing the aspirations of the indigenous people. French philosophers had also long expressed the belief that self government is always preferable to good government, but it was to be over 150 years before the territories around the Niger basin were to test the truth of this for themselves.

In 1805 Mungo Park was drowned in the rapids near Bussa while exploring the Niger and in 1823 Clapperton, Oudney and Denham reached Bornu overland from Tripoli. Denham explored the River Shari area near Lake Chad and, two years later, Clapperton returned to Sokoto with Richard Lander via the coast at Badagri.

Early explorers and traders penetrating West African rivers in the late 18th century and the first half of the 19th century compiled charts which showed settlements and trading posts, and recorded local geographic information. In accordance with her policy of abolishing the slave trade Britain established settlements around the coast. Small bases to support naval activities were established at Lagos, Brass and Bonny and they moved inland up the River Niger. Beyond these watercourses little was known.

In 1830 Richard Lander and his brother reached Bussa and completed Mungo Park's quest by following the Niger to the sea, but Richard died with many others two years later on an expedition with Macgregor Laird when going up the Niger to its confluence with the Benue, which at that time was known as the Shari. Another ten years were to go by before a small settlement was established on land beside the river, purchased from the Ata of Igala, at a site later known as Lokoja, but again many died and West Africa was gaining the title "The White Man's Grave".

Missionaries also moved into parts of what was to become south-west and south-east Nigeria in the early 19th century and pidgin English became established as the lingua franca in these areas.

In 1854 Dr Baikie went up the Benue (which is navigable up to Garoua in the Cameroons) nearly as far as Yola and by 1857 he and Lt. Glover (later Sir John Glover, Administrator of Lagos) had reached Jebba on the Niger.

In the latter half of the nineteenth century, when the industrial revolution in Great Britain was developing fast, overseas trade and an increasing desire to export manufactured goods resulted in pressures to explore and develop British commercial markets in as yet unknown and uncharted lands. Limited funds for exploratory mapping were forthcoming from organisations such as The Royal Geographical Society, the African Association and the British Association but, in the end, it became a military task in Nigeria when the British government was persuaded, somewhat reluctantly, to back up the growing commercial interests in this part of Africa.

To strengthen their trading position on the coast the British took control of Lagos in 1861.

In 1866 a consulate was established at Lokoja but closed three years later, again because of health problems, although trading continued along the rivers.

In 1880 the Emir of Kontagora was known to be conducting a policy of slaving against the pagan people of the area.

Commerce and Administration

In 1884 Sir William Wallace, who was opening up trade along the Benue, was able to purchase 'straw' tin from traders on the river at Ibi, of the kind which had been traded in the ports of North Africa by Hausa merchants. This gave rise to speculation about possible local sources of tin ore, the eventual discovery of which was to prove of considerable significance, in the years to come, to the economy of the developing country and the work of the Survey Department.

A year later the British negotiated a treaty with the northern emirates for the grant of trading rights and the administration that went with them. George Taubman Goldie, founder of the Royal Niger Company, extended his administration into this area, centred on Lokoja, through a Royal Charter originally granted when the company was called the National African Co. Ltd.

An international conference was held in Berlin in 1884 in an attempt to settle many of the issues which were arising out of the competition amongst European nations to establish trading rights in various parts of Africa.

In 1886 Goldie, who had become established as the leading merchant in the Niger and Benue valleys, said that in the uncharted regions of the interior he knew of a large area which he would like to see coloured red on the early map of Africa. Legislative power was vested in the governor and council of the company in London. Its area of effective administration was centred on Lokoja. It encompassed Onitsha and Asaba to the south and Bida in the north. There was no map on which a widening sphere of influence was defined but had there been it would have included Kaiama and Ilesha to the west, Sokoto and Gwandu to the north-west, Kano to the north and Yola to the east; in other words, virtually the whole of what was to become Northern Nigeria. Added to the trading lands he already controlled around the Niger basin, the Oil Rivers Protectorate, the area might well have been called Goldania. Instead, the name Nigeria was later chosen.

Lugard, an employee of the Royal Niger Company, became involved in the negotiation of treaties with local rulers. He set about establishing a defensive imperial force, the West African Frontier Force, based on Lokoja, which prevented the French from obtaining concessions downstream from Bussa, and claimed territory on Britain's behalf. This was done not because it was of any great strategic concern but because Britain had for some time encouraged its own nationals to trade there at their own expense and thought it should protect their interests by preventing them becoming dominated by the French and Germans. Realising that conquest for conquest's sake was an indefensible, unsustainable and extremely expensive concept, the British presence came about in the interests of trade and their early armed struggles were undertaken to protect that trade. *Map 12 shows West Africa in 1895.*

By 1897 Ilorin and Bida had come under the influence of the Royal Niger Company, railway construction had begun, Lagos was expanding, and the first Survey Department was established there.

Following an investigation into its monopolistic tendencies, and its unpopularity amongst the people it administered, the Royal Niger Company surrendered its charter to the Crown in 1899, but continued its trading activities.

Protectorates

On 1st January 1900 the flag of the Royal Niger Company, which bore a Y-symbol depicting the Niger-Benue river system and symbolising its sphere of influence, was lowered for the last time and the Union flag was hoisted simultaneously over the Protectorates of Northern and Southern Nigeria. The West African Frontier Force absorbed the Royal Niger Constabulary. Nigeria became a new name on the maps of the world.

The South included the lands of the dominant local peoples, the Ibos and the Yorubas. Boundaries were demarcated for the new colony of Northern Nigeria. The British Government took over virtually the whole of the ill-defined Hausa, Fulani and Kanuri homelands, a much bigger area than had ever been effectively administered by the Royal Niger Company, much of it controlled by the Sultan of Sokoto and the Emir of Kano. Although Britain's knowledge and experience of Northern Nigeria was very slight, it was proclaimed a protectorate under a high commissioner (Sir Frederick

Lugard), in whom legislative authority was vested. Much of the territory was unknown and such knowledge as there was had been acquired through the earlier commercial, scholarly, exploratory, religious and political missions. If little was also known about its inhabitants, the people of the north knew even less about those who purported to rule them and who would have such a profound influence over their future development. Many trading centres in the north were destined to be brought under closer supervision, including Nassarawa, Bida, Yauri, Kontagora, Argungu, Ilorin, Borgu, Bauchi, Yola and Bornu.

The declaration of the Protectorate of Northern Nigeria had far more meaning in the capitals of Europe than it did to the emirates of Kano, Sokoto, Bornu and the rest of the north. The creation of artificial internal boundaries often exacerbated antipathies which existed, and still exist to this day, between the 300 or more ethnic groups of tribes, clans and families. It was, at the time, regarded as a laudable attempt to bring together a large number of people who might otherwise have remained as warring tribal groups. Critics cite Nigeria, as a whole, as one of the poorest examples, in Africa, of the imposition of random national boundaries to create a spurious nation-state; but if the boundaries were so wrong, why, it has to be asked, in the 40 years since independence, has the country and its neighbouring states not changed them ?

In the following year work began on a steam tramway to link Zungeru with the Kaduna River while the British were busy confronting the northern rulers. The West African Frontier Force captured Kontagora to end the slaving which was still going on, but both Sarkin Musulmi at Sokoto and the Emir of Kano remained uncompromising.

In 1902 Lugard moved his headquarters briefly to Jebba and then Zungeru. He was contemplating action against Sokoto partly because information had reached him that the Sultan had, in breach of the early treaty, allowed French convoys through his territory and had even permitted observations for latitude and longitude to be conducted in Sokoto itself.

In 1903 Lugard, with a small force, overcame the strongholds of the Emir of Kano and the Sultan of Sokoto, the last of the emirates to fall. The British restated their policy of non-interference with religion, customs and law but insisted that slaving, oppression and extortion would have to cease everywhere. They then put in train the establishment of properly controlled treasuries and systems of taxation, which would permit the grant of salaries to the emirs, and the introduction of methods of local government in the form of Native Authorities.

In the meantime the quest for tin ore had continued and Wallace obtained samples from the Delimi River near Naraguta. In 1903 H.W. Laws was the first to reach the Bauchi Plateau and confirmed its valuable tinfield; commercial mining started at Naraguta almost straight away.

Railway construction was in progress and between 1903 and 1904 a survey was completed for the line from the River Niger to Kano.

In 1908 the High Commissioner for Northern Nigeria was replaced by a Governor and Provincial boundaries were established in the North. Construction of the railway from Jebba had reached Zungeru.

Provinces

With the suppression of slavery, Lugard attempted to strengthen local economies with the development of industries and the laying of the foundations for better rail and road communications. The arrival of the railway north of the Kaduna River in 1913 allowed the planning and the founding of the future Northern capital to get under way.

In January 1914, the Colony and Protectorate of Nigeria was formed by the amalgamation of the Northern and Southern Protectorates, which were renamed the Northern and Southern Provinces, with Lugard as Governor-General. He introduced indirect rule under which chiefs and officials in native administrations controlled their own areas under British supervision, saw that local rulers resisted the temptation to keep their hands in the till of the local treasuries and tried to ensure that local taxation went wholly to the financing of public projects.

To all intents and purposes these authorities, which consisted of a chief and his council, were self-governing and the British Provincial administrators were to become advisers rather than absolute rulers. Ultimately there were 64 such Native Authorities in the north, with 76 subordinate N.As, 41 town councils and 574 district or village councils.

The emirates had long had a system of tax gathering, a system which had been open to abuse, but it was now brought under control. Local revenue was raised by an annual tax known as *haraji*, a system based on Koranic law, which had been in force, but sometimes abused by the chiefs, for many generations. Under British administration this method of taxation was placed on a more controlled and equitable footing and amounted in total to about a tenth of local income, and was based on the ability of individuals to pay. Tax gathering became the responsibility of *hakimai*, or district heads, whose areas of responsibility were defined on very roughly drawn sketch maps.

Local taxes and funding from central government were in due course to enable each Native Authority to administer a judicial system, to maintain a police force, to undertake public works including buildings, roads and water supplies, to run schools, health facilities, and other services, and to administer land transactions. Emirs held the land on trust on behalf of the people and there was no land ownership as such. People were allocated sufficient for their agricultural and residential needs. Lugard recognised the need for a land policy which would remove oppression from the ordinary people but allow rapid economic development. He assumed control of the land and issued Crown grants for specified uses which were required to be registered under a Land Registration Ordinance.

By 1914, construction of the eastern branch of the railway from the coast at Port Harcourt had reached Enugu and in 1916 Lugard moved his Northern capital from Zungeru to Kaduna.

Also in 1916, German forces surrendered at Mora, 100 miles east of Maiduguri, an event of considerable significance to the future of the Cameroons. At the end of the first world war in 1918, the German colony was divided into northern and southern parts and administered as League of Nations mandates by Britain and France. Dikwa Emirate, under its own chief, became a part of Bornu Province.

The Jebba bridge over the River Niger was completed during the war, the first fixed link across the major rivers between North and South *(Photo.129)*. Until then trains had been ferried across.

The 'Land and Native Rights Proclamation' of 1910 was replaced by the 'Land and Native Rights Ordinance'. It declared that all lands were 'native lands' and were controlled by the Governor and that the greatest interest that it recognised was a 'Right of Occupancy'. This right took two forms, the first a Statutory Right which could be granted to natives and non-natives alike, and the second a Customary Right which was the title of native communities. It had the effect of protecting the people from exploitation and made provision for the growing number of outsiders who needed land for development and commerce.

Between the Wars

In 1919 Lugard left on final retirement and in 1920 W.H.Lever acquired the Royal Niger Company in continuation of Britain's trading interests.

In 1922, in his book the *Dual Mandate in British Tropical Africa*, Lugard declared that Britain had a responsibility to improve the material and moral position of colonised people to enable them to rule themselves at a future date. Britain also had a duty to lay the foundation of a sound economy for the colony, based upon development of its natural resources and the marketing of its products abroad. The administrative system set up was intended to allow local people to maintain their own customs, laws and culture, overseen by British provincial and district officers.

In Lagos in the same year the Nigerian Council was replaced by a partly elective legislative council for Southern Nigeria but a governor retained legislative powers for the North.

1923 saw the formation of Nigeria's first political party, the Nigerian Democratic Party, by

Herbert Macaulay.

In 1927 the Kafanchan to Jos branch of the Nigerian Railway was opened, and the first boat train arrived in Jos.

In 1929 W.H.Lever's trading companies were amalgamated and renamed the United Africa Company (UAC).

In common with other parts of the world, Nigeria went through a difficult financial period in the early 1930s, but there was something of a return to prosperity by 1936. Railway construction had continued and in 1932 the Makurdi bridge was built. The Colonial Development Fund gave aid to education.

Political forces were at work in the south of the country and in 1934 another party was formed, the Lagos Youth Movement, which later became known as the Nigerian Youth Movement

Ahmadu Bello, cousin to the Sultan of Sokoto and great grandson of Shehu Othman Dan Fodio, was appointed Sardauna of Sokoto in 1938. This was the title given to a traditional war leader in the Fulani army and was bestowed by the Sultan upon one of his close relations. Ahmadu Bello was then 29 years old, had been a schoolteacher, having been educated at Katsina College, the only full secondary school in the North at the time.

By the outbreak of the second world war over 200 pupils were turning out from secondary schools each year to provide the foundation for a new professional class of Nigerians.

The Southern Provinces were divided and renamed Eastern and Western Provinces. There was a suggestion that each group of Provinces should be called a Region with its own House of Assembly.

Many expatriates, including surveyors, departed for war service.

Post War Politics

Toward the end of the war there was an increase in political activity as colonial territories around the world began actively to seek independence and in 1944 Dr Azikwe launched the NCNC, the National Council of Nigeria and the Cameroons, with Herbert Macaulay as President, receiving enthusiastic support in the east of the country.

By 1946 anti-British feelings were being voiced in the Lagos press by people who had hoped for a German victory in the war, which they had thought would be an opportunity to set up an independent republic. Independence for India sparked off more agitation for Nigerian independence from people living in the south of the country.

Nigeria was given a new constitution, the Richards constitution, which created Regional Legislative Councils for Northern, Western and Eastern provinces. There was an increase of Northern self-awareness and the strides it would have to take to keep pace with the rest of the country.

The Colonial Development and Welfare Act, which had been passed in the British parliament in 1940, began to permit grants to Nigeria which allowed staff increases and the implementation of a ten year plan to improve public services and infrastructure and for agricultural development schemes such as large scale cotton and groundnut production. This was the first time that Britain had diverted from its economic policy of Colonial self-sufficiency. Inevitably this went hand in hand with an increased demand for maps and survey.

In 1947 a partly elective council was established for the whole of Nigeria and Houses of Assembly were set up in Eastern, Western and Northern Nigeria with a Houses of Chiefs in the North and in the West.

Regionalisation

The principle of Regionalisation was developed in successive constitutions. Sir Arthur Richards retired as Governor and Sir John Macpherson took over. In 1948 another constitutional change devolved power to the Regions. The Sardauna of Sokoto took his place in the House of Chiefs where he was destined to play a dominant role for many years.

The Northern Region covered about three quarters of Nigeria, roughly 500 miles from north to south and 700 miles east to west, a land area about 3 times the size of Britain. Southwards a strip of land only 120 to 180 miles wide separated it from the sea, and this area contained the Eastern and Western Regions. *Map 11 shows Nigeria in the mid 1950s, Map 13 the 1960s and Map 14 the Provinces of the North.*

The most powerful political unit of the North, and therefore of the whole country, the NPC (Northern People's Congress), had it beginnings in Kaduna and Zaria. Also in 1948, perhaps as an indication of future events and as a localised revelation of underlying ethnic relationships, Ibos and Yorubas clashed over political issues at Gusau.

One of the new members of the Northern House of Assembly, Abubakar Tafawa Balewa, spoke in favour of a modern Northern Nigeria at its first meeting. He was an ordinary man from a village in the remote hills of Bauchi Province, who was destined to be Nigeria's first Prime Minister. As a student in London he had earlier expressed the prophetic view that Nigeria's historical, cultural and religious diversity would not permit a western-style democracy to work and he had doubted whether English justice could survive there without English law. He argued that Nigeria was little more than a geographical expression and its unity only a British notion. He could see the rate at which things were beginning to change and expressed the view that as Nigeria progressed towards independence it would for some time need the support, patience, and experience of serving British officers.

In 1949 the Northern House of Assembly first met at Lugard Hall in Kaduna with Bryan Sharwood-Smith as President.

Two years later the new Macpherson constitution, which was Nigeria's first step towards independence, established a Council of Ministers and a House of Representatives.

Regionally based political groupings gained strength and in the North the NPC was led by the Sardauna of Sokoto. Its only rival in the North was a radical organisation based in Kano which was known as the NEPU, the Northern Elements Progressive Union.

The Northern Executive Council, which still had three principal British members, was sworn in at Lugard Hall on February 6th 1952.

The Nigerian constitution did not work well and during 1953 it became difficult to reconcile the vastly different viewpoints coming from the Regions. The results of the previous year's national census indicated that the Northern Region contained more than half the population of Nigeria with about 8.3 million males and 8.6 million females. About 60% were Moslems, a third spoke Hausa, a sixth Fulani and a twelfth Kanuri. Over 4 million were from 'pagan' tribes, some groups as small as 500 people, and none with more than 60,000, living in the hilly country of the Plateau and the Cameroons borders. About 750,000 Tivs and 250,000 Idomas lived in the Benue area, 400,000 Igalas and Igbirras in Ilorin and Kabba and 330,000 Nupe and 250,000 Gwari were mostly in Niger Province. There were about 176,000 Ibos and Ibibios living in the North and 535,000 Yorubas, mostly Northern Yorubas in Ilorin.

Until 1953 the old Emir of Kano had conducted the affairs of the local administration in an outdated and almost feudal, secretive manner and key positions were awarded to those he favoured, or to members of his own family. His administration was at odds with new democratic thinking and when he died these practices were denied to the incoming Emir who was obliged to conduct his affairs in a much more open manner, including the operation of a publicly accessible land registry.

The Western Region began pressing for self-government for Nigeria within three years, but the Northerners felt they could not be ready so soon. They felt they had an insufficient number of educated men to run the North and had little desire to replace British rule for alien rule of another kind. 95% of the Civil Service came from outside the Region. There was an urgent need for education and training in all fields. The political differences led to unrest in Lagos and there was rioting over two days in Kano, when southerners, principally Ibos living in the *sabon gari*, were attacked. With the suggestion that the uniting of the Protectorates of Southern and Northern Nigeria in 1914 had been a mistake, there were calls from the NPC for complete regional autonomy and they were so concerned for the future that there was discussion of constructing a new rail link to the sea through the neighbouring French territory of Dahomey.

Another constitutional conference was held in London with a view to providing greater regional devolution and in 1954 a revised constitution came into force. Nigeria was declared a Federation under a Governor-General, and the Regions became largely self-governing with their own Executive Councils, Governors and Premiers. Lagos became Federal territory. The Sardauna was installed as Premier of the North, and advocated a policy of Northernisation of public offices.

Northernisation

The policy of Northernisation was to train and appoint enough skilled and semi-skilled people to replace the outgoing expatriates without having to replace them with southerners, who might secure permanent positions, dominate and exert unwelcome influence. Differences between North and South were seen by some as at least as great as the differences between Northerners and expatriates. The Northern Premier, a staunch feudal Moslem, had declared that he wanted a Hausa-speaking policy for the Region's civil service. All junior posts which required no special qualifications were to be the exclusive preserve of Northerners. Those which did require special qualifications or experience and for which no Northerner was available were to be filled preferably by expatriates who would eventually return to their homelands or, as a temporary measure only, by people from the other Regions. The application of this policy certainly gave impetus to the establishment of better training facilities and greater opportunities for training abroad. There was to be no lowering of educational standards and outright rejection of any tendency to regard being a Northerner as a qualification in itself.

Northernisation could not however be applied to the Federal departments operating in the Region, nor could it apply to transport, banks, communications, trade, commerce and in the various statutory corporations where Ibos were often predominant.

In some parts of the North, particularly the rural areas, there was disquiet about the prospect of premature British withdrawal as well as a realisation that there was unlikely to be available very much more money to fund state and personal aspirations. The Emir of Bauchi *(Photo.4)* was, for example, very concerned and had grave doubts about *mulkin kai* (self government) and wanted to know why the British were apparently prepared to pull out before the country was fully ready to look after itself. These sentiments were not however reciprocated in the southern regions.

In 1955 the Federation's first budget, augmented by grants from the Colonial Development and Welfare Fund, gave the opportunity to go ahead with many proposed development schemes, the more high profile being meat canning at Kano, a textile factory at Kaduna, the construction of airstrips in remote areas, improved river trade facilities and fish farming at Panyam.

In February 1956 the Queen visited Nigeria, accompanied by Prince Philip, the first British Royal visitors for over thirty years, and arrived in Kaduna where a great durbar was held. One of her equerries was Major Johnson Aguiyi Ironsi who had recently passed out of the Camberley staff college and who was destined to become Nigeria's first military governor after a coup ten years later. The Royal party flew to Jos and, after visiting other parts of Nigeria, returned to Kano and visited the Emir's Palace and watched a parade of over 4,000 traditionally robed, turbaned and veiled horsemen *(Photo.5)* and camel riders from all parts of the Emirate and the desert country to the north. Their presence was not of course spontaneous. They had been commanded by the Emir to attend. Few of them had felt any particular loyalty to the Queen, nor to any other outsider, whether in Africa or further afield, for they had never been accustomed to look up to anybody but their own local ruler. In their closed society the concept of Empire and Commonwealth was nothing to them, but they responded to the respect that their own ruler had shown to the foreign Queen with a huge surge of genuine excitement and enthusiasm, and, for some at least, an understanding that her visit symbolised the international recognition that their long isolated country was destined to receive.

In 1956 the Colonial Service was renamed Her Majesty's Overseas Civil Service.

In August 1957 the first Federal Prime Minister, Alhaji Abubakar Tafawa Balewa, was appointed. The Eastern and Western Regions became self-governing following a constitutional conference in London, but it was decided that changes in the North would be more gradual. The Southern Cameroons became a Region while the Northern Cameroons remained part of the North. A movement began to delegate more power to the twelve Northern Provincial authorities.

Sir Gawain Bell succeeded Sir Bryan Sharwood-Smith as Governor of the North. Northern Ministries were reorganised and some new ones formed, which led to some problems of staffing them.

All three Regions were seeking independence for Nigeria in 1959 but it was decided that a decision would not be made until after the Federal elections, which were to be held in that year, when a formal request could be made by the newly elected House of Representatives.

In the regional Public Service staffing by Northerners, although increasing, continued to be a problem and less than 20% of the names in the staff list were Nigerian, and many of them were not Northerners. The North was still only providing a very small number of recruits for the Federal service upon which the North was becoming increasingly dependent for its revenues.

Self Government

Northern Nigeria attained self-government in 1959. A plebiscite offered the people of the British Cameroons three choices, to join the Republic of the Cameroons, to remain part of Nigeria or to become a British dependency. The southern part opted to join the Republic of the Cameroons, but the two northern parts, which had been administered as parts of Bornu and Adamawa Provinces did not. They chose firmly to remain under British administration. The possibility of such an outcome had not been envisaged by the Trusteeship Council of the United Nations in New York and the impracticability of such a future was realised and the people were denied their democratic decision by the staging of a second plebiscite in which the British option was not included.

With its strong masculine culture, Northern Nigeria was self-confident enough to go its own way because it had developed over many centuries remote from outside influences; but what was unique was that it was now looking southwards for its future in a national alliance with radically different people. There was some justification for the traditional rulers adhering strongly to their old ways because, bred to the ways and good customs of Islam, they were unable to come to terms with the thinking of a new generation of politically motivated, acquisitive young men who had acquired a level of materialistic western values and who had been elected to represent the local people in regional and central government. Returning to their constituencies many had blatant ideas of reform and self aggrandisement. These new people were first generation democrats but, being born Moslem in the local community, they appeared to have difficulty in applying to their everyday lives the principles that had elected them. They had brought about a new thinking but, for the vast majority of people surveyors generally met in the course of their work; the chiefs and their representatives, the village heads, the people about town, the traders, the ordinary country people and junior surveying staff; a change from the traditional feudal control of the emirates to a democracy had few attractions. These people still had a broad confidence that their religion and their government, with continuing expatriate participation, would see to their well being; self government was not something to get very excited about because they had always governed themselves without undue interference from the British.

Politicians in the Western Region campaigned before independence for the transfer of large parts of Kabba and Ilorin Provinces from the North because of the large numbers of Yorubas who lived there but the Governor decided there was insufficient justification for a change.

In 1960, the Prime Minister introduced a motion in the House of Representatives formally requesting Britain to legislate Nigeria's independence, and the last constitutional conference took place in London in May.

Economy

In Africa, Nigeria is said to be only second to South Africa in terms of its economy. Its wealth is today very heavily dependent upon its oil revenues.

In terms of per capita income, education and industrialisation, the north compares unfavourably with the south of the country. Agriculture was the backbone of the northern society and economy during the 1950s and the 1960s; rural land was not in short supply and its tenure was based on rights of usage. The greatest constraints on its development were water supply and labour. Over vast areas the dry season was its greatest handicap. There was the opportunity to use sub-surface water in the flood plains more efficiently. Sugar and rice schemes on the Niger demonstrated this and there were also schemes for rice in the Sokoto-Rima Valleys and east of Kano in the Hadejia area, and for wheat in two areas close to the western side of Lake Chad.

The groundnuts, the principal export item, and the cotton of the north used to form a major share of Nigeria's economy. Great pyramids containing 9,000 sacks each were spectacular seasonal features at Kano, Gusau, Zaria and other northern railway towns. 715,000 tons were marketed in 1957-58. 124,000 tons of cotton (Nigeria today produces less than half of its own domestic requirements), 16,000 tons of beniseed, and 14,000 tons of soya beans, were also produced in 1957-58. Tobacco was grown in commercial quantities around Sokoto, Gusau, east of Kano and Zaria.

The dominant soils were of the tropical ferruginous type, low in nutrients, prone to drought and sensitive to erosion. Little fertiliser was used and Nigeria had no fertiliser factory, although there was thought that natural gas or basic slag from an iron and steel industry could supply sources of raw materials. The mid belt of the country was relatively sparsely inhabited, with better soils and a wetter climate and offered opportunities for considerable development for agriculture.

There were enormous herds of cattle, sheep and goats (about 5 million head in 1959). The famous Sokoto red goatskin is the source of "Morocco" leather. 120,000 cwt (approx. 6,100 tonnes) of hides, 50,000 cwt (approx. 2,500 tonnes) of goatskins and 11,000 cwt (approx. 560 tonnes) of sheepskins were produced in 1959. Nomadic Fulanis owned about 90% of the estimated (in 1970) 8 million cattle which migrated to the tsetse free grasslands in the north during the wet season. Dry season grazing can support only 20% of the wet season capacity. More than half the 750,000 culled each year went to northern markets and the rest went south. The half that went by rail lost 5% of their weight en route and the other half, sent on the hoof, if they survived, arrived much lighter and very emaciated. There was a clear need to establish slaughterhouses in the north and frozen meat transport to the southern markets. An experimental Fulani settlement scheme was established at Katsina as a trial for ranching and better husbandry but flew in the face of local nomadic traditions.

Conscious of the fundamental importance of agriculture to the future of the north, land was set aside by the government for experimental farms for improved and disease resistant strains suitable for use under local conditions, for stud farms and cattle farms, irrigation schemes and for forestry reserves and nurseries. As the population increased, and the numbers of grazing animals began to put more pressure on a land coming under the increasing influence of the northern desert, it was vital to take steps to prevent soil erosion. The precious few inches of topsoil are so easily permanently lost at times of flood in the wet season. Goats, with their habit of eating anything green that starts to grow, have been blamed for the steady southward advance of the dry arid and infertile lands. Time and education were needed to convince local people of the need to adopt a different approach to land use.

The only significant metalliferous deposits other than those principally associated with the Plateau Minesfield were the oolitic ironstones and Jakura limestone of the Agbaja Plateau near Lokoja, the development of which depended upon the location of a proposed iron and steel industry along the Niger, using Eastern Region coal.

Nigeria's economy was transformed by oil revenues. Industrialising of the north was important to raise the economy and increase employment, since it was politically undesirable for the workforce to move south to work. Hydro-electric power from the Kainji Dam on the Niger and other places promised to be the key to northern industries. Nigeria's economic future may lie in its natural gas reserves, which could last 100 years. They are worth more in energy terms than its oil reserves.

Independence

On 1st October 1960 the Federation of Nigeria became a sovereign independent state within the Commonwealth.   Princess Alexandra of Kent represented the Queen at the ceremonies in Nigeria. The Cameroons ceased to be part of Nigeria.

On the racecourse at Lagos, just before midnight, the Union flag was lowered in the presence of the Prime Minister and Sir James Robertson and the British anthem was played for last time. The lights were then switched off briefly and when they came on again the new Nigerian flag was flying in its place and the military bands played the new unfamiliar anthem. Sir James Robertson was succeeded as Governor-General of the Federation by Dr Azikwe.

By now there were a few more Nigerians in the Civil Service, but for ordinary people, and those engaged in professional, technical and commercial work, everyday life went on much as it had always done. Nothing changed in the country districts; few realised that independence had been achieved and they had no concept of its implications. Some expressed disbelief and sorrow that many expatriate Europeans might be leaving for good.

Colonialism has its critics but, in the case of Nigeria, rule by foreigners had the merit of removing many abominations and brought the concept of respect for law and democracy. Some senior Nigerians, in fact, thought Britain had imposed a very humanitarian imperialism and had, in difficult circumstances, created a nation of very diverse peoples who might otherwise have remained as separate warring groups. Perhaps the experience of imperialism was not long enough. A mere 60 years was insufficient to establish strong democratic systems and, as the troubles of 1966 and later years were to show, the antagonisms between tribal groups were by no means a thing of the past.

The first Minister of Land and Survey was Musa Gashash; one of the new progressives and a prominent Kano businessman. On one notable occasion he accompanied the Emir of Kano and the Sardauna of Sokoto on the holy pilgrimage to Mecca and was the first of a new educated class to be admitted into a circle which had until then been a preserve of the Fulani and Kanuri aristocrats.

In a plebiscite, held in 1961, the Northern Cameroons voted to become part of Nigeria again and formally joined the Federation.   The Southern Cameroons opted to join the Republic of Cameroon.

In the following year Provincial Commissioners replaced Residents in Northern Nigeria. Another national census was conducted, the results of which decided the proportions in the House of Representatives in Lagos. The rigged result led to immediate accusations of falsification, and disagreements about the allocation of central development funds, and underlined the fact that relations between the three Regions were no better than they had ever been.

Independence had brought about the establishment of many foreign embassies and delegations and a competing inflow of foreign investment, expertise, voluntary assistance, development grants and loans began to bring about temptations to those new to power and big business. Bribery and corruption on an unprecedented scale became commonplace and there was a decline in the quality of government. It is sad to recall that much aid was wasted, failed to reach those for whom it was intended and was often ill advised or poorly managed. Some schemes and projects, though sound in conception and very well intended, were eventually found to be uneconomic and unworkable, but there were success stories. A tin smelter was constructed near Jos, a textiles mill at Gusau, cement works at Sokoto, a sugar refinery at Bacita near Ilorin and new industries in several other locations, and work was in progress on the greatest project of all, the Kainji Dam on the River Niger, to supply hydro-electric power over a very wide area.

Ahmadu Bello University at Zaria began conferring its first degrees.

1963 marked the completion of final stage of construction of the Nigerian rail network, the Bornu extension from Kuru on the Plateau to Bauchi, Gombe and Maiduguri.

In 1963 Sir Kashim Ibrahim was appointed Governor of Northern Nigeria on the departure of Sir Gawain Bell, the last British Governor. Alhaji Ali Akilu, a relatively young man at 34 years of age, succeeded Bruce Greatbatch as Secretary to the Premier and head of the Northern civil service. The Federal Republic of Nigeria was inaugurated on 1st October, the third anniversary of independence, with Dr Azikwe as President and, following a long period of agitation, a new Mid-West Region, Nigeria's fourth, was excised from the Western Region.

The previous year's census was cancelled, and a new census, although accepted, was generally believed to be very inaccurate. Each region had exaggerated its own numbers to improve its representation in Federal Government and to obtain a greater share of the national budget. The loyalty and respect amongst northerners for their traditional leaders meant that none of their seats would fall to southern opposition and they would be assured of a majority in the House. The subsequent election was partially boycotted in the West, where there was severe rioting, and totally in the East. After much dispute a broadly based government was formed and Sir Abubakar was re-appointed Prime Minister. With corruption all around him, where the needs of the State were taking second place to personal considerations by politicians and ministers, he faced a nearly impossible task.

The Sardauna became more religiously oriented in 1964, led a campaign for conversions to Islam, and reverted to a more traditional lifestyle. He used his influence and prestige during his extensive travels in Europe and elsewhere to attempt to diversify external technical aid instead of being tied exclusively to British, US, German and French sources. He successfully sought investment capital from Kuwait and found teachers in Egypt, Pakistan and elsewhere in the Moslem world.

The Northern Government commissioned a three year study by Max Lock and Partners to produce a town plan for Kaduna as a Regional capital.

By 1965, in the absence of Northerners in government, clerical, technical and artisan positions were very often taken by the resourceful, capable and go-ahead Ibo people. Some of them also found domestic employment with expatriates because of their ability to speak good English, their longer period of familiarity with western ways and perhaps, to some extent, their religious persuasion. In Eastern Nigeria there had been no obvious form of organisation above village level until the British took over. They had quickly responded to western ways and education. It is probably true to say that the Ibos did well in the North because of the willingness of expatriates to employ them and to provide them with a measure of encouragement and protection. At the same time they were not slow to protect themselves if their positions and their livelihoods were at risk. Their loyalties to their own people went very deep and they were not keen to see Northerners replace them.

In the North, people from other parts of Nigeria tended to live in the separate areas known as *Sabon Garis*, or new towns, where their religion and way of life would not interfere with that of the local townsfolk. They brought families with them, or sometimes intermarried with local people, and adopted the local religion. Many such communities were respected by the local people, were settled and peaceful, but as they were succeeded by a younger, more aggressive and opportunistic generation with less toleration of what they saw as backward and unprogressive Northern ways, tensions began to build up.

Many decent people, including high ranking civil servants, were becoming very concerned by the internal and external effects of the rising tide of corruption and violence but the Prime Minister declined to use military force to control the situation. The situation was soon to be taken out of his hands.

By 1966 the higher levels of the Northern civil service and most other key positions were completely indigenised.

Military Rule

On 15th January 1966, in a swift and bloody coup, the Premier of the North, Sir Ahmadu Bello was assassinated and his Kaduna house destroyed by aggrieved rebel soldiers organised by Acting Commandant Chukwuma Nzeogwu, who was Chief Instructor of the NMTC in Kaduna, on operation *damisa* (leopard). *(Photo.6 shows the site)*. A political effort was made to obliterate Sir Ahmadu's memory by destroying thousands of his files, and photographs of him at the New Nigerian newspaper offices. Sir Kashim Ibrahim, the Governor, was taken into custody. Kano airport was occupied by the military.

Similar events took place in the Western capital, Ibadan, but, significantly, there was no violence in Enugu in the East.

The Prime Minister of the Federation, Alhaji Sir Abubakar Tafawa Balewa, was assassinated in Lagos.

Two days later, a Military Government took control, headed by an Ibo, Major-General J.T.Aguiyi Ironsi, and a few days after that Nzeogwu was imprisoned in Lagos. Ministers handed over government to the armed forces. Nigeria's first experiment with parliamentary democracy had come to an abrupt end. Legitimate opposition had proved to be an alien concept. Those in power had not been able to accept that they might have to surrender it by the will of the people and to those in opposition, force was seen as the only way to secure change.

The conduct of affairs in the North was handed over to Ali Akilu, the Head of the Civil Service.

There was a widespread sense of shock in the North at the loss of the elected and traditional leaders and the high ranking military personnel who lost their lives in the same actions. During the months which followed, the Northern people slowly took stock of the situation and were resentful that the perpetrators were not brought to trial; while in the East they were regarded almost as heroes. Ibo soldiers manned roadblocks and adopted a swaggering and arrogant attitude with their new found power, but Northerners, particularly the Hausas, were not slow to remind them that retribution awaited them.

The following statement was issued by the British High Commission in Lagos as reassurance to the expatriate community:-

BRITISH HIGH COMMISSION
KAJOLA HOUSE,
CAMPBELL STREET
LAGOS.

29 January, 1966.

Dear Sir/Madam,

The authorities in the period immediately following the events of 15 January, took vigorous measures to maintain law and order and restore conditions to normal. In the subsequent week there has been complete calm throughout the Federation. The disturbances in the West have come to an end, and travel has become safe again on roads that have long been dangerous. The North, East and Mid-west have been tranquil with life proceeding as usual. The Federal and Regional Departments are functioning normally and the new machinery of government seems to have slipped into gear smoothly without disruption. You will have observed what widespread and hearty applause and support has been given to the new regime throughout the country. If the Military Government succeeds in its object of proceeding effectively and quickly with economic and social development with attention to the needs of the under-privileged, it is likely to retain great popularity.

The Military Government has emphasised its desire that relations with Britain should be maintained on the usual cordial basis, and the British Government reciprocate this wish. We can therefore all proceed on the basis that business will be as usual, and that the value of the contribution of expatriates in the life of Nigeria will continue to be recognised.

The Military Government have indeed on several occasions emphasised the value that Nigeria continues to attach to the contribution of expatriate interests to the economy, and the Government's appreciation of the services of expatriates in other fields remains unchanged. Business and other expatriate interests will benefit from the achievement of the Government's policies of eliminating abuses and the authorities can justifiably look to us for all possible support. The British Government for their part will continue to give all possible backing to the Nigerian Development Plan. It is helpful that the transition should come at a time when economic conditions are fairly buoyant, the danger of loss of the cocoa crop in the West having been averted.

I hope that relatives of yourself and members of your staff and of your wives have not been made unnecessarily anxious by some of the more sensational press reports that appeared at home. I arranged for the BBC to broadcast that there had been no attack on expatriates and the Commonwealth Relations Office has been giving general reassurance in reply to enquiries.

We are fortunate in Nigeria in the friendly and relaxed relationship which expatriates enjoy with Nigerian citizens. I know that you will agree that this legacy of the good relations of the past underlines our obligation to take special care not to offend susceptibilities in any way by careless talk.

Now that conditions are restored to normal, it is no longer necessary to restrict journeys. There are still a number of road blocks to help in the apprehension of wanted persons: and care should continue to be exercised to comply with the requests of those manning them.

Yours faithfully,

(Sgd) FRANCIS CUMMING-BRUCE
(British High Commissioner)

By April the Military were in firm control and Hassan Katsina was appointed Military Governor of the North, with Sir Kashim Ibrahim as his adviser.

In May 1966 Ironsi announced that Nigeria would cease to be a Federal Republic, Regions would be abolished and replaced by groups of provinces, the Civil Service would be unified, political parties were to be abolished, and land and jobs throughout the country would be open to anyone. This was interpreted in the north as an invitation to Ibos to take control.

Anti-government rioting which began in Kano and Zaria spread to other northern cities. Many Ibos lost their lives and others began returning to the Eastern Region, where the Military Governor, Lt Col Odumegwu Ojukwu gave assurances that they would be protected.

There was widespread talk of *raba* (separation) at grassroots level in the North and talk of the need for a new state called **AREWA**.

On July 29th Major-General Aguiyi Ironsi and many Ibo officers all over the country were killed in a counter-coup and Lt Col Yakubu Gowon, a Christian from a minority tribe in the Plateau area of the North, emerged as the new head of the National Military Government. He had fortuitously been in England at the time of the January coup otherwise he too might have been a victim. Ojukwu condemned the new government and made a broadcast which included reference to the splitting up of Nigeria. Gowon announced plans to return Nigeria to a federal structure and called for a national conference designed to seek some form of reconciliation by bringing the conflicting interests together.

As constitutional debates took place over the next few months there was a massive return of indigenes of the Eastern Region to their home areas and non-easterners were expelled from the Eastern Region. Small groups of Northerners living in the East were the subject of retaliatory attacks and many were killed.

Toward the end of September rumours were being put around of a possible strike by Ibos in the North against key civil servants and even expatriates. As if to pre-empt this, there began, on the 29th of the month, the most massive civil uprising that the North had even seen; a collective, barbarous attempt to exterminate the Ibos, an action which the army and the police were either unable or unwilling to contain. Ibos were sought wherever they might be and were killed in revenge for the loss of the Prime Minister, the Northern Premier and other prominent Northerners, and in resentment of the domination they had achieved over the years, and their continued threat to Northern interests. The Hausas went about the slaughter as if it was just some everyday event and the victims not human. In this act of extreme tribalism they showed no remorse. Whilst there was obvious provocation there were no excuses for such inhuman action. Those who were lucky enough to escape fled or were escorted back to the East, leaving behind their possessions and their property, much of which was stolen or destroyed. The massacre was over in three long days, an amnesty came about, and the police started offering limited protection to any Ibos, or those who had been mistaken for Ibos, who had survived and to offer them safe passage out of the North. Led by Lt Col Ojukwu, they began demanding secession from the Federation.

Acrimony continued over the following months, Ojukwu assumed control of Nigeria's oil reserves and supplies, appropriated federal revenues, took over various Federal institutions and began building up and equipping his armed forces with assistance from abroad.

For expatriates this was a period of considerable and unaccustomed mental strain, disillusionment, disappointment and uncertainty, the like of which those who had previously served and departed the North could never have contemplated or experienced.

In May 1967 Gowon had to declare a state of emergency, announced that the regions would be abolished and Nigeria would be divided into twelve states, six of them in the north and six in the south. Ojukwu rejected this and sought, generally unsuccessfully, international recognition of his declaration on 1st July, of independent nation status for 'Biafra' the Eastern Region. Federal troops invaded a few days later and Nigeria was engaged in civil war. Nzeogwu, the assassin of the Sardauna of Sokoto, was killed in battle at Nsukka.

There was no general administrative breakdown in the rest of the country and the civil service continued to function more or less normally.

Break-up of the Northern Region

Between July 1967 and April 1968 senior civil servants were engaged in an exercise to divide the assets of the former Northern Region. Sokoto and Niger Provinces were to be joined to form the North-Western State; Borno, Adamawa, Sardauna and Bauchi to become the North-Eastern State; Kano would stand alone; Benue and Plateau were to be linked; Ilorin and Kabba would become the Central-West State or Kwara; and Zaria and Katsina would form the North-Central State. *(Illustration 7 and Map 15)*. Of the 30 million people said to be living in the Northern Region at the time of the 1963 census 26% were in the new North-Eastern State, 20% in Kano 19% in the North-West, 14% in North-Central, 13% in Benue-Plateau and 8% in Kwarra. The North-Eastern State replaced Northern Nigeria as the most populous political unit south of the Sahara.

The Regions, and hence the Northern Nigerian Survey, ceased to exist on 31st March 1968. The six new northern states became fully functioning on 1st April, each with its own Survey Departments. The former Kaduna Survey headquarters in Kaduna South became part of Kaduna Polytechnic. For a while it continued in limited production as a Survey Unit within an Interim Common Services Agency which had responsibilities in other areas such as broadcasting and the press, the former Northern Nigerian Development Corporation, marketing boards, and Ahmadu Bello University.

Kaduna was to be the site of major Federal departments and branches and the six northern states would continue to assume financial responsibility for Kaduna Polytechnic.

The civil war lasted until January 1970 when federal forces reunited the country and the Federal Government enforced its rule through a series of military and increasingly dictatorial governments.

General Gowon's administration lasted until July 1975 when he was removed in a bloodless coup and General Murtala Mohammed from Kano took over as Head of State. He further divided the country into 19 states to satisfy local and tribal aspirations, 10 in the north and 9 in the south, and set in motion the removal of the capital from Lagos to a new site near the geographical centre of the country, at Abuja.

Murtala Mohammed was assassinated in February 1976 and was succeeded by General Obasanjo of Ogun State.

In 1979 power returned to the civilians under a presidential constitution, which was the foundation of the Second Republic, led by President Shehu Shagari from Sokoto.

Still not content with civilian administration the powerful military took over again on December 31st 1983 under the leadership of General Muhammed Buhari from Kaduna, and in August 1985 General Muhammed Buhari was replaced by General Ibrahim Babangida from Niger, in Nigeria's sixth coup. In 1990 an attempted coup failed. By 1991 Nigeria consisted of 21 semi-autonomous States and a Capital Territory.

And so the story went on. More and more states were created until many of them were smaller than the Provinces inherited from pre-independence days. By 1999 there were 36 of them. The former Western Region, which had been divided into Lagos, Ogun and Ondo States, became Lagos, Ogun, Oyo, Osun, Ekiti and Ondo. The former Mid-West which had been broken into Bendel and Rivers, became Edo, Delta, Bayelsa and Rivers. The former Eastern Region, which had attempted to break away as Biafra, was instead broken into Imo, Cross River and Anambra, and later Cross River, Imo, Enugu, Ebonyi, Anambra, Abia and Akwa Ibom.

The former Northern Region which had been broken into North-Western, Kano, North-Eastern, Kwara, North-Central and Benue-Plateau States in 1968; into Niger, Sokoto, Kano, Borno, Bauchi, Gongola, Kwara, Benue and Plateau in 1976; and later into Niger, the Federal Capital Territory, Kebbi, Sokoto, Katsina, Jigawa, Kano, Yobe, Borno, Bauchi, Taraba, Adamawa, Kwara, Kogi, Kaduna, Benue and Plateau; eventually became 19 States; Niger, Sokoto, Zamfara, Kebbi, Katsina, Jigawa, Kano, Yobe, Borno, Bauchi, Gombe, Taraba, Adamawa, Kwara, Kogi, Kaduna, Benue, Nassarawa and Plateau, plus the Federal Capital Territory (Abuja).

This is not the place to delve further into the complex story of political intrigue, military and civilian rivalries, international relations, ethnic unrest, and economic instability which have continued to dominate headlines about Nigeria. The country has endured numerous military dictatorships which failed to make optimum use of a rich oil-based economy. Corruption, lawlessness and nepotism were rife in spite of proclamations and openly expressed desires for improvement and reform.

Rightly or wrongly Nigeria acquired the reputation of a militaristic pariah, an outcast amongst nations, and one of the few countries which, by its political attitudes and reputation, effectively closed its borders to the outside. This was a great pity because it has a wonderfully rich and diverse cultural heritage, and geographical interest, a land with proud and likeable people, spoiled only by the political ambitions, avarice and corruption of the few. Isolation has, on the other hand, spared the country the indignity of the excessive tourism experienced elsewhere in Africa. Under the mature civilian leadership of recent years there are encouraging signs that the political situation is improving and that Nigeria will assume a respected and influential role in sub-Saharan Africa.

PART 2

SURVEY DEPARTMENTS

PART 2

PART 2

SURVEY DEPARTMENTS

The Concept of Mapping

As late as the 1980s cartographic appreciation was still not a generally developed skill in Northern Nigeria and even today it is unlikely to be so. Many quite educated people were confused when a map was placed before them. This is not surprising because large scale maps of their country had not been available to them when they attended school and the use of symbols and shapes to represent the physical and geographic features all around them, and the inter-relationship of scale and direction, were concepts to which they had not been exposed. Quite senior government officers were known to resort to a random search of a map to find the name of their hometown written somewhere, and then search all parts of the map again for the name of an adjacent village, rather than use the logic of distance, scale and direction. To people like them, the map was just a random collection of names, written anywhere on the paper wherever there happened to be a space. The primitive maps which some northern emirates used in the early days were not unlike that and there was, therefore, no established indigenous cartographic culture to be displaced by the arrival of the European concept of scaled mapping using symbols to represent detail.

Such drawings as existed usually attempted to be a portrait of the district, centred on the chief's palace and the main buildings, with no attempt to show boundaries. Although some emirates recognised conspicuous boundaries on the ground, the geography of these 'maps' was invariably confused and inaccurate. Areas were not seen as shapes as on European maps and the relationship between settlements, rivers and topographic features, which were placed in apparent random and unrelated order, was seldom reliable.

It is little wonder, therefore, that so many people had scant appreciation of the usefulness and value of the products of land surveying, no knowledge of the processes involved and, even when occupying positions of influence and responsibility, gave such low priority to the surveyor's needs.

Exploration, Charting and Military Mapping

Early explorers and traders penetrating the rivers in the late 18th century and in the first half of the 19th century compiled charts which showed settlements and trading posts and recorded local geographic information; but beyond the watercourses little was known.

European international competition for the acquisition of trading rights gave impetus to the accumulation of geographical information and, as the 19th century progressed and interest in securing trading lands increased, there was growing interest from commerce, from the military, and from various learned societies in Britain, in the areas coming under British influence. In the North such activity was at first confined to the navigable parts of the Niger, up to about Jebba, and the Benue.

For many parts of the world, military considerations have been the mainspring for topographic mapping and the lands which were to become Nigeria were no exception to this general principle. Some funding for charting was provided by organisations like the Royal Geographical Society, the African Association and the British Association, but surveying and mapping were primarily military inspired activities; indeed the legacy of military influence continued in the methods and discipline of surveying until quite recent times.

This mapping went hand in hand with military expeditions into the interior of the country. Information concerning townships and settlements, areas of influence of local rulers and trade routes were noted and sent back to the Geographic Section of the General Staff (GSGS) in Britain because so much information of this nature is best recorded in graphical form on map sheets. For example, as early as 1889, the Intelligence Division at the War Office had produced a map sheet at about 1:2,500,000 scale showing some detail as far north as Sokoto, some seven hundred miles from the coast.

The British had long appreciated that maps could be powerful weapons in the hands of the military and maps had often achieved strategic significance, imagined or otherwise, and could thus be endowed with security labels. The Nigerian army of the post-independence years was certainly to think so *("Where there are maps, there lies power")*; some maps were regarded as having strategic significance and persons passing cartographic information to imagined enemies were not regarded as acting in the country's interests. In consequence, Nigeria's central government mapping organisation of the 1950s and 1960s became very protective of its national mapping.

In 1890 France, Germany and Britain agreed on their spheres of interest in West Africa but the informal arrangement was inadequate because it was not very long before British and French trading areas began overlapping. Over the next few years crises continued with the French, who had military backing, regarding the demarcation of the western border of the British area. This led to the need for formal and sometimes ill-considered demarcation of boundaries and the production of definitive maps. Such commercial considerations were sometimes known to ignore the existence of the fixed boundaries of Islamic states, for example on the Anglo-German boundary between Bornu and Adamawa, and adjustments later became necessary.

In 1898 an Anglo-French convention agreed the frontier of Bornu on a roughly drawn map, and Stanford's of London produced a general map of West Africa, at a scale of 30 miles to an inch, which included the Niger Coast Protectorate and part of the Royal Niger Company's territory.

....

SURVEY DEPARTMENTS BASED IN LAGOS

The Formation of Survey Departments and early Small Scales Mapping

The earliest Survey Department was established in 1897, in Lagos. Local surveying started in the Works Department and was mostly related to government needs like setting out headquarters, residential and commercial layouts, railway routes, etc.

The **Southern Nigeria Survey** Department was set up in 1900 to deal in the first instance with the Nigeria-Cameroons boundary and in 1906, with the merging of the Colony of Lagos with Southern Nigeria, the Lagos Survey Department was amalgamated with the Southern Nigeria Survey under its first Director, a Canadian, Major F.Guggisberg CMG RE.

On January 1st 1900, Sir F. Lugard took over the administration of the territory from the Royal Niger Company. His annual reports 1900-1905 *(Appendix XIV Ref. 64)* show a pressing need for exploration and mapping; as the following two extracts from his 1902 Report show most vividly.

> *".......... I cannot speak too highly of the ability with which this most difficult task (the occupation of Bornue Province) was carried out by Colonel Moreland and his officers. An enormous area, some 60,000 square miles in extent, was brought under administrative control, with little bloodshed. The difficulties encountered were unusually great owing to a lack of water and of supplies but the whole expedition, including Major Cubitt's later operations, was concluded in about four months. Over 1,000 miles of country were traversed and mapped during this period. "*

The inference is that when not fighting, mapmaking was a priority occupation for the soldiers and because in this case the fighting was mercifully small the map making was correspondingly great. Again, towards the end of the 1902 report we read:-

"*Surveys*".
96............Considerable progress has been made in surveys and the map of Northern Nigeria is now beginning to be filled up with some degree of accuracy. I have a separate map of each province on a scale of 1:250,000 and upon this has been traced every route surveyed since February 1901, when the existing data was last incorporated. Maps of a portion of the Protectorate on scales 1:500,000 and 1:1,000,000 have been compiled by the Intelligence Branch of the War Office, and these will be corrected and brought up to date by the recent information in the large scale maps. I also have had made a map on a scale of 1: 2,000,000 ....from which will be seen the tentative division into provinces, the boundaries of which have in many cases been surveyed and fixed in accordance with tribal jurisdictions."

The survey methods used by the military at this time would be of rapid techniques based on compass traversing and plane tabling, mostly carried out on horseback. According to a well known survey manual of the period   "*... in open country and with a good horse about 60 square miles of country per day can be surveyed by simple plane table methods. "*

The Provincial maps referred to in the Lugard report covered most of the Northern Region, and resulted in the production by the War Office, in 1902, of eight sheets at a scale of 1:1,000,000 covering a large portion of the Region. They were reproduced and printed by Messrs W.&A.K. Johnston and put on sale through the agency of Edward Stanford of Long Acre in London. They were numbered in the following way: Sheet 50 (Sokoto), Sheet 51 (Kano), Sheet 52 (Lake Chad), Sheet 61 (Nikki), Sheet 62 (Central Nigeria) *(See Map 16)* and Sheet 63 (Yola). They included no boundaries except parts of the Anglo-French boundary in the west, which had been demarcated by a joint commission in 1900. The important Jos Plateau area was as yet undiscovered and so was shown only in vague outline. An area to the north west of Wase was also more or less unknown and so was labelled "Moffat (Cannibals)" - a change from the Jonathan Swift (1733) formula:-

" *So geographers, in Afric-maps,
With savage-pictures fill their gaps,
And o'er inhabitable downs
Place elephants in place of towns".*

An ancient map of Africa after Ptolemy (c.1500) that illustrates the above comment quite well was reproduced from one of the rare originals by the Lithographic Section of the Northern Nigerian Survey Department in 1966 as a training exercise in colour separation and four colour printing. *(Map 17).*

Apart from the military input, these sheets would have been compiled from all available sources of information and that would have included, for example, reports or notes made by any traders and travellers passing through the region. Hence the sheets were not the results of accurate systematic surveys or observations as we understand them today and so depicted a very small amount of the total detail. They were of necessity simply the best possible sketch maps that could be produced at the time.

With so many other commitments in the many British colonies, the GSGS was unable to devote resources to systematic mapping. Local departments everywhere were being encouraged to take charge of mapping produced to GSGS standards and specifications, uniform in scale and accuracy, but drawn and printed in Britain. Despite the obvious pressing need for surveys of all kinds, the financial and logistic support necessary for an enlargement of the work and remit of the existing Survey Department in Lagos was slow in coming.

From 1901 to 1909 local activities were concentrated in the western part of Nigeria. Theodolite traversing with steel bands provided positional reference for later mapping, checked by observed latitudes and telegraphic longitudes, the latter based on Lagos which was fixed telegraphically from Cape Town in 1903.

Better mapping produced in the early years was for specific projects, for example between 1903 and 1904 a survey was completed for the railway from the River Niger to Kano.

In 1905 Stanford's Geographical Establishment in London published a map of the country at a scale of 1:2,000,000. This was another subject of a lithographic training exercise by the Survey Department in Kaduna in 1969 and an extract from it is given as *Map 18*.

In 1905-06, Captain R. Ommaney RE carried out astronomical observations to obtain correct latitudes and longitudes for 15 towns: Ibadan, Ilorin, Jebba, Pategi, Lokoja, Zungeru, Kontagora, Yelwa, Zaria, Kano, Lere, Bauchi, Ibi, Keffi and Loko. Prior to this, and before the introduction of the telegraph land line to Lagos, earlier astronomical determinations of longitude had been somewhat inaccurate because of poor estimates of Greenwich Mean Time. From this work the previous assumed positions of Zaria, Lere and Bauchi were found to be 16 miles too far east, Zungeru was 8 miles east, Loko and Keffi 13 miles, and Ibi 22 miles too far west.

A Colonial Survey Committee was set up in London in 1905 to advise the Secretary of State on surveying and geological work in the colonies and protectorates. It made no attempt to set up systematic mapping but aimed to assist exploration and provide a graphical record of journeys, information about trading stations, routes, settlements, rivers and topography, and provide a base for recording boundary demarcation, the whole resulting in a useful archive of military intelligence. The Committee produced specifications for surveys, recommendations on circumstances when mapping should be carried out, the content of maps, including rules on the spelling of local names, and the training of those recruited for overseas service. It was not granted funds to enable it to assume an executive role. However, the West African Frontier Force had gathered enough information using instrument traversing to lay the foundation for a sixty-one sheet 1:250,000 series of maps which was published by the Topographic Section of the General Staff. Later more detailed mapping would provide tools for general administration, development schemes, communications planning, minerals exploitation and cadastral charting for land use and development

By 1906 there was still no effective Survey Department in Nigeria. Lugard left Lagos for Northern Nigeria and from an early date he had pressed for an active Survey unit to be established in the North. Among other things, he pleaded embarrassment at the much better mapping being produced in the neighbouring French and German territories. However, funding was scarce and nothing but minor expenditure could be justified and had to be raised locally if needed. It was not until 1908 that some recognition of his arguments prevailed with the Colonial Office in London and then only to the extent that he was allowed to employ one RE officer to carry out astronomical observations for latitude and longitude to collate the topographic information being provided by administrative officers, travellers and others.

In 1907 a 1:1,000,000 scale map of Lagos and Southern Nigeria was printed by the GSGS in London and although incomplete, served as the best guide yet to the colony. Maps at 1:250,000 scale of the North were revised and a political map gave information about districts and population. A demand for other maps was also beginning to be felt and the Secretary of State was, for example, calling for a map showing the tsetse-fly belts.

The existing map sheets at scales of 1:500,000 and 1:250,000 were constantly being revised and up-dated and reprinted by GSGS, and for the first time, on a map of Northern Nigeria at 1:2,000,000 scale dated 1909, coloured information as to ground relief was introduced, together with the new Provincial boundaries of Borgu, Sokoto, Kontagora, Ilorin, Niger, Kabba, Kano, Zaria, Nassarawa, Bassa, Bornu, Bauchi, Yola and Muri. It also showed that the railway had progressed as far as Maikonkele east of Zungeru near the Baro line junction. This map, an extract from which is given as *Map 19*, was compiled from boundary commission surveys and road traverses, adjusted on certain towns fixed by latitude and telegraphic longitudes and partly engraved by Messrs Philip & Sons. A similar map, but without the coloured relief, was produced in the following year, covering the whole of Nigeria.

Apart from its boundary activities the work of the Southern Nigerian Survey was mainly of a cadastral nature. However it was finally realised that a much larger unit was required if the territory was to become independent of the GSGS for serial mapping. And so, on the first of April 1910, the then Governor, Sir Walter Egerton, instructed Major Guggisberg to reorganise the Southern Nigeria Survey Department and bring into being a unit capable of producing maps in its own topographic section. (Guggisberg had previously been Director of Surveys, Gold Coast Colony [now Ghana] and was a well informed and experienced topographic surveyor. At a later date he was to return to the Gold Coast and became a distinguished Governor of that country). From 1910, and this milestone in Nigeria's surveying history, the story of mapping is taken up in Part 3 of this work in the section entitled 'Topographic Mapping'.

The Formation of a Survey Department in Northern Nigeria.

Due to an increasing amount of survey work being carried out in areas remote from Lagos, Major Guggisberg proposed to the Colonial Survey Committee (CSC) in 1914 the formation of a northerly survey department. This was agreed and Lugard proposed that the head of the combined southern and more northerly units should be designated Surveyor-General. An Assistant Surveyor-General was duly appointed to the Northern Provinces, with the principal function of organising cadastral work. When Lugard moved the Northern capital from Zungeru a small drawing and clerical office was established in Kaduna and work was done in connection with township and trading layouts all over the North. This work, and later small-scale mapping, by touring surveyors, gathered pace over the next two decades. At the time there were only about 30 survey officers in the British Colonial Service based in Nigeria. This was a very modest number compared with the total of about 600 other officers involved in the setting up of educational, transport, administrative and other technical services.

Surveying by Administrative Officers

It has been asserted by academic critics that the British stuck to the ideal of disciplined surveying not in spite of how hard it was, but **because** it was so hard. Anyone, as was demonstrated by the District Officers, who, as part of their basic training, learned the elements of simple surveying, could sketch an ordinary map using a compass and a chain; but a full topographic survey demanded the high-minded, rational, mathematical, co-ordinated discipline of experts working within an enlightened administration.

Maps were not produced as cartographic tools of colonial appropriation and acquisition; rather they came about as a consequence of these activities, for few things could warm an administrator's heart and better provide a medium for development planning than a map of his domain prominently displayed in his office. The early Residents were, in the main, military officers with a knowledge of basic surveying techniques and some of the plans they produced bore evidence of military terminology like *bariki* (barracks), stations, transport lines, etc. As yet there was no association of surveying with menial work and in some respects it still had the reputation of being a respectable and gentlemanly science in which many had bettered their social status. British officers sometimes undoubtedly performed an elaborate play of what it was to be British., involving arduous performances and the emergence of some idiosyncratic personalities. Charles Lindsay Temple for example, who was a Resident in Northern Nigeria from 1901, and was Resident at Bauchi in 1903, was not only a competent geologist but during his early travels in the North did a certain amount of records-keeping as a contribution to early mapping and had a reputation as a surveyor who undertook astro-fixes.

In 1909 the Colonial Office set up a 2 - 3 months training course at the Imperial Institute in London for the African Administrative Service. In this short period the course covered accounting, tropical economic products, hygiene and sanitation, criminal law, international law, Islamic law, African languages, ethnology and elementary surveying. The period devoted to surveying must have been extremely short. The limited surveying knowledge acquired obviously had a direct bearing on the quality and quantity of the surveying which these officers carried out.

Until the 1930s, District Officers were usually taught the elements of simple architecture, public works, road engineering and surveying in the course of their basic training at Oxford or Cambridge and at the Imperial Institute in South Kensington, before setting out for Nigeria. The more enthusiastic of them might use their surveying knowledge to produce simple sketch maps of their headquarters towns and districts, to assist in general administration and minor public works. These skills were also useful in implementing locally planned improvements to some of the old congested townships, marking out lines for widening roads, demolishing some walls and houses and establishing new rectilinear layouts, with avenues of shade trees. Such activities were necessary while surveying specialists were few on the ground and did not often extend into the vast expanse of country which lay between the widely scattered small townships. As an example, however, of what could sometimes be achieved, Rex Niven spent about two years around 1923 carrying out mapping work over an area of about 5,000 square miles each side of the Niger near Kabba and Koton Karifi, where nothing but a primitive sketch map had existed before. An idea of the precision of the work can be gained from the fact that some of his sight-lines were to a "drum beat"; using a measuring wheel; pacing; and a "very straight path" about 25 miles long which formed a "baseline". The approximate heights of hills were obtained using a barometer. He did, however, make use of a war surplus artillery theodolite for angular measurements from some of the hills to the roofs of houses and to the smoke from fires in remote villages and, although not a trained surveyor, covered the area in some detail, visiting many places which had never been seen by a white man. This was no doubt an outstanding example of the kind of useful work which D.Os sometimes undertook, and a copy of his map was deposited with the Royal Geographical Society; where no doubt it still resides to this day. As was the case in many other parts of Northern Nigeria, it remained the only detailed map of the area, apart from locally detailed work done by the Forestry Department, until mapping from aerial photography came along over thirty years later.

The need for maps soon reached a stage where their production called for a higher degree of specialist skill and training than that given to Administrative Officers. For these officers to have achieved anything better would have called for the expenditure of considerable time and effort which could only be provided at the expense of their other responsibilities.

The Survey Department of Nigeria

The Survey Department of Nigeria, or Nigeria Surveys as it was sometimes called, arose from a coming together of separate surveying activities in the three original parts of Nigeria; Lagos Colony; Southern Nigeria; and Northern Nigeria; and was based in Lagos. In 1921 the Surveyor-General and his staff were based with several other offices such as those of the Chief Secretary, Attorney-General, Solicitor-General, Crown Counsel, and Medical HQ, in the Secretariat. An indication of the size of the Survey Department can be gained from the fact that in 1925 only about 0.02% (just under 40 officers) of the expatriate Colonial Service posts in Nigeria were held by surveyors.

The Survey Department produced annual reports of its work and progress. Copies of most of them up to 1939 are available in British archives. No reports were produced for the war years 1939-46 and for 1955-58, which was a period of reorganisation for the Federal Survey Department following the hiving-off of Regional Departments. After independence in 1960 few annual reports were sent from Nigeria and none was produced after 1963.

The Department was responsible for national and local framework control (triangulation, traversing and precise levelling networks - lines of precise levels generally followed the main roads and the railways); topographic mapping, lithographic printing and drawing; national and internal boundary surveys; cadastral surveys; and survey training. The Survey lithographic section in Lagos, as well as printing maps, produced many publications and reports for other government departments.

For many years up to World War II the Department was the official collector of meteorological statistics all over the country and supplied information for aviation, forestry and medical use. In 1929 a series of daily observations of the upper air were carried out at the request of the Air Ministry for the use of the first non-stop RAF flight from England to Cape Town, which unfortunately ended in disaster near Tunis. Observations were made to balloons released at intervals and the force and direction of winds at varying altitudes were recorded. Reports were cabled to England and a monoplane was eventually successful on its flight to Walvis Bay in 1933. The introduction of the Empire Air Mail service in 1933 necessitated the expansion of meteorological services.

A Surveyors Licensing Board, for which the Director of Surveys had responsibility, was authorised under the Survey Ordinance 1918, subsequently by the Survey Ordinance of 1952 and later by Item 20 of the Nigeria Constitution Orders in Council, 1954. The responsibilities of the Board were the examination and licensing of surveyors who wished to practise cadastral survey work in Nigeria. The registration and examination of the pupils of licensed surveyors who may be responsible for boundary surveys of valuable property, and their status and qualifications were a major concern of the Board.

National surveying organisations are primarily responsible for triangulation, levelling and mapping, but, from the earliest days, the Department was also responsible for government layouts, the setting out of residential, commercial and trading areas, and surveys for the grant of statutory rights in land. Surveyors based in the North produced township plans, which were printed in Lagos. Offices were maintained in the major administrative centres for this purpose. The principal one in the Northern Provinces was at Kaduna. This Cadastral Branch, with its drawing and clerical offices, was destined to continue its uninterrupted work through to the formation of the Northern Nigerian Survey nearly thirty years later and beyond to the break-up of the Northern Region in 1968, and thereafter became the nucleus of the Survey Department of the new North-Central State.

It could be argued that Lagos, in one corner of the vast undeveloped country, was, in spite of its access to communications and supplies, not the best choice as a location for Survey headquarters. It was no more Nigeria than London was Britain, and like all capitals it developed an insular attitude, absorbed with its own affairs, and it was felt that it too often had insufficient understanding and sympathy with the hard and harsh lands to the north.

The staff list of the Nigeria Survey Department at 31st December 1928 read as follows:-

Surveyor-General:	**Capt. T.J.Water**
Deputy Surveyor-General:	**Capt. J.Calder Wood**
Assistant Surveyors-General:	**Capt. T.H.Galbraith** (Cadastral Branch, N.Provinces, Kaduna)
	Capt. C.Gilbert Evans
	Capt. H.Morphy (Permanently seconded to Kano N.A.)
Senior Surveyors:	**W.K.Robertson** (Cad.Branch, N.Provinces Townships)
	Capt.A.W.N. de Normann (Cad. Branch, Minesfield)
Surveyors:	**Capt. R.Buckingham** (Cad.Branch, Minesfield)
	J.F.Morris (Cad.Branch, Minesfield)
	A.E.Thomas (Cad.Branch, Minesfield)
	H.Isherwood (Cad.Branch, Cameroons)
	J.A.Bentley (Cad.Branch, Minesfield)
	A.E.Lee (Cad.Branch, Minesfield)
	G.J.Humphries (Cad.Branch, Western Division - Survey School)
	W.E.Mooney (Cad.Branch, N.Provinces Townships)
	W.B.Hewitt (Cad.Branch, Minesfield)
	W.D.C.Wiggins (Cad.Branch, Eastern Division)
	F.W.Sutton (Cad.Branch, N.Provinces Townships)
	T.Russell (Cad.Branch, Minesfield)
	C.W.Malyan (Cad.Branch, Minesfield)
	W.B.McNab (Cad.Branch, Lagos)
	A.S.Paterson (Cad.Branch, Minesfield)
	D.L.C.Anderson (Survey School, Ibadan)
	M.D.Wimbush (Cad.Branch, Eastern Division)
	K.H.Hunter (Cad.Banch, Eastern Division)
	C.S.Barron (Cad.Branch, Kaduna)
	G.V.Ashton (Cad.Branch, Minesfield).

Stationed on the Minesfield was a special R.E. party led by **Capt. B.T.Godfrey-Faussett**, with **Lts S.W.Joslin, H.E.Pike, J.D.Newman** and **F.G.Clarke** and 18 non-commissioned officers.

K.H.(Keith) Hunter, who was destined to become the 'father' of the Northern Nigerian Survey, was appointed to the Nigeria Colonial Survey Service on 7th November 1928. Much of his service until 1939, when he was called up for war service, was spent on primary triangulation reconnaissance in preparation for the subsequent mapping of the country. From 1948 onwards he was stationed in Jos and then in Kaduna as the first Surveyor-General of Northern Nigeria until his retirement in 1959 .

The growing strength of the Survey Department meant that it was able to expand work on such basic activities as the observation of networks of triangulation points that would provide the essential pattern of control points required for the systematic production of map sheets. This mapping began as soon as some control was in place.

1934 was noteworthy because the Lands Department, whose entire staff were based in Lagos, and the Survey Department were amalgamated under the direction of the Surveyor-General J. Calder Wood, who was then known as the Commissioner of Lands and Surveyor-General. A Survey Section had been operating in Kano to handle the increasing amount of cadastral work there, although it had to close in 1934 because of staff shortages.

In 1935 the 'Registration of Titles Ordinance' passed its third reading at a meeting of the Legislative Council. New Survey Regulations came into force and a new Survey Manual embodying all Ordinances and Regulations was printed and circulated.

With increasing activity throughout the North, trading and residential layouts were surveyed in Sokoto, Bornu, Bauchi, Zaria, Kano, Ilorin, and Niger. This was at the time of the introduction of air services and the Survey Department set out airfields and building-free zones around them at Kano, Kaduna and Maiduguri. The promulgation of the 'Township Amendment Ordinance' 1935 meant that the depository office for signed and approved plans of townships for the Northern Provinces changed from Lagos to Kaduna. 61 plans of trading layouts were deposited there in 1937.

It had long been the aim to set up Provincial Survey Offices throughout the North but this did not start to become a reality until well after World War II when financing and staffing permitted. Until then, surveys were undertaken by touring officers working out of Kaduna, Jos and Kano.

The headquarters building was improved in 1938 to house Lithographic Printing, Computing and Meteorology, and Lithography was the only one still left in the hutments on the old golf course (then King George V Memorial Park).

The Second World War

150,000 Nigerian volunteers joined the 81st and 82nd Divisions which served with success in the Arakan and Burma. Many of the older Survey headmen and messengers of later Northern Nigerian Survey days were among them. The Survey Department was seriously depleted.

Triangulation had been pursued as vigorously as possible until 1940 but it was not possible to continue the observing programme during the war. Work continued on government, residential and trading layouts and detail surveys, albeit at a much reduced rate.

To illustrate the sort of work which was done during the war, K.M.(Keith) Sargeant, who ultimately joined the Northern Nigerian Survey, and who had worked on the topographic survey of Chafe and Gusau sheets at 1:125,000 and triangulation work in Sokoto Province in 1939, was one of a small group of expatriate surveyors to remain during the war. He was seconded to the censorship branch in Lagos, and the Aviation Department, as Aerodrome Control Officer-cum-Meteorologist at Maiduguri, Minna and Kaduna airfields from 1940 to 1942 . He was engaged on the inspection of all primary trig points on the Bauchi-Yola chain between January and April 1943 and went on to carry out a contour survey near Maiduguri aerodrome for a proposed anti-malarial drainage scheme. From January 1944 until December 1945 he was in charge of the Oyo Survey School.

There had traditionally been very little, if any, collaboration and interchange of survey information with French authorities; perhaps a hangover from the days of territorial acquisition; and it was an embarrassment to administrators that the allied forces in Nigeria could not call upon the Survey Department for plans of the towns in the territories surrounding Nigeria.

Post-War Resumption

Major W.G.Wookey, Capt. M.D.Wimbush and Hunter came back from military service and in 1946-47 work on primary triangulation and its breakdown into secondary and lower orders was resumed, and a start was made on more accurate topographic mapping based on aerial photography.

As in so many other fields, there was little precise levelling done in the war years, but by 1948 a 1,200 miles loop from Oshogbo to Akure, Benin, Onitsha, Umuahia, Makurdi, Kafanchan, Kaduna, Minna and back to Oshogbo revealed an unacceptable misclosure but checks observed in the following year located a gross error in the Makurdi-Umuahia section.

After the war, the Director of Surveys in Nigeria at the time, N.S.Clouston, was very critical of some of the proposals for the establishment of the British Directorate of Colonial Surveys (DCS) in London, its domination by military officers and its intended role in national mapping. He opposed the idea that all geodetic surveying should be completed before a start was made on systematic topographic surveying, saw a possible weakening of his department when the reverse might be required, and thought Europeans were trying to take financial and career advantage of the Colonial Development Welfare Act. Brigadier Hotine of the DCS had a great influence on triangulation in many countries, including Nigeria, though it has to be said that the Nigerian programme was well planned and advanced before he came on the scene. He had a hand in initiating new schemes, filling gaps in existing work, replacing lost and inadequate stations, was an advocate of the integration of neighbouring systems and of a common projection and grid reference system. Clouston was justifiably proud of the achievements of his own organisation to date, in spite of the staffing and financial constraints it had always suffered; confident of its abilities; sought more support for it; and wanted map production to be done in Nigeria. He sought an increase in his establishment, thought that DCS personnel should be directed and supervised by him and wanted the appointment of training instructors for Nigeria. He accused the DCS of 'poaching' two of his surveyors, Lt.Cols G.J.Humphries and W.D.C.Wiggins and of making its conditions of service more attractive, thus depriving Nigeria of candidates. He also wanted full participation in aerial survey and insisted that Nigeria would be responsible for its own geodetic and topographic surveys and for preparing its own maps from photographs of the country. In 1946 the Directorate started to become involved in extensive and systematic aerial photography and some aspects of mapping in Nigeria.

1947 saw the end of the amalgamation of the Lands and Survey Departments. There was a great increase in the amount of work for both, due to the development programme, and it was decided they would work more effectively if independent of one another with their own departmental heads.

The Department reported resumption of mapping activities in the North and, in 1948-9, 1:1,000,000 scale maps of Sokoto Province and the Kontagora area were drawn in Lagos. Work was also in progress on the 1:2,400 Kano township map series, an unusually-scaled 1:6,250 map of Lokoja and 1:12,500 maps of Jos, Kaduna and the Mokwa-Zugurma road. In the following year the 1:125,000 Kakuri and Kushaka standard sheets were printed, together with a 1:62,500 Geological Map, PAN I, covering part of Plateau Province.

It is interesting to look back at the prices of maps on sale at the time to the public. Survey maps could be purchased at the Survey Department offices and in Church Missionary Society (CMS) Bookshops, both of which were reporting rising sales. A 1:5,000,000 map of Nigeria cost 6d; 1:1,000,000 scale maps in 4 sheets at 5s each, or mounted as a single sheet on linen for £1 2s 6d; 1:500,000 Provincial maps at 2s 6d each; 1:125,000 Standard Sheets at 2s each; 1:12,500 Town Plans at 3s each and 1:4,800 and 1:2,400 sheets at 2s each.

1949-1951 saw an improvement in the post-war supply of paper and other materials and made it possible to greatly increase map production but the number of printing machines was inadequate to meet the rising demand. Two new power driven machines were included in financial estimates for

1950-51 and provision was also made for the appointment of a dedicated Map Production Officer. Work was done towards the production of 1:500,000 *(example: Map 23)* and 1:750,000 maps of all the northern Provinces, 1:125,000 sheets of Abuja, Bida, Funtua, Paiku, Maska and Shaki, the Kano area at 1:25,000, a 1:12,500 map for Ilorin, the 1:2,400 series for Ilorin, Kano, Katsina, Sokoto, Kaduna, Jos and Minna, a 1:62,500 Geological map of Neil's Valley and the Jema'a, Minesfield and Jimaku Composite sheets at 1:125,000. Maps were produced from aerial photography for Utachu in Niger Province, and for Bauchi town, while three members of the section, training on Multiplex, contoured an area of four square miles at 1:5,000 for the proposed Shiroro Gorge Dam Site in Niger Province.

Forest Reserves had always been surveyed in detail by the Forestry Departments, though their large scale maps, intended for internal use, were seldom of value for systematic map production by the Survey Department. They showed boundaries, physical features, watercourses and all major stands of trees. P.A.Daley, a former Forestry Officer, has provided the following brief account of some of his own surveying work:-

> *'I served in Plateau Province (based on Jos) for two spells, first from January to August 1949, then again from January 1952 to April 1953. Then I was Provincial Forest Officer, Niger (based on Minna) from September 1953 to January 1959.*
>
> *Much of my time, and that of colleagues in other provinces, was spent on surveying the boundaries of new forest reserves. The published Survey maps at that time provided only sketchy information about many of the areas in which we were operating. Our own surveying was very basic chain-and-compass stuff but provided the definitive maps to accompany the Gazette Notices by which the reserves were legally constituted. I do not know if our efforts ever contributed to the filling in of blanks on 'your' maps.*
>
> *During my second spell in Plateau I was able to borrow from the offices of Amalgamated Tin Mines of Nigeria, near Bukuru, some of the air photographs which they had commissioned previously, and use them to construct maps of the irregular patches of high forest (Hausa: 'kurmi') from which timber was being logged in Jema'a district, just south of the main plateau. We had no machinery for compiling these maps, but the application of simple methods which I had learned in 1951, during a course at the Forestry Institute in Oxford, gave results infinitely superior to those attempted by driving traces through the bush.*
>
> *That reminds me that during a bush trip to Ilorin Province in 1950 (with a class from the Ibadan Forestry School) I discovered some RAF personnel who were, I understand, manning a beacon which controlled the major air survey which was being carried out at that time, the aircraft following a circular course.'*

In Lagos the Air Mapping Section was gradually being built up for mapping from departmental photography. 13 junior technical officers were under the supervision of the Chief Computer. It had Casella slotted template apparatus for mapping horizontal detail and Multiplex, consisting of two 7-projector tables and one 3-projector table, for contouring. The slotted-template method was quickly mastered by the junior technical staff. The rate of output was lower for areas of close detail but the relative time was still good compared with ground methods. For example, the individual buildings of a 20 square mile town with a population of 57,000 people, were mapped from air photographs in four weeks by two junior draughtsmen. The services of several highly skilled surveyors would have been necessary for some months to complete the same amount of mapping by ground methods. Later, a Williamson enlarger was installed in Lagos and this allowed an attempt at revision of some town plans by direct projection of the photograph at the appropriate scale.

In 1948-49 the Kaduna staff comprised an Acting Assistant Director of Surveys, five junior service surveyors, a senior draughtsman, four junior draughtsmen, a computer, a sunprinter and four clerks.

Aerial mapping control work in progress in the North included Bauchi town, the River Nadijin, the River Sokoto irrigation, Zaria town, the Maiduguri-Bama rice area, the Yola-Wukari road reconnaissance, the River Niger (Jebba-Komi) commercial area, the River Benue navigation, the Nguru-Maiduguri railway route reconnaissance, Makurdi town and Bijim Hill geological mapping. With a widespread and increasing demand for maps in the Regions the intention was announced to transfer, as far as possible, the preparation of line maps from departmental aerial photographs to the Regional Departments as soon as sufficient staff for the purpose had been trained.

Reorganisation of the Department

Reorganisation of the Survey Department was begun in 1950 in order to cater for economic and political developments in the country, with a need for regionalisation and decentralisation from Lagos. Recruitment of more expatriate officers made it possible to commence the systematic mapping of 150,000 square miles photographed by the RAF. Ground control was commenced in November 1951, and in a significant move towards future development, a small topographical mapping drawing section was established at the Kaduna Survey office. This embryonic unit, accommodated in a mud hut, consisted of only one fully trained senior draughtsman and three partly trained juniors, plus one Nigerian surveyor and 3 Survey assistants-in-training in the field. They were initially engaged on the use of aerial photographs to produce maps for the construction of the new Kaduna-Keffi road and for ground control for geological mapping at Gombe.

In 1950-51 Provincial Offices were in operation at Jos, Kano and Minna and a fourth was added, in Benue, in a new building at Makurdi.

With the introduction of the new constitution during the latter part of 1951 there was a further devolution of authority to the Regional organisations. The Director of Survey, A.P.Mitchell, became Inspector-General and the three Regional Assistant Directors became Directors. The Inspector-General exercised important inspecting and advisory functions in respect of the Regional organisations and in addition retained executive responsibility for the central organisation which had four principal functions:-

1. National Triangulation and Precise Levelling.
2. Air Survey operations by the chartered Dove aircraft.
3. Map Production
4. Policy in connection with photography carried out by the RAF and map production by the D.C.S.

Staffing Matters

During the 1930s the economic recession in Europe had an impact abroad. Nigeria suffered as a result of the world depression and the slump in the prices of agricultural products which followed. In 1931, retrenchment (a 28% reduction, which included 15 surveyors and one draughtsman) and early retirements were imposed and these, together with a virtual embargo on recruitment of expatriate staff, inevitably meant a slowing down of progress. The North, with few indigenous survey staff, was left at a great disadvantage. These shortages and an apparent unwillingness of Nigerians to take up the profession, were always a major constraint. In Nigeria generally, the recruitment of indigenous staff had been disappointing and it was some time before the expatriate staff realised that the work carried out by professions such as civil engineering and surveying did not appeal to the Nigerians in the same way. 'Boy scouting' activities were not for them and this was particularly true in the North where a strong conservative cultural background produced an even greater reluctance to take up many European practices. In 1932 there were 39 European officers, 56 Nigerian surveyors, 7 Nigerian computers, 37 Nigerian draughtsmen and 7 lithographers and sunprinters, of whom 8 European and 16 Nigerian surveyors plus 16 draughtsmen were on cadastral work in the Northern Provinces.

1933 saw more retrenchments and European staffing was down 46% on the 1930 level and the Nigerian 17% below. The strength of the department remained constant in 1934 while, at Kaduna, the Cadastral branch had 11 European surveyors, 14 Nigerian surveyors and 12 draughtsmen. The Lagos Lithographic section in 1935 consisted of 2 European officers, 6 Nigerian lithographers and 2 apprentices.

Like most other colonial departments, Survey still had insufficient staff and money to go ahead with the development it could see was needed but 1936 saw something of a return to prosperity and an increasing demand for services in every branch. There was no increase in staff in 1937 but nearly every branch showed an increase in production. There was a total of 23 European surveyors at the end of the year. The same economic strategy continued in 1938 with no increase in the numerical strength of European staff. There were 3 in Lands, 23 in Survey, 4 in Reproduction, and 3 probationers in training in the UK, and 49 Nigerian surveyors.

Almost inevitably the post-war period repeated the former problems of staff shortages and lack of recruits, but in 1947, as more money became available, staffing levels began to show signs of improvement. Then, as always, serious disruption to work could be caused by leave, local crises, climatic events and illness. The number of draughtsmen was small, equipment meagre and methods and processes antiquated. The British Ordnance Survey provided two technicians, and then Brig. F.O.Metford retired from the O.S. and came out to transform the map reproduction section. When N.S.Clouston left Nigeria in 1947-48 and A.J.Morley took over in an acting capacity his establishment consisted of 24 senior service surveyors, but there were 13 vacancies. This situation was unlikely to change in the short term because of the world-wide demand for graduates. He had 55 junior surveyor posts but 20 of them were vacant. In the drawing section was O.Kanno, who was later to serve with the Northern Nigerian Survey.

The new establishment post of Survey Assistant in the junior service was introduced during the year to meet the continuing demands for Government surveys. They were employed as technical assistants in the field, were required to possess School Certificate qualifications and were given every measure of assistance possible to enable them to obtain full qualifications for appointment as Surveyors.

Mitchell, the newly appointed Director, and late Director of Surveys, Palestine, assumed duty in 1948. Two junior service surveyors, F.M.Wey and W.Gascoyne were promoted to the senior service. Mitchell was not one of the most admired of the Survey Directors. The late John Pugh expressed the following opinion and had strong views on the attitude of others members of staff in Lagos:-

> 'I do not know the details of Mitchell's background. In the Staff List, he gave his qualifications as CMG FRGS - the latter, as you know, is available to anyone who pays an annual subscription to the Royal Geographical Society, so I assume he had nothing else. I had the impression that he did not know very much about surveying but had probably spent most of his time in Palestine dealing with land tenure (much the more likely to be rewarded with a CMG !)
>
> The Nigerian Department was then officially the Department of Lands and Survey. The Lands side was self-contained, run very efficiently by Buckingham (Assistant Director, Lands), Hewitt and Hunter, who kept very much to themselves. All three left after Mitchell arrived - apart from anything else, they were all very obviously from a very different social stratum.
>
> When I joined the University College (Ibadan) it was with the expectation of transferring eight years of pension rights, that being the normal arrangement for Government staff who moved across. I later found that this had been stopped by Mitchell, and I protested to the Civil Service Commissioner, who was also Chairman of the College Council - that got me nowhere.
>
> Mitchell was one example of difficulties not attributable to Nigeria or Nigerians. There were others. I had one senior colleague, a canny Scot, not a graduate, who served his probationary three years, mainly, on cadastral work in the Lagos area, I believe. Once confirmed in his appointment he developed recurrent knee trouble which cut short all attempted postings to work in the field. Too junior to be an Assistant Director in West, East or North, and too inexperienced for the office job in the Minesfield, he was made officer in charge of "X" Section in Lagos H.Q., dealing with all the non-technical aspects of the Department - running the clerical staff and testing for promotion, coping with labour, arranging leave and passages for senior staff, handling transport, keeping staff records, looking after

instruments, etc. This became his permanent position, with a Government house in Ikoyi and his wife and daughter always with him - a nice social life, which included tennis with the Governor twice a week (his knee, oddly enough, never gave trouble in Lagos). He was excellent company, and popular with everyone. For some months in 1944 I was pulled out of bush to take over the Computing Section in H.Q. from another Senior Surveyor, and shared a room with O.i/c "X" Section. At that time he was also running the Drawing Office while the Chief Draughtsman was on leave, and he would appear in our shared office at about 10.00 sit down to a desk with usually three tall piles of files in the in tray, clear the lot by 11.00 and say "What about coffee ?" I marvelled at his efficiency. Then one day he came in, said that as he had done his 18 months (I had then done 2½ years) he was sailing that afternoon, going on leave. I was to take over "X" Section as well as my own. I soon discovered how he had coped so rapidly with files - he just kept them moving around!'

The high level of vacancies in 1948, 9 in the senior service and 27 in the junior service, continued to have very serious effects not only on the progress of development, mining and other surveys, but also on the Nigerianisation of the department. Junior staff needed senior staff guidance if they were to assume greater responsibilities.

In 1949-50 two expatriate probationers joined the department and the Survey Assistant establishment was increased from 25 to 50, with further increases envisaged. The total establishment consisted of 26 senior service officers, 275 junior service, 137 other employees and 380 skilled labourers. Typical salaries were Director of Surveys £1,750; Senior Surveyor £1,170 - £1300; Surveyor £660- £1300;Chief Draughtsman £985 - £1,075; Junior Service Surveyors £170 - £600; Survey Assistants £96 - £250; Chainmen £72 - £108; Messengers £42 - £64; and skilled labourers 11d to 2s 8d per day.

A.J.Morley was Acting Director of Survey in 1950-51 and there were 32 senior service officers in post, 313 junior service, 148 others and 61 skilled labourers.

In 1951-52 expatriates were still in charge of the Lagos mapping and printing operations. Brig. F.O.Metford was Map Production Officer, a post he continued to hold right through to 1959, J.W.Hewish the Chief Draughtsman, E.Gresty the Chief Lithographer and N.Fisher the Chief Photographer. In 1952 they were responsible for the introduction of 'scribing' using the new plastic drawing medium, Astrafoil; the installation of a new press; a Rotaprint machine; a "Crabtree" offset machine; and for ordering a new process camera.

Shortage of Nigerian Surveyors for bushwork

In her memoirs of the year spent in the bush with her husband Keith in Sokoto in 1946-47, Nora Hunter remarked that a promise had been made by the Director of Surveys that all Nigerian surveyors returning from the services, all of whom had served for long periods without leave in Burma and East Africa, would be allowed to do a tour in Lagos before going to bush. These people obviously made personal and domestic arrangements which it was unfair to expect them to forego but used these arrangements as arguments for not being posted to remote places. Those who had not served in the services reported sick in order to avoid unpopular postings and some left the service to set themselves up as freelance surveyors which would give them a life in or near the large towns. The result was that expatriates were left to do the arduous bushwork. Fears were raised even then what this might mean in the future when Nigerians would have greater responsibility for Survey. Few were ever likely to go willingly to enjoy the discomforts of bush life and many of them, being townsmen, were more out of their element in the bush than the Europeans. Such concessions were not available for ex-Service expatriates. The Director had said quite categorically that he had every intention of sending expatriates to bush, and he kept his word.

Funding for Survey Work

It has long been the opinion of surveyors that governments will more readily finance work which can be seen to have some immediate tangible benefit than commit expenditure to systematic and protracted survey for mapping which may appear to serve no immediate purpose, other than to keep pace with man-made and natural changes. Governments seem to be reluctant to accept that the work of a Survey Department is **never** finished. Financing of surveying and mapping in support of specific development schemes, for geological survey, and for construction work, is generally more readily approved than work which serves as a long term information resource. Map users with little understanding of the mapping process were heard to complain about the time it took to produce maps after aerial photographs had been obtained; most thought it was a simple tracing process easily performed by low paid junior staff with a minimum of training. The inevitable consequence of this attitude was that surveys were often carried out in too much of a hurry and schemes might be inaugurated with inadequate or poor quality ground information, leading in turn to poor planning and costly mistakes. Nigeria was only an exception to this common experience when, with considerable technical and financial assistance from abroad, combined with the post World War II efforts of its later North Regional and Federal Departments, it was provided with the wherewithal and the infrastructure to embark upon a sustained programme of systematic topographic and townships mapping.

There had been no salary revisions for anyone in government service between 1922 and 1950, survey instruments had fallen into a bad state of repair during the war and surveyors in the field were sometimes issued with equipment that was far from satisfactory and were obliged to use their skills to carry out essential repairs. There had been no replacements since the war, and since the slump in the 1930s, the department had been unable to afford to buy very much new field equipment. Theodolites needed continual, careful and intricate adjustment in order to achieve the accuracies expected. Major repairs to survey instruments had traditionally been done in Europe but this was becoming increasingly expensive and inconvenient and long delays could be experienced. A proposal was made to establish a repair workshop in Lagos, sponsored by private enterprise. Such a facility was established by F.Steiner, the Wild agent.

On schemes begun before the war many beacons had been tampered with or destroyed by local people, which resulted in yet more expense, sometimes amounting to thousands of pounds in re-establishment and re-observation. Provincial administrations and District Chiefs were asked to use their influence to ensure that beacons were not interfered with, but there could never be a guarantee that sufficient protection could be provided, especially if local people were convinced in their own minds that the surveyors had, in the course of their 'mysterious' work, concealed money in the ground beneath their beacons.

The benefits of the British 1940 'Colonial Development and Welfare Act' were not felt in Nigeria until after the war when grants were made which permitted staff increases and the implementation of a ten year capital development plan for agricultural development schemes and the improvement of public services and infrastructure. This assistance was augmented with earnings from agricultural exports to fund many general improvements such as better water supplies, markets, irrigation, health services, education and, amongst many other things, surveying. In 1947-48 a surveyor was engaged at Damaturu with a soil survey team investigating a ground-nut scheme; a year later there was levelling for a Rice Mission near Bida; and aerial photography, with ground control by D.M.(Donald) MacPhee and A.D.(Denis) Willey, was started for the Kontagora Groundnuts Scheme (later known as the Niger Agricultural Project).

The Kontagora scheme covered an area of 6,500 square miles, bounded in the west by the River Niger, in the south by the railway, in the east by the Tegina and Jimaku 1:125,000 standard sheets and extended to the north as far as 10° 30'. It was photographed by the RAF 82 Photographic Recce. Squadron, improving the quality of photographs obtained on an earlier sortie, between the end of November and the end of January 1949. Students from the Survey School at Ibadan worked there during their summer vacation under the supervision of a School Instructor and another senior surveyor. Normal survey parties then took over and by early 1949 five secondary trig points and 300 miles of tertiary theodolite traversing had been done. Preliminary 1:62,500 uncontoured maps of the project area were prepared by the Directorate of Colonial Surveys and printed in Lagos.

In 1951 O.Arikpo, the Minister for Land, Survey and Local Government remarked that Survey Departments have been regarded as 'Cinderella' organisations for many years and the first to suffer severe cuts at times of economic difficulty. It had only recently been fully realised that adequate and accurate surveys were essential if there was to be no delay to the 10 year Development Plan for

Nigeria, and funding was being improved. One of the problems was that as much as 10% of the Survey Department's annual expenditure went towards the cost of free services to other Government Departments from whom reciprocal services could not be expected. Such expenditure was always difficult to plan and placed a considerable burden upon departmental production and staffing.

The total cost of running the department in 1947-48 had been £121,440, of which £26,112 was for field surveys and £23,682 for drawing. Revenue receipts for 1947-48 were £3,438, rising to £5,842 in the following year and £11,440 in 1949-50. By 1952-53 it had reached £13,000, largely due to increases in Minesfield work and the growing efficiency and increased output of junior technical staff. By 1953-54 it was up to £18,637 and increasing. Revenue continued to grow in 1954-55 and reached £20,004, and £21,000 in 1956-57. By 1958-59 revenue and expenditure were still not large in comparison with overall Federal Government figures.

Britain has been criticised for not doing enough to aid the development of the country until the last few years before independence, but this ignores the fact that local progress had always been declared as dependent upon its fiscal capacity, aided by considered special injections of aid when necessary. In the North, remarkable progress had, however, been made from the feudal, peasant-based economy of the past to the arrival of roads, railways, water supplies and commerce of the 1930s and the remarkable progress after the second world war. Inevitably much of the national revenues had been absorbed by Lagos and the other important centres and there was little left for the remote areas and the smaller departments like Surveying where much resourcefulness was needed to make any sort of meaningful progress.

Progress and development in Nigeria had traditionally depended much on the agricultural and mineral wealth of the North. The nation was unable to finance its own development from its taxation system and the days of oil revenues and international aid and finance had not arrived. Inadequate finance had always restricted the recruitment of expatriates to train local people. It has to be admitted that over the years the British surveying effort failed to meet the needs of colonial administration because of the low priority given to investment and staffing. It was therefore greatly to Nigeria's credit that, as independence was attained, it heeded the needs of developers and appreciated the benefits which would accrue from a comprehensive base of topographic mapping.

The Establishment of Federal and Regional Departments

In 1952 a revised Survey Ordinance was enacted which had the effect of transferring from the centre to the Regions powers to make regulations on all Survey matters other than fees and the licensing and discipline of surveyors.

Up to independence in 1960 the Survey Department of Nigeria had about ten heads and each one of them had made attempts at reorganisation, but mandatory changes did not take place until the Richards Constitution in 1952, the Federal Constitution in 1954 and Self Government in 1957. The changes of 1954 were those which resulted in the creation of the **Northern Nigerian Survey** (the title, preferred by Hunter, which first came into official use in the 1955-56 Departmental Annual Report) and the **Federal Survey Department**. In 1960 the Northern Nigerian Survey, and the other Regional Survey Departments, became independent of Federal Surveys, when surveying and mapping were placed in the concurrent legislative list.

Elsewhere, the Western Region's Survey Department was established in 1952 with W.G.(Gordon) Wookey as Director. Wookey was a pre-war Bristol graduate who arrived in Nigeria just before the war, then served in the West African Frontier Force, and attained the rank of Major. In 1953 W.B.(Brian) Till, who has contributed to the section of this work covering Survey Training, joined the staff of the Department which included Gordon Arnett (also a war-time Major who served under Bomford - *"we all wondered what he was always working away at and then his book came out")*, S.A.Ishola Bucknor (who was a Sergeant-Major in the West African contingent in Burma and who sadly suffered a stroke and died whilst Acting for the Director), William Gascoyne (who succeeded Wookey as Director) and Oluwole Coker, recently returned from the U.K. with an Honours Mathematics degree and Professor Thompson's post-graduate Diploma in Surveying. There were several other of the older generation of Nigerian surveyors who had joined the Nigerian Survey as young men in the 1930s including Adebayo Morgan, Ola Bamgbose, Omorogie and Arubayi; also several veteran draughtsmen and a specialist computer. Later, J.R.(Jim) Smith was on the staff of the Department, serving for three years from 1962 in Ibadan and Oyo.

Initially the Western Department's headquarters in Ibadan was located in premises rented from an Italian construction company but moved into a custom-built two-storey building at Agodi near the main Western Nigerian Government Secretariat buildings. A year or so later, in 1956, the Department also took over the top floor of the new Ministry of Lands four-storey block.

Much of the Department's time was taken up with cadastral matters, mainly Government acquisitions and layouts, processing of Licensed Surveyors' title surveys and land dispute surveys. It was a time of hectic development in Western Nigeria and a great deal of such work was undertaken. Provincial offices were established at Benin, Warri, Ikeja, Abeokuta, Akure, Ijebu-Ode and Oyo, each undertaking cadastral and township surveys. In 1956 Gordon Wookey obtained funds for and initiated a topographical programme; secondary framework traverses between existing primaries were run by Brian Till, Alan Haugh (on secondment from Federal Surveys), Olu Adebekun (later Federal Director) and others, whilst a photogrammetric section was established within a specially-designed extension to the Departmental building.

The last published Nigeria Surveys staff list before the regional departments were hived off was for 1953. Most of the senior staff were expatriates, many of whom had served in the North. Several of them elected to transfer to the North when they were given an option to do so. The Inspector-General of Surveys was H.A.Stamers Smith who had previously served for 21 years in Ceylon and 6 years in Kenya. There were three Directors of Surveys, K.H.(Keith)Hunter serving in the Northern Provinces at Kaduna, J.H.Keast at Enugu, and, as mentioned above, W.G.Wookey at Ibadan. Hunter became the Surveyor-General of the Northern Region. Of the six Senior Surveyors, two were transferred to the North. They were K.M.(Keith) Sargeant, originally appointed in 1939, and who was serving at Jos at the time, and D.C.(Douglas) Eva DFC *(Photo.21)*, who was one of those who attended Bristol University for survey training after his distinguished war service in the RAF. Eva had arrived in the North in 1949. Under Hunter's leadership he became the driving force behind the establishment of the topographic mapping unit of the Northern Nigerian Survey, and became Surveyor-General when Hunter retired in 1959.

J.F.A.(Alan) Lees, who served in the Navy during the war, arrived in 1947. He served for a while in the Northern Provinces in the early 1950s but remained in Lagos after the split. *(Photo.8 shows the staff of the Kaduna office in 1950, marking the transfer of J.F.A.Lees to the Minesfield Division at Jos.)* There were 22 surveyors in post in 1953 of whom 10 transferred to the North. They included the veteran Nigerian surveyor F.T.M.(Frank) Wey, who had been first appointed as a junior service surveyor in 1926; A.D.(Denis) Willey *(Photo. 229)*, a contemporary of Eva, who served in the Army and who eventually succeeded Eva as Surveyor-General in the North; R.W.(Roger) Pring who had arrived in 1948; and J.P.W.(Paul) Ward who was also in the Army during the war, attended Long Survey Course No.4 at the School of Military Survey in 1950, arrived in Nigeria in 1951, and was posted to the North. He succeeded Willey as Surveyor-General of Northern Nigeria and was still in that position at the time of the dissolution of the Northern Nigerian Survey in 1968.

Other names on the list who later joined the Northern Nigerian Survey, or worked in the North, were K.J.(Kevin) O'Shaughnessy, who had arrived in 1950 and went to serve in the Cameroons; V.T.(Trevor) Brokenshire, D.(Derek) Woolhouse and D.R.Jones who arrived in 1951 and were posted to Jos, where, at the time, D.M.(Donald) MacPhee was in charge; the Dutchman H.W.(Harry) Rentema *(Photo.11)*, a contract surveyor appointed in 1952, and T.A (Thadeus) Moszynski *(Photo.206)* and the Dane N.K.V.(Kjeld) Hansen *(Photo. 16)* who both arrived in 1953, were all posted to Jos. W.B.(Brian) Till did not join the Northern Nigerian Survey but moved to Kaduna Polytechnic from the West after 1968. O.(Olu) Kanno *(Photo.21)* was a Nigerian Assistant Map Production Officer, based at Jos, who transferred to the Northern Nigerian Survey.

Federal Survey Department

Federal Surveys inherited the responsibility for survey work of national interest in the following broad areas:-

-Control surveys
-Topographic (including aerial) survey
-Map reproduction
-Liaison with other Survey organisations
-Control of the Survey profession as specified in the Survey Ordinance 1918 and subsequent
  legislation
-Survey of international boundaries

The Department comprised the following sections:-

-Field
-Air Survey
-Cartography
-Photographic
-Lithographic
-Cadastral (for Lagos Territory)
-Computation and Clerical
-Stores and General

In the first annual report (for 1958-59) to be produced since the new organisation came into being in 1955, the Director of Federal Surveys explained that organisational difficulties had prevented the publication of reports in the intervening years. It contained a foreword by Alhaji Inuwa Wada M.H.R., the Federal Minister of Works and Surveys who reiterated the familiar story about Survey being essential to development and the difficulties of attracting young Nigerians into the profession. He said *"The work of a surveyor is an exacting one. He must spend long periods under camp conditions and his work depends on a high standard of professional integrity. This, however, should be regarded by young Nigerians not as a deterrent, but as a challenge............"* He repeated this message in the 1959-60 report when recruitment was still at a much lower level than was hoped and when resignations remained fairly high, which meant a great wastage of effort in training. In the senior grades, three officers had been recruited, but five had left, and amongst the juniors 63 were recruited, but the same number retired or resigned.

The lag in recruitment between 1939 and 1949 had given rise to a gap between experienced staff and relatively inexperienced or newly recruited staff, and there was a serious danger that the wastage of expatriate staff would exceed the rate at which new staff could be recruited and trained. The establishment was by no means adequate for the existing and future programmes and increases were proposed, including posts requiring experienced and specialist officers for instruction and supervision. It was also recognised that with advances in methods and equipment for mapping since 1945 there might be a reduced requirement for junior staff in some fields.

Cartographic production remained high in spite of training and recruitment difficulties. There were problems too with insufficient staff in the computing section, where a disincentive was the fact that the computers were classified and paid as clerical staff, an issue which was being addressed by making them interchangeable with field assistants.

Staffing problems even extended to the labour force. Long distance travel obviously made vehicular transport essential and more commonplace, though there seldom seemed to be enough vehicles available. Labourers and carriers were no answer to long distance travel and in many areas were difficult to obtain anyway.

H.H.Stamers Smith, the Director, retired in 1958 and was replaced by R.B.(Brook) McVilly; T.A.Bankole retired a year later; D.M.Y Armstrong was seconded to the Eastern Region as Acting Director of Surveys; D.Woolhouse, Senior Surveyor, was seconded to the Southern Cameroons in 1959, as were T.L.Butler and N.J.Field. There were 18 posts in the senior establishment of which six were filled by Nigerians, eight by expatriates, and four were vacant.

Exemplifying the work carried out by expatriates, Colin Emmott made a significant contribution to the Federal surveying programme in Northern Nigeria. He worked on secondary triangulation and geodetic levelling in the Borgu Division of Ilorin Province and did a pre-construction survey for the Kainji dam site on the River Niger. He completed part of the Nigeria-Dahomey boundary survey and provided control for the 1:50,000 scale mapping programme in Ilorin Province. He used a Wild T4 theodolite for observations to strengthen the primary triangulation at Sokoto and Jos, did photo-pointing and levelling for the 1:50,000 scale mapping of the Zungeru-Minna-Abuja area, and ground control for 10,000 square miles of contoured topographic mapping in Sokoto Province, and similar work in Benue based on the Federal field office at Makurdi.

Kaiama and Makurdi were in use as field headquarters in 1960-61. *(Photo.9 shows a Federal Surveyor, E.R.(Dick) Rogers being entertained by Sarkin Kaiama.)*

D.Woolhouse, who became Acting Director in 1961-62 after the departure of McVilly, retired in 1963 and the incoming Deputy Director R.O.(Oluwole) Coker declared this event *"the end of the expatriate regime in the Survey Department"* It was appropriate, and of course entirely expected that he, as Nigeria's first graduate surveyor in 1952, should become the first indigenous Surveyor-General. In his striking attire, his flamboyant, cordial and slightly arrogant figure was seen at international surveying meetings in many parts of the world for several years to come. Neil Field remarks:-

> *'He was the right man in the right place at the right time, no doubt about it. At about the same time as putting this declaration on the public record Olu called a meeting in his office of all the expatriate surveyors in Federal Surveys, there were still quite a lot of us, to reassure us that we were needed, would be promoted when appropriate, and given our due responsibilities. A pledge that he honoured. I retained my post as o/c of a Field HQ, as did Colin Emmott, and Laurie Butler remained number 3 in Lagos, none of us was ever made to feel unwelcome. It needed a strong personality to deal with the transition from colonial to representative government, and to reassure expatriate staff while encouraging Nigerians. Considering the baggage that he had to carry and the already emerging tribalism of government it is surprising that he managed so well. It was fashionable at one time to mock at his idiosyncrasies, which included always wearing the agbada even in deepest Cambridgeshire. But as Pat Carmody said to me once (I paraphrase), people can mock Chief Dr R.Oluwole Coker but he is listened to and respected by academics and heads of other survey organisataons as the personification of Nigerian Surveys. Few others could have done as much.'*

For over 50 years Survey had been pushed ahead as fast as finance and manpower had allowed by the devoted efforts of three or four generations of British surveyors. Much of the essential groundwork had been done and much more was now known about the problems of mapping and surveying. Money and assistance, which started to come in from western governments and private investment, allowed advances which had not previously been possible, and much better educated young people were beginning to come out of the schools, but field activities were being restricted by the departure of expatriates. Senior Surveyors in post were J.D.Willis, T.L.Butler, A.C.Ogo, A.J.Bull, N.J.Field, D.A.Omoigue, and D.E.Mbata. Surveyors were M.A.R.Cooper, C.Emmott, J.O.Daramola, P.A.O.Adeleye, and V.A.Obafemi. M.J.Miles was Principal Surveyor (Photogrammetry).

Part 4 of this work contains an account written by Jennifer Cooper of her experiences in bush in 1963 while accompanying her husband M.A.R. (Michael) Cooper engaged on re-defining the scale of the Nigerian primary triangulation.

In 1963-64, as the shortage of field staff continued, the Director appointed seven Philippine surveyors (J.L.Nicomedes, L.S.Sinsioco, X.B.Valerio, E.M.Dayrit, R.Y.Lacandola, J.Sacrimento, and V.Libranda) to join his staff of three Principal Surveyors (O.A.Adua, T.L.Butler and M.J.Miles), five Senior Surveyors (N.J.Field, D.A.Omoigue, C.T.Horsfall, D.E.Mbata and C.Emmott) and 21 Surveyors including J.O.Daramola and M.A.R.Cooper.

The last Federal Report was produced for the year 1963-64. Intended later reports were victims of the situation in the country from 1966 onwards, when the Federal Survey Department went into serious decline as an effective national mapping organisation. As Nigeria gradually divided into more and more semi-autonomous States, each looking after its own cadastre, the Federal Survey Department continued its responsibility for geodetic surveys, national mapping, national and inter-state boundaries and Survey policy generally.

....

KEITH HUNTER

In 1928, when Capt.T.J.Water was Surveyor-General of Nigeria and J.Calder Wood was his Deputy, K.H.Hunter, who was destined to become the 'father' of the Northern Nigerian Survey, its first Surveyor-General, was appointed as a surveyor and worked first of all in the Cadastral Branch in the Eastern Division. In 1930 he carried out a survey for the Yola trading layout, but he was already involved in primary triangulation reconnaissance on the Yola-Bauchi chain and went on to complete the Yola-Naraguta chain in 1931.

He was remembered by B.A.Babb, a former Education Officer, who met him at Yola:-

> '................a surveyor arrived having completed the first mapping survey from the north of Adamawa Province to the Provincial HQ at Yola. I was very interested in his account of the work entailed and of the long periods without contact with fellow Europeans. I myself had just spent long periods on anti-locust work, (little good did it do !) without European contact, but his time knocked mine into the shade.'

Photo: Nora Hunter

In 1934 he was on the eastern end of the Minna-Naraguta chain, and also on the Ilorin-Sokoto-Chafe chain to cover the Niger and Sokoto mining areas. Until 1939 he spent nearly all his time on triangulation, much of it in reconnaissance, and resumed this kind of work when he returned from military service. In 1946 he worked in the Sokoto area, providing ground control over a little known area of about 14,000 square miles for mapping from RAF photography. Maps of the area were in demand for Forestry, Geological and Administrative use but, more importantly, on account of its potential mineral wealth. It was said that diamonds, gold and other precious metals had been found there.

His wife Nora accompanied him on this tour and kept a detailed diary, which she later produced as "*Where my caravan has rested*", a graphically written, human and non-technical reminder of what it was like to work in remote areas. Her descriptions of everyday events, the 'nasties' and the weather bring back vivid memories to all who did the same sort of thing.

From Sokoto Province he moved to Jos in 1948 and then on to Kaduna where he was promoted from Senior Surveyor to Assistant Director in 1950. As the head of the branch in Kaduna, he continued his interest in triangulation and his staff were still carrying out this work until the end of the 1950's. It was under his leadership that the Northern Nigerian Survey embarked upon its remarkable growth and developed its reputation and ability.

It was Hunter's inspiration which produced the Northern Nigerian Survey logo, and the brass badges for the uniforms and caps of chainmen and messengers, which remains the symbol of the organisation for those who remember it *(Photo. 10)*. Quoting Paul Ward:-

> *"Hunter, off his own bat, got the politicians to accept the NORTHERN NIGERIAN SURVEY logo on vehicles, paper heads, etc. from the very start."*

His own practical experience gave him sympathy for the man in the bush, though he had his critics because of his demanding, perhaps dated, and uncompromising ways. He was a very strong character and did not suffer fools gladly. Some were in awe of him; others disliked his authoritarian, strict and intolerant attitude; but there can be no denying that he was responsible for setting the Northern Nigerian Survey on its successful path.

His retirement, and final departure from Nigeria in 1959, coincided more or less with the completion of the last chain in the Nigerian primary network, work on which he had been occupied for much of his career; the 'P' chain along the Benue valley from Lokoja east towards Makurdi and beyond.

He continued to show an interest in Northern control and demonstrated a good retention of detail when enquiries were made in 1963 about his thoughts on the extension of control into the flat lands of the North-East. He died in 1988, 29 years after his retirement.

Hunter produced his first Northern Region Survey Report for the year 1952-53 when the title *NORTHERN NIGERIAN SURVEY* had not yet come into use. This, and his subsequent reports until 1957, found their way to Britain and are available in some principal reference libraries. The only report which has come to light for the period 1957-60 is a combined one covering those years and can be seen at the Ordnance Survey Library at Maybush, Southampton. It seems very unlikely that the annual reports produced by his successors after Independence were sent to Britain and, if they still exist, are likely only to be found in the older archives of Kaduna Polytechnic, the Federal Survey Department, or Nigerian National Archives at Kaduna or Lagos.

THE NORTHERN NIGERIAN SURVEY

Early Developments in the North

Surveying in connection with the grant of mining concessions had commenced on the Bauchi Plateau in 1905 and some time after the establishment of the new town of Jos in 1912, a branch office was set up there to deal with Minesfield surveys. Thereafter the Plateau continued to receive a great deal of attention from surveyors involved in operating the Minesfield cadastre, and the office at Jos remained second in importance only to Kaduna right up to the dissolution of the Northern Nigerian Survey in 1968.

It has long been assumed that the name *Kaduna*, Lugard's chosen site for his new northern headquarters, derives from the Hausa for "crocodiles". No settlement with that name was marked on the very early War Office maps and in 1902 it was shown only as a crossing point of the River Kaduna, or Lafun as it was otherwise then known, of a caravan route which came up the Gurara River from the Niger through Abuja on its way to Zaria. Although Lugard is said to have chosen an empty site, it is now the view of the Gbagyi (*Gwari*) people that it had never been uninhabited. They maintain that it comes from their own word *kadudna* meaning "crossing the river of snails". '*Gwari*' is a Hausa term which refers to a category of non-Hausa and in 1979 it was agreed that 'Gbagyi' is the correct term and is now used by the people themselves *(Photo. 217)*.

In 1927 Kaduna Junction, or Kaduna South as it later became known, had been the headquarters of the Northern Division of Nigerian Railways, then a Government department. Simple houses for Railway staff such as for plate layers, engine drivers and permanent way inspectors had been built in a curve, some with lawns sloping down to the river. Some of the bungalows stood on Eaglesome Road, named after Sir John Eaglesome, a member of the Public Works Department at Nigeria's creation in 1900, who worked on the Baro-Kano railway in 1907 and who was Director of Railways and Works from 1912 to 1919. Many of these old buildings were in the course of time destined to be taken over by the Survey Department for use as offices and houses for senior staff *(Photos. 17 and 213)*. A large bungalow by the river was to become the Surveyor-General's residence *(Photo.212)*. It had two wings with a central dining-room and lounge and was therefore very convenient for guests. It had a large, cool verandah on which were pots of flowers. The compound too was large and well set out with shady trees, one of them a magnificent Flamboyant, and many fruit trees, orange, grapefruit, lime, guava, mango. A path ran down to the edge of the river, a wide, swirling brown torrent during the wet season but a shallow braided stream flowing between large rocks in the dry season *(Photos. 220 and 221)*. The river was said to contain many crocodiles, though they were not often seen, and mosquitoes were, inevitably, quite a problem.

It was long felt that the spacious layout of Kaduna had an air of impermanence about it but it was obviously there to stay, botanical gardens were planted and an Army swimming pool was installed before the war and was used to train African troops, en route to Burma, how to swim.

Regionalisation

The Survey Department at Lagos passed through a transitional stage of reorganisation and expansion in 1950 to enable it to fulfil the considerable survey requirements arising from the economic and political developments of the country. It was considered neither feasible nor desirable, with greatly expanded activities and staff, to maintain detailed control over all the departmental ramifications from the centralised headquarters in the capital. Arrangements were therefore begun for full decentralisation or 'Regionalisation' from 1st April 1950 and, to facilitate this, some structural alterations were made to the Survey buildings at Kaduna South.

H.Isherwood had been Director but left in 1950. The Kaduna staff at the time consisted of an Assistant Director of Surveys, an Assistant Director plus a Senior Surveyor for seven months, six or seven junior service surveyors, three survey assistants, a senior draughtsman, six junior draughtsmen, one or two computers, one sunprinter and eight clerks.

By 1950-51 the land surveying activities of the central department were rapidly being decentralised and, with the imminent introduction of a new Constitution for Nigeria, distinct Regional Departments for purposes of Regional autonomy were being established in order to develop a systematic approach to regional land problems. With decentralisation in mind, the new Provincial office was built in Makurdi, while offices at Minna and Kano (the N.A. Survey School) were housed in temporary buildings.

The Northern Region Department became controlled from Kaduna by an Assistant Director of Surveys, K.H.(Keith) Hunter, assisted by a Senior Surveyor, with responsibility for Regional administration, finance, map sales, stores, records, plan production, surveys in the Kaduna area, and the Survey Training Centre and the Provincial Offices.

In 1951-52 a start was made on the new administration and drawing offices in Kaduna South and they were completed in 1952-53. Alterations were then commenced to the old cadastral drawing office and a new store was begun.

In September 1952 a revised Survey Ordinance was enacted which had the effect of transferring from the centre to the Regions powers to make regulations on all Survey matters, other than fees and the licensing and discipline of surveyors. Revised regulations were prepared and submitted to the Northern Government.

In 1952-53 Mallam Isa Kaita, Minister of Works in the Northern Region, said:-

> 'The Survey Department used to consider itself rather neglected ....little attention was paid to the need for surveying...............when funds were short the Department was the first to suffer ....it is necessary to build up an organisation for the Region almost from nothing for an area so vast that the surveying still required is almost limitless.'

Although the Department was not much in the public eye, its services were considered a vital component of Regional development. The emergence of the Northern Nigerian Survey as the most effective surveying force ever to exist in the North began as Colonial Development and Welfare funds started to provide the wherewithal for projects which had always been beyond the Region's capacity, but the familiar handicap of staff shortage was ever present. There was recognition of the great quantity of fieldwork to be done as the office work for the Minesfield and for Certificates of Occupancy rapidly increased and occupied most of the available personnel. The Department could only deal with the needs of two or three Provinces at a time, so while in some areas work may have been substantially up to date, unavoidable delays would pile up elsewhere. Plans to provide large scale cadastral plans of all the larger towns were thwarted. Gusau, Bida, Makurdi and Oturkpo were being mapped from aerial photographs and there was some revision of the Jos and Minna mapping but most staff were still engaged on individual property surveys. Cadastral efficiency would have been enhanced by more extensive and up-to-date large scale maps and ground control networks.

In 1953-54 the Survey Department in the North became part of the Ministry of Social Development and Surveys under its Minister Shettima Kashim, a Kanuri. He said that it was clear from recent speeches in the Legislature that the importance of the Survey Department was becoming more appreciated by the general public. He reiterated that accurate survey was an essential preliminary to the development of the natural resources of the Region and the extension of its communications. A number of projects planned which would materially increase the production of export crops and food hung fire because staff was not available to undertake the necessary survey. The flow of junior technical assistants was adequate in number but most of them had insufficient basic education to allow them to become surveyors. It was therefore a matter of concern that the recruitment of qualified survey staff still lagged, and it was important that every step was taken to recruit senior staff, preferably Northern Nigerians, to supervise the training of juniors. This statement appeared not to recognise the reality of the fact that senior Nigerian staff needed not only to be recruited but needed lengthy training and experience themselves before they would be in a position to supervise others. As the future was to show, few Northerners were destined to rise to this position, indeed surveying continued to be a career which, because of its arduous, even degrading, nature would never appeal to the educated and qualified

Northerner. In the early days of Northern Nigeria, the strong chiefs and the Islamic organisation had given the North an advantage over the more primitive and anarchic tribal societies of the South, but by the 1940s the situation was largely reversed. The European approach to commerce and education had been absorbed by the Southern cultures and had given the area far more competence in trade and political organisation than the North. The absorption of these influences by the North was much more slow in coming. When Regional self-government came in the late 1950s this process had advanced little and the mode of administration which evolved was inevitably more like an advanced Native Authority, led by a sprinkling of educated and capable aristocrats.

The work and the administration of the Survey Department had always been relatively free of direct political influence. It was now accepted that Ministers, although perhaps unable to fully understand the technical activities for which they had been given responsibility, and who were a little suspicious of the independent outlook and professional pride of Departmental heads, nevertheless had the power to inspect and comment on the work of the Department. In about 1954-55, constitutional changes meant Ministers needed to become more involved in professional matters, take more responsibility for the departments which lay within their portfolios and, through the appointment of former Administrative Officers as Permanent Secretaries, exercise more control over technical and professional affairs. Many surveyors, especially those who had served for long periods in the bush, had gradually developed interests in the country and its people which extended beyond their professional duties, but most felt that politics were almost irrelevant to what they were doing and none of their business. For them the production of maps and plans continued to take pride of place, and they accepted that Ministers had the right to inspect, comment and exert more influence upon the work of their department, in fact they rather welcomed such attention and the strengthening it might bring.

When asked to comment on Northernisation, Trevor Brokenshire wrote:-

> 'My only involvement with "Nigerianisation" was visits with Keith Sargeant to the Ministry of Land and Surveys' Permanent Secretary. As far as I can recall the main object of our visits was to discuss and agree budgets. When, at the end if my time in Nigeria, I was in sole charge of the Survey Department (while more senior surveyors were on leave) I had little, if any, contact with politicians or their civil servants; the Department simply carried on as usual'.

Progress and Expansion

The Director of Surveys at Kaduna was assisted by a Deputy Director who was responsible for the Topographic Mapping Section, the Minesfield Division, Provincial Surveyors, the Cadastral Branch and the Administrative Section. A Senior Surveyor in the Topographic Section looked after the field parties, the computing and records and the drawing office and another Senior Surveyor, based on the Minesfield at Jos, was in charge of field parties, the drawing office, the examination section and the clerical unit there. Provincial Surveyors controlled Topographic, Minesfield and Cadastral staff placed under them. The officer in charge of the Cadastral Branch at Kaduna controlled field parties, an examination section and a drawing office, while an Administrative Assistant looked after the clerical unit, finance and stores. The emerging department enjoyed a relatively high degree of freedom from external control, and serving officers were given substantial independent discretion. Attitudes, experience, interests and talents all had a bearing on the way the different sections were run.

Until 1953-54 there was no provision for **original** mapping by the regions; only revision work. Regional departments had not had the capability or the technical staff, so the Federal Survey Department inherited the responsibility for national topographic mapping, aerial surveys and map reproduction. But with barely 20% of Nigeria mapped at a scale larger than 1:500,000, and wastage of staff starting to exceed the rate at which recruitment and training of senior staff could take place, more work was delegated to the North because of the strength, capability and dedication of senior staff there.

Protracted discussions took place as to the future of the Regional Survey Department vis-à-vis the Central (Federal) Department under a new Constitution. It was at first suggested that many of the responsibilities of the Regional Department should be transferred back to the Central Government, but eventually a compromise was reached and it was decided that the existing organisation of the Regional Department should remain and that the Central Department should hand over to the Region many of the duties for which it had been responsible since 1951.

In early 1954 the supervisory grades consisted of the Director, two Senior Surveyors, 12 Surveyors, one Map Production Officer, four Surveyors Grade II and four Surveyors Grades III & IV, giving a total of 24. There were vacancies for a Deputy Director, seven Surveyors, four Surveyors Grade II and 16 Surveyors Grades III & IV.

Shettima Kashim was much impressed by the rapid progress made with the construction and adaptation of Survey Headquarters buildings and recognised the need for improvements to the offices on the Plateau at Jos. At Kaduna in 1953-54, a large new store for technical equipment, of mud construction and using Survey labour, was completed, and the size of the printing shop doubled. An old building was gutted and reconditioned as a clerical office, the reconditioning of another old building to be occupied by the Cadastral section was begun and a mud building for the Town Planning unit was built. An old mud-built drawing office was re-roofed and reconditioned by the Department's own staff and its life thereby extended for a number of years and by June 1954 reconditioned drawing offices were occupied by the Cadastral and Topographic divisions. Plans were also in hand for the reconditioning and conversion of the remainder of the old buildings at Kaduna, and for the extension of the Minesfield branch office at Jos, but no new Provincial offices were built during the year.

The Minister was also pleased with the reduction of the arrears in the areas awaiting survey on the Plateau and the amount of fieldwork that had been done in the mapping of the Region, though concerned at the delays in map printing in Lagos. The planned installation of lithographic equipment would do much to speed up the production of the simpler maps in Kaduna and he thought it important the requisite buildings should be erected as soon as possible.

Shettima Kashim welcomed the co-operation of the British Directorate of Colonial Surveys (later to be renamed the Directorate of Overseas Surveys and commonly referred to as the DOS) in the drawing of maps. The support which the British government gave to the Northern Nigerian Survey in pre and post independence days, much of it through the DOS, reflected its sense of determination to assist the development of Nigeria. *An outline of the work of the Directorate is given at Appendix VII.*

The Director attended a conference in Lagos to decide, following Nigeria's constitutional changes of 1954, the division of the staff of the central Survey Department into the Federal , Western, Eastern and Northern Regional Departments. Paul Ward remembers:-

> *'Hunter always wanted to hive off the "Dry North" from the "Wet South" of Nigeria. There was also a political push in this direction. In 1954, I think, all members of the old Nigeria Surveys had to state, in writing, in which Region they wished to serve.'*

With very few exceptions, the staff serving in the Northern Region on 1st October were taken over by the Regional Department. Only a few members at first refused to accept transfer to the Regional services and all had done so by the end of the year. Under the degree of regionalisation in force between 1951 and 1954 the Regional Department had not been in full control of it staff, so that a key man was always liable to be transferred away at short notice, with disastrous results to continuity and efficiency. Complete regionalisation was therefore seen as a great benefit, in that staff and equipment were no longer liable to be moved away at a critical moment.

The decision to decentralise was aided by the fact that, as a result of the revolutionary effect of post-war air survey methods on topographic mapping, it was no longer necessary for the central department to maintain a very large national ground organisation for the production of topographic maps. In consequence much more effort and field staff could be directed to regional surveys in connection with town planning, local development schemes, land transactions, etc. At the same time provision was still made for the establishment of framework control points to be used throughout the country, not only in connection with the topographic mapping programme, but also for the co-ordination of the regional surveys. It was also considered desirable to provide the regional Assistant Directors with certain of the statutory powers vested in the Director of Surveys under the Survey Ordinance. There were already well established offices at Kaduna and Jos, and smaller offices at Yola, Sokoto, Maiduguri, Minna, Ilorin and Kano (the N.A. Survey School) but it was feared that until surveyors could be posted to all Provinces, the Department would be unable to give other government departments the survey assistance which should be available to them when needed.

Although the constitutional changes which came into effect on 1st October 1954 increased the work of the Regional Department, they did little more than regularise a state of affairs which already existed. Since 1951 all survey work in the Region had in fact been done by the Regional Department, so the changes merely provided the establishment within the Region to enable the Regional Department to do what it previously had perforce to attempt to do with inadequate staff. In common with most other government departments, Survey expanded considerably soon after regionalisation. Not only was the complement of surveyors increased but headquarters in Kaduna benefited greatly by the appointment of an expatriate senior executive officer, Donal Baragwanath, to oversee the administrative and clerical staff.

It was decided at the London Conference on the Nigerian Constitution that Survey should be a "concurrent" subject, so that on 1st October the staff of the Regional Department passed to the absolute control of the Regional Government. The Federal and Regional Governments agreed to accept certain responsibilities and principles and this agreement is briefly as follows:-

1. The Federal Department was to be responsible for the national triangulation which was estimated to be completed within 5 years, for precise levelling, for the compilation and drawing of the national map series and for the printing of all maps.
2. The Federal Department was to be principally responsible for aerial photography, though it was expressly agreed that it was open to the Regions to make such arrangements for photography as they thought fit.
3. The Federal and Regional Departments were to be jointly responsible for topographic surveys.
4. The Regional Departments were to be responsible for the compilation and drawing of all topographic maps not forming part of a national series, for all cadastral surveys, for the compilation and drawing of all cadastral maps and plans and for the supply of topographic information to the Federation.
5. Staff of the Federal Department, when working within the Region, should come under the administrative control of the Regional Director.

The shortage of supervisory staff remained the greatest obstacle to development and progress. It was found difficult to fill all the new vacant posts with suitable British surveyors and a number from Holland, Denmark and Poland were recruited on contract terms *(Photos.11-16)*.   The Director remarked that they were all competent surveyors, and therefore of great value as individuals, but difficulties due to language and unfamiliar instruments greatly reduced their usefulness to the Department and although they could and did increase field output, they could do little to assist the few experienced surveyors with the much needed supervision of the junior staff or in the growing administrative work of the department. Though well qualified, these newcomers had problems in adapting to British methods - feet and inches, acres, degrees Fahrenheit, etc. Some even had difficulties with angles, being used to 100 grades, instead of $90°$, in a right angle.

The Town Planning Section was transferred from the Public Works Department to the Survey Department in 1954 and necessitated further office extensions in Kaduna South. The design and construction was undertaken by the Survey Department's own staff and the building neared completion by March 1955. As a result of piece work and close supervision, construction costs were far below normal. Additional accommodation was needed for the storage of technical records and equipment and for the installation of modern equipment; and an extension to the mapping office was completed by the PWD; while a large building for the accommodation of a slotted template assembly platform and various map plotting machines was designed and erected entirely by Survey staff, thereby doubling the capacity of the cartographic office. Four more bungalows were built in Kaduna South, thereby making possible for the first time the housing of all senior staff.

There was an overall improvement in the staffing position in 1954-55, a trend which was to continue in the years through to 1958, helped by the arrival of new recruits and the growing ability and experience of officers in all the technical grades of the very young department. In particular, the non-

English expatriate surveyors, whose usefulness had at first been to some extent impaired by their unfamiliarity with the administrative and technical methods, overcame their initial difficulties and showed themselves during the year to be not only highly competent surveyors but in all other respects very useful members of the department.

The annual Ministerial comment for 1954-55 was a familiar one, remarking on the very satisfactory progress in some aspects of the Department's work, such as production and buildings, and paying lip service to the surveyor's *cri de coeur* for more support, recognition and recruitment. Although there was substantial improvement in the recruitment of expatriate surveyors, and in this regard the department had started to reach its peak, it continued to be a disappointment that so few Nigerians were coming forward to fill vacant senior posts or even to replace wastage in the junior grades. It had not proved possible to open any more Provincial offices, but a full time Provincial Surveyor was posted to Kano. The amount of work for operational Provincial offices was growing steadily and there was increasing demand in all Provinces in which there were none.

At the time of the reorganisation in 1951 the department was badly equipped. The lack of money before the war and the difficulties of getting replacements after 1945 meant that the instruments in use were 20 years old and many were worn out. By 1954-55 replacements of a modern type were arriving in adequate quantities, the best of the old ones were reconditioned, and most equipment was in good order. All the old unserviceable material, some of it dating from before 1914, was disposed of. Plans were afoot to issue a theodolite of a suitable modern type to each surveyor as a personal issue. It was intended that this arrangement would encourage surveyors to treat these costly instruments with greater care, for it had to be admitted that in the past some had not been as careful of their instruments as they ought to have been. It was inevitable that accidents and damage would occur from time to time, but great care was normally exercised, especially in remote places, for the loss of a fundamental piece of equipment like a theodolite or a level could seriously delay the progress of an observation scheme. Some of the earlier theodolites could be repaired and adjusted by surveyors themselves, or attended to by a trained storekeeper. But these skills were lost as precise optical instruments became more sophisticated. Considerable use was made of Wild T2 1 second Universal theodolites; each senior service surveyor was issued with one for his use and personal safekeeping. Periodically, if necessary, these instruments would be sent for repair or overhaul to the Wild agency, F.Steiner, in Lagos.

Mention of instrument repairs brings to mind an occasion when the writer took a recently overhauled T2 from the Kaduna store and was surprised in no small measure to see, just out of the plane of focus of the cross-wires, a spider sitting in its small web, almost hermetically sealed inside the telescope. It appeared to be awaiting the arrival of passing flies. Surely spiders must be amongst the most optimistic creatures on earth ! It was a reminder of the days when a surveyor would gather fresh spider's silk from the hedgerows to dextrously mount new cross-wires in his instrument ! Here was a spider ready to do the job unasked ! Obviously an adventuresome stowaway from Steiner's repair workshop in Lagos.

During 1955 fieldwork for future mapping was completed in eastern Kano and continued in Bornu, Bauchi, Zaria, Niger and Sokoto Provinces. By the end of the year 23,000 square miles of mapping had been completed, a big increase over previous years. Revision parties were engaged on existing maps in Bauchi, Sokoto and Niger Provinces.

In the large towns fieldwork was done in Kaduna, Kano, Maiduguri, Gusau and Bida; the last two were completed and mapping was planned for 1956-57. Part of Bida was mapped from air photographs and, although this method as applied to large scale mapping was new to the junior staff, considerable saving in time was evident in the plotting of detail in the old town and in other areas where ground survey would have been slow and difficult. It was planned to do as much as possible of Maiduguri in the same way, but it was seen that it was not always possible to map built up areas by this method because some ground was obscured by buildings, shadow and trees.

The large scale survey of Kaduna by ground methods continued but many errors and omissions, blamed on the poor supervision of junior staff, were found and a fresh start under close supervision was required in some parts.

Better progress had been made in Kano township where triangulation for ground control for aerial mapping was carried out by the Provincial Surveyor, but this fieldwork was sometimes spoiled by inaccurate plotting by inexperienced staff in the office and he had to resort to plotting his own work, thus achieving better results, but more slowly.

With the arrival of more expatriate surveyors, the opportunity was taken to undertake some infill triangulation, such as in parts of the Minesfield where height control was needed for contoured 1:50,000 mapping.

Recruitment of Nigerian Staff

At March 1955, the establishment was a Director and a Deputy Director, four Senior Surveyors, 16 A Scale Surveyors and 10 vacancies, a Map Production Officer Grade I and a vacancy for an MPO Grade II, one Administrative Assistant and one vacancy, a vacancy for a Surveyor Grade I, three Surveyors Grade II with five vacancies, three Surveyors Grade III and IV with 17 vacancies, and a vacancy for a Senior Computer. 54% of supervisory posts were vacant. Five new expatriate surveyors arrived during the year, and a senior surveyor left on retirement. Regrettably, for the sixth year in succession, no Nigerian recruit came forward with an academic background sufficient to make possible his appointment as a surveyor, while the number of Survey Assistants passing through the Survey School was barely sufficient to replace normal wastage and a shortage of efficient and reliable clerks meant that technical officers had to spend more time on clerical work.

In 1955-56, with headquarters staff of 112, it was stated in the annual report, in which the title **NORTHERN NIGERIAN SURVEY** appeared in records for the first time, that the main obstacle to progress remained the lack of recruits from the Region for the higher technical and professional posts. All Ministries in the North were looking for Secondary VI candidates but Survey was getting none at all. The Minister of Land and Survey, I.M.Gashash, said in 1958:-

> *'Our young men appear to be unaware of the advantages of the profession of surveyor, of the chance to travel and work out of doors, to have one's own organisation to run from an early stage of one's career and the satisfaction of achievement on completing a map or drawing. I intend to have these advantages brought to the notice of 6th form boys who are on the point of choosing careers. There may also be the lingering fear that survey is still regarded by government as a luxury, to be the first to be dispensed with as soon as economies are necessary. It is now realised that if land is to be used to the best advantage and if there is to be planned development in the way of constructing roads, water supply systems, hydro-electric schemes, etc., the first requirement is survey and prospective recruits need not fear that it is an insecure profession.'*

The familiarity of such high-minded Ministerial pronouncements, containing evidence of prompting by the Surveyor-General or the Permanent Secretary, did little to improve the overall situation and appeared to ignore the fact that most educated Northern people just did not want to do this kind of work, and were perhaps temperamentally unsuited to what they saw as a difficult, menial, degrading, servile and arduous way of earning a living which would be unlikely ever to gain them the respect and standing of their office and city-bound contemporaries. It was clear to many that Northern people were not well enough prepared to man and run Survey, an occupation with an unattractive image, in the short period of intense preparation for Independence. Surveying was an alien, technically obscure and even pointless operation in many local inexperienced minds. Highly qualified and highly paid expatriate surveyors were therefore employed on simple work which could have been done more economically by less well qualified men if they were available and this situation made it necessary to increase the number of professional posts in what had become a rather top heavy establishment.

Staffing and Accommodation

Provincial Offices were still maintained in Plateau, Kano, Niger and Benue and new ones were opened in Bornu and Ilorin In spite of staff shortages, there was continued hope of being able to open offices in the remaining Provinces. It was felt that this was the only satisfactory way to administer the Department. Time was found, however, in November and December 1955, for two surveyors and a number of assistants to lay out the Durbar Camp at Kaduna and assist in other preparations for the visit of H.M. the Queen. Paul Ward remembers:-

> 'Hunter brought me in to Kaduna to lay out an enormous zana village; rumfas, horse-lines, latrines, et al, beyond St. John's College, down towards the river. I worked up there from dawn till dusk, with the S.D.O. i/c the durbar breathing down my neck all the time.'

Five Surveyors and a Draughtsman-Instructor were appointed during 1955-56, but this was partly offset by the loss of two surveyors, including the instructor from the Survey School. Recruitment to junior and clerical staff was consistently bad throughout the year. The establishment then consisted of a Director, a Deputy Director, three Principal Surveyors, six Senior Surveyors (three posts vacant), 25 Surveyors (10 posts vacant), three Town Planning Officers (two posts vacant), two Administrative Officers, a Draughtsman-Instructor, a Lithographic Instructor (post vacant), a Senior Computer (post vacant), two assistant Chief Draughtsmen, a Surveyor Grade I, eight Surveyors Grade II (four posts vacant), 20 Surveyors Grade III & IV (19 posts vacant). 53% of supervisory posts were vacant.

Continued growth had led to housing difficulties in Kaduna Junction for senior staff. Funds were made available for the renovation of two of the old railway quarters of 1915 vintage and for the erection of six new Kaduna-type bungalows *(Photo. 214)*. By March 1956 two new houses had been completed and two more started. Unlike touring surveyors, all survey staff in Kaduna South enjoyed the facilities of electricity and running water.

After the production of topographic maps of Plateau and the Minesfield in 1954 by the DCS many requests were received from both Regional and Federal Government departments for contoured editions. In consequence the Regional Government authorised the Northern Nigerian Survey to enquire from various air survey companies their estimates for contouring about 10,000 square miles covering the Minesfield. Replies were received but, before any decisions were made, at a conference in Lagos in December 1955, the DCS offered to help to place a contract for the photography of an area of 13,000 square miles to be paid for out of Colonial Development and Welfare funds. The DCS would then produce the contoured maps provided the necessary fieldwork was carried out by the Northern Nigerian Survey. The Northern Region Government was in full agreement and in February 1956 the aircraft arrived in Jos to commence the photography of the Plateau. Unsatisfactory weather and cloud prevented photography until the end of the year. A test strip of photographs to calibrate the camera was taken however and proved so successful that it was proposed that the ground strip, which had clearly marked points, fixed and heighted by the Northern Nigerian Survey, should be used for the calibration of all cameras to be used on West African aerial photographic projects.

During 1956-57 fieldwork was carried out to provide ground control for the contoured mapping of Lere (Sheet 147) and Jos (Sheet 168). Fieldwork for other mapping was less than in the previous year but ground control was provided for 8,000 square miles in Bornu, Niger and Zaria Provinces and field revision of 8,000 square miles of the 1952-54 mapping in Bauchi, Bornu and Plateau was done. Output of topographical maps from the Kaduna drawing office was down on the previous year and no maps arrived from the DCS, which had been involved in a 1:50,000 uncontoured programme, because of the heavy demand upon the Directorate for maps from other territories. The fall in output was due partly to the need to concentrate more on the production of large scale town plans but also because of the emphasis being placed upon training by a newly appointed Draughtsman Instructor. It was considered that the improvement in quality and eventually in the speed of production would make the temporary drop in output well worthwhile.

Following the poor visibility experienced during 1955-56, the DCS.contract aircraft arrived to make a second attempt at photographing the Minesfield and 11,500 square miles were successfully flown. The aircraft of the Federal Survey Department photographed gaps in the photography of the Sokoto area, some 2,000 square miles in Adamawa Province covering the Benue Valley east of Yola, as well as other gaps between the areas covered by the post-war RAF photography.

Field parties working on the survey of the larger towns, in particular Kano, Kaduna and Ilorin, continued work being done in the previous year. Progress was slow owing to the shortage of competent field personnel, a problem which was being addressed by the reopening of the Survey School to train Technical Assistants. Six sheets of Bida and four of Gusau at 1:4,800 *(Map 28)* were fair drawn at Kaduna and sent to Lagos for printing, and at the same scale a plan of Maiduguri was produced from air photographs and sent for field verification and revision. A 1:12,500 plan of Kaduna was completed and prints produced in Kaduna.

The 1956-57 annual report noted a continuing improvement in the staffing of the upper cadres and an increase in output, but still no sign of Northerners coming through. It was feared that Survey would be the last department to be Northernised but that this would not be due to lack of encouragement of school leavers to enter, or of vacancies for them to fill. Six expatriate Surveyors and two Town Planning Officers arrived during the year.

Keith Sargeant was Acting Deputy Director from January until November 1957, then became Chief Surveyor, a post he held until June 1959, finally serving as Acting Surveyor-General until his retirement in February 1960.

The building of a new store for tentage and tools was completed. The Minister congratulated the Department on the way in which it had undertaken some of the office and residential building programme itself, rather than wait to come to the top of the Ministry of Works priority list. The offices then comprised five main buildings with ancillaries in the way of stores, garages, etc.

A Divisional Office was opened in Kaduna, independent of the headquarters office group, the idea being that the surveyor in charge should function in the same way as a Provincial Surveyor, dealing with all surveys in the Kaduna Capital Territory and Zaria Province. A Provincial Surveyor was posted to Yola in January 1957 to deal with the survey work in Adamawa Province, leaving only Sokoto, Katsina and Kabba without permanent Survey staff, though Katsina and Kabba were dealt with from Kano and Ilorin respectively. Sufficient houses were allocated to allow the proper housing of senior staff in some Provinces.

An important contribution to the technical operation of the Department was completed in 1957, when Keith Sargeant, Trevor Brokenshire and others completed the first publication of the Departmental "bible", the *Technical Instructions for Field Parties,* an essential reference booklet which was aimed at reducing the need for extremely detailed instructions, and defining standard procedures and standards for every survey undertaken, particularly for junior staff.

Between 1957 and 1960 the Topographic Section made much technical progress in spite of staffing difficulties. Increased field survey production and an expanding mapping programme began to place heavy demands upon the Section's Computing and Records Office. J.F.(Derick) Bell was given responsibility for this aspect when appointed in 1958. By the time he left in 1962 he had not only established an orderly system of checking, cataloguing and storing survey data but had trained Nigerian staff to carry out check computations on a range of tasks including least squares adjustments of traverse networks, astronomical position fixing and calculations associated with aerial triangulation.

The DCS (by then renamed the Directorate of Overseas Surveys) continued to provide great help with mapping and provided surveyors for ground control work. Over the period, 43,700 square miles of small scale maps were produced by the Topographic Section and added to this were 25,300 square miles compiled by the DOS from ground control provided by the Northern Nigerian Survey, and another 1,100 square miles compiled by Federal Surveys also from NNS ground work. Over a quarter of the Region was thus accurately mapped between 1957 and 1960. The total mapping in Northern Nigeria prior to 1957 was 81,250 square miles, much of that done prior to 1939 and out of date. During this period Nigeria became noticeably more map conscious, with the Nigerian Military Forces beginning to show more interest and putting pressure on Federal printing resources.

Topographic Section field parties completed 47,000 square miles of control, which permitted the compilation of 28,500 square miles of mapping at the Kaduna office and 18,500 by the DOS. Also, 2,200 square miles of the Minesfield had been contoured by the DOS and another 4,400 square miles was to be ready by 1962. Elsewhere in the North, Federal Surveys were involved with the Niger Rivers Project and completed 9,000 square miles of control in Borgu. All this mapping was scheduled for completion by 1962, meaning that 80% of Northern Nigeria would have detailed and accurate mapping cover. Few new countries of comparative size could match this achievement.

From 1957 to 1960 57 maps at 1:2,400 or 1:4,800 scales were provided for Kaduna, Kano (outside the city), Ilorin, Jos, Lokoja, Maiduguri, Katsina and Bukuru and ground control surveys were done for contract mapping from air photographs for Nguru, Kano City, Minna, Gombe, Bauchi, Samaru, Makurdi, Mubi and Offa.

Organisation

In the past, the Survey Department had been a section of two government Ministries, the Ministry of Social Development and Surveys and the Ministry of Social Welfare and Co-operatives; but it settled into becoming a Division of the Ministry of Land and Survey. The Heads of the two Divisions, Land and Survey, were responsible individually to the Permanent Secretary but, in fact, worked in close harmony at their own level, with a tendency towards more integration, since the separation of Land and Survey was artificial and mainly for administrative convenience. The Lands Division was located separately in the administrative offices of the Ministry in Kaduna North. The Survey Division, however, operated as an integrated unit in Kaduna South and although Lands matters began to enter into the daily life of the survey staff to a greater extent, the prime function of the Division was still the measurement and mapping of the land, albeit frequently for Lands purposes.

The Division was divided into three Sections:-

(i)   Cadastral and Town Planning;
(ii) Topographical
(iii) Minesfield

Each of these three sections had its own field parties which were self contained and virtually self administering and were capable of moving to practically any part of the country as required. In addition to these mobile parties, each of the thirteen Provinces in Northern Nigeria should ideally have had a Provincial Surveyor.

1958 saw the start of an 8-year period of construction by the Public Works Department of new offices, production and specialist buildings and by the efforts of a direct force of Survey labour. A new printing building started in 1958 was completed in 1959. For quality, low cost and speed of erection, the results were to reflect great credit on J.P.W.(Paul) Ward for the considerable personal effort he put into arranging the work to be carried out by departmental artisans. Their efforts continued right up to the 1966 coup with the improvement and expansion of specialist buildings for Cadastral (Photo.18), Records and Stores.

The Approach of Independence

A close-knit, efficient and progressive surveying, mapping and planning organisation had developed rapidly from its inception in the mid 1950's and in eight short years had reached a pre-eminent position amongst the Regional and Federal surveying departments in Nigeria, led and manned by enthusiastic, capable and professional expatriate and Nigerian staff. An exodus of Europeans from the North on the scale that had occurred in the Eastern and Western Regions of Nigeria, which had the advantage of a large number of trained Nigerian officers, would have caused problems, because British departmental heads like Hunter still had responsibility for their staff and the internal running of their organisations. Hunter continued for a while, watching the departure of many of his contemporaries in other departments, and even when he did go there was no Nigerian technical successor.

All Northern Provinces had Survey staff in 1958, but this was not so by 1959, but it was hoped to recover the situation by recruitment and training by 1962. The period from 1957 to 1960 had begun with high hopes but some expatriates were apprehensive about conditions after independence and the feared exodus was noticeable in 1959, one which included the Surveyor-General himself. As mentioned in the previous section, K.H.Hunter retired and left Nigeria for good. His position was taken by D.C.(Douglas) Eva who remained in charge until his own departure in 1961. Of the 36 senior staff 15 left on retirement.

In an attempt to stem the tide, "Special Lists" of the colonial-recruited expatriate staff were set up in order to encourage them to continue to assist on anticipated development and training programmes. A "Special List B" granted immediate part-advances of lump sum compensation for which they might eventually be entitled on retirement, together with an opportunity to hold or 'freeze' the amount payable at its maximum point. For some this was sufficient inducement to commit them to continued service.

In anticipation of Nigeria's approaching independence a Royal Durbar was held in Kaduna. Keith Sargeant remembers :-

> *'May 15th 1959 was a great day in the history of Northern Nigeria when the attainment of self-government (two months earlier) was celebrated with considerable pomp and ceremony. A huge Durbar took place on Kaduna racecourse in front of the Duke and Duchess of Gloucester. Some 11,000 horsemen and footmen, and more than 3,000 horses, from every province took part in the procession in front of the royal couple. The construction of an extensive temporary encampment to accommodate all these people and horses was quite an achievement in itself.*
> *Each Government department took part to a greater or lesser extent in the celebrations which included not only the march past of the Chiefs and their men in the Durbar itself, but also an extensive exhibition and several pageants. The Northern Nigerian Survey's contribution at the exhibition included large murals of a survey camp by J.W.(Jimmy) Dickson, a Senior Surveyor, and aerial photography by P.H.S.(Peter) Redwood (Photo. 19), a model township by the Town Planning section, and a life-size model of a survey beacon.'*

Paul Ward recalls that Richard Barlow-Poole, the Permanent Secretary, asked him to do something for the exhibition and 250 tons of earth and laterite nodules were shifted (labour was no object) to raise a 'hill' for the construction of the beacon in order to get a heliograph sight-line to the triangulation point on Kajuru Hill *(Photo. 20)*.

From 1957 to 1960 all activities continued to be handicapped by the lack of staff. There were only just enough surveyors to carry out the essential administration at Headquarters, leaving none for field duties. Young, inexperienced staff members were therefore left without supervision. Young expatriate surveyors on their first tour were sometimes tied to offices when they should have been engaged on technical duties in the field, where they could have acquired experience both of their profession and of the country. The quality of work, and in many cases the output per surveyor, fell rapidly, and training virtually ceased. The department was in fact so reduced in the supervisory grades that it was scarcely able to overcome its own inertia and was rapidly ceasing to function. Until the shortage of senior staff was remedied it seemed almost impossible to provide the training necessary to carry out rapid Nigerianisation, let alone Northernisation. If the Northern Region was to have an efficient Survey Department in years to come the seriousness of the situation could not be overemphasised. Serving officers had to try to be optimistic about the future but they were also realistic and held very serious personal doubts about the North's ability to operate an effective Survey Department without external assistance. Five surveyors arrived during 1957, three came on loan from Federal Surveys, but they were not English, so their usefulness in the supervision and training of junior staff was limited by difficulties arising from language and technical methods. One senior service officer arrived from Sierra Leone but his arrival was offset by the loss of a more experienced officer. There were plenty of applicants for the junior grades from the North but no really promising young men had yet joined the Department. In 1960 only Kano, Jos, Ilorin and Sokoto had Provincial Survey Offices.

At Independence, the department went to some considerable trouble to organise a special celebratory exhibition at Kaduna South, to which the Premier was invited, and the new green and white flags and bunting were much in evidence *(Photo.22)*. But that apart, the change was a gradual, matter of fact and peaceful event, because the new Northern Regional Government after 1960 had neither the staff nor the money to make immediate far reaching changes. British methods, standards and thinking had become deeply ingrained in the everyday conduct of routine Government affairs and administration in Northern Nigeria and this was as true in the Survey Department as anywhere else. Many heads of departments, including Survey, continued to be allowed considerable scope for individual initiative. It was reasonable to assert at the time that nowhere in Africa south of the Sahara was the European imprint more durable than in Northern Nigeria.

The Northern Nigerian Survey, and the Survey Departments of the other Regions, became independent of Federal Surveys when surveying and mapping were placed in the concurrent legislative list.

Into the 1960s

With independence achieved, everything was in place for a sustained and comprehensive programme of mapping in Northern Nigeria. The primary triangulation network was fundamentally completed, new electronic methods of distance measurement permitting greater use of traversing in the northern flatlands were emerging, and high order levelling lines were being extended to all parts of the country.

A very experienced Lithographer/Instructor, William Stopforth, arrived in the middle of 1960 and was soon busy assembling printing and photographic equipment. It was planned to train young Nigerians in lithography and, with funds allocated for a new press to supplement the existing one which was used for training, it was hoped there would be no need in future to depend upon Lagos for the printing of maps.

Two expatriate Senior Assistant Surveyors were recruited in 1960, primarily to assist in the mapping programme, and by 1961 15 Assistant Surveyors, six of them Northerners, had been added to the field staff. The total number of A and CT scale surveyors which had stood at 42 in 1959 was about the same in 1961, but many of them were lacking in experience.

In 1961 Douglas Eva departed and was replaced as Surveyor-General by A.D.(Denis) Willey. DOS assistance continued and Malcolm Anderson was seconded to join their party *(Photo.23)* on triangulation and Tellurometer traversing to provide aerial mapping control for the Jakura Limestone/Agbaja Ironstone area near Lokoja. The towns of Sokoto, Malumfashi, Malamaduri, Potiskum, Lafia, Kafanchan, Kuru, Jebba, Kaura Namoda, Funtua, Bama, Anka, Wudil, Dikwa, Wamba, Keffi, Challowa, Hadejia, Gwoza, Omu-Oran, Bichi, Damaturu, Numan and Kabba were photographed for mapping. 13 of them were scheduled for mapping in Kaduna on the newly arrived Wild A8 plotters and the remainder by contract; and all were to be drawn by the Northern Nigerian Survey.

In 1963 the writer arrived in Survey HQ from another spell in the bush to find the place.......

' .....*in a depressing and unwelcoming state. Both Willey and Ward were despairing about the future as the local political scene showed evidence of deterioration. Britain was being blamed by many for some of the failures of post-Independence aspirations. There was a beginning of more vociferous discontent amongst the junior and support staff throughout government and the almost unheard-of situation of strikes was threatened; indeed these strikes did take place in September of that year.'*

In spite of the progress which had been made, particularly in topographic mapping, there was a feeling of increasing uncertainty and unease about the future. In the years following Nigerian independence, senior expatriate staff began drifting away from the Department and, although there was a reserve of strength from below to allow the Survey to function efficiently, the high point had been reached.

In 1965 Denis Willey retired and was replaced as Surveyor-General by Paul Ward, who remained until the end of the Northern Nigerian Survey.

Between 1959 and 1967 the Department was led by the Surveyor-General. His second-in-command was for some time called Chief Surveyor, then Deputy Surveyor-General and, in 1966 two Assistant Surveyors-General were appointed to this position. Until the end of 1966 there were three Principal Surveyors and this was increased to five (with two of them vacant) in 1967. Senior

Surveyors ranged from five to 11 (four vacancies), reaching a maximum of nine in post in 1961. The table below gives a broad picture of the staffing position of the Northern Nigerian Survey from 1959 to 1967. Where the number of vacancies is not given the number is unknown. "Survey" includes all Survey staff except those in the Topographic and Lithographic Sections.

	1959	1961	1964	1965	1966	1967
Survey	40	49	41	68 (42 vacancies)	82 (43 vacancies)	82 (50 vacancies)
Mapping, Carto and Printing	10	19	25	35 (8 vacancies)	34 (3 vacancies)	39 (17 vacancies)
Town Planning	4	4	3	5	5 (2 vacancies)	5 (2 vacancies)
Valuation & Lands	3	3	5	7 (all vacant)	8 (all vacant)	7 (all vacant)

With a background of budgetary limitations from 1959 to 1967, the task was always to maximise the size of the establishment in order to cope with the ever-formidable workload, trying at the same time to encourage the recruitment and training of Nigerian staff as expatriate numbers declined. Published staff lists show total establishment figures of 57 for 1959, rising to 75 in 1961 and dropping to 74 in 1964, but over the critical years of the coups, total establishment figures rose from 116 in 1965 to 129 in 1966 and 133 in 1967. Total vacancies stood at 60 in 1965, falling to 54 in 1966, but rising sharply to 77 following the exodus of staff of Eastern Region origin during 1966.

Although the Survey Department had a Valuation and Lands establishment the only Principal Valuation Officer had departed by 1961 and nobody else was ever appointed. Establishment posts of Cadastral Lands Officer and Technical Officers (Land) existed from 1964 onwards but these posts were never filled.

The official Staff Lists for 1959 and 1961 make no mention of a Lands Division but the wholly Nigerian-staffed Division in Ministry headquarters in Kaduna North developed as follows:-

1964	1 Valuation Assistant Grade I

1964   1 Valuation Assistant Grade I
           1 Senior Deeds Registrar (with a vacancy for an Assistant)
           1 vacancy for a Senior Assistant Lands Officer
           20 Assistant Lands Officers

1965   The situation was much the same but the number of Assistant Lands Officers rose to 30, with 11 vacancies

1966   1 Valuation Officer
           1 vacancy for a Valuation Assistant
           1 Senior Deeds Registrar (with a vacancy for an Assistant)
           30 Assistant Lands Officers (11 vacancies)
           15 Assistant Lands Officers in training

1967   1 Senior Valuation Officer
           1 Senior Deeds Registrar
           30 Assistant Lands Officers (1 vacant)
           5 ALOs in training.

The Events of 1966

"Soldiers have killed Sardauna. May God help us "

If the Northern Nigerian Survey had been in decline, then these words, uttered after the military coup on 15th January 1966, marked the moment when everyday work began to take second place to open inter-tribal discontent and the political disruption which within two years was to bring an end to Northern Nigeria as a political entity and with it the break-up of the Survey. A dream which began in the pre-war years and became a reality in the 1950s under the leadership of the first Northern Region Surveyor-General, Keith Hunter, fell apart with undignified and disastrous haste just eight years after his retirement.

In the 1960s Nigeria had well trained military forces and it was within the ranks of the army that the opportunity was seen, backed by the force of arms, to intervene in what was alleged by some to be a national government dominated by Northern interests, which appeared to be doing little to stem the rising tide of corruption and violence. The swift and bloody military coup, amongst other things, resulted in the assassination of the Premier of the North, Alhaji Ahmadu Bello, Sardauna of Sokoto, and the Federal Prime Minster, Alhaji Sir Abubakar Tafawa Balewa. The State and the Regions came under the immediate control of a military government headed by Major-General J.T.Aguiyi Ironsi.

These events at first had very little effect upon the everyday work of the Northern Nigerian Survey but there was a widespread sense of shock in the North at the loss of the leaders and deep unease about what the future reaction of the Northern people might be. They became increasingly and vociferously resentful that the perpetrators were not brought to justice and that in the Eastern Region the rebel soldiers were regarded almost as heroes.

Paul Ward recalls:-

'As an early aftermath of the January 1966 coup, Richard Barlow-Poole, our last expatriate Permanent Secretary, thought it better to tender his resignation and prepare to leave Nigeria finally. His successor was Yahaya Gusau, a man with a mind of his own (and probably educated at Katsina College, where only Oxford graduates taught !). I remember compiling the annual Northern Nigerian Survey Crown Agents indents in the following April, 1966, and forwarding them to him for the usual checking and approval. In the list I had put in for a supply of brass chest plate and cap badges (which had been designed originally by Hunter) - 100 of each from Gaunts of Birmingham. Yahaya called me over to the old Kaduna North Post Office building, which was the old Ministry of Land and Survey headquarters until 1968. He suggested that in the then present political climate these specifically designated NNS symbols were as dead as the Dodo.'

Although trouble had been brewing for some time, the first military coup marked the beginning of the decline of the fortunes of the Northern Nigerian Survey. Ethnic differences and animosities which had always been a major constraint to the internal harmony of the Nigerian state had become exacerbated by the emergence of regionally based political parties which formed the first post-independence parliamentary democracy. Disagreements, sometimes resulting in violence of a relatively minor nature, had from time to time arisen between the people of the North and 'southerners', principally those from the Eastern Region. Although conscious of the differences of opinion between the peoples of Nigeria, expatriate surveyors had seldom, until then, become intimately involved with the problems which from time to time arose and had been able to perform their professional duties without undue disturbance.

There were great problems and sensitivities in a Department which had traditionally employed a great mixture of peoples, many of them from the southern parts of Nigeria. Expatriates were at times very uncertain of where they stood and local reactions to what they did were open to misinterpretation. Many felt unsure of themselves and the future, and made plans to leave. Those that remained wished to be seen to be acting completely above board and were reluctant to openly express any personal feelings they might have about what was going on around them and certainly had no wish to commit their experiences to paper for fear of their misinterpretation. Diaries contained virtually no entries for what was a very trying time.

The writer comments:-

'From the time of the first of the military coups in 1966, when I assumed responsibility for running the Topographic Mapping Section upon the departure of Cliff Burnside, it was no longer just a matter of personal survival in wild places, but survival of the profession itself, and political events began to have immediate and dramatic consequences.'

By April, when the Ministry of Land and Survey changed its title to the Ministry of Town and

Country Planning, the Military were in firm control and senior staff were invited to events where there was always a prominent military presence; like the cocktail parties given by Lt Col Hassan Katsina, the Military Governor of the North. Soon after that the intended abolition of the Regions was announced and the well documented civil strife was under way.

In May 1966 the Federal Military Government announced its intention to dissolve the Federation, abolish the four semi-autonomous Regions, unify the civil service and ban all political parties. At once there was realisation that what had hitherto affected only the highest levels of administration was likely, if these changes took place, to impinge quite soon on the work and the lives of everybody, expatriate staff included. There was widespread consternation about the sweeping changes being mooted, rumours became rife, work began to take second place to matters of personal concern. Ethnic differences became more openly expressed, anti-government rioting took place in Kano and Zaria and spread to other Northern towns, and there began to be some attempt by southern staff to seek transfers to nearer their homelands. In one tragic incident, a very experienced and capable Nigerian surveyor, Godfrey Oraeki, engaged on topographic work in Katsina, lost his life during an outbreak of violence in the town.

In July there was a second military coup, this time principally in the Western Region, and the head of the Federal Military Government, Major-General Ironsi, and many Ibo officers, were killed. Lt.Col. Yakubu Gowon, a Christian from a minority tribe on the Plateau, emerged as the new head of the Federal Military Government and attempted to put in hand some form of reconciliation, but was bitterly opposed by the Military Governor of the East who was in favour of splitting up the Nigerian state.

A massive return of indigenes of the Eastern Region to their home area got under way and small groups of Northerners living in the East were subjected to retaliatory attacks.

In September came an unpleasant and threatening atmosphere and the worst of the disturbances. The writer recalls:-

> *'During September 1966 I was in charge of field and office staff numbering perhaps 100 people. Some of the surveyors and many of the office technicians were Ibos or other people of Eastern Region origin. Victimisation of people from Eastern Nigeria was taking place all over the North and, fearing for their lives, surveyors were abandoning their parties of northern labourers and all their equipment wherever they happened to be. I went to Minna, which is some 170 miles south of Kaduna by road, to 'rescue' what remained of A.O.Archibong's party.*
>
> *I reported what I had done to the District Officer and told him I was setting off back to Kaduna. He said that he didn't advise it. He had just received a message saying "Kaduna in flames. Everybody murdering everybody else. Mayhem. Travel to Kaduna not recommended". "Well" I said, "I have to go, I have a lot to do, more field parties to rescue and, besides, I'm due to go on home leave in a few days". Three other Europeans, each with his own car, had equally good reasons for wanting to reach Kaduna as soon as possible. Having given his advice, the DO suggested that if we did go it was our responsibility, we should travel together, and strongly advised us to arrive before nightfall. So I set off in my car, a powerful Mercedes, and, knowing I had to reach Kaduna before dark, and with the day already well advanced, I drove very fast like the others, sometimes reaching 90 to 100 miles an hour. Only small parts of that road (the A 1 Lagos - Kano main road) (Photo.145) had a good tarmac surface and we took the rough parts as if in the Safari Rally.*
>
> *We reached the outskirts of Kaduna without mishap, as the light began to fade. There, however, was an unofficial roadblock, made of tar barrels lined across the road. I stopped my car and was at once surrounded by a number of men armed with sticks and machetes. They searched the car and the boot looking for Ibos and, finding none, to my great relief, rolled away two of the barrels allowing me to drive on through the centre of Kaduna, the only way to reach Kaduna South. I drove down what used to be called Lugard Avenue, the main commercial road, now strewn with debris, with blazing buildings on either side and people running in all directions,*

until I came to the bend and the Queen's Hotel, owned by Paulina Okon (Photo. 228). Her bar had been ransacked and hundreds of bottles of beer and spirits had been thrown across the road and smashed so that I was faced with a sea of broken glass. There was no way around it. There was nothing for it but to drive on with my fingers crossed, but both rear tyres blew simultaneously and I skidded to a standstill.

Attracted by what sounded like gunshots, a gang of wild-looking men armed with knives and machetes then ran towards my car. I was very scared. I really thought this was my end. But seeing that it was not a gun, but a T2 tripod, on the roof-rack of my car, a voice from within the crowd said in Hausa "He is one of our surveyors. For God's sake help him ! Let us help you, sir !" and, with that, they picked up the rear of my car and replaced the wheels with my spares without using a jack. Then they cleared a way for me and I drove on to my house, which I was relieved to find was untouched. That incident exemplified to me more than any other the character of the ordinary Northern people with whom I had worked for the previous ten years.

I arrived home just in time to see my elderly cook (Photo. 132) leaving the house armed with a long knife. "Where are you going, Momo ?" I asked. "To kill Ibos, Sir" he replied. "Maybe you are, but you're certainly not going to do so with my kitchen knife. Put it back !"

I spent a few hours that evening sitting with Jack Ashton on the verandah of his house, sharing a beer, and aware of the unusual atmosphere and the sounds of disturbances coming from the town. At the time, with occasional gunfire and the passing of police and army vehicles, I was personally not at all convinced that we might survive to drink very much more Star beer.

It was a very disturbed night in Kaduna, with fires, shouting and the sound of gunfire. But when I went to my office the next morning I found that of approximately 30 technical staff I had left there only a few days before, only about half a dozen, all Northerners, remained. All the others had fled, some had taken a chance and driven south in their own cars, and some had been taken into safe custody by the police and given asylum in prison pending transportation to the Eastern Region in escorted railway trains.

Meanwhile, Jimmy Dickson and his wife, living at Jos, hid their Ibo cook in the loft of their house where he escaped detection when a mob came searching. In Jos he survived. In other places he might not have been so lucky.

In 1967 I took over the Minesfield Cadastral Section at Jos for a year and was to preside over its subdivision. The civil war with "Biafra" began in July and, warned of the possibility of Biafran air-raids, particularly on account of the Survey office being located close to a fuel storage depot, I was apprehensive when a suspicious, dark painted and unmarked DC3 aircraft flew unusually low over the town. We were used to seeing jet war planes from time to time but this was strange. But there was no bombing and the plane landed at the airport. It being a Saturday lunch-time, I made a hasty departure in the direction of the club to discuss the matter. Three South Africans in flying overalls walked in, drank a pint apiece, got a lift back to the airfield and took off again for a destination unknown. ....Biafra was said to have employed South African mercenaries on reconnaissance and bombing missions...........cool customers who didn't think twice about landing in enemy territory when they were thirsty !

In another incident it was reported that a Biafran plane attempted to bomb Kaduna Airport and the military installations nearby, but the raid did no damage because the altitude fuses on the bombs had been wrongly set, or they were merely hand grenades, and they all exploded in the sky at 5,000 feet. It is hard to believe that South Africans would have made such a mistake. It was more likely to have been the fault of a fledgling and rather inexperienced and ill-supplied Biafran munitions industry.

Not long after that incident, and still a little edgy, I was woken by a loud explosion but again the mercenaries were blameless. My house had just been struck by lightning.'

Reorganisation: New States to replace Nigeria's Regional Structure

In 1967 Gowon declared a state of emergency and announced that the Nigerian regional structure was to be abolished and would be replaced by a new States structure, based on groupings of Provinces, and the North would be divided into six States. **This was to be implemented on 1st April, 1968. The Northern Nigerian Survey would therefore cease to exist on 31st March of that year.**

Staff were to be posted, so far as possible, to their States of origin, and assets, records and equipment divided in such a way that embryonic Survey Departments could be set up in each new State, functioning primarily as cadastral units. As soon as these intentions were announced the heart fell out of the NNS, and it was left very largely to the expatriate staff to maintain order and cohesion while the Nigerians focused on their personal prospects and concentrated on work which would benefit the State to which they were to be posted.

Preparations for the break-up of the North were in full swing during 1967 and for some time loyalties of the staff had been switching from the sort of Northern unity where *"Arewa, Arewa !"* was the cry, to new found allegiances. Almost overnight the long established regionalism was changed and from the instant of announcement, interest and ambitions switched to new loyalties as civil servants were told they would have to return to their homelands. Neglected birthplaces far from Kaduna were suddenly of national significance and there were noticeable efforts on the part of some Survey staff to further the interests of their own home areas in the work they did. With the removal of the threat of southern domination, and with no other overall respected leadership, it was almost as if the people of the North, who hitherto had been largely united, wished to take the revolution a stage further by reversion to their age-old tribal loyalties. This would inevitably leave many northern States extremely poorly manned by Survey staff. The Northern Civil Service, including the Northern Nigerian Survey, was asked to preside over the division of the assets of the Region and the dissolution of all it had helped to build and to which it had maintained such loyalty. This task was undertaken with a mixture of qualified optimism, integrity and dedication but, inevitably for some who saw the rapid breaking up of a system which had taken so much time and painstaking work to establish, a sense of disappointment and foreboding for the future. Many did not rejoice at the passing of the giant Northern Region but they accepted it as a necessary sacrifice for the long term unity of Nigeria. Staff deployment was a major exercise. With the exception of Kaduna, none of the new State capitals had the necessary housing, office space and infrastructure to cope with the influx; some were better off than others. 36,000 people were destined to leave Kaduna in April 1968.

It was impossible and undesirable to divide and allocate to the States much of the specialised mapping and printing equipment in the Kaduna Survey headquarters and for a while after 1968 it continued in limited production as an Interim Common Services Agency Survey Unit, printing and distributing topographic and townships mapping, continuing liaison with British and Canadian technical assistance mapping programmes and Federal Surveys, and providing a centre for the training of junior surveying and cartographic staff for the Northern States, partly financed by them and which became the surveying arm of Kaduna Polytechnic which exists to this day.

The four most northerly States' Survey Departments were to be run by senior expatriate surveyors, while Kwara State (Ilorin and Kabba Provinces) with its capital at Ilorin, and Plateau-Benue State run from Jos, were to be under the control of senior Nigerian surveyors.

The Permanent Secretary of the Ministry of Town and Country, Alhaji Yahaya Gusau retired and became the Federal Commissioner of Natural Resources.

Kaduna Polytechnic

Describing the situation regarding the residual assets at Kaduna South, Paul Ward wrote:-

'*Another piece of writing on the wall came with the arrival of Ibrahim Argungu, Yahaya Gusau's successor. He told me not to get too involved with the School of Surveying in Oyo. Although a Federal institution, it was, de facto, a Western Region set-up. I had tried to continue the training of young Northern school certificate leavers there after the demise of the Northern Nigerian Survey training facilities.*

There were others straws in the wind, and one soon began to realise that Hunter's great 'empire' (and it was an extremely efficient one) was rapidly being confounded and it became obvious that I had better find a 'home' for the rump of the Survey that was to be left behind by the approaching formation of the individual Northern States Survey Departments.

To prevent a reverse take-over bid from Federal sources (and then close us down), we had to find a 'home' for the static buildings and equipment, after the States had split up the 'moveables'. A period of intense lobbying took place, visiting Military Governors, Secretaries to the Military Governments, and State Surveyors-General.

My first requirement in the prolonged exercise of setting up the six Northern States Departments and the Interim Common Services Agency (ICSA) Survey Unit was that I was told to find a set of offices for the North-Central State Survey Department. The North-Central Lands set-up, wily as ever, were determined to carry on the old administration ploy of keeping themselves completely separate from the plan cadastre. Colin Emmott took over the Chief Surveyor post, based in the former Cadastral Section offices, but when he left to lecture in land surveying at Ahmadu Bello University, that new State department was left in the hands of a newly-made Surveyor of Kwara State origin, A.K.Alabi. He was not particularly co-operative with ICSA or later with Kaduna Polytechnic and he was ultimately sacked for incompetence and corrupting the State cadastre in favour of his friends and himself.

At this time one felt that Federal Surveys were only biding their time and waiting for a complete vacuum to appear at the former NNS headquarters compound so that they could take over the rump; lock, stock and barrel. Fortunately they dithered and prevaricated so much (apparently nobody wanted to come to the North) that I managed to put my case to the Northern States Military Governors. When Federal did send up a surveyor (Ekpenyong of Calabar origin) he was more than satisfied with the old railway house and large compound at the bottom of Keffi Road. As far as I could see, he had been given no specific orders but was just sent up to mark time and liaise with the American 12th Parallel Survey Team led by Earl Bishop.

The break-up of the former NNS personnel, records, stores, etc., had gone smoothly enough thanks, in the main, to the expertise and the professional goodwill of the respective States' Surveyors-General. Stan Klepacki was however not happy with his posting to Kano, but I had no choice, the Permanent Secretary was breathing down my neck and there was no compelling reason for continuing the computing section, which he had been running.

On personal reflection, I seem to have had a very easy passage; co-operative State Surveyors-General, understanding Northern Permanent Secretaries who 'left me to it', and a laid-back ICSA set-up. This all gave me time to formulate the future of the old NNS, the only unfortunate thing for me being that Jack Ashton and Jacob Daramola had intimated their desire to leave as soon as it was convenient.

Jack Ashton and Jacob Daramola's request to be transferred to State Survey Departments precipitated my request to Mike Sharp, the ICSA Secretary, to have a personal hearing, if possible, with the Northern States' Military Governors, at one of their early meetings in Kaduna; otherwise, as I was to point out to them later, nearly all the former NNS headquarters complex could fall like a ripe plum into the hands of Federal Surveys, with half of the buildings being closed down and with no apparent gainful use to the Northern States Survey Departments.

I did a very large public relations exercise, with much reading matter and diagrams for the Secretaries to the Military Governments in the new States, suggesting our absorption into the Kaduna Polytechnic, as a campus in its own right, with the possibility of future technical educational departments, such as land, survey, town planning and printing.

Mike Sharp sent out all the 'propaganda' material in good time to the respective SMGs, and gave a longish slot at the next meeting in Kaduna for a personal hearing. Jacob Daramola agreed to come with me and we had a long discussion with them. At the end of the hearing we were asked to wait outside for a decision. Audu Bako, Military Governor of Kano, walked out with us as a gesture of solidarity, and gave his full backing to the project, saying "They're silly if the rest of them don't give their full backing to your proposals". They called us back in again after their discussions and wanted to know who would oversee the implementation of these proposals of absorption into the Kaduna Polytechnic. In a rash of enthusiasm I said I would stay for a period of time to see the job done. They then voted for money to be made available for the conversion to a technical campus in its own right.

I was fortunate, again, in that Gerald Summerhayes, an ex-D.O., on temporary attachment as Acting Principal, was a self-stated, full-blooded 'Northerner'. He welcomed us into the Kaduna Polytechnic, though Alan Martin, ex S.D.O. Gombe and the then Secretary of the Polytechnic, wasn't so sure. It was only when Dr Bernard Hawes arrived, as the substantive Principal, under U.K. Technical Assistance terms, that our future as an educational establishment was fully assured (after all, it was U.K. money that had built this Northern Polytechnic as a 'dash' to the North).

As I have stated, Jack Ashton and Jacob Daramola wished to return to production survey, and without them I began to have misgivings as to whether I had bitten off more than I could chew in this rapid movement towards the setting up of an educational campus. Not only was I faced with modifying physically the specialist field survey/mapping and reproduction buildings into academic usage - classrooms, canteen, library, etc., but where was I to find the relevant and professional lecturing staff?

The turning point was the early recruitment, following my contact with him when he was working in the Delta, of that excellent professional and well-practised surveyor from the 'wet south', William Brian Till. I was to find that education was an incessant procession of committee meetings at all times of the day and night. The detailed preparation for the Board of Governors, the Academic Board, and other such meetings had to be dealt with, as well as the ever-growing demand to modify buildings into classrooms. Money was no object in equipping classrooms and laboratories, fortunately, but the necessary administration time had to be found, too. It was Brian's early arrival that gave me someone at the contact end of lecturing. He had been at some time the officer in charge of the Survey School at Oyo, and this, allied to his intense practical work for Hunting Surveys, and earlier in the Western Region Surveys, made him a 'sine qua non' in the ultimate, long-term evolution of the NNS compound into the College of Environmental Studies.

My other main problem, a political one, was to placate Federal Surveys. I managed to unload our former, extensive and well-stocked Northern Region map store into their jurisdiction. Again, Oluwole Coker, the Director of Federal Surveys, had his hands full with his new job, while the civil war had been getting ever closer with the invasion of Benin. Also, I must say this, that when he saw survey training in the polytechnic context was taking off the ground he encouraged it from the Federal end.

Other factors came to my rescue. Yahaya Gusau, our first Northern Permanent Secretary, had by now become a top-end Permanent Secretary in the Federal Government, and he made sure I got overseas scholarships for professional training for any suitable Northerners I could find. (Hence James Dashe went to the University of New Brunswick, Canada, and, incidentally, returned with First Class Honours). Umaru Fika, as the last Secretary, ICSA, always made sure we were not forgotten, either.'

Paul Ward eventually left the College of Environmental Studies and moved across to the main campus of the Kaduna Polytechnic in Kaduna North as Director of the College of Technology, ultimately becoming the Principal of the Kaduna Polytechnic. He severed his relationship with the Polytechnic in 1978 and joined a private water resources enterprise in Kano.

Surveying had its roots in the responsibilities of efficient government administration but it should not be a surprise to learn that it received scant attention and funding in the excitement of establishing the new State administrations. The unique and successful experiences of the late 1950s and the early 1960s were not repeatable in the new environment and political circumstances prevailing under the first of Nigeria's military governments. Mapping was placed on the back burner and surveying only came to the fore when sensitive issues like boundaries and land ownership arose. Those who had been with the Northern Nigerian Survey during its best days found it impossible not to regret the dissolution of such an active and progressive organisation and the abrupt end to the department's *esprit de corps*. That spirit only travelled to the new states in the form of some backward glances and continued slight dependency for a while on some of the residual services which were provided by an Interim Common Services Agency and later the Kaduna Polytechnic.

....

SURVEY DEPARTMENTS IN THE NEW STATES

The evolution, structure, programmes of work and ultimate capability of these new organisations was left very much in the hands of 'Chief Surveyors' and each Department developed in a slightly different way, reflecting local needs, the extent of previous surveying work in the area, the ability and experience of available staff (some States were very poorly manned), the attitude to and awareness of surveying by the State administration, and the experience, ability and interests of the senior surveyors themselves. A report written by Malcolm Anderson in the mid-1970s, which is reproduced as *Appendix IX*, gives a broad outline of the situation in the North-Eastern State in the years which immediately followed the dissolution of the Northern Nigerian Survey. *(Photo.24 shows the N.E.State Survey Office)*. It cannot be considered entirely representative of the surveying and mapping programmes of the other northern States. But what they all had in common were rapidly expanding townships, demands from ambitious administrations, huge and chronic shortages of manpower, and formidable and overwhelming backlogs of cadastral and planning work. Mapping services were no longer available from Kaduna, and Lagos lacked the resources and interest to become involved in township work. The coverage of NNS large scale mapping for most towns was inadequate, became outdated very quickly, and alternative fast means of depicting the ground had to be found.

In a short period of time, some of the new departments, especially those in the more remote areas which had received little attention in the days of the NNS, now found themselves faced with the problems of burgeoning populations and huge problems of maintaining effective cadastres, for which modern and innovative solutions were needed. The cadastral workload for some of them was soon running to at least ten times the highest levels ever seen in the whole of the former North, and rapid and extensive mapping of many places, hitherto only regarded as small towns or villages, was soon in demand for cadastral charting and planning. How these problems were addressed and the extent to which each of the new States' Surveyors-General were able to replicate the services provided by the former Northern Nigerian Survey is a story which must be told elsewhere.

These new surveying units strengthened and diversified over a period of eight years before the next major upheaval when, after another military coup in 1975, some of the Northern States which had been formed in 1968 were themselves subdivided. *(Photo.25 shows junior staff obliged to retire under the new arrangements)*. Since then, political and military upheavals have followed at frequent intervals and the States which make up the former Northern Nigeria are so numerous that they outnumber the original Northern Provinces.

There can be no topographic mapping role for such small units and the responsibility for this work has to be a Federal one. 'Topo' was the stuff of traditional surveying; all the processes in the field and in the office that contributed to the production of small scale maps; the sort of thing that featured in all the textbooks. In the Northern Nigerian Survey, between 1954 and 1960, the Topographic Mapping Section took priority in expenditure on instruments and equipment. The field surveyors involved were given a large measure of independence in their work, with adventure, exploration, bush-work, risk, hardship, the chance to lead and prove themselves, and an opportunity to make a significant mark in the department. Maps at small scales of vast tracts of nearly empty country were printed by the thousand, but there was never a big demand for many of them. Few infrastructure developments depended upon mapping at 1:50,000 and 1:100,000 scales, although maps were occasionally required to serve specific needs, before they were available from the Survey Department. (The Associated Tin Mines of Nigeria, for example, made arrangements to produce their own topographic maps from aerial photographs around 1952.) Infrastructure such as roads, railways, telecommunications, and agricultural and irrigation schemes usually required site-specific up-to-date surveys and aerial photographs. As a result of the considerable topographic mapping effort large stocks of these small scales maps were distributed to the new States in 1968 and later, where, unless efforts were made to distribute them free of charge to schools, training institutions, government offices and local authorities, they often did little more than gather dust and take up valuable storage space in the local survey offices.

It was natural that the new States' Surveyors-General, who had previously been committed to the Northern Nigerian Survey enterprise, should feel regret at its demise, but the years of struggle with inadequate funding and staffing resources equipped them well for the even more demanding struggles which would follow. Democratic government goes hand in hand with good cadastre, hence the political importance of surveying and mapping, but corrupt regimes, imbued by nepotism, are likely to lead to abuse and degradation. And so it proved. The short-sighted manipulation and neglect of these services by the new State governments started having potentially disastrous and costly consequences for equitable and orderly land administration.

....

PART 3

TASKS AND RESPONSIBILITIES

PART 3

TASKS AND RESPONSIBILITIES

Most land surveying is an investment in the future. Land information and maps are fundamental to successful planning, design, construction, setting out, land and property administration, education, defence and a number of other activities. The task in Northern Nigeria was to make maps, rather as the Ordnance Survey does in Britain, but in addition, to define the extent of property so that legitimate rights could be protected. Boundaries between administrative districts, divisions and provinces were surveyed and described, and plot boundaries were measured, to satisfy the requirements of the relevant laws for grants of title for different kinds of land use. It was the surveyors' job to install permanently marked, interconnected points throughout the country to provide a reference framework of precise positions and relative heights for national and local mapping and development. The resultant maps have become monuments to the past. Many have not been revised since and still represent the country as it was seen 30 or 40 years ago.

Today, measuring to within a few millimetres and determining relative or absolute three dimensional positions instantaneously virtually anywhere on the surface of the earth can be achieved quickly by the use of electronic self-reading instruments, automatic data recording, computing and plotting, and receivers using the GPS satellite system. It is tempting to look back at the days of toil and sweat, recalling the diligence required to achieve acceptable results, and wonder, in the light of what has happened in Nigeria in the intervening years, whether the time and effort expended on arduous field surveying and mapping was worth while. Only a few far-sighted individuals could guess at Nigeria's tumultuous future, and none could predict the rapid advance of science.

Just after World War II, survey field instruments were not markedly different to those in use a hundred or more years before and surveying was being done using methods which had not changed fundamentally for over 200 years. In Nigeria, surveyors used the best methods and technology that local finance could afford, to achieve what, by today's fast, modern, automated standards, appear to be quite modest results. Instruments required skilled and meticulous operation and maintenance if acceptable results were to be achieved. Slowly, over the next two decades, changes occurred, but it was not until the advent of the electronic calculator that surveyors could start leaving behind their heavy books of logarithms and trigonometric tables. During the 1970s, electronic distance measurement had still not completely replaced the measurement of distance with steel tapes and chains in Northern Nigeria. Party leaders, usually qualified surveyors, needed the support of teams of organised people; labourers and porters to carry heavy equipment and perform the manual tasks of ground clearance and site preparation; and trained assistants to work as chainmen, heliograph operators and bookers. Later, back at the office, the products of their efforts, the fieldbooks, calculations and drawings, would be checked, and those skilled in other mapmaking processes would convert the verified data into finished maps and plans.

Major F.G.Guggisberg produced a Handbook in 1911 containing the rules for the conduct of surveys by the Southern Nigeria Survey. This remained the standard reference for a long time, gradually changed and augmented by procedural pamphlets and booklets from the central Survey Department. In October 1956, Keith Sargeant, with the assistance of others, was given the task of producing the Northern Nigerian Survey's own booklet, *"Technical Instructions for Field Parties"*, giving instructions for all kinds of survey likely to be undertaken. It included chapters on triangulation, traverses and sun azimuths, town surveys, minesfield surveys, lists of stores required in the field and a chapter on topographical survey (written by Douglas Eva, then in charge of the topographic mapping section). It was found useful not only for field surveyors but also in headquarters, saving the need to compose separate detailed instructions for routine jobs. The resultant booklet was, for the next 12 years, regarded as the surveyor's 'bible', a useful companion and guide, particularly for junior staff.

When the new State departments were created, following the split-up of the North in 1968, these 'T.I.s' became in need of revision. New electronic instruments, changed surveying and computing methods, the incorporation of new sections for aerial photographic control, township mapping and the multitude of changes to take account of metrication and the alteration of mapping scales, had to be taken into consideration, and in the North Eastern State, for example, the original instructions were completely revised.

The activities of the "Geographic Labourers" of Northern Nigeria were principally:-

- Control Framework surveys (triangulation, traversing and levelling)
- Mapping (at a range of scales) and aerial photography
- Town Planning
- Cadastral surveys and layouts
- Minesfield surveys (Cadastral surveys for mining concessions)
- The survey of Administrative Boundaries
- Miscellaneous surveys for special projects
- The training of Nigerian staff

A notable omission from the list of services provided by the Northern Nigerian Survey and its successors was that of Engineering Surveying. On large infrastructure schemes, such as railways, irrigation projects, dams and major roads, engineering surveys were generally carried out by appointed private sector contract surveyors. But as time went on and the major towns began modernising, industrialising and expanding more rapidly, requests were made for more detailed information for site development and setting out, for detailed large scale plans, levelling control and ties to the cadastral reference framework. Lines of precise levelling were pushed out by the Federal Survey Department to link the widely scattered Northern towns and to provide a common height reference where arbitrary or approximate trig heighted information had hitherto been the best available. Telecommunication routes, highway construction, factories and commercial sites, ambitious drainage and irrigation schemes, expanding residential areas and institutional sites all began to underline the fact that if the Government surveyor was to function effectively in the future, he needed to update his methods and provide an enhanced service to the public and the developers.

SURVEYS FOR THE CONTROL FRAMEWORK

The Importance of Control Points in Making Maps

C.D.Burnside wrote:-

"Most people reading this account will appreciate the fact that systematic mapping of an extensive area cannot begin until a satisfactory network of control points covering the whole area has been put in place by one means or another. Some readers will also know that today such a task, although still a major one, is nowhere near as formidable as it was in earlier times, before the arrival of what might be termed 'electronic surveying'. Before the electronic age, the methods for providing control then available to the topographic surveyor were; triangulation, both instrumental and graphical; high quality traversing; and astronomical observations. All had certain characteristic advantages and disadvantages.

Triangulation was always regarded as the best solution if this was possible. But covering a region with triangles with side lengths of, say, 20 miles or more required hills or mountains in more or less the right places. Sometimes when the topography becomes uncooperative about this surveyors would resort to increasing the elevation of selected high points by building circular towers of mud, brick or stone. Sometimes, platforms built into the tops of high trees were another possibility. Such activities were all attempts to increase the length of the sides or make the shapes of triangles more equilateral and by so doing reduce the number of triangles needed to cover an area. The aim was to maintain the highest accuracy possible and minimise costs.

If there was a dearth of hills, and triangulation was not an option, then traversing might be resorted to, but this was even more expensive. And this only provided a thin line of control at points, not readily seen from round about, and therefore not so useful for many surveying purposes. For example many parts of Ghana and some areas in southern Nigeria posed control problems that could, at that time, only be overcome using the traversing method. The Survey Department of Ghana became particularly expert at providing high grade traverse control at comparatively high speeds and low costs. But here again unfavourable topography and tall vegetation might severely limit the lengths of the lines of sight along the traverse and hence reduce the final accuracy of the survey and increase its costs. To get above the vegetation some form of portable elevated observing platform was needed and for this purpose metal towers (such as the Bilby tower) were introduced. But such towers were of limited height and 100 ft was a good height for a Bilby.

All of the above comments relate to small scale mapping (i.e. of the order of 1:50 000 scale) but if the area to be covered was not too extensive - such as that of a large scale urban area and the map required was of much larger scale (say about 1:2,400) then in fact traversing was most likely to be the best answer to the control problem.

The third technique listed above, that of the astro fix, was at the other end of the spectrum in the provision of control points. It was comparatively cheap and fast but the accuracy obtainable was very low in comparison with the other two methods. Possible errors were of the order of a few hundred feet instead of a fraction of a foot and their nature was such that they could not easily be reduced by the field surveyor.

In Northern Nigeria the favourable topography made triangulation the most obvious overall technique to employ, but, as one moved further north, towards the

Sahara desert, the terrain became more open but also flatter. Hills became infrequent features, with heights much reduced, and eventually the size of any possible triangles became too small for practical surveying purposes. In these conditions the use of low towers was employed to keep the trig going for a little longer but greater and greater effort only resulted in smaller and smaller triangles. So, in the more northerly parts of Sokoto, Katsina, Bauchi and Bornu Provinces, theodolites had to be turned to the night sky for the observation of astronomical fixes".

TRIANGULATION

Great things are done when
Men and mountain meet -
These are not done by
Jostling in the street

William Blake

A Foundation for Surveying and Mapping

Triangulation was, and perhaps still is, the most familiar of all surveying operations and the application of its principles served not only the establishment of networks of permanently marked reference stations but was used as an everyday method of positioning, scaling and the determination of heights for mapping, cadastral, minesfield, boundary and other surveys *(Photo. 29)*.

Surveyors recognised three orders of triangulation; in order of accuracy, *Primary* (or Major) *(Map 20), Secondary* and *Tertiary*. Standards and methods for Primary work were laid down in 1933. Major triangulation was of Primary standard and was established in order to cover the wider gaps between the primary chains and to provide control for lower orders of triangulation, being a net of simple well conditioned triangles or chains of quadrilaterals or polygons with average side lengths of 20 miles. Secondary triangulation provided control points for topographic and cadastral surveys, and a reference framework for the establishment of Tertiary triangulation with points about three miles apart which in turn was used for cadastral, minesfield and mapping control surveys *(Photo.44)*.

In spite of the fact that a control network was an essential prerequisite for the processes of national mapping and positioning it was commonly perceived by the controllers of government purse strings as serving no practical administrative need, giving rise to the constant problem of justifying resources for the operation.

To those involved in surveying during the colonial period, however, primary triangulation was of fundamental importance to their task and their greatest challenge. Surveyors went into remote, unmapped areas, and explored hills and mountain ranges and at their summits enjoyed endless panoramas seldom if ever previously seen by white men. To some this was what surveying was all about; pioneering, adventure, and a chance to explore and experience the whole country in a way that few others ever could.

While far below men crawl in clay and clod
Sublimely I shall stand alone with God.

Mary Sinton Leith. The Summit

The arrival of a survey party in a remote area was undoubtedly a dramatic and historic moment for local people who could have had no notion why these strangers had come *(Photo.183),* why they climbed hills and cut down trees, built cairns of stones, erected strange timber constructions on the hill summits, left concrete markers on the ground and then went away having apparently derived no obvious benefit from their visit. Their curiosity was even more aroused because triangulation was a multi-stage process and survey parties might return time and again.   First of all there was a reconnaissance to select the particular summits to be included in the scheme, hills and mountains anything between 20 and 80 miles apart, then the station marking or beaconing, and finally the observation, each sometimes separated by lengthy intervals.

Reconnaissance

Everywhere in Northern Nigeria long range visibility was impaired by the dust-laden Harmattan wind of the dry season, so triangulation was invariably a wet season activity with all its attendant problems. Reconnaissance *(Map 21)* was demanding, often the first penetration into virtually unknown and unvisited areas, known only to a few local guides, selecting the best hills, which might mean climbing every prominent summit and rejecting half of them, establishing intervisibility of their highest points by clearing obstructions and vegetation, and leaving behind a marker cairn *(Photo.28)*. In the vast areas to be covered it could be demanding work, trying to identify distant hills in monotonous landscape, the light, the haze, the heat shimmer and the appearance of hills changing from different aspects. Over much of the North the establishment of chains of triangulation was a fairly straightforward task but in the forested areas of the south and amongst the low flat hills it was a different matter. Then, at a distance, many hills could look alike, especially under difficult atmospheric conditions.

The plane table was the most useful tool of reconnaissance and the surveyor would build up his scheme as he went along, plotting and confirming intersected and resected points. If a wooded hill was used as a station the policy was to clear all vegetation right down to the ground, perhaps leaving a single tree to allow the hill to be identified from a distance. In flatter country, tree stations or permanent observation platforms raised by the use of rock and laterite, were often used.

Beaconing

After selection came the emplacement of permanent concrete ground marks at the chosen site *(Photo.31)*, and the erection of observation targets and station platforms if needed. A typical day starting from a base camp near the foot of a hill on a beaconing job would involve following a guide to the hill, perhaps a difficult climb to the top because there were no tracks and nobody ever had cause to go there. Local people quite sensibly went around rather than up the hills so there were generally no paths to the summit except those made by hunters and the ascent could be a very rough, tiring and hot undertaking. There would be lots of stumbling through tall grass, cutting away at undergrowth and thorn thickets or bushes, grabbing at branches, keeping half an eye open for rare but unpleasant hazards like snakes and scorpions, and contending with the eternally attentive 'sweat bees' which were forever trying to crawl into the eyes, nose and ears. On the summit would come the clearing of trees *(Photo. 27)* and the preparation of the survey marker; drilling a hole in the summit rock and placing inconspicuous witness markers, preferably without being watched by local people (to aid re-establishment if the station marker itself should ever be destroyed); the taking of measurements for the station description, and the construction, from natural materials, and centring, of a tripod beacon. The beacon was unlikely to be later taken by curious local people or disturbed by locally resident baboons if it was made from straight tree trunks and grass thatch *(Photos. 30 and 32-35)*. Vines or grass "ropes" might be trailed from the beacon tripod to make baboons think it was a trap. A detailed beacon record was prepared for each chosen point, fully describing the location, station marks; a panorama drawn of the horizon with compass bearings to adjacent detail and the next trig points, and details given for the approach to the hill and local facilities such as water supply and resting places for survey gangs.

Keith Sargeant recalls:-

> *'Periodically it was necessary to inspect trigs which had been established many years before - to ensure that the actual mark was still there and its position correctly described in the beacon record. I was once given this task - to visit all 38 trigs in the Bauchi - Yola chain. This involved about 1, 100 miles of trekking, moving camp every second day, and was the only occasion when I found a horse invaluable.*

The job was made more interesting as I was also required to observe the magnetic declination on certain hills by comparing compass readings with sun azimuths.'

Today, surveyors working in remote and wild places will, if at all possible, seek access by air. Such a luxury, overcoming weeks of arduous overland trekking and hill climbing, was an unfulfilled dream in Nigeria in the 1950s. John Street recalls:-

'When we observed the Mambilla Plateau from over 100 miles away, the summit area appeared to be 'dead level'. One part of my brief was to identify suitable sites for helicopter or aircraft landing. I was given a reconnaissance flight in a Dakota (with a bubble in its side, from which to observe) prior to our two-year stint on the hills. It all proved 'in vain'. The 'level area' was hopelessly eroded, most hollows were filled with peat, and the idea of using aircraft was abandoned.

Marching through the swamp and plains in the foothills of the high areas of southern Cameroons and Adamawa was like another world when compared with Jos and the minesfield. We walked for hours in water where the leeches burrowed into our skin. At night we slept on 'dry' islands and everyone helped to locate the leeches and burn them out. Those that went in deep could be very painful and dangerous and, 40 years later, I still carry scar tissue where they exited.

It was an incredible contrast to walk in these conditions for two or three days, then suddenly reach a hill mass. The scouts then went out to find a way up onto the plateau and after a day's steep climb we were walking across level turf more akin to the golf courses of England.'

Cliff Rayner recalls his experiences on the beaconing of the 'C chain' *(Illustration 42(1) and Photo. 42(2))* in 1957:-

'My next task took me to Yola, Adamawa and beyond. Tales of Adamawa were rife; if you survive that you will survive anything. And so it seemed to be. In truth, tales from 'old Mambilla Plateau' were even more hair raising. My mentor in Yola was Peter Redwood, another Bristol man! Peter was in Yola as Provincial Surveyor, Adamawa, and was therefore concerned with all survey matters in that province. The first job was beaconing of the newly reconnoitred 'C Chain' of the national primary triangulation. It was also a familiarisation exercise, in preparation for the observing programme which would start with the onslaught of the rains. I was briefed to observe the north-eastern portion which tied into the 'E' chain, whilst Bassey Ekanem observed the south-western portion tying into the 'U' chain. Strangely, although we were working on the same project, we did not meet until I was on my second tour two years later at Makurdi.

The beaconing was expected to be a three week assignment and as we went by car there was very little trekking involved. Beaconing is decidedly unexciting unless line clearance is involved, especially when lines are restricted by massive boulders on the top of the station. Such was the case at 'E 13' seven miles from the village of Jauromanu on the Garba Shege to Mutum Biu dry season road. A massive typically tropically weathered boulder about twenty metres by ten with another lesser boulder precariously standing on the top was the scenario for our labour (Photo. 36). The designation 'E' indicates a well established station but it was not situated on the highest aspect of the hill and thus there were obscured sight lines to the newly established C chain stations. The solution - build a tower or have a satellite station from which all sight lines would be clear. Or, remove the offending boulders.

The story goes that at Avebury, Wiltshire in the middle ages the pagan standing stones were regarded with no little embarrassment or tolerance by the local clergy. A suggestion to bury the offending stones was put into action until what time the practice was abandoned for whatever reason in favour of an improved and more permanent solution. The new improved solution to the problem of the remaining standing stones was launched which had the added advantage of providing valuable building stone for the resident builders. The method was basically as follows; build a fire around the offending standing stone and allow to bake overnight. Next morning dowse liberally with cold water. Miraculously the stone will split into many pieces admirably suited for building works which incidentally can be seen to this day in the older buildings of the village.

And so it was at 'E 13'. Wood was gathered all day and at night a mighty fire was lit in the crevices of the rock and all around it. By virtue of the coolness of the nights during the dry season there was no necessity for a morning watering ritual, for to everyone's delight an early morning visit revealed massive fracturing of the rock. It was but a small task, (which took two weeks!), to remove the pieces and open up the required sight lines. A terse telegram sent to H.Q. in Kaduna indicated - "E 13. All sight lines now open" or words to that effect. Keith Hunter, the Director, wanted to know more! In good time, all was revealed.'

Observing

As soon as possible came the observation stage to measure with great precision all the horizontal and vertical angles of the triangulation network *(Photo.37)* and Keith Sargeant recalls:-

'Observing meant measuring the horizontal and vertical angles from each trig point to up to seven or eight other points which might be 60 miles or more distant. A great degree of accuracy was required, using a Wild T3, the most accurate theodolite available (Photo.38). The sum of the internal angles of each triangle had to be correct within about one second of an arc; this meant allowing for the curvature of the earth - the so- called spherical excess which had to be added to the 180° of a plane triangle. Observations were taken to heliographs on the distant hills which reflected the sun's rays and had to be adjusted continuously to allow for the movement of the sun. These distant points were manned by heliomen who had been previously briefed on their future programme - where to go next and to which trig to give light. The surveyor communicated with his heliomen by light flashes and it was remarkable how few problems arose.' (Photo.41).

J.C. (John) Pugh, who was appointed in 1941, also observed Primary triangulation:-

'We were allowed up to one second of arc as the difference between the total of observed angles in any one triangle and the calculated expected total. I finished the chain with an average of 0.23 of a second of arc per triangle, which I thought pretty good until I heard that the Survey of India had one chain in the Himalayas with an average of O.1 of a second.'

Many problems could arise to cause failure and frustration and prolonged and repeated effort. Visibility was usually the greatest problem, especially if the Harmattan was late to clear or early to arrive or, as happened to the writer amongst the very low flat hills and long rays north of Makurdi on the 'P' chain, the Harmattan returned for several weeks, after having apparently cleared in April, leaving heliograph parties stranded for long periods on distant and remote summits. Under such circumstances the success of the observation programme was greatly dependent upon the alertness, reliability and intelligence of heliograph operators. Wild T3 geodetic theodolites were used in primary and major triangulation *(Photo. 38)*. Heliographs were also used on the longer rays of secondary work and during periods of reduced visibility on lower order work. T2 theodolites *(Illustrations 43(1) and 43(2) and Photo.46)* were generally used for secondary and lower order schemes.

Cliff Rayner continues with his experiences of observing on the 'C chain' in 1957:-

'While the chainmen and labourers were finishing off the hill we returned to Yola to prepare for the observing season. Instructions to heliomen concerning what to do, when and where to do it were prepared. Operating in an area about 2,400 square miles in extent meant that smooth co-ordination between observer and heliomen was essential for a successful outcome. That was the dream and it remained a dream. The painful experience learned in Adamawa was well applied later in my professional career. Supplies were also obtained and checks made on tents etc.

For my part, primary observations consisted of observing rays to distant helios in combinations with individual angles being quoted to 0.01 second of arc. Triangular misclosures were to average 1.2 seconds with no single triangle exceeding 2.5 seconds misclosure. Spherical excess had to be taken into account and in almost all triangles it exceeded the observing misclosure. A Wild T3 geodetic theodolite was the instrument used. Being already familiar with its smaller brother, the T2, it was a joy to use the T3. But with the intermittent availability of helio signals it was a lengthy process. By no means the longest stay at a station in Nigeria, my enforced stay of seven weeks at Jauromanu, the infamous E 13, was not something to be repeated. Least squares station adjustment had to be made at each station before departure and with one station having nine rays the calculation by Gauss elimination was a lengthy business. However the worst chore by far was the monthly preparation of the labour work sheet. It was a physical effort to ensure that, using layers of carbon paper, the fifth copy was still legible!

Peter Redwood accompanied me to station 'C34' at Zaga about 200 miles from Yola at the very end of the motorable portion of the new Yola to Takum dirt road which was currently under construction. We were therefore literally at the 'end of the road' and were very isolated. It was soon to become apparent that we would become even more remote as we trekked off the road into the flood plain of the River Benue. Routines were established at C34 and on completion we moved north-east up the road to C 35 named Gidan Ali. This was a hill about 2,500 feet above the river plain, the summit of which was noticeably in a different vegetation zone (Photo.165). More remote than Zaga, wild life there was abundant. The usual dog faced baboons were plentiful on the tops of the hills and kept me company, at a distance fortunately, during observation sessions. Although we did not see any leopards there was plenty of oral evidence not very far from the camp. The maigardi had a restless fortnight for it seemed that he spent all day collecting kindling and all night burning it! He for one was taking no risks. Colobus monkeys were around us, spoor of bush cow and wild dogs were also seen. The camp site was a lonely clearing at the highest available water point and still about 35 minutes climb to the summit of the hill. By this time the rains had set in with a vengeance. The storms in this area, the foothills of the Cameroon mountain range, were dramatic and spectacular. It was possible to collect rainwater from the fly sheet of the tent occasionally, thus providing the small luxury of fresh potable water.

In a letter to home I wrote:-

'The water we thought would be quite a problem, for although it rains quite often it is not enough to give us a regular water supply by collecting it from the tent. However we discovered the tiniest stream about 10 mins down from here and just below its source we placed a kerosene (4 gall size) tin into the bed of the stream, having made plenty of holes in its base. The water thus seeps into the tin from the bottom and as a result is very clean although it does taste a bit brackish. Especially as it's running water it should be quite pure as well.'

A few days at Gidan Ali and Peter returned to Yola. By this time I had become well acquainted with the observing and camping routines and also what *came to be in some cases a rigorous calculating process, that of station adjustment by 'least squares'. At the time, the Facit manual calculating machine was considered to be the latest aid in field computing! We certainly would not have been without one.*

And so on to trig point C39, Dalli, on the west bank of the river Taraba. The village of Dalli was on the east bank and fortunately at the early part of the rains it was still possible to ford the river Taraba. Later, when in spate, it was quite a different matter. We camped on the extensive summit of the hill for convenience, but this became a liability when one storm really did approach too close for comfort. At its height I left my tent and the cash box and all the instrumentation to put distance between me and what was effectively the most efficient lightning conductor within a mile. Thankfully the lightning did not strike and the upshot was that I had an extended natural shower. It was also here that the word got around that that big green box, that only a special labourer was allowed to carry (Photo.26), was a money making machine and that it functioned best on the top of the hills. By this time the 5 shilling note had been introduced and at the month's end, when the labourers were paid, new 5/- notes were a plenty in the local market. There was only one place they could come from ... a fairly plausible deduction.

At C40, Sabon Gida, about 15 miles east of Dalli,, now two days trek off the road, life progressed without undue excitement until it was announced on the BBC World Service towards the end of our stay that the Russians had successfully launched their first satellite, Sputnik, thus igniting the space race. The labourers were not overly impressed by the news! On to C 36, Maifula, a most pleasant situation with wonderful views in all directions. It is on the main road and we were able to 'camp' in the village within walking distance of the hill. However hot it was in the village, on top of the hill it was always reasonably cool. The next hill on the schedule was C 37, Kankane, the biggest of the hills - a good 3,000 feet from the plain. Near the summit is a huge rock overhang and I decided to have a break from the confines of the tent and settled in under the overhang. Often we were above the cloud base and it was definitely sweater and long trousers weather at the summit. We were soon finished and moved to E 13, Jauromanu, of splitting rock fame.

E 13 was infamous in another way, for it occasioned my longest stay at any hill seven weeks in all. Not a departmental record but certainly my personal worst! My monthly receipt of mail and supplies were a life saver, as was the wireless. It was a great temptation to read all one's letters and newspapers in a single frenzy of avaricious greed and delight. Most times I resisted. The BBC test commentaries were high points. I remember well the exciting record breaking 4th wicket stand of 411 by May and Cowdrey in the first test at Birmingham, which finally loosened the stranglehold on English cricket that West Indian spin bowlers Ramadhin and Valentine had had for so long.

But it was also at E13 that the frustrations of primary triangulation observation were beginning to take their toll. The reliability of the heliomen was less than it might have been and because there was no communication between us we worked every day. Sooner or later the deprivations of life in the bush in the rains and the boredom of enforced inactivity would begin to have adverse effects. The following from a letter to home conveys some of the frustration:-

'2 August: .... And I'm still at Jauromanu. Have now been here about two weeks and done practically nothing, 9 days so far without working. Last night we had a terrific rainstorm so maybe it will clear up later to day. At the moment its sort of drizzling.
... Yes still waiting for heliomen to shine their lights at me. I have actually seen all of them on one occasion or another, but never all at once. This would happen as we are so near the end. I expect they are getting a bit browned off after 4 months sitting on the tops of hills, is there any need to say that I am?

11 August: .... Still wasn't able to get any of the work done yesterday as it was cloudy all day with scattered rain showers everywhere. I only saw 3 of the helios in any case.

16 August: .... Its raining again and it never clears up before 4.00p.m. By that I mean enough to start thinking about working. Such a change from Kano during the rains last year when there wasn't a day when the sun wasn't brilliant at some time or other. The rain usually fell during the night or was limited to short (3 to 4 hour) thunderstorms. Peter (Redwood) wrote saying that the troublesome ray is 50 miles away - Bath to Gloucester approximately.'

I remained at E 13 for another 3 weeks but seemed not to be in the right spirit for letter writing. By the end of our seven week stay at Jauromanu I had been 'out' 21 weeks. To add to our troubles and discomforts was an affliction beyond our control. Reports on the wireless that Asian 'flu was spreading from Mecca to all parts of Nigeria were not exaggerated. Within about a week of the epidemic arriving at Kano with returning pilgrims, it was evident in the remotest bush in southern Adamawa. Although not particularly fatal, it was nevertheless very debilitating. Every one of the helio parties went down with it at one time or another and that caused no end of frustration to the observing programme. The 'flu also caused much sickness in all the small villages which no doubt made them wonder what on earth had hit them. At the same time letters from home told of the new sensation in the pop world - Elvis Presley!

And so to what I had hoped would be the last station, Kamberi on the north bank of the Benue. By dry season road, then in a dugout canoe to Mutum Biu, and on to our destination. On completion we returned by way of another canoe trip for two days up the Taraba, making very slow progress until we finally landed at Gassol. It was here that the delights of a UAC canteen were promised. After much speculation the reality was rather different. There was certainly a huge shed to mislead, but inside the choice of merchandise was extremely limited. The display comprised a large pyramid of bagged cement, which I did not need, a large pyramid of NTC Bicycle cigarettes and a large pyramid of Harvey's Bristol Cream! And nothing else! I was informed that the establishment was primarily a centre for buying local cash crops, peppers, cotton, skins and groundnuts. Needless to say, I replenished my dwindling supplies (a monthly grocery supply, along with my mail, from Peter Redwood in Yola had been supplemented by buying local produce whenever it was available.) with ample portions of sherry and fags!

For whatever reason, some of the results were not without error, and I never did know why. Triangular misclosures were not acceptable and re-observations at Kankane and Zaga were requested. Far from being near the end of my sojourn, the re-observations and the addition of two more trig points at the south-western end of the area delayed my finishing and indeed my leave. At one time I thought that the onset of the dry season and the Harmattan would frustrate matters even further and prevent completion of the programme. By way of relief I travelled to Jalingo, met Peter Redwood and rested up for a week before moving back to Kankane. The break was very necessary as the letters to home testify.

'27 October: ....'Well Peter's been with me the last week and I reckon I am just about back to normal. Whilst in Jalingo we had a pretty gay time and knocked back lots of beer and booze and had dinner out a couple of times. We also spent an evening with the Project Engineer at Beli bridge and all in all I have spent a pretty civilised week. We are now at Zaga. I went back to Kankane earlier in the month and re - observed the station there. After this one we move about 10 miles away and the last one is at Donga - quite a metropolis for the area. Otherwise I don't seem to have any interesting news. As I said in my air letter, I've ceased to find interest in bush life, at least to recount it, the novelty has indeed worn off. Anyway I can say I'm in much better spirits than I was when I last wrote.'

Second time around it was all much easier, although by the time we reached Donga we had had some atrocious weather again. It was at Donga where I came across sand flies for the first time in any number; much more of a nuisance than mosquitoes. Once I had made camp and settled in I sent a messenger off to market to buy fresh fruit and gave him half a crown. He returned some time later with a sack full of oranges, bananas, paw paws, grapefruit and pineapple. Jungle juice was rapidly back on the menu. A gift of chickens and a bowl of rice from the local chief was very acceptable. The rice was the nicest I have ever tasted! There's a saying that 'appetite is the best sauce', perhaps that had something to do with excellence of the rice. During my stay I planted some paw-paw seeds on the top of the hill - I wonder if they ever germinated and grew?

Once the work at Donga was completed we all made our way back to Yola, and for me another step nearer to my delayed leave From leaving Yola on the 7th April to start the observing it was 33 weeks plus before I completed the task with just a week's respite in Jalingo in late October. I returned to Yola, job completed, on 25th November. The labourers and heliomen had been 'out' even longer, 40 weeks, for they did not return to Yola on the completion of the beaconing in February. Most of this time I spent in isolation from other surveyors. It had been a baptism by fire but I guess my efforts were not unappreciated for on return from leave and towards the latter half of my second tour I was sent off to Benue province to complete the observation of the Primary 'P' chain. With my Adamawa experience behind me I was well prepared. The area was less remote and I made good progress. The 'P' chain was the last systematic establishment of primary triangulation in Nigeria; what remained were fairly undulating areas in Sokoto and Bornu which were best served by tellurometer traversing. The new age of electronics had dawned. I was privileged to have been a part of the era when primary triangulation was the preferred way of establishing national control. Today the solution, by GPS, would take less than a tenth of the time!

And so my first tour came to an end. My relief was total and I needed a leave to recharge my batteries. The adversity was soon put in its proper place and I soon looked forward to returning. Leave was all that one might imagine, Tozer's and Wilkie's weddings, skiing, theatres, a trip to Sweden in February to get really cold and a whirlwind of socialising. My first tour had been more of an adventure than I dared imagine and in retrospect it was a period, the memories of which remain to a surprising degree, largely intact and vivid.'

The History of Triangulation

A triangulation survey of the Oban Hills carried out by Capt. A J Woodroffe RE in 1905 was one of the earliest recorded examples of this type of survey carried out in the territory. The Cameroons Anglo-German boundary from Yola to the Cross River rapids, a pioneering trigonometrical survey carried out by Major G F A Whitlock RE. between 1907and 1909, was possibly the first such survey in any part of the north. Some work had started as early as 1910 in the more open areas of economic significance in the south, to aid topographic mapping, but in the north it was limited to the tin mining areas of the Bauchi Plateau, as it was then called, and the densely populated agricultural area around Kano. None of this work was of primary standard. The Survey Department was too small to undertake more than localised triangulation until the late 1920s.

No work was done between 1914 and 1923 because of the first World War, although thoughts turned to the systematic establishment of a national network of primary triangulation and traverse when Cleminson, the Director of Surveys, submitted a memorandum on triangulation and topographic surveys in Nigeria to the Colonial Survey Committee in 1920.

Early in the previous century, British endeavour in India had set an outstanding example of how triangulation, carried out under military discipline, could provide an orderly structure for a geographic archive, a reference framework for future mapping, and a better knowledge of the shape of the earth. (In his book *'The Great Arc'*, John Keay gives, for the layman, an excellent description of the processes of triangulation). This example had subsequently been taken up in other parts of the world and 1926 saw the start of systematic triangulation in Nigeria. The programme was destined not to be completed for well over 30 years. It was not undertaken because it was high science, indeed the standards achieved at first showed that it was indeed at times far from that, but rather because it was the only known means of providing an accurate and reliable framework for future mapping and local development. Even so, the quest for precision, the elaborate instruments, the intensive labour, arduous living and travelling, and complex calculations brought mysterious foreign activities to primitive surroundings, much as they must have done in India a century and more before. In the first year 98 stations were established and observed on a loop running from an invar-taped baseline at Kano to another on the Plateau at Naraguta.

In about 1929 Capt. J.N. Calder Wood, the Surveyor-General, started to plan the primary triangulation as it came to be. He reviewed the existing sub-standard and piecemeal work, and proposed much re-observation using better instruments and the increased use of heliographs to replace the hitherto-used opaque tripod beaconing. As a first step he sent Keith Hunter to carry out a reconnaissance from Yola to the Gongola River bend at Nafada and on to the Plateau, and to investigate the northern limit of triangulation possibilities in the north-east. David Anderson, the author of *Surveyor's Trek*, later emplaced the station markers along the arc of large triangles through the sparsely inhabited country stretching north-west from Bauchi, with Bauchi on its southern side, through Darazo and Nafada, then turning south towards Gombe and Biu towards Yola. In this area shade temperatures up to 120°F (49°C) were not uncommon and lions were occasionally seen.

Much of the forested south of Nigeria had to be traversed, but the open country of the North with its sharply defined hills and mountains and seasonal good visibility lent itself to triangulation. The principal task was the progressive establishment of a network of chains of triangulation and every year up to 1939 saw a programme of reconnaissance, beaconing, base line measurement and observing, much of it in the Northern Provinces. Up to the start of the second World War this geometric foundation for the future systematic mapping was painstakingly laid down, and the areas between the chains were being broken down into secondary triangulation schemes for 1:125,000 scale mapping of selected areas of economic significance, and to a lower order for township and minesfield cadastral control.

In 1928 the Minna base was established and measured and a wireless framework party took observations for latitude and longitude on points on the primary chain to Jos. Work was in progress on the Bauchi Plateau primary and the north and south Mada Districts. By the end of 1929, the tinfield to the south of Jos was provided with a framework of tertiary points linked to the Jos-Minna chain. There was discussion about the type of beacon which should be used. It would be of a permanent nature and as impervious as possible to damage by local people, termites and lightning strikes, while being constructed of easily obtainable material and cheap to erect. It was finally decided to erect standard concrete pillars, of the type with which we are familiar in Britain, on a concrete platform with a 3½ inch iron pipe down the centre to serve as a centring device for the instrument and signal.

Work was done on the Kano-Minna chain in 1928, 1929 and 1932 and re-observed in 1935, while the Kano-Naraguta chain was in progress between 1929 and 1931. The Minna-Lokoja-Udi (just south of Enugu) chain, through difficult forested country, and the Birnin Gwari-Naraguta chain were observed in 1930 and 1931. Work on the Minna-Eruwa chain went ahead in 1932.

Reconnaissance for the Yola-Bauchi-Naraguta chain was completed during 1930-31 and observed by Hunter in 1933. A measure of the effort required on this sort of work can be obtained from the account given by D.Anderson in *Surveyor's Trek* where between January 12th and April 2nd 1933 he and Dawnay completed the beaconing of this chain. In all they covered 870 miles, half of that distance on foot, and established 32 beacons. One hill took a whole day to climb. 9 days would have been spent in hospital if such an amenity had been available ! They were accompanied by 60 labourers working in an area of famine and drought. These are by no means exceptional figures but such efforts were the norm on triangulation work.

The survey framework prior to 1930 was not of a quality and precision to be classified as primary triangulation. This was ascribed to inexperienced and unsuitable personnel, old and worn instruments, asymmetrical signals and interrupted programmes of work. Much difficulty had been experienced in effecting a satisfactory adjustment of the net in the Northern Provinces and its connection to the base at Eruwa and Udi in the south. The greater part of the triangulation personnel therefore became engaged in a re-observation programme.

Between 1931 and 1935 Nigeria suffered acutely from the prevailing world economic depression and the survey estimates for personnel and equipment were gradually reduced by some 45%. This entailed constant revision and curtailment of the programme, and surveyors had to take a 10% salary cut. Triangulation was however pressed forward and it was a tribute to the loyalty and enthusiasm of the field and computing staff, the latter almost entirely Nigerians under European supervision, that so much was accomplished.

The precision of the work done with old 6" theodolites (which only yielded secondary order standards) was improved following the purchase of three 5½" Wild Geodetic theodolites and the use of 5" heliographs. The heliomen were an assortment of young men from schools in the North, ex-signallers and others from the Nigeria Regiment of the Royal West African Frontier Force (RWAFF), and some of the more reliable people from the survey gangs. The success and speed of observation programmes were always heavily dependent upon their skill and attention to their thankless work.

The Ilorin-Sokoto-Chafe reconnaissance and the eastern end of the Minna-Naraguta chain was done by Hunter in 1934 and observed in 1935 using a Wild theodolite. It was a good year for observations and a total of 105 stations were observed by three surveyors with a maximum triangular misclosure of 0.94 seconds of arc. The Ilorin-Sokoto-Chafe chain was important because it provided mapping control for the Niger and Sokoto mining areas. M.D.Wimbush and G.J.Humphries were engaged on the beaconing of this chain. The Chafe base, 6.1 miles long, and the Rijau base, 7.5 miles long, were measured that year, using 150 feet x ¼ inch tapes standardised at the National Physical Laboratory in England in 1934.

Beaconing and observation of the Rijau-Chafe chain and re-observation of the Minna-Kano chain were carried out in 1935. The former was very arduous, with difficult communications and much head-loading of cement and sand. Two men died of smallpox and the whole party had to go to Gusau for vaccination. On the Minna-Chafe chain some of the trig stations were damaged by local people and had to be re-established. The azimuth of the Kano base was re-observed (it had previously only been observed by the Kano N.A. survey institution) using a CTS 8 inch 3 micrometer theodolite by east and west stars near the prime vertical. with a Helleson lamp as a reference object. A Connolly Standard Compass was purchased in 1935 and in the north observations were taken at Kaduna, Kano, Jos and Maiduguri. The compass achieved a precision of about 1 minute of arc. The observations were repeated on an annual basis and were still in progress after the war and into the 1950s.

Some idea of the costs of survey in those days can be obtained by looking at the costs of triangulation between 1932 and 1935 for the Ilorin-Rijau and Rijau-Chafe chains, a total of 580 miles. Reconnaissance cost £2109, beaconing £1382 and observation £4059, a total of £7550 or £93 per station. These sums included salaries, labour, transport, materials, passages, an allowance for leave pay, pensions and depreciation of instruments.

A new 6 miles long base was laid down on triangulation 10 miles from Ilorin, to help solve disparities which arose through using a Wild theodolite on the Ilorin-Rijau portion and the old 6" theodolites which were used on the Ilorin-Eruwa portion to only secondary accuracy. The new base was measured in 1936 and the base extension figures established and observed, and part of the Minna-Ilorin chain re-observed. At Yola, the reconnaissance, beaconing and measurement of a new base was done, and computation of the Bauchi-Yola chain was in progress at Lagos. In the following year part of the Rijau and the Ropp-Yola primary triangulation were observed and there was rearrangement and re-observation of part of the Ilorin-Minna and the Eruwa-Ilorin chains. Reconnaissance and beaconing of the Yola-Cameroon-Udi primary chain was done in 1937 and observations started in 1938. Also in 1938, reconnaissance and beaconing of the Ogoja-Lafia chain was done and secondary triangulation was carried out for the Ikara, Funtua and Chafe standard mapsheets.

The results of trig computations on the five primary loops, Minna - Kwongoma - Naraguta - Minna, Naraguta - Chafe - Kwongoma - Naraguta, Rijau - Chafe - Kwongoma - Rijau, Minna - Ilorin -

Rijau - Kwongoma - Minna, and Bauchi - Yola - Ropp - Bauchi, gave average fractional misclosures of 1:260,000 or 1 foot per 50 miles of triangulation. Figures of 1:193,000, 1:91,000 and 1:242,000 have been quoted for the eastern part of the US, India and South Africa, so in view of the fact that these three countries had a high reputation for precise surveying, it is apparent that the trig survey of Nigeria was of the highest class.

Although primary triangulation was pursued as vigorously as possible until 1940, and most of the main chains were completed, none was done during the war. Nothing had been done in the far north-east of Nigeria. Its remoteness and general backwardness meant a very low priority in the scheme of things.

Extension of the network, re-observations, and its breakdown into secondary and lower orders was resumed after the war. Hunter, Wookey and Wey were engaged on the provision of triangulation and traverse control for mapping the Sokoto gold fields (12,000 square miles) during 1946-47. The area had been photographed by the RAF in October 1946 around a radar tracking station at Funtua. Keith Sargeant *(Photo.37)* carried out primary triangulation observations on the Lafia-Ogoja and the Udi-Cameroon chains during the observing season of 1946. In April 1947 the observation of the Lafia-Ogoja chain was resumed, and J.C.Pugh was engaged on this work. This required the occupation of stations N22, N24, N25, N 26 and H 15 at the northern end.

Hunter was in Kaduna from 1951 and when staff became available he carried the trig east from Biu to the Gwoza Hills and north from Kano and Ningi as far as possible into the plains towards the Hadejia river valley, which was not very far !

In 1950-51 the Lagos computing section recalculated the heights of 418 primary trigs using a least squares adjustment and compared the results with the unadjusted heights obtained from precise levelling:-

> Chafe-Kaduna 2.70'
> Kaduna-Jos -0.36'
> Jos-Kano 4.36'
> Kano-Chafe -1.39'
> Jos-Minna -3.03'
> Minna-Kaduna -2.14'
> Chafe-Rijau-Kwangoma-Chafe -4.46'
> Chafe-Minna-Ilorin-Rijau-Chafe -0.52'
> Ropp-Yola-Bauchi -1.05'
> Minna-Ilorin 2.64'
> Ilorin-Oshogbo 0.77'
> Oshogbo-Abeokuta 1.79'

None of the medium scale topographic and large scale townships mapping during the late 1950s and early 1960s would have been possible without more survey control and the policy of extending the primary triangulation, and breaking it down into secondary schemes, was ably kept up by K.H.Hunter.

Trevor Brokenshire has provided the following description of work on a typical breakdown scheme carried out during 1954 and 1955:-

> *'...........it was decided that new fixed points should be provided over an area of 1,000 square miles, and not more than 4 miles apart. The selected area covered four of the Minesfield Priority sheets.*

> *Almost all of the area was already covered by a network of primary and secondary trig. points. Topographical maps, based on aerial photographs, were in course of preparation at Kaduna, but not even a 'preliminary, preliminary' map was available and it was therefore necessary to carry out a plane table reconnaissance in order to plan the proposed new points. Immediate plans were made to beacon all existing primary, secondary, and the very few tertiary trig. points; and after a quick*

reconnaissance by car; those hills which might usefully be included in the new tertiary scheme. There were therefore two survey parties in the field; the advance beaconing party and the plane table party. Work commenced in November 1954 and the plane table reconnaissance was completed by February 1955.

The plane table reconnaissance was carried out at a scale of 1:100,000, with the positions of most of the existing trig. points plotted onto the table. However, the positions of 6 existing tertiary points could only be plotted some time after the reconnaissance commenced; their co-ordinates had to be obtained from the Survey Department in Lagos. During the reconnaissance the plotted positions of the existing trigs were tested by triangulation, intersection, and resection and a number of points appeared to have been wrongly plotted - God forbid ! - or to have had incorrect co-ordinates. Where existing trig. co-ordinates were correct it proved possible to resect and intersect from them, and to check their positions to within 150 feet. A total of 75 new tertiary points were identified and 'fixed' on the plane table - despite the effects of the Harmattan, which caused a few problems.

The original instructions for the work required all new tertiary trig. points to be marked with a distinctive concrete block beacon, but as the plane table reconnaissance progressed it was decided that as time was of the essence, and in order to ensure that the point itself could be 'occupied', non-permanent signals should be used. The actual point to fix was, on rock, a 6" deep drilled hole, with a ring of cement bearing the trig. number around it, and in soft ground, a 6" cross-section concrete pillar sunk to a depth of 2 feet, with a 3" projection above ground level. Except in two cases, non-permanent signals erected over the drilled hole or concrete pillar were either stone cairns around a straight pole with brush or long grasses tied around the top; or tripod signals constructed of straight trees, again with brush or grass at the top (versions of these given in illustration 30). The exceptions were on the two hills which already had Ordnance Survey type pillars in situ; it was presumed that these had been built for but not used in the previous tertiary trig. scheme.

The next step was to plan the theodolite observations. Many of the new points were on relatively low-lying hills which might be difficult to locate when observing from much higher distant trig points. The ideal solution would have been to use heliographs on many of the new points, but only four trained heliomen were available. Party organisation was a major problem; due to the seasonal migration to farming there was an acute shortage of labourers and for most of the observing period a force of only 14 men was employed to do the work of at least 20. The whole party consisted of four heliograph parties (where necessary), consisting of one helio-man and one labourer, two advance marking and beaconing parties, augmented whenever possible by local labour, and supervised by a Nigerian surveyor, and the observing party of a headman, two experienced labourers, and myself. It was periodically necessary to suspend the observation programme while clearing of hills was completed.

The labour problem had some effect upon the method of fixing points. Ideally all points should have been fixed by observation of all three angles of each of the triangles, but, having regard to the need for as many points to be fixed in the shortest possible time, three methods were employed:-

1. by fully observed triangle, to a tertiary accuracy of 10" angular misclosure

2. by semi-graphic resection (setting up at the new trig. point and observing at least 3 existing trig points, with one or more reciprocal rays observed as a check).

3. by semi-graphic intersection, with at least three rays observed (in this case there was no need to visit the new point).

All observations were carried out using a Wild T2 glass arc theodolite, reading to the nearest second of arc. At most points, including many of the existing trig. points (where permanent beacons were often, and in at least one case, regularly destroyed by lightning - I wonder how many of the new *tertiary beacons have survived) the instrument was set up on a standard weight tripod. In high winds it was necessary to wedge the tripod legs with large rocks; where available, O.S. type beacons gave a much better set-up.*

Theodolite observations were carried out to provide tertiary accuracy, i.e.. on 3 or 4 zeros, with rounds closing to the first observed point to 5", and with the 3 or 4 sets of observed angles agreeing within 10". Vertical angle observations were taken after those for horizontal angles had been completed.

Because of the advance clearing problems, computation of the co-ordinates of new points was carried out on days when it was not possible to observe. During the period from the end of February 1955 to the beginning of April, 29 new points were cleared, marked,, and beaconed and theodolite observations were completed at 11 points. Due to the continuing Harmattan, observation was not easy, and the provisional co-ordinates of only 5 points had been calculated. By the beginning of May, 52 points had been beaconed, and when observations were suspended at the beginning of July, enough observations had been made to enable the computation of the co-ordinates of 54 points.

As already mentioned, resection and intersection co-ordinates were obtained by using a semi-graphic method. The approximate co-ordinates of the point to be fixed were taken off the plane table and two approximations were used to obtain the final co-ordinates. After the final co-ordinates had been determined by a resection, the bearing of the observed reciprocal ray was calculated and used as a check. Co-ordinates obtained by the semi-graphic method were within limits of + or - 2 feet, and in most cases were better than + or - 1 foot. Computations were carried out using 8-figure log. tables of trig. functions and a manually operated calculating machine (a Brunsviga, I think).

No astronomical observations were made or were necessary for the calculation of co-ordinates but some very long rays were observed and in such cases a 'torsion' or (T-t) correction was applied to observed bearings. Nigeria used a modified form of the Transverse Mercator Projection, known as the Colony Projection. The country was covered by three separate strips, each 4° of longitude wide with central meridians at 4° 30' E, 8° 30' E, and 12° 30' E (The area covered by the tertiary trig. scheme is in the Mid Belt at a longitude of about 9° E). Lines of longitude on the projection are curved, and a rectangular grid was superimposed over it. If astronomical observations had *been made a 'convergence correction' would have had to be made to correct observed bearings to 'Colony' bearings. A similar, but smaller correction for 'torsion' is often ignored, but the tertiary trig calculations applied the correction where it was considered necessary. Maximum corrections were of the order of 5" of arc, but in every case application of the calculated correction narrowed down the probable position of the point obtained from the numerous rays on the semi-graphic plot.*

Some of the first batch of computations confirmed that there was a problem with the co-ordinates of some of the existing trig. points. One resection was re-observed and re-computed without any increase in the expected accuracy and it was necessary to spend several days in the Minesfield survey office examining co-ordinate registers and all related files. It was obvious that many of the figures in the registers could not be relied on. Files from which the registers had been compiled showed 'unadjusted', 'provisional', 'preliminary' and 'final' values. In one case five different co-ordinate values were found. It was therefore necessary to contact Lagos again, and, after some delay, new co-ordinates were supplied. Use of the new figures in computations showed that the co-ordinates of all the new tertiary points could be fixed to the desired accuracy. It is interesting to compare old and 'new' co-ordinates of some of the primary and one of the secondary trig. points.........

		N	E
K45 (Primary)	original	2 210 899.0	2 342 581.1
	new	2 210 909.6	2.342 586.3
	difference +	10.6	5.2
K40 (Primary)	original	2 322 791.3	2 366 447.6
	new	2 322 802.2	2 366 452.8
	difference +	10.9	5.2
XK255 (Secondary)	original	2 279 846.1	2 304 481.6
	new	2 279 847.6	2 304 482.0
	difference +	1.5	0.4

.........evidence, I think, that the primary chain co-ordinates had been re-computed some time before 1954; that the secondary chain co-ordinates had been computed using the new primary co-ordinates, but that nobody in Lagos had bothered to tell Jos about the new K-chain co-ordinates.

Of far greater moment, as far as the Minesfield was concerned, was the fact that the co-ordinates of one <u>existing</u> tertiary point, had, as a result of my observations and the new primary and secondary chain figures supplied by Lagos, changed by 154 feet in eastings and 144 feet in northings (a displacement of over 210 feet) and in a second point by 428 feet in eastings and 327 feet in northings (a displacement of 538 feet). As far as I am aware no explanation of these errors was ever given.

As a matter of interest, the heights of many of the new tertiary points were determined by observations of vertical angles from and/or to existing trig. points. In most cases the mean figure was within + or - 1 foot of the calculated heights. This standard of accuracy relied upon one or both of two corrections. If only one vertical angle is observed, a correction must be applied for the curvature of the earth, and also for refraction in the atmosphere; in that case the coefficient of refraction must be known or assumed. 'Reciprocal' vertical angles were observed on some rays, though 'reciprocal' only in that rays were observed in both directions, but not at the same time. By observing 'reciprocal' vertical angles, corrections for curvature and refraction are avoided. A coefficient of refraction was determined from the vertical angles observed, and was 0.05 (the mean coefficient for the UK is 0.075). When used in height calculations there was a better correlation between the figures for the height of a new tertiary trig. point which was determined from existing trig. points."

Staff shortages after the war had delayed completion of the primary triangulation but there was resumption after the new regional survey Departments had become established and the network was substantially completed by 1960. Although this work was a Federal responsibility, the Federal Survey Department was not in a position to complete the entire programme of full national coverage and under Hunter's leadership the Northern Nigerian Survey completed four important primary chains.

During 1955-56 it was decided to begin to establish nets of major triangulation to fill in the gaps between the chains of the Primary frameworks in order to control medium scale mapping but also for further breakdown for cadastral and other purposes. This major triangulation was to be observed to the same standard as the Primary. By the end of the year reconnaissance of 2 nets covering 9,000 square miles had been successfully completed and sufficient observations completed for computation of provisional co-ordinates of nearly all the new points. Further triangulation to Secondary standards was begun in the Ririwai area and observations were completed at all the new stations on mapsheet 126 (Ririwai). This was particularly important since it provided height control needed for the contouring for one of the sheets in the Minesfield 1:50,000 series as well as for the re-plotting of the Minesfield priority diagram. The Lafia-Ogoja chain of primary triangulation was observed between 1955 and 1957.

In 1956-57 the reconnaissance, beaconing and the greater part of the observing of a primary chain extending from the River Gongola across southern Bornu to the hills east of Gwoza was successfully completed. The reconnaissance of a primary chain from Yola southwards to southern Adamawa, which had been established as far as the Taraba River in 1937, was continued southward, and the reconnaissance of another primary chain extending across the Benue valley from near Takum to northern Muri, and linking two previously observed chains, was also successfully completed. The reconnaissance of a net of major triangulation covering southern Bauchi, which was started in 1955-56, was continued eastward but was held up by the difficulty of the terrain east of Yuli. Work was continued on the major net covering some 5,000 square miles in central Zaria and southern Kano Provinces between Kaduna, Zaria and the Plateau, and the observing was finished before the end of the season. Yola-Nkambe (in the Bamenda Highlands of Cameroon) was observed between 1958 and 1960 and Nkambe-Takum and Biu-Madagali in 1958-59.

During 1956-57, work done in connection with the re-plotting of the cadastral diagrams of the Minesfield around the Bauchi Plateau highlighted once again the fact that, as Trevor Brokenshire had already discovered in 1954-55, many of the trig. co-ordinates, contained in lists supplied by the old Nigerian Survey Department shortly before regionalisation, were not in sympathy with each other. The minesfield happens to be at the junction of four primary chains. Of these the K, N and B series had been adjusted in sympathy but the E series had not, and the secondary net covering the same area had not been adjusted to any of the primary. This fact had apparently been overlooked when the lists were prepared and although there was discordance amounting to as much as 20 feet in places between the values of primary and secondary stations, the co-ordinates of all had been included in lists without any note as to their lack of sympathy. An adjustment by graphical methods was therefore undertaken to provide temporary values for all stations in an area of some 5,000 square miles which would be in sympathy with the adjusted values of the N primary chain and therefore of use to the cadastral field parties working in the area.

Towards the end of the year, a register containing the co-ordinated values and heights of all the triangulation points in the Northern Region was printed. Triangulation diagrams showing all the known rays between primary and secondary triangulation stations, and covering approximately half the Region, were also prepared during the year, and work continued on the remainder.

In 1957, an investigation was conducted into confusion which existed concerning the identification of a primary triangulation point on the summit of Ningishi Hill in Jema'a, followed by a reconnaissance for the extension of secondary triangulation to the west of the Jos Plateau towards Kwoi and Nok hills and south to Wamba, Akwanga toward the Mada Hills.

Primary triangulation had always been Hunter's forte and he was very anxious to complete the last of the Northern chains, the 'P' chain from the east of Makurdi to Lokoja, before he left Nigeria in 1959. Kjeld Hansen, a Danish surveyor, carried out the reconnaissance *(Photo. 16)* and Cliff Rayner and Malcolm Anderson, the writer, carried out the observations *(Photos. 39 and 40)*. Anderson started work at the eastern end in April when many of the long grazing rays from his first station, P16, situated on a low rise in the Doma Forest Reserve, rather than on a hill, were still not fully cleared of obstructing trees. This start proved to be too early when a return of the dust-laden Harmattan combined with the increasing humidity of the forthcoming rains in the Benue valley to produce many weeks of very poor visibility. It was 73 days before he was able to leave the site and trek to his second station. When Rayner started at the western end in June the rains had cleared the air and observations continued normally through to the end of the observing season in November, just about in time for Hunter's retirement.

Federal Survey Reports had little to say about triangulation between 1955 and 1959 but its overall responsibility for this work remained and there was progress on the improvement and rigorous adjustment of the network, and the computation of the results of the Northern field observations. In

1958-59 special parties made observations on the Minna base in conjunction with the Northern Nigerian Survey; a Tellurometer was brought into use and a Wild T4 theodolite obtained for revision work and scale checks in various parts of the North. Many of the very earliest control points from the pre-1930 work still existed but were excluded from the high order national framework which was fully established following traverse extension, EDM scaling work and rigorous adjustments processes during the first half of the 1970s.

TRAVERSING

Unlike the centre and north of Nigeria, where the more open country was often ideally suited to chains of primary and infill networks of secondary and tertiary triangulation, the nature of the terrain and the high forests in the south meant that major control was provided by traversing. High order theodolite traversing in the far north did not come along until electronic distance measurement was introduced. Lower order traversing, using steel bands suspended in catenary, was, however, the everyday method for the establishment of short range control for mapping and township control, while measurement on the ground was generally sufficiently accurate for cadastral, minesfield, boundary and other surveys.

Until the advent of airborne and satellite instrumentation during the 1980's and the 1990's, and in spite of the sparse vegetation in the very far north, the notable absence of topography meant that traversing was the only practical way of providing major control. The flat land to the east of Sokoto Province, the Zamfara valley, Katsina Province and the vast area of the plains of eastern Kano and Bornu Provinces were entirely unsuited to triangulation and the penetration of major control schemes for aerial mapping could not get under way until rapid traversing and trilateration using electronic distance measurement between observing towers became feasible from the mid 1960s onwards. The first experimental traverse of this kind by the Northern Nigerian Survey was conducted by Frank Waudby-Smith and Malcolm Anderson from Kano towards Nguru using 'home-made' Mills scaffolding towers and Tellurometers in 1961 *(Photos. 51-53)*. Malcolm Anderson recalls:-

"Reconnaissance for the Kano East (Kano-Nguru) Tellurometer traverse control started in July 1961. It was here that we first used 'Mills' scaffolding to construct towers for traversing in flat country. An inner instrument tower stood independently of an outer tower which supported the observer. Both towers were secured by guy-wires fixed to the ground with buried anchor-plates. It was found that stability of the instrument could be improved by replacing the inner tower with a column of portable lengths of 4" water pipe to which flanges were welded to allow them to be bolted together. They could swiftly and safely be erected to a height of about 50 feet, which was adequate for country with low scrub. On one occasion a tower was erected to a rather precarious observing height of 83 feet, but even at this height long sight lines could not be achieved and the instrument tower was never as stable as we would have liked, particularly in strong wind. These metal structures were at risk of lightning strikes and we were at pains to keep well clear during thundery weather. They were, however, very convenient and inexpensive. Their modular construction allowed a reconnaissance tower to be carried on the back of a Land Rover and a full height double observing tower with all necessary guys, anchor plates, braces and foot-boards to be carried on the back of one of our standard Bedford 3 ton trucks. By using small elevations at the Kano end of the traverse, and by zigzagging along the narrow corridor of the railway track further east, we were able to prove that we could reach Nguru using this method, but the reconnaissance was eventually halted by floodwater at the Nguru end.

While this work was in progress we transported one of our towers and our Tellurometer equipment to Kaduna for erection and display at the Survey Exhibition, which was witnessed by the Sardauna of Sokoto."(Photo.22).

Tellurometers *(Photos. 49 and 50)* were later in regular use for the establishment of traverses for the control of mapping in Kano, Katsina and eastern Sokoto Provinces, up to the time of the dissolution in 1968. The tower equipment was later passed on to the Directorate of Overseas Surveys parties for their ongoing mapping control programme in the north *(Photos. 53 & 54)*.

After the wind-up of the Northern Nigerian Survey, the Americans (Coast & Geodetic Surveys) observed a first order Geodimeter traverse, using Bilby Towers *(Photo. 55)* where necessary, along the 12th parallel of latitude across the North, part of the trans-Africa traverse from Senegal to Eritrea. It connected to the national trig. network at eight points, the last of which was one of Hunter's points to the north-east of Bauchi.

The highest order of cadastral control traversing, using Wild T2 theodolites and 1/8" steel bands suspended in catenary, formed the first break-down from the main framework (usually triangulation) of a township area or was itself the main framework. It aimed at a linear accuracy of 1:15,000, though this requirement was commonly greatly exceeded without difficulty by fast working and disciplined teams. Azimuths were controlled by astronomical field observations to east and west stars. Major loops of primary traversing were broken down into secondary order work with a specified accuracy of 1:8,000 and tertiary or topographical order at 1:3,000, for which sun azimuths sufficed. Secondary order work also used 1/8" bands in catenary but lower order traverses were done using ¼" bands flat on the ground. It was sometimes hard to justify the need for maintaining traverse accuracies of 1:3,000, perhaps just the width of a nail head, for the definition of property boundaries out in the bush, but it can be important on valuable land in developed town centres. The problem sometimes was, where did the bush start and where, in a rapidly developing country, will the next town centre be built ?

Trevor Brokenshire provides a description of typical cadastral control establishment:-

"My involvement with primary and secondary cadastral traverses was in September 1961. By 1959 Jos was a rapidly expanding town and it became necessary to provide additional control points as an aid to mapping and planning. This was accomplished by fixing a number of new minor trig. points about one mile apart, incorporating, in the south, the primary trig. point N6 and tertiary trig. points YK490 and YK2476; in the west, the primary trig. point N3; and in the north, tertiary trig. point YK455. The new triangulation was then broken down by a primary cadastral traverse running in a northerly direction from N6 to the approximate mid-point of the minor trig. scheme, with a second primary traverse running in a southerly direction from a minor trig. point in the north-western area of the scheme and a secondary traverse off the primary and between two of the minor trig points. The original traverses, in early 1960, were carried out by an expatriate contract surveyor, who, since the traverses were not up to acceptable standards for primary traversing (an angular misclosure of not more than 3" per station, and a linear accuracy of better than 1:15,000) shall be nameless. I do not know, or cannot recall, why it took so long to discover that the traverses would have to be checked (possibly because a later traverse using the control points proved the error), but the need to check gave me the opportunity to tape distances in catenary for my first and last time. My checking involved horizontal angle observations at 21 stations in that part of the primary traverse connecting to N6; using a Wild T2 theodolite; and measuring distances by using a 300' x 1/8" steel band. Horizontal angle observations were taken to plumb-bob strings suspended over the forward and rear stations. I am pleased to say that my angular misclosure was 1" per station. Taping in catenary involves supporting the steel tape at the 100' and 200' marks, applying a 15lb pull, measured by a spring balance, and reading the distance to the nearest 1/1,000th of a foot (0.012 of an inch, an easy task). Corrections to measured distances were applied for 'standard' (the exact length of the tape when measured on a standard base length at the Minesfield office), slope (measured as a vertical angle by the theodolite), and temperature (since the whole of the tape is supported off the ground it is possible to assess its temperature with reasonable accuracy by measuring the air temperature

close to the tape. I see from my calculations that the tape had been standardised at 85° F and that the largest correction, over an approximate length of 300 feet, was 0.030 feet for a temperature of 69°). The temperature range over the period 27th to 29th September was from 69°, the first reading on 29th, September, to 90° on 27th September. It took two days to observe the horizontal angles, and three days to measure the distances. On computing the traverse the linear accuracy turned out to be 1:44,500. The story does not end in 1961. In November of that year Mohammed Baba Kolo checked the other parts of the primary, and the secondary traverse but the computations were rejected because of a "faulty standard". (I wonder how that was discovered ?) Mohammed Baba Kolo re-observed in June/July 1962 and achieved satisfactory results. His computations were checked by A.A.Musa".

PRECISE LEVELLING

Early determinations of the height of the land above sea level in Northern Nigeria were by rough and ready methods using barometric pressure and road traverses, but as the primary triangulation chains spread their way through the country the vertical angle observations from each point carried forward heights to the hill summits and thence, by local observations, to ground control points.

Although of a much lower order of priority than triangulation in the early days, the establishment of a national network of accurate levelling, based on sea level at Lagos, was a departmental aim.

The central Survey Department of Nigeria always retained responsibility for national precise levelling, the routes of which generally followed the main roads and the railways. In 1935 levels had been run along the railway from Ilorin to Minna, a distance of 150 miles, producing an apparent difference between triangulation and precise levelling of 1.24 feet. In the following year work continued towards Kaduna where a Fundamental Bench Mark had been built, and the difference was 2.0 feet. In 1937, both the Minna-Kaduna and Kaduna-Zaria lines had been levelled to another FBM at Zaria, and progress was made towards Kaura Namoda. By 1938, work had been completed as far as Chafe, giving a 1.71 feet difference, and was also in progress on the Kaduna-Kafanchan-Jos line. As has been mentioned earlier, little precise levelling was done in the war years, but by 1948, a 1,200 miles loop had been completed from Oshogbo passing through Akure, Benin, Onitsha, Umuahia, Makurdi, Kafanchan, Kaduna, Minna and back to Oshogbo.

The Northern Nigerian Survey did not become involved in precise levelling; but Federal Surveys continued the extension of levelling lines, principally along the main roads, gradually and intermittently extending the network to cover the whole country over the next 40 years or so.

The North was, however, responsible for an ongoing programme of local and township levelling networks, and for long lines of low order levels to control topographic mapping. This levelling was connected to the precise network whenever possible.

TOPOGRAPHIC MAPPING

Introduction.

This brief account of the mapping of Northern Nigeria is an attempt to trace the processes by which almost the whole of the territory was eventually mapped at a scale of 1:50,000 *(example: Map26)* or 1:100,000 *(example:Map 27)* with contours at 50 feet vertical intervals. In addition to this, most of the towns of the territory were mapped at the much larger scale of 1:2,400 with contours at five feet vertical intervals. Other than this serial mapping, there were of course many special areas mapped at a variety of scales for projects such as the construction of dams and railways, and for agricultural schemes and so on.

The overall period of time for these works was approximately some seventy years from 1900 to 1970 but the main purpose of this account is to provide a detailed record of the achievements of the Topographic Section of the Northern Nigerian Survey Department and in particular of its 'golden age' from about 1953 to 1966. During this rather brief period of time the Department made a substantial contribution to the mapping of the Northern Region, despite very limited resources of finance and expatriate manpower.

In order to appreciate better the scale of this achievement, and to set this in the appropriate context, a brief history of the earlier years of charting and mapping up to about 1910, when a decision was made to bring into being a Nigerian unit capable of producing maps in its own topographic section, has been given in Part 2 of this work. An outline of the achievements since 1910 is now given and provides an opportunity to acknowledge the often considerable contributions of other external agencies in providing the country with much needed map sheets.

The beginning of Serial Mapping

A photograph of the European staff of the department at the start of their first field season in 1910 indicates a total expatriate force of some 15 persons, comprised of four commissioned officers, five NCOs and six civilians. Under Guggisberg, the Southern Nigeria Survey rapidly went into action. In that first April a 1:500,000 map of the Central and Eastern Provinces was compiled by Capt. W H Beverley, Intelligence Officer, from a variety of sources, including some work from the department itself and published by Stanfords of London.

The enactment of the 'Land and Native Rights Proclamation' in 1910 gave the Government responsibility to administer land on behalf of the people, and with it a consequential need for better mapping. 1910 was a milestone in Nigeria's surveying history when the first attempt was made to establish a local mapping unit. In the more open parts of the Western Provinces the reorganised Southern Nigeria Survey Department employed localised triangulation as the control basis for the first systematic mapping of six sheets at 1:125,000 scale. These maps, based on a general specification for topographic mapping that was to be used for all British territories in Africa, were the first to be produced by a local government organisation, but the control proved to be poorly recorded and inaccurate and much re-survey was later necessary.

A prime aim of the new Department was to up-grade the existing traverse control framework and then revise the maps as soon as possible. The stated over-all aim however was to map the whole of the colony with these standard map sheets as soon as possible. The prospect of mapping Nigeria's huge unknown territory was a daunting one and the accumulation of the geographical record would be an incredibly slow and laborious business. The early surveyors began this great task with amazing foresight and determination.

Within a matter of months, Guggisberg had produced and issued to his staff cyclostyled copies of a 'Handbook of the Southern Nigeria Survey' *(Appendix XIV Ref. 44)*. This textbook was almost entirely concerned with the procedures for topographic mapping current at that time and pertinent to the work in hand in Nigeria. Its production and distribution was considered to be an essential factor because of the lack of experience in this type of work by the majority of his staff. The volume was later printed and published in book form in 1911 by W & A K Johnston Ltd. of Edinburgh; a firm which was to take on the compilation and printing of maps from the field sheets produced each season by the Department. In addition to its technical content the book provided very detailed instructions for all aspects of field work and some 28 pages, for example, from a total of 238 pages, were devoted to lists of stores required for various field activities, together with details of the cost of each item and the supplier. One theme that permeates the early chapters of the book is the need for the highest possible accuracy, despite the demanding circumstances. Officers were warned of putting speed of production before accuracy in perhaps a bid for early promotion. However, as always, money was scarce:-

> "... 5. (a). To begin with, the accuracy aimed at in carrying out the various processes of construction depends not only on the nature of each individual process but also on the monetary resources of the survey. This last fact is sometimes lost sight of, for accuracy means time and money and there is no profession in the world in which there is more temptation to enter into minute niceties than that of the surveyor.
>
> The guiding principle of every surveyor, therefore, should be to cut his coat according to the cloth available .... a fair mean should be struck between the conflicting demands of accuracy and economy. "

The Department in Lagos was also responsible for other aspects of surveying, such as cadastral work and meteorology and this work, together with the production of large scale plans and maps of towns and so on, were in the hands of the Cadastral Section, unless they were to be carried out as specific projects by some other agency. However, the impression is that the main thrust of the Department was to be smaller scale topographic mapping.

Progress was slow but, by 1911, 64 provisional map sheets of Northern Nigeria at a scale of 1:250,000 had been compiled by Capt. H.N. Kempthome. He was also responsible for a 1:62,500 map of part of the Jos Plateau; an area of growing economic importance due to the presence of alluvial tin in good commercial quantities. In addition, because of its elevation (about 4,000 feet above sea level) and therefore more temperate climate, its value as a 'hill station' had been quickly appreciated even in 1905 when first discovered. Although all this work came under the jurisdiction of Guggisberg and the Southern Nigeria Survey, Capt. Kempthorne can rightfully be regarded a the true pioneer of mapping in the Northern Nigeria.

Surveying During the Inter-War Years.

After the first world war, there was a much increased interest in the extraction of minerals in Nigeria. In the north the prospecting was mainly for tin and to a lesser extent gold. This led to the formation of the Geological Survey of Nigeria and the need for accurate base maps. Hence in the north, the Jos Plateau tin fields and the Zungeru gold bearing areas were systematically mapped at a scale of 1: 125,000 by the Royal Engineers.

The need for reliable base maps for a wide range of activities, geological surveying being just one example, was now becoming a pressing issue. In 1920 Cleminson, Assistant Surveyor-General, Southern Nigeria, had made a case to the CSC for an extension of the triangulation control network and topographic mapping in Nigeria. The immediate impact was less than considerable but eventually the need for additional resources to carry out these important works was recognised and a significant increase in the recruitment of surveyors commenced; so much so in fact, that the ship that brought Keith Hunter to Nigeria in the November of 1928 had 19 other surveyors aboard. Hunter, who was later to become the first Surveyor-General of the autonomous Northern Nigerian Survey Department in 1956, modestly claimed that his success was mainly due to the fact that most of the others had died of ill-health along the way.

All the achievements of those surveyors who worked in the country during the years up to the second world war will not be catalogued but the following examples are typical of the type and extent of the work undertaken in the North:-

- In 1928 the Survey Department produced a 1:500,000 uncontoured map of Plateau Province on which ground revision had been carried out by Administrative Officers. The increasing numbers of such officers, together with other government personnel, such as Ministry of Works civil engineers, geologists and so on, meant that valuable map completion and revision material was now forthcoming in greater quantities from a wider range of sources.

- In the same year, records show that extensive large scale township mapping at a scale of 1:2,400 was in hand in several Northern towns, which included Azare, Bida, Bauchi, Damaturu, Dutsin Wai, Funtua, Gusau, Kafanchan, Katsina, Katsina Ala, Lokoja, Minna, Potiskum, Sokoto, Yola, and Zungeru.

- Also in hand were smaller scale compilations of Bida and Kaduna township mapping and in 1931 the township maps of Kano were revised and brought up to date.

- A standard sheet system based on sheets ½° in size (about 34 miles square) was adopted. Small scale mapping was being carried out as fast as conditions would allow *(Map 22)*.

A topographic map at that time was produced by plane table surveying; a slow but satisfying job, in which the surveyor, with simple instruments and his drawing board (the plane table), constructed the map in the field as he progressed through his allotted area. The scale chosen for the map sheets was 1:125,000; that is about 2 miles to the inch. Ground shape was depicted using contours or form-lines at 100 feet intervals. When the maps were finally fair-drawn and printed from the surveyors' original field documents they were in the four colours: black, blue, brown and red. The Survey of India is perhaps one of the best known examples of systematic mapping by plane tabling of a large region but it needed for its success a large number of well-trained and dedicated indigenous surveyors. Such a solution did not develop in Nigeria.

- In 1932 the first comprehensive gazetteer to accompany the 1:500,000 map sheets was published.

- The Nigerian Handbook for 1933 noted that only about 10% to 15% of the country had been "accurately mapped" and that most of the survey staff were engaged in the surveying of townships, government lands, acquisitions and leaseholds. However some small-scale topographic work was still being carried out on the standard sheets (1: 125,000 scale) of Kaduna and Kakuri. The Harmattan, a dust laden wind that blows strongly throughout northern areas in the dry season, together with the dense vegetation, meant that plane tabling was difficult. Much work was therefore the result of compass traversing and aneroid barometer heighting, so progress was slow. The control points for this work came from the previously established triangulation stations. Records indicate that by this time there were only four European surveyors and six Nigerian surveyors engaged on this type of work. It was further stated that the mapping was costing £2-19s-6p per square mile.

- 1935 saw the publication of the 1:500,000 sheets of Benue, Kabba and Sokoto Provinces and a revised edition of the 1:2,000,000 Northern Provinces map. In addition, nine of the Zaria township sheets (at 1:2,400 scale) and 13 Kano sheets were printed in three colours. A smaller sheet compiled at 1: 12,500 scale was also produced for the Zaria township area.

- By 1936, mapping of Ilorin township had been produced at scales of both 1:2,400 and 1: 4,800 and a revised standard sheet for the Minesfield area at 1: 125,000 had been reprinted.

- 1937 saw the production of 1:4,800 scale maps of Lokoja; the Paiko standard sheet was completed in the field, mainly by compass traversing and aneroid barometer work; and field work was also in progress on the standard sheets for Bida, Maska and Zaria. The completed Abuja sheet was also published about this time and revised editions of the Kano and Katsina Provincial maps were also published.

- Provincial maps of Bauchi and Bornu (1:500,000) appeared in 1938 and nine large scale (1:2,400) sheets covering parts of the Jos Plateau area were also produced.

- At the outbreak of the second world war in 1939, field work using plane table, compass traversing and aneroid barometer was being carried out on the Chafe *(Map 24)* and Gusau standard sheets by field parties, one of them led by Keith Sargeant, under the control of D Wiggins, who was based in Funtua *(Photos. 56 and 57)*. (After the war, Wiggins was to became an Assistant Director of the newly formed Directorate of Colonial Surveys (DCS), while Sargeant remained in Nigeria throughout the war and later became Assistant Surveyor-General in the autonomous Northern Nigeria Survey Department).

- Keith Sargeant recalls his work in 'the bush' at that time on the plane table sheets of the Gusau area:-

> *'Topo proved to be an interesting job. As one progressed over the allotted area, moving camp about once a week, the original plane sheet, with just a few trig points dotted here and there, gradually grew into what one hoped was a fairly accurate map with the addition of villages, paths, rivers, form lines and other detail Some parts were virtually unexplored. An extract from my diary:-*
>
> *"Evening gramophone recital to the whole village - many shadowy dark figures wrapped in grey blankets sit motionless, listening intently. Apparently only one white man had been here before, and he had no gramophone. "*
>
> *One kept in touch by messenger with any surveyors working in adjoining areas and the completion of a quarter-sheet was an excuse for a small party ostensibly to compare sheet edges. This could be quite interesting and a certain amount of give and take was necessary to make the detail coincide. '*

In the early days, before air conditioning, the heat and humidity of Lagos caused considerable problems for the drawing office, particularly with regard to matching mapsheet edges. Tracing paper could change by as much as ½" in half an hour. The only thing to do was to rush the contracted sheet edge to a special hot room, stretch it to its correct length, and hurry back to the drawing office before it had time to shrink again. Original drawings were hard to preserve, tracing paper would go yellow in 2 years, and zinc plates would oxidise rapidly.

The Second World War

As might be expected, during the war, many of the routine tasks of the Survey Department were suspended whilst other more pressing matters were attended to. Schemes which had been started, for example control for mapping in Sokoto Province, were held over. Many surveyors were called away for military surveying duties in Europe. However, sometimes there arose a need for some survey work to be done when, for example, the pilots ferrying military aircraft northwards over the country from Lagos to Kano and beyond discovered that their flight maps were none too accurate. John Pugh, was one of the few expatriate surveyors (along with Keith Sargeant) working in the Survey Department during the war, and recalls the state of mapping:-

> *'......... In those days, of course, (1943) one did not really know where one was ...... I walked 60 miles to Rijau, our nearest fixed point, doing a running theodolite traverse as I went. When plotted, it left a 40-mile gap to the west of Sabon Birni, and so the Department decided to ignore it ! In those days only about 10% of Nigeria was properly mapped (at 1:125,000) and the 1:500, 000 series for the whole country showed towns anything up to 40 miles out of position, did not show them at all, or showed them twice, up to 30 miles apart, joined to themselves by footpaths, as on Sheet 6. It was the result of fitting together rough sketch maps produced by D.Os. in adjacent divisions. I also recall in southern Nigeria the Idare Mountains (3,000+ feet) which were not on the map at all.*
>
> *During the War, fighter planes were crated to Takoradi, put together and flown to the Middle East in groups. The pilots had strip maps en route, including Nigeria, where the stretch from Lagos to Kano initially showed land below 600 feet, and when they found mountain peaks whizzing past they complained loudly. The maps were hurriedly altered ! '*

Until the basic control framework of trigonometrical and traverse points had been established such errors would be difficult to avoid. Hence that first and most important rule of land surveying - *'work from the whole to the part'* . A very sound dictum, but unfortunately one that cannot always be adhered to in every circumstance.

The Immediate Post-War Period.

In many ways the end of the second world war marked a cardinal point in the development of mapping world-wide, but particularly so in the mapping agencies of the U.K. Wartime experiences had clearly shown the great value and potential of aerial photography as a much better and quicker method of mapping terrain at almost every scale. In fact, war-time and immediate post-war developments indicated that the limitations of the method were no longer technical but mainly human in the correct identification of topographic features of the photographic imagery. And so photogrammetry, as it was called, now became recognised as a new powerful mapping technique.

As a direct consequence of the above, a number of events occurred in the U.K., in the late forties, that changed profoundly the course of mapping in the then Colonial territories. The first of these and, perhaps the most important, was a statement issued by Sir Arthur Street of the Air Ministry, who, in a response to requests from the Colonial Office that a number of RAF photo-reconnaissance squadrons be retained after the war for mapping purposes, made the following statement:-

> *'........and in these circumstances it seems to us to be very much in the interest of all concerned that the survey requirements of the Colonial Empire, as well as of this country, should be undertaken by the RAF.'*

Rather interestingly, later in the statement, he goes on to suggest that if the RAF did not prove to be the best agency for the provision of aerial photography for the Colonies then the right approach would seem to be the setting up of a special part of BOAC to carry out this work. (British Overseas Airways Corporation and British European Airways were the two organisations set up after the war as the national carriers).

As a result of this policy statement, it seemed logical to two different organisations in the UK that if there was to be a central agency responsible for aerial photography then they would be the obvious choice of central agency to produce the maps from it; the two contestants being the Ordnance Survey and Military Survey. Both put forward their claims in a most forceful matter and to say the least, the exchanges of correspondence between Brigadier Hotine, Director of Military Survey, and Major-General A M Macleod, Surveyor-General O.S., were somewhat 'robust'. Perhaps as a result of this strong difference of opinion, in 1946, a completely independent organisation was set up – The Directorate of Colonial Surveys with Brigadier Hotine as its first Director. However, the organisation was not given quite the universal remit as first proposed because although it was welcomed by the great majority of Colonial Governors, and particularly those with weak or non-existent Survey Departments, it was opposed in the strongest terms by the Governor of Nigeria who stated *'.....the proposed centralised scheme should not be imposed on a territory which has an organisation built upon a sound foundation because the majority of Colonies, which have no organisation, are in favour of it'.* He was particularly unhappy about the impact this centralisation would have on local computing sections, drawing offices and map producing facilities which, in his opinion, would be much better done locally. He went on further to say somewhat prophetically that

> *'...any assistance which is to be granted to this territory should be made available not only for the performance of certain branches of the survey work, but also to assist in enlarging the existing Survey Department so that as soon as possible it will be strong enough to undertake all the work necessary in this country...'*

There were of course some reservations from some Colonies in favour of the scheme but the overall favourable response persuaded the Colonial Secretary to accept the general principles of the scheme and it went ahead. However, the comments of Nigeria were well noted. That independent stance, so firmly expressed by the Governor, persisted in the colony thereafter and was nowhere more strongly upheld than in the Northern Nigeria Survey Department under the directorship of Keith

Hunter. An outline of the eventual contribution of the Directorate to the mapping of Nigeria is given at *Appendix VII.*

Early Aerial Photography in Northern Nigeria

RAF Photography

The RAF units deployed in Africa on mapping projects were No. 82 and No. 541 Photo-Reconnaissance squadrons. They worked under the direction of the newly established Directorate of Colonial Surveys (DCS). This was just one element of the resources that were to become available under the provisions of the Colonial Development and Welfare Act passed by Parliament just after the war. The intention was to provide good topographic maps of the whole of Nigeria in the shortest possible time. At that time that meant, in fact, most of it, because up to the outbreak of war, only about 15% had been covered by standard sheets.

However, some priority tasks were not serial mapping but were connected with specific projects such as the Volta Dam in Ghana, the Kariba Dam in Southern Rhodesia (now Zimbabwe) and the infamous ground nut scheme of Tanganyika (now Tanzania). There was a proposed groundnut scheme in Nigeria in the Kontagora area, extending over more than 6,000 square miles, and this also was an early target for the RAF photography. Nevertheless, between the Aprils of 1946 and 1951 some 189,700 square miles of priority areas in Nigeria were photographed and most of this was for serial mapping purposes.

The aircraft used on these missions were converted Lancaster bombers fitted with wide angle Williamson F49 cameras using the now standard format of 9"x 9" (230 mm square). The operational ceiling of these aircraft was about 20,000 ft above sea level and this, together with the fact that the cameras had a focal length of 6" (152 mm), meant that the photographs taken had an approximate scale of something just under 1: 40,000; depending on the average height of the terrain. Flying times were limited in the north by the dust of the Harmattan wind that blows in the dry season and any clouds under 20,000 ft in the wet season, which in fact was the practical flying season, roughly from April to July.

Each photograph at the scale mentioned above would cover an area of a little over six square miles. However, the requirements of aerial photography for map making are quite stringent such that all points on the ground need to be viewed stereoscopically from adjacent photographs, so the gain per exposure is about half the above. To achieve stereoscopic photograph cover, the aircraft is required to fly in straight lines taking photographs at a set interval so that they overlap each other by some 60%. At the end of each flight line the aircraft makes a controlled turn to start a new strip of exposures that overlaps the previous one by about 20%. This is not a trivial operation and requires great concentration especially when no navigational aids are available.

At the time of the RAF photography there was a simple radar device that was a good aid to the flight crew but meant that, instead of flying in straight lines, the flight lines were in fact arcs of a large circle. The accompanying flight cover diagram *(Map 25)* clearly shows the pattern of photographs produced by this process because much of this photography (flown in the wet season of 1950-51) made use of the radar beacon located on Gubi Hill just to the east of Bauchi town. During the sortie, the receiver in the aircraft continuously monitored the distance of the plane from the beacon, hence the pilot navigated to maintain a fixed distance between beacon and aircraft and thereby flew along an arc of a circle. At the required time, he turned and flew back along another arc at a computed distance greater than the first so that the resulting overlap of flight strips was the required 20%. As can be seen, a large area of the country was covered using the Gubi Hill beacon, covering in all about 150,000 square miles of the north east with photography of about 1:40,000 scale. (i.e. practically all land lying within 200-250 miles of Bauchi, excluding an area lying within 35 miles of the hill itself). Another radar beacon situated on a hill near Funtua was also employed in the same way to produce similar photography but this was not used to the same extent as the Gubi point..

In addition to standard aerial photography DCS also commissioned some trimetrogon photography over parts of the country, but little or nothing worthwhile resulted from this as the additional pairs of oblique photographs produced at every air station were difficult to use for anything other than rapid sketch mapping. The RAF deployment came to an end in the early 1950s but not before a very large part of the Northern Region had been photographed. The existence of this large amount of material gave a great kick-start to the post-war mapping programme and the new photogrammetric methods that were to be adopted.

Aerial Photography by the Survey Department

In 1949, to supplement the work of the RAF, the Survey Department in Lagos chartered a Dove aircraft from the West African Airways Corporation based in Lagos. This required the cutting of a hole in the floor of the aircraft to accommodate the Williamson Mk.2 camera. When not engaged on survey duties the aircraft was used normally as part of the carrier fleet. Because the operational ceiling of this aircraft was lower than the Lancasters (a little over 12,000 feet) the resulting photo-scale was larger. Hence it was used mainly to obtain photography for township and special projects mapping as requested by the three Regions. It is interesting to note that the aircraft was used to obtain photographs of the Benue River basin (at 1: 20,000) from Amar to Lokoja. For many years it had been impossible to obtain satisfactory photography of this area because of persistent cloud cover that never seemed to rise much above the 12,000 feet level. Hence, although rather a large scale for economic small scale mapping, it was better than nothing. In the Northern Region, examples of the Dove's contribution include 1:5,000 photographs of Zaria township, 1:20,000 photography of the Ririwai Hills and Neil's Valley areas in Plateau Province, and strip photography for a proposed railway extension from Nguru to Maiduguri. The above are just three examples from the many sorties flown by the Dove on behalf of the Northern Region. However, towards the end of the 1950s and the early 1960s, when other outside agencies began competing for aerial photography, and contractors in Nigeria and a number of other countries were offering aid programmes, it was decided that the heavy expense entailed in chartering the Dove aircraft could no longer be justified. In 1949-50 it was chartered for 182 days and achieved 469 flying hours, producing about 19,000 photographs covering an area of 18,761 square miles at an average cost of £1 5s for each photograph. In the following year it flew 49 projects covering 3,907 square miles and included the Jebba Dam site at a scale of 1:3,000 for a proposed hydro-electricity scheme, the River Gurara in Niger Province for hydro-electricity and navigation, the Zamfara Valley and Lake Zaru in Sokoto Province.

Agency Photography

The other agencies referred to above included Hunting Surveys Ltd. and Fairey Surveys Ltd. Both of these companies were based in the UK and their first entry into Nigeria was when contracts were awarded to them for large blocks of small scale photography and new large scale photography for important townships in the north, such as Kaduna and Kano. These contracts were first awarded by the DCS, Federal Surveys in Lagos and (later) the Northern Nigerian Survey Department in Kaduna South. The photography taken on behalf of the Northern Nigeria Survey Department differed slightly in its specification from most others in the fact that the fore-and-aft overlap was stipulated at 80% instead of the more usual 60%. The cost of this change was minimal and produced no additional work for the contractor but it resulted in the situation that either the odd numbered photographs or the even numbered photographs would provide the necessary cover for stereoscopic mapping. The subtle difference was in the location of the super-overlaps on the ground (i.e. the overlap of models as opposed to photographs). Cliff Burnside had realised that by selecting either the odd or even numbered photographs of two adjacent strips the super-overlaps could be made to coincide in almost every case. Hence, a minor control point selected on one super-overlap would also fall on the super-overlap of the adjacent strip. This avoided the doubling up of points as so often was the case with the more usual flying specification.

The aircraft used for most of this work was the Dakota, with a slightly higher ceiling than the Lancasters of about 1:23,000 feet; hence this new photography was at a slightly smaller scale of about 1:45,000. The photography produced by these civilian contractors was of a better quality than that previously provided by the RAF; the flight lines were better controlled by the new navigational aids that had been developed. Hence there were fewer gaps in the photography and there were fewer exposures outside the overlapping specifications. In addition, the cameras and their object lenses had also improved greatly; images were sharper and easier to interpret correctly. Furthermore, the geometric properties of the lenses had greatly improved, to the extent that the Aviogon wide angle lenses used in the Wild cameras were almost distortion free. (i.e. image points on a photograph fell within a few microns of their positions predicted by the rules of mathematic perspective projection.). Finally, the photographic emulsions used in these cameras had also been much improved, resulting in finer grain emulsions and a choice of sensitivity for infrared and panchromatic wavebands.

The change over from RAF photography to that provided by outside contractors was very significant in quite another way. It marked a watershed in the way the photographs were to be used to make maps; as will be clearly seen in later paragraphs. In essence, the shift was from producing planimetric maps, almost devoid of height information, to accurately contoured maps with a good distribution of reliable spot heights. An additional contracting agency that appeared in Nigeria towards the end of the 1950s was a Canadian company - Canadian Aero Services. Their Dakota arrived in the country at this time to carry out a large area of 1:50,000 small scale topographic mapping as part of a Canadian funded aid scheme.

The above comments relate, in the main, to small scale work but large scale photography was also being provided under contract for the renewal of important township mapping for towns such as Kano and Kaduna. In the Northern Region, work was put out for these towns under separate contracts but the "20 town" contract for other important towns was the first of two such contracts scheduled to provide cover for most towns of any size in the Region. In addition, very small townships were often photographed on an 'ad hoc' basis whereby if a contractor's aircraft happened to be flying over a small town then it was photographed and then paid for on a fixed price of £50 per town. Most of this work was carried out by Canadian Aero Services Ltd.

Small Scale Topographic Mapping of the Northern Region

An end to field mapping

As stated above, the availability of aerial photographs after the war had a profound effect on the outlook for the topographic mapping of, not only Nigeria, but the whole of the Colonial territories. Their availability meant that there was now a possibility of providing maps of the whole of the Northern Region within a foreseeable period of time. The old graphical field methods of producing standard sheets at a scale of 1:125,000 using the plane table were both slow and expensive. It took from six to eight weeks for a good surveyor and his field team to complete one quarter of a standard sheet covering about 250 square miles. Over difficult terrain the time required could be much longer than that, while the work would be very strenuous and the end product usually not as accurate as that now possible using photogrammetric means. However, the problems of finance and cost had not disappeared, because to make the very best use of the photography, costly plotting machines would be needed in large numbers if a useful rate of production was to be achieved.

An advantage of the graphical field method of mapping by plane tabling was that 'field completion', an operation at the end of the plotting process, was generally unnecessary. The names of places, rivers and features were collected in the course of the work and not, as in the days of aerial mapping, as a separate job. 'Field completion' of aerial mapping was sometimes much delayed and not always very thoroughly carried out. In the haste to map the country as quickly as possible this process tended to be overlooked and many maps went to press with very sparse information, sometimes gleaned from earlier, out-of-date maps. In an ideal world, aerial photographs, and every new map, would be taken to the field and fully annotated by surveyors moving around on foot and accompanied by knowledgeable guides fully conversant in local languages. This ideal was seldom achieved. Many small places off the beaten track were missed or included from directions and names inaccurately supplied from adjacent villages and vantage points and, in the absence of local people, it was difficult to avoid misunderstandings and miss-spellings. It was not unusual, therefore, to find names translating as "Far away", "Behind the hill", "That one", "The Chief's house", "I don't know", etc.

A quotation from Frank Waudby-Smith:-

> *" I remember doing place names on Sheet 29, Denge, and coming across the last place where the Brits formed a square, the Battle of Sifawa, 1906, which they lost, also known as the Satiru Massacre. After the "fighting" the blind Mahdi who had caused all the trouble was led to the Maxim gun, round which the square had not formed, and he stabbed the water jacket with a dagger. "Look," he said, "I have turned their bullets to water." And the correspondent of the Daily Telegraph was not there to hear him ! A very bon mot. If one makes such a brilliant comment one ought to ensure that some reporter hears it, but when I talked to Michael Sharpe, then SDO, about finding and questioning the locals about this strange, bare area of otherwise good farmland, he told me what had happened, why the land was never used again and what had been said. I sometimes wonder if the crossed swords I marked on the map and on my notes ever got into the final printing of sheet 29."*

Plotting Machines

From about 1935 onwards, countries such as Germany, Switzerland and Italy had all developed analogue plotting machines capable of producing good quality mapping from both aerial and terrestrial photographs. But the majority of those in charge of mapping policy in the UK were not so enthusiastic about the capabilities and economics of using such machines. It therefore proved to be most unfortunate that at the beginning of the second world war there were only two first class instruments in the UK, as opposed to the hundreds available for military purposes in Germany and Italy. On the other hand, because of this lack of enthusiasm for these machines, simpler graphical techniques had been developed to make some good use of aerial photographs. These methods worked quite well but they had the very great disadvantage of being unable to produce the accurate contours that can be obtained using stereoscopic plotting instruments.

Planimetric Mapping by the Directorate of Colonial Surveys

With the war over, some surveyors returned to Nigeria but these in fact were few in number and included Keith Hunter, John Pugh and Keith Sargeant who, as mentioned earlier, had remained in the country throughout the war. It was therefore part of government policy under the Colonial Development programme to recruit surveyors as quickly as possible. Even so, with the great post-war need for development and the corresponding demand for maps, it was quite clear that Nigeria would not be able to meet this demand unaided. It was therefore agreed that under the Colonial Development Programme, the DCS should commence the compilation of planimetric mapping from the RAF photography and also carry out the fair drawing and printing of the resulting map sheets, provided the Nigerian Survey Department would carry out all the field work; that is, the provision of the necessary ground control points and the 'finalising' of the printed maps.

Brigadier Hotine, the Director of the DCS, was a great advocate of graphical methods of map compilation from aerial photographs and, bearing in mind the financial constraints imposed upon him, began developing such methods for colonial mapping. It is not the intention in this text to describe these methods in any detail, although more than 80% of the North was provided with 1:50,000 and 1:100,000 scale planimetric maps by these methods in a little over ten years. A great deal of this work was done in the UK by the DCS but much was also done in Kaduna South by the staff of the Northern Region Survey Department and a particular aim of this text is to highlight that achievement.

In the immediate post war years the Nigerian input into the first phase of the new mapping activity was field work for the new style map sheets at scales of 1:50,000 and 1:100,000. These were initially printed in one colour and were often marked as 'Provisional'. Later, when more expertise had been acquired by all concerned, better quality work printed in four colours became the norm. The standard sheet size of ½° x ½° and map specification were the same for all Colonial territories.

Sometimes a sheet area would be covered using four quarter sheets at 1:50,000 scale but in the North, where there was often a paucity of hard detail, cover at 1:100,000 might be sufficient initially. This smaller scaled sheet was often the more practical end product.

The graphical techniques of map compilation from aerial photographs, as developed and utilised by the DCS and later Northern Nigeria, are explained in some detail in the textbook of that name written by Clifford Burnside, as a result of his experiences in the Northern Nigeria Survey Department *(see Appendix XIV Ref. 24)*. The basic assumption behind these techniques is quite a simple one. Namely, that an angle measured about the central point on a near vertical aerial photograph to any two points of detail on the photograph is the correct ground angle, provided the camera axis was vertical at the moment of exposure. This assumption remains true enough for graphical mapping purposes even if the aircraft was not in fact flying exactly straight and level but had a small tilt of no more than about 3° when the photograph was taken. The photograph can therefore be regarded as a form of plane table record at the ground point corresponding to the central point of the photograph. This property can be utilised to carry out a form of graphical (aerial) triangulation with the aid of a set of cheap and simple 'slotted templates'. There is one template per photograph and the radial slots cut in it replicate eight angles to eight minor control points selected on each photograph. When assembled on a laydown board these templates provide a regular distribution of minor control points on every stereoscopic overlap of the photography. These minor controls can then be used to scale and orientate each individual overlap and locate it in its correct position on the map. After that, all points identified as required map detail can be accurately plotted in their correct positions by a simple method of graphical intersection from a base line composed of the two photo centres of the overlap. When the laydown of all templates of the block has been successfully carried out the six points of control on each overlap were then transferred to a plotting sheet on which the required map detail could then be plotted.

Photo Control

A slotted template assembly, such as the one illustrated *(Photo. 58),* could be assembled on any flat surface without any constraints involving known ground points in the form of photopoint control. Unfortunately, such a laydown would be at some arbitrary and unknown scale, of uncertain orientation and of unknown geographical position. Hence the importance of introducing a number of photopoint control points into the block of templates to remedy this unsatisfactory state of affairs. Such a photo control point is a small point of photographic detail that has been positively identified on the ground by the field surveyor *(Photos. 64 and 65)* and then 'fixed' by him using observations to the national control network. From these, its national grid coordinates can then be calculated and plotted to provide the required number of fixed points on a laydown board upon which has already been drawn an accurate map grid.

From the above brief outline it might now be realised that the process of topographic mapping has changed almost beyond recognition and no part more so than the role of the professional ground surveyor. Instead of working in the small area of a particular standard sheet for many months on end with his plane table, constructing upon it the definitive map as he worked over the area, a slow but satisfying job in many ways, he was now to be engaged on providing isolated photo control points that might be up to something like 33 miles apart. The observations to the national network to fix the selected photopoint would use traditional methods involving a theodolite and 300 ft steel tape. The work often provided the surveyor with some interesting surveying problems and gave much scope for ingenuity, especially when it was realised that the accuracy required of any 'fix' was about five feet (i.e. 0.03 mm at map scale). (The words of Major Guggisberg in the quotation given above are particularly apposite to such work). However, the selection of the photopoint itself - the positive identification on the ground of a small photographic image point - was a new skill and could be very demanding in some circumstances. For example, the RAF photography might be five or more years old before being used in the field, not of good quality and taken during a different season. (i.e. wet as opposed to dry). Problems were particularly great in areas almost devoid of obvious natural features and with no permanent man-made objects. In such areas the time lapse between photography and field work was a particularly serious one and the rather poor quality of some of the exposures did nothing to help the situation. Frustrated surveyors were known to have described some of the poorer quality photographs as 'moonlight photography'!

To be most effective a ground control point should fall on as many photographs as possible; that is, in the super overlapping of the strip and also within the lateral overlap of the adjacent strip. This is quite a small area, perhaps a square inch in area on the photograph. Within this restricted area one hoped to find a small, sharply defined feature that could be identified both on the ground and on all the photographs. Having decided upon a suitable photopoint, its ground coordinates in the national framework had then to be determined. Nowadays, with the availability of global positioning systems (GPS), this can be an easy task, but in the past it could be a most challenging but rewarding exercise. Just how difficult mainly depended on how far away the nearest triangulation point was and the nature of the intervening terrain. The Northern Region was well provided with a series of chains of triangulation covering most of the country - due to the enthusiasm of some of its senior members for this kind of survey work. When connections to the existing trig control became difficult, surveyors in the field could resort to a variety of ingenious ways to make this possible. The main point to bear in mind here was that, at this time, the measurement of accurate distances over the ground was difficult, and therefore slow, and so indirect methods using short bases or subtense methods were often resorted to. When connections to the control network were not possible then the Department resorted to astronomical methods of fixing the points.

As a new recruit to the Department, Trevor Brokenshire recalls some early control work he carried out using the RAF photography. Fortunately, that first area south of Jos was not too bad for selecting the control points – but there were other little difficulties !

'In 1951 I was to provide photo-control on or close to existing roads and tracks in an area to the south of Jos; from Panyam, through Pankshin, and off the Plateau to Shendam and as far south as I could get.

I was issued with a 4½" vernier theodolite, a 300 ft x ¼" steel tape, a set of arrows, ranging rods, machetes for clearing where necessary; but, "sorry, we don't have any umbrellas". Could they have known that in the 120° summer heat of Iraq all I had worn was a beard, a turban, shorts and sandals ? In addition there was cement for making up survey beacons, with various other odds and ends of field books and forms, and, last but not least, a specie box with chain, padlock, keys and a supply of cash to pay my labourers their weekly wages. In addition, there were my metal trunks with spare clothing, etc., my 'chop box' full of tins of this and that, and basic cooking items, including two empty kerosene (paraffin !) tins and a piece of expanded metal for the 'oven', a water filter, hurricane lamps, a Tilley lamp, and a canvas bath and hand basin. With all that lot, and now including a substantial wood and canvas 'canopy' which had been made up on the back of the kit-car; the cook and his paraphernalia; a jerry can (ex-Army, dated 1941) and a 44 gallon drum, both full of petrol; the springs were groaning before the journey started..

The only maps available in 1951 were those which had been produced from time to time by the Forestry Department so I had to rely almost entirely on the sets of aerial photographs (flown, I believe, in 1947) which had been issued to me. After settling in at the first of many mud-built, grass roofed rest houses I did a quick reconnaissance by car and the terrain was such that I thought I would be able to establish a chain of minor triangles and fix my photo-control points from the triangulation points. All went well at first, but soon the weather overcame my well-laid plans; within days it was impossible to observe over even the shortest of triangle sides because of the onset of the 'Harmattan', a dust laden north-easterly wind. Now my only method of fixing photo-control points was from a topographical traverse, tied whenever and whenever possible to existing triangulation points.

By now my trusty headman (I wonder who he was ?) had fashioned a Heath Robinson 'umbrella' from sticks and grass, and off we went a-traversing. That was many years ago, and I can only hazard a guess that I traversed for about 100 miles. I see that the 1957 Technical Instructions for Field Parties prescribe the placing of groups of three tertiary cadastral traverse type beacons at 4 or 5 mile intervals. I guess that is what we did - we had to lighten the load by using up the cement - I wonder whether any of the beacons are still there. I suppose I must have fixed my starting point and starting bearing from existing triangulation points but after every 30 stations or so it was necessary to observe the sun, either in the relatively early morning or relatively late afternoon. I must have obtained reasonably reliable *latitudes from existing maps, since I do not recall having any problems with azimuth computations or unacceptable corrections to bearings. I had no problems with finding and fixing photo-control points.*

My wife, Joan, arrived in Jos in June 1952 and that marked the end of my traversing. I spent the rest of my first tour in Jos, living in the "Doll's House" (Photo.87). We left Kano, on leave, on 23rd May 1953 and returned to Kaduna, on 13th November. I was to undertake more photo-control work in an area some way south of Kaduna. Doug Eva was then in charge of the Topo. section and Keith Hunter was still around.'

It is difficult to estimate the number of surveyors engaged on small scale photo control work at this time because, although some work was assigned to surveyors as a specific task, some was also carried out by Provincial Surveyors and Minesfield staff and fitted in with their other duties as convenient. However, it was probably not greater than three or four surveyors at any one time. This figure can be compared with the pre-war era when in seems, again, about four surveyors might be simultaneously engaged on topographic work. The great increase in speed of production was due to two things: the limited nature of the field work now required and the large number of technical staff now engaged on map construction in the drawing office (in fact carrying out a form of 'office plane tabling'); working on a production line basis.

Just how many ground control points were provided for a particular block of photography varied and to some extent was dictated by the availability of trigonometrical and traverse control points in the area. In some areas, where there was little or no control of this nature, astronomical observations for latitude and longitude had to be resorted to, and often the control in such places dropped to about four points; one in each corner of the standard sheet. However, if this was located within the block then one point might effectively serve as the corner point for four adjacent sheets. As a standard ½° sheet was about 33 miles square this resulted in a control density of one point every about 1,000 square miles or so for internal areas of a block ! Because astronomical fixes were of a much lower accuracy than other work it was counter productive to provide too dense a distribution of points when the only method of adjustment available was a simple graphical one. In some ways astronomical field work was rather like altimeter work in that it is an activity 'on its own' and is not directly connected with other instrumental observations. Hence movement about the countryside from one point to the next is not inhibited in any way.

In 1956, Frank-Waudby-Smith was providing astro. control for the future mapping of parts of Sokoto Province where he was the Provincial Surveyor. It was only a part-time job for him and therefore progress was inevitably slow. Hence Clifford Burnside and Clifford Rayner were posted into the area in December 1958 to carry out a programme of astro. control work for the large block of photographs covering the far north and north western parts of the Province It took them over three months to complete this programme and Clifford Rayner recalls some aspects of the project:-

'When Mr Wey returned from leave I was posted, with Cliff Burnside, to Sokoto. The job this time was astro. fixed photo control for slotted template controlled 1:50,000 mapping from air photographs, of an area about 100 miles by 150 miles in west and north Sokoto Province. We were based in Sokoto where Frank Waudby-Smith was Provincial Surveyor. The routine was to select points where an astro-fix was required on a leap frog basis and Cliff and I were to meet up once a month to compare notes, submit work, get drunk and generally have a break. Most of the time we were trekking, especially as we got nearer to the Dahomey and Niger borders. We found one or two of the old boundary markers and connected them to the nearby astro-fixes. Back at HQ the markers were found to be so far from the perceived and accepted position that the new positioning was ignored lest a controversy be ignited!

Technical details. All fixes were to be the result of observations taken over at least two nights. A minimum of four sets were to be meaned, the spread in latitude and longitude for the four sets being less than 2.5" arc. After an initial period of skill acquisition it was not difficult to achieve the specification. One was however working to the limit of the instrumentation. That is to say a 1" Tavistock theodolite, a 0.1 second stop watch and a half second chronometer. Time was received from BBC pip signals via a reliable wireless. All computation was undertaken using a Facit mechanical calculating machine and Peters 8 figure tables. The chronometer was allowed to settle before observations commenced and remained undisturbed until the end of observations two, three or even four days later.'

When the Northern Region Department started to produce planimetric maps in Kaduna it was soon realised that the control being provided by the field surveyors using the standard method was not the best that could be obtained for a commensurate amount of effort in the field and particularly so in the case of the astronomical work. The positional errors that build up in a slotted template laydown are due to errors in scale and orientation of the laydown, but this can easily be reduced considerably without the need for position fixing of identified points on a photograph. In fairly open terrain it is a simple survey task to determine the length and orientation of an identified line on the photograph. A sun azimuth can provide the required orientation, while quick ground taping or sub-tense measurement can determine the length of the line to the rather low accuracy needed. A line on the photograph greater than about 4 inches in length is required to obtain the best results from this method. Having determined the two parameters it was found that these data could be introduced into the laydown quite simply. (This was first introduced over part of the West Sokoto astro block). At a later stage in the development of analytical aerial triangulation this same idea proved to be of good value.

Planimetric Mapping by the Northern Region Department

Nigeria was divided into three Regions: the East with a capital at Enugu, the North with a capital at Kaduna and the West with a capital at Ibadan. Each Region had its own set of Government Departments, including Survey Departments working under the general direction of the Federal Department in Lagos. These departments eventually became autonomous in 1956, with the various responsibilities allocated between them and the core Federal Department. Small-scale mapping was not a matter of great concern to the East and the West because of their relatively small areas. But for the Northern Region, because of its considerable size, mapping was an important requirement and hence there was some emphasis placed upon this. The North was anxious to make greater and greater contributions to its mapping programme and no doubt was looking forward to a time when the Survey Department was sufficiently large and capable of looking after most of its mapping requirements without outside help. Because of this aspiration, a small topographic unit was formed by Keith Hunter in 1952 and Douglas Eva was put in charge of this in 1953.

Eva had noted the various experiments being carried out in Lagos but was not impressed by their potential for serial mapping. For example, Lagos had tried a number of ways for the rapid production of planimetric maps by using photo-mosaics. One such method was to compile and annotate photo-mosaics as map sheets and to photograph these for the production of lithographic printing plates. Such photomaps can only give an acceptably accurate result if the photography used is truly vertical and there is an absence of ground relief. (Both these factors, if left uncorrected, can produce unacceptably large scale changes over the extent of the photograph which will therefore result in errors on the photomap). This method therefore requires a great deal of ground control to limit just some of these errors and this was not usually available.

After a visit to DCS in Tolworth, Eva became convinced that the way forward was to adopt and adapt its slotted template method to the conditions in the North. Some of the best draughtsmen from the drawing office were therefore recruited for training in this new method. The start was not exactly from cold, because a certain amount of good work had been done in Kaduna with aerial photographs, but this had always been project based and over limited areas. In order to produce serial planimetric mapping in the DCS style the Nigerian staff were split into a number of sections, each trained to carry out a specific operation in the map making process. Very briefly these were as follows:-

(i)   mark up each photograph using four water colours to highlight the details to be included on the map (red for roads, blue for water courses and etc.);

(ii)   mark up the three photograph centres that appear on each photograph (i.e. the centre of a photograph plus those on either side in the strip) and select the other six minor control points on the photograph;

(iii)   transfer minor control points onto a thin plastic template, one for each photograph and cut the radial slots in it using a special cutter;

(iv)   plot all ground control points as accurately as possible on the laydown board;

(v)   assemble templates on the laydown board and when satisfied mark the positions of all the minor control points on it;

(vi)   transfer positions of all control onto individual plotting cards, one for each overlap;

(vii)   carry out the plotting of all detail onto the plotting card using graphical intersections to the inked up detail on the photographs;

(viii)   compile individual plots onto a master compilation sheet at 1:40,000 scale;

(ix)   fair draw the sheet with one sheet for each colour.

Many of these tasks were of a completely new nature to the Nigerian staff but they seemed to cope very well with the new techniques. Mistakes were made of course but the learning curve was a steep one, possibly because this new mapping section was a prestigious place to work and staff were not anxious to lose their place working in it.

For final completion, the following further steps were required to be carried out by the lithographic printing section:-

(x)   reduce the fair drawn sheets to either 1:50,000 or 1:100,000;

(xi)   prepare a printing plate, one for each colour;

(xii)   print each sheet in its various colours on a semi-automatic proving press;

(xiii)   after proving, print a limited number of copies of the sheet (about 20) for the Kaduna map store;

(xiv)   send printing plates to Lagos for bulk printing on rotary presses.

It must be noted that, after training, only two expatriate officers were involved in all of the above processes – the Principal Surveyor (Topographic Mapping) in charge of the map making process, and the lithographic printing officer in charge of the printing process.

From small tentative beginnings, the topographic section rapidly began to make progress, and with four standard sheets completed and work on a second block of some further 16 sheets in progress, Keith Hunter in his annual report for 1953, was able to make the following observation:-

> 'The topographic branch, although still far too small to meet the needs of the Region, is none the less rapidly growing both in size and efficiency and can be regarded as the one bright spot in the Survey department which otherwise presents a drab and disappointing picture.'

However, that same report anticipated that, with the arrival of additional equipment from the UK during the coming year, the topographic branch would be capable of producing somewhere between 20 and 25 standard sheets per annum. Control for these sheets, together with a similar number for mapping by DCS, would be provided by Departmental ground survey parties.

Harry Rentema *(Photo.11),* from Holland, was one of a number of surveyors recruited from outside the UK. because of the lack of suitable recruits at home and, on arrival at the beginning of 1953, was posted to the North to join the field parties engaged on photo control work. Some of his comments recorded below give an idea of the nature of the work and also show that not everything went too well at first !

> *'At the end of January 1953 1 collected my car from Lagos and was transferred to Kaduna to work in the recently established Topographical Survey section; pinpointing on air photographs.*
> *My area was about 110 x 90 km, situated on the south-west side of the Jos plateau; Gudi, Jema'a, Kafanchan, and Wamba. I laid out the photographs on the mud floor of the resthouse to locate the available trig points. They were curling badly in the heat and I kept them down with stones. Identified photo-points were connected to the trig points, and numbered on the photographs and the coordinates computed. The scale of the photographs was about 1:50,000 and maps were to be*

produced in Kaduna, using the slotted template method. Photo-points were about 25 km apart.

It was hot and humid and there were plenty of sweat bees to bother us as we climbed hills, waded and swam through rivers and sometimes I could not resist taking a sip of river water.

My headquarters were Kaduna but I also came to Jos for new supplies, and I bought a football for the boys.

Later, I had to verify the maps which were made from the air photographs and the photo-points which I had established. Unfortunately they showed some big distortions and had to be re-plotted.'

The rate at which the Department could compile and fair-draw maps was limited by the trained staff available to do this work. By the end of 1952 there were 15 draughtsmen and 4 field parties were providing field control. Good progress was made through the quite excellent work of the one fully trained Senior Draughtsman, Mr G. N. Igbodo, whose interest and enthusiasm was infused into the junior staff to a remarkable degree. His untimely death in 1953 was a setback in the training process because he was one of the few highly skilled people able to carry out air photo work. Hence, in the early days, there was always a need for a balance to be made between training and production when allocating experienced staff. In these circumstances the offer, made by DCS following a visit by its Deputy Director to Kaduna in 1953, to compile and fair draw a large number of sheets was especially appreciated by the Northern Region Department. With this aid the production of maps surged forward. For example, in May 1954, field control for the mapping of 13,000 square miles of Katsina and West Kano were sent to DCS and by the end of that year the 1:100,000 sheets of these areas were received back in Kaduna. Meanwhile, in the Kaduna drawing office, some further thirteen 1:100,000 sheets and five 1:50,000 sheets were compiled, fair drawn and sent to Lagos for printing. (At that time it was estimated that the cost of each of these fair-drawn standard sheets, covering about 10,000 square miles, was some £200 and took 3 months to compile and draw). This rate of mapping is close to 30,000 square miles for the year, with about half of it being done in Kaduna - quite a remarkable record for a Topo Section that was little over three years old !

In the November of 1955, Brigadier Martin Hotine, Director of the D.C.S. and Advisor to the Secretary of State, visited the Northern Region and inspected the Survey Offices at Kaduna and Jos. It was possibly as a result of this visit that a further boost to the production potential of the Northern Region Department was given by the arrival of a draughtsman instructor in Kaduna at the end of the year; seconded from DCS as a further item of the UK aid now being provided from the Colonial Development and Welfare Fund.

A further result of this aid programme was the secondment of a lithographic printing instructor to the Department. Unfortunately, his rather strict adherence to union regulations and practices did not altogether engender a happy and successful stay in the country; which was brief. A few years then elapsed before the recruitment of William Stopforth M.B.E. who proved to be a most valuable member of the Department. Stopforth had retired after long service with the Survey of India but had decided to take up the post advertised for the Department in the UK. In the new print building, with the new flat bed printing press and other new printing equipment that had been received just prior to his arrival, the training of lithographic staff and the production of multi-coloured map sheets began to make great progress.

Without going into great detail as to when each map sheet was produced, it is perhaps sufficient to record that the topographic branch continued to expand, so that by the end of the 1950s most of the Northern Region had been provided with 1:50,000 or 1:100,000 sheets. Nearly half of these were produced in the Department with the remainder being done in Tolworth by the DCS. In addition, some of the earlier Provisional sheets had been the subject of field revision and second editions were printed. But with manpower always at a premium, this revision and correction in the field never had the highest priority; instead, priority was always given to the production of new mapping. However, by 1957, the pressure for maps had eased to some extent and so Clifford Burnside was detailed to carry out an extensive revision programme of the 1:50,000 sheets covering Katsina Province. Copies of the maps were printed in blue on Whatmans heavy duty drawing paper. Detail was inked-up after confirmation in the field. Names of towns, rivers and etc., were also added, together with any new detail discovered.

The Production of Contoured Topographic Maps in the Northern Region

The value of a planimetric map, while somewhat limited, was of course very much better than no accurate map of any sort. However, the lack of topographic information in the form of contours and/or spot heights had always been acknowledged as a serious deficiency that needed to be addressed if and when resources became available to remedy the situation.

The late 1940s and early 1950s were a time for experimentation both at the DCS headquarters at Tolworth in the UK and in the Nigerian Survey Headquarters in Lagos. The lack of height information on the planimetric sheets being produced by DCS for Nigeria (and other territories) was a cause of concern. The potential for contoured mapping using the stereoscopic photography available was there but was not being exploited. In Tolworth, early experiments with parallax bar readings, and the rather laborious calculation of approximate height values from these, gave a distribution of spot heights of some sort but depended very much on the distribution of any height data available. From these results, tentative form lines could be provided with the aid of a skilful stereoscopic inspection of the overlapping area of two photographs using a simple stereoscope. But, like all approximate methods of working, to achieve results of even tolerable accuracy a great amount of ground control was needed and of course this was not usually available. Hence, whilst occasionally such methods might solve isolated requirements, it was not a viable method for serial mapping of large areas.

Multiplex Plotters

The DCS solution was therefore to equip the department with cheap stereoscopic plotting instruments of the Williamson Multiplex type, both long bar (for aerial triangulation) and short bar (for stereoscopic plotting). At the peak point of utilisation the DCS had a total of 148 instruments – probably the largest collection in the world ?

The earliest contributions of DCS to contoured mapping in the North were concerned with specific areas of high priority such as the tinfields of the Jos Plateau. These maps were at a scale of 1:50,000 with contours at 50 feet intervals. Because of the importance of tin mining to the economy of the North, the Plateau and Minesfield areas of the Region were usually the first to benefit from any improved photogrammetric techniques that might become available. Now, for the first time, outside contractors (such as Fairey Air Surveys Ltd. and the Air Operating Company Ltd.) were employed in Nigeria to provide the necessary aerial photographs. One of the earliest examples is illustrated *(Map 26)* and is a part of the second (1959 contoured) edition of the Naraguta NE area of the Minesfield (Sheet 168 NE). Other special project areas mapped by D.C.S. from photography provided by Hunting Surveys Ltd. (previously known as A.O.C. Ltd) were the Shiroro Gorge Dam area, the Kainji Dam area and sugar plantation, and agricultural areas in the vicinity of Lake Chad.

The characteristics of Multiplex instruments (and many others) are described in the text book by Burnside *(Appendix XIV Ref. 24)* and in a series of nine articles written for the Photogrammetric Society *(Appendix XIV Ref. 25)*. However, in brief, these instruments cannot make the best use of the photography because the stereoscopic images produced by them are poor and much inferior to that produced by other plotters of much higher cost. Over the years, DCS produced great quantities of good small scale mapping from a very large set of these instruments but it must be said the results were due to the quality of the observers rather than the quality of the machines themselves.

For many years the DCS used Multiplex exclusively for its small-scale work and in fact this type of instrument is not suitable for anything but small scale work. The Survey Department in Lagos also acquired such a machine – a three projector short bar instrument. With its poor imagery and the need for dark room conditions this type of instrument is not easy to use and so it is not at all surprising that it did not appear to make any great impact on the mapping situation. As Trevor Brokenshire remembers below in his brief encounter with material produced by it:-

> *'...........On completion of the photo-control work in early 1954, we moved eastwards into an area adjacent to the foothills of the Jos Plateau. The proposed task was to contour the DRESS SW quarter sheet, using a Multiplex-plotted 1:50,000 scale base map prepared from aerial photos, at the same time providing revision data, such as names of villages, rivers, streams and hills. The original instruction,*

(born of desperation to produce at least <u>one</u> contoured quarter-sheet ?) was to use a plane table and clinometer to contour, with the assistance of form-lines which had been shown, from the aerial photos, on the provisional map. As far as I can recall, all details and form lines were shown in blue.

Several days were spent in checking the accuracy of the base map, and it soon became obvious that the position of detail did not correspond to the positions of triangulation points which had been plotted on to the base map by their correct co-ordinates. Detail was only 'correct' relative to the next adjoining detail and it was impossible to scale distances accurately from the map to calculate differences in heights where slope angles had been measured. My 1954 report to Doug Eva refers to positional errors of approximately 500 feet on the southern edge of the sheet, with the errors becoming progressively worse to greater than 1,500 feet on the northern edge. This seems to have been due to the lack of any photo-control points, poor interpretation of photo-detail and slap-dash, 'let's get it done quickly', draughtsmanship

The Survey Department base map was not the only one which was incorrect; an aerial survey map of adjoining land, privately produced for the largest tin mining company on the Plateau (A.T.M.N.) also had errors in both horizontal and contour detail. The error in detail on the A.T.M.N. map was greater in the south than in the north, and although the heights of almost all of the hilltops were reasonably correct, contours in lower parts of the map had errors of approximately 150 feet..............

Since it was not possible to use the plane-table method, I provided height control with altimeters and contoured by form-lining in the field and by stereoscopic inspection of aerial photographs.

*..........Having regard to the large shift of detail in the northern part of the quarter-sheet I decided that there was no point in adding contours. With hindsight of over 40 years, it could have been contoured, since the contours were related to detail which, in small sections, would not have been dramatically changed in position after re-mapping with adequate control. The work was completed on 11th June 1954. I guess I was the first person in Northern Nigeria to find such large errors in newly produced 1:50,000 scale maps, aptly called "Provisional"; but probably not he last, and probably also **the last surveyor to produce a contoured map in the field ?'***

These experiences of Trevor Brokenshire with the products of the photogrammetry were not unique, many other surveyors had similar experiences that had made them quite sceptical about the 'new wonder' method of surveying. The problem was that too many untutored people were being far too optimistic about the capabilities of the photogrammetry generally and especially the abilities of anaglyph machines such as the Multiplex and Kelsh plotters.

Advances in Photogrammetric Techniques

In the Northern Region Department, Douglas Eva had noted with interest the successful use of Multiplex at Tolworth by DOS (the name was changed to the Directorate of Overseas Surveys in 1958). The North was now anxious to expand its mapping capabilities as funds for development were now slowly becoming available. The problem was a simple financial one: to make a significant contribution to the provision of contoured maps of the North at least six instruments would be required. But six instruments of better performance than the Multiplex would be beyond any available budget. Also, it was obvious that the Multiplex was a difficult instrument to use and required great skill on the part of the operator to produce decent results. To train-up sufficient Nigerian staff would therefore take an appreciable time. As a tentative alternative solution he therefore bought, in 1959, an approximate solution instrument, of roughly the same price as a short bar Multiplex, for £1,000. This instrument, a Santoni Stereomicrometer SMG Mk 1 *(Photo.61),* had recently appeared on the market and is described in references 24 and 25 in *Appendix XIV.* The most obvious advantage of this Santoni approximate solution instrument was its remarkably good optical viewing system in which full-sized 9"x 9" inch (230 x 230 mm) diapositives were observed using transmitted light. The images produced were both bright and clear and 'the floating mark' used to determine the height of ground points in the stereo model was easy to see and use. In addition, the instruments did not require the dark room conditions necessary for Multiplex use.

The disadvantage was the fact that the stereo model produced in the machine was not distortion free, as in more expensive instruments. These distortions were corrected for by a number of ingenious but rather complicated correctors. To make use of these, and reduce residual errors to an acceptable level, more control points were required to set up each model – a minimum of six, in fact, as opposed to the three of the superior machines. This however did not necessarily mean more ground control work had to be done in the field. Each model covered about 10 square miles of ground and so any instrument would require a tremendous amount of surveying if it were to be controlled directly from the work of field surveyors. Clearly this was not a practical proposition and so small scale models of this nature were invariably supplied with their control by a technique known as aerial triangulation (described below). Unfortunately, this process cannot be carried out on instruments such as the Santoni model and in fact a large first order instrument is required for the purpose. Fortunately, additional funds became available and two Wild A8 first order plotting instruments were purchased in 1961 at a cost of some £8,000 each *(Photo. 62)*.

These instruments are much easier to use, produced results of the highest possible accuracy and are ideally suited to large scale mapping of townships at scales such as 1:2,400 or greater. In addition, a method of using them for aerial triangulation had just been developed at the I.T.C. (the International Training Centre for Photogrammetry, at Delft in Holland). To take advantage of this development Clifford Burnside, then acting as Principal Surveyor (Topo), spent some months of his home leave at the I.T.C. studying the technique of aerial triangulation using plate bubbles. (Doug Eva had been promoted to Surveyor-General on the retirement of Keith Hunter in 1960). The intention was that, initially, both A8s would be used for carrying out the triangulation process and fulfil the same role as the slotted template laydowns had done for the planimetric work. In the long term it was envisaged that the instruments would also be used for large scale plotting and contribute to the township mapping programme as described in the next section.

On first delivery, the characteristics, potential and limitations of the Santoni instrument for contour mapping in the Northern region were not fully appreciated and Clifford Burnside was given the job of looking into this matter. (This work later became the subject of a successful thesis submitted to the R.I.C.S. in 1962). His conclusions were that the instrument was better suited to the Department's requirements than Multiplex instruments and would provide better and more reliable results if its limitations were fully appreciated and the required extra density of model control was always provided. However, there would be a limited number of models on which even 6 points per model would not suffice - perhaps something like 5% of models, but depending entirely on the quality of the flying. This adverse situation arose when, in the orientation procedure, the difference in fore-and-aft tilt on an overlapping pair of photographs was greater than about 3°, but this could be detected during the aerial triangulation process on the Wild A8. In this case a further 3 points would be needed down the centre of the model. The initial Santoni SMG Mk.1 Stereomicrometer purchased had a corrector that dealt directly with this situation but the seven additional instruments purchased over the next few years were Mk. 4 models, in many ways superior to the first, but with that particular corrector omitted. This suggested that, with the better flying aids that were becoming available, the problem would not arise in the future, and this proved to be the case in Nigeria. Whichever plotting machine is used for plotting small scale work (Multiplex, Santoni SMG, B8 etc.) the control points required to set up each model will need to come from a process of aerial triangulation. Hence, the fact that a few additional points are required in the case of the Santoni instrument was not of any great consequence. (Note: The technical details of all the techniques and equipment mentioned above can be found in reference 24 of *Appendix XIV*).

Having decided to go ahead with the use of Santoni plotters, the matter of training Nigerian staff in these totally new fields needed to be resolved and this was done in the first instance by sending the two best team leaders in the Topographic Section, Messrs Onyile and Oloyede, to the I.T.C. under the Netherlands aid programme. They were there for just under a year and undertook a general course in aerial photogrammetry that included theoretical studies but also required students to become proficient operators on a range of plotting instruments. Both acquitted themselves well at Delft and on return immediately began training staff in the use of the Santoni instruments whilst they themselves practised the method of aerial triangulation using plate-bubbles. The training process went well and a number of topo. staff quickly learned to use the plotters. Furthermore, because of the clarity of the optical system, the contours they began to plot after a comparatively short time became accurate and reliable. In later years the best of these operators were also sent to Delft under the Netherlands training aid scheme.

Aerial Triangulation

Aerial triangulation is a technique used in photogrammetry to reduce drastically the amount of ground control required to scale and level up the set of stereo models produced from a block of aerial photography.

In large scale work, such as township mapping, it is quite feasible to provide the control requirement for each individual model directly from field observations because the distances involved in traversing and levelling are not too great (this kind of operation is described in a later section concerned with township mapping).

However, the above approach would be very time consuming and not really a practical proposition for controlling a large block of models such as those needed to cover a 1:50,000 standard sheet. The minimum control needed to scale and level up a stereo model in a plotting machine (such as a Wild A8 or B8) would be two plan control and three height control points, but in practice twice this minimum would be preferable and especially so when using inexperienced staff and the Santoni type of instrument. Also of course in the case of the small-scale mapping the distances involved are some twenty times greater than in township work and each standard ½° sheet needed about 120 stereo models to cover a ground area of some 1,000 square miles. The prospect of controlling each of these stereo models directly from ground observations could not be contemplated, hence the need for the aerial triangulation.

The process is made possible because of two factors:-

i.   the 60% overlapping of adjacent photographs in the strip produces a 10% overlapping of adjacent models,
ii. two adjacent models make use of a common middle photograph.

The first factor means that the location, scale and orientation of the first model can be transferred with accuracy to the next model and so also can the levelling across the model at a right angle to the line of flight - this joining-up is therefore in the form of a hinge connection. Some errors must be involved with this model joining process and the transfer of information but these are small and random in nature and can be treated very much in the same way as the misclosures of traversing or levelling.

The second factor is utilised in an obvious way in large plotting machines that have the ability to retain the middle photograph within the instrument in its correct position in space after the correct setting up of the first model (i.e. absolute orientation). The third photograph is then inserted into the instrument, joined to it to form the second model that must then also be in correct orientation and scale with only the effects of small random errors that must occur in the relative orientation process. Unfortunately, such instruments were expensive and outside the range of the financial resources of the Northern Nigerian Survey Department in 1961. However, a recent development had occurred that made aerial triangulation possible on less expensive instruments such as the Wild A8. This technique, employing sensitive inclinometers to record and then reproduce the tilts on the middle photograph as required, was investigated and taken up by the department and later used with great success.

The main source of complication with the aerial triangulation process is the accumulation of errors in height values along the strip - a factor that made it prudent to limit the number of models in a strip to a maximum of about 24. Although the individual observational errors made were small and random in nature, the propagation of errors in height along the strip could not be treated by a linear form of adjustment because analysis indicated these particular errors produced a form of weighted summation of error that in turn resulted in a strong systematic effect in the propagation of height errors along the strip. Fortunately, a quadratic form of adjustment was adequate, provided the strip was not over-long. Hence, height control was needed down the middle of the strip as well as at both ends. A simple graphical adjustment using a thin spline was a common way to deal with such errors, but in fact the Department adopted a more complex device known as the Jerie Analogue Instrument (Height) to provide a more effective mechanical adjustment of all height values. When set up, the device provided a simultaneous least square adjustment of all height values of points within the block.

The inventor, Dr Jerie, had also produced a companion device for carrying out a similar rigorous adjustment of planimetric values, but this involved a much more complex process requiring a number of reiterations. In consequence it was a time consuming operation that the Department decided not to incorporate in its system. (The Ordnance Survey in the UK decided at that time to use the planimetric but not the height version of the Jerie devices). Because planimetric errors within a block do not propagate in such a drastic way and are usually smaller in value anyway, the Department decided to opt for Stereo Templates as the most appropriate form of adjustment for the planimetric errors. In appearance and use they are similar to the ordinary slotted templates mentioned earlier but, instead of being produced from individual photographs, these templates are produced from individual stereo models as they are generated in the plotting instrument. Hence they utilise model, not photograph, geometry and so are less complex in nature and deal with much smaller errors. They very rarely gave any problems on the laydown board.

As a consequence of the above situation it will be realised that the control requirement for a block of models covering a standard sheet is mainly one of the provision of a satisfactory distribution of height control points over the area. The accompanying diagram *(Illustration 63)* shows a distribution of plan and height control points that was considered to be an optimum by the Department.

From an examination of the diagram it can be seen that the height control lies within three narrow bands that run down the centre of the block as well as the two edges This control is confined, therefore, to points situated on the first, eighth and fifteenth models on every other strip. On each of these models there is a distribution of six height control points. When these models are levelled up in the A8 there are twice the minimum number of points required for the process. Any gross error in one point could be detected and that point eliminated. In addition, when such a model is set up, the best mean fit using all satisfactory points should enhance the overall accuracy of the height values to some degree.

The planimetric control requirement is far less demanding and is located only at the four corners of the block. This is provided in the form of two points per model because this then ensures that, at the commencement of the operation, the first model of strip 1 can be accurately scaled and orientated. The same provision in the last model means that there is a ready check on how well these parameters had been carried forward along the strip, and this provides some measure of the accuracy with which the triangulation had been carried out. A similar comment can be made concerning the downward transfer of scale and orientation from one strip to the next.

Finally, it should be realised that if the sheet lies within a block of sheets being mapped then the planimetric control requirement can be as low as one pair of points per 1,000 square miles because in some cases the corner control will be common to the other three adjacent sheets. The problem in small scale work is therefore how to provide a satisfactory pattern of height control points for the aerial triangulation.

Height Control using Altimeters

As seen above, the major problem was how to provide the pattern of height control points as quickly and economically as possible, bearing in mind that an accuracy of the order of +/- 3 feet would be quite adequate for the purpose. It was decided that even low order levelling or height traversing would not provide a practical solution to this problem. When presented with a problem of this nature the use of barometric heights was often put forward and indeed had been used on occasions by DCS and Northern Nigerian Survey field parties in a number of ways. Unfortunately, although often good, the results could be erratic with errors of perhaps as much as 15 feet appearing in the results for no apparent reason. However, articles appearing in the Empire Survey Review in the early 1960s written by Desmond O'Connor seemed to suggest a way forward on the matter and it was from this work that the departmental method using Wallace and Tiernan altimeters was evolved. The method is well described in the R.I.C.S. thesis submitted by Dominic Moss in 1965 *(Ref.78 Appendix XIV)*. The important features of the method can be summarised as follows-

1. base altimeters are placed at the top and bottom of each band of required height control points at the end of each strip;
2. on a given day, some eight or more instruments are placed in line between the two base stations on the identified photo control points;
3. all the altimeters are read and the readings recorded by trained observers every 15 minutes for as long a period as possible during the day – usually four to five hours;
4. on the next day the altimeter parties move to the second line of required points some two miles to the east or west;
5. the party moves about 15 miles east or west to the next double line and the regime of observations is repeated.

By this means all the points within a narrow band of terrain can be observed over two days with every other model down the strip being provided with six control points. It took about a week to prepare for this operation and so over the period of one month each field party could provide the three bands of height control points for a block of models; i.e. about 1,000 square miles of mapping. Of course, many bands would in fact be an edge of two adjacent sheets, hence internally, the control density can be regarded as somewhat under two bands of control per sheet. By this means each sheet could be provided with 72 height points in three bands in a remarkably short time and with a certain flexibility not always possible in other methods.

It was found that the accuracy of the height values calculated from these observations was rather better than the +/- 5 feet accuracy required. After some experience in the field the following points were noticed:-

1. the atmospheric gradient along a line of points could occasionally be as great as one foot per mile, but of course in this method this possible source of error was eliminated – unlike all other methods of using altimeters;
2. it was also noticed that a small local atmospheric disturbance would sometimes cross a line and cause perhaps two or three readings to be in error by five or more feet. Again not often detected in other methods unless readings were taken over a sufficiently long period;
3. because six points could always be provided on certain models set up in the A8 instrument any serious error in any one point would show up as a discrepancy when levelling up that model and could therefore be tracked down and disregarded - a valuable stop on possible error propagation. In addition, in theory at any rate, with a 100% redundancy rate in the control provision, the accuracy of the height values could be enhanced using a mean square error adjustment;
4. atmospheric conditions were most stable during the long dry season which was also the best time for moving field parties about the countryside;
5. although described as 'points' this type of control in fact takes the form of a large patch of flat ground and was much easier to find and document than a planimetric point;
6. the provision of a much less dense array of planimetric control points could often be provided within the period taken to carry out the height work.

The only remaining constraint on the smooth running of the system was to ensure that ground height information in the form of triangulation points or road bench marks were available for use by the base altimeter stations. This was a responsibility of the Principal Surveyor (Topo.) to ensure that, where necessary, the road levelling programme that placed third order bench marks at one mile intervals along selected roads was running ahead of the topographic mapping programme. This height data was also required by the Geological Survey Department in their survey of gravity anomalies.

This method of controlled altimetric heighting called for regular and careful calibration of the Wallace and Tiernan altimeters before, during and after the control observations for each mapping block. An ideal place for this exercise was along the road which descended from the Jos Plateau to the Jema'a plain. All the instruments were placed together on a suitably padded floor of a pick-up vehicle and each read at 100 feet vertical intervals from approximately 4,000 feet above sea level on the plateau down to about 1,000 feet on the plain, thus covering their normal full operational range during the control work.

Compilation and Plotting

On the completion of the plotting, all detail was transferred to the master compilation sheet but only after edge comparison with adjacent plots to ensure that minor discrepancies were averaged out and any major ones investigated and reconciled. As with the planimetric mapping, the master compilation was carried out at a slightly larger than final plot scale; the reduction to 1:50,000 or 1:100,000 only taking place just prior to the production of the lithographic printing plates.

The first contoured sheet produced by the Department was Sheet 123 from aerial photography taken by Hunting Surveys Ltd. in January 1962. The planimetric control was derived from existing triangulation points in the area and the height control provided by the altimeter method described earlier. The sheet was printed in four colours and three stipples in January 1962. This printing was carried on a semi-automatic flat bed proving press that had recently been imported. Much to their surprise, Clifford Burnside and Dominic Moss were detailed to collect the large packing cases containing the various parts of the machine from the railway sidings, assemble it and get it into working order – it took about a month for them to do this.

On checking the finished map against the existing 1:125,000 sheet no serious anomalies were detected and there was good agreement of plan detail and contour shapes. Other tests carried out later confirmed that the quality of the work was satisfactory. At this point, 20 copies of the sheet were printed in Kaduna for local use, after which the lithographic plates were sent to the Federal Department in Lagos for bulk printing on their rotary presses as required.

Map Production

Having proved that the many aspects of the new production process were providing the correct results, the Department was now able to set in motion a mapping procedure that would become a major part of the routine work of the Department. The first block of sheets to be undertaken was the Kaduna-Zaria Block comprised of nine sheets, in the following configuration, covering an area of about 10,000 square miles:-

101	102	103
123	124	125
144	145	146

This area, apart from sheet 123, was photographed by Fairey Surveys Ltd. at about 1:45,000 scale between December 1962 and January 1963. All the control point work was completed by the end of December 1963 by field parties working under Malcolm Anderson, working through two dry season field seasons of about six months duration. In the mapping office, all the aerial triangulation, plotting of overlaps and compilation onto standard sheets was completed by the end of 1965. Also, by the end of 1965, the following 16 sheets had been fair drawn and published at a scale of 1:50,000:-

	102 (all quarters)
123 (all quarters)	124 (all quarters)
144 (NE & NW)	145 (NE & NW).

Fair drawing was in progress on the other 20 quarter sheets.

Having now been in production for some time, the following rates of progress were noted at the time. In the aerial triangulation process it was found that one strip of 15 models could be observed in a working week. Hence a block with 8 strips would take about two months to complete. If both A8 instruments were engaged on the work the capability would therefore be for 12 sheets per annum. In the case of the Santoni plotting section, they could plot between 50 and 60 models per month – the amount depended to some extent on how much training was being carried out in the section. As a sheet contains some 120 models, this suggested a mapping rate of 6 sheets per annum.

In the early days, all plotting was done on Santoni Stereomicrometers instruments. Eventually, eight of these instruments were in use. However, in 1962, two better plotting machines were purchased to increase the plotting capability of the unit still further. These were Wild B8 and B9 second order instruments using an exact solution to the photogrammetric modelling process. Difficult models that were the results of rather large tilts of the aerial photographs therefore no longer needed to split into two narrower models. Also, because of their superior performance and ease of use, model orientation and plot times on these instruments were shorter.

The second block of sheets, the West Kano Block, was photographed by Hunting Surveys Ltd in December 1963 and was comprised of six sheets in the following configuration:

$$55 \quad 56 \quad 57$$
$$78 \quad 79 \quad 80.$$

By the end of 1965 the situation was as follows:-

- field work had been completed for the four sheets: 78,79 80 and 55 with field work in progress on sheets 55 and 56,
- in the mapping office plotting was in progress on sheet 76, with aerial triangulation in progress on sheet 55,
- ground control reconnaissance and aerial photography at 1:45,000 scale was in progress on the third Departmental block of mapping, the Katsina-West Kano Block:

$$14 \quad 15 \quad 16$$
$$33 \quad 34 \quad 35 \quad 36 \quad 37$$
$$58 \quad 59$$

- In addition, contract details were being prepared for the fourth block of photography for the following sheets to be photographed early in 1966:-

$$165 \quad 166 \quad 167$$
$$187 \quad 188$$

It is important to note that the work of the mapping and drawing staff was greatly facilitated by the fact that they were working in good conditions provided by the purpose built accommodation *(Photos. 59 and 60)*. These were funded and built from resources within the Department and were designed and built under the supervision of Paul Ward, a senior member of the Department. The buildings housing the expensive instruments such as the A8s and Wild B8 and B9 were air conditioned.

Contoured Mapping of Townships in the Northern Region

Large Scale Mapping

As indicated in earlier sections, large scale mapping of one kind or another had been going on in the territory, particularly the south, from very early days because of urgent requirement for maps, plans or diagrams of government areas, military quarters and important township areas. Usually, they were essentially planimetric in character, although the provision of spot height information was provided where necessary. Unfortunately, this work was often delegated to local staff, many of whom had received minimum training and often had to work with little or no professional supervision. It is therefore not surprising that some of those early efforts were found to be inaccurate and inadequate and especially so in the larger northern towns such as Jos and Kano. Improvements and revisions seemed to take place at frequent intervals.

In the Northern Region, the situation was finally remedied by the awarding of contracts to outside surveying companies to produce the up to date and accurate maps required, most of which would be at a scale of 1:2,400, with spot heights and contours at five feet intervals. The source material for this work would be aerial photography taken with the normal wide-angle cameras with a photo scale of about 1:10,000. Among the towns dealt with this way were the following:-

- Kano was mapped at the standard scale in a contract awarded by the Department to Hunting Surveys Ltd in 1962; the control being provided by Hunting's surveyors.

- Jos was mapped at the scale of 1:2,400 under a contract awarded to Fairey Surveys Ltd in 1963 with control being provided by the Department.

The Northern Nigerian Survey Department was always wishing to be more directly involved with the production of township mapping by photogrammetric means but, as resources were much taken up with the small scale mapping programme, the approach had to be a cautious one. The first real involvement occurred when the Department embarked on its 'Twenty Towns Programme'. This was the contoured mapping at 1:2,400 scale of twenty major towns other than those listed above. This contract was awarded to Fairey Surveys Ltd. in 1961. Ground control would be provided by the Department for the 1:10,000 photographs (taken this time by a rather ancient DeHavilland Rapide aircraft belonging to the company). All plotting would be done in the UK by the company and all fair-drawing would be done by the Department in Kaduna.

Great care was taken with the Departmental input into this work and especially the selection and documentation of the photopoints themselves. This was a new type of work for the Nigerian Survey Assistants who were now becoming involved with photo work and they were sometimes uncomfortable with it because, unlike traditional field work, there could be no 100% check on the correctness of the work. Problems, when they did present themselves, were always in areas of sparse firm detail outside the built-up areas of townships where development was being anticipated. Nevertheless, there were very few problems and the contractor's comments were highly favourable concerning the quality of the data being sent to them. The few cases of error in identification that did occur were always investigated in the field and usually proved to be due to undetected changes in detail that had occurred in the time interval between photography and fieldwork.

Because the distances involved in this type of work were comparatively short, all models were provided with full height and planimetric control. National control was usually available in or near the township area and, from this, height control points were often supplied by ordinary levelling, while the coordinates of the plan control points were supplied by the use of catenary taping. This latter technique involves the use of a 300 feet tape suspended above the ground and therefore taking up a catenary shape. The method requires little ground clearing and the procedure evolved by the Department, using only basic survey equipment, produced results of high accuracy at a good speed. After allowing for any predicted growth of a township area, a set of closed traverses would be agreed upon that would enable all the photopoints to be readily coordinated from the permanent survey beacons put in prior to traversing. The specification for the misclosure of these traverses was 1 part in 100,000; i.e. a tolerance of just over 0.5 inches per mile of traversing. After some experience, the expatriate surveyors doing this work sometimes managed to achieve a misclosure of half this value. Malcolm Anderson and Cliff Rayner did a great deal of this work and became very proficient at it. They certainly had plenty of practice as the following remarks from Cliff Rayner makes abundantly clear:-

'1961 was a touring year. After a welcome break in Kaduna I was posted to Funtua to undertake photo control for township mapping. This did not take very long and I was soon off again to southern Sokoto to do some astro control for topographic mapping at a scale of 1:50,000. I had hardly got more than a single photo point completed when I developed an abscess under one of my wisdoms. I was lucky to meet a doctor on tour who was fighting a meningitis epidemic. He gave me some antibiotic and suggested that I return to Kaduna and have it out! John Evans relieved me and sent my kit back to Kaduna. I had the tooth out courtesy Mr Fox. I was out of action for about two and a half weeks and was then posted to Kafanchan, Bama, Mubi, Gwoza, Dikwa and Bauchi in turn. All the work was photo control for township mapping at 1 2,400 scale. I enjoyed the work and for much of the time I made Maiduguri my base.......

....Gwoza was a ten day job and Dikwa not much longer. After Dikwa I was posted to Bauchi where I had an Education Department house (very comfortable). The job was a bit frustrating - trying to put right somebody-else's work.

Next posting was Katsina on the other side of the country, about 200 miles north of Kaduna. Katsina was a big assignment, to provide photo control for the whole town from scratch, and was expected to last me to the end of the year and the end of my tour. I made about 160 pillars and completed scores of miles of catenary traversing. With the rains at an end, and the Harmattan dry season closely following it, could be quite cool at night. One day having started work at sun rise, the temperature rose 20°F within the first hour! By mid-day it was quite warm.'

Rayner went on leave at the end of that assignment and, in his absence, Malcolm Anderson carried out the control work for Gusau Township and then went on to carry out the control work for Bauchi Township (March 1962).

The control and mapping situation in Gusau was not unlike that in many other towns in the North. The first plans of Gusau had been produced in 1925 by the Native Authority, at a scale of 1: 4,800 and depicted the old town and its pattern of completely random building along routes radiating from the centre. These plans were followed in 1928 by a Resident's Sketch Plan, concerned mainly with the residential area. The town was given considerable commercial impetus when the railway arrived in 1929 and control surveys, based on True North, were carried out in residential and commercial areas, and provided the basis for a series of layouts and proposals made by Government and Native Authority surveyors right through until 1940. In 1950 thoughts turned to air mapping and 5 strips of photography were flown, comprising 77 photographs of the town and its environs. Control for this was carried out in September 1952, but the existing ground control network was not extended. Later, the five resultant 1:4,800 scale mapsheets, produced at the Survey Department in Lagos in 1953, provided inadequate coverage for an expanding commercial area. In 1955, the area came under review for future development and the maps were revised in December of that year, from traverses based on the old cadastral control *(Map 28)*. A small amount of primary and secondary Cadastral control for a light industrial area was added in January, 1958, but further expansion was visualised, and proposals were made to revise and extend the entire system of cadastral control in the town. The control register in Survey headquarters listed 73 old primary points, 54 of them with heights based on a lost railway datum, 17 secondary points and eight tertiary points. A decision was made to reject all these unreliable old control beacons unless they could be found, renumbered and adequately tied into and adjusted to a new system. The opportunity to do this came in 1961 when it was decided to extend the network with a comprehensive survey based on Colony North, and replace the old, out-of-date and very misleading air maps still available to the public *(Map 29)*.

It was on the Gusau project that the Computing Section queried the 'accuracy' of Anderson's work when he submitted a catenary traverse that closed only to something a little better than 1:100,000 – his more usual misclosure was of the order of 1:200,000!! The Section even suggested where the small blemish might have occurred and this indeed proved correct. The speed of working overall was about 10,000 feet of traversing per day.

As the pace of the development of certain Northern towns increased, it was realised that many large scale maps were becoming in need of urgent revision. In large areas of new development, usually on the fringe of the existing detail, the best plan was to completely re-map. However, within towns where there was a great deal of hard detail already plotted, such as Samaru - Zaria, it was thought that the task might be reduced by simply adding to the existing mapsheets using the old detail as control. It was therefore decided to re-photograph this area and carry out experiments to determine how best the revision might be done. In 1965, one of the A8 instruments was taken off aerial triangulation and used for large scale mapping work.

Training and Recruitment

With regard to training and recruitment, promising junior technical staff of the mapping office were selected to attend the six months long technicians training course at the I.T.C. in Delft. This course provided sufficient theoretic knowledge and much practical training to enable students to operate most types of photogrammetric plotting instruments. In addition, the department had been most fortunate in recruiting Mr Gabriel Obenson into the Topographic Section. He had completed the full course of study at the I.T.C. with the highest possible grades and began working as assistant to the Principal Surveyor (Topo.) in 1965. His sudden departure at the end of 1965 had not been anticipated and was a most un-welcome event.

The lack of recruitment of young Nigerians into the professional grades in the Department had been the subject of a number of campaigns, all with little or no success. There were other competing professions that young people found much more appealing than field surveying. (It was soon realised that many of the factors that made the profession of land surveying a most attractive way of life to young expatriates from western Europe did not apply to young African graduates!).

A Sad and Unexpected Conclusion.

By the end of 1965, the Topographic Branch of the North Nigerian Survey Department had made remarkable progress since its inception in 1953. It was by now a modern, well-equipped section capable of meeting many of the surveying needs of the Northern Region. In fact, with the bulk of the 'de novo' mapping of the countryside and townships scheduled to be completed in the near future it was anticipated that it would be able to maintain this mapping and also deal with any new special projects work that emerged.

A regular stream of visitors from the United Nations and elsewhere commented most favourably on its work and the fact that, apart from two expatriate officers, all mapping office work was being carried out by Nigerians. The only weakness to this scenario however was not apparent to such visitors, but it was nevertheless a most crucial one, - the all important field control work was being carried out expertly and expeditiously almost entirely by young expatriate surveyors. (Idle or much under-used expensive photogrammetric equipment, usually supplied under some aid programme or other, was a familiar feature in many third world countries at this time). The Department had been aware of this weakness for a long time and with the coming of self-government, and the slow but steady stream of expatriates retiring from government service, the situation was becoming more acute. Unfortunately, as indicated earlier, the recruitment and training of professional Nigerian surveyors had not met with any great success. However, one science graduate had been recruited in later years and had been sent off to the School of Military Survey in the U.K. for survey training.

On 12th January 1966, Clifford Burnside retired from the Department and left Nigeria after 12 years in the Department with rather more than half of them being involved with topographic work of one sort or another. His successor was Malcolm Anderson, a Senior Surveyor who had also acquired much experience in control and mapping work. Just two days later the military coup occurred in which the Sardauna of Sokoto and other Northern senior ministers were assassinated. This was to be the first blow in the events that were to bring to an abrupt end the work of the Department before the end of the year.

The 'Handing Over Notes: Burnside to Anderson January 1966' are reproduced below, almost in their entirety, because in this way they most clearly indicate the health of the Department, the breadth and diversity of its work programme and the firm plans for the future.

At first, work in the field and in the offices continued as normal, with Nigerian and expatriate officers at work in many parts of the country. Topographic staff were at work in Kano, Katsina and Zaria Provinces; township work was going on in Bama, Bauchi, Keffi, Mubi and Yola. But the after effects of the coup began to show themselves almost immediately and with growing intensity. After escalating unease, these culminated in the civilian backlash of September. Rumours of a possible strike in the North by Ibos from the Eastern Region against key civil servants and even expatriates were prevalent. Further rumours threatened the lives of any Nigerians of Eastern Region origin and many of Western origin and even the southern-most parts of the North itself. These threats were very real and there was even a date promulgated for the start of this action against these people and their families if they continued to stay in the North. In consequence most non-Northerners departed in great haste and indeed carnage did break out in many Northern towns as threatened. For some days in September chaos reigned and all things came to a standstill. Afterwards, when work finally resumed it was with a very depleted workforce with many of the most experienced, skilled and reliable Nigerian staff departed never to return. It was then apparent that the years of effort to establish an enviable and efficient mapping unit in the Northern Region had suddenly come to nothing. That section and the whole North Nigerian Survey Department had suffered blows from which it would never recover.

From September 1966 and on through 1977 survey work, map compilation and reproduction did not completely cease in Kaduna but there was no capability for any recovery. A tidying-up activity was all that could be achieved and considerable effort was put into printing outstanding maps; bearing in mind the considerable administrative requirements that would arise from the division of the old Northern Region into smaller States. None of these new States was ever destined to have a mapping capability of its own and so future mapping work would have to be done by outside contractors.

HANDING-OVER NOTES: TOPOGRAPHIC SECTION
BURNSIDE to ANDERSON   JANUARY 1966

Because you have been working in the section for about six weeks we can skip some of the more routine matters and concentrate on specific subjects.

1. *LARGE SCALE MAPPING:*

(a).   *Ilorin.*
        As you know, the field work is near completion. The staff there are comprised of one senior surveyor, two assistant surveyors and one technical assistant. On completion of the work, i.e. the submission of all field work and any checks or additions required by Comps., the two assistant surveyors should be posted to the altimeter party to gain experience of this work. The T.A. can go on to road levelling, field revision or the Keffi Town survey party. The posting of the Senior Surveyor, Mr.Laurberg has not yet been decided upon.

        On completion, part of the Ilorin area will probably be put out to contract mapping in the usual way, in the financial year 1966-67. Just how much, if any, is put out to contract depends on two factors:

        (i)   How much of the £10,000 will be used for flying contracts in the year, (small scale and large scale for revision purposes).

        (ii)   How much work have you got for your own machines, (at present only Samaru-Zaria revision, and the prospect of Keffi Town, available in about September 1966). More money spent on revision flying would mean more work again.

        I would suggest spending about £2,000 on mapping Ilorin central areas. There are about 10 overlaps in 3 strips covering this area and the cost should not be more than about 30 x £70 = £,2100.

        The remainder of the control can be used as a stock job for our own A8 machines. There will be close on 70 overlaps remaining. Any, at any time, could be plotted immediately if any priority requests were made. Each overlap should take the average operator 1-2 weeks to complete, depending on the amount of detail.

(b)   <u>Samaru-Zaria</u>

Samaru and part of Zaria were re-photographed in March 1965. The area was covered by 3 strips. Mr Ekanem has put in ground control such that the top and bottom strips (17 overlaps in all) can be plotted direct and this I think should be done. The central strip is for the most part covered by existing mapping and we have been experimenting with methods of revising these sheets from the new photography. I have written a separate note on this revision work as it is important and will become the major large scale job in the future.

In the near future, the area between Samaru and Zaria townships requires to be mapped from the Canadian Aero Services photographs. To do this the following extensions to the primary network will be required. The next available surveyor should be put on this work if possible:-

(i)   *North traverse along the top edge of the mosaic PP 131-953,*
(ii)   *South traverse along bottom edge of mosaic PP204-847,*
(iii)   *Line of PP required along Redwood traverse,*
(iv)   *Line PP 42,43,44 along lateral overlap to P840 (about).*

Apart from this, part of Zaria Town could be revised from the Canadian cover as far as it goes. Also you might consider the 1:4,000 cover of Zaria native town that was flown in 1963.

There is a Samaru-Zaria key diagram in the drawer with a proposed mapping programme marked up on it.

At the present moment, Mr Ekanem's field work is being checked by Comps. When final coordinates have been supplied, plotting on the northern and southern strips can be started on the A8 machine. At present the A8 is engaged on revising the mapping covered by the central strip and Sheet 19 has just been completed. Revision of Sheet 14 should start next.

(c)   <u>Keffi</u>

The original Keffi township control work was a mistake. The photography was too old and too large a scale to be economic. (In fact all that early large scale Dove township photography was the result of ignorance). Some of the points, particularly the height points, could be transferred and used on small scale photography. A list and a mosaic have been produced to show what could be salvaged. I recommend that you only use them as check points.

There is little doubt that Keffi Township will be re-photographed in January along the same flight lines as before with 80% fore-and-aft overlapping. (This will enable you to keep your ground control to a minimum if you select your photographs carefully).

I have indicated with dotted blue lines my proposed extension of the Keffi network to provide the necessary photo control and we have talked about this..

Mr Eyamba is scheduled to undertake this work and, as he has never worked alone on this type of work before, it is rather difficult to estimate just how long it will take. In the first instance I would provisionally allocate 6-7 months- but see how things progress.

It is intended that the plotting will be done by us.

(d)   <u>Maiduguri.</u>

For some months a field party has been operating in Maiduguri under John Evans. The party consists of Mr. E. and two survey assistants. The object of the survey was to check the existing maps, to add to them all detail missed because of trees etc. and also to add all new detail that has appeared since 1962.

This has turned out to be a bigger job than expected, for much detail was obscured by the many neem trees in the town and much new detail has appeared, particularly near the railway station. There appears to be more interpretation errors on the maps than one might have expected and I think this was due to the fact that Messrs Fairey Surveys Ltd. used anaglyph machines [Kelsh plotters] for this work?

The revision was carried out using Pagrafoil cards as intended, with deletions in green and additions in red ink. New detail was supplied using the existing detail as a framework.

Unfortunately John Evans had to be recalled from this very important job to supervise the altimeter party for a time – another important job. At the end of October therefore he handed over to the M.P.O. four completely revised Pagrafoils i.e. Sheets 12,19,20 and 52 (not quite completed ?). The other sheets are in your office. It is hoped that this party can start up again shortly. I have written a short note on the revision of large scale maps.

(e)   <u>Bida.</u>

The sub-master copies of the pencil plots of Bida were received from Hunting Surveys Ltd. not long ago. Arrangements have been made to pay the Invoice (£1,230) submitted. To date, the original pencil plots have <u>not</u> been received. Give them a month and then write to them.

2. *LARGE SCALE PHOTOGRAPHY.*

(a)   <u>Negatives of Various Large Scale Photography.</u>

When making out the card index system for our negative film stock I noticed that certain films have not been returned to us – Maiduguri, Gusau, Katsina, Lokoja, Kano (two scales). Also of course the new Kaduna photography is being used in the U.K. at the present moment. I have written to the various companies requesting their return and a note has been made in the Negative Stock Issue book.

(b)   <u>Prints of Township Photography.</u>

I have had made two lists of prints held by the Photo Library. The first covers the older pre-1959 photography, mostly Dove, and at very large scales. The other lists 1:10,000 and 1:12,000 photography taken since 1959. 1 have also made a list of the A..C.D s we have and of the photo indices so far produced. You will notice that there is neither an a.c.d. nor a photo mosaic for some township photography - see the pencil list on the back page.

<u>A card index system for prints</u> needs to be made, similar to the one we now have for the negative stock. This one should also note the number of sets originally supplied.

(c)   <u>Future Programme of Large Scale Photography</u>

At this moment the prospect of re-flying Keffi township is the only thing in hand.

During the year we photographed ten small towns. Unless there is a definite demand I do not think this programme is worth pursuing much further – although at £50 each (Canadian price) it is not an expensive pastime.

For the future, I have proposed in my note on Revision that a systematic programme of flying is carried out to re-photograph all towns for revision purposes. How much photography for this purpose should be done per annum really depends on how much one A8 (or perhaps two?) can handle in a year. To date, experiments have proved that progress is slow but I would have thought that one sheet per week was not unreasonable as an average speed. (There is little or no contouring to be done). At the moment, with one A8 utilised for this purpose, we could only cope with about 50 overlaps per annum, i.e. two medium sized towns per annum, i.e. about £1,200 worth of photography. This would leave a clear £8,000 for small scale photographs and perhaps a little more plotting of outer Ilorin or Keffi?

In future the re-plotting should be geared to the finalisation speed of one or more field parties. From our present experience I would say that one field party could handle more than two averaged sized towns per year if they were finalising the plotting from recent photography.

3. SMALL SCALE MAPPING

(a) Field Work.

Completion of the field work, altimeter line No. *** , is now under way on Sheet 56. The only sheet remaining on the West Kano Block is therefore Sheet 57 with its three altimeter lines. In the past we have averaged two lines per month. I think therefore you have sufficient field work to last till the end of February; by which time the prints of the Katsina - E.Kano Block will, we hope, be available.

If these photographs of the new block do not appear then you should consider switching to something like Sheets 165 and 167. But note there is £6,000 to be unloaded before the end of the financial year.

Assuming the photography will be available, altimeter work can proceed on Sheets 33, 34 and most of 35. The Tellurometer traversing and plan photo-control will have to be done in the wet season. On completion of the boundary traverse by Bob Walker, the photo control can be easily extended to the border, i.e. to parts of Sheets 14, 15 and 16. For the remaining sheets, i.e. those of East Kano, more plan and height control will be necessary. The height control will be in hand when Mr Agbu starts his road levelling party when he returns from leave.

It was not my intention to put in control for Sheets 37 and 59 in the present programme but rather hold them in reserve. According to the present provisional programme all but these two sheets should be completed by early 1968. In the season November '67/January '68 it has been proposed to photograph the area south of the Kaduna-Zaria Block.

(b) Mapping Office Work.

Apart from a few overlaps on sheet 101, all the Kaduna-Zaria Block has been compiled at 1:40,000. Sheet 103 will be passed to you for reduction (to 1:50,000) sometime soon and 101 will follow later. I have written quite a long note on the various processes that take place in the Mapping Office.

At the moment Sheet 78 is being plotted on the Santoni machines and the aerial triangulation of Sheet 55 is about half completed. After Sheet 55, the next sheets for triangulation are 79 and 56 (the field work for 56 should be ready by then; and after that 80 and 57. After tha,t work will commence on the Katsina sheets 34 and 35.

The times taken to carry out the various operations are roughly as follows:-

i) Our best triangulator can do about 3 models per day, i.e. one strip per week. As there are eight strips to a sheet, it means you can reckon on about 2 months to observe a sheet for aerial triangulation. Hence when the ground work of sheet 56 is ready for use, there will be about seven months work in hand. (Sheets 55(Part), 79, 56 and 80).

ii) You can expect the Santoni operators to complete about 50 - 60 overlaps of plotting per month. The amount varies a lot according to the terrain and how many trainee operators there are. As a sheet contains about 120 overlaps it means that at the above rate they will produce three quarters per month, i.e. the same rate as the triangulation. As the plotters are one sheet behind the triangulation team it means that they have about nine months work in hand. The completion of work on Sheet 57 will yield two more months, thus taking them up to near the end of 1966 before the field work of the Katsina block is required.

During 1965 the Drawing Office did not draw as many sheets as we plotted. One of the reasons for this was the delay in having compilations reduced and overlay traces produced after compilation. Hence they were not being supplied with material as quickly as possible. In 1966 we should try to avoid this delay

4.   *FIELD WORK – GENERAL*

(a)   *Road Levelling.*

Mr Agbu, on returning from leave, will take up road levelling. It has been decided that he will commence work at Kano and work north of the Kano-Maiduguri road.. In cases where our lines coincide with the Primary level lines (being carried out by Federal Surveys), we have agreed to put in Primary Beacons. When this is done, only two of our beacon type will be put in – one either side of the primary point. ALL three beacons should be levelled over. Thus, preliminary values of the primary beacons are obtained which might be of use to the Federal Department.

Although our programme of levelling will be of use to the Geological Department, the work should be organised with our own future mapping programme in mind. Note a connection is still required in Adamawa between the end of Mr. Whiley's work at Gulak and the primary beacons at Jiberu, near Yola.

Sometime in the future we will re-map the sheets covering Bornu Province (but only when accurate plan control is available to make this worthwhile) and, because the terrain is so flat, no contouring can be contemplated because to photograph at a scale large enough for this to be possible would be a highly uneconomic business. Hence it is anticipated that the only level data that will appear on these sheets will be spot heights and/or bench marks derived from the road levelling.

A road levelling party should be regarded as a stock job that should operate all the year round.

(b)   *Extension of Plan Control.*

As you know, we have been considering the extension of plan control into the flat northern areas for some time now. It seems that towers and elevated signals are at last going to be available and so in future seasons some progress can be expected. The scheme of last year for Aerodist control under Canadian Technical Aid seems to have come to nothing.

It is my view that the present mapping of the N.E., when revised and brought up to date, is quite adequate and there can be no reason for re-mapping it unless accurate plan control can be used. I think that survey work can best be justified for this purpose if it can be linked to the provision of control points on or near the international border so that, when the time comes, the boundary beacons there can be located accurately with little or no trouble.

5.   *REVISION and FINALISATION of TOWNSHIP MAPPING.*

(a)   *Field Work.*

When the first twenty towns were mapped, it was intended that the mapping would be checked and finalised on the ground before fair drawing was completed. It did not work out that way unfortunately and so now, with the end of the primary mapping in sight, the next big task is to revise and bring up to date the mapping of about 40 towns. There is so much work to be done in this field that I think there should always be a township revision party at work and that it should take priority immediately after any topo. mapping considerations. However, the staff position so far has never been favourable and this aspect of the work has suffered in consequence.

(b)   *Mapping Office Work.*

By re-photographing, most of the existing mapping can be revised in the office without recourse to any fieldwork (but with the usual limits on visibility). Usually, this work will be a revision of the planimetry for in the majority of cases the contours will remain unchanged – other than in the case of major civil engineering work.

Very briefly the method of office revision using an A8 machine would be as *follows...... ... ...*

6.   *INSTRUMENTS, TOOLS and STORES*

(a).   *Diapositives*
We recently (October last), received 600 diapositives. These are now half consumed. We use between 700 –800 per annum and so a further 200–300 should be ordered quite soon. Present stocks will last for no more than five months and it takes a long time for them to arrive after ordering.

(b).   *Altimeters*
After a lot of shopping about we have decided that the Wallace & Tiernans are about the best. It was agreed that some should be bought this year. I would say in all we need four more-

- *2 calibrated in metres for doubling up at base stations,*
- *1 to be kept always in office for calibration purposes*
- *1 spare.*

I wrote to W. & T. some months ago and received details of prices and delivery dates. Note that we decided to keep to the 0 – 7,000 ft. range in preference to a smaller 0 – 4,000 ft. with a different (and therefore possibly confusing) read-out.

C D Burnside
January 1966.

TOWN PLANNING

Orderly Development and Reconstruction

Town Planners will question the inclusion of their profession in a list of surveying activities and may take rather less kindly to being described as "Geographic Labourers" but it is a fact that the design and improvement of low cost settlements in the early days of the development of Northern Nigeria did not call for professional town planning skills. The straightforward and commonsense requirements for low density residential areas, the layout of Government stations, trading plots, unsophisticated township extensions and access roads were easily enough satisfied by administrators, engineers and surveyors; and trained local officers in the Native Administrations could soon acquire the skills for simple layouts.

The old randomly built towns and cities, some more than a thousand years old, originally consisted of a cluster of mud buildings built very close together and through which disease and fire could spread. During the 1930s administrators persuaded local authorities, or native authorities as they were then called, to think about more orderly development and reconstruction of their towns to create broad avenues, planted where possible with shade and fruit trees and spacious gardens, in an open rectilinear form of layout, to ease the squalor, to provide space for services and easier access to the town by vehicles. Such spacious suburbs became known as Nassarawa and to encourage this sort of thing the chief would sometimes go to live there in a new palace of his own.

A law making provision for the re-planning, improvement and development of different parts of Northern Nigeria came into force in 1946. The objective was to empower planning authorities to draw up schemes for the control of the development and use of land, to secure proper sanitary conditions, amenity and convenience, and to preserve buildings, objects and places of special interest.

Planners join the Survey Department

With the establishment of regional government, the Town Planning Section in the North was transferred from the Public Works Department to the Survey Department in 1954. The change gave Town Planning Officers easier and more convenient access to aerial photographs and plans held by the Survey Department and closer liaison when transferring schemes to the ground.

David Ball remembers:-

'In March 1956, having been appointed Town Planning Officer in the Survey Department, I accepted an invitation from the Colonial Office to go and talk to a surveyor who was on leave from the Department. This was John Adshead (Photo. 69), who entertained me to tea and told me all about Northern Nigeria and the Survey Department. He apologised for the fact that, having spent most of his time in bush, he could not tell me much about the planning division. "What 'Rolly' (the Senior Town Planning Officer) seems to spend his time doing," he said with a grin "is drawing little squares representing house plots". I was sure he was exaggerating his ignorance of and lack of interest in town planning. Six years later, after I came home for the last time, my old town planning division, somewhat enlarged, was absorbed into John's cadastral survey section and when he eventually retired from Northern Nigeria he, like several other surveyors, took his Town Planning Institute examinations. He eventually retired from the Department of the Environment as Deputy Chief Planning Inspector. Irony first and last.'

David Ball went on:-

'A residential neighbourhood must be pleasant to look at when you live in it or pass through it and not just have everything in the right place.   I was therefore somewhat taken aback when I was shown the sort of housing layouts prepared for Nigerian towns and villages: blocks of house-plots on a strict grid system of streets:-

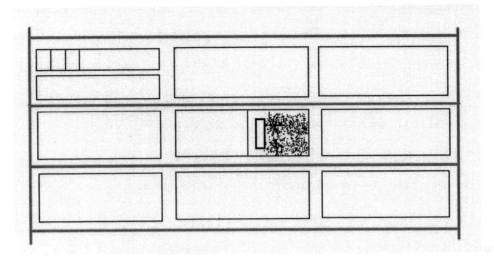

"Why?" I asked. "Because that gives them the best chance of being set out by the Native Authority! " said my boss. "Fancy angles and curves might look better on paper but will never get built." Nevertheless we reached a compromise: oblong blocks still, each with up to about twenty plots, or compounds, back to back (though separated by a "night soil" alley), but oriented in such a way that small open spaces and closed vistas could be incorporated, something like this:-

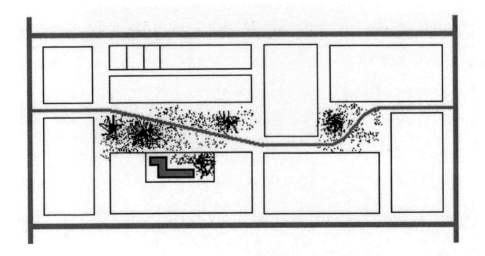

I soon discovered that there was rather more to the work of the Town Planning division than I had been led, albeit jokingly, to believe. My first job was to propose improvements to the road system in Katsina city, 170 miles north of Kaduna, and redesign the market. There being no base map, my first task was to make one, from 1/10,000 (roughly six inches to the mile) air photographs and cadastral survey plans which the survey division had produced for the GRA (government residential area) and the commercial area, a plan of a forest reserve and plans of one or two other plots outside the eastern walls of the old city. Rollison (the Senior Town Planning Officer) had previously compiled by the same means a plan of greater Kaduna, which the Surveyor General, Keith Hunter, had strongly criticised on the grounds of inaccuracy. "It's as much as five per cent out in places!" he said.

"Well," said Rollison, "Until you do something better it's all we have!" - and, indeed, many government and commercial offices relied upon it and had a copy on the wall. The fact was that, at that time, the Survey Division had not the time, nor was it in their brief, to produce town maps. In order to complete a base map for a plan for Greater Kano and to plot extensions to the city carried out since the official air photographs were taken, I once borrowed the government plane and photographed them, as near-vertical as possible, myself.'

Planning Responsibilities

The senior Town Planning Officer was responsible for providing plans and advice throughout Northern Nigeria for GRAs, commercial and industrial areas and related roads and railway connections; as requested by Residents of Provinces or the Administrator of Kaduna Capital Territory. For land administered by Native (later Local) Authorities, requests for plans came from the Emir-in-Council, through the Resident for town extensions, new roads and markets. Plans for government land had to be approved by the Governor – in practice the Lands Secretary.

Until the Survey Department produced accurate township maps, plans produced by the town planners were, of necessity, sketch plans, not very accurate and usually based on air photographs, pacing and compass surveys, and estimation. Once approved, however, the boundaries of the designed plots were accurately set out and beaconed by cadastral surveyors. Inside the townships and the Capital Territory rights of occupancy automatically existed for government plots, and land could be leased under the terms of a Certificate of Occupancy by non-government bodies like companies and missions. In other areas, Native Authority agreement was required for such development and leases were granted by the Governor to government and non-government users alike.

A Kaduna Town Planning Advisory Committee was established in July 1955. Town Planning always suffered from staff shortages and, as with Survey, was not taken seriously until it was found necessary to invest a lot of long-term money. Two Town Planning Officers left the service in 1955-56 and the remaining officer was left alone, until April 1956 when David Ball joined him, with an ever increasing volume of work. In spite of this, much was achieved including the preparation of plans for extensions and development in Bauchi, Gusau, Jos, Kano, Makurdi, Offa and Zaria. O.W.(Bill) Attoe was the Nigerian senior town planning draughtsman at the time. In Kaduna work included detailed plans for the "Whitehall" area, industrial sites, commercial and trading plots and a Government Residential Area extension. In Kano, following the preparation of an outline plan and the convening of a Greater Kano Planning Committee, a consultant (previously Chief Planner in Ghana) was appointed to prepare a more comprehensive plan for the period 1963-1983.

By 1956-57 many of the initial difficulties had been overcome but the demands for planning services were more than could be met and much of the year found one, or at best two, qualified officers available to deal with an ever increasing demand for services from the more remote Native Authorities. A final outline planning scheme for Kaduna was completed and approved and the newly formed Planning Advisory Committee proved useful in co-ordinating the various services and Departments. Similar plans were set in motion for Kano and Zaria, but their operation was dependent upon the availability of staff.

Town Planners' Recollections

David Ball has produced a small book of personal memories and anecdotes entitled *Into Africa (And Out) Northern Nigeria 1956-62* in which he gives an entertaining insight into his travels, his work, life in Kaduna and the people he met. He worked under H.S.A.Rollison from 1956 to 1958 when he followed him as Senior Town Planning Officer (later Principal Town Planning Officer) until 1962. He recalls his planning work for the new town at the Kainji Dam:-

'One day in 1960 in my office in Kaduna I got a telephone call from the Resident, Ilorin. He said: "You've heard about our dam on the Niger. We shall need a new town. We think about 30,000 people. Can you come down next week, find a site and plan it?" I found he was a bit premature. The consultants had drilled

over 100 feet below the river bed and still not struck solid rock so were not even sure yet that the (£80m) project was viable. I heard this from the chief geologist the following week when I made a short visit to get the lie of the land. About a year later the designs for the dam, the hydroelectric installations and the 75-mile long lake which would displace several villages were complete and approved and I did go down and find a site - with the luxury of large scale contoured maps (supplied by the Dam Consultants, Balfour Beatty, and probably produced by Hunting Surveys) of the search area - and, after several meetings in Ilorin, Kaduna and London, prepared the plan. At a meeting in Kaduna of the New Town Sub-committee of the Niger Dams Committee one of the members said: "What are we going to call this new town? It's being referred to, variously, as Wawa, Kainji and New Bussa." Someone else said: "Ball planned it: let's call it Ballsville" and [Peter Gibb] the chairman said: "That's not a bad idea! There might be a High School there. Ballsville High and Balliol would look good on anybody's cv!" It was nearly my moment of glory. But it never happened. New Bussa township was created as part of the Kainji resettlement scheme.'

.............and on a special task in Kaduna:-

'Kaduna's town engineer - the first Northern Nigerian professional engineer, it was said - came to see me in my office one day in 1961. He asked if I could come and help sort out a problem and we drove to a point on the Zaria road on the northern outskirts of Kaduna, a few hundred yards from Lugard Hall, the parliament building, where a cul-de-sac served two rows of large plots called the "Emirs' plots" where several Emirs had built their town houses. There was an open space about seventy yards wide between the main road and the first house. The town engineer's problem was that a large borrow pit which had been started inside the plot had now been extended well beyond its boundary towards the road and was still growing in that direction. "Not only is it illegal," said the town engineer, "but it is very unsightly at the entrance to the Capital Territory and close to Lugard Hall. What can we do?" "Tell the owner to fill it up again, surely" I said. "Yes. Good idea. But we can't!" "Why not?" "Because the owner, the Emir of....., is Minister for Public Works." I could see the problem. After some thought I said: "Perhaps the only answer is to suggest to him he digs no further in this direction and you build an eight-foot wall, nicely designed, to screen the pit from the road." "That's what we will do!" exclaimed the engineer. "And we will call it 'Ball's Wall' - with your permission." "I should be honoured," I said.'

The Dane, Mogens Vejby (who was known as Mogens Vejby Christensen during his time in Nigeria) worked for two tours in the North between 1957 and 1961 and was originally a surveyor but transferred to the Town Planning section. He has written an account of his experiences in Northern Nigeria which he entitles:-

" A Letter from one of the Danish Surveyors in Northern Nigeria 1957 - 1961"

'The period 1951 to 1956 when I was studying in Copenhagen to become a chartered surveyor was poor indeed. Not only did the recovery from the world war take much longer than hoped and expected, but also the situation in one of the corners of Europe with a soft , unchangeable currency meant that the urge to travel abroad could not be satisfied with resources to do so.

Not long after I started my studies in 1951 it was clear to me that I had chosen the wrong career - I simply disliked the millimetre accuracy required - and was disgusted with the thought that my working life should entirely be occupied with setting out plots for the middle-class to build middle-class houses on, and to plant hedges around. Hedges that would be planted exactly on top of the exact line, that I had wasted my life in laying out for my middle-class man. But finances didn't allow a change of study and the loss of one valuable year.

And what was there to change to? Civil engineer - much the same, less survey and certainly not cadastral, but more bridges and sewers, which had to be accurate down to the same hated millimetres, not worth a wasted year.

Architect - yes that would be a relief - but in my case such a change of study would be impossible. I was born left-handed. Nothing wrong in that - except for my mother. She had the very firm idea, that one did eat with the knife in the right hand and the fork in the left, the result being that I didn't enjoy food for the first 15 years of my life. In 1946 when I finally was bigger than she was, I took the knife over in the right (left) hand and started eating with pleasure !

Mother also had the very firm opinion that one wrote with the right hand - so she taught me a year before I should start school. A bitter year. Every time she left the room I switched the pencil over in the other hand and wrote with ease, and much more beautifully, only she could not read it, unless she brought out a mirror. The outcome of this was that I never learned to draw - didn't have a hand to do so, so architecture was out , and surveyor it had to be. Here it is necessary to mention, that a town planning education was not, and still is not given in Denmark. It comes as part of the architect's, civil engineer's, and surveyor's education.

It was with interest therefore that I, for one, listened to the rumours about former students like lb Mathiassen and Keld Hansen (Photo.16), who had gone to Nigeria, and had great adventures there - at least compared to what could happen in Denmark at the time.

So in April 1956 I sent my application to " The Colonial Office". Being clever, I thought, I did so three months before my final examination, so I would be ready to go immediately after a short summer holiday. I didn't know about red tape at that time, but it meant that there was no interview until September.

But there was a positive reply and I should be ready to go in mid November 1956. But!! English and French politicians suddenly forgot which century we were in and attacked Egypt - these two countries always were too fond of channels. Russians made use of the turmoil to spank naughty Budapest, and the Colonial Office thereby caused me to stay for a long, long, cold winter in Copenhagen as a schoolteacher, since no survey jobs were obtainable in Denmark at that time, with short notice and unknown duration. I made an important observation on schoolteachers health during that winter. My job was to ring the central office for school education in the capital, Copenhagen, each morning at seven o'clock, to learn where I should go on my bike to replace a sick schoolteacher. We lived in the very centre then. There was never a sick teacher in the central schools but always in one of the schools in the fringes 8 miles away. It was odd to find out that living in the pleasant village areas is much more a risk to health than living in the old run-down flats in the centre.

Finally, in March 1957, I arrived in Kaduna and was put to work under Senior Surveyor Trevor Brokenshire. It was my task to begin the making of 40 exact township maps covering the Kaduna capital area at a scale of 1:2,400.

The first three months were wonderful. I had a chainman, a Kanuri called Mallam Gana - wonderful man, and three labourers who taught me Hausa, and our little team produced three mapsheets in three months. Then everything went wrong. The new survey school had produced 16 young schoolboys, who could measure along a given line, and four better-educated men who could handle a theodolite and make the lines for the boys. I was put in charge of all these people, and when you include four labourers for each of them, we were quite a team - about 100 men and it turned out, that we were able to produce one sheet a month. I went out of "production", spending my time on counting pencils and erasing gum, dishing out weekly pay and checking the final results, and came to hate it.

I now understand, but didn't at the time, that getting all these people into meaningful work, and educating them more and more, was far more important than the cost in time and money of producing township maps.

When the first year in Kaduna had gone, and after many talks with Senior Town Planner Rollison and Surveyor-General Hunter, I was permitted a transfer to the Town Planning section, where Rollison gave me my first job in Nguru.

There had been a request for a planning officer to go to Nguru for a long time, nobody knew what they wanted in Nguru and nobody wanted to go because the town could not be reached by car, it required an eight hour dreary train journey from Kano. The line (Photo.66) being famous for having the next longest stretch without a curve in the world (the longest being somewhere in Australia). On that train ride I saw the poorest part of Africa, almost desert, no variations in landscape and lots of poor people and beggars at the few stations. The number of lepers was enormous. When my coins were finished , I drew the curtain and slowly drank the bottle of whisky which was meant to last for the duration of the three day tour.

Late at night the D.O. poured me into the government rest house and next morning I set out to do my first, and it so happened my most successful, piece of town planning work ever.

At the morning's meeting with the local authority, the D.O. had left me to do this on my own in Hausa, it turned out that they didn't need a town planner at all. The problem was that in the short, but fierce, rainy season the centre of the town stood under water(Photo.67). Not that it mattered so much; the people were used to moving out, but the dreadful thing was that at the lowest point, at the very centre, where the water sometimes rose 3 feet, just there, was just where the Emirs palace was situated, and that even a planning officer could understand this was serious indeed.

I suggested digging a ditch to a lower point. Yes they said, they had had a P.W.D. engineer working there for six months, finding out that the nearest lower point was 14 miles away - far too long and expensive to build, even for the head of Nguru.

Then I got the big idea - DIG A WELL AT THE LOWEST POINT........ AND LET THE WATER RUN DOWN

Of course I had no idea about the underground structure but it could be assumed that a clay layer stopped the water from quickly sinking down to the layers of desert sand beneath. The locals told me the wells were very deep and that they met different sorts of material as they dug down. It even turned out in Kaduna, that Geological Survey had boreholes showing how deep they should go down to meet a layer of coarse material and a drawing of a 'silt trap' to shoot in before the water was let into the well. I sent these two pieces of information to Nguru, and I never heard about the matter again. But personally, I believe that my first town planning job helped to keep an Emir's feet dry.

I spent the last three months of my first tour doing a planning survey job for the extension of the Zaria Sabon Gari.

During my second tour which started in 1959 I worked as a Town Planning Officer living in Kaduna, Zaria and Kano and acted for David Ball from June 1960 to January 1961 (Photo. 68).

My last planning job in Nigeria was really a survey job, equally as successful as the first one, and has become one of the stories I enjoy telling my grandchildren.

The time is late 1960 and the place is Idah on the east bank of the river Niger. After an earlier visit to carry out a rough survey, I had prepared a plan for a much needed town extension. I loved that trip - wonderful landscape, very different to the usual Northern Nigeria - and a lot of good mileage at 10d a mile in the old Standard Vanguard.

David Ball was home on leave and I was acting S.T.P.0, sitting one fine dry season morning in the office near Eaglesome Road. Outside the door sat a messenger, who I did not know originated from Idah. Suddenly this man throws himself on the ground, face literally in the dust. I had seen many acts of courtesy before, but never this one.

It turned out to be the Emir of Idah, who had had another meeting in Kaduna, and came over to say that he liked my plan, but his local surveyors could not set it out on the ground and that the Survey department could not spare a surveyor to do so.

I promised to come down for two days - not more - and do the most important lines and leave the rest to his own surveyors. But what about labourers to clear lines? I was promised as many as I would like.

Two weeks later, in Idah, I discovered that I had travelled 800 miles only to find the field covered in 3 metres tall elephant grass, and I needed to get a 2 km. long line through, just in order to get started. The choice was to go home or really get hold of man power. They solved the problem by opening the prison for 60 robbers and murderers, each with chains around his feet and a long machete in his hand.

A little team was sent up to one end of the line to make all the noise they possibly could. All the others were down the other end cutting grass. After a couple of hours we had the line, finely marked with red and white poles, a beautiful sight. Now for the secret of the Danish surveyor- the optical square. One man went into the grass with a pole as far as he could be seen and the line was cleared to his pole. Then cutting was done backwards along the intended roadside. Another man went backwards along the next streetline, and so on. When all the streetlines were being cut - I went back to the first one making a longer and more accurate right angle, then correcting the next and so on. By evening the prisoners were marched home tired and happy after an eventful day compared to daily prison life. I went to the club for some much deserved servicing.

There I got to talk with a P.W.D. engineer, who happened to have a grader. It only took that big machine a few hours to drive through all the streets where both sides were cut in grass and the whole town plan stood out for all to see. Streets in red soil, the interior squares in three metre tall elephant grass all ready for the local surveyors to divide into plots, which the Emir could sell. So everybody was happy.

The journey home to Kaduna became very special. The old Standard Vanguard was as ready as I to go home for good. There had been no hand-brake for a long time, the parts still working were only doing so on the understanding that they were only going to last one more month - only this long trip home plus a few short ones to Kingsway and the club. The gearbox on such a car is attached to the chassis with a thick rubber pad, which found it appropriate to give up just there in Idah 800 miles from home. That meant that there was no chance of shifting gear from the inside of the vehicle, but still possible with two fingers when laying on one's back full length under the car. The place where this operation had to take place was on the right side of the car, but it could not be reached from the right side, since the way was barred by the glowing hot exhaust pipe, so one had to crawl under - full length- from the left side - and remember, there was no hand brake !

So the way to travel was: Start the car on flat road in top gear, spinning the wheels and burning the clutch - which was only going to last one month anyway; remember to have two labourers sitting in the back with two big stones and ready for action; drive happily until hills arrive - and they did; many; drive uphill as long as the car would go in high gear; shout; the men drop the stones behind the back wheels; I get down under and change into first; the car starts slowly uphill; stones up; men up; drive up to just over top; men down; stones under front wheel; bature - also called "Mai Gemu" (The bearded one) down under full length; change to top gear; stones up; men up and running again. I reached Abuja by dark.

Funny to think, that Abuja now is the Capital of all Nigeria. Then, it was small.

I asked around for a European, preferably P.W.D., and was shown a house on a hill top. Once more down under but I reached the top, entered the house, and heard a man singing in his bathroom - in Danish!! Keld Gommesen, civil engineer, road builder - P.W.D.

Going to Nigeria and there getting the chance to get out of survey into planning turned out to be a lucky strike in my life.

Back home in February 1961, I was appointed planning officer in our Ministry, as the first surveyor. Before that this office was manned solely by architects.

Ten years later I started a consultancy firm, which I closed down in 1995 to become a farmer.'

....

Jean Burnside, spent one tour working with the Lagos Executive Development Board. The maps which she had to work with in Lagos were not very satisfactory as they were very much out of date and there were many disputes over land ownership. An applicant for planning permission to build would send in a site plan which might be overlapped by two or three other so-called ownership plans and on site there could be several conflicting sets of pegs and pillars to be sorted out.

She had two weeks local leave during her spell in Lagos (in July 1960) and took the opportunity to go on a tour of part of the Northern Region with friends who had flown out from the UK. When her two friends, who were both teachers, arrived at the Hill Station, they got into conversation with a doctor, who asked why on earth they had come to Nigeria for a holiday. One of them replied in a lordly manner that 'All the cathedrals in Europe were the same and all the beaches were the same so they thought that Nigeria would be a change'! The doctor replied 'Yes, Miss Rothschild'. They toured the Plateau, visited Kaduna, Zaria and Kano (where they stayed at the Old Residency) and always found someone to show them around colleges, schools, agricultural research stations, factories, trading stations and the old parts of Zaria and Kano etc. The trip made Jean keen to see more of Nigeria, which was clearly a lot more interesting out of Lagos.

Having completed her tour in Lagos she then transferred to the North and describes her work in the Planning Section there in the early 1960s:-

> 'The climate in Lagos could be rather trying because of the high humidity, and I was, therefore, glad to have the chance to move to the north on my second tour with a better climate and a chance of more varied work both in urban and in rural areas.
>
> I returned to Nigeria from leave by sea in April 1961. I arrived in Lagos and after a couple of days there visiting friends and arranging to sell my small Fiat, I headed up north by train. I had decided to buy a larger car in Kaduna, more suitable for northern roads. The journey by train was not ideal as the engine was fuelled by brown coal which gave off thick black smoke. I found that you could wash your face and hands only to find that you were covered with soot again within another ten minutes. Then the train broke down somewhere in the Western Region and remained there for 1½ days. The scenery was not very inspiring and it was very hot. My new employers at the Northern Nigerian Survey must have thought that I was still enjoying the nightlife in Lagos!
>
> I was put into the rest-house for about a week and then moved into a bungalow in Kaduna South near the Survey Department. It was one of the old railway houses, very different from my flat in Lagos but very pleasant with a beautiful flame tree in the compound. I bought a fairly new Hillman Minx with the advice of Paul Ward and Cliff Burnside.
>
> The Planning Section was very small, consisting of David Ball, the Senior Town Planning Officer, myself and a half qualified Nigerian plus about five draughtsmen. This was not many to deal with the whole of the Northern Region! However, most of the work was in the main towns - Kaduna, Kano, Zaria and Jos, especially Kaduna. All we could do with such minimal staff was to respond to requests from different parts of the Region for e.g. a small housing layout extension to a village; a road improvement scheme; an industrial estate; a scheme to try and sort out an area of haphazard unplanned shanty development; or a layout for some petrol filling stations (much loved by Ministers).
>
> There could be a considerable difference in scale, as I once had to produce a plan for a whole new town of 15,000 rising to 30,000 population at Bacita to house the workers at the local sugar factory. At the other end of the scale the Kaduna Parks Department made a request for us to plan some more roundabouts so they could plant flowers on them !
>
> The large scale mapping of the main towns in the Northern Region was very good and made it easier for the Town planners David Ball and myself to operate.

Some smaller settlements were in the process of being mapped at this time, but for very small villages we relied on aerial photographs to use as a base. These we obtained from the Topographic Section where Cliff Burnside was in charge. The low level photography did actually give quite a good image of settlement patterns in remoter areas and sufficed for sketch layouts to be drawn up.

I probably spent most of my time in Kaduna doing plans for new housing areas and for sorting out the rash of illegal mud houses at the edge of Tudun Wada; for the redevelopment of the Mogadishu Barracks area as a new shopping and office area with a new hotel, public hall and cinema etc.; and for the traffic improvement of Ahmadu Bello Way. We made a study in 1962 of the increase in the volume of traffic due to the building of the road bridge across the Kaduna river in 1957 (Photos. 218 and 219) and the development of industry in Kaduna South - mostly textiles and brewing at that time. Studies were also made of the volumes of turning traffic at the main junctions. It was recognised even then that sooner or later a second bridge would be required across the river linking Tudun Wada with the industrial area in Kaduna South. I eventually produced a Draft Development plan for Kaduna for a 20 year period from 1962 - 82 which included suggestions for phasing of the new development but it was never approved and was soon superseded by Max Lock's Plan.

Towards the end of my time working for the Northern Nigerian Survey I was involved in getting some preliminary surveys done in Zaria with a view to the preparation of a Development Plan for the town. These included a Land Use Survey, a survey of age of buildings and type of construction etc.'

Kevin O'Shaughnessy, who had been in the Cadastral Section, took over the Planning Section from David Ball in 1962. During the year the expansion of all existing urban areas continued, leading to demands, many of which could not be met, for rapidly produced plans for commercial and residential development. Regular lectures, mainly on village planning, were given at the various courses held at the Institute of Administration at Zaria, and it was hoped that they would prove of value in guiding village growth along the correct lines.

Major Development Plans

As the major towns throughout the North expanded, populations grew dramatically, and finance for major high cost developments began to appear. Infrastructure, land use, and more complex design considerations called for comprehensive plans, and professional consultants were appointed. Indeed things eventually changed to the extent that the Ministry of Land and Survey was renamed the Ministry of Town and Country Planning, with surveying and mapping as its major component. The stage was reached when, for want of local expertise, experienced and professional overseas assistance was sought for the long term planning of Kaduna as Northern Nigeria's capital. In 1964 the Northern Government commissioned the well known London-based Max Lock and Partners to prepare a comprehensive development plan for Kaduna. In 1965 Max *(Photo.229)* and his partner Gerald King went to Kaduna for a preliminary reconnaissance, and later worked from the Planning Office in the Northern Nigerian Survey compound in Kaduna South. In the course of the study it was arranged for Sir Desmond Heap, one time president of the Royal Town Planning Institute, to visit Kaduna and meet senior members of Government and to underline the importance of adoption of serious and well researched planning schemes. Heap (later President of the Law Society and Comptroller of the City of London, who had been much involved in the drafting of the Town and Country Planning Act, England & Wales 1947) drafted the detailed planning ordinance included in the Lock plan.

Jean Burnside comments:-

'In 1965 Max Lock & Partners were invited to produce a much more elaborate and detailed plan for Kaduna, something which could never have been done with the very limited planning staff at the Northern Nigerian Survey

Department. They produced an excellent and very ambitious Development Plan including such schemes as the transformation of Ahmadu Bello Way (formerly Lugard Way) into a two-mile limited access ceremonial avenue from Lugard Hall in the north to a new Civic Centre near the Administrator's office at the south end including a new Town Hall, Civic buildings and a Capital Mosque. It went into considerable detail over planning new housing areas, new industrial estates and the provision of services - the supply of adequate water resources and proper sewage disposal etc. It was a very impressive scheme and if it could have been brought about, it would have produced an exceptional town. Unfortunately, it was planned as the Capital of the whole of the Northern Region and with the fragmentation of the Region into so many separate units there was no chance of the money being available to carry it all out. However, some of the important proposals were implemented such as the construction of a proper dual carriageway main road system. Also implemented were the proposals for improving the water supply on the lines suggested in a report by Scott Wilson & Kirkpatrick. The barrage constructed across the River Kaduna to the north of the Capital school was estimated to eventually provide 40 million gallons of water per day. Although Kaduna has not developed into a Capital city, there has been more industrial development, notably in the development of a car industry which has resulted in increased industrial employment and a further increase in total population. Kaduna is, therefore, a major industrial town rather than an administrative town as in the past.'

The plan was not completed until after the first military coup. Sometime after the impressive book (*"A Survey and Plan for the Capital Territory for the Government of Northern Nigeria"* by Max Lock and Partners, London. 1967.) was published, Max told David Ball over tea in Max's house in London of the 'night of the long knives'. He was an accomplished pianist and, having shipped his grand piano out to Kaduna, was giving a recital one evening in the Hamlada Hotel, the Parliament building. He said he heard a lot of gunfire and thought "This is a bit thick! I'm going to complain to the military authorities tomorrow about holding an exercise while I'm giving my recital !" - only to find out the next day that what had been going on close by was the murder of the first Premier of the Northern Region, the Sardauna of Sokoto and of all Hausa army officers of the rank of Major and above.

The services of Max Lock and Partners were commissioned again after the break-up of the North when long term structure planning was considered desirable for some of the former Provincial towns, now capitals in their own right, - Maiduguri, Bauchi and Yola.

A Backward Step

Even for everyday routine work there continued to be very few local people with the requisite skills and experience, and some recruitment of planners from other developing countries took place in the 1970s. Well intentioned as this policy may have been, it was not always very successful. Some recruits, from countries little more developed than Northern Nigeria, were obviously opportunists with mythical qualifications from doubtful sources and clearly incapable of reading, or unwilling to use, a contoured map or to interpret an aerial photograph. The simplest of geometrical designs, produced in the office without reference to maps, totally ignoring the topography, and without visiting the sites to carry out ground investigations, were a standard product from such people. They side-stepped the serious problems their designs created, which were pointed out to them by the setting-out surveyors, by saying "That's the job of the construction engineers."

CADASTRAL SURVEYING

Property Rights and Development

Legally enforceable property rights have provided the basis for economic development in all the major successful countries of the world. The resources, the size and the burgeoning population of Nigeria gave the country the potential to be a prosperous leader in Africa but there was a need to awaken the dormant capital that lay locked up in its land resources. If rights in land are not properly documented, assets cannot be turned into useable capital, cannot be used as an investment and cannot be traded other than locally amongst those who trust each other or who have traditionally exercised control over that land. There is a risk of a weakened or black economy based on untrustworthy businesses conducted without proper documentation. The key to a system of secure and demonstrable rights in land which cannot be held in freehold, with little risk of counter claims, and which can be used as collateral, is an efficient cadastral system backed by fast and efficient land surveying and an open and dependable land register. Obtaining rights of occupancy swiftly, and with permission to develop, has to be within the reach of ordinary people, free of any burden of bribery and corruption. The operation of such a system was the aim of those who worked in cadastral surveying.

Land Tenure

From 1916, in the Northern Provinces, through regionalisation in the 1940s to Independence in 1960, all land was, by the Land and Native Rights Ordinance, held in trust for the people by the Governor. Its disposition was under his control and no title to the use and occupation of any land was valid without his consent. The alienation of land to non-natives without his permission was prohibited. Building and agricultural "rights of occupancy" were granted by Government with conditions as to improvements, and revision of rent at stated intervals.

The Land Registration Ordinance No.36 of 1924 prescribed that every instrument (which was defined briefly as any document whereby right or interest in land was acquired) must be registered. The Land Registry in the north was, at the time, at the office of the Secretary of the Northern Provinces at Kaduna.

With the enactment of the Land Tenure Law in 1962, all land in Northern Nigeria was declared to be 'native lands', to be held and administered for the use and common benefit of the 'natives' as therein defined. No title to the occupation and use of any such lands by a non-native was valid without the consent of the Ministry of Land and Survey.

Two titles to native land were recognised. They were :-

(i)   the customary title of a native or native community using or occupying land in accordance with native law and custom. This was defined in the Law as a customary right of occupancy; and

(ii)   a statutory title granted by the Permanent Secretary or by a public officer or native authority, under the provisions of the Law, to any person. This is defined in the Law as a statutory right of occupancy.

For expatriate companies and individuals, the form of title under which land was held in Northern Nigeria was a statutory right of occupancy. This was granted on prescribed terms for periods of generally between 20 and 99 years, according to the improvements offered by the applicant and the status of the land, and was evidenced by a Certificate of Occupancy. In general, rights of occupancy were usually re-granted for further periods on the expiry of the first term. The terms of the grant included the erection of buildings ('improvements') to a stipulated sum and the payment of a ground rental which varied according to the locality and the use to which the land was put. In government residential areas, in the larger centres where the expatriate community normally resided, rentals were at the rate of £50 per acre per annum. Rights of occupancy to expatriates were not granted outside approved Government layouts except for certain specific purposes.

Native or Local Authorities had a parallel but subordinate existence to the Regional Government. Land in certain areas, particularly outside the main towns and within the ancient walled cities, was administered entirely by the L.A. and unless an area had been specifically excluded, there was always consultation before a statutory R of 0 was awarded. The Local Authorities had procedures for their own Cs of O which were broadly similar to those used by Government, except that a demarcation survey was not usually required. The certificate would include a plan which was often the same unchecked sketch which accompanied the application. There was often no form of demarcation, although concrete pillars were sometimes placed at the corner points and had numbers on them which, less often, were recorded in a register at the L.A. office. Some security of tenure was given, but not against government development and the certificate was not acceptable for a financial loan. Most people, particularly in the rural areas, had no formal certificate for their land at all. For them their farmland was their only form of security. They relied on the unwritten customs which had been followed by their people for generations, usually without the benefit of written agreement of any kind. A farmer always knew how much land he had and where its boundaries were, the measurements having been done by pacing or even with the aid of a rope, usually of undetermined length. Boundaries were marked by planting shrubs such as henna, by leaving strips of grass, or even, in contentious places, with a fence, hedge or ditch. But, except in the intensively cultivated Kano hinterland, a map was not made and a surveyor was unknown.

Rights of Occupancy

The principal task of the Cadastral Section of the Survey Division was the processing of applications for statutory Rights of Occupancy (Rs of O), granted by the Regional Government. Before approval was given to alienation of land by this means, a strict procedure of examination of the application and definition of the site was followed. Survey was involved from the beginning because, unless the application was in an approved layout, it had to be accompanied by a sketch plan showing the boundaries of the land, its relationship to adjoining plots and the location of nearby survey control pillars.

The application for a Right of Occupancy was charted on master plans (intelligence charts), based on the best large scale maps available, held in the Survey Division. Any conflicts or overlaps with adjacent grants or established land use were noted and ironed out at this stage, after which comments were routinely required from the local authority and the Town Planning Section, plus other interested departments, before approval was given by the Minister for Land and Survey, who increasingly liked to keep the sensitive subject of land under his direct control. When approved, the application file came back to the Survey Division and was added to the pile awaiting demarcation and plan preparation. Cadastral surveys were generally carried out by supervised junior surveyors and assistants, touring parties working from Provincial stations, from Jos and Kano, and from a Kaduna unit concentrating on this sort of work, the Kaduna District Survey Office. Eventually concrete property beacons (PBs) would be placed at the corner points of the plot and the dimensions and corner angles measured using the applicant's sketch plan as a reference. The PBs would then be connected to the nearest cadastral control pillars *(Photo.70)* by a theodolite and steel tape traverse made to a linear misclosure of better than 1:3,000. Details such as existing buildings within and just outside the plot would be surveyed by compass and tape. The surveyor computed his traverse, adjusting it by the Transit method, and drew a plan at a suitably large scale. His work was checked in the office for compliance with technical instructions; the co-ordinates of the corner beacons were registered and a tracing made from the plan. The tracing was used to print copies of the plan (usually by sunprinting) which were then attached to the Certificate of Occupancy deed (the Certificate was the document which evidenced the Right of Occupancy) which was registered by the Lands Division of the Ministry. There was a slight variation to the procedure if the plot was in an approved layout which had already been surveyed; but in all other cases a ground survey was required.

Survey work was carried out under the Survey Law which specified that plans attached to registrable instruments must be signed by a government-appointed or licensed surveyor and countersigned by the Surveyor-General, and that unlicensed persons were not to undertake professional surveying. Survey Regulations specified technical methods to be employed, traverse accuracies, connections to control beacons and previous and adjacent surveys, the positioning of plot boundaries, the information to be recorded in fieldbooks and methods of computation. They also defined the methods and materials for beacon construction, their positioning and numbering, and the requirements for the survey of areas subject to the Minerals Act. They laid down the methods of drawing plans and their content, the plans and work to be produced by licensed surveyors, the conditions which applied to private applications for survey; and the assessment of charges. All in all a fairly rigid set of rules, designed to produce uniform and reliable, if at times costly and laborious results.

Township Mapping and Survey Control

Hand in hand with the fieldwork for mapping went the establishment of networks of township framework control points *(Photos. 71-73)*. Primary Cadastral Control traverses formed the first break-down from the main framework of a township area, or themselves formed the main framework. They either ran between triangulation stations of at least national secondary accuracy or were traverses that closed upon themselves. The linear accuracy was at least 1:15,000 and a Wild T2 one-second theodolite or instrument of equivalent accuracy was used for observation of angles taken to plumb-bob strings or traversing targets, to achieve angular misclosures not exceeding 3 seconds of arc per station. In the absence of azimuth control from triangulation stations, astronomical observations were taken to the sun in the morning and evening or to stars in the east and west. Measuring of the distances was done with a 300 ft x 1/8th inch steel tape suspended in catenary with readings taken to the nearest 2nd decimal of a foot, corrected for temperature, slope and sag. The co-ordinates of each control pillar were calculated from network adjustment to provide northings and eastings based on a local origin to the nearest second decimal of a foot. Secondary order control traverses ran between points on the primary traverses, using similar techniques, but a lower order of accuracy was sufficient, with linear misclosures not exceeding 1:8,000. Tertiary control was the final breakdown of the primary and secondary network, instruments of a lower order were acceptable and ground taping using 300 ft x ¼ inch steel bands sufficed to achieve the required accuracy of 1:3,000.

Beacons

The law permitted access to any land for the purposes of public surveys and the placing of marks and beacons, and the payment of compensation for any crops or trees damaged in the process. Owners, occupiers and chiefs were required to preserve such markers placed on their land. Nominal fines or imprisonment were specified for the wilful obliteration of or damage to survey markers and the obstruction of surveyors in the course of their work, but it was virtually unknown for these powers to be invoked.

Amongst surveyors, 'beacons' were inevitably a common topic of discussion and their preoccupation with them is the theme of the following contribution by David Ball, a Town Planner:-

> *'When it came to large scale survey, the Surveyor General was concerned almost entirely with cadastral survey: surveying and setting out land titles called Rights of Occupancy, in effect government leases or subdivisions of government owned land. Part of our job in the Town Planning Division was to prepare "layout" or site plans for such areas, for government residential areas, commercial and industrial areas, road and rail connections etc. These were essentially sketch plans, though based on compass-and-tape or compass-and-pacing survey. Once approved (before Independence by the Civil Secretary; afterwards by the Minister of Land and Survey), these were set out by the Cadastral Survey section, by theodolite, to a high standard of accuracy. Corners of plots and changes in direction of their boundaries were marked on the ground by means of short concrete posts known famously as "beacons" one of which was "tied into" a conveniently placed "secondary or tertiary trig point", one of a network of topographical survey beacons*

covering the whole of the country.

Though lacking the glamour of Geodesy and mapmaking there can be no doubt that the most fundamental and publicly visible work was that of cadastral surveying, the work to which over the years the greatest effort was put, and perhaps one of the few survey processes in which the man in the street could begin to understand (the surveyors')standards of accuracy. The Certificate of Occupancy (C of O) issued by the government in respect of each such title contained a cadastral plan, at up to 1:100 scale, or possibly (since, even after Independence, measurements were still imperial) 1:120 or 10 feet to the inch, showing the bearings and lengths of each leg of the boundary and the bearing of and distance to the trig point. Thus the precise boundaries of every plot could be identified even if all the beacons were destroyed, as often happened, usually by the Public Works Department's graders when they graded the roads. Nevertheless, displacement of cadastral beacons understandably caused some consternation among the surveyors, so much so that "beacons" was a favourite topic of conversation among them.

A Greek friend in Kano told me one day that he was having a drink with the Provincial Surveyor when another surveyor dropped in. "They started talking" said George, the Greek, who worked for a commercial firm, "about beacons. After a bit I said: 'Excuse me, but what is a beacon?' They looked at me as though I were from outer space and then went on again about beacons. I was getting bored so I looked round at the garden in which we were sitting, when I found I was looking, through a shrubbery, into a bedroom window and in that room the Provincial Surveyor's wife was undressing. Just then I realised that things had gone quiet and the Provincial Surveyor was looking at me. I turned to face him. 'What was that you were saying about beacons?' I asked, all ears."

A few days after hearing this story I was sitting with some friends on the terrace of Kano Club when I found that George was sitting nearby at another table. His companions were in deep conversation but George was looking round with a bored look on his face. "They are talking about fishing," he said to me quietly. "It's like beacons".'

Progress

From the earliest days the Survey Department of Nigeria was responsible for government layouts, the setting out of residential, commercial and trading areas, and surveys for the grant of statutory rights in land and cadastral and clerical offices were operated in the major administrative centres. The branch set up in Lugard's new Northern capital, Kaduna, was destined to continue its uninterrupted work through to the formation of the Northern Nigerian Survey in the early 1950s and beyond to the break-up of the Northern Region in 1968, and thereafter became the nucleus of the Survey Department of the new North-Central State.

The concentration of cadastral surveying effort during the three years following the second world war had been on the developments in Kaduna such as the Government Residential Area, the Secretariat, the Catering Rest House, the Technical Training Centre, the Public Works Department Yard and the Radio Diffusion Centre, but surveys were carried out all over the North in places as far apart as Minna, Kano, Ringim, Damaturu, Nguru, Zaria, railway land in Gusau, the GRA and radar station at Funtua, Bauchi GRA and airfield, and at development sites in Igala, Kabba and Badeggi. As a measure of cadastral survey production in 1950 the drawing office produced 290 tracings, 2542 sunprints and lithoprints, 350 Certificates of Occupancy, scrutinised 28 Forest Reserve Plans, completed 9 layouts for Government stations and 59 sites for Government departments.

Reorganisation of the central Survey Department was begun in 1950 in order to cater for economic and political developments in the country, with a need for regionalisation and decentralisation from Lagos. An aspect of this decentralisation was the establishment of a small topographical mapping drawing section at the Kaduna office and such was the push for mapping in the 1950s and the 1960s that the Cadastral Section seemed, almost throughout the days of the Northern Nigerian Survey, to take second place to the newly introduced needs and priorities of topographic mapping. As the urban areas embarked upon rapid expansion and development, it started to become apparent that topographic mapping was not really the most important aspect of surveying so far as the opening-up and development of Nigeria was concerned. The really important bit was the cadastral work and the urban mapping at the large scales of 1:2,400, and later 1:2,500 and 1:2,000 scales, which were the foundation for town planning, for the grant of title for public use, for industrial and commercial development and to the ordinary people for private development.

As the workload increased, 1953-54 saw the production of 347 deed plans, 597 other drawings, and 757 site reports. 742 Certificates of Occupancy were charted in the drawing office, 250 surveys dealt with in the examination section, and 361 certificates issued, with plans and descriptions.

An increasing number of Certificates of Occupancy were being issued every year without survey. The practice arose as a result of the shortage of survey staff and caused no harm other than a considerable loss of revenue, so long as they were for isolated plots where no other development was taking place or was likely. But it had to be remembered that in a country developing as rapidly as Northern Nigeria, a plot which was isolated one day might no longer be isolated in a year or so. It was therefore highly desirable that the practice of issuing Certificates of Occupancy without survey should cease as soon as sufficient staff became available. An attempt was made to start production of large scale plans of the larger towns and revision of the existing plans, most of which were 20 years or more out of date. Kaduna was used as a training ground for Survey Assistants in this sort of work and some progress was made but staff shortages hindered progress.

A total of 151 large surveys and 104 surveys for Certificates of Occupancy were carried out during 1955-56. A number of Certificates of Occupancy applications had been outstanding for a very long time and in distant or isolated areas not yet served by Provincial Surveyors the work was being undertaken by small roving parties from Kaduna.

Statistics for 1956-57 showed that 374 deed plans were produced, 779 other drawings, 6405 prints made, 609 reports on Certificates of Occupancy and Site Boards were made, 751 Cs of O charted, 323 surveys dealt with by the examination section and a total of 384 Cs of O issued, complete with plans and descriptions. In all a total of 193 large surveys and 138 surveys for Cs of O were carried out during the year. Although a total of 370 surveys, yielding revenue of £4,600, were done in 1957-58, the cadastral branch was not in a satisfactory state. The standard of much of the fieldwork had been deplorably low for years, owing to the lack of basic education of the junior field staff, many of whom had no real understanding of what they were doing; while the office records were inadequate and in many cases inaccurate and unreliable. As development of townships gathered pace it became obvious that overhaul of the Section would be necessary. Plans were afoot for a complete reorganisation, similar to one already in progress on the Minesfield; but little could be done until staff had been trained in sufficient numbers to make the necessary large scale surveys, and until adequate office accommodation became available.

Clifford Rayner recalls being posted to Kaduna in 1958 where temporarily he took over the Cadastral Office from Frank Wey, a Nigerian surveyor. Wey, whose first appointment was in 1926, had been assisted in the office by Victor Williams who, having been first appointed in 1917, had reached the normal age of retirement but had been retained on temporary terms because he was something of an oracle on cadastral records, and the continuity of his knowledge was invaluable. Rayner was given the task of trying to sort out all the Railway properties in the North as a result of the reorganisation of the railways, a rather frustrating operation, not assisted by the paucity of information and assistance available from the Ministry's Lands Division.

The much needed reorganisation commenced in early 1959 and resulted temporarily in a reduction in the number of surveys completed. The writer joined the section for a while in late 1959 and found the office 'chaotic', and being run by Norman Herring who, through his technical competence, productivity and uncompromising views, was beginning to contribute to the radical reorganisation required. He was succeeded by Paul Ward who continued the reorganisation and through to 1962 by a succession of Senior Surveyors including John Adshead, Frank Waudby-Smith and Kevin O'Shaughnessy, interchanging responsibilities during periods of leave.

During 1958-59 production had fallen to a total of 220 surveys yielding £3,500 and was down to 211 and £3230 in 1959-60, but in the first 8 months of 1960-61 261 surveys yielded revenue of £3,930. This varying rate of cadastral survey production directly reflected the changing supervisory staff position during the period and began to reflect the benefits of the reorganisation.

In 1962, 2 years after independence, Northern Nigeria enacted the Land Tenure Law, which amounted to adoption of the principles of land tenure established by the British, with the fear of exploitation switching from expatriates to other Nigerians. The continuation of control was justified by the fact that the Government was the only agency with sufficient resources to undertake large scale development but it wished to ensure that as the economic well being of private individuals increased, they would have access, particularly in urban areas, to development land and alienable rights over it. In urban areas there was a disincentive to develop land held under relatively short term Rights of Occupancy because alienation to non-natives without the consent of the Minister was unlawful, development loans could be hard to obtain, building covenants might be too onerous and with no guarantee of renewal, improvements could vest in the Minister on expiry. But such short term grants did have the merit of freeing up land for new and much greater development within relatively short periods of time. In later years the system was seen to be at risk of abuse by corrupt officials prepared to accept bribes for the grant of long term rights.

In renovated offices and new ones built by Paul Ward using 'in house' masons, carpenters and labourers, the efficiency of the Cadastral Section continued to improve during the mid 1960s under the control of John Adshead (1962-66), Frank Waudby-Smith (1962-65) and Clifford Rayner (1963-66), but their departure within a short period of time heralded potential problems for operation and efficiency of the Section.

Development continued to gather pace and the demand for rights in land increased. With its limited resources, the Survey Division faced an increasing backlog of work. With no relaxation of established standards, the solution was always seen as an increase in the number of junior surveyors and assistants and the opening of Provincial Survey offices all over the region.

Colin Emmott took over the Cadastral Section in 1967 when it produced over 1000 tracings, 520 Certificates of Occupancy, 10 layouts, 142 sites for Government Departments and scrutinised 43 Forest Reserve plans.

Break-Up

With the dissolution of the Northern Nigerian Survey in 1968 Cadastral records and assets were divided, sent off to the new State capitals where the number of applications for rights to occupy land were destined to rise to undreamed-of levels. The Cadastral Section offices became the headquarters of the new North-Central State Survey Department, run temporarily by Colin Emmott until his resignation and departure for Ahmadu Bello University where he was to establish a Land Surveying degree course.

Alternative Methods of Cadastral Surveying

Alternative methods of cadastral surveying involving less rigorous and demanding methods, cutting out the need for precise survey and training, and perhaps making use of low-level aerial photography and necessitating amendments to the Law, did not, over the years, receive the consideration they merited. In his 1965 RICS paper, John Adshead described how, aided only by assistants trained in elementary survey techniques and equipped with the absolute minimum of photogrammetric equipment, he was able to obtain very reasonable results, quickly and effectively, in spite of difficulties with the terrain, by making use of aerial photographs. He demonstrated how he provided a form of documentation for Rights of Occupancy held under Native Law and Custom and for restrictions imposed under the Native Authority Building Restrictions Regulations; to act as an interim solution to registration until a more sophisticated method could be used; techniques which may well have found application for statutory Rights of Occupancy too. He prepared an uncontoured plan at a scale of 1:2,400 of a native town composed to a large extent of walled compounds of irregular shape and of too intricate a pattern and juxtaposition for the junior staff to be able to survey by ordinary ground methods. He demonstrated that with a shortage of capable and experienced surveyors it would be possible, using junior staff trained to interpret large scale aerial photographs, to satisfy many of the urgent mapping and cadastral requirements of a rapidly developing country. Many land applications did not need the high precision of controlled mapping. Aerial pictures accompanied by witnessed ground identification of boundaries would be sufficient to satisfy many records and ground information purposes.

The application of such methods was to be even more justifiable in later years as the demand for land reached explosive proportions and the staffing problems became even more acute, but it is regrettable to have to record that such innovative solutions were never seriously considered during the life of the Northern Nigerian Survey. Rigid adherence to the methods required by Survey Regulations meant that the use of aerial photography for cadastral purposes did not to form part of the curriculum of training in survey schools which catered for the expressed requirements of their patrons, the government. Radical solutions to township mapping and cadastral records were proposed and at least temporarily adopted in the North-Eastern State during the 1970s, making use of rectified and enlarged photographs and orthophotomaps in screened positive transparent form to facilitate inexpensive local reproduction.

Land administration and cadastral problems for Local Government after 1968

New regulations governing land administration by Native Authorities were introduced. The Land Tenure (NA Control of Settlements) Regulations of 1962 had concerned the powers of local government to lay out, for example, a residential area and then grant plots to natives and non-natives for a fixed term and rent.

The same principles applied to existing settlements under the Land Tenure (N.A. Rights of Occupancy) Regulations of 1962 and 1969, ensuring that the number of people holding land under Rights of Occupancy would increase, and such rights would not be held under customary law. Under these Regulations the term 'settlement area' could be held to include grazing, forest and agricultural areas, reservoirs and water catchment areas, thus paving the way to placing all NA land under statutory Rights of Occupancy.

Even in the days of the Northern Nigerian Survey it was recognised by the Native Authorities that, as the development of the country accelerated, the need for all kinds of surveys would increase in the areas under their control which had not been alienated for Government or for statutory title and which lay outside township, and settlement areas. Rights over land in the NA areas were held by the people occupying the land and granted by the Emir, or his local representative, in Council, together with the NA. Allocations were made fairly and not until every facet of the need for allocation was examined and discussed in great detail with all interested parties. As a result, litigation and disputes were very rare and in many places almost unknown. The land was allocated physically and almost ceremonially, and witnessed by many local people in a process of literally "beating the bounds". No one was left in any doubt as to what had been allocated, the boundaries were marked by pointing out bushes, trees, bounding footpaths, and by cutting shallow trenches. The allocation was then entered into a register held in the NA Office and seldom referred to again.

The system worked and was basically good because it did not result in disputes, but the problem was that it rested entirely on the honesty and integrity of the people concerned. This was because it was quite impossible to locate with any accuracy the boundaries of a piece of land from the NA registry entry, unless it happened to be a numbered rectilinear plot in a township area pegged out by a local Land Settlement Officer. Up to 1965 this had not mattered, but the Region's leaders were getting concerned that the system might break down as the country developed, as local people aspired to properly defined rights to support applications for development loans, and as tribal loyalties and integrity were replaced by urban sophistication and individual aspirations. A form of registration was sought which not only said who had been granted what but also defined its boundaries unambiguously. With a population of millions holding land rights in this customary manner it was clearly inconceivable that universal adoption of the Government system of statutory survey and definition could ever be successfully introduced. A programme of large scale mapping on which every field boundary would be shown was also out of the question because of the staffing, financial and technological issues involved.

A possible solution lay with the use of aerial photographs, provided the assurance could be obtained that it would always be possible to successfully operate the necessary aircraft and, presumably, pay hard currency to the overseas contractors who would probably have to provide the service. With plenty of large scale coverage available, some 1:4,000 scale coverage of Zaria was enlarged to 1:2,000 and the feasibility of using it tested with local people, using quickly trained primary school leavers to read the photographs. Boundaries were pointed out to them on the ground by an NA representative in conjunction with the land holders and their neighbours and ownerships numbered on an overlay trace. These numbers were then recorded in a book with details of the land holder and a boundary description. The system was far from perfect but no alternative offered such good results so cheaply and effortlessly, with such little need for survey supervision. A legal and Cadastral Surveying criticism was that it would be impossible to re-establish a boundary from such a description on an uncontrolled photograph but this was irrelevant because the boundaries existed physically on the ground in nearly every case and could easily be marked if they did not. Land holders could even be obliged to plant small bushes, excavate a shallow trench, or leave a narrow uncultivated strip to define their land. Deliberate obliteration could not be carried out without leaving traces or witnesses and would in any case be unheard of in this kind of community, especially if it was known that the NA kept a photograph. In most cases a precise area was not important, because taxation was not based on land holding. If things were to change, an estimation of area would be feasible without the need for precise surveying. If all else failed, there would still be the option to carry out more sophisticated survey and mapping for special cases and difficult situations.

If adopted earlier, such uncomplicated and unsophisticated solutions would not only have solved some of the increasing problems of unmanageable workloads of Provincial Surveyors but would have gained local acceptance and given encouragement and example for systems of the post NNS days when the fears of the country's leaders began to be substantiated and when surveying workloads were magnified a hundredfold.

Cadastral Postscript:

The Statutory Right of 0ccupancy was originally designed to control the acquisition of land by foreigners, mainly trading companies. The same survey procedures were applied when setting aside land for government projects. Throughout the days of the Northern Nigerian Survey this was its main purpose but during the 1970s the situation changed. The demand for Rights of Occupancy increased greatly in the towns where customary rights were found to give insufficient security and, even more importantly, because the bank would accept the certificate as security for a development loan.

The effective operation of a cadastral system supporting statutory rights, which uses co-ordinated boundaries, depends very much on the existence of satisfactory cadastral control from which the boundary pillars of the plots may be surveyed and of a survey profession with high integrity and good local knowledge. The provision of control generally went hand-in-hand with establishment of traversing networks to provide control for the large scale aerial mapping of township areas. With some notable exceptions this control work was relegated to the background after the dissolution of the Northern Nigerian Survey and manpower resources became devoted primarily to the immediate demands of plot demarcation. When the number of applications became overwhelming, the job of extending the cadastral control was often abandoned entirely. In 1968 nearly all the main towns had cadastral control schemes and large scale maps, but the break in continuity of staff, records and survey programmes was thereafter never completely mended.

The system, which had been established long before independence, had changed very little, and started to come under strain as the pace of development rose to levels which could not have been foreseen. At the same time the effectiveness of the survey staff showed little sign of improvement to the levels which would be needed to sustain the system. In general the calibre of persons joining the land survey profession mirrored the rewards available. Whereas quantity surveyors, for instance, could expect to gain handsomely from development, land surveyors were, and remained, technicians performing a mundane task. In some of the new States, applications for statutory Rights of 0ccupancy by members of the public were coming in at the rate of 50 per day and with the production of the Survey Department standing at about 30 surveys a month, some idea can be gained of the problems that were arising in coping with the demand for demarcation. The backlog of surveys would take over 10 years to clear in many of the urban areas.

At the end of the 1980s and into the early 1990s a programme was under way at Ahmadu Bello University to examine the state of cadastral control networks in major towns, work which could not be done by the State Survey Departments because they were too busy coping with the ongoing demands for plot surveys. Graduate students were assigned to towns, preferably ones they knew well, and the Survey Departments co-operated by giving them access to all their cadastral control records. Visits were made to the field to assess the condition of the network on the ground, how many pillars remained, and whether the town extended far past the original outer traverse, which it generally did.

The old walled town of Katsina was such a town investigated. It lies on the border between Nigeria and Niger and was a terminus of the trans-Sahara caravan route and a Provincial headquarters. It became a State capital and an industrial and educational centre. The history of the cadastral control was traced, partly by interviewing the surviving staff, and partly by examining records showing the establishment of the control network which had been completed in 1962. The township itself was well covered but new expansion had taken place to the east which was outside the cadastral network. However, in the thirty or more years since the control pillars were buried there had been a great deal of loss and damage inflicted upon them by weather, traffic and passers-by. Within the walls of the old city only seven control pillars could be found and only two of these appeared to be undisturbed. Obviously the traverses within the built up areas of the old city were in need of complete renewal.

Towns like Katsina and Kano show the extreme difficulty faced by surveyors demarcating for statutory Rs of 0 in an old city where traditional buildings and compounds form a continuous mass broken only by very narrow twisting lanes *(Photo.74)*. The old compounds are being broken up as people try to secure their tenure and build better houses with the aid of loans from the bank. The surveyor has to negotiate one or more *zaure* (gate houses) to enter the compound. As many as 20 intermediate stations have been used to co-ordinate one property beacon in these circumstances. The message about employing alternative methods of cadastral survey using aerial photographs to overcome such problems, suggested in the North-Eastern State during the mid 1970s, had still not been heeded. The idea was to use rectified and enlarged aerial photographs as 'deposited plans' to allow demarcation of properties, particularly if applicants were required to mark their boundaries in such a way that they were visible from the air.

The Nigerian cadastral system has been going through a period of great change, during which the methods which sufficed for several generations are being applied for purposes which were not considered when they were laid down. It is in need of major overhaul, and radical changes in procedure are required. A more flexible choice of survey methods, particularly the use of photogrammetry and GPS, would help the situation. Attention needs be given to the maintenance and extension of the cadastral control networks which are vital to the accuracy of plot surveys, because the demand for statutory Rights of Occupancy has increased greatly in the towns where customary rights are found to give insufficient security. The introduction of GPS and Land Information Systems could provide a long term solution to many of the problems of the cadastre but it has so far met with little support from cadastral surveyors who continue to be poorly equipped and badly financed.

In the light of the way things have developed it is tempting to ask whether it was a mistake to have introduced an inflexible system of statutory land administration in the first place, and then later attempt to use it to serve burgeoning local everyday small scale needs It was natural enough for the early European administrators and the developers to introduce methods effectively employed in most parts of the developed and developing world, but was the later perpetuation of an underfunded cadastral system, involving disciplined surveying, **really** appropriate where the demand for land was so great, the attraction of surveying as an occupation so weak and, in consequence, the calibre of its recruits so low ? In cadastral terms, perhaps Nigerians didn't know what they wanted, or were not in a position to do anything about it, but in retrospect it can be considered a waste to have introduced a system and standards which they could not or did not want to adopt in perpetuity. On the other side of the coin there can be no denying that at times they were apt to blame everyone else for the condition in which they found themselves, their lack of progress, and various man-made or man-induced disasters, and tended to overlook their own failure to take advantage of the examples that were set and the chances that were given.

MINESFIELD CADASTRAL SURVEYS

The Jos Plateau
(Refer to Maps 30 - 36)

The scenery, climate and general atmosphere of the plateau contrasted dramatically with the rest of Northern Nigeria. At over 4,000 feet (1,220 m) above sea level (Jos stood at 4,300 feet (1,310 m) and the peaks of the Shere Hills at about 6,000 feet (1,830 m)) it could be cold and wet like England in the wet season with temperatures in the low 60's (approximately 16°C) quite common and rainfall of about 56 inches (1,422 mm). For surveyors, the rain washed away the pleasures of trekking and camping, and for most people life was lived indoors with closed windows more than in other parts of the country. The skies, the colours and the scenery could be magnificent in the brilliant clear air of September, a surveyor's dream come true *(Photo.75),* but it was desolate and colourless in the Harmattan. After a clear, still night during the dry season at Bukuru a shallow tin containing a little drinking water, left on the ground outside for the dog, might have a thin skin of ice by morning.

The topography made the plateau a great breeding ground for storms. Here the rain would start sooner and end later than in other parts of the north. The Bukuru area had the world's second highest electrical potential after Venezuela and it could be a hazardous place to live, especially in the Survey Rest House *(Photo.86)* which sat on the crest of a hill with high Eucalyptus trees in the garden.

The plateau has the appearance of a high, open green plain, sloping away gradually down to lower country on its north-eastern side, scattered with spectacular granitic inselbergs standing dramatically several hundreds of feet out of the plain, and treeless except in mining reclamation areas and where planted for amenity in gardens and camps. Many of these trees were Eucalyps, claimed to have been planted originally by Tasmanian tin miners. From most directions the approach to the plateau was quite abrupt. The first glimpse was a wall of distant blue hills, then came a steep climb and an immediate and refreshing drop in temperature. The Plateau edge was a spectacular place; deep ravines filled with blue shadows and cascading streams in the wet season *(Photo.78).* Electricity came from the hydro-electric source at Kurra Falls off the plateau edge to the south-west of Jos. To many expatriates the plateau was the most comfortable and the loveliest part of Nigeria with its open, rock-strewn grassland with wandering herds of white Fulani-owned cattle followed by white egrets, its miniature red canyons and colourful heaps of mining spoil, and groups of round, quaintly-roofed Birom houses and cultivated enclosures surrounded by hedges of cactus or *karena*. It was wonderful country for horse riding and outdoor sports like tennis and golf. There was a strong polo-playing tradition amongst the expatriates. Europeans made permanent homes for themselves on the Plateau and spent years of hard work and devoted care in cultivating the loveliest gardens full of English and tropical flowers, shrubs such as Bougainvillaea, Poinciana, Cassia and multi-coloured Frangipani and fruit trees. The beautiful blue jacaranda trees were a feature of Jos for they did better there than anywhere else in Nigeria where the climate was probably too harsh for them. For most Europeans there was good living in the luxury and comfort of the Plateau *(Photo. 88)* where it was cool and often under familiar grey skies and almost free of flies and mosquitoes. However, a common affliction was 'Jos Tummy'. There seems to have been no medical explanation for this common complaint but it might have had something to do with the surfeit of fresh vegetables, potatoes and strawberries !

Most of the expatriate community of the plateau was not in Government employment and consisted very largely of like-minded and congenial people with a common interest in mining. In her memoirs Nora Hunter was delighted to arrive on the Plateau after a year in the harsh bush of Sokoto Province and she said *".......Government officials are very much in the minority, and it is a relief to escape from a government-only atmosphere, with its inevitable talk of 'shop', its seniorities and priorities, and to breathe a wider, freer air."* Compared to other parts of the north the community was much more settled and hence better developed socially, with two semi open-air cinemas *(Illustration 80),* several clubs, and better homes, food, luxuries and climate, all conducive to longer stays without the need for home leave. In the residential area of Jos stood the small St.Piran's Anglican Church, built by the European mining community. St.Piran is the patron saint of Cornish miners, who were always strongly represented on the Plateau. Several of the mining stations had social clubs. Perhaps the best known of all were the Plateau Club near the golf course in Jos, the Gold & Base Anglo-Jos Club just outside Jos on the road to Bukuru, the ATMN (Associated Tin Mines of Nigeria) Yelwa and Barikin Ladi Clubs and the Foley Memorial Theatre at Rayfield, venue for the annual gathering of the Scots at the Caledonian Society Ball. The area was well served by its government and mission-run hospitals and was also a popular maternity centre for those expatriate women who chose not to be at home for the birth. Jean Burnside recalls:-

> *'During my second tour I found that when I was visiting Jos, I always shared a room with someone's pregnant wife who had come in from a smaller station or the bush to await the arrival of the baby. However, I was never inconvenienced by the premature arrival of the expected baby !'*

The writer found respite in the government hospital there:-

> *'Three or four months after my return from bush, while I was working as an area supervisor of mining surveys on the Plateau, I started feeling progressively unwell and the undulant fever of malaria began. After a week or so I still felt well enough at times to drive, so I went to the hospital where I was immediately admitted and given intensive treatment, about which I remember very little except the needles. I was very sick for three days and virtually unconscious for one of them, but the main recovery, when it came, was fairly swift, although I was very weak for a fortnight. I awoke from the three day serious part to find the bed alongside mine occupied by a PWD road engineer who seemed to be quite cheerful. As soon as it was dark and the nurses had gone I heard "Psssssst ! Fancy a beer ?" "What me ?" I asked. The way I was feeling with my terrible feverish head I think a beer would have seen me off for good. "Come on" he said "I'm going to have one". And with that he climbed out of the low window, got into his car which was parked outside, and drove down to the Plateau Club. I was vaguely aware of his return through the window some hours later. I could not imagine what affliction had brought him to hospital, he seemed well enough to me, apart from his hangover the next morning. And that, as it transpired, was his problem. He had become addicted to alcohol out at one of his lonely road camps and had been sent to hospital for a 'drying-out' session !'*

Jos was a popular leave and recuperation station with its thatched Hill Station Hotel *(Photo.85)*, Catering Rest House *(Photo.84)* and other accommodation *(Photo 83)*. The Hill Station was, for a long time, run rather like a private country-house hotel where only the more senior officers were allowed to stay. Casual visitors needed an invitation (readily provided by Denis Willey, the Principal Surveyor, who was no snob), presumably to keep out the riffraff. Set amidst beautiful gardens, with lawns and roses, it exuded an atmosphere of quiet comfort, with immaculate and polite Nigerian staff, a rather superior but very pleasant elderly Nigerian bar-man, thick carpets, English hunting scenes on the walls, easy chairs, curtains and chandeliers; a nice place for dinner or genteel afternoon tea on the lawn. It also possessed a luxurious, well kept and wood-panelled billiards room where quiet attendants unobtrusively chalked the players' cues and fetched drinks from the bar. It remained the best place to stay in Jos until well into the 1970s, though its exclusivity declined. It was destined never to recover its former glory after suffering a disastrous fire in 1969, when the thatched roof was ignited from a garden bonfire which went out of control, and all its furniture and fittings were destroyed.

Jos was also one of the best places for shopping in Northern Nigeria and most of the main stores, or 'canteens' as they were called, were represented there. The main streets *(Photo.79)* had familiar names like G.B.Ollivant, Paterson Zochonis, UAC (Kingsway), John Holt, CFAO *(Compagnie Française de l'Afrique Orientale)*, the SIM Bookshop, Syrian traders' shops selling cloth, and the Indian stores T.Kahale and K.C.Chellaram and an excellent small Lebanese-owned bakery, and dairy produce and dried milk were available from the Government run creamery at Vom.

The Birom People

The real soul of the original Jos Plateau lay within the small undisturbed villages and hamlets of small mud-built round houses, surrounded with fences of living cactus perhaps 15 feet high, with grass roofs, hidden away in the hills, rocks and white stemmed euphorbia bushes. There lived a tough, virile and independent people, little changed in their way of life and customs for many centuries *(Photo.77)*. Archaeological finds, sometimes in the mine workings, indicate a culture well developed 2000 or 3000 years ago. There was a huge contrast between the lifestyles of the wealthy expatriate and Nigerian mining community and these Birom and other 'pagan' people who, unless they were actually employed in mining work, scratched a meagre living from the poor soil, a great deal of the best land having been lost to mining in the valley bottoms of the tin-rich areas *(Photo.93)*. Over the years most of the able bodied men found manual employment in the mines, but the Birom were fundamentally hunters and agriculturists. Hunters could sometimes be seen in remote areas armed with bows and arrows and hunting dogs or would sometimes pass by leading packs of tethered dogs to market where dog meat was a delicacy. There was little left to hunt on the open Plateau but it produced a range of crops grown on a small scale for local consumption including *acha* (a grass-like cereal crop), millet, kokoyams, Guinea corn, groundnuts, rice, tiger nuts, pumpkins, gourds, spinach, gauta, okra, peppers, cassava, sweet potatoes, cotton, hemp and tobacco. Many of them lived a primitive life of poverty, the womenfolk *(Photo.82)* half naked and dressed only with bunches of leaves, in small hamlets with fences of cactus for defence and protection of their crops against grazing livestock. These people, like the pagan hill tribes of other parts of the north and the areas bordering the Cameroons, were probably the descendants of those who sought refuge from the northern Islamic invaders in high, inaccessible places. For some time the British administrators found it difficult to control the banditry, head-hunting and slave dealing which went on but there are well documented accounts of how District Officers attempted to do so with the assistance of quite small detachments of armed policemen. By evading the influence of Islam they became the subject of conversion by the Christian missions and schools, and often took very successfully to western ways of life, producing strong political leaders to represent them in independent Nigeria.

Pagan areas were, and probably are to this day, still rife with superstition. Offerings were made to deities of the bush, the forests and the rocks - dried bones, skins, bits of old clothing and food offerings could be found in the most unlikely places or in shrines in the vicinity of the village. The high ground often sought by surveyors for their work was sometimes regarded by the local Birom people as sacred 'juju' or *tsafi* land used traditionally for ceremonies connected with their beliefs. Such ceremonies were normally the province of the men, and women were known to have been put to death by stoning for illegal attendance and thus the ceremonies were frowned upon by authority. Such places did however retain local importance, mining within them and within protected farming areas was generally not allowed unless local interests were placated by appropriate compensation. Some sites used for survey beacons were not known to be sacrosanct until the beacons were destroyed after the departure of the surveyors; a number of prominent triangulation stations suffered in this way. As a newcomer and unaware of the significance of such places, Harry Rentema experienced difficulties on his first tour of the Plateau in 1952:-

> *'Although we had some authority as "white men" we had to respect the local customs and religious beliefs.*
>
> *I was working near Miango, a large pagan village, surrounded by a cactus hedge and had left my labourers there and went with two Hausa boys as guides to look for a place to pitch my tent. They took me to a rocky place with trees, but I discovered a level place with big shady trees which I preferred. The boys were arguing but I did not understand them and decided to let the labourers put up the tent there.*
>
> *I had just taken my bath and changed my clothes when four people and a young boy appeared to tell me that I was standing on "Tsafi" ground, which was not allowed. I did not take that too seriously and bluffed that I was a government officer and could stay. I was asked by the young boy who was acting as interpreter if I could write that down and sign it. I began to feel uncertain. I argued that my labourers were far away in the village and it was getting dark. That was (correctly) considered a very different argument and they went back to the sarki in the village to convey the message.*

I tried to forget the problem but after 1½ hours the four elders and the sarki's son appeared again in the light of my Tilley lamp. I was asked to leave the next day early in the morning, otherwise a cow should be slaughtered in front of the tent and I should have to pay £8 for it. Never had a European camped there before and although the sarki understood my problems and was willing to help me, he could not justify this for his people. If they did not offer a cow, an epidemic would break out and I would be responsible. I got rather fed up. I said that I had selected this place with the help of the two Hausa men and that we had some arguments about "here" or "over there", but I did not understand their Hausa, in which case the Hausa men should pay for the cow. Things were getting more and more complicated. In the end I said that I would not get the sarki into trouble and would move my tent provided that he would help me with labourers. This was a very different point of view and caused much commotion on the other side, while I started packing. At midnight it was decided that I could stay. The sarki promised to come next morning to find out whether I had had a good night. I told him not to come too early.'

The Kagoro Hills, a miniature version of the plateau to the south-west of the main mass and isolated from it, appears like a wall of granite from all sides and there was no road to the summit. The ascent was an energetic, hot climb on foot along narrow, wet defiles between huge exfoliated boulders up on to wild, indented, unspoiled grassy tableland. Two primary triangulation points some miles apart made this an interesting, and from the surveyor's point of view essential, place to visit *(Photo.171)* and, until the 1950's, a slightly risky one because of the antipathy to outsiders of the local people who had lived there in splendid isolation, undisturbed by the outside world for many hundreds of years. Comparatively few Europeans had ever visited the hills, though it later became a popular excursion to climb the steep path from Kagoro town which lay on the northern side of the hills. On maps still in use at the time it was designated an 'Unsettled' area and official advice was still to travel with local guides, contact local chiefs and be accompanied by an armed policeman. The local people lived in small hamlets of conically roofed houses and huge pot-like vermin-proof granaries standing on stilts, concealed in defensive positions amongst the rocks. Defensive because these people were driven into the hills by the Fulani slave raiders before the arrival of the British. With little to fear from the British they sometimes ventured out from their hilltop fastnesses and did some pillaging of their own until police and military action was taken against them. In sharp contrast to the wild hills, the small town of Kagoro with its mission station, schools and busy weekly market lay on the railway line a few miles east of Kafanchan Junction and the station burst into a frenzy of sales activity when the daily up and down local trains or the Plateau Limited pulled in.

Prospecting for and mining cassiterite and other minerals

There is mention on some of the very earliest navigator's maps, which displayed only the most rudimentary knowledge of the West African interior, that tin was one of the trading commodities of the inland tribes, some of it reaching the ports of North Africa via Hausa merchants, though nothing was known of its origin. The usefulness of the heavy black grains of sand found in the beds of the streams had been known for centuries by the indigenous people who long had a 'tin industry' of their own, and used it for tinning their brassware.

That tin ore existed somewhere in the northern part of what was to become Nigeria was contained in a report by Sir William Wallace in 1884. He was opening up the River Benue for trade on behalf of the Royal Niger Company and was able to purchase tin ingots from traders on the river at Ibi. It was in the form of 'straw' tin, so called because it was produced in small furnaces by the side of streams and poured into moulds made from course grass stems set in a hardened clay base. Wallace was Political Agent to a party sent to subdue the Emir of Bauchi and took the opportunity, in 1902, whilst on the Bauchi Plateau, to obtain an ore sample from the Delimi River near Naraguta. It was sent to England where the company was so impressed that it organised a prospecting expedition which got no further than Loko on the Benue, but a Mr G.R.Nicolaus discovered a clan near Badiko producing ingots consisting of a number of coarse wires uniting at one end to from a block of metal. Its source was said to be an impure black sand from the Delimi River at Tilde Fulani.

H.W.Laws was the first prospector to reach the plateau, then known as the Bauchi Plateau, approaching from Jagindi, and discovered its valuable tinfield in 1903. He went on to Tilde Fulani which became a prospecting base and then moved on to Naraguta. He lost his two assistants to sickness and as a solitary European in their midst, was harassed by the local people, thinking he was a slave trader, until he was relieved by a military expedition from Zungeru in 1904. For some time the area remained beyond the pale of the administration, especially in the outlying areas and protection was needed for exploration. In 1905 a Government station had been opened at Bukuru under the control of the Resident of Bauchi Province, but administration was not easy and communications continued to be unreliable and dangerous until 1909 and it was not until 1929 that there was a year entirely free of disturbances somewhere or other in the plateau area.

Cassiterite is tin oxide and is usually found as water-worn grains ranging from a coarse gravel to fine sand. It is usually black, but ruby and grey or almost white varieties are also known. Minerals commonly associated with cassiterite are topaz, ilmenite, magnetite, rutile, zircon, monazite, garnet, and more rarely, columbite, tantalite, wolframite, corundum and gold. Columbite yields niobium, a metal which allows steel alloys to withstand the very high internal operating temperatures of jet engines. Nigeria was the world's main producer from the 1930's onwards. In the 1950's its use in engines led to great demand as the USA stockpiled, prices doubled and Nigeria experienced a three year boom. During the 1960s Nigeria led the world in columbite production.

The economic deposits are almost entirely of an alluvial nature (although some lode and pegmatite working is done) lying either in the more recent river beds or in ancient ones which are concealed by volcanic layers. These deposits of cassiterite owe their existence to the breakdown of the stanniferous lodes associated with the Plateau Granites, a series of Younger Granites intruded in the old Pre-Cambrian complex of igneous and metamorphic rocks. After the close of igneous activity there were long ages of denudation which resulted in the removal of much old rock and the upper mineralised parts of the Younger Granite batholith. Tinstone became concentrated in the valleys which were later buried by a Fluvio-Volcanic (mid-Tertiary age) series of alluvial and volcanic accumulations. New drainage lines then developed, the older superficial deposits were gradually removed, and the tinstone was rearranged along the floors of the Tertiary valleys. But much of the Fluvio-Volcanic material still remained when geologically recent volcanic activity broke out again and large areas, especially of the Plateau, were flooded with basaltic lava, covering the valleys and burying the tin.

By the 1970's the geologically modern placers were very rapidly being used up and the 'deep-leads' in the Fluvio-Volcanic formations were becoming more important though they were harder to work on account of the difficulty of locating the old drainage patterns beneath an overburden sometimes consisting of basaltic lavas.

The tin was won by a variety of methods ranging from simple small scale digging *(Photos.89 and 90),* sluicing and hand-washing, to pressure hosing, bucket dredging, and utilisation of heavy earth-moving vehicles *(Photo.91),* draglines *(Photo.92)* and floating dredges by the large mining companies. The tin strata generally lay 20-60 feet below the surface and mines usually took the form of large pits. During the dry season water supply could be a problem and it was generally stored in old workings *(Photo.93).* and used over and over again. The product was generally a high grade concentrate, with a 70% tin content, which for many years was bagged and exported in this form for smelting in Europe. Security in the mining tin stores and on the trains taking it to the ports of the south had to be high and stealing was rife. It is now converted into tin metal ingots at a smelter at Jos.

By far the greater part of Nigeria's tin has been produced on and around the Jos Plateau, but there have also been workings in parts of Benue, Bauchi, Zaria , Kano and Ilorin Provinces. The small Ilorin field was about 350 square miles in extent lying about half way between Ilorin and Baro near the Niger.

Interaction of Mining and Surveying

Tin was the mainstay of the mining industry until it was ousted by oil production from the southern part of the country and, as one of Nigeria's most important industries, from an early date the administration of the land for mining purposes demanded considerable Survey support.

Cadastral surveying for prospecting and open-cast mining purposes applied throughout Nigeria but the greatest concentration of this work lay in and around the Plateau, especially the country around Jos, which was destined to become one of the most walked-over, measured, beaconed and mapped parts of the whole Federation. Contrary to popular belief these surveys were traditionally conducted by government surveyors but, particularly between the two World Wars, a significant proportion of the work was in the hands of private Licensed Surveyors.

Only 59 lbs of tin ore were won in 1903 because the emphasis was on prospecting, but the Niger Company demonstrated the opportunities for success and attracted outside capital for development. The necessity for the definition of mining concessions on the ground was immediately apparent during the great outburst of interest in prospecting and mining in the very early years of the century and the site of the first mining beacon, which is preserved by the Department of Antiquities as an Ancient Monument, was established in 1905 near Tilden Fulani. Surveys were at first rudimentary and based on True North or Magnetic North azimuth control. Leases were surveyed to what amounts to present day tertiary cadastral standards with heights carried forward along traverse lines, and contours or form lines were drawn on each title deed plan. The resultant plan was a useful working diagram for the miner and a tool for the map maker in a gradual build-up of topographical information.

Apart from rough maps compiled from road reports by administrative officers, no survey work for mapping was carried out until 1908 when a company of Royal Engineers, working under the direction of the geographical section of the War Office, produced a rough map of the Bauchi Plateau area at a scale of 1:250,000.

By 1909, largely through the efforts of the Niger Company, production had risen to 458 tons, to 774 tons by 1910, and by 1912 the mining industry had reached a stage which made necessary some form of control for the survey of prospecting and mining areas. The town of Jos was being established and a Jos Native Authority formed. A party of Royal Engineers measured a base line at Naraguta and began the observation of chains of triangulation, northwards towards Kano, and southwards as far as Jama'an Daroro. The outbreak of war in 1914 prevented the completion of their work although it gave tin production a considerable boost. Subsequently it was found that the triangulation was insufficiently accurate and their work, with the exception of the actual measurement of the base line, had to be remodelled and re-observed. This was started in 1924 by the Nigerian Survey Department, when the primary triangulation from Naraguta to the south was re-observed and the chain carried on to Minna in the following year. The other chain, from Naraguta to Kano, was re-arranged in 1929 and completely re-observed in 1930 and 1931. Full trig control over the area became possible as the Primary chains met the plateau, indeed the base line on the 'N' chain ran right across what is now a part of Jos township *(Photo.103)*. Breakdown of the Primary control into Secondary and Tertiary nets was carried out with the assistance of the Sappers in the inter-war period.

As mining activity became more widespread and extended off the plateau locally established trig control was also extended and used as a framework upon which to build up the earliest 1:62,500 maps whose initial purpose was the plotting of existing holdings and new applications. The intelligence charts in due course became known as 'Priority Sheets' since a master version of each was used to plot new applications which were treated strictly on a 'first come, first served' basis. From 1912 onwards the Survey Department was kept very busy dealing with the survey of areas over which prospecting and mining rights were applied for or granted. The discovery of the Jema'a tin 'lode' brought interest in tin in Nassarawa Province to a maximum since it was conveniently located for transport to the Benue. The main tin producing district was situated south and south-east of Jema'a as far as the Arikia River and including Mada as far south as the South Mada Hills.

The Bauchi Light Railway linking Bukuru with the main line track at Zaria was opened in 1915 when tin production was of the order of 7,000 tons and worth about £1,000,000, thus greatly facilitating the export of tin ore. It brought greater emphasis to plateau tin and interest in Jema'a declined, though the area was still being worked in the 1960s, and some tin was still being found in underground working in the lode bedrock near Jema'a. By 1919 there were 80 companies and syndicates at work producing a total of over 8,000 tons.

In 1924 and 1925, when the mining industry was in its heyday of prosperity, applications for leases became so numerous that available Survey personnel were insufficient to prevent an increasing accumulation of arrears of work. In 1926, therefore, another party of Royal Engineers came to their assistance and in 1927 their numbers were increased, enabling them also to undertake trigonometrical and topographical work on the minesfield and elsewhere. Geologists had produced technical reports covering the principal tin mining areas of Nigeria and their bulletins contain maps which appeared to be based on sketchy RE 1:125,000 scale maps showing the principal drainage and positions of triangulation points.

Plateau Province, the smallest of the Northern Provinces with an area of about 10,560 square miles, was brought into existence as one of the measures of the reorganisation of the Northern Provinces in 1926 and was divided into five Divisions, Jos, Pankshin, Jema'a, Southern and Shendam. It was created out of the Provinces of Bauchi (Jos and Pankshin Divisions, Gindiri Village area, Plains, Angas and Kanam Districts), Muri (Shendam Division, less Awe District and Wase District proper) and Nasarawa and Jema'a Divisions, and Lafia Division less Lafia Emirate). Muri and Nassarawa disappeared entirely. The tribal units of Moroa, Kagoro and Jaba later joined Zaria Province. The Jos N.A. inaugurated a system of registration of the holders of plots in the Jos Native (Hausa) Town. Delimitation of parts of Plateau-Benue and Plateau-Bauchi inter Provincial boundaries took place.

A Lands and Mining Section, part of the Northern administration, had offices in Kaduna and Jos. It dealt with all mining titles under which land was held by non-Nigerians. The Lt-Governor was empowered to grant Certificates of Occupancy over such land. New public offices (Provincial, Mines, Survey and Treasury) were opened at Jos. The system of application for Mining Titles and of the 'Lands and Mines' branch of the Provincial Office was inaugurated.

The railway continued in importance until the Kafanchan to Jos branch of the Nigerian Railway was opened in 1927, allowing the use of labour-saving machinery using coal brought from the Enugu coalfield and tin production had passed the 10,000 tons mark. Deforestation of parts of the Plateau during early mining had created a fuel shortage. The first boat train on the newly opened Kafanchan-Jos line arrived along the track which reached its highest point near Kuru at 4,324 ft above sea level. This year was also memorable because it marked the opening of the Jos telephone exchange and the first visit of aeroplanes to Jos. Two RAF aircraft from Egypt landed in Kaduna and went on to Jos and left for Bauchi the next day.

During 1928 there was a tin boom in Nigeria and not enough surveyors to cope with the demand for prospecting licences. In his book *Surveyor's Trek*, David Anderson said that he had come out to West Africa with romantic notions of charting the unknown but quickly found himself surveying mining leases. There were 136 mining leases and 99 exclusive prospecting licenses awaiting survey at the end of the year. 50 leases, 3 mining rights and 59 EPLs were surveyed yielding revenue of £4,089. A peak of employment was reached in the tin industry with 40,000 Nigerians and 363 Europeans. Annual tin production then stood at over 15,000 tons and was worth over £2,000,000.

During this period of intense mining activity it became apparent that the control of mining surveys by primary triangulation was inadequate, and in 1928 it was decided to establish a close framework of secondary and tertiary points over the whole minesfield. This work was undertaken by the Royal Engineers and by 1930 an accurate framework of trigonometrical points, based on primary triangulation, had been established, sufficiently close to enable practically any area to be connected with at least one triangulation point. This secondary and tertiary triangulation was extended into the Nunku District of the Southern Division. After the completion of the triangulation, the R.E. Special Survey Party made a topographical map showing all mining camps and other detail to the scale of 1/125,000 covering the area enclosed by latitudes 9°12' 30" N and 10° 00 00" N and longitudes 8° 40' OO"E and 9° 02' 30"E. Surveys for the layouts at Kafanchan and Bukuru were also carried out.

A Minesfield Survey Office was being maintained at Jos though it never had many expatriate surveyors. Licensed surveyors then did much of the minesfield surveying. Nigeria Surveys had long concentrated on the provision of triangulation to control the jig-saw of mining leases and in 1928 there were more expatriates working in this area than in any of the other survey branches, 11 surveyors plus the special R.E. party of 5 officers and 18 non-commissioned officers.

A reconnaissance was carried out for the first stage of a proposed new railway which was to run from Lafia to Lake Chad but the line was never built; an alternative route from Kuru, 20 miles from Jos, on the plateau being chosen some 30 years later. The Bornu railway extension started in 1958 and construction of the 400 miles of track to Maiduguri via Bauchi and Gombe took 6 years at a total cost of £20 million.

In 1931 the value of tin went into decline and so did output and there was international agreement on enforced reduction in output in order to maintain prices. In 1932 the Nigerian quota was a mere 3,431 tons. The population of Plateau Province stood at about 533,000 Nigerians, with just 308 Europeans, including a few Syrians. There was something of an exodus from the tinfields to the gold mining areas.

In 1933, after 3 years of comparative inactivity, the Minesfield Division once again became one of the most important and busy sections of the Nigerian Survey Department owing to the exploitation of the gold-bearing areas of Niger, Zaria and Sokoto Provinces. Much of the work of surveying the leases was carried out by licensed surveyors. 1934 saw revived interest in mining applications as the tin quota rose to 4,340 tons. Sterling had depreciated and there was a great demand for gold. As well as the work of licensed surveyors the officer in charge at Jos had 9 European officers to help for an average of 4 months each, and 6 Nigerians for an average of 7 months. A further increase in the tin quota in the following year and a demand for columbite gave an impetus to the industry and there was a rise in applications. Possible gold lodes were located in the Bin Yauri and Mailele districts.

In 1936 goldfield applications were reduced but were offset by an increase on the tinfields. 310 mining leases and 85 EPLs were surveyed. Very little was done by licensed surveyors who now preferred to employ freelance surveyors to carry out this work. There were 737 new tin applications in 1937 and an average of 18 gold applications per month and 15 for tin in 1938, the latter a figure well below normal. 248 MLs and 77 EPLs were surveyed leaving 135 MLs, 2 MRs and 56 EPLs outstanding. Jos aerodrome and the township boundary were demarcated

The loss of Malaya as a source of tin for the war effort meant attempting to step up production in Nigeria and other unoccupied territories, and this in turn implied the need for a continuing Survey service on the Minesfield. Under Mooney, the officer in charge, J.C.Pugh was engaged on mining surveys in 1942 where the war effort required tin, tantalite, columbite, wolfram and gold (which was then £9 an ounce). This work took him to Plateau, Bauchi, Kano and Sokoto Provinces and elsewhere.

He remembered being brought in from triangulation work:-

'At my last station, at Tof, on the southern edge of the Plateau, I received an urgent message to go to Jos and take over the Minesfield Office. My senior officer there had been galloping his horse when it put one foot in a hole and he was thrown, and he was in hospital with badly broken bones. I finished the last observations on the chain, and moved to Jos, where I found an empty gida on the Bukuru road. I knew the general workings of the office. What to do after office hours ? I no longer knew anyone in Jos. I looked at the very faded notice-board outside the office yard, which said NIGERIA SURVEYS - MINESFIELD DIVISION - barely legible, not having been repainted since before the war. So I took it away at the weekend, bought black and white paint and brushes, and replaced it on the Monday in its original glory. What else to do ? I realised the monthly report to Lagos would have to be written in a fortnight. The basic details of surveyors and their output, new applications and surveys completed, were all straightforward. I looked back, over many months, and all had figures for outstanding applications awaiting survey - over 700 in each case. I asked the Chief Clerk for a list of them, and was told that no list existed - each officer in charge took the previous figure, added the new applications and deducted the completions. I asked where all the outstanding applications were located, and he showed be a long shelf of files, clean at the new end and very dusty at the other. I started to explore and found it intriguing, so much so that I stayed in the office every day until dusk. The dusty end included over 60 applications for Exclusive Prospecting Licences, Mining Leases, Mining Rights dating back to 1923, for mining diamonds (after one diamond had been reported as found - probably stolen and brought in from elsewhere). All were time-expired, given up before survey. There were many other applications for tin, etc., similarly given up before

survey. There had never been a category of lapsed or withdrawn before survey. By the time I wrote the monthly report I had reduced the 'outstanding" applications to 300+ . My senior colleague was out of hospital but content to "recuperate", leaving the office to me. Finally a message came from Lagos instructing me to report there as soon as possible, so my colleague returned to work. He found a letter just arrived from HQ asking for an urgent explanation as to how the "outstanding" figure had suddenly dropped from 700+ to 300+. I explained. He was furious, charged me with deliberately trying to make him look inefficient, and told me to get on the train due to leave that evening.'

Post War

In 1946-47 323 mining applications were received and about 134 surveyed, 72% of them by Licensed Surveyors. The minerals being sought were cassiterite, tantalite, columbite, wolfram, gold, silver, galena (lead) and sphalerite (zinc). In the years which followed, the annual figures for mining applications more than doubled, rising to 885 in 1948-49 and reaching a high point of 1,037 in 1952-53 before falling back to 685 in 1956-57. The number of mining areas surveyed and titles prepared and the revenue earned from them kept pace, peaking at 746 in 1953-54 but there was always a significant number, of the order of 200 or so, awaiting attention.

In 1947-48 work was done on the Jos township 1:2,400 mapping, some of the mapsheets were printed in Lagos, and a 1:12,500 scale map of the Jos area was being drawn.

The proportion of work done by Licensed Surveyors, many of them expatriates, gradually diminished to about 60% in 1949-50 and continued to decline as more Survey Assistants were appointed by Government to carry out this kind of work. The Survey Act 1958 defined a surveyor as either 'an officer of the Survey Department authorised to undertake surveys' or as 'the holder of a Survey Licence'. In colonial times the Licence was the reward for long service in the Government survey department under a 15 year rule. Most Nigerian licensed surveyors were elderly and content to make a comfortable living in the large cities by employing assistants to demarcate small plots or to map areas in dispute. Their numbers were small and their relationship with the Government close and subordinate, not only because many of them were ex- employees of fairly lowly status, but because of the legal requirement for any cadastral plan to be checked by the Survey Department and countersigned by the Surveyor General. A short clause inserted in the Law stated 'No person shall without the written permission of the Surveyor General demarcate or survey the boundary of any area the subject of a right of occupancy '.

Compared with his colleagues in private practice the government surveyor enjoyed a relatively stable and unchanging existence. In the North the surveyor tended to be looked upon as a minor government employee engaged on technical work which required him to spend most of his time in someone else's backyard. Where this attitude prevailed recruits to the profession were naturally much harder to find and candidates with the required qualifications in scientific subjects were attracted to more prestigious professions.

Staffing levels had been very low in the late 1940's with 2 senior service officers, 5 junior service surveyors, 1 Survey Assistant, 8 draughtsmen, 2 computers, 4 clerks, a type-printer and a sunprinter. By 1951 however, as the demands of the Minesfield increased, there were increases all round with 5 senior service officers, 6 juniors, 20 Survey Assistants, 14 draughtsmen of various grades, 3 computers, 10 clerks and other junior office staff.

This expansion was facilitated by the erection of new office buildings at Jos during 1949-50 *(Photo.102)* at a cost of £2,500 to house the whole of the Minesfield District Headquarters staff *(Photo.101),* allowing them to move from the Provincial Administration offices, where drawing office production had been limited by the number of draughtsmen that could be accommodated. The Provincial Administrative Offices at Jos continued to maintain a Mines Section which handled the lands affairs of the Minesfield. This was not to be confused with the Mines Department of Central Government which had inspectors in Jos, working under the Chief Inspector of Mines, responsible for the technical and legal side of mining activities.

The Jos Survey office also acted as a branch office for other types of survey work, rather like a Provincial Survey office, but on something of a headquarters scale. Surveys were done for example for Rights of Occupancy in Bukuru, for the setting out of Jos Radio Diffusion station, Mai-idon-Toro Veterinary station, Veterinary land at Vom, and other surveys at places like Bokkos, Gudi and Ganawuri. The layout survey of Jos township was in progress and for general mapping the roads on the Minesfield were revised for the 1:125,000 series topographic maps.

During 1953-54 the high number of mining applications, 124 in the month of September alone for example, placed a heavy strain on the administration and the drawing office at Jos which could not be increased because of the shortage of men and the inadequacy of the accommodation. Licensed surveyors were doing less and less survey on the Minesfield and the burden on the Department was increasing accordingly. Reorganisation of the Survey Section was begun but this placed a heavy burden on staff.

In 1954-55 routine work was at much the same level as in recent years but was handicapped by inadequate office accommodation, particularly drawing space and records storage for the vulnerable and virtually irreplaceable records of over 20,000 surveys. A new Plan Inspection Room, for Priority Sheet inspection by the mining community and others, was built and opened for use by the public in 1955-56, and work on other buildings was started. Construction was started on a new headquarters building at Jos consisting of a new drawing office and offices for the Principal and Senior Surveyors, together with an extension to the old drawing office and internal reconstruction of the old buildings, greatly reducing congestion and making possible an increase in the technical staff. A new fire and vermin proof record room was also started and promised at last to make possible the safe housing of the valuable cadastral records of the minesfield.

The number of outstanding surveys increased in the early part of 1955-56 but 80 were completed in March 1956, the second highest monthly figure ever recorded, bettered only by the figure of 83 for May 1953.

Minesfield triangulation control had been neglected for many years, many beacons had disappeared, and the triangulation had not been extended as the mining area expanded. Detailed secondary and tertiary triangulation infill of the fringe areas of the Plateau Minesfield was carried out in the outburst of survey activity which followed the establishment of the Northern Nigerian Survey. The peak of surveying activity in the area was probably reached during this period when there were as many as 15 survey parties in the field based on Jos and fully occupied on triangulation extension and repair, the revision and replotting of Priority Sheets, providing new mapping control, as well as the 'bread and butter' Mining Lease surveys. 54 new tertiary triangulation points were fixed in the first half of 1955.

It was during this period too that the Surveyor-General, Keith Hunter, conceived the idea of marking tertiary triangulation points with tall white masonry beacons, of inexpensive breeze block construction *(Illustration 45 and Photo.95)* using relatively unskilled labour, to avoid the constant necessity for hill climbing and beaconing and to provide a dense network of prominent hilltop reference points to which angular observations could be taken by theodolite for the fixation of a surveyor's position, using a computational method known as resection. The intention was to permit identification of the control points not only by survey parties but also by prospectors and would enable the latter to pin-point their application plans more accurately. By March 1956 16 of these had been erected.

It was decided to extend the triangulation and increase its density so that no Mining Lease was likely to be more than 2 miles from a fixed point. The new beacons were fixed by intersection from secondary stations but were criticised for their size, their square sectional shape (which could give rise to 'phase' errors when bisecting at close range with the vertical crosswire of the theodolite), and the fact that they created the necessity for satellite computation should the need arise to occupy the point; but for general survey use and a source of constant wonder for the unenlightened, they proved invaluable. In an attempt to make the higher of these beacons visible against a bright or white sky some of them were painted red, but the decision was later made that white would in fact make them more distinct in most lighting conditions and they were repainted. More than a hundred were eventually built and new visitors to the country around Jos would remark about the piety of the local people because of the white 'madonnas' which appeared on many of the bare and treeless hilltops *(Photo.96)*. But the saintly, nine feet tall, figures of Laminga, Dogon Dutse, Kassa, etc., the topmost part of which from a distance might be mistaken for a head, were in truth the very visible trademarks of the Survey Department. As any metal or other valuable material used in the construction of beacons on the minesfield was almost invariably stolen, these new concrete block pillars offered less temptation to the local inhabitants to break them up. It was expected that about ten percent would be destroyed each year by lightning. A bolt from a violent thunderstorm would strike like a high velocity artillery shell and scatter the beacon in tiny pieces over the hill top. Copper lightning conductors were installed as an experiment but these were stolen immediately by the Biroms. In the end, an annual rebuilding program had to be included in the budget.

Concurrently with the extension of the triangulation, field parties started to refix, from the triangulation, a proportion of all the old cadastral surveys, in preparation for the accurate replotting of the cadastral diagrams. At the same time, a computing and drawing section was planned, to begin the work of replotting, completely, the more congested and inaccurate Priority Sheets at a scale at 1:50,000, 1:25,000 or, if necessary, 1:12,500. The old sheets had been plotted with very sparse ground control on a scale of 1:62,500 in the early days of the Minesfield. Many of them had become so congested as to be almost indecipherable *(Map 37)*, while as a result of lack of skilled staff and supervision, and of slipshod field work during and immediately after the war, they were in many cases inaccurate and unreliable. Although there was never any concrete evidence, it was often suspected that some distortion was introduced through 'outside' influence by mining applicants on some of the Survey draughtsmen. Surveys had not been subjected to sufficient checks to ensure that errors were always detected and some surveyors' work, Government and Licensed, was not as trustworthy as it should have been. The matter was becoming more serious and would have to be put right, even at the expense of other survey activities. Here and there no better example could be found of how a mass of loosely connected surveys have the effect of a task carried out from the part to the whole ! Also, as they showed little or no topographical detail, the Priority Sheets were not easy to use in the field. For clarity of cadastral detail the new sheets showed cadastral information printed in colour on a grey topographical background. They were a great improvement on the old sheets but their production entailed a vast amount of work and promised to take years to complete. Steps were taken to ensure that from then onward Survey Regulations were complied with, field checks made on a proportion of the work done by all surveyors, government and licensed, and the rules for government surveyors were tightened up.

In 1955-56 the tertiary triangulation on the Northern Minesfield was extended and 52 new points beaconed, 26 observed and 22 computed and connected to the existing primary and secondary triangulation. Some of the old secondaries were found to be lacking in consistency. Old primary and secondary triangulation had been readjusted and recomputed several times but co-ordinate records had not always been kept up to date. The co-ordinates of all points had to be checked and new lists prepared showing the final or most recent values for each point. This revision was undertaken with the co-operation of the Federal Survey Department and new lists were drafted and printed by the end of the year.

Trevor Brokenshire was involved in this work and has contributed the following:-

'Jos was 'home' to Joan and me; we were there in part or all of 1952(Photo.87), 1954, 1955, 1956, 1959, 1960 and 1961. In 1952 I worked in the Minesfield survey checking section, checking the surveys of government and licensed surveyors and I carried out some surveys of mining leases myself to see what problems there might be.

In general, Minesfield work was straightforward, consisting of the placing of cement beacons at the corners of mining leases (ML's) and exclusive prospecting licences (EPL's) which had been applied for, traversing by theodolite and steel band between those beacons to a misclosure of better than 1 in 3,000 and, where necessary, ensuring that a new lease which has a common boundary with an existing lease properly adjoins the old lease. This would involve a traverse between the beacons of the old lease and pegs marking the approximate positions of corners of the new lease; computation of the traverse, and shifting the pegs to their correct positions on the common line. If the corners of the ML or EPL were not intervisible, line beacons would be placed so that they were intervisible and not more than 1,320 feet apart. This would also involve computation of the boundary traverse and shifting of the traverse pegs onto line. All surveys of mining areas would be shown on a plan and should be connected to triangulation points or control traverse points.

When surveys had been checked and accepted, title deed plans were prepared and the position and extent of the lease or licence plotted on to a Priority Sheet, a map at a scale of 1:62,500 which showed, in pencil, the positions of applications for grants of title for mining purposes, and, in ink, the surveyed position of the title.

By 1954 it had been recognised that the positions of many of the MLs and EPLs on the Priority Sheets were not correct, and there were several instances of apparent overlaps of proposed MLs on existing leases plotted on the Priority Sheets, where, on the ground, there was no overlap. A re-drawing of selected congested mining areas to a scale of 1:25,000 had shown up various errors in previous work, mostly due to faulty connections to triangulation points, but occasionally due to a faulty boundary traverse.

The connection of leases to "a Government survey beacon" was, in 1954, governed by a Regulation:- "Surveys shall wherever possible be connected by closed traverse or triangulation to a Government Survey Beacon or beacons......to an accuracy of 1:3,000". Connections to triangulation points were the exception rather than the rule and "Government survey beacons" had come to mean any beacon, including those on MLs etc., which had been placed by a Government or Licensed Surveyor. It was therefore decided that the Regulation should be considerably strengthened by requiring that if a triangulation or control traverse point was within 3 miles of the site of the survey, connection must be made. In order to give the Regulations some 'teeth' it was also decided that a network of tertiary triangulation points should be provided over the greater part of the Minesfield.

Before reaching a decision as to the best solution of the problem of inaccurate Priority Sheets a considerable amount of research on the fixing of existing MLs etc., was done. In some case, leases were tied to leases extending for large distances along an alluvial tin-bearing stream or other deposit; some were tied to existing triangulation points whose co-ordinates had become suspect; and some had been tied to triangulation points by methods which invited inaccuracies. For example, one lease was tied to a trig. point 20,000 feet away by observation of the base angles of a triangle which had a deduced apex angle of 3°. A lease not far away had been tied to a trig. point 50,000 feet away, using a triangle with a deduced apex angle of 6°. A traverse between the two leases revealed a fixing error of about 100 feet. Another lease had been fixed by a three point resection to trig. points; but the co-ordinates of one or more of the trig. points were now suspect; and a further lease had been fixed by using an apex angle of 2°.

It had become obvious that there was need for drastic action and the decision was taken to undertake the initially daunting task or re-fixing every ML or EPL where trig. points existed within a reasonable distance. A Nigerian surveyor, with my occasional assistance, started on this task, and did some sterling work.

The next task was to commence re-plotting of the Priority Sheets. All existing sheets were of linen-backed paper mounted on zinc plates; it was decided that opaque astrafoil (plastic) sheets should be used for the new work. The plotting scale was also changed from 1:62,500 to 1:50,000, the latter being the scale at which new topographic sheets were being produced at the Survey Department office in Kaduna. After an initial hiccup over gridding of the new sheets, where drawing office staff had 'constructed' the grid by stepping off grid squares with boxwood scales, set squares, and protractors, I did the construction myself with a beam compass and long steel straightedge. I also insisted that plotting of points fixed from trig. points should be plotted by co-ordinates rather than the previous method of bearing and distance. After a little practice, the drawing office staff took pride in being able to plot to 1/200th inch (equivalent to about 20 feet on the 1:50,000 scale). Such a degree of accuracy should, in the future, show up gross errors in new fixes, and any substantial overlap of existing and proposed leases.

Subsequent tours in Jos were mainly administrative, ensuring that up to 16 field parties produced acceptable work and that the survey checking and drawing office staff kept up to a high standard. I could occasionally do some surveying *myself, but usually only to overcome problems or to check suspect surveys. One of the latter which I still remember was the Nigerian surveyor's attempt to pull the wool over our eyes by inserting a slope correction for 10° in a line which ran beside a level gradient railway line ! There was also one occasion when I was called as a witness in a case involving the moving of survey beacons into the area covered by an adjoining lease, with a subsequent allegation of the theft of someone else's tin. The beacons <u>had</u> been moved, but I have forgotten, or never knew, the outcome of the case. I do remember thinking whether I had fallen into any trap set up by a wily English Q.C., but I believe not; I had no doubt about my findings.*

Talking of mining reminds me of the Jos Minesfield story of the one-eyed English opencast mine owner who closely supervised his usually hardworking labourers. Whenever he left the site, he would take out his glass eye and place it on a post; reminding the labourers that though he was not there, he was still keeping watch. Little did he know that as soon as he was off the site, the eye was covered with a tattered hat ! Talking of labourers, I must say that I never had any problems, in all my time in Nigeria, with mine. They worked cheerfully and well for as long as I worked; often from before dawn until after dusk; and every headman was a character to be remembered - even if I cannot now remember their names !'

In 1956-57 work on the fireproof records room was completed and extensions to the main office buildings were also completed. Staff losses affected the Minesfield Survey Division in 1957-58 but, whenever they were available surveyors continued on the repair and extension of the triangulation. This effort was scaled down in 1959-60 but there were hopes of improvement in 1961. Between 1957 and 1960 a total of 1165 mining surveys were completed yielding revenue of £27,790.

In an RICS thesis entitled *The Rehabilitation of the Jos Minesfield*, written after his experience there in 1958, John Street described the processes of turning a rough and inaccurate Priority Sheet into a real tool for planning, mining operations and commerce. He described earlier revision operations, their limitations, and the special conditions under which they were attempted. His account dealt with the programme of fieldwork for triangulation improvement and extension for the production of more accurate base maps; the retying of existing leases to the framework, and the associated problems; a review of legal and administrative procedures; and training for office and field staff in techniques and recording. The thorough operation extended to office reorganisation to permit accuracy control during computation allowing two full-time computer men to overhaul a complete Priority Sheet in about eight months.

Mineral prices and quotas always had rapid effects upon mining activities and at times of high prices of tin and columbite there would be a rise in the demand for mining surveys. It was then necessary for Survey to react by moving in extra staff, sometimes at the expense of other branches and provinces. Between 1957 and 1960 there was something of a recession in tin mining. The Jos Plateau produced 5% of the world's tin (13,577 tons in 1959) and most of the world's columbite (1,145 tons).

The following is an edited extract from the personal memoirs of Kenneth Toms, who describes his work at Jos in 1957-58:-

'The term "Minesfield" took some getting used to. At first it conjured up images of large areas laid with land mines from some forgotten war. The term simply referred, however, to that part of the region favoured by the extensive mining industry. It included most of the workable country of the Plateau itself and some of the nearby lowlands.

The Plateau country was unique in Nigeria. At an average altitude of some 4,000 feet above sea level, it consisted of a mixture of high grassy plains drained by many rivers and smaller streams and more rugged mountain terrain (Photo.76). The many hills were grass-clad and easily climbed. It was a trigonometric surveyor's dreamland.

The climate, for ten degrees north of the Equator, was mild. For one half of the year the Harmattan (the great desert wind) would blow down from the Sahara. Then, as if regulated by clockwork, it would die away and the monsoon would come up from the Bight of Benin, bringing the rain to the Northern Region.

Tin, in the form of cassiterite, had been mined on and around the Plateau since well before World War II. Developments in space technology and high speed aircraft design and construction had led to a high demand in the fifties for the rarer minerals such as rutile and columbite. There were deposits of these associated with Plateau tin, and the miners were busy exploiting them as well as the traditional minerals. Some companies, including very small ones, were doing very well indeed.

The industry was regulated by the mining ordinances. These provided for companies to apply for mining land titles, the major forms being Exclusive Prospecting Licence (EPL) and Mining Lease (ML). Our operations were mainly concerned with the office examination of application documents that included a map or plan showing the pegged application area and the formal marking and survey of the boundaries of the area after approval.

Most of the survey work of my office was concerned with MLs. The surveys were carried out by African survey assistants under my supervision. Technical standards were reasonable, as theodolite and steel tape were utilised in regulated procedures. Boundary corners were marked with concrete beacons resembling mushrooms. If more useful objects such as wooden or concrete pegs were used, the native people, the Birom, would steal them. It was for this reason also that the tertiary triangulation control points were marked with the massive permanent concrete structures that stood like phallic symbols on many of the hilltops.

The most common mining technique involved hydraulics, as the minerals occurred mainly in the alluvial plains of the many streams that intersected the Plateau. Consequently, the typical mining lease took the form of a relatively narrow strip of land that encompassed a long stretch of river. All surveys had to be tested by mathematical "closure" in the office before the plan was plotted. This was to ensure the absence of gross error that could, and often did, occur through a miss-reading of the tape by a foot or even ten feet. Long, narrow parcel surrounds in which the sides were approximately parallel in many cases lent themselves to a "fiddle" by the survey assistant. Instead of returning to the field for a tedious re-measure, he would be tempted to "adjust" the error by "cooking" the close in his field book.

When running my random check surveys on the work of my African assistants, I found it useful to survey short connections across the lease at several points. A quick calculation in the field would reveal the presence of a gross error that may have been due to genuine compensating chaining mistakes, or to a fiddle by my man. After picking up one or two such anomalies and reading the riot act to the assistants, my checks revealed remarkably accurate work by all concerned.

On one occasion, Kaduna had requested us to traverse and co-ordinate some twenty miles of new road to enable them to plot it on the topographic map sheet. One of my men was a Mr Jas. Ononye, an older Ibo survey assistant from Onitsha. I instructed him to commence at a known trig point near the start of the stretch of new road, traverse the new formation with theodolite and steel tape and close the work on to another control point. Back in the office, Mr Ononye's traverse would just not close. The co-ordinate summation was in imbalance to the tune of hundreds of feet. I checked his field book and calculations thoroughly, but the misclosure remained. It was obviously due to some very gross systematic error in the linear measurement.

I questioned Mr Ononye on any recent damage to his tape. Yes, there had been an incident just prior to his start on the road traverse. On another survey, he had to run a connecting measurement line across the Jos-Kaduna railway. The inevitable had happened. The Jos Mail had run over the tape. But his chainman had repaired it with sleeves and solder. Had he checked the repaired tape on the standardisation base at the office? No, he had forgotten; in any case the chainman was very reliable.

We put the tape on the base, and there it was. It was three and a half feet short. The very reliable repairer had left out the severed section. After applying the equivalent correction to each measured distance, Mr Ononye obtained a very good close, and I breathed once again as the spectre of having to arrange for the re-measurement of that long length of bush road dispersed.

All in all, I found the work of Provincial Surveyor (North) to be interesting, if not onerous in the technical sense. Importantly, it gave me the feel for the management of human resources in a new and fascinating environment.

Paul Ward went on leave and on his return to the Colony, he was to be posted to Kaduna. I was appointed Acting Senior Surveyor, Minesfield Cadastral Office in his place. My new duties would be interesting, as they involved the co-ordination of existing and new cadastral surveys and the revision and reprinting of the Minesfield "Priority Sheets". I would have a competent staff of field survey assistants and draftsmen. Things looked good.

With the new assignment came the necessity to move into the senior surveyor's house. It was a relatively new dwelling set amongst enormous granite boulders behind the Plateau Club. Paul had supervised the building operations, and it was bigger and generally better than the Doll's House.

The old "Minesfield Priority Sheets" were black and white maps plotted at a scale of one mile to an inch. They depicted triangulation control points and the positions of the boundaries of all mining titles as determined by cadastral survey and located by simple triangulation or traverse connections to the control network. Under the Ordinances, all applications for mining title had to include a sketch map showing the pegged area and a connection to a control point or a previously surveyed title boundary. The information thereon was then plotted in the Jos drafting office on the relevant master Priority Sheet. If it showed no overlap on another title, the application would be approved for cadastral survey. If encroachment was indicated, further information would be required of the applicant.

The system was inefficient, as the actual position of existing mining parcels was not known to an appropriate degree of accuracy. My new job was to continue the establishment of a co-ordinated cadastre that had been commenced by John Street and Paul Ward. This entailed a systematic approach to the accurate co-ordination of new and existing title boundaries through fixation, usually by the technique of "resection" from co-ordinated control points, and the plotting of a new series of Priority Sheets at a scale of 1 to 50,000. The new sheets were to be based on the planimetric topographic maps series produced by the Directorate of Overseas Surveys in London. In my drafting office we produced the colour separation plates for the first of the new maps that would be printed in four colours.

The printing was to be done by the Federal Survey Department in Lagos. Travelling by road with my wife Susan, my son Stephen and my cook Hassan, I personally took those precious plates to the Superintendent of Mapping in the Federal Department of Lands and Survey, Brigadier Metford, R.E.(Retired). He was impressed with our work and organised a trial printing. It was very rewarding to see the maps come off the printing press in black, red, blue and grey tones. I felt that our people in the North would be pleased indeed. During those few days in the Federal Department, I learnt a lot about advanced cartographic and map reproduction processes. I saw scribing in progress. It would soon displace hand line drafting for fine cartography. I was introduced to the art of the printer and the operation of large presses. I owed much to the courtesy and interest of Federal Surveyor-General McVilley and his staff.

On the social side, Alan and Marion Lees entertained us at dinner and John Bull, a young surveyor and one of Malcolm Anderson's class mates from Newbury, took us to a night-club on the seamier side of the city. The entrance was via a gap in an old iron fence, the drinks were watered but the African band was good.

On our last day in that steamy city, we took Hassan to Victoria Beach on the ocean side of the island. He was thunderstruck by the vision of the limitless open sea and raised his arms to heaven, muttering "Allah, Allah." He then posed a good question, "How do ships know where to go?"

Before 1961 all tin ore had been sent to the UK but in 1961-62 two smelters were built near Jos, one by the Nigerian Embel Tin Smelting Company and the other the Makeri Smelting Company. Only the latter remained in permanent operation *(Photo.94)*.

In 1961 Plateau Province produced 8,685 tons or ore, Bauchi 1021, Zaria 418, Kano 241,

Benue 131, Niger 7, Ondo 6 and Kabba 3. Proved and indicated reserves amounted to 137,000 tons. It was estimated that the minerals were likely to be substantially exhausted by the end of the century. EPLs covered a total of 156 square miles and MLs covered 272,000 acres. The industry employed 255 expatriates and over 34,000 Nigerians.

Tin production was primarily in the hands of UK companies and about 45% of it was produced by Associated Tin Mines of Nigeria (ATMN) with its large scale mechanisation. It had introduced draglines during the second world war which quickly resulted in the creation of the huge red spoil heaps of overburden which were such a feature of the plateau landscape. In 1961 this large company, with its headquarters at Rayfield and its main yards at Bukuru, produced 4,649 tons, and the other principal producers were Gold and Base with 804 tons, Bisichi with 678, Ex-Lands with 550, the Kaduna Syndicate with 315 and Naraguta Extended Areas with 275.

The Minesfield Survey Division continued to be very busy throughout the first half of the 1960s and further improvements were made to the drawing, records, storage and administrative offices facilities, a new building was added for the Principal Surveyor in charge and facilities for the public inspection of Minesfield charts were improved *(Photos.104 and 105)*. Tin ore production stood at 12,855 tons in 1965, dropped a little in 1966 but rose again in 1967 after the disturbances.

Mining Concessions

The entire property in, and control of, all minerals in Nigeria was vested in the State and no person could prospect or mine on any lands (though there are a few Customary exceptions), or divert water for these purposes, without authority as provided for in the Minerals Act. Mining development was controlled throughout Nigeria by the Ministry of Mines and Power. The survey of mining concessions was necessary in order to define for cadastral and fiscal purposes the area of land over which a lessee had the right to prospect for or extract specified minerals or to collect, store and convey water for mining purposes.

A Mining Lease (ML) was granted for a maximum of 21 years, was renewable, and its size and shape was governed by the restriction that it must not be greater than was necessary for the mining of the minerals contained in it. An Exclusive Prospecting Licence (EPL) which was not often, in the 1960's and afterwards, the subject of field survey, was limited to covering an area of eight square miles. An accepted offer of exemption from survey postponed and exempted, was granted for a definite period, and might be revoked. The Title Deed Plan was made from the applicant's sketch plan or from existing survey data, whichever fitted the case more completely. Special Exclusive Prospecting Licences (SEPL) were seldom surveyed but were defined by natural boundaries or geographical co-ordinates. They were EPLs of unlimited size, occasionally granted in uncongested areas to companies able to prospect in a short period of time. Mining Rights (MR) were areas along streams or rivers of a total width (including the width of the stream) or not more than 100 feet. Within this area the holder had the right to extract specified minerals. They were only granted for a year but were renewable. Generally they were not surveyed and their total length along a stream had not to exceed one mile. MRs became increasingly rare as the well known and easily worked surface deposits were exhausted. A Water Right (WR) was a narrow strip of land or part of a stream along which the holder was allowed to collect, store or convey water for mining purposes.

Mines Reclamation Areas (MRAs) were worked-out areas which had been reclaimed for agricultural purposes and were permanently closed to mining. They were surveyed like Rights of Occupancy (Rs of O) and were given property beacon numbers. It has been said that mining operations in any part of the world seldom bring beauty in their train, and tin mining in Nigeria was no exception but, perhaps concerning surveying more, is the fact that they have a habit of both temporarily and permanently changing the face of the countryside, sometimes in a short space of time. The mining towns of Bukuru, Ropp and Barakin Ladi were largely ugly ill-assorted collections of utilitarian buildings and housing, and galvanised iron working sheds often standing close to derelict mine workings. The large operators on the Plateau were in their way landscape architects creating new leats, ponds, reservoirs, waste tips and excavations almost overnight. These often affected drainage, communications and farming patterns of extensive areas, thus giving rise to the constant need for map revision. The policy of Government called for the restoration of mined land to bring it back to a condition fit for agriculture or afforestation. Immediate re-establishment for agriculture was not very successful and a number of these Mines Reclamation Areas were restored by the Mines Reclamation Unit and planted out with eucalyptus saplings. Most of the minerals worked were found below the water table so excavations soon filled, especially during the wet season, to make ponds. In the right location such ponds could be useful for irrigation, as was demonstrated by a European company at Makeri, where fruit, (particularly strawberries), flowers, potatoes and other vegetables were grown commercially.

Concession Application Procedure

If suitable topographic mapping was not available from the Survey Department prospectors had no choice but to make use of whatever information was available. In later years the larger companies might have access to aerial photographs, but for a long time there was nothing better available to them than the old small scale maps derived from information supplied by administrative officers containing little more than the sparse information they needed for their own purposes.

An area intended for mining development was pegged out by a qualified and licensed applicant. Full details of the area on a specified form accompanied by a plan were sent to the Mines Department where the application was given a priority time stamp and then passed to the Survey Department for charting on the 'Priority Sheet' and for reporting in accordance with the provisions of the Minerals Act. The Lands Officer of the Provincial or Divisional Administration arranged an inspection and the Local Authority was consulted for details of land ownership and compensation if appropriate. The Forestry Department was asked for its comments and recommendations when proposed mining activities impinged upon established Forest Reserves.

Having considered all aspects of the proposed working and received favourable reports from all other Departments interested, the Mines Department passed a 'Notification to Survey' to the Survey Department. The Surveyor-General prepared an 'Instruction to Survey' for one of his own surveyors or for a Licensed Surveyor if the applicant had nominated one. A number of surveys were allowed to accumulate in any given area to be completed when a touring party *(Photo.100)* visited and it was then sometimes found that in areas of intense mining activity a number of leases could be surveyed in a single survey operation to avoid duplication of effort and excessive travelling.

If the survey was done by a Licensed Surveyor his charges were made direct to the applicant and his field records were passed to the Surveyor-General for scrutiny, Title Deed Plan preparation and retention in Records. It had in the past not been the practice for Government to make any charge against the Licensed Surveyor for this and the applicant paid separately for all aspects of Title Deed preparation actually carried out by Government.

After finalisation, Title Deed plans were sent with a report to the Mines Department, the accepted boundaries were inked on the Priority Sheet, replacing the original pencil charting, and the Register of Mining Titles completed. The Survey Department was kept informed at all times concerning the history of extant concessions in order that it could maintain its files, charts and registers completely up to date. The system was well established and with a few minor criticisms worked very well. (See *Appendix VIII* for a 'Guide to Procedures' for the survey of Mining Titles).

Priority Sheets

These were 'intelligence charts' of mining applications and leases based on the standard mapping sheets but containing only a grid, control points and water features. The latter were the only important topographical features because the great majority of mineral working were along the recent and buried channels of rivers and streams. Areas excluded to mining activities such as building zones, forest reserves, Rights of Occupancy and protected areas (*tsafis*) were charted. A busy Priority Sheet looked like a vast patchwork quilt of small rectilinear areas for prospecting and open-cast mining *(Map 37)*. Some leases were worked more than once as methods of ore capture improved.

The production and revision of the original 1:62,500 scale Priority Sheets, which bore a letter indexing system distinguishing them from the national topographic sheet system, continued until DOS 1:50,000 basic mapping became available. The planimetric base of the new 1:50,000 series then began systematically to replace the older sheets as a basis for Minesfield charting, and continued into the less congested areas away from the Plateau proper. As old Priority Sheets were replaced by new ones there appeared to be a reasonable case for the discontinuation of the old sheet referencing system, which was understood by few outside the mining and minesfield survey fraternity, with the new one based on the nationally recognised Standard Sheet system using National or Geographical Co-ordinates, but it was possible to see that it might be just as difficult to impose any new ideas on the established procedures of the mining world as a new system of metrication on the public generally.

In areas of congested mining activity Priority Sheets were constantly revised to show mining information such as surveyed M.Ls, approved EPLs, WLs, MRs, and Rs of O overprinted on a revised grey base of topographical detail, using a series of conventional colours. A master copy was kept in the Jos Survey office and maintained completely up-to-date daily, whilst an attempt was made to revise and publish annually an edition for public sale. Clearly, as much as if not more than any other map, the usefulness of a Priority Sheet, particularly with regard to administrative charting, depended upon constant maintenance of its accuracy with regard to cadastral, topographic and control information. There was a need for a well established and efficient process of revision by a procedure combining systematic field observations, checking by co-ordinate plotting and constant vigilance in office charting which would never fail to show up deficiencies and inaccuracies in previous field survey, in office charting and interpretation of topographic detail.

In less congested areas there was not perhaps a strong case for the publication of a separate Priority Sheet as such, provided an intelligence chart on an accurate 1:50,000 topographic base was maintained. With a very small demand from the public in the little used areas, especially some of those away from the Plateau, there was a deliberate policy of combining the normal cadastral country intelligence charts, which showed all applications for land use including Rs of O, Forest Reserves, Grazing Reserves, on a single chart together with the mining information. Printed overlays on to standard published topographic maps could from time to time be made, not so much for public sale, but more for use in the chart rooms of the Mines Department and the Survey office where they were in any case open to public inspection.

In some areas, principally around the township of Jos, there was an attempt to maintain a series of 1:25,000 scale Priority Sheets. In areas of heavy congestion caused by R of O grants this scale of charting proved invaluable and there was, in view of proposals to commence the mapping of certain parts of the country at this scale and the rising value of land for development purposes, a good case for the consideration of the 1:25,000 scale mapping of all the congested parts of the Minesfield both on and around the Plateau.

At times of staff shortage not enough attention was paid to the revision of topographic mapsheets (and hence Priority Sheet base material) in areas of mining activity. There was a suggestion that traditional methods of Priority Sheet revision should give way to regular and systematic revision by aerial survey and photogrammetric methods. The open country of the Jos Plateau lent itself admirably to the emplacement of permanent revision control markers and the detection of minor changes in ground detail, and regular photography would provide a ready reference medium for those concerned with mining statistics, excavation progress and quantities, leat construction, reclamation proposals and even the activities of illegal miners !

Survey Fieldwork

The 'Instruction to Survey' given to the surveyor contained a copy of the latest published Priority Sheet, a revised portion of the same sheet covering the working area, a copy of the applicant's sketch, details of adjoining mining areas and Rs of O and a completed form of specific survey instructions which made special mention of any known problems, missing beacons, triangulation ties required, etc.

The surveyor met the mining representative at a pre-arranged time and walked around the boundary of the area locating each temporary beacon or, if the applicant's representative did not appear, as was frequently the case, used all available information at his disposal to locate the temporary beacons. He then replaced these temporary beacons with 'mushroom' type survey corner beacons emplaced and numbered serially around the area. In the case of MLs the applicant's Location Beacon was replaced by a permanent Location Mark and CB1, CB2, CB3, etc., replaced his temporary corner beacons. Where for any reason, such as excavations, it proved impossible to emplace a CB in its correct position a Witness Beacon was located on each of the two boundary lines as close as possible to the corner.

If after inspecting the boundaries the surveyor noticed a small area of land had been left between it and a nearby extant lease, action was taken on the inclusion of the land in the new application, provided there were no objections.

The usual method of survey was by a closed tertiary cadastral traverse and ground taping. Initial bearings were based on a sun azimuth or taken from a tie to a triangulation point. In order to retain acceptable and achievable accuracy, and uniformity and economy of operation, this method was rigidly adhered to by generations of Survey Assistants, trained up to a certain level of ability. It was sometimes felt that the methods laid down did not give sufficient latitude for the more versatile surveyor. As long as alternative methods could be proved to be of equivalent or higher standard it was felt that there was a case for attempting to speed up the work by using separately, or in combination, processes of traverse, triangulation, tachymetry or electronic distance measurement. It had to be borne in mind however that in country where lines had to be cleared they gave the applicant and other interested parties a visible indication of the exact delimitation of the surveyed concession.

Between any two surveyed points a magnetic bearing was observed and the magnetic variation indicated on the final plan. For many small scale miners the only angle measuring device available was a compass, and more often than not it was a very old and inaccurate one !

Steel bands were regularly standardised on a baseline at the Jos office, especially after a period of intensive use in rough country and of necessity after any breakage.

All surveys were soundly connected to one or more triangulation or control traverse points if such points were within 3 miles of the survey, or of it was reasonably possible to connect them even when the range exceeded that distance. The versatility and experience of a surveyor was very frequently demonstrated by his ability to connect his work to control by reliable methods capable of independent check.

The area of each Mining Lease was computed in acres to four significant figures from the final co-ordinates of the corner beacons. The areas of Exclusive Prospecting Licences were generally given in square miles.

When a Mining Lease had to adjoin or touch the side of a previously surveyed lease it was necessary, if any of the corner beacons concerned were not intervisible, and after initial emplacement of traverse pegs, to resort to a simple method of corner shifting to ensure that the leases did not overlap and the corner beacons were co-linear. A certain amount of care was called for and fieldbooks had always to contain sufficient observed proof that correct emplacement has been carried out.

On long lines or in rugged country intermediate beacons known as Line Beacons were placed on line between Corner Beacons so that consecutive beacons were intervisible and not more than a quarter of a mile apart. This involved a great deal of extra traversing and line clearing in some places because after emplacement of the Line Beacons it was required that the boundary line of the lease be cleared and the LBs proved on line by observed and recorded checks. It was sometimes felt that this expensive operation was a waste of time, especially in the fringe areas of leases where mineral values were very low and where the ground would probably not be excavated. In such cases it may have been more economical to break down long ML sides, provided the applicant was in agreement, into shorter sides with more CBs emplaced initially so that successive beacons were intervisible and did in fact form the traverse stations. Care had to be taken to ensure that large differences did not occur between requested and surveyed areas.

A lease might surround areas which had for one reason or another to be excluded from it. Such exclusions, normally outlined by low order traverse, sometimes by compass, were other extant mining leases, Rs of O, WRs, areas prohibited to mining such as basalt zones and sacred ground. Until the enactment of Regulation 21 of 1950 the interior detail of mining leases was surveyed and included on the survey drawing, providing a piecemeal approach to the maintenance of the topographic record of the Minesfield. Thereafter it was only necessary to carry out this work at the specific request of the Director or the applicant.

The surveyor was required to draw a plan on good drawing paper, normally on a scale of 1:5,000, plotted from his co-ordinates, adhering to specified style, content, colours and conventions. This was a demanding and time consuming aspect of the work for some Survey Assistants and it became acceptable in later years for them to do no more than careful plotting and annotation in hard pencil which was then subject to inspection and correction prior to fair drawing by drawing office staff, on tracing cloth. This created more uniformity of Title Deed Plan style, saved surveyor-time and took advantage of the higher standard of drawing expected of full time draughtsmen.

A survey report was carefully prepared and, since it formed the basis for costing and reference during examination, had to include an outline of the survey method, connection to control and details of azimuth observations. It had also to include a statement of time spent on each stage of the work, travelling required, the nature of the country, beacons emplaced, and any comments relating to the survey of neighbouring areas, adjacent beacons or control.

As mentioned earlier EPLs were, from the 1960s onwards, seldom surveyed because their life was often limited to a year only and in fact conveyed no rights over the land other than prospecting. Applicants were given a Title Deed Plan constructed from their own inspected and checked plan based on Magnetic North or a plan constructed from Survey data. A nominal charge was made for exemption and plan preparation. Very occasionally however, in very congested areas, where applicant's plans were ambiguous and in areas of potential dispute, it was necessary to implement the provisions for survey. When this was done the boundary traverse was accepted provided the linear closing error was less than 1:1,000. The areas were quoted in square miles to three decimal places and a plan drawn at 1:25,000 scale. Priority Sheets at the same scale would simplify the process of plan preparation, application and charting.

A cadastral tertiary order traverse connected to triangulation control was run between 'upper' and 'lower' beacons marking the extent of a Mining Right along the watercourse. Offsets were taken to the stream in order to produce a 1:5,000 scale plan which was required to show both the traverse lines and the watercourse.

The survey of Water Rights was only undertaken after construction of the water channels and there was therefore a delay of some years between application and preparation of final plans. A low order (1:1,000) theodolite or compass traverse was run along the watercourse and short offsets were taken to provide a detail plan. Initial and closing bearings for the traverse were generally taken from the corner beacons of the mining leases which the WR served or through which it passed. Since the WR was accurately described in relation to streams, dams and mining beacons throughout its course, and because it was clearly visible after construction, beacons were not emplaced. Its starting and finishing points were tied to triangulation or to mining beacons. It was regarded as having an arbitrary width of ten feet for the purpose of determining its area when it had to be excluded from a lease.

Survey Staff

Most of the senior service field surveyors of the Northern Nigerian Survey worked at one time or another in the Minesfield Division. Douglas Eva was an Assistant Surveyor there in 1948-50. Donald MacPhee was the officer in charge in 1951. In 1953 the official Staff List, the last to cover the whole of Nigeria, Keith Sargeant was the Senior Surveyor in charge assisted by Surveyors J.A.G.Worlledge, D.R.Jones, E.G.J.Eisinga *(Photo.12)*, H.W.Rentema *(Photo.11)*, M.Nickel, T.A.Moszynski *(Photo.206)*, and N.K.V.Hansen *(Photo.16)*, and Assistant Map Production Officer O.Kanno. A.D.(Denis) Willey, a contemporary of Douglas Eva, was there in the field in 1949-50, as officer in charge of the examination section (OCX') from 1951 to 1953 and served as Principal Surveyor in charge of the Eastern Survey Area (when the North was divided into East and West for field survey administration purposes) between 1956 and 1958. Other expatriates who served there were K.O'Shaughnessy (1950), C.D.Burnside (1954), J.D.Adshead (1954), J.Street (1957-59), V.T.Brokenshire, I.Gilfoyle, J.P.W.Ward, J.Tozer, H.Peake (1958), P.Upperman *(Photo.14)* (1958-59), A.Voshaar *(Photos.13 and 97)* (1957), A.G.Wright, J.Jensen *(Photo.15)*, K.Toms (1958), F.Waudby-Smith, F.E.Larsen, M.G. de Vries, K.L.G.Terrel, J.W.Dickson and the writer M.F.Anderson

(Photo. 98) (1957-59) and, as the last officer in charge, and the person responsible for the division of the staff and Minesfield records when the new States came into being (1967-68).

After a period on secondary triangulation in the Jema'a area in 1957 the writer worked for a year as a 'Field Supervisor' controlling the work of up to eight Nigerian assistants on the Minesfield including S.E.S.Nwosu, E.E.J.Eyamba, A.O.Ita, Joe E.Umunna *(Photo.100)*, J.U.Adimoha, and Bello Usman. The work involved keeping them supplied with materials, minesfield and cadastral work instructions, money, supervising and checking surveys, checks, checking instruments, standardising tapes, and running a party involved with triangulation beacon construction and repair, and in addition producing at least as many surveys as any of his assistants. None of them had motor transport of their own. For long distances between their bases, usually in mining towns and villages, they were moved by Survey lorry, the writer's 'kit-car', or public transport (lorries) or walked with their parties of labourers *(Photo.99)* if distances were less than about 10-15 miles.

Licensed Surveyors.

For a long time, especially in the inter-war and post-war period, Minesfield surveying provided a lucrative, full time business for about a dozen Licensed Surveyors at a time. It would perhaps be more correct to refer to them as Private Surveyors rather than Licensed, since none of them held a licence as such. Most of them were Europeans who had personal links with the mining industry and who used personal contacts to obtain the work. During the 1950s their numbers dwindled to a mere handful and they ceased being involved in this sort of work by the end of the 1960s. It was a pity that Nigerian Licensed Surveyors did not see this as an opportunity, for there was never a shortage of work which they might have undertaken on behalf of Government. It would certainly have given them the opportunity to practise skills which were seldom called for in other parts of the Federation. The Survey Departments of the new States, limited as always by staffing shortages, would have welcomed, with certain reservations, the opportunity to pass this kind of work on, to release their own staff for work on control, mapping and other Government surveys. These reservations related to the problems of the maintenance of standards and procedures. There were on record a rather large number of examples of low standard and slapdash work which had been carried out by Licensed Surveyors. The writer has personal recollection of at least four different kinds of handwriting in a fieldbook presented as the work of one man, of a theodolite being used without a horizontal plate bubble, of compasses which needed an occasional good kick to make them work at all, and of that unforgettable old individual, Wilfred Miles, who at the age of about 80 was still trundling around the Plateau in his 1920s vintage kit car in which there was no floor on the passenger's side and where the battery had to be held in place by the passenger's feet. He used a steel band, a good bit over 300 feet long, constructed from the remnants of seven other bands he had salvaged over the years (largely from the sale of unserviceable Government stores). On account of its consequent complicated graduation he was the only person who could read it and when questioned about the requirement for periodic standardisation on the Jos base replied "What do you mean, standardisation ? I know the tape's length because I made it myself - besides, my traverses always close ....!"

Subdivision of the Minesfield Cadastre

The writer recalls:-

> *'On my return to the country in February 1967, I was posted to Jos to assume responsibility for the running of the Minesfield Division from the retiring Jimmy Dickson. This was a quieter and more agreeable posting than amidst the administrative and political manoeuvrings then taking place in Kaduna, though with depleted staff and a continuing heavy workload of Minesfield work it was a busy office to run.*
> *I was promoted to Assistant Surveyor-General a few months later and had, as well as operating the day to day work of the Minesfield, to almost single-handedly start arranging for the subdivision of the assets and records of the office for distribution amongst the States where mining activities were still carried out. The Plateau, of course, was to retain the bulk of these records, but a large number had to*

go to Bauchi for the North-Eastern State, some to Kaduna for the North-Central State, a small number to Kano, and Sokoto for the North-West, and a few to Ilorin for Kwara. In some case these records, and the plans and charts, had to be duplicated where they overlapped State borders. Staff, equipment and transport all had to be readied, and a large amount of administration and finance completed in time for the start of the new State administrations on 1st April 1968.

While I was engaged in all this work at Jos, preparing the ground for the incoming Surveyor-General of Benue-Plateau State, Mohammed Dauda Alayo, the first indigenous officer to assume control of the Jos Survey office, who had no experience of Minesfield or any other major office administration, I also had the responsibility for setting up my own new Survey Department in the North-Eastern State Dauda Alayo's appointment was destined to be quite short-lived, for he was drafted into the Army to take charge of military land requisitioning and was temporarily replaced at the request of the Military Governor, by Donald MacPhee, a former Government surveyor and Licensed Surveyor, who had long since left the service to run his own private tin mining company on the Plateau. He was joined by Denis Willey, the former Northern Surveyor-General, who had returned to Survey administration after a spell in the academic world of Ahmadu Bello University and the University of Glasgow".

Mining Surveys and Inter-State Boundaries Post-1968

The division of Nigeria into States with individual responsibilities for their separate systems of land administration, survey and revenue collection focused some attention on the question of MLs which overlapped State boundaries. This was quite a common occurrence along the border between the Benue-Plateau and North-Eastern States and gave rise to consideration of possible problems concerning rent division, revenue derived from tin working, survey fees, labour employment, mining regulations, title deed plan preparation and document registration, as well as giving attention to disputed parts of the boundary itself which might otherwise have remained dormant. Generally speaking the boundary was ill defined on the ground, inaccurately surveyed or not surveyed at all, and plotted with ambiguity on existing maps and plans. Furthermore there was no compatibility between the low order boundary surveys of the past and the accurately traversed and tied MLs. The need to show the boundary on a plan, especially one which was to be registered, created the need for accurate survey of the boundary itself and its attendant political implications. Any attempt to make a lease coincident with a boundary would imply definition of the State boundary at that point, work which could only be undertaken with the consent and approval of higher authority in both States' administrations.

The immediate solution was to allow extant concessions which straddled the boundary to continue until expiry, but upon renewal each case would be considered on it individual merits and in certain circumstances applicants might be asked to divide their leases. New applications straddling the boundary were not processed and applicants were asked to submit separate plans falling entirely within one State or the other.

From both administrative and practical points of view there were very strong arguments for retaining a unified system of mining surveys after the creation of the States. The Jos Minesfield Cadastre was a well organised, very experienced and efficient unit and it was regretted that politics had deemed it necessary to decentralise its records, processing and surveying, and to establish parallel units in other states. This was particularly noticeable on the eastern side of the Minesfield where most of the N.E. State surveys, administered from nearly 400 miles away in Maiduguri and out of the reach of the mining community, lay within an hour's easy drive from Jos.

ADMINISTRATIVE BOUNDARIES

When administrative boundaries are created it is adviseable to mark them on the ground with bold and permanent intervisible beacons, accurately described, and surveyed in such a way that they can be reliably retraced should the beacons be disturbed or the boundary disputed at any time in the future. Regrettably, at the time of establishment of the original internal Provincial and District boundaries by administrative officers in the north in 1908, financial and manpower resources did not afford the luxury of permanent markers and comprehensive survey.

International boundaries

International boundaries marking the limits of Anglo-French and Anglo-German interests did, however, receive much more serious attention, indeed one of the principal reasons for the establishment of the Southern Nigerian Survey in 1900 was to demarcate the Nigeria-Cameroons boundary, using military personnel. Triangulation for this task was carried out between Yola and the Cross river in 1909. In spite of this, a section of this boundary was still in dispute at the time of writing, in 2002. It was acknowledged in a treaty signed in 1931 that a part of the boundary running along a particular watershed was incorrectly shown on a German Moisel map made in 1908. An attempt was made to transfer the line to the latest available map (a compilation of topographic maps produced in the 1960s) but there were considerable differences between the old and new maps, made about 60 years apart, and Nigeria and Cameroon had not been able to agree on a common interpretation.

The Anglo-French boundary to the west of Nigeria was demarcated in 1900 and to the north, covering a narrow strip of terrain some 850 miles long stretching from the River Niger to Lake Chad, between 1906 and 1908. This was compass work, carried out by three officers and four NCOs and required points fixed by observed astronomical altitudes and chronometer longitudes. The work took 15 months in the field and was completed at what now seems an incredibly low cost of £12 16s per mile. This, and the work done on the Anglo-German boundary, produced some of the most accurate mapping carried out so far.

The Nigerian Survey Department carried out a survey of the Anglo-French Cameroons boundary starting in 1937, starting at Victoria.

In January 1959, the Director of Surveys was instructed by his Permanent Secretary to implement an agreement entered into between Nigeria and Dahomey, Nigeria's neighbour to the west. This was that, after Nigerian independence in 1960, some 200 miles of their common boundary would be adjusted, demarcated and surveyed. The stretch of boundary in question ran from Illo on the Niger, southwards to the upper reaches of the River Okpara and coincided largely with the western boundary of Borgu Division of the Northern Region. This was an important task for Federal Surveys in the delicate political climate of the day. The survey would involve reconnaissance and observation of secondary triangulation some 150 miles westwards from the primary chain running from south to north along the western side of the Niger valley. But the department was small, its remit large; geodetic and other control surveys as well as mapping over the whole country and the Cameroons, and the few relatively experienced surveyors were already committed. This job, therefore, was given to a young surveyor, now Dr.Colin Emmott, who had arrived in the country three months before, fresh from Newbury. The following extracts from his diary, which illustrate travel in Nigeria at the time, were prepared for the Biennial Conference of the Royal Institution of Chartered Surveyors at Nottingham University in September 1999:-

'Sunday, January 3rd

Eight o'clock on a perfect Lagos morning, not yet hot and the streets are empty and quiet. Why though do we go to bush on Sunday? Two Bedford 3-tonners are being loaded with camp gear, survey equipment – plane table and T3, and two survey gangs, thirty men in all under the direction of Headmen Musa and Isa. Things are sure to go well with Moses and Jesus each of which has over ten years army service behind him as well as a deep knowledge of the ways of the survey labourer.

Over Carter Bridge and across the causeway, the road leading to Ibadan and Ilorin is tarred and a pleasure to drive on, particularly on Sunday when the mammy wagons are few. The first stop is Fiditi. This roadside market is the place to stock up on fresh fruit, particularly ripe oranges that are dark green, and bright yellow bananas that can only be cut with a machete.

The road cuts through high rain forest until, at Ibadan, this is replaced by dense secondary growth after generations of slash and burn farming. Once beyond Oyo the farmland on both sides of the road becomes continuous until the border between the Western and Northern Regions when scrubland begins. Why I wonder.

We arrive at Ilorin in mid-afternoon. This is the Provincial Headquarters and an important southern staging post en route to Kaduna, Zaria, Kano and the rest of the 'Holy North'. The men go off to find lodgings in the town and I book into the Catering Resthouse (Photo.210). Ilorin CRH is well known in the North for its comfort and food. A group of chalets set under shady neem trees amidst beds of canna lilies and fifty yards from the club, it is ideal for the dusty traveller. Dinner then early to bed.

Monday, January 4th

Up early, breakfast (full English) then to the Beach for some last minute shopping in the canteens. The main item is beer. Experiments have shown that Becks is the most palatable of those available when drunk warm, and since Federal Surveyors do not have fridges, this is a most important consideration. Furthermore it comes in cartons of twenty-four and two of these cartons form a head load.

By mid morning the lorries are ready and we head northwest along a good but corrugated laterite road towards Kaiama, which is to be home and field headquarters for the rest of my tour. The road carries on to Bussa (the nemesis of Mungo Park on his way to the sea after discovering the source of the Niger) and then, crossing the Niger by ferry, to Kaduna, the Regional Capital.

Arriving in Kaiama, by mid-afternoon I have moved into the bush resthouse, unpacked and taken stock of the surroundings. The house itself is large and built of stone with a pan roof covered in thatch. This is slipping off at one end but still keeps the place cool. Meanwhile the survey gangs have gone off to the town. The impact on the local economy of these men, with salaries of 3s 3d a day as compared to the northern rate of 2s 4d, is likely to be great.

Tuesday, January 5th

The main object today will be to pay a courtesy call on the Emir of Kaiama. Until the relatively recent establishment of Bussa, 68 miles up the road, as the Divisional Headquarters, the Emir had been the most important leader in the Division. Borgu is the largest Division in the Region, and one of the most sparsely inhabited. Kaiama is situated at the crossing of a main trade route from Yorubaland in the south to the important centres to the north, and the old east-west route between the Niger and Dahomey. The Emir's palace is surrounded by red mud walls with an impressive entrance hall which is the focus for ceremonial occasions. We exchange greetings and presents, then it is time to view the town.

When he passed through it in 1826 on his way from the coast to Sokoto, Hugh Clapperton described the town as a straggling and ill-built city with a population of 30, 000 people. Now it is neat and well built with a population of no more than three thousand. The east-west trade is long gone but Kaiama is still important in the trade to the north and between Dahomey and Ilorin.

The road leading south west to Yashikera on the Dahomey border will be *important for the trig reconnaissance and even more so for the observations, which will involve moving light-keepers and heliomen around. This road, marked on the only map available, which is at 1 in 250 000 scale and of doubtful accuracy, had been improved and surveyed by Joyce Cary when he was ADO Borgu here in 1917. As well as road building, Cary had written his best Africa novel, Mister Johnson, based on his life in Kaiama.*

Wednesday, January 6th
        I decide to climb the rocky ridge just north of the town. This will be a start to the recce. The climb is easy but finding a viewpoint more difficult. When I do, I can only see about a mile because of the dense haze and realise now what was meant in Ilorin when I was asked how I would manage to survey in the Harmattan which was thick this year and would last until March.
        Crikey, what now? I had better send a telegram to Lagos........'

With the depletion of human and material Survey resources which followed the creation of Nigeria's new States in 1968, Federal Surveys retained responsibility for the survey, demarcation and mapping of international boundaries and had also to assume responsibility for inter-state boundaries, but not much had been done right up to 1994.

Internal boundaries

Taking cognisance of geographical and cultural realities, the novelty of Provincial boundaries was imposed on the north in 1908. A 'Resident' ' (usually a military officer) was posted to each Province and a District Officer was put in charge of Divisions of those Provinces. At this time, surveys for Provincial and territorial boundaries, such as the southern boundaries of Northern Nigeria where compass work was checked by observed latitudes and chronometer longitudes, were carried out by special commissions set up for the purpose.

Until regionalisation took place, the responsibility for surveying disputed and previously ill-described and measured internal boundaries lay with the central Survey Department. In 1935, for example, it worked on the preparation of a full description of the boundary between the Northern and the Southern Provinces. In 1937 surveyors based in the Northern Provinces carried out a compass traverse survey in Ninzam District to define the boundary of Jema'a Division and the Wamba District of the Southern Division.

After regionalisation, some internal boundaries in the North were redefined and clarified by the Northern Nigerian Survey, but only when serious disputes warranted investigation.

The most precisely surveyed administrative boundary of all was that which defined the boundary of Kaduna Capital Territory, carried out by theodolite traversing between control and co-ordinated property beacons with distances measured to a tenth of a foot and bearings to the nearest minute of arc. The aim was to provide unambiguous definition of the area subject to the Kaduna Capital Law, and planning and other regulations affecting customary and statutory land holdings. Clifford Rayner describes a court case involving this boundary :-

        'From time to time Cadastral personnel were required to act as expert witnesses in matters relating to land disputes. An experience, in the early 60's, was both educational and amusing. The case involved an interpretation of the existing land law concerning a land holding in the vicinity of the Kaduna Capital Territory. The land holder had Native Authority title to a plot that had been developed as a petrol station. His title had been questioned because it was thought that the plot in question was outside the gazetted area of the Territory and therefore unlawful. The holder disputed this and had been advised to take the matter to court.

And so this particular dispute went to court. From the information available I was asked:-

'Was the plot within or without the Kaduna Capital Territory ?'
I replied that it was outside the designated area.
'Can you describe the designated area ?'
'It is that area delineated by a red verge line on the plan numbered KAD 629 which is deposited in the office of the Survey Division of the Ministry of Land and Survey at Kaduna'
' Can you be more specific?'
'Starting at beacon marked PBZ 2206 the co-ordinates of which are 36450.55 feet North and 11155.33 feet East of beacon marked KDCS P. 61 origin of Kaduna Cadastral Surveys the boundary runs for a distance of 660.1 feet on a bearing of 199° 19' to Beacon PBZ 2207 thence of 660.0 feet on a bearing of 199° 18' to Beacon PBZ 2208 thence................... there are another hundred or so markers, do you wish me to continue ?'

At this point there was confusion in the mind of the questioning lawyer over the subtle variations in tenure under the law as displayed by my replies.

'You are being very elusive'
To which I responded, 'it is not my fault that I am more familiar with the law of the land than you appear to be!'
'I call the Minister of Lands and Survey to witness'
Of course there was no response, upon which I was asked ,
'Where is the Minister?'
'I don't know'
'Do you mean to say that you do not know where your head of Ministry is ?'
'I do know where he is not'
'Yes ?'
'He is not in this room!'

By this time I think the judge had had enough of the farce and suggested that the case be adjourned. A date was suggested which was not convenient for one of the lawyers, an alternative was suggested, again not convenient for another of the lawyers, a third date was suggested, not convenient for me - I was due to play rugby! The clerk to the court was requested to organise another time but I assume that reason prevailed and the case was dropped. I heard nothing more.

A sad farce it was, for the poor plot owner should never have been persuaded to have brought the dispute to court, he had no case at all."

Attempts to resolve internal boundary disputes

Disagreements were always likely to arise in areas where insufficient evidence had been gathered at the time of the original boundary declaration, where surveying and beaconing work had been hastily or inadequately done by the administrative officers responsible, and where straight lines of convenience had been drawn through what was then empty, unused (but not necessarily unclaimed) territory. Populations moving back later into such previously abandoned areas had no concept or knowledge of the invisible dividing lines now passing through their lands. To avoid prolonged and otherwise non-existent disagreements there was obvious merit in leaving some boundary descriptions deliberately vague, and not attempting to mark them too obviously on the ground, nor to define them by accurate surveys; but disputes about responsibilities for the payment of local taxes and the ownership of trees or farmland were bound to arise in the course of time between adjacent Native Authority areas, or when compensation was to be paid when the land was acquired for development purposes. The attention of the surveyor was then required.

"Surveying on behalf of the King"

> *"The professors of this science are honoured with a more earnest attention than falls to the lot of any other philosophers. Arithmetic, theoretical geometry, astronomy and music are discoursed upon to listless audiences, sometimes to empty benches. But the land Surveyor is like a judge, the deserted fields become his forum crowded with eager spectators. You would fancy him a madman when you see him walking the most devious paths. But in truth, he is seeking for the traces of lost facts in rough woods and thickets. He walks not as other men walk. His path is the book from which he reads. He shows what he is saying; he proves what he has learned; by his steps he divides the right of hostile claimants; and like a mighty river, he takes away the fields of one side to bestow them on the other. Wherefor, acting on our instructions, choose such a land surveyor, whose authority may be sufficient to settle this dispute, that the litigants may henceforth cultivate their lands in peace".*

Cassiodonis (died AD 595)

Definitions of International, Northern Region and Native Authority boundaries and detailed descriptions of the gazetted inter-Provincial boundaries were printed in the Handbook of the Ministry of Town and Country Planning in the Northern Region in 1966. Most of them were those declared by the original administrators, sometimes referring to impermanent features such as blazed trees, footpaths and streams with distances perhaps to the nearest mile on coarse compass directions. The following is an example of such a description covering part of the southern boundary of Bauchi Province:-

> *"From a baobab tree 3 miles from Kombo on the Kombo-Bangu road, the boundary runs for 6 miles in a southerly direction to a point 4 miles north-east of Bangu; thence 3 miles in a south-easterly direction to a point 1½ miles south-west of Tiu; thence 7 miles in a south-south-westerly direction to a point 3½ miles west of Falwe; thence 4½ miles in a south-easterly direction to a point 7 miles west of Gunda; thence 4 miles in a south-westerly direction to a point ½ mile from Gumshi leaving Gumshi to the east; thence 7 miles in a south-south-westerly direction to a point 5 miles south-east of Nyuar, thence 10 miles in a south-westerly direction to a point 5 miles east of Mannari; thence 7 miles in a westerly direction to a point 2 miles south-west of Mannari; thence 4½ miles in a south-westerly direction to a point 2 miles south-west of Boleri; thence 15½ miles in a westerly direction to a point 1 mile south-west of Borok; thence 2 miles in a north-westerly direction to a point 1 mile due south of Kashi; thence 4½ miles in a south-westerly direction to a point 1½ miles south-south-east of Dilla................."*

Attempts to resolve major disputes might involve a gathering together of village chiefs, district heads and administrative officers and the presence of a surveyor with his instruments. What then took place was a major event in local history, witnessed sometimes by hundreds of local people and committed to memory for the rest of their lives and then perhaps passed on verbally to their children.

Having performed the necessary introductions and urged diligence and honesty upon the litigants the administrative officers would generally beat a diplomatic retreat. The surveyor would remain to listen to the conflicting stories and claims from each side (often very exaggerated and untruthful but firmly believed for all that); with strict impartiality suggest a solution or a compromise; or, if there was no agreement, simply go ahead and attempt to re-establish the boundary from the vague previously gazetted description. His task was to produce a much less ambiguous description using taped measurements, and a theodolite to determine bearings.

Permanent markers or cairns had seldom been used for the original demarcation and it was only when surveyors became involved that properly numbered and referenced ground markers with precise bearings and distances were used on sections of inter-Provincial boundaries. For example, work done by Ian Gilfoyle in 1956, and the writer in 1957, resulted in detailed amendments to the Plateau-Benue boundary. The following is an example of a surveyed section of that boundary:-

"............thence downstream along the Rafin Feferuwa in a general north-easterly direction for a distance of approximately 27,547 feet to Beacon PLA-BEN No. 14, situated on the left bank of the Rafin Feferuwa; thence on a bearing of 24 degrees 30 minutes for a distance of 6,253 feet to Beacon PLA-BEN No. 15, situated approximately 2,100 feet north-west of Gidan Kake and beside the footpath from that village to Arugwadu, thence on a bearing of 24 degrees 30 minutes for a distance of 5,627 feet to Beacon PLA-BEN No. 16 situated beside the marsh at the headwaters of the Rafin Ige, thence on a bearing of 24 degrees 30 minutes for a distance of 5,617 feet to beacon PLA-BEN No. 17 situated on the left bank of the Rafin Limbele; thence on a bearing of 25 degrees 30 minutes for a distance of 5,483 feet to Beacon PLA-BEN No. 18 situated approximately 3 miles east of Arugwadu village; thence on a bearing of 355 degrees for a distance of 6,990 feet to Beacon PLA-BEN No. 19; thence on a bearing of 355 degrees for a distance of 7,911 feet to Beacon PLA-BEN No. 20 situated approximately 7,920 feet east-south-east of Arikia Bissa Hill; ...."

Such end results look neat and orderly but they disguise a host of residual disagreements and in no way reflect the unpleasantness and the toil which went into achieving what was sometimes a very unrewarding exercise.

Present by the roadside at the start the survey done by the writer were R.C.Loadsman, the D.O. Wamba, accompanying the Chief of Nassarawa Eggon from the Plateau side, and Vic Ashwell the D.O. Lafia, with the Emir of Lafia from Benue, and N.A. policemen from both sides. The attendance of the dignitaries was a necessary formality and they soon departed leaving behind a great entourage of village heads, hangers-on and bystanders, some bearing arms, all of whom had vociferous and strongly held views on a dispute deepened by being a disagreement between a Moslem and a 'pagan' area *(Photo.106).*

'Having spent the entire wet season under canvas on triangulation work, it was very unpleasant and exhausting still to be in bush as the hot, dry season began. There was always a great deal of uncertainty when trying to retrace a boundary which had never been properly surveyed or adequately described. Everybody was irritable and argumentative and the chances of arriving at an amicable solution to the dispute were remote when there were so many widely held opinions and myths about when and where the original line had been drawn, many years before some of the litigants were born.

My survey gang spent exhausting days cutting lines through the tall grass and light woodland along the boundary traces and there was fighting in the villages at night.

The exercise created more problems than it solved and resulted in a lot of confusion in the minds of local people, especially when 'trial' traces, which appeared as good clear lines through the bush were abandoned in favour of some other boundary line which placed villages on the 'wrong' side of the line. Occasionally, however, this line clearing did the local people a favour when one of the tortuously winding paths which meandered through the bush from one village to another was intercepted, providing them with a much more direct route from A to B. Traces several feet wide might be cleared of vegetation and obstructions to obtain sight lines, and these would become the preferred new route.

The 'pagan' Eggon chiefs of one side were anxious to gain my favour and supplied my party with generous gifts of food, potent village beer, and the services of some of their surplus womenfolk, hence the fighting ! The effect of the alcohol, which resulted in many of them dancing to mouth music in the village square, was an amusing evening diversion.

Some of my walking on that job was alleviated by the use of my messenger's bicycle, but to add to my discomfort it broke clean in half while I was riding it. Then the Harmattan dust arrived. Sources of water in the drying stream beds were turning stagnant and green.........

Boundary surveying was not my preferred work'.

Similar work was done on other boundaries, notably between Sokoto and Katsina and Niger Provinces and, in 1957, Trevor Brokenshire and Clifford Rayner attended to a dispute between Sokoto and Ilorin Provinces *(Photo. 107)*. Clifford Rayner, who was on his first tour in Nigeria remembers :-

'Christmas 1956 was an opportunity to take stock, and as Alan Wilkie was the only member of the Bristol quartet who was living in a house, he invited us all to Katsina for the holiday. And a good break it was too. But all good things come to an end and I had instructions to return to Kaduna to join Trevor Brokenshire for a 13 mile boundary re-establishment survey between Ilorin and Sokoto Provinces. By now we were in the middle of the dry season with the occasional period of Harmattan making everything as dry as the proverbial bone. Once ready, we took off for Yelwa on the east bank of the Niger and 250 odd miles from Kaduna, and apart from the first 10 miles or so all on a dirt road. Could this be the reason why I have never really enjoyed driving? A short stay of two days in Yelwa to meet up with the admin: representatives and then by boat down the river Niger to Rofia and then onto Mogo by car to the vicinity of the disputed boundary.'

Trevor Brokenshire recalls :-

'............... getting to it involved using dug-out canoes on the River Niger, and horse-back riding into and around the area.

I remember that we took a good supply of Star beer; and managed to persuade the District Officer that this was an essential element of bush life; he left us to get on with our job for some days; but when he returned he replenished our beer store !'

Cliff Rayner continues:-

'The ends of the stretch of boundary in dispute, some 10 miles apart, were identified by a cunning reference to a 3D air photo model of the location. This after a futile attempt to locate their positions by reference to the relevant Gazette description. I recall that 'blazoned trees' figured largely in the description and the fact that numerous slashed trees were identified did not really put a truly scientific perspective on the matter in hand. So, in the spirit of the task, a solution provided by reasonably up to date (war time moonlight [?]) RAF photos did not seem too unreasonable!

However all agreed upon our interpretation of the Gazette entry and all that remained to be done was to establish a straight line between the two ends and cut a swathe of about 20 feet wide through the bush so that all and sundry could be aware of the boundary, where before there had been some confusion. The cause of the problem had been a village, in the vicinity of the boundary, which whilst paying taxes to Sokoto Province was convinced that it should be paying taxes to Ilorin Province, or vice versa.

To determine the relative positions of the ends of the disputed boundary, marked by two well built stone beacons 6 feet by 2 feet by 2 feet, a third order traverse was surveyed via the most convenient route between the two. Orientation was controlled by sun azimuths and a 45° check ensured that the traverse computations were without calculation error. The bearing and distance, of the initial boundary marker from the terminal beacon, were duly calculated and off we went! But not before Trevor observed latitude and longitude by position line astro-fix. This latter event is memorable only in that on the same day the news on the wireless, used for time check, informed the world that Princess Grace of Monaco, formally Grace Kelly of Hollywood, had given birth to Caroline, her and Prince Rainier's first offspring.

With the excitement over, we steadily, and with hired local labour, cut the boundary line on the determined bearing, praying to any god of surveying that might be listening that no gross error had been made and that we would meet our initial boundary marker. Traversing through elephant grass ten or so feet high was nigh on impossible. One match and a lunch hour break was the solution! The ensuing bush fire (Photo.s 108 and 200) was very effective and after a while we had perfect ground level visibility. The downside was that the area was now thick with charcoal. The pyrotechnic display had been impressive as was the drama of survival between predator and preyed upon as the fire drove the bush wildlife from, what had been minutes previously, an ordered state of existence.

From a letter to home: -

'1 Feb.: .... After leaving Mogo we stayed at a place called Shafashi about 9 miles away. This we walked and all the loads were carried by' head' - the labourers'. I set off about 8.30 and arrived at 11. 00. We had one tent up and also a straw house built. I stayed in the straw place and Trevor had the tent. The weather had changed by then and it was very hot during the day and fairly warm at night. In fact while the hot weather was with us we'd get up at 5.30 and start work about 6.15 before the sun had risen. It was quite pleasant until about 11.00 and it was very hot (103°). We stayed in Shafashi for 4 nights then moved on again walking to Tungan Bube where we both had tents..'

We also stayed at:-

'...... Tungun Abashi, a small place and really the whole object of our efforts as nobody was quite sure in whose province it was and so there was a difference of opinion of who should receive its taxes. Nearby we relied on there being decent water to hand so took our kettles and teapots in readiness for the lunch break. Well the water was very thick but after a thorough boiling we made tea (a not too pleasant light grey colour) drunk it and enjoyed it. I suppose we drank about one and a half pints each, not without its after effects though. Trevor it seems was unturned by the revolting brew but I had a bit of a stomach after and it will be a long time before I drink any more unfiltered dirty water. The bath water at camp was even worse - very muddy but with bottles of Dettol poured into same it was hygienically clean at least. '

Eventually the end of the line was reached and thankfully homing in on our original beacon, what error there was, was within acceptable limits and well within the extent of the trace that had been cut through the bush. What was disturbing or another example of the universal nature of Murphy's law was that within three-quarters of a mile of the end of the trace we passed through the middle of a formerly unknown village and nowhere near the village which lay at the centre of the dispute! But we, the surveyors, had completed our mission and were enthused to depart as quickly as possible. Trevor had a wife to go back to and I had another bush assignment awaiting, the observation of the primary 'C' chain of triangulation in Adamawa.'

TRAINING

The Importance of Training

It was satisfying for senior officers to achieve a high level of efficient production and there were considerable pressures for them to do so during the period of rapid development and political change, but there was also a need to impart their experience and knowledge to those who would soon be replacing them. Somehow it was necessary to combine the two responsibilities, because there could be little justification for the employment of anyone who did not regard the training of local staff as of prime importance.

A perpetual shortage of suitable Nigerian staff meant that a very great deal of surveying, especially in the early years, was carried out by expatriates only. Demands meant that, after basic training, new Nigerian recruits coming through went immediately into productive survey work, but supervised whenever possible by senior and experienced officers who were encouraged to provide 'in-service' training, equally in field and office.

Northern Reticence

The ever-present problem, especially in the North, and one which for that matter applied equally to expatriates at home, was of trying to convince potential recruits of the good career prospects in the profession of the land, and of making what appeared to be an arduous, challenging, outdoor occupation attractive and worthwhile. The aim was to build a department of well trained and enthusiastic Nigerian surveyors, stronger and more effective on the ground than any foreigner could be, and armed with sufficient technology to permit favourable comparison with their counterparts all over the world. It was impossible to achieve this by disregarding local attitudes and blindly substituting imported ideals. Over the years considerable effort was put into vocational training, but there was always a shortage of capable students for this unappealing and 'obscure' profession. The reticence of the North towards technical education was in part due to the feeling that the moral component of their traditional learning was not included, or was being substituted by an alien alternative. Many young people, who may well have made good surveyors, were thus denied knowledge of the profession. It was difficult to influence them. Surveyors were seen to be doing things for reasons which concerned them alone. Although Northerners might sometimes be persuaded that the profession could provide a satisfying and lucrative career there was always a risk of slipping into traditional ways and values. European concepts of order were sometimes little understood, especially when, as in land surveying, they were of a regimented, meticulous and rigidly systematic nature. It was a matter of concern that the radical changes being introduced as necessary to progress and development were in fact proving too much to absorb in so few generations, hence the apparent lack of interest in surveying and mapping and the refuge sought in (as it sometimes appeared) humanities and religion.

Training Abroad

During the days of the Northern Nigerian Survey the recognised educational and training route for expatriate staff was via a relevant university degree course which, preferably, included a land surveying or related specialism, followed by an intensive period of more advanced and practical land surveying training at an R.E. establishment up to the level of the Intermediate examination of the RICS. Those recruited from continental Europe and elsewhere were required to have commensurate qualifications and experience.

Before the war, before the RICS requirement had been introduced, broad-based intensive post-graduate theoretical and drawing training for at least six months was provided by the Ordnance

Survey at Southampton and at a Royal Engineers' facility at Bembridge Fort on the Isle of Wight or elsewhere. With the resumption of survey training for civilians after the war, courses were provided at the RE establishment at Warminster and later at the School of Military Survey at Hermitage near Newbury.

From the late 1940's into the 1960's, one of the main sources of surveyors for overseas survey service was Bristol University, where land surveying became one of the options of the final year of the Geography Honours Degree Course. This course provided a sound introduction to the Officer's Long Survey Course at the School of Military Survey. Denis Willey and Doug Eva were amongst a group of post-war ex-military personnel to attend this course at Bristol before going on to Nigeria. Kevin O'Shaughnessy and Frank Waudby-Smith came later, Alan Wilkie, Cliff Rayner, John Tozer and Ian Gilfoyle graduated there in 1955, Malcolm Anderson, Alan Wright and John Bull (Federal Surveys) in 1956 *(Photo.110)* and Michael Cooper (Federal) a year later.

The RICS Intermediate level examinations, with the backing of a degree, became the accepted standard for appointment as a surveyor, but it could take a Nigerian without a university degree up to six years to become a senior service surveyor, including two years abroad to obtain RICS Finals. Two of the most promising Survey Assistants were sent for advanced training to the School of Military Survey in England in 1954-55, where they took the training course normally taken by new entrants to the Colonial Survey Service who have just left university. It was feared the course might be too advanced but, since the training there was as good as if not better than anywhere else in the world and was more practical than going elsewhere, it was thought the advantages outweighed the disadvantages. A year later they returned with good results. Two more were sent in 1956.

Having completed lower and intermediate level training in Nigeria, progressive cartographers were given the opportunity to enjoy excellent training to the highest standards available anywhere in the world at the Directorate of Colonial/Overseas Surveys at Tolworth, and at the Ordnance Survey at Southampton. Until lithographic training later became available in Lagos and Kaduna, it was also provided at the Ordnance Survey. Other overseas technical training for Nigerians was available through full time courses at South-West Essex Technical College (which in 1958-59 was dropped in favour of the Nigerian College of Technology at Enugu) and the Delft International Training Centre for Air Survey in Holland.

The Development of Training in Nigeria

From its inception in 1900, the Southern Nigerian Survey had a declared object of training young Nigerians to become professional surveyors, in addition to those trained for technical and lesser tasks. Surveying education began in 1906 and a survey school was set up in Lagos in 1908. Those who attended the course were amongst the first trained professionals to emerge in the new country. Not only was it perhaps the earliest technical profession to emerge in Nigeria but, in the south of the country, it was a much respected one too. Lugard pressed for such opportunities to be extended to his people in the Northern Provinces. When he reorganised the Southern Nigerian Survey in 1910 Major F G Guggisberg was in strong support of its training role.

The Lagos school moved to Ibadan in 1927 and was housed in old buildings vacated by the West African Frontier Force, and in 1928 was being run by G. J. Humphries (who served with the Directorate of Colonial Surveys following the Second World War) and D. L. C. Anderson. The school closed in 1933 because of the economic situation but was re-opened in 1935 at Oyo and joint training of surveyors was arranged with the Yaba Higher College, which had been established three years earlier; a liaison which, because surveying was introduced late in the programme when the students had begun to see other career options, was not entirely successful. In 1937 the school moved temporarily to Bida to assist with the mapping of the Bida standard mapsheet at 1:125,000 scale, and returned to Oyo in 1938.

The school continued to operate for at least part of the war and during 1944-45 was run by K M Sargeant *(Photo.109)*. N S Clouston, the Director of Surveys, sought the secondment of survey instructors from the Directorate of Colonial Surveys when it was established after the war, but in this he does not appear to have been successful.

The training in the sciences at Yaba was transferred to the new University College at Ibadan in 1948 and the Survey School moved there from Oyo. The intention was to handle the full training of surveyors at the university, but some students saw the opportunity to free themselves from the ties of in-service training by severing their attachment to the Survey Department. Others agitated for better conditions of employment, and with declining support from the Department, the course decayed and no degrees in surveying were awarded at Ibadan.

Keith Sargeant recalls the post-war situation:-

'Before regionalisation there was only one Survey Department school for the training of African surveyors. This was at Oyo in the western provinces, near Ibadan. The students came from Yaba Higher College in Lagos and had a good grounding in mathematics (sometimes correcting their Instructor!). The two-year course covered virtually all branches of survey, and the students - all from the southern provinces - became the elite of the department's African staff. Some, however did very well, Oluwole Coker, for instance, who was the first Nigerian graduate surveyor in 1952 eventually became the first Nigerian Director of Federal Surveys in Lagos. Nevertheless Survey was not a popular career with the educated Africans; too much bush-work and the majority preferred a more sedentary (and more lucrative) life as a lawyer.'

The following is a quotation from the post-war experiences of John Pugh :-

'The Department had for years run a Survey School, training Nigerians for junior surveying grades, usually about four students at a time for a two-year course. The surveyor in charge, who had run it for years, retired early in 1946 and I had taken over for that year. In 1947 the British Government decided to set up universities in West Africa. Ibadan was the first. The Principal-designate, Kenneth Mellanby, arrived to explore the situation and to see where the students would come from. At that time Yaba Higher College was the only school in Nigeria that took students to "A" level, and Mellanby realised that he would have to recruit students with "O" level only. The Deputy Director of Surveys, Joe Morley, who was the best brain in the Department, realised that Nigeria would become independent in the not-too-distant future, and that we should be training Nigerians for the Senior Service grades. He persuaded Mellanby to take into the Survey School, as part of the University College, students to do one year of survey training, followed by two years working for a degree, with a fourth year of advanced professional training. 27 students were recruited to start in 1948, and I was ordered to move everything from Oyo to Ibadan and to run the first year of the course. The College was housed in the huts of an abandoned Army camp pending new buildings on a permanent site. College students initially were all working for B.A. or B.Sc. General External degrees of London University, taking three subjects, and it was found that some of them had chosen Geography as one subject, although the College had no Geography staff. It was discovered that I was a Cambridge Geography graduate, and I was asked to take over the College course. As I was not paid by the College but by the Survey Department, this was a private arrangement : in return for my lectures in Geography, the Maths Department taught my students spherical trigonometry and other useful mathematical techniques. All went well. For two months in the Long Vacation I had the students working in pairs, each with a labour gang, running traverses for ground control for air surveys, spread between Jebba, Mokwa, Bida, Kontagora and westward. My erstwhile colleague from Jos was sent to take overall control. He sat in the Rest House at Kontagora, making model railway engines, and even refused to supervise the party working on the road outside. I had to drive up from Mokwa to cope. He subsequently sent Lagos a damning report on my performance.

In August or September we had a new Director, Mitchell, ex-Palestine, and in October he came up to inspect the Survey School. He told me he would be shutting it down at the end of the year, as he certainly did not wish to recruit graduates. "The trouble with you graduates, Pugh, is that you get ideas. I do not want men with ideas.

The best man I had in Palestine started as a labourer - never had an idea in his life. Did exactly what he was told, nothing more, nothing less. That is the sort of man I want ". I began to get the message. He then said that he wished me to spend 1949 in 'Iboland', running a training school for chainmen and senior labourers - put as a request, but clearly a command ! I had to agree. However, the Government had introduced a rule after the war: normal tours of duty would still be 18 months, but anyone would have to obtain a clear medical certificate before going on over two years. As I would reach two years in the December I asked the local Medical Officer for the appropriate clearance certificate. He examined me for five minutes, diagnosed a tired heart, and told me to go on leave as soon as possible. I reported this to Mitchell, and received a rocket - my original agreement to do a third year had been, he alleged, a deliberate lie, and I had bribed the M.O. to help me. He also wrote to the M.O. ticking him off for being bribed, and the M.O. sent the letter to the Director of Medical Services, who carried more weight than Mitchell., who was given an ear-full. I heard this from Morley and realised I had no future, so arranged to go on leave to South Africa, in January 1949, thinking that the chance of obtaining a surveying position there was better than in the U.K. Half an hour before I left Ibadan, Mellanby offered me a Lectureship in the College, which I accepted on the spot (subsequently finishing as Professor and Head of Department at King's College London). Mitchell had a staff of 22 senior grade officers, 16 of them graduates, most of whom he got rid of in one way or another - I was the first to go. In due course Morley protested to the Chief Secretary that the Department was being wrecked, and was told to get on a ship leaving three days later.'

1949-51 saw the beginning of training in the use of photogrammetric plotting instruments in Survey headquarters in Lagos, with three Nigerians experimenting with productive mapping work on recently acquired Multiplex equipment.

In 1952, a survey school was re-established at Oyo, offering one year basic training for school-leavers with a West African School Certificate. Emphasis was on practical training but with a considerable amount of background theory. Candidates were taken from Lagos and the Western and Eastern Regions. The course, aimed at producing Survey Assistants, was not, however, very successful because of the large number of dropouts and those deciding to seek alternative careers. Some went on to join licensed surveyors' practices or even took advantage of lax controls to carry out surveys themselves and came to an "arrangement" with a licensed surveyor to certify their plans and their work to obtain payment

This school was first run by David Okagbue, who later became Surveyor-General of the Eastern Region, briefly by Oluwole Coker in an 'acting' capacity, and subsequently by Brian Till, Les Howells and then a succession of Nigerian surveyors to the present day. Coker initiated an Advanced Course with a syllabus written by him closely following the requirements of the Nigerian Survey Licence. Major practical projects were run from a surveying camp organised annually at Iseyin some 30 miles west of Oyo.

New buildings designed by Patrick Gordon, architect in the Western Nigeria P.W.D. and financed by the Western Nigeria Government, were erected in 1956 and still form the core of the campus which later became the Federal School of Surveying, Oyo. The school, now having strong links with the Regional Training Centre in Photogrammetry at Ife, is one of the principal centres for training in land surveying in Nigeria.

When the Federal Survey Department was set up in 1954, it started another survey school at Okene offering a basic nine month advanced course. This school was destroyed in a violent storm and was moved to Oyo under the control of the Western Region government and an advanced course inaugurated in addition to the existing basic course. The school remained under the control of the Western Region until 1968, and the Western State until 1976, but when the latter was divided into three new States the school reverted to the Federal Survey Department.

In 1956, a 4 year course in land surveying up to Intermediate RICS standard was started at the Enugu branch of the Nigerian College of Arts, Science and Technology, and the only Northern Survey

Assistant possessing a suitable basic education was granted a scholarship to the College.

Federal Surveys were still reporting a high resignation rate and a great wastage of effort in training in 1958. The net gains in staffing were insufficient to sustain the demands being made for map production.

Before Independence the policy of 'Nigerianisation' began to further underline the problems of Survey staffing. European surveyors started to withdraw, creating vacancies, but no university in Nigeria was producing surveyors. Training was still a long process and was much shorter for other professions, which offered a softer post-qualification career, better remuneration and advancement prospects, and without the need to spend long periods outdoors in inhospitable places. Some of those who did persevere were attracted by offers from the commercial sector, especially in the southern parts of Nigeria. With the prospect of the departure of Europeans after Independence, what was particularly important was a willingness and enthusiasm from Northerners to join the profession. There was no shortage of training facilities for those who did decide to join, whether it was as surveyors, draughtsmen, photogrammetrists or lithographers.

Up to Independence in 1960 survey training was available for all Nigerian staff at the Survey School at Oyo, the Kano Survey School (mostly Local Authority personnel), and the Northern Nigerian Survey School at Zaria and Kaduna. If suitable recruits had been available, courses were also available at the Yaba Higher College, the Nigerian College or Arts, Science and Technology and the University of Ibadan.

Branches of the Nigerian College were established to form the nuclei of three universities; the University if Nigeria, the University of Ife, and Ahmadu Bello University at Zaria. A degree programme in surveying at the Nsukka branch of the University of Nigeria was introduced in 1962 and five graduates passed out in 1966, but there were no Northerners amongst them. Ahmadu Bello University started its degree programme in 1969, a year after the dissolution of the Northern Region. Colin Emmott left his position in charge of the North-Central State Survey Department to establish and teach the B.Sc. Land Surveying course at Ahmadu Bello University at Zaria from September 1970. By this time the need for an RICS qualification had been dropped as a requirement for appointment as a senior service surveyor.

Survey Schools in the North

The earliest elementary surveying taught in the North was in 1910 when a Government school for about 300 pupils opened at Nassarawa just outside Kano City and ten boys began studying the subject, the start of the Kano Survey School. It was run by a former Church Missionary Society worker, the Swiss-born Hans Vischer, then a government administrative officer, acting on instructions from Lugard.

Commencing as early as 1912, the Kano School was only ever intended for the training of Native or Local Authority personnel and high technical standards were neither necessary nor sought. The course generally lasted for a year and included a high proportion of practical work, measuring and preparing simple plans of the peasant farming small-holdings around Kano, for local taxation and settlement purposes; the so called *taki* surveys. The training was mostly in simple chain and compass work. Most of those trained were neither interested in, nor suitable for, further advancement in surveying and were not very effective when later tried on formal cadastral surveys, mining lease surveys and topographical work. They had a low, non-technical educational background, were not up to the standards being taught in the southern School and were taught in Arabic and Hausa to Moslem traditions. Unlike the people of the south of Nigeria, those in the north had not had any strong desire for Western education and technology. British policy had always been that of non-interference in religious matters and, in the 'Holy North', Christian missions, which were for a long time the main instrument of Western education, were only permitted to proselytise with the permission of the Emirs, and the North inevitably fell far behind. At the time, there was no education in the north capable of producing students of the requisite calibre to absorb survey training and there was no inclination amongst the educated few to face the rigours of a surveying life. Henry Morphy, a surveyor from the Nigeria Survey Department, took over the school in 1914 and teaching continued in Hausa until 1920. He was the sole instructor and the school closed when he went on leave; the students were attached to field parties during his absence. In 1919 the school had introduced a preparatory course of reading, writing and arithmetic before starting the survey course. During the 1920's, graduates of the school started taking part in triangulation and topographic surveys of mining areas but they proved to be inadequate and the school reverted to its original purpose in 1926 under the Kano N.A., which remained in control until 1951. Morphy, who was ranked as an assistant Surveyor-General, was still at the school in 1928. The school produced a map of Kano in 1930, a useful achievement, of which it was very proud. It had good colour lithographic machines for printing maps and official forms. The entire Emirate of 10,000 square miles was covered by maps showing all farms and villages *(Photo.182)* and was under constant revision.

In 1947-48, a junior service surveyor from the Survey Department started instruction at Kano for the Native Authority Land Settlement Officers training courses, and these courses were still running in 1950-51. Their administration was however taken over from the NA on 1st April 1951 and the school became staffed entirely by Survey Department personnel when 12 LSOs and 10 Chainmen attended courses. In 1952-53 a senior service surveyor and a junior technical assistant were based in buildings lent by Kano N.A. and were also looking after production survey work in Kano and Katsina Provinces. A batch of Survey Assistants passed out during the year. A second batch of 11 which started in May 1952 were a bit of a disappointment, two of them leaving for other work and another two resigned when they were unable to reach the required standard. This left seven Survey Assistants and two Land Settlement Officers in training, plus four chainmen who were undergoing simpler training. The school had a capacity of 12 in each class. The school continued to be based at Kano through 1953-54 but it was recognised that it was not the ideal location because the terrain is too flat for training and for several months the presence of growing crops is a major hindrance to fieldwork.

Although the Survey Assistant and LSO training continued at Kano, it was not very satisfactory. With their low standard of education, the recruits could only absorb the simplest instruction and were unable to acquire a real understanding of what they were doing. Also, the officer in charge was on call for other duties. The location was also unsuitable and, in 1955, was moved to join the Survey School at Kaduna, in buildings vacated by Keffi Secondary School. This allowed closer supervision by HQ and allowed the officer in charge to be freed from all duties other than teaching. During the following year 12 Survey assistants satisfactorily passed out and 15 LSOs were trained for various N.As.

In 1949, Survey Department Schools had been established, at Kakuri near Kaduna Junction and at Enugu in the Eastern Region, to provide training for Survey Assistants on a six months basic course for appointment as government junior technical staff. Entry level was School Certificate but this standard was lowered in the North. 34 Survey Assistants attended the training course at Kakuri and 22 of them successfully completed the course which was run by a senior service surveyor assisted by two junior service surveyors. The Kakuri course trained men for all regions, but at first there was a shortage of candidates from the Northern Provinces and particular efforts were made to recruit them. A shorter intensive training course was organised for Survey Assistants at a tented encampment at Eke some 12 miles west of Enugu. The recruits had a lower academic entry standard than those at Oyo and, though all were southerners, many later became useful members of the Northern Nigerian Survey.

Training in survey techniques was not only provided for the internal requirements of the Survey Department. Periodically, instruction was given to the technicians of other departments who needed a knowledge of elementary surveying in their everyday work. Between 1949 and 1951, for example, a junior service surveyor was posted to Sokoto to assist the Irrigation Engineer in the training of levellers for the Agricultural Department, and Agricultural and Marine Department assistants were attached to the Kaduna courses.

During 1950-51 the training centre at Eke in Enugu was merged with that at Kaduna, where training for Survey Assistants was concentrated on 7-8 month courses. A new classroom was built at Kaduna South to replace a building previously lent by the Keffi Secondary School. Special efforts to recruit candidates from the Northern Provinces were proving more successful. Of 14 recruited during the year, eight successfully completed the course. Of 49 Survey Assistants attending the Survey School, 15 were successful and 22 continued in training. Another 23 Survey assistants passed out of the school in 1951-52, six of them for service in the North.

One of the more pressing needs of the North was the provision of large scale plans of the rapidly growing town areas. If this kind of work was to be done quickly it demanded a large number of junior staff which, to be efficient, needed close supervision and much careful training in the early stages. The main problem was finding enough supervisory and training staff. Many survey assistants engaged on this kind of work had little real understanding of what they were doing and their work was often of very poor quality. It was also regrettable that some of the surveyors in intermediate grades, who should have been useful instructors, showed little interest in helping the younger men. In 1954-55 the school was temporarily closed because of the resignation of the surveyor in charge and a refresher course for some more senior Survey Assistants was suspended before its completion. A more permanent instructor was expected to be appointed to permit continuity and more ambitious training schemes.

As the Northern Nigerian Survey became more firmly established, with increased responsibility for the training of staff to meet the development needs of the Region, greater emphasis was placed on this aspect of the Department's work. The Survey School was re-opened in October 1956 with a course for 20 LSOs from N.As from all over the Region, followed by courses in large scale township surveying for a total of 24 Technical Assistants. A course for 12 Survey Assistants was started in March 1957.

In September 1957 a Senior Surveyor with previous military and Ghana survey experience, Jack Ashton, began a four-year attachment to the school and ran advanced courses for staff to Intermediate RICS level, assisted from time to time during that period by other senior staff of the department, including Ian Gilfoyle. Names remembered from the course of 1958 are M.A.Onigbanjo, E.E.Essien, F.C.Okoli, S.A.Aje and D.Alayo. During 1959, of a departmental total of 22 surveyors, three were employed on survey instruction, assisted by two junior officers. Courses were being run for field and office staff, Survey Assistants, Assistant Surveyors, Draughtsmen, LSOs from the N.As, and personnel from the departments of Agriculture, Animal Health and Forestry and from the Southern Cameroons. Between 1957 and 1960 24 Survey Assistants (all Northerners), 14 Assistant Surveyors, 59 LSOs, 86 Technical Assistants and Tracers, 15 Draughtsmen and 24 Draughtsmen from outside Ministries had been trained. Survey instruction was also given to members of the Nigerian Army, which collaborated with transport support for the annual wet season field camp for the Advanced Course near Kachia *(Photo.111)*, about 80 miles to the south of Kaduna, where survey fieldwork assisted with the topographic mapping of the area for a military firing range.

In 1960 the quality of in-service training for lithographers at Kaduna showed a marked improvement with the arrival of an experienced Lithographic Instructor, William Stopforth. Also, at this time, great strides were made in the training of operators in the use of modern instruments for the plotting of maps from aerial photography, details of which have given earlier in the Topographic Mapping section of this text.

By the early 1960's most of the in-service junior Nigerian staff of the Northern Nigerian Survey capable of benefiting from further training had attended courses at the school. With long term plans for the regional concentration of higher educational facilities at Zaria, including the establishment of a university with which higher survey training might be associated, and with increasing demands upon staff resources and office facilities at Kaduna for survey production, it was decided to move the Survey School to Zaria *(Photo.112)*, where for a while a newly appointed expatriate Survey Instructor, G.N.D.Beale, and Senior Surveyor J.D.Adshead, took responsibility.

The writer took over the third and last of the department's Advanced Courses, at Zaria, in January 1964, when Nigerian Assistant Surveyors were running the junior courses and Bassey Ekanem was dealing with the administrative aspects of the School's operation *(Photo.113)*. Instruction began with field astronomy during the very cool Harmattan nights, and triangulation instruction followed in March. As in the past, practical training was carried out as a production exercise, this time to provide a secondary triangulation scheme for the control of topographic mapping in the Kagarko area off the Keffi road, about 80 miles south of Kaduna. A camp of 19 tents, for students, chainmen, drivers, labourers, stores, instructor and with one as a classroom, was set up three miles east of the village *(Photo.114)*. This provided a good taste of bush life for the students, becoming more realistic as the wet season progressed when roads became at times impassable, limiting visits to Kaduna HQ to about once a month. The work involved all aspects of triangulation over an area covering more than one standard mapsheet of about 1,000 square miles, from initial reconnaissance to beaconing *(Photo. 115)*, observing and computation. Breakdown of the triangulation then went ahead to fix photo-control points for the mapping, which was to be done by the topographic mapping section in headquarters. To speed the production process towards the end of the scheme, the course was joined by Dauda Alayo, a very capable Northern surveyor, who demonstrated the efficiency with which Northern people could, if they were so inclined, work and move through rough areas without the large parties of carriers needed by expatriate surveyors. The camp was occasionally visited by other surveyors, notably Jack Ashton, who had much previous experience with courses at this level at the Survey School, Baba Kolo who was engaged on levelling work in the area, and John Evans who was surveying in an adjacent area.

The following quotation from the writer's diary gives some detail of life in the Survey School camp :-

> *'A strike of labourers and drivers took place and HQ was more or less paralysed for a fortnight. Jack Ashton came to stay and he and I drove the lorries to keep the training going. Peter Redwood and Paul Ward also came down at that time, bringing a new lorry with them. Other visitors were the Catholic fathers from the nearby missions (who, incidentally, always kept a supply of cold beer in their fridges!), and the D.O. from Zaria. I managed to contract some sort of virus and spent a short time in Kaduna for treatment. When I returned I had to cope with frequent minor emergencies - a Land Rover without battery or drive shafts had to be rescued and pushed by my men for several miles along rough bush tracks before being loaded on to a 3-tonner and sent to Kaduna - we reconstructed a bridge in the country around Jere - and we had some interference from elephants. I became known locally as a repairer of vehicles and found myself looking after Army Land Rovers, the Chief's Taunus, the N.A's American car, a priest's Simca and a Zephyr belonging to a local which we found nose down in a flooded ditch. Life in camp was comparatively uneventful, but I was kept very busy on reports, plans, checking fieldbooks, logistics, making 'History Books', vehicle maintenance, dealing with the needs of students, and instructing in the 'Lecture Tent'. Whenever possible, I visited the parties at work in the field, and as many trig points as I could, and also did some practical survey work myself, including reconnaissance, demonstration, the establishment of lower order trig stations, road levelling, and the inspection of baselining and astrofixing operations. Our link to the main road became more and more of a quagmire and many streams in the area became difficult to cross as the wet season progressed. Kagarko is a particularly wet area and some of the thunderstorms were very severe and the lightning quite intense and frightening. It goes without saying that we were bothered all the time with insects in their teeming millions ! Several snakes were killed around the camp and monkeys were a source of food for Joe Onugha with his gun. Some parties ran across elephants and buffalo, but without serious incidents. The usefulness of the Kagarko camp declined as the work progressed and the whole camp was eventually transferred to Kachia.'*

On completion of this work, the Advanced Course moved to Kaduna, instruction resumed in one of the former Railway houses on Keffi Road in Kaduna South *(Photo.116)* and practical work included traversing for the extension of township control *(Photo.117)*. In spite of the weak performance of half of the students on this final Advanced Course, a political decision was made, in support of 'Northernisation', that all had done well enough to be awarded passes and thus take an upward step in their career progression regardless of their actual ability.

No further local training at this level was available until the training role of the Department was absorbed by Kaduna Polytechnic College well after the break-up of the Northern Region, though the training of junior assistants continued at a much reduced rate.

Kaduna Polytechnic

The remnants of the Northern Nigerian Survey in Kaduna South became, in April 1968, a temporary Survey Unit within an ICSA (Interim Common Services Agency) with responsibility for the indivisible and common aspects of the former service, for mapping and printing, and for the continued training of junior field, and office-based cartographic and lithographic staff. Part 2 of this work contains a description of how the remnants of the ICSA Survey Unit became part of Kaduna Polytechnic, with Paul Ward as Principal.

Brian Till ran the survey courses at the Polytechnic between 1971and 1982, and between 1986 and 1990, and in the interim period, 1983-1986, was Principal of the School of Technology in the Institute for Higher Education at Kano. He had first arrived in Nigeria in 1953 and worked until 1965 as a surveyor with the Government of Western Nigeria, and then with Huntings Surveys until 1971. Although never a member of the Northern Nigerian Survey, his experience at Kaduna during a period of great change and progress placed him in a good position to provide a first hand account of what became of the former Northern Nigerian Survey headquarters. Those who remember the quiet, peaceful and spacious environment in Kaduna South will be interested to read about the changes which took place there, and what became of the equipment inherited from the Northern Nigerian Survey. The remainder of this section on Training is taken up with extracts from his account.

'Kaduna South' since 1970

In 1969, with the abolition of the regions of Nigeria and the creation of States, staff and equipment of the Northern Nigeria Survey were deployed to the six northern States. Part of the Kaduna South premises was occupied by the newly-created North Central State (subsequently Kaduna State) Survey led by Chief Surveyor Colin Emmott, whilst the remainder was vested, together with residual staff and equipment, in the Interim Common Services Agency of the Northern States (ICSA) as the 'Survey Unit'; under the former Northern Region Surveyor-General J.P.W.(Paul) Ward. In 1970 Colin Emmott left the North Central State and moved to Ahmadu Bello University(ABU) at Zaria.

In April 1970 the Northern States' Military Governors, needing to dismantle ICSA and appreciating the need for training in the land-based disciplines, merged the Survey Unit within Kaduna Polytechnic, an existing institution jointly-owned by the Northern States. Paul Ward was in charge of this unit. Over the years he had taken on the task of designing, modifying and constructing many of the buildings on the Survey site in Kaduna South. He also undertook many building modifications which made an excellent job of transforming the fabric of the Northern Nigerian survey premises from a production role to an academic role.

At this time the Survey Unit with its two in-service courses taken over from the NNS - one for land settlement officers and one for cartographic draughtsmen - and the Ahmadu Bello University, Zaria (ABU) with its degree course in land surveying, written and established by Colin Emmott, were the only providers of such training within the Northern States There was quite a lot of inter-action between the ABU course and Kaduna Polytechnic during the years. Colin Emmott's successor, Neil Field, ran it. He became the external examiner for the Professional Diploma (Post-HND) and ABU used the Polytechnic's Kajuru field camp on several occasions, whilst several of the Polytechnic's Nigerian staff obtained ABU M.Sc (Surveying) under Neil Field's tutelage. So what was initiated by Colin Emmott produced considerable 'positive feedback' for Kaduna South.

It was clear that the ambitious development plans of the States required a great expansion in training in surveying and allied techniques. Foundations for this expansion were laid in 1971. Existing buildings were modified for academic use, progress was made on the completion of outstanding production commitments, notably the township mapping of Okene, and preparations made for the inauguration of the first polytechnic-style diploma course - the Diploma in Land Surveying.

This commenced in January 1972 with an intake of 30 WASC (West African School Certificate) holders, almost all from the Northern States. Since some of these did not have the credits in mathematics and physics required for direct entry into the two-year Diploma course, this was preceded by a two-term 'Introductory' course with a strong element of these subjects. This was in keeping with the Kaduna Polytechnic policy which was essentially to provide 'tertiary' education for Northern students with an initial remedial bias where necessary.

The syllabus for the Diploma course, the first such course in Nigeria, was evolved within the Unit with the help of a professional advisory panel - it was later adopted by other polytechnics and eventually adopted for the (Nigerian) National Diploma in Land Surveying. Whilst providing a sound theoretical background it stipulated a series of practical tasks to be completed by each student. The Diploma was internally assessed but externally moderated - the pioneer external examiner was a former Assistant Surveyor-General of the Northern Nigerian Survey and Map Production Officer of the ICSA, Jack Ashton, then transferred to Kano State.

Every effort was made to provide realistic practical training. The resources inherited from the NNS, coupled with the recruitment of experienced surveying staff, made this possible. Vernier theodolites were used to give the students an introduction into theodolite techniques and an understanding of the inherent geometry of theodolites and their adjustment. The eleven Wild T2 theodolites inherited from NNS (each with its former assignee's name inscribed on the case !), together with several smaller optical theodolites and a number of levels, a good deal of plane-table equipment, and much ancillary equipment, enabled the practical requirements of the syllabus to be met (to a far greater extent than later when student numbers greatly increased within the Unit and surveying courses proliferated around the country within institutions ill-equipped for them).

In 1973, realising the need for students of the pioneer Diploma course and their successors to gain more extensive practical experience, a survey camp was established at Kajuru some 30 miles south of Kaduna and three miles in from the Keffi road. This was within the area used earlier by the NNS Advanced Survey Course and their tertiary triangulation served as a basis for some of the students' exercises (helped by the unearthing of the relevant file with computations in the unmistakable hand of the former instructor, J.Ashton).

Some of the old hands of the NNS proved invaluable in establishing the camp and in assisting the students in their work, running the communal catering, etc. Names that come to mind include: Usman Bornu, Shehu Azare, Haruna Bauchi II, Bala Chinuku (headmen/chainmen); Yusufu Alao, Momoh Katsina, Tsofo Kano (drivers); Usman Mubi (cook).

Access to Kajuru from the Keffi road involved crossing a drift over the Kajuru stream, the bridge having collapsed some years earlier. This was never easy and became impossible during the flash floods caused by heavy rain upstream, much of the catchment being rock outcrops. A Polish engineer from the Department of Civil Engineering of the Polytechnic with the help of artisans from the Survey Unit notably Usman Egba (mason) and Itodo (carpenter), rebuilt the bridge with steel beams and wooden decking. This lasted for some 15 years until it was replaced by a reinforced concrete bridge built by German engineers as a gesture to the people of Kajuru and also to improve access to the German-owned Castle which eventually graced Kajuru (see below). The Survey Unit artisans also rebuilt several of the culverts along the access road. These access improvements and the very existence of the annual survey camp (later used by several other institutions offering surveying courses) did much to open up the Kajuru area ,and the present Serikin Kajuru praised this contribution during the ceremony marking Kajuru's recognition as headquarters of the Gwagwada Local Government Area.

For the first ten years or so, the Kajuru camp was 'under canvas' using the large ridge tents inherited from NNS with a large space, roofed with canvas, doubling as dining room and office-work room; but in the mid-1980s on the initiative of James Dashe the camp-site was formally acquired by the Polytechnic and single-storey dormitories and stores erected. Some of the 'romance' of living under canvas may have been lost by this but it saved the annual hassle of erecting the camp with ageing tents etc., and in any case, as it happened, much of the camp equipment was lost in a fire in the camp equipment store of the Unit.

The pioneer Diploma in Land Surveying class graduated in July 1974. By then firm links had been initiated by Paul Ward with the Canadian International Development Agency (CIDA) who not only provided two land survey staff (George Wallace and Greg Castleman) but also sponsored six of the 1974 graduands for the degree course in Surveying Engineering at the University of New Brunswick. All but one of these returned, after graduating at New Brunswick, to join the staff. Of these, long-term members of staff included Mustapha Sanni, Winston Ayeni, Shaibu Abdu and Ahijah Enjugu. Another 1974 graduand, Nathaniel Ogah ,after obtaining the ABU degree and some years of experience, also joined the staff. Further CIDA sponsorships to the New Brunswick degree course included 1975 graduands Ebenezer Dania, Samuel Boye and Ibrahim Jahun and staff Member Wasiu Salisu all of whom returned to serve on the Departmental staff.

Following on the success of the Diploma in Land Surveying course, similar courses in photogrammetry and cartography were started. The Unit's legacy from NNS in respect of photogrammetric equipment included the two A8 and two B8 Wild plotters, still regularly maintained by Steiner of Lagos, slotted template equipment, the large photo-laydown platform, a contact printer, and much air-photograph material including original films, diapositives and prints. Cartographic equipment included a considerable number of light-tables, scribing equipment, drawing equipment and materials.

Ex-NNS map production technical staff deployed to the Unit included Alhaji Abdul Mamman and Mallam Sadiku Okino (photogrammetry), Mallam Salihu Angelu, Abraham Odeyemi and Ayo Peters (cartography). [Sadly it has to be recorded that, after playing key roles in the development of the Diploma in Photogrammetry course and subsequent Higher Diploma course, both Alhaji Abdul Mamman and Mallam Okino died - Alhaji Abdul Mamman in a car accident and Mallam Sadiku Okino from cholera ,both in mid-career and leaving young families.]

Cartographic staffing was greatly strengthened by the recruitment of three recently-retired officers of the Federal Surveys namely, Messrs. C.O.Audifferen (the first Nigerian Federal Map Production Officer and, later, the founding President of the Nigerian Cartographic Association), Jelili Salimonu and George Gberevbie and also by the recruitment of Fred Dada, a graduate of Professor Petrie's Topographic Science course at Glasgow University. An approach to Voluntary Service Overseas (VSO) yielded, amongst others, Dorothy Hunter (photogrammetry) and John Ward (cartography).

With the continued improvements in staffing, and quite generous provision for capital and recurrent expenditure, and as the Diploma graduands gained work-experience, Higher Diploma courses in all three topographic science disciplines were mounted together with one-year in-service courses in surveying and in cartography.

The re-naming of the Unit took account of its potential for offering training in 'environmental' disciplines other than topographic science. In 1973 an experienced town-planner, Ms.Janet B.Whitehead joined the staff to head the proposed Department of Town Planning and Estate Management.

Also at about this time faltering steps were being made for training in printing techniques based on the resources of the former map-printing section of the NNS. Following contacts made with Manchester Polytechnic by Paul Ward this was put on a firm footing with the secondment of David J.Searles from Manchester Polytechnic to head the proposed Department of Printing Technology whilst a request to CIDA for printing personnel resulted in the long-term assignments of Frank Williamson and Murray Donaldson. Other staffing improvements in the mid-1970s resulted from Kaduna Polytechnic recruitment tours to India - V.P.Sharma, K.S.Singh and Mangroo Ram (surveyors) and D.N.Sharma (photogrammetrist) - and to Poland - Messrs. Zapolski and Sobierazski (surveyors) and Mr Leon Wieckowski (photogrammetrist) amongst others, and as a result of advertisements of posts in U.K. several appointments were made e.g. Paul Barber (surveyor), Mr.Nakjevhani (estate management), R.I.Chard (town planner). Also about this time Mr.A.B.Ojo, ex-NNS staff member, returned after successful completion of his M.Sc. course at Ohio State University.

Significant local recruitments included Mr.J.D.J.Dashe (ex-NNS, recently returned from the University of New Brunswick with a first-class honours degree), Mr.Jehu Gwani (town planner), Mallam Ja'afaru Ago (town planner) and 'Pa' Salako (land officer).

As a result of this improved staffing, rapid progress was made by the two new Departments of the College and the 1977-78 Prospectus listed , in addition to those for Topographic Science, courses in Town Planning and Estate Management and Printing Technology.

The College was by now undertaking virtually all the printing requirements for the Polytechnic as a whole - ex-NNS technical staff including Ayo Enock, Ahmadu Oudah, Johnson Kolade, Roland Aremu being largely responsible for this. It was however becoming increasingly difficult to accommodate both printing production and printing education within the same set-up as each expanded. After very considerable debate and much heart-searching it was eventually decided that the proposed new building for the Department of Printing Technology should be erected, not within the College premises, but at the Tudun Wada campus of the Polytechnic.

With the sum of N3,000,000 allocated for building and equipment (a generous amount in those days when the Naira was almost at par with the pound sterling) detailed planning was instituted by a team led by David Searles. [It is amusing to note that at a subsequent Academic Board meeting when the Department was firmly established at Tudun Wada an Acting Director of the College of Science and Technology (of which the Department was now a part) claimed credit for the creation of his new department!]

Unfortunately David Searles returned to Manchester Polytechnic before he could witness the fruits of his labours, now just about to begin to take shape on the Tudun Wada campus. Neither Andrew Dimsey (David Searles' successor from Manchester Polytechnic) nor Ivor Powell, newly-recruited from U.K., remained long enough either and, following contacts made by Paul Ward, the running of the department within the new building fell eventually to a German Technical Aid (GTZ) team led by Martin Ziegenhorn (who remained as head of department until 1986) and the growing Nigerian staff.

As a quid pro quo for the loss of Printing Technology from the College of Environmental Studies (now termed 'CES', always with a humorous, semi-derogatory zest by the Secretary of the Polytechnic, Isaac Olarewaju, and even by the Rector Hamman Tukur, both of whom, together with most of the hierarchy of the Polytechnic, regarded the College as a rather impudent, albeit interesting, upstart), it was agreed that the Department of Building should ultimately be transferred from the Tudun Wada campus to Kaduna South.

That this transfer was effected earlier than had been anticipated was due to three events. Firstly a visit to the College by Borini Prono engineers looking for 'fill' material for the reconstruction of the Keffi road through Kaduna South resulted in the removal of the lateritic 'hills' within the College compound and subsequent terracing [additional terracing work was later done by the Nigerian Army Engineers] (the hill from which astronomical observations were undertaken by the surveying students was left intact). Secondly the chairmanship of the Polytechnic's Academic Planning Committee charged with drafting the 1980-85 Development Plan again fell to the writer (the 1975-80 Plan had been produced virtually in a week to meet a suddenly-imposed Federal deadline, largely due to blitzkrieg methods employed by Messrs. Ward, Till and Searles (this was perhaps the earliest example of the 'usefulness' of CES as compared with the purely-educational character of the other two Colleges of the Polytechnic)). It was a simple matter to give top priority in the Plan to a Building Technology Workshop to be located on the lower (excavated) terrace of the newly-landscaped CES campus. Thirdly it had already been agreed in principle by the Academic Board that the 'School' system should be introduced. This was laid out in detail in the 1980-85 Plan resulting in both the Department of Building and the Department of Architecture moving to Kaduna South and joining the, now re-named, Department of Urban and Regional Planning within the 'School of Environmental Design'. (The Plan, which was approved without amendment by the Board of Governors, also merged the Department of Topographic Science, the Department of Land Economy and the new Department of Environmental Monitoring within the 'School of Geodesy and Land Administration').

Further manifestation of the usefulness of CES to the Polytechnic included the acquisition of land for the third campus of the Polytechnic, known as the '1000 Acre Site', for the Polytechnic Farm and for residential and academic extensions to the Tudun Wada campus. Prolonged perseverance by Paul Ward and 'Pa' Salako utilising their intimate knowledge of the intricacies of land administration led to the securing of titles to many smaller parcels of Polytechnic land.

Again, in compliance with a request from Alhaji Salihi Iliasu, Commissioner of Education, Kano State and the then Chairman, Board of Governors of the Polytechnic, the final-year students of the Diploma in Land Surveying provided ground control for the contoured mapping of ten educational areas within Kano State from new photography flown for this project

A later set of final-year Diploma students undertook the expropriation survey of the impoundment area of the Bakalori dam for the Sokoto-Rima Basin Authority. Plane-table methods were used to chart farm boundaries throughout the impoundment area onto the authority's large-scale map sheets. The Bakalori reservoir is perhaps the fourth largest in Nigeria (after Kainji on the Niger, Shiroro on the River Kaduna and Tiga on Kano River).

Other surveys, undertaken on a 'consultancy' revenue-earning basis by the Department of Topographic Science, included Certificate of Occupancy surveys of some 100 school premises in Kaduna and the production of a number of map sheets for the Federal Capital Development Agency, Abuja, which involved staff and students of all three sections of the Department for periods spread over several years

A further source of revenue, and at the same time a unique service to the State Surveys and other surveying organisations in the North, was the instrument repair shop. This was run by Mr.Winston Ayeni (one of the 1974 graduands), who benefited from the Polytechnic's staff development bursaries by spending two periods of attachment to the Steiner workshop in Lagos.. During his last few years of service Mallam Usman Borno (headman) assisted Winston Ayeni by carrying out running repairs on prismatic compasses, instrument tripods and the like. The successive use of any given piece of equipment by many different students brought plenty of grist to the mill - a far cry from the days when each T2 had its owners' name on the metal case !

Each Higher Diploma student was required to undertake a project. In the case of surveying students this would typically involve control survey work with a least square adjustment and a topographical survey based on this, usually two or three students working in a syndicate. Kajuru village became the most surveyed village in Nigeria !

As early as 1982 a draft syllabus for the proposed Professional Diploma in Land Surveying had been drawn up with the help of an advisory committee with representatives of the Surveyors' Licensing Board, the Nigerian Institution of Surveyors, Federal Surveys, the States' Surveyors-General and relevant polytechnics, chaired by the present writer. The objectives of the course were stated as: (a) to provide a channel to the attainment of professional status (b) to alleviate the current dearth of professional staff in the (Northern) States' Surveys. The syllabus was closely modelled on that of the Survey Licence Part II Examination and the final examinations, thesis and practical task were to be assessed by an examination panel which included a representative of the Surveyors' Licensing Board.

Prior to the drafting of this syllabus a discussion had been raging (about the right word) between the senior Dean of the Polytechnic (the present writer) on the one side and the six remaining Deans as to the nature any post-HND course should have, the former advocating a profession-related course and the latter an M.Tech. course, fortunately with the Rector (a COREN (Council of Registered Engineers of Nigeria) registered electrical engineer) favouring a professional course.

The appendices to the draft syllabus indicated the staffing of the Department of Topographic Science as at 1st April 1982 as comprising 41 full-time lecturers (20 land surveying, 10 cartography, 11 photogrammetry), 5 senior technicians and 4 National Youth Service Corps (NYSC) members (i.e. Nigerian graduates in their one-year period of national service) and listed the equipment and other facilities available for use. The equipment included (in addition to items inherited from NNS, mentioned earlier): 3 Wild T3 theodolites (also inherited from NNS), 8 1'' theodolites (in addition to the 11 inherited from NNS), 2 geodetic levels, 5 EDM instruments, 20 altimeters (partly inherited from NNS), 2 HP 85 computers, 60 programmable calculators, 5 chronometers (3 from NNS), 4 stereo-plotters (in addition to the 2 A8s and 2 B8s inherited from NNS), a Zeiss SEG5 rectifier, much ancillary surveying and photogrammetric equipment and a wide range of cartographic equipment. A visit to the College by the Rector involving a discussion with Mr.C.O.Audifferen led to an unexpected windfall for the purchase of additional cartographic equipment including a Klimsch ULTRA KT 80 map reproduction camera with ATMOPLAN extension, contact printer, printing down unit, Cromalin colour proofing equipment, photo-typesetting equipment and a Posigraph Coordinatograph (in addition to the Coradi coordinatograph inherited from NNS).

The Professional Diploma course finally commenced in October 1986 when, after a four-year absence, the writer returned to CES as the Polytechnic's first Senior Principal Lecturer. It was the first Post-HND course in any Nigerian polytechnic, none of the proposed M.Tech. courses in other Departments of the Polytechnic having seen the light of day (if they have yet).

Additional 'firsts' achieved by the Department of Topographic Science (headed by Mr.J.D.J. Dashe since 1982) included three national seminars on surveying subjects held in 1988 ,1989 and 1990. The 1989 seminar on the theme 'Surveying and Mapping in the 1990s - A Strategy for Nigeria' also attracted two overseas participants namely, Professor D.G.Pöhlmann of the Technische Fachhochschule, Berlin and Dr.J.C.Iliffe of University College, London. Professor Pöhlmann gave a paper on 'Map Production Today and at the End of the 1990s' and Dr.Iliffe on 'Terrestrial and Space Geodesy in a Three-Dimensional Framework'. (On an outing later in the week both distinguished themselves - Dr.Iliffe by climbing Kujama Hill (XJ 352) and Prof.Pöhlmann by failing to climb it, but 'reaching the highest point ever reached by a cartographer'). There were a total of 102 participants, from all over the country and 25 papers were presented. Consequent upon the proceedings of the seminar, ten resolutions were adopted and published in the press etc; all, of course, ignored by the powers that be, including regrettably by Federal Surveys and the States' Surveyors-General.

The 1990 seminar, on GPS applications, was notable for the active participation of a full team, including their Chief Surveyor, from Shell - the first organisation in Nigeria to adopt the widespread use of GPS control - and a team from Federal Surveys, both bringing their equipment and enabling delegates to undertake GPS observations in and around Kaduna.

The Building Technology workshop lies behind the other large building which marked the transition from the older direct-labour single-storey buildings. This is a four-storey block containing 48 classrooms and studios, offices, toilets, etc. With student numbers rising to over 2000 by the early 1980s and building land limited, even after the terracing mentioned earlier, relatively 'high rise' styles were needed. Two three-storey staff office blocks were also built utilising the identical design which had proved successful on the Tudun Wada campus of the Polytechnic. Other building included six bungalows fronting Keffi road and a single-storey (utility, stop-gap) classroom block on the highest of the CES terraces. The Printing Technology building (on the Tudun Wada campus) also served a dual purpose for a time. It had been designed with the printing workshops on the ground floor, the classrooms and offices on the top floor and the intervening floor empty except where it contained the lower reaches of a lecture theatre straddling it and the top floor. The empty floor with supporting pillars but without walls or windows provided an ideal space for exhibitions, evening events and the like and was in fact used for the CES exhibitions on several successive Polytechnic Open Days. The popularity of the CES exhibitions had begun from our first participation in the Open Day when the combination of a surveyors' camp and a Bilby Tower stole the show with a never-ending queue of small boys waiting to climb the tower. By contrast the College of Science and Technology seemed to trot out the same stale exhibits year after year - including a set of animal skeletons in glass cases known as 'Goyal's Children' (after the then Head of Department of Science). Unfortunately the middle floor of the printing building was later enclosed and partitioned to provide more classrooms and, in any case, the Open Days were discontinued (unilaterally, without reference to the Academic Board; could it have been sour grapes ?)

Mentioned earlier was Professor Pöhlmann's outing to Kujama Hill; amongst other pearls of wisdom during his brief stay with us was his remark (to the writer) when being shown around the German-built (and owned) 'castle' at Kajuru - a fantastic multi-storey structure on one of the smaller inselbergs with a swimming pool on one of its open terraces, 'en-suite' accommodation with tiled bathrooms on each floor of the main tower, private borehole etc., etc. - "typical rich Germans". [Recent BBC reports subsequent to the death of General Abacha stated that he spent much of his latter time in a similar castle near Abuja "built by German engineers"]

The initiative taken by James Dashe in acquiring the Kajuru camp site proved timely because soon after all the adjoining 'buildable' land was taken up by a new technical school, part of the Kaduna State's moves to bring about more development in the rural areas and stem the tide of urban inflow. What with this school, the Germans' castle and their re-building of the access road bridge, our survey camp buildings, new local government offices and the building of 'country-seats' by the now-numerous Kajuru people who had prospered in the outside world, Kajuru, a village said to be older than Zaria was being transformed. Strange that only a mile or so away, the picturesque Kadara village lying beneath one of the larger inselbergs (with its tertiary trig point), a favourite outing from Kaduna to view the Pagan Village, was almost unchanged. [It was a fine balance as to who got most out of these visits - the visitors viewing the 'pagans' or the 'pagans' viewing the visitors (Photo. 82, taken in the 1950s, shows that this was not a new question)].

By the late 1980s the economic situation in the country was worsening, at least in its effect on the many. The World Bank's 'Structural Adjustment Programme' soon became known by all the lower orders, including university and polytechnic lecturers, as the 'Stomach Adjustment Programme'. The Naira depreciated rapidly and the ordinary worker's wages were insufficient even to buy the very basics for the family. Things have not got better and it is a tribute to the staff in Kaduna South that what was put together in somewhat better circumstances still has a degree of integrity and there is still 'esprit' [an example being the outright winning of the Rector's Cup by the Topographic Science staff football team (manager James Dashe, coach Wasiu Salisu, star-player Ebenezer Dania) after three successive victories in the annual competition between the Polytechnic's 37 departments]. It is also pleasing to note that at the time of writing (September 2000) James Dashe is Acting Rector of Kaduna Polytechnic and Mustapha Sanni, the best of the 1974 graduands, heads the Department of Topographic Science.

Kaduna South, i.e. CES, still has the potential to be a 'centre of excellence' for the land-based disciplines - the way ahead for Nigeria, rather than its present tendency to proliferate the same course in innumerable State institutions loosely supervised by the National Board for Technical Education. Kaduna Polytechnic, in its heyday as an autonomous institution jointly owned and governed by the Northern States (it has now been taken over by the Federal Government), was the leading polytechnic in Nigeria. Let us hope it may still be.

PART 4

THE GEOGRAPHIC LABOURERS

PART 4

THE GEOGRAPHIC LABOURERS

DESTINATION NIGERIA

An Unappealing Profession

Surveying (*Aikin safyo* to Northerners), was never an attractive profession to young Nigerians setting out to find a career and a comfortable living. For a long time the country was heavily dependent upon expatriate recruitment and leadership for its surveying services. Surveyors have a habit of assuming that everyone else knows exactly what they do, but their activities were often cloaked in suspicion and mystery. The profession was as unappealing in Nigeria as it tended to be in very many other parts of the world, as exemplified by the following description of a surveyor which is quoted from an unknown source in South Africa:-

> *"A Sirvayur is something that grubs around in the woods looking for little sticks and stones. When he finds them he does some kind of weerd dance around them with a funny-looking three-leg crutch which he leans on and looks at. When he don't find them he walks around all day like he's lost. Sometimes you see them squashed by cars along roads, espeshelly in the summer when all the other bugs are out.*
>
> *A Sirvayur has one big eye and one little eye like Popeye. He usually walks bent over all the time which is why he always looks so stopped. His face looks like old lether. He cusses terribul. He can't read because he measures between things and then puts down a number in a littel book which is defrint than wat his littel map says. He always measures to a stick or stone, stops neer it, and puts in another stick or stone. He is not too brite because he is always making marks on side-walks and rodes to find his way home. His pants are allways tore from rock salt and his shoes look like they was made of mud. People stare at him, dogs chase him and he always looks wore out.*
>
> *I don't know why anyone wants to be a sirvayur."*

Motivation

The European "geographic labourers" went to West Africa because they were individualistic, adventurous and ambitious, and wished to experience exotic sunny lands and remote places. The romance of far horizons and the prospect of distant unknown mountains kindled a primal urge to travel. Some had scarcely ever been a hundred miles from home, but had studied geography and map making, had inherited a curiosity about foreign places from forebears who had served abroad, and saw the opportunity of a worthwhile, hopefully lucrative and exciting alternative to a predictable, unrewarding and unadventurous life under the grey and drizzling skies of home. In general they were enthusiastic about their work and convinced of the value of their maps and plans to the developing country. Some had travelled abroad on military service, and as a result, fancied a life in tropical surroundings. The fact that they were prepared to go and survey in Africa indicated that, in some, there may have been a remnant of the pioneering spirit which had begun to open up the colonies more than half a century before, but it is probably true that none of them went to Northern Nigeria out of political or purely philanthropic concern. They all sought a career, the achievement of personal goals and appropriate financial gain. In addition to a background of technical and mathematical training, they needed a good measure of physical fitness and had to be prepared to live a tough itinerant life. They needed to be self-sufficient, and able to cope with emergencies and crises. The majority didn't know what they were letting ourselves in for; they had little idea what demands the life might make upon them; had little regard for the possible loneliness, repeated hardships, sudden illness in remote places far from medical aid; had not thought about the effects of disagreements and jealousies amongst fellow Europeans, and the homesickness and privations of an unaccustomed way of life. They had never experienced the discomforts of tropical weather and they had no inkling of how they would cope with the monotony and uncontrollable irritability and discomfort of enervating days. The dangers were pointed out to them before they left home, but, in a way, the major risks acted as an incentive and tended to be blindly ignored, as indeed they would be by the young of today; the minutiae they were to experience first hand.

> *'When you have made up your mind to go to West Africa the very best thing*
> *you can do is to get it unmade again and go to Scotland instead.'*

> *Mary Kingsley 1897*

Something of the approach to working overseas can perhaps be seen in the following reply by Keith Sargeant when he was asked why, in 1938, he elected to go to Nigeria:-

> *'......after graduating in geography (specialising in survey in the third year),*
> *I felt I would like a job overseas involving some kind of surveying, so I applied to*
> *join the Colonial Survey Service. The application form asked for my choice of*
> *colony, and I gave Malaya or East Africa - but the only vacancy offered was in*
> *Nigeria and this, somewhat reluctantly, I accepted. I had never met anyone from*
> *Nigeria, and it was still regarded as the White Man's Grave.'*

'The White Man's Grave' reputation of West Africa no doubt deterred many from considering working there. From the early 1950s, together with the other documentation issued by the Colonial Office to newly appointed officers before their departure, was a small, green hard-backed booklet, guaranteed to give rise to some apprehension. It was entitled *"Hints on the Preservation of Health in Tropical Countries"* and was seized upon by those who scorned the idea of working in remote and inhospitable parts of the world. For a start, inside the front cover, pasted as if in dire warning, was the note "A poisonous insecticide has been used in binding this book". The writer recalls the occasion when the more 'entertaining' parts of it were read out loud in a students' bar in Bristol, to the uproarious amusement of all present, particularly the sections on the very detailed rules for the construction of privy pits and the use of the 'pail and bucket' system.

In spite of the dire warnings, the words of Mary Gaunt were worth recalling:-

> *'A land of immense possibilities*
> *Heat, fever and mosquitoes*
> *Gorgeous nights and divine mornings*
> *A white man's grave -*
> *but live wisely and discreetly*
> *and it is no more likely to be there than anywhere else.'*

A Colonial Service recruitment memorandum dated February 1936 illustrated improving conditions by comparing the European death rate of 1.73% in 1909 to 0.65% in 1934, and the invaliding rate from 5.65% to 1.33% during the same period.

Appointments

Applicants were generally able to express their personal preference of the country to which they were posted, and this was usually accepted, if vacancies existed, but temperament and ability were sometimes taken into account. Although no longer the 'White Man's Grave', expatriates liked the title as a reason for having shorter tours and more generous leave than the healthier parts of East Africa. Length of tours was a factor, certainly for the writer:-

'I was not at all sure I wished to stay in Africa and thought that, initially, two tours of 18 months each as Nigeria approached independence might be enough for me. The fact that I did in fact serve for twenty years says a lot about me, but probably says more about Nigeria and Nigerians.'

Although full colonial administration had decayed before the Northern Nigerian Survey came into being, most expatriates started their careers by recruitment to the large body of technical and administrative expertise that was the Colonial Office. *(Conditions of Colonial Office appointments are given at Appendix V)*. Appointments were made by the Secretary of State, but once attached to Northern Nigeria, surveyors became staff of that territory and paid by it at agreed rates from Northern Nigerian revenue. They certainly did not think of themselves as colonialists or imperialists. They went to work in a country which was a British creation and responsibility, but which was known, as pressures mounted for independence in many other colonial territories, to be heading rapidly towards self-determination.

West Africa was essentially a place for bachelors. Some people, married or not, left quickly. Others were trapped by their own situations and had to stay for the money and counted the days to leaving. Those who stayed on could be hooked for life. They enjoyed the novelty, the excitement, the opportunity for the exercise of responsibility, and the freedom. The eccentrics among them could find a place there. In the early days of surveying in Northern Nigeria, a surveyor was not expected, nor for that matter was he allowed, to take his wife to Nigeria. Permission had to be obtained (and was rarely granted) for wives to accompany their surveyor husbands in bush. Such a distraction would hamper his mobility and production and would make unacceptable demands for additional carriers and camp equipment. Furthermore, before the Second World War, there was a distinct lack of suitable housing accommodation for married officers accompanied by their wives, especially in the extreme conditions likely to be encountered by surveyors, and quite rigid restrictions to ensure, for the sake of all, that wives and families stayed at home.

'There is no place where a wife is so much wanted as in the Tropics; but then comes the rub - how to keep the wife alive.'

Richard Burton   1863

The situation became more relaxed after the war, when facilities and medical services improved, but the corollary was that the husband would inevitably spend much less time on trek in the bush. No doubt on account of her long pre-war experience and knowledge of Nigeria, and the character of her husband, a notable exception was Nora Hunter, who in 1946 spent a year in the Sokoto bush, scarcely using a motor vehicle, and recorded her experiences in her diary *"Where My Caravan Has Rested"*.

The introduction of more effective vaccines, antibiotics and improved prophylactics to combat malaria, made Nigeria a healthier place after the war. The rules concerning accompanying wives were relaxed in about 1952 and it was left to the surveyor to decide, though newcomers were not encouraged to bring their wives out until they had familiarised themselves with the conditions of bush life *(Photo.193)*. This was not a problem for officers posted to a station and a lot of married men were accompanied by their wives for part, if not the whole, of a tour. Numbers of European children came out to Nigeria too, an event almost unheard of in earlier years. When the Northern Nigerian Survey came into being in the mid 1950's, there were over a hundred white children in Kaduna, for whom schooling up to the age of about six was organised. As they grew up, it was sometimes very difficult for a wife to decide whether to stay at home away from her husband, or whether to join him in Nigeria and face the expense and separation of sending their children to a boarding school.

The benefits for married surveyors were often that postings were likely to be to the more comfortable stations and tours to more remote parts would be of shorter duration, unless his wife was of that rare kind who was prepared to become involved in his work. It also ensured that priority was given to those with wives and families when it came to optimum times for taking leave in England.

Winter leaves were the inevitable consequence of remaining a bachelor ! In 1961, Clifford Rayner was firmly intent on leaving Nigeria for good - having had enough of touring and feeling rather victimised as a bachelor. But he was getting 'acting' pay and a promise of a permanent promotion to Senior Surveyor changed his mind !

The arrival of wives and children brought about increased domesticity, improvements in living conditions, in health and diet, more emphasis on home entertainment and leisure activities, and social changes to the previously male-dominated society, with less focus on the club; though for many the latter remained the centre for station social life throughout their Nigerian days. A small minority were of a school of thought that blamed the decline of the British Empire on three things; one, swimming pools; two, air conditioners; and three, white women, but not necessarily in that order ! At the same time, surveyors who had experienced the rigours of military service or who were trained in the post-war period brought in new thinking about their work, new attitudes towards the people for whom they were to work and more flexibility in the interpretation of the rules. They were less narrow-minded and more ready to adapt the colonial formality and traditions of the past to the needs of an emerging and rapidly changing and modernising country.

Some surveyors, especially in the pre-Northern Nigerian Survey days, endured physical hardship and separation from their families for surprisingly small remuneration, but with improvements in transport and station amenities, these problems diminished and those who spent very little time or no time at all in the bush were able to live a life which was at least as comfortable and remunerative as they could have expected to enjoy at home. For those who had to endure the exacting hardships, there could be tremendous personal satisfaction and sometimes the excitement of undertaking work in extraordinary circumstances and amongst people with whom, when all was said and done, it was pleasurable and fulfilling to work.

Preparations

Gullible new recruits and impoverished ex-students, who were dependent upon the Colonial Office kitting-out grant (an initial Clothing Allowance of £45 and a Touring Equipment Allowance of £40 were given in 1957) for their essential equipment, were easily persuaded into parting with every last penny of it by the London tropical outfitters and their displays of 'essential' equipment, with the result that many arrived in Nigeria virtually penniless. Camp baths with basket linings, airtight black uniform cases which they would letter with the owner's name (examples have lasted well over 40 years and are still immaculate inside), palm beach suits, filters, mosquito nets, camp beds, Tilley lamps, folding chairs, mosquito boots, folding canvas hand-basins and much more were stacked in endless array in the showrooms of F.P.Baker of Golden Square and Griffiths McAllister. In the words of Clifford Burnside:-

> *'This old-world firm* (Griffiths McAllister of Farringdon Road) *specialised in supplying such gear to missionaries and had no doubt supplied the likes of David Livingstone in his time. In fact much of their range seemed to have changed little over the years. Certainly the tropical linen suit I found I had bought (but never ever wore) came into this category. However, the folding camp bed complete with mosquito net, the water filter, the five foot zinc bath, the Tilley lamps, the charcoal iron (for ironing the linen suit) and the Roorki folding arm chair all proved invaluable in the days ahead.'*

Voyage to West Africa

The passenger/cargo ships of the Elder Dempster line, usually sailing from Liverpool, were, until the 1960s, by far the most common way to travel to Nigeria *(Photos. 118-125)*, especially for newly appointed officers carrying heavy baggage and an assortment of bulky equipment, but a significant number used freighters of other lines from different ports. Most sailings, until about the mid 1950s, included an assortment of 'old coasters', mostly bachelors, who would spend the greater part of the voyage in small groups in the bar, but sailings in the later years catered much more for women and children, travelling to join their husbands and bringing the heavy baggage. Some preferred the tradition and style of the journey and would always prefer to travel this way.

The first port of call was Las Palmas in the Canary Islands, the last opportunity for shopping for luxuries. Beyond the belt of the trade winds, off the coast of north-west Africa, the sea became pale grey and lifeless, and the atmosphere started turning hot and sticky. The Gambia was the first real contact with Africa. In the port of Bathurst (now called Banjul), there was a great mixture of races and it was there that most first set foot on African soil, felt the heat of the land, mingled with African people and experienced the genial confusion. The ship took on a different character as disembarking Europeans, with their supplies and luggage, were replaced by African passengers, with a colourful assortment of possessions, most of them heading for Lagos. Many of them travelled third class, on the foredeck, with huge canvas sheets erected to protect them from the hot sun and the rain. Freetown in Sierra Leone was a regular stopping place. Launches and canoes came alongside, young men dived for coins thrown overboard; contacts with the real Africa had begun. The writer's lasting memories are of the activity and noise of the town and the Central Hotel, where a vulture watched attentively from a nearby window-sill as a very large Lebanese gentleman tucked into an enormous and colourful mound of West African curry. Ships would sometimes call at Monrovia in Liberia, a rude introduction to West Africa, and at Accra in Ghana. In both, the ship would anchor offshore and cargo and passengers would be loaded into surf-boats and barges. The first sight of Nigeria was a low flat horizon of grey-green palms.

Keith Sargeant describes his journey by sea in 1939:-

> 'In those days there was no regular air service to Nigeria, and Jack Spicer and I duly sailed on the "Abosso" - one of Elder Dempster's liners which plied a regular fortnightly service from Liverpool to West Africa. All four of Elder Dempster's liners were destined to be sunk during the war, but were subsequently replaced and provided the same regular service until 1972. Nearly all our fellow passengers were "Old Coasters" who enjoyed recounting tales - some true, some apocryphal - to the new boys about the life awaiting us. The fourteen day voyage was an entirely new experience for Jack and me, and I well remember being off-loaded by "Mammy chair" into a tossing surf-boat at Accra (Photos. 126 and 127). During the voyage we were told our posting by the ship's radio: Jack to go to the Minesfield office in Jos, and I to join a topographical survey group in Katsina province after a few days in Kaduna, survey headquarters of the northern region.'

After 1950, a number of very likeable and capable Dutchmen and Danes served with the central Survey Department and with the Northern Nigerian Survey. Their education, sense of humour and their ability to speak very good English made them excellent working colleagues and friends. Their motives for seeking employment in Nigeria were very much the same as those who came from England and elsewhere and their attraction to West Africa was perhaps a reflection of their own countries' past when the Dutch established the castle at Visscher Fort at Accra and the Danes built Christiansborg Castle in 1610. Two Dutchmen, Harry Rentema and Arnold Voshaar, have bravely and painstakingly, after many years of absence from everyday use of English, recorded some of their memories, asking for the correction of any serious grammatical irregularities. Arnold comments:-

> 'The British and the Dutch have in common a kind of humour that enables them to regard a problem as a challenge. My Dutch colleagues and I, as continentals, enjoyed living and working together with Englishmen, Scotsmen and so on. Several times I was asked, due to my pronunciation of my English, if I was a Scot. I took it as a compliment.
>
> In Holland we were trained in several languages. Maybe that was why I felt pronunciation of the Hausa language was easier for the Dutch than the British.'

Harry Rentema *(Photo.11)* joined Nigeria Surveys in 1952 and completed one tour, working mostly in Northern Nigeria. Later, after experience elsewhere in Africa, he returned for one more year, in 1963-64, with the United Nations Food and Agriculture Organisation. With the aid of letters written to his parents at the time he recalls his appointment and journey:-

> 'It is almost 50 years ago since professor Roelofs from our Technical University in Delft, who had contacts with his colleagues in England, investigated whether there was interest amongst the students in a job in the British colonies. I had always dreamed of Africa and this seemed to be my chance.

In 1952, when I finished my geodetic engineering studies in Delft, we got visitors from the Colonial Survey Dept in Tolworth, who had a talk with some candidates, which resulted eventually in a medical test and a formal offer of appointment for a job at the Directorate of Colonial Surveys, to be sent on short missions in the colonies. Because of my eyesight (Lazy eye) this was later changed to a contract with the Colonial Survey Dept in Nigeria. Because of long delays with the paperwork some of us got other jobs in the meantime but I was rather fixed on Africa.

From the Colonial Office in London I got a long list of recommended bush-outfit items which I ordered from Holland, in good faith, from Griffith McAllister in London.

On lst November 1952 I was waved goodbye by my parents and left by boat and train for London where I found a room in the Tuscan Hotel in Shaftesbury Avenue at £1 a day including breakfast. It was my first visit to England and I discovered that spoken English is different from school English. Nevertheless I found my way to the Colonial Office, met Mr. Morgan, got lots of paper and £120 outfit allowance which I spent at Griffith McAllisters; bath £10, camp bed £10, mosquito net £5, mosquito boots £4, 3 airtight boxes £18, palmbeach suit £13, evening dress £14 etc. I enjoyed the colourful mix of people in the town: Indians, Africans and the rather conservative looking Englishmen: moustache, bowler and umbrella and striped suit; good looking ladies of different origins; and old cars. Everything plentiful compared with Holland where things were still rationed. I got my first class ticket for the train to Liverpool and ship to Lagos - an unusual luxury after my modest life as a student in Delft where I used to move about hitch hiking.

The departure from Liverpool was on 6th of November with a day's delay because of heavy weather. My cabinmate, Charlie, was to be an administrator in Nigeria. He had been in Holland until he was 15 and spoke fluent Dutch. This was quite a relief for me sometimes. Another land surveyor on first contract, Ted, 24 years old, and a Danish civil engineer, Jos, also on first contract, completed our bridge group.

The "Accra" was a fairly small ship, 11,000 tons, to allow it to enter the West-African ports. It accommodated 500 people, including 250 first class passengers. It had all the essentials for a good life on board (swimming pool etc.) Many old timers met old friends and colleagues. Some left their wives and children behind, single ladies were to rejoin their husbands.

Going south and getting warmer it was interesting to see people gradually change into tropical clothes and mood. The ship had to take fuel in Las Palmas which took about 7 hours, time to celebrate farewell from Europe for the coming years. It was difficult to get everybody aboard again. Games and dances were organised. First chance to use the swimming pool and our 'black and white". The crew members, in their smart white uniforms, were by far the favourites with the ladies.

On 16th November we reached Freetown. The mountains in the far distance in the clouds. The harbour was not deep enough for our boat. We anchored and were surrounded by dugout canoes with pennydivers. They sang on request whisky songs or negro spirituals. Their leader used to dive in evening dress but he had recently been eaten by sharks.

Between Freetown and Takoradi we had been informed about our future stations. I was lucky; Jos, Nigeria's holiday resort I was told. Charlie should go to East Nigeria, the Dane to Kaduna.

In Takoradi there was the same ceremony, but here we could moor at the quay where a dance was given to celebrate reunions with family and friends. The night before arrival in Lagos there was a farewell dance aboard. Somebody played the bagpipes and there was a lot of drinking.

On arrival in Lagos, a happy welcome, tea for the whole family on board and exchange of news. There were many black porters to take our luggage ashore. Ted and I were guests of the Director of Surveys in Lagos. He had spent most of his life in Egypt. His son was killed during D-day in Normandy. He was a very hospitable man. We had an evening walk on the beach.

The next day we boarded the train to Jos. Ted was going to Western Nigeria and travelled on the same train. Charlie waved us goodbye. We left at midday, travelling at about 30 km per hour. The windows were open and it was very dusty and dirty with soot from the wood-burning locomotive. There were many villages along the line, it was very, very colourful, palm trees, fruit and vegetables for sale. Vultures sat on the roofs and in the trees.

Northwards there was more scrub. The next day we reached Kaduna and I was picked up by Mr. and Mrs. Hunter for a cup of tea. The next morning I arrived in Jos and met and stayed some nights with the Sargeants. There I met my colleague and countryman Evert Eisinga, who had arrived a month before me. He had malaria.'

Arnold Voshaar *(Photo.13)* tells a similar story:-

'In Delft, the Netherlands, I signed in 1952 a letter of intent with the representatives of the Crown Agents for Oversea Governments and Administrations, 4, Millbank, London, with the aim, after finishing my study at the University of Delft, of being available to expatriate to one of the British colonies for geodetical activities. The final date I had to be ready to do so was 31st December 1953.

I was living with a couple of students in a manor house at Delft. It was not a very suitable environment in which to complete my studies successfully in time for this deadline so I moved in to another house in Delft and finished my studies in July 1953. As a student however I needed a lady companion for a students-soirée. Next to my new address there lived a girl, and what a girl ! So after some hesitation, I invited her. After some time we became close friends and were engaged just before I left Holland for my first tour of two years. Ria and I had agreed to marry during my first leave and she would travel out with me for my second tour(Photo.81).

Then I had to wait for several months before confirmation of the Colonial Survey appointment. Looking back I realise that if there has been no conditions in my contract with the Colonial Department I would, probably, never have changed my landlord and would never have met my present wife.

I had the choice of several British Colonies. Finally I chose Nigeria, and for just one reason. At that time the Royal Dutch K.L.M. flew once a week from Amsterdam to South Africa with a stop at Rome and another at Kano airport. So I had, in the event of an emergency, a preference for Northern Nigeria.

On the 31st December 1953 I left Holland, on New Year's Eve, taking a ferry from Hook of Holland to Dover. The ferry, at night, was almost empty. Dover-Liverpool was a pleasant journey and my destination "the Accra", a passenger ship of the Elder Dempster Line.

I had a list of articles to be bought. I needed equipment for use on tour in "the bush". In Holland I had already bought a Palm Beach suit and a dinner jacket to use when in station. In Liverpool everything was tax free and delivered on board by the firm of Griffith McAllister. For several years afterwards I used, during my holidays, the Houndsfield camp bed they supplied.

I remembered my first breakfast on board (Illustration 124). I was sitting next to an older person. In my best English I asked him: "Sir, from which part of England are you coming?" His face stiffened. "I am Scottish." After I had explained that I just had left my home country, Holland, and that it was my first contact with Britain, he accepted it as a joke. The rest of the cruise to Lagos, Nigeria this Scotsman was a good companion.

Eventually I arrived at Lagos. The train to Kafanchan and from there to Jos was not a pleasant journey at all. Once we stopped in the middle of nowhere. The "fuges" had broken down. It took half a day for somebody, on a bicycle, to collect a new one. A "fuge" was, apparently, a fuse. It was the first time I heard the use of pidgin English.

In Jos I had the opportunity to take over a Studebaker 'kitcar' from a geologist. The car was in good condition and I bought it for a fair price.

The director, Keith Hunter, and his wife, invited all the surveyors for an afternoon drink to get me acquainted with my colleagues. I remembered that a young surveyor entered with a beard and a moustache. Hunter got angry and shouted: "If you, after one week in the bush, are too lazy to shave yourself you'd better go". After half an hour the youngster came back well shaven.'

After completing his first tour of duty, Arnold Voshaar returned for a second tour, again travelling by sea:-

'During my leave in Holland, I married my present wife Ria van Neerijnen. One week after our marriage we left Amsterdam on the cargo-boat "van Linschoten". We were, with a missionary nun, the only passengers.

During the second night I fell out of the upper bed and bruised my ribs on the back of a chair. In the harbour of Bordeaux, our first stop, a medical man came on board. First he asked for his honorarium and after the steersman had paid, he looked after me. For the rest of the journey the crew was wondering why I, only just married, had left my bed in the middle of the night !

We called at several harbours and had chance to visit the towns of Dakar, Conakry, Freetown, Monrovia and finally Accra.'

Clifford Rayner recalls his departure and journey to Nigeria:-

'In the April of 1956 the Royal Engineers 'Long Survey Course' No.15 at The School of Military Survey, Hermitage and my eight month stay in digs at 114 Craven Road, Newbury, with Mr and Mrs Durbidge as landlord and lady, came to an end. Good-byes were said to Mike Smith, another surveyor from Bristol, who went to Tanzania, and Mr and Mrs Durbidge. Although the innumerable tales of pre-war Nigeria from Mr Durbidge, who had worked on the railways, and Mrs Durbidge gave us some idea as to what to expect in colonial service, my departure to join Northern Nigeria Survey (NNS), was nevertheless a great adventure.

Before too long, with fellow Bristol graduates Alan Wilkie, John Tozer and Ian Gilfoyle, I was off to Liverpool, with a reasonable amount of kit consisting of two cabin trunks, to make acquaintance with the Elder Dempster Line and in particular the M.V.. Accra. Twelve days at sea with reasonable weather which got better i.e. hotter, with each passing day soon convinced the 'Bristol four' that we had definitely made the right choice. The alternative being a stint in Her Majesty's armed services by way of National Service.

The food on board was excellent, and we, being young and fit, made full use of the ample menus three times a day at least. The days of war-time and post war austerity had definitely disappeared; and we hoped for good. First stop was Las Palmas. A short trip ashore to see the sights and another step in our inexorable acclimatisation to Africa and then we were off again, next stop Freetown, Sierra Leone where we met up with Peter Gardner (L.S.C. No. 14) who was now an 'old timer' of six months standing! One more stop at Takoradi and then Lagos, twelve days and nights from Liverpool. It seemed, and indeed we had, landed in another world! It was very hot and there was an air to the place that I came to love. Even now, more than forty years later, the scent of Africa conjures images which are indelibly printed on my memory. And so at the age of 21 years and 8 months a real African adventure had begun.'

In the following extract from his personal memoirs the Australian surveyor Kenneth Toms, who had been teaching surveying in the U.K. describes his appointment and journey to Nigeria:-

'In the fifties the British Empire was still largely intact. The "political" colour scheme of my copy of the 1952 Concise Oxford Atlas allocated pink (of all colours) to the United Kingdom, her Dominions and her colonies. Consequently, large areas of the earth's surface depicted in the ninety-six pages of small scale maps contained in the Atlas carried that distinctive tint of Empire. The Colonies, as distinct from the Dominions, were still ruled from Westminster by the Colonial Office through the medium of Her Majesty's Colonial Service. My time with the Condominium Government of the New Hebrides had opened my mind to career possibilities in that Service. So, I applied to the Colonial Office for an appointment thereto.

I was interviewed in London by the Deputy Director of Overseas Surveys, Lt. Colonel G.J.Humphries and a rather pompous person from the recruitment division of the Colonial Office. I was questioned on my work in the New Hebrides and my Australian background. Later in the interview, I was invited to indicate my preference for posting. I said that I would like to serve in the Pacific, it would get us closer to Australia to begin with. Fiji was my first priority, with Hong Kong a close second.

"Hum", as G.J. Humphries was generally known in the Service, was sorry to say that there was no vacancy in either my first or second choice. There was, however, a position available in Nigeria.

Geography had always been my long suit, hence I knew that Nigeria was situated on the western hump of the African continent just above the Bight of Benin. I was also a fan of Edgar Wallace and was thus aware that it contained a great river or two, grew oil palm and cocoa in great quantities and its inhabitants were very black. Hum pointed out that I would be posted to the Northern Region of the Colony, and he waxed eloquently on what a wonderful place the North was. Had he not spent an early part of his own overseas career in that part of the world before the War?

A month later, I received a letter from none other than the Secretary of State for the Colonies, offering me appointment to the service of the Northern Nigerian Government as a Provincial Surveyor. The salary was a great advance on the College stipend, Africa beckoned and Susan, after some persuasion, agreed to go. I accepted the appointment.

I submitted my notice of resignation to the College. It was received well enough, with some polite expression of regret at my leaving. Professor Thompson thought that it was a retrograde step, but he did not elaborate. If I had ever created any ripples on the pond of British academia, they were quite minor. I had nevertheless benefited by the experience. There is nothing quite like a teaching commitment to force one to update one's knowledge. I was not sorry however, to leave those hallowed halls to return to professional work in the field.

As with any move, let alone an international one, there was the inevitable upheaval involving the sale of the house, finding temporary accommodation, storage of household effects and the general preparation for departure from an established way of life.

From the information provided, it appeared advisable for me to go first to ensure that adequate accommodation was available before the family came out. The logistics of colonial appointments were the prerogative of the Crown Agents for the Colonies. I arranged with them for the organisation for sea passage for myself to take up appointment, and for my wife Susan and son Stephen to fly out later.

In due course my ticket arrived. I was to sail from Liverpool on Thursday, 2nd May 1957 in Elder Dempster's MV Accra for Lagos via the Canary Islands, Sierra Leone and Ghana. My posting was to a place called Jos on the Bauchi Plateau in Northern Nigeria. The trip from Lagos to Jos would be by rail. It was all very stimulating.

Elder Dempster passenger sailings departed from the big port on the Mersey. In a way I was quite attached to Liverpool and felt a touch of nostalgia as the twin Liver birds were lost to view as Accra slipped down the river to the Irish Sea.

M.vs. Accra and Apapa (Photo.122) were the pride of the Elder Dempster fleet at the time. They were handsome vessels in their light grey paint and yellow *funnels. Accra displaced a gross tonnage of 11,599 and her length overall was 471 feet. On that voyage her passenger list comprised 271 men, women and children in the first and third class. There was no second class.*

Shipboard friendships can be struck up very quickly. Often the catalyst is the purser's allocation of seating in the dining room. Pursers seem to have the knack of creating a good mix of personalities at meal times. No doubt it is an art acquired through long experience. On this voyage it led me to meet two remarkable people, who were also on their way to Northern Nigeria.

Gordon H. Colton was a Devonshire builder on his way to take up appointment as a public works inspector with the Northern Nigerian Government in Kaduna. Gordon was a man with a most infectious laugh. He was bored with life in England, and like many other of the "new boys" aboard, he was in search of adventure in Africa. Britain was still outward looking in 1957, and the Colonial Service offered a reasonably well-paid avenue to see something of the world in a more or less meaningful manner.

Dr Crkvenak was a Yugoslav medico who had taken British nationality. He had been offered a position as a medical officer in the Northern Nigerian Service. His posting was to a remote station on the Plateau some distance from Jos. I always had difficulty in pronouncing Crkvenak. It sounded something like "Susquernas". Whatever, the good doctor was a great chap. His prime ambition in life was to hunt elephant, even though it seemed that he was going to the wrong side of the great continent for that purpose. Crkvenak, Colton and I became good friends through that voyage.

The Atlantic had always been kind to me. On this trip it was the same; the weather was perfect, with calm seas right across the Bay of Biscay and right down to Las Palmas in the Canaries. The passengers were drawn either from the colonial service in one or other of the West Coast territories, or from the staff of large commercial houses such as the United Africa Company. Some were officers still serving in the newly independent country of Ghana that was formerly the Gold Coast Colony. The passenger list included one Knight of the Realm, Sir John Verity KT, an Air Commodore, S.H.C. Gray, OBE and a Judge, The Hon. Mr Justice H.S. Palmer TD. There were a large number of families. The nice thing about Accra was that she was not a tourist ship. West Africa was not on the tourist trail in those days.

Our first port of call was Las Palmas. In the nineteen fifties, it was a busy port on the northern side of Grand Canary Island. A Spanish colony, the Canaries have an interesting history. They even got a mention by Pliny in 40 B.C. We found the town a pleasant enough place to wander through. The fish markets were extensive and sold the largest snapper that I had ever seen. At the main street intersections, a traffic policeman was ensconced in a little pergola to shield him from the midday sun.

A few more days of perfect Atlantic weather, and we berthed in Freetown, the capital of the then Colony of Sierra Leone. Within minutes of the ship being secured, a horde of small boys arrived in dugout canoes to dive for coins in the murky waters of the harbour. They were incredibly adroit at that sport, and they must have done very well by fetching many English florins and shilling pieces.

Ashore for a few hours, we sat on the verandah of an elderly wooden hotel, drinking local beer and listening to squeaky tunes rendered on an old and battered bugle by a small African in a tattered military uniform. I ate my first mango since leaving the New Hebrides three years before.

Our last port of call before Lagos was at Takoradi in Ghana (formerly the Gold Coast). Ghana had received its independence from British rule only three months before our visit. I had wondered, before leaving Britain, whether the Nigerians might wish to emulate the Ghanaians and make an accelerated bid for their own independence. In 1954, the British, under pressure from the leaders of the major ethnic groups, created a federation of three autonomous regions and the federal district of Lagos. The names of the leaders involved in these early moves towards independence were already well-known to the world in general. There was Dr Nnamdi Azikiwe in the Ibo-dominated Eastern Region, Chief Obafemi Awolowo in the predominantly Yoruba Western Region and Abubakar Tafewa Balewa in the essentially Moslem Northern Region. Even to a tyro like me, there seemed to be the elements of a political powder keg in the tribal mix of the country.

There were few signs of self-rule fervour in Takoradi. The place seemed to doze under a sun of immense power. A number of passengers, nearly all Britons returning to work in Ghana, disembarked. They seemed to think that there would be little change for quite some time in the way the new country was run.

The next day Accra entered Lagos Harbour. The pleasant fourteen day voyage was over. Africa suddenly became very real to Colton, Crkvenac and myself.'

Lagos

At Apapa, the leisurely and comfortable voyage came to an end with the bustle and turmoil of disembarkation and the assembly of luggage as it came ashore. The humidity which had been felt on board as the ship moved along the coast had been tempered by the breezes at sea but, upon arrival in the oppressive heat of Lagos, the atmosphere suddenly became airless and heavy with the rich, ripe smells of damp Africa. This was not the gentle heat of England, but an enveloping and clammy air which was almost difficult to breathe. Out at sea the sky blackened and rapidly approaching clouds flashed with spectacular lightning as the afternoon rain approached. The noisy and sweaty time spent in the customs shed was a first taste of things to come.

'In the beginning God created the Universe. Then he created the moon, the stars and the wild beasts of the forests. On the sixth day he created the Nigerian. But on the seventh day, while God rested, the Nigerian invented noise.'

Anthony Enahoro 1966

Keith Sargeant recalled his arrival in Lagos in 1939 :-

'The first day in Nigeria was a very busy one. Between docking at Lagos at 7.45am and catching the boat train at 10.00pm, Jack and I visited the survey headquarters offices, ordered quantities of tinned food, drinks and other essentials from the John Holt's store, were lunched and dined by Captain Buckingham (a senior surveyor known as "The Duke") and were taken on a trip round the harbour in his motor boat.'

Trevor Brokenshire remembers his wife Joan arriving in Lagos by sea in the early 1950s and attempting to clear Lagos Customs:-

'She had brought quite a lot of things with her, many packed by the Army and Navy Stores in London, and Elder Dempster had, with great efficiency, gathered all her belongings together in one place. Amongst the belongings was a sewing machine in its locked carrying case, and a long roll of carpet. Even in those far off days, the Nigerian Customs officer was looking for a 'dash' (a gift) for clearing the 'luggage'. He insisted that there must be GUNS in the carpet roll (it was pretty heavy) and that the cotton reels rattling around in the bottom of the sewing machine were, in fact, AMMUNITION ! No amount of persuasion worked and, by now, Joan was the only passenger in the customs shed. Luckily it had been arranged that Alan Lees, of the Lagos Survey Department, should meet Joan off the boat, preparatory to sending her on her way to Jos, by air. He was, at last, allowed into the shed; what he said, or how he said it, we know not now, but Joan was quickly released. All of her heavy baggage arrived safely in Jos; presumably by train.'

As an introduction to the oppressive climate of Lagos the writer's first night in Nigeria was spent at the Ikoyi Catering Rest House under a monotonous, squeaking fan which moved warm air lethargically around the room, just enough to keep the mosquitoes in flight:-

> *'Unable to sleep very well on account of the noise I decided I would brave the heat and humidity and turn off the fan. I did so, but the noise continued. I was experiencing, for the first time, what was to became a very familiar sound, the relentless nocturnal chorus of frogs and ground crickets.'*

Air Travel

After the war, there was rapid development of air services to West Africa by BOAC. By the mid 1950s it had become the standard way to travel to and return from leave in Europe, though many would take the sea route for their first journey out, or their last journey home, in order to accompany their heavy baggage.

The first aircraft seen in Kaduna had been in about 1930. It was a small, private aeroplane and the pilot took people up for 10 shillings a flight. Not long after that the intrepid Duchess of Bedford was flying in Northern Nigeria and caused a stir when she landed at Potiskum market. In 1936 there was an Imperial Flying Boat Service down the Nile to South Africa and a weekly link to it, by de Havilland 12-seater, to Nigeria and the Gold Coast. Proposals were being made for internal air services and the formation of Kano and Lagos Flying Clubs, but the austerity which accompanied the approach of World War II put a stop to the plans.

The Avro York, a development of the Lancaster bomber, was the first on the trans-Sahara route to Kano in 1947 and was succeeded by the Hermes. From London it flew to Frankfurt, Rome or Madrid, then on to a stop at Tripoli in Libya before going on to Kano. Argonauts, British versions of the Douglas DC6, went into service after the Hermes, and by 1958 Boeing Stratocruisers *(Photo. 131)*, which had an intimate little bar down a winding staircase, and flying at a stately 180 knots, were in service with BOAC. By 1960 the elegant turbo-prop Bristol Britannia was in use on the service, followed by the finest of them all, the Vickers VC-10, the first jet to operate the London-Kano-Lagos route, the range and speed of the last two making the stop at Tripoli unnecessary.

Unlike the journey by sea via Lagos, the problem with flying to Northern Nigeria direct was that there was no gradual transition. After the coolness of the flight across the desert the aircraft descended through the hot turbulent air, the doors opened, and heat, dust and smells of a very different world burst in. Suddenly, there was Kano, a faraway place, where at first it appeared nothing had changed for centuries. From there the usual destinations were Kaduna or Jos, by internal flights using smaller aircraft. BOAC and later Nigerian Airways operated Herons and DC3s on internal services and these were superseded by turbo-prop Fokker F27s and twin-engined jet aircraft. There is something legendary about internal flying in the extremes of the seasons in Nigeria and aeronautical tales of hair-raising experiences abound.

Up-country Journey by Train

For those arriving in Nigeria by sea and heading directly for the north, the journey was more transitional, generally made by train *(Photo.128)*; a journey of about 24 hours to Kaduna, and another 12 if the destination was Jos. Leaving Lagos by boat-train, the scenery for hour after hour was of deep forest and very thick green bush, interspersed with plantations of palms and bananas and farm clearings, and small villages with palm-thatched roofs. Reaching Ibadan, capital of the Western Region, a vast, low, undulating sprawl of rusty tin roofs appeared; the most populous of all cities in Africa bar Johannesburg. During the night the train travelled out of the forests into less dense bush into the Northern Region at Offa, then crossed the River Niger on the Jebba Bridge *(Photo.129)*. By dawn the savannah country had been reached, thinly populated and with views of distant, spectacular inselberg-like mountains, most of them already explored by surveyors. Occasionally the train stopped at a small station, which would immediately burst into life with a crowd of jostling food sellers, several at each window of the train, all apparently offering the same articles to the passengers. The noise of animated exchanges would not abate until the train moved out, some transactions still in progress as it gathered speed. Many felt that the true North wasn't reached until the train pulled into Minna or Kaduna Junction.

Keith Sargeant recalls his up-country journey in 1939 :-

> 'After two nights on the train we reached Kaduna Junction in time to have breakfast with Tavener (Assistant Director for the Northern Region) and then Jack continued his train journey to Jos on the Bauchi Plateau. I stayed with Tav (as he was affectionately called) for three days, collecting survey instruments, tent, etc., and engaging the steward boy and cook who would look after me. By now, I was becoming embarrassed by all the hospitality received which I was unable to return, but when I mentioned this to my host I was told not to worry - "Your turn will come" (and it did many years later).'

Clifford Rayner writes of his introduction to the North in 1956:-

> 'We spent two nights in the Ikoyi Rest House, during which time we all received our 'marching orders'; Gilfoyle to Jos, Tozer to Zaria and Wilkie and me to Kano approximately 700 miles to the North and taking 37 hours, by train. In the event the train journey was quite enjoyable, hot but by the time we reached Kano and ready to disembark discovered that Kano was even hotter. We were met by Henry Cotton, formerly an O.S. surveyor, and for two weeks we sweated it out at the Airport Hotel; air conditioning in the bar only. It was still very much the 'dry season' and the daily chore of 'smalls washing', with no exaggeration, dried in about 10 to 15 minutes.
>
> After two weeks I moved out of the Airport Hotel and into No.3 Ikoyi Terrace. Its previous resident, Hugh Peake, had been posted to Maiduguri. The house was mud built and consequently was refreshingly cool during the daytime. But at night it was a different story. Alan stayed on at the Airport and eventually was posted to Katsina.'

Kenneth Toms continues his memoirs with the following account of his arrival in Lagos and his journey up-country:-

> 'With immigration business completed on the upper deck, we disembarked and passed through customs in one of the large wharf sheds. Crkvenac had the necessary routine for gaining entry for his collection of big game rifles well organised. Apart from the standard tropical kit purchased at Army and Navy Stores in London, I had nothing much to declare and passed through quickly.
>
> Situated on two islands connected by causeways and bridges, Lagos is Nigeria's chief port. In its early days it was a notorious slave market. In 1957 it was a steamy crowded city. I was not to get to know it until the following year, as we were taken by the Northern Region agent straight to the railway station. There we boarded the train for the 600-mile trip to Jos.
>
> During the colonial age the British had made a great thing out of building railways in the territories under their control. Nigeria was no exception. The line from Lagos ran northwards to the border with French West Africa on the fringe of the Sahara Desert. It linked Lagos to Ibadan and Kaduna, the capitals respectively of the Western and Northern Regions. Branch lines ran from Kaduna to Zaria, Kano, Kaura Namoda and Nguru in the far north. A southbound line from Kaduna reached down to Enugu, the Eastern region capital and on to Port Harcourt in the Niger Delta. The branch to Jos forked from the Enugu line at a place called Kafanchan at the foot of the Plateau.

The Nigerian Railways were not in the same speed league as the European systems. They ranked well enough though, with their Australian counterparts. It took us two days to reach Jos from Lagos. The ten-coach train, hauled by a handsome steam loco, was comfortable enough. We had sleeping berths, and there was a restaurant car for meals.

There can be no doubt that rail travel is the best way to be introduced to a new country. We passed thorough the tropical forest and cocoa and coffee plantations of the coastal hinterland, stopping at countless village sidings, towns and Ibadan, the largest city in West Africa. Indeed, with a population of half a million, it was supposed to be the largest negro city on the African continent. At a tiny whistle stop named Itori, pot-bellied children gazed at us in awe. I was later to learn that their condition was countrywide and is due to malaria, a disease endemic to that part of the world.

We crossed the Niger at a place called Jebba. The great river flowed deep and green below the massive steel bridge that served both rail and road (Photo.129). From thereon we entered the savannah lowlands typical of the Northern Region. Yellow rivers ran sluggishly across the lightly treed plains. Villages of mud huts and grass thatched roofs were a common sight. Although the sky was overcast with heavy cloud, it was very hot as we traversed the long route to Kaduna.

Gordon Colton left us at Kaduna. It was to be his home for two years. Crkvenac and I were met at the station by senior officers from our respective departments. My man was Douglas Charles Eva DFC, an expatriate Australian who held the post of Principal Topographic Surveyor in the Northern Nigerian Survey, as our Division of the Ministry of Land and Survey was known. We shared a Star beer from the restaurant car refrigerator, and Doug filled me in on some of the details of my posting to Jos. My superior officer would be Principal Surveyor Denis Willey and my appointment would be as Provincial Surveyor, Plateau Province. It seemed that this was a plum posting. Although only ten degrees north of the Equator, Jos was at an altitude of some 4,000 feet above sea level. It thus enjoyed the best microclimate in a very hot country.

Early the next morning the train, after lumbering up the steep grades to the top of the Plateau (Photo.130), pulled into Jos Station. Denis Willey was there to meet me. The long journey from England was over.'

The writer recalls his journey to the North in 1957:-

'At Minna station a man was busily at work with a hacksaw, cutting a large, hard yellowish-brown object which was held firmly in a vice. It took me a while to realise it was dried fish ! The journey was slow and dirty, and there was a three or four hour wait at Kaduna Junction. Surveyors before me had memories of being met by the Director with the offer of having a bath and a meal during this waiting period, and I was no exception. I was met by Keith Sargeant and Frank Woods. Keith took me off to his bungalow where he and his wife Alicia served very welcome and civilised tea. My destination was Jos, an overnight journey from Kaduna.'

Arrival

A newly appointed surveyor usually ended his outward journey at Kaduna, Jos, or perhaps Kano. After a fortnight of relaxation as a cosseted passenger on board ship, his new life began in earnest. New experiences came crowding in as the up-country train jolted to a halt at its destination. Pandemonium, confusion and shouting broke out as a throng of excited people surged forward to meet their friends and relations; the new arrival's first experience of the people amongst whom he would be working, and perhaps his first personal encounter with Africa.

Amidst the crowd meeting the writer's train at Jos at 5.30 in the morning there was, understandably at this early hour, no white face to provide a welcome and initial support:-

'Help was at hand in the form of a small, ragged group of wiry-looking men, indistinguishable to me from the rest, apart from the fact that they seemed to be under the limited control of a khaki-uniformed headman wearing a brass Survey Department badge on his grimy bush hat.

"Welly-come, sah" he said, with a big smile.

Obviously he had a greater command of English than any of his men. Their greetings came in Hausa, a language I had never heard before. English seemed of little use. I felt vulnerable and an obvious and easy target for the unscrupulous.

It was, therefore, with some misgiving that I saw, first my hand luggage, and then from the baggage car at the rear of the train, my shiny boxes and packages, bearing the tropical outfitters' labels, lifted with surprising nonchalance to the heads of these men. They made off with them at speed, steering a passage through the throng, shouting something that sounded like "Gafara ! Ku ba mu hanya !" (Look out ! Make way for us !).

My apprehension turned out to be totally unfounded. In less time than it used to take to hail a British Railways porter at Liverpool Street station, everything and everybody were aboard a decrepit old Survey Ford pick-up truck, driven by a notorious scoundrel called Ishiola, which then rattled and wheezed its way through the unfamiliar, but surprisingly colourful and spacious town and park-like residential area, to Paul Ward's house where another welcome and a good breakfast were waiting. Later that day I met the other expatriate staff of the Jos office, Denis Willey, Ian Gilfoyle, John Street and Henry Wythe'.

As for so many others before, the writer's chosen itinerant lifestyle now began. Four days were spent in the basic, but comfortable Jos Catering Rest House; three days in a flat as the guest of John Street; ten days in an unfurnished rest house at Bukuru, ten miles from Jos, sleeping on a camp bed for the first time; seven days at the Jos Leave Camp *(Photo.83)*, a compound of 'rondavels', originally established as a military camp; and then off to bush for more than six months in a tent.

MAKING A START

Health

Having arrived safely, and with reasonable luck in good health, not yet perhaps having noticed any mosquitoes or suffered any of the ailments about which so many warnings had been sounded, it was important to take precautions, not the least of which were to ensure that drinking water had been boiled and that ice cubes had not been made from water which had come straight from the well.

Quoting Keith Sargeant:-

'During and after the war, there were still many hazards. Inoculation against yellow fever was essential and all Europeans were required to take a prophylactic against malaria - at first quinine, then mepacrine (which turned one's skin yellow) and subsequently paludrine. Other precautions included mosquito nets and, after dark, long sleeves, trousers and mosquito boots. The last named were long leather or canvas boots, usually worn without socks, to protect the ankles which mosquitoes particularly liked to bite. It was advisable to shake the boots before putting them on in case a scorpion was hiding inside!

In spite of all precautions some Europeans seemed to succumb to tropical ailments more readily than others. I recall on my first tour, after only two weeks in bush on topo survey, I had arranged to meet another surveyor (Biddlecombe) working on the adjoining map-sheet - we hoped to spend Easter together. When I mentioned this to my headman (Jatto) he said, "Massa, you no go see um, he done die." He had heard by bush telegraph, and later I was told officially that he had died very suddenly from cerebral malaria. The poor chap was nearing the end of his first tour and was due to go on leave within a few weeks. It was a significant object lesson and afterwards I never once omitted to take the malaria tablet.

The attitude to the tropical sun changed over the years. Before the war, a pith helmet - worn between 10am and 4pm - was regarded as absolutely essential. During my first few days in bush I remember being severely ticked off by my senior officer for not wearing my helmet when leaving the shelter of my tent for a few minutes to "see Africa" (euphemism for spending a penny!). During the later stages of the war, the sun became regarded in a more friendly manner and helmets were very rarely worn by Northern Nigerian Surveyors, being usually replaced by felt hats.'

In addition to malaria, the most common risks, some much more common than others, came from dysentery, hepatitis, cholera, prickly heat, sunstroke, solar keratosis, and skin cancers, but the days of sun helmets and spine pads had gone forever. 'Bush sores' (caused by infected bites from the wide variety of aggressive insects and the constant exposure to minor cuts from cutting grass, poisonous fronds and thorn bush) were a common problem for the surveyor in the bush and iodine and Dettol were essential constituents of his medical box. There were inevitably concerns about poisonous snakes, spiders, centipedes and scorpions *(Photo.197)* but, although everyone has stories to tell, few were ever victims. Much more dangerous and common were parasitic insects and, in the bush, dangerous plants, bees, wasps, sandflies and tsetse flies. The cantharides, or blister bug, was extremely common in some parts, especially amongst tall crops at harvest time in the far north. The chief potential killers were mosquito-borne diseases like malaria and yellow fever and those carried in water or by flies, sleeping sickness, tick fever, sandfly fever, typhoid, bacillary dysentery and amoebic dysentery, together with blackwater fever, the final result of cumulative attacks of malaria and of the massive doses of quinine which in the past had been used to deal with each one. There was exposure to elephantiasis, also carried by mosquitoes, smallpox, cerebro-spinal meningitis, rabies, tumbu-fly and Guinea worms, though they were generally avoidable with slight care and common sense. It was unwise to walk through streams in bare feet. To do so was to court the real danger of contracting bilharzia, a particularly nasty disease transmitted by water snails.

There was also something commonly known as 'Harmattan sickness'. It might be imagined that the relief from the heat and humidity of the wet season would be welcomed, but for many the dry wind from the desert brought its own discomforts. Lung infections and inflammation of the eyes were caused by airborne dust and parasites.

A monotonous diet could be a debilitating hardship and could make life difficult and dangerous. Insufficient importance was perhaps ascribed to this aspect of a new surveyor's life and little advice and assistance was offered or available. In the bush, diet was apt to consist of scraggy hens, small eggs, onions, yams, and corn-on-the-cob, but often little in the way of fresh meat, fruit and green vegetables. Both meat and milk could be unhygienic and dangerous. 18 months of eating largely canned food could make one tired and debilitated. The recovery when on home leave was usually swift and dramatic. It was extremely important to pay attention to the boiling of water and the use and maintenance of water filters.

It was important to maintain good health in remote places where medical aid was unobtainable and surveyors needed to maintain physical endurance, mental stability and concentration. Those who could not withstand a certain amount of heat and discomfort were very unhappy, but very few such people opted to go to Africa in the first place. It was important either way to conform conscientiously to the basic rules of health but, inevitably, there were numerous occasions when, for the sake of convenience, one 'took a chance'. Arnold Voshaar recalls:-

> 'Once when I was crossing, at mid-day, a wide river, sitting on three big calabashes, which were tied together, I fainted. I had sunstroke. The boys swam swiftly and brought me to the riverside. They threw a lot of water over my head. I set up a camp and after one day I felt recovered, but with a headache.
>
> Ever since my time in Nigeria, I have been using Marmite on my slice of bread every morning. I was told vitamin B is important, in particular in the tropics. Two sources were advised. Beer or Marmite. It was impossible to carry beer into the bush, so I decided to take many pots of Marmite with me. At first I did not like the taste at all.
>
> Other than these two incidents and some problems with malaria, I was lucky to have no trouble with my health.'

It went almost without saying that it was vital, for the man who spent the greater part of his working day walking, to pay great attention to the care of his feet and his footwear. Psychological needs received scant consideration, the demanding lifestyle, the frustrations and the pressures of work schedules could lead to stresses for individuals and in family relationships. If it was assumed that the warnings sounded in the little green Colonial Office booklet applied largely to those working in the bush, then those in the towns were asked to note that *"In the tropics small and perhaps trivial things have a tendency to loom into disproportionate size when the mind is tired, and it is a good rule to cast away all office cares before retiring for the night. Anything short of this often spells disaster".* Justification indeed for some of the drinking which went on. Surveying work in the field, or in an office environment, called for self-denial and attention to fitness and general health. Surveyors in the bush had good opportunities for a sane and sober existence, or quite the reverse if they so wished, free of many of the risks and pressures of the conventions of life in the towns.

Introductions and First Jobs

Introductions to expatriate working colleagues and their wives were probably the first part of the settling-in process for new arrivals and an exploratory first round of evening drinks the first introduction to social life. The first few working days invariably involved a visit to the Survey Office, meeting Nigerian colleagues and junior staff for the first time, the appointment of a survey team, task briefing, drawing instruments and equipment from the store, arranging personal banking, store accounts and transport, and even a little surveying. Public transport was virtually non-existent and departmental vehicles, which could only normally be driven by Nigerians, were not available for private use.

The newcomer would be the subject of polite curiosity by junior staff, with greetings spoken in the Hausa tongue to which, at first, nothing but an English "hello" could be given in reply, or perhaps a simple "Sannu", the first word of Hausa learned by many. It was at this time, without it being realised, that his Hausa nickname may already have been decided by the labourers and chainmen; something descriptive, but not always very complimentary, which they would keep to themselves ! (*mai gemu* - the bearded one, *mai lofi* - the man with the pipe, *yaron ba hankali* - the careless boy, *mai fuskan jaki* - him with the donkey's face, *mai dogon wando* - he who wears long trousers, *dan iska* - the troublemaker, *mai tashin hankali* - he who makes careful preparations, etc.)

Familiarity with the names, ranks and other details of members of the Department, and all the other Government Departments, could be gained from the current copy of the officially published Staff List. These annual government publications were and still are a useful key to seniority, date of appointment, and date of birth. Quoting Keith Sargeant:-

> *'One of the more interesting Government publications was the annual staff list. This listed all the "senior service" officers for each department in order of seniority, giving dates of first appointment. promotion (if any), posting and dates of birth. Actually, the dates of birth of the relatively few females were always omitted except on one famous occasion when the compiler made a mistake and printed this confidential information . . .   The issue was quickly withdrawn but some copies escaped and became collectors' pieces!'*

Appendix III lists senior and junior colleagues in the Northern Nigerian Survey and others who spent much time in the North in the post-war period, while *Appendix IV* lists ranks.

Harry Rentema's first work in 1952 involved the surveying of mining leases, moving around mostly on foot:-

> *'I prepared for my bushwork: survey of mining leases on the Jos Plateau. I inspected my bush-outfit, got my tent demonstrated by my 15 labourers and chainman Liman Zakare (Photo.135), the only member of my gang who spoke English.*
>
> *I engaged a cook and a steward and bought a book "Helps in the study of Hausa". After some days a truck took my labourers, equipment (theodolite, umbrella, chain, maps and fieldbooks) and tent to my first job. Keith Sargeant introduced me to a tin-miner.*
>
> *The work was simple: traversing and closing with a sun-azimuth. And so we moved from one opencast mine to another, mostly walking, sometimes by the tin-miner's car. I learned that it was wise to send a messenger ahead to the next mining lease to act as a guide for us because the maps were very poor and incomplete and during one of my first moves I lost my way. Once a month I came to Jos to bring my work, get new instructions, and buy new supplies. Keith came to see me sometimes. After work I spent most of the time working out the observations, having contact with the miners and the Sarkin Gida, paperwork, learning Hausa and enjoying silence and the drums in the distance. Also new to me was the medical care for the labourers and the villagers. Sometimes terrible swellings caused by accidents or former operations by the local barber/surgeon, or somebody who stepped in a leopard trap and came bandaged with an old dirty cloth and leaves. Iodine, ointment and white bandage or aspirin and paludrine did wonders, and I always had a lot of patients.*
>
> *Jos is well situated on a plateau, at an altitude of 1300 m, and had all the essential shops for the 1,000 Europeans: a club for the Colonials, tennis courts, swimming pool and a bar of course, but no music or other cultural happenings. It was always nice meeting people again in Jos but after some days I longed to go back to my tent and my own men.*
>
> *My kitchen was made from two empty kerosene tins and an iron plate and my cook managed to make excellent bread and cake. We bought our firewood, and water was carried from the river. The steward looked after me well: tea in the morning and a lot to drink after a day's work, and a warm bath. In the evening my watchman (Photo.133) settled himself in front of the tent, with his bow and arrows (poisoned) standing by and lighting his pipe.*

In the north we had Moslem Hausas who were usually farmers and traders; Fulanis, who were nomadic cattle people, and primitive pagans, whose women wore little but leaves (Photo.82). Their jobs were collecting firewood, carrying water, cooking, farming and raising children (a woman cost about £10). The men wore penis sheaths and spent their time farming, hunting (although there was not much left to hunt) and sitting under the palaver tree in the village. '

John Street remembers how work began for him:-

'It was less than a week after I arrived in Jos, and already my new De Soto was parked in the bush with a watchman to look after it. I was supposed to start re-establishing, identifying, preparing and extending a set of trigonometrical points in this wilderness.

The tent went up and nobody asked me anything about that; the cook went to work and it was clear he and the 'small boy' would get fed but, since we had no common language, my position appeared ambiguous.

I unpacked my personal things and placed them in a row, trying to ignore the heat. Suddenly, there was a sharp explosion as my shaving brush (made from stressed plastic ?) disintegrated.

I was hungry, but worse, very dirty and dusty. Where and how to wash ? With some trepidation I went to my new fat Hausa dictionary, compiled by Bargery - (bring: 'kawo', bath: 'wanka'), called Bayero, my cook, and said it. Then, heaven; a huge smile and a large tub of hot water arrived and a table was set on which food magically appeared - so I could survive.

Audu Gora, my headman, arrived later to talk about tomorrow. It was a triangle of two strangers and me, which I learned to trust completely, and which for years never let me down. Within a week I was part of a team.'

Clifford Rayner recalls his early experiences after arriving in Kano in 1956:-

'Henry Cotton was an excellent mentor. First things first; awaiting our arrival in Kano were a brand new Wild T2 theodolite and a Facit calculating machine. We signed for these even before we were settled into a house! These two items without which a surveyor could not exist were our responsibility for as long as we remained with NNS. And so it was; the T2 became a trusted 'friend' and was indeed a most excellent instrument. I recall meeting someone who joined NNS after I had left and on introduction remarked "Ah.... Cliff Rayner... I was issued with your T2 ! " Such was the regard with which these Universal 1" instruments were held.

Henry taught both Alan and me to drive and we soon had our own vehicles, De Soto kit cars. These served us well. I sold mine nine years and about 90,000 miles later. He also dissipated the awe with which I held any kind of sun or star observations. One morning, on arrival at the office, during my early shadowing days prior to having a vehicle of any kind, Henry declared "I need to get some gin from Kingsway store , but before I do that I have a morning sun azimuth to observe, it won't take long." It was like going to the hardware counter for some minor purchase, it was so matter of fact. Witnessing the routine convinced me that there was nothing to it! How true that was became a reality later. However, no sooner than we were mobile we could get down to some serious work. I was given some chain survey detailing at Tudun Wada, adjacent to the airport road. Next followed the setting out of a small residential sub-division at Nassarawa. Both good experience with attention to detail which would become essential for my later assignments.

When Henry went on leave he was replaced by Frank Waudby-Smith another ex-Bristol man, who had recently been in Benue with a precise levelling team. He was glad to be in station and promptly, well almost promptly, sent me to bush for the first time. I made my way to the government rest house at Funtua. Isa Mura was my chainman and he stayed with me for most of my days in bush. What was required in and around Funtua was the beaconing and surveying of Cotton Seed Store sites. Bearing in mind that most of these were in places more remote than I had ever experienced, it seemed a trifle pedantic to set concrete beacons in positions to the nearest 0. 1 foot and 1' arc. Such are the ways of government and I remember to this day the plot dimensions of 60.5 yards by 80.0 yards to give a plot exactly one acre in extent. I was later to learn on numerous occasions that common sense logic does not always determine policy decisions reached by administrators! However these surveys gave me good experience in setting out and stood me in good stead for later photo control surveys of a much more extensive kind and required me to take off to remote villages, make camp and generally learn to be more self-sufficient.

I remember we had a bit of a job sorting out the bits and erecting the tent for the first time, at Maska, - practice makes perfect!

From a letter to home at about the time:-

....Well I didn't know a thing about Maska so I took the tent and hurried to the place. We got there about 5.20 by what time it was getting very near sunset. Having never in my life ever put up a tent, I wasn't really qualified to either direct or even assist operations. So I left it to my head man. We had 3 bundles any one of which may have been the 'guts' of the tent. However we laid <u>everything</u> out and had a good look at it before deciding what was what. If the truth were known I believe the labourers were at a bit of a loss. Anyway we were able to get the one bundle sorted out and began putting it up. The other two were a ground sheet and something else which I still can't fathom. The labourers used the latter as a bed cum blanket! By this time of course it was dark and no moon! Here the sun sets very fast and there is precious little dusk. So with the help of a Tilley lamp we completed the erection of the tent. We pitched camp on the cotton seed site - so I was really on the job. It was very fortunate to be able to have the car with us for its side lights (remember its an American thing) gave plenty of light for Ali to work by. To save kerosene I cooked by wood. After about 1.5 hours after sun down we were all settled. I had the wireless going and was feeling very relieved that everything turned out OK. Incidentally there were no pegs with the tent so one of the boys had to go and cut about 30 by the light of an ordinary oil lamp. Of course I christened my camp bed and chair as well. Life in the Rest House is comparative luxury - its amazing how one's standards drop!

I was soon to get very used to pitching camp! '

In his personal memoirs Kenneth Toms describes his arrival and settling into his new post at Jos:-

'Newcomers to a station in Nigeria were usually accommodated in a government rest house while their housing was being sorted out. There were two such establishments in Jos; the Catering Rest House itself and the Hill Station. Hill Station was more like a three star country hotel with all modern conveniences. Only very senior officers were temporarily accommodated in Hill Station, I was told. Consequently, Denis Willey had booked me into the Rest House for a fortnight. I had no reason to complain. It was a modern building, the rooms were spacious with ceiling fans and the food was good. Crkvenac had gone straight off to his station, and apart from several transitory guests, I had the place to myself.

I was a little disconcerted to be told by the manageress that a previous occupant of my room had died of polio not so long before. I rummaged in my kit for the little green book entitled "Hints on the Preservation of Health in Tropical Countries" that had been issued to me by the Crown Agents before leaving England. That excellent publication led off by stating that it had been prepared with a view towards giving candidates appointed to the Government services of the tropical and sub-tropical territories some acquaintance with the principles to be observed in avoiding the more common diseases to which they are likely to be exposed. It was silent on polio, but it dealt at length with a whole array of other communicable diseases, malaria, blackwater and yellow fever, sleeping sickness, dysentery, typhoid, the list went on and on. According to an "old coaster" in the Rest House, all of these maladies were rampant in Nigeria. Obviously, we would have to be very careful.

Amongst other general hints was included "Alcohol in moderation is neither essential nor harmful ... it is wise to take no spirits before sundown ... The cocktail party prolonged till nine o'clock and later, improves neither the dinner nor the digestion."

Jos was a pleasant African township. Its main street was lined with giant trees that made me feel a little homesick. They were eucalypts that would have graced a Gippsland forest. The shops included a "supermarket" called Kingsway and Chellarams', an Indian general store. There was a post office of some magnitude and a movie theatre (Illustration 80). On a prominent rise at the end of Tudun Wada Road was the Hill Station. That side of the town contained most of the expatriate housing, both government and commercial. To the south was the African quarter. There was a European hospital and an African hospital. Some way out the Bukuru Road was Jos airport.

Most of the "white collar" jobs in government and commerce were held by either Yoruba people from the Western Region or Ibos from the Eastern Region. One would be served in the Post Office, for example, by a smiling person from Enugu. The senior clerk in the Resident's office could be a gentleman from Ibadan in the Western Region. This situation had arisen from the lower standard of education in the North, where colonial policy had favoured the continuation of Islamic education procedures in the school system. While the Hausa or Fulani child was wise in the ways of the Koran, he lacked the "three R's" that had been brought to the southern part of the country by the missionaries. The imbalance was to lead to grave problems in the sixties after the independent Federation of Nigeria had come into being.

The Survey Headquarters in Jos was a large establishment. Overseen by Principal Surveyor Willey, it included the Minesfield Cadastral Office under Senior Surveyor Paul Ward and the Provincial Surveyor's Office. The operations of the latter were divided geographically. The Provincial Surveyor (North) was a lanky Dane, Jorgen Jensen (Photo. 15). The southern part of the Province was looked after by Arnold Voshaar(Photo.13), a Dutch surveyor. The Minesfield Cadastral Office staff included a young Britisher named John Street. John was in charge of the development of a scheme of revision of the mining cadastral maps of the whole Region.

So we had a real league of nations as far as the expatriates were concerned. It seemed paradoxical that the British Colonial Service should employ so many people from the Continent. The African staff included a number of survey assistants, chainmen and labourers for the field operations. The office support staff (all African) included draftsmen, clerks and messengers. I noted that the great majority of skilled and semiskilled people were Ibos or Yorubas.

Denis briefed me on the role of Provincial Surveyor (North), Plateau Province. I would take over from Jensen, who would be going on transfer to Yola on Nigeria's second great river, the Benue. My main responsibilities would lie in the supervision of cadastral (boundary) surveys for mining land titles. According to Denis Willey, this was a most important function of his office. Not only did tin and rare mineral mining contribute largely to the Nigerian national income, the associated survey fees helped to pay our salaries. Denis made a big thing about that. Of course there would be other duties. These could include provision of photogrammetric mapping ground control, detail survey to fill in existing topographic mapping, triangulation break-down, it was a long list.

Nigeria was on the way to emancipation. All African subordinate officers in the Service had to be addressed as Mister. Thus I had to remember to call the storeman, Mr Yoheziwe, the chief clerk, Mr Gomez, my senior survey assistant, Mr Ononye and so on. The chainmen, as befitting their rank were addressed by the Hausa honorific of Malam. I was assigned an elderly senior chainman, one Malam Buka. He, in turn, addressed me as bature (European). The labourers went by their full names; Idi Yola, Dan Asme and so on, the second name denoting the person's place of origin. In retrospect, the formality was not out of place.

A decision was finally made by the Provincial administration on my housing allocation. The process was, of course, ruled by a seniority pecking order. New appointees, generally, were low on the list. I was no exception. I was allocated a

Survey quarter in the township of Bukuru, on the railway a few miles south of Jos township. When I saw the house, I was very glad that Susan had bided a while in England. It was a large African mud hut with a thatched roof that leaked badly. I had never lived in a round house, and although there were a number of rooms, a circumscribing verandah, electric light, a refrigerator and it was reasonably clean, it was a bit of a shock to the system. And, for the time being, I was stuck with it.

The next thing to do was to engage a cook. The word gets around that a new bature is in town, and a white-robed Mohammadu Zaria duly arrived at the Rest House with a sheaf of tatty references. Momo was a small Hausa man with a disarming grin and some English. I took him on as cook and set up house in Bukuru.

There was another Survey house in the same district, about half a mile from mine. It was occupied by Arnold Voshaar and his wife Ria(Photo.81). Arnold was about to complete his tour and return to Holland on leave. It was very pleasant to walk across to the Voshaars in the late afternoon, and sip Bols gin with them on their front verandah.

Headquarters occupied a site that looked out onto the Plateau across the railway line. The buildings were substantial enough. It seemed that Paul Ward had built the most recent of them with Survey labour and the African masons. The main duties of the latter were to construct the cement block pillars on the minor triangulation points that were scattered about the Plateau countryside.

Outside each office door squatted a messenger. To see one of those people in action for the first time was quite an experience. On being handed a document for delivery from say Denis to Paul, he would remove his cap, place the sheet of paper on his head, secure it by weighting it with a stone and trot the few yards to Paul's office where he would remove the weight and hand over the missive with due ceremony. I was soon to learn that the African, male or female, if he or she had to carry anything whatsoever, it would be carried as a "head load".

Next to a house and a cook, the most pressing need of the new appointee was the acquisition of a vehicle. All officers were required to provide their own transport. To that end, Government would advance an interest free loan. A reasonable mileage allowance was paid for duty running. It was a good arrangement for the officer and Government, but the loan would only be approved for the purchase of a conveyance appropriate to the officer's rank and duties. For surveyors like myself, the approved vehicle was a "kitcar", or what we would call in Australia, a "utility".

There was always a fair turnover of used vehicles as Government and commercial people came and went on the relatively short duty tours. I decided to buy a new vehicle and opted for a Standard Vanguard kitcar. The chief engineer of the United Trading Company assured me that the Vanguard was second only to the Peugeot 304 in coping with the corrugated laterite roads of the Northern Region. I took his word for it, and discovered later that, by and large, he was right.

Then there was the matter of applying for membership of a club. Much of the social life of the expatriate community ranged about club activity. There was the Plateau Club in Jos itself. It was rather a formal establishment, and on someone's advice, perhaps Paul Ward's, I applied to join the Anglo-Jos Club that was situated out of town in the mining area. It was cheaper than the Plateau Club. Importantly, for expatriate males at least, it possessed two excellent snooker tables. In addition it offered the Government officer the opportunity to meet people from the extensive mining community.

Some weeks after my arrival, I awoke one morning feeling distinctly queer. Before the day was out, I was stricken with very severe diarrhoea known as "Jos Tummy". The following day I drove with some difficulty to see Dr Ralph Branch, the Senior Medical Officer in Jos. Without further ado he admitted me to the hospital, where, after a few days of good treatment, I recovered and returned to work. It was a most unpleasant ailment.

While in hospital I met Hugh Peake for the first time. Hugh was an English surveyor whose posting was Maidugari, an out-station near the shores of Lake Chad on the eastern side of the country. Hugh had been hospitalised in Jos for some minor operation. I learned that his father, Brigadier Peake, had been the Director of

Military Survey in the United Kingdom. More recently, Peake senior, had served as military attaché in the British High Commission in Ottawa. Hugh had worked with the London-based Directorate of Overseas Surveys in out-of-the-way colonies like the Gambia and Basutoland. He was quite a character and proud of the fact that he was regarded by the Surveyor-General and some of the Resident Commissioners as an "enfant terrible". That, apparently, was the reason for his posting to the most remote station in the region.

I met Hunter, our Surveyor-General, on one of his visits to Jos when he was "on tour" inspecting his minions. He had the reputation of being a hard task master. Any disagreement with the great man, it was said, would lead to a bush posting. Hugh Peake was a good example.

I received some good news from Denis. John Street was to "go bush" on triangulation work in the British Cameroons. His relatively modern flat in Jos would then be allocated to me, and my family would be able to join me forthwith. Life on the Plateau was beginning to shape up.

Later we became friendly with the Jensens and were sad to see them off on transfer to Yola. Their departure meant one thing for us though, and that was a move to the Survey dwelling known as the "Dolls House". On the Tudun Wada Road, it sat nicely amongst huge mango trees in a large compound. It was a real house, and we were very happy to move in from the flat.'

Kenneth Toms' mention of his membership of the Anglo-Jos Club reminds the writer of an occasion when he was invited there by Ken and his wife Susan, and the sense of humour of one of the Ibo waiters:-

'We decided to order omelettes for lunch.
The waiter returned from the kitchen to inform Ken,
"Very sorry, sah, dere no be enough egg for three omelette, only two "
"Oh, that's O.K." said Ken "I'll have a sandwich instead"
A while later the same waiter appeared at our table carrying a tray with three delicious omelettes.
"I thought you said there weren't enough eggs" said Ken
"Sah, de cook ee done squeeze de chicken".'

Domestic Staff

For those who had never previously lived and travelled abroad, let alone in the tropics amongst strange cultures, there was a lot to do in a short period of time soon after arrival, many adjustments to make, and much to learn. Many of our Nigerian hosts knew little of the expatriates' background, expected too much, too soon, but were very capable of spotting a greenhorn when one appeared, and not slow to take advantage ! Decisions which could have a major influence on comfort, efficiency, health and general well-being, were usually aided by those who had similar experiences themselves not so long before. One of the most important was the engagement of a reliable cook, preferably one who spoke a little English, who could make all the difference between harmony and perpetual discomfort, particularly if there was to be little opportunity to find alternative domestic help after an early departure for a lengthy spell in remote places in bush. In town, or in bush, bachelor surveyors inevitably employed a cook upon whom great dependence would be placed. The 'old faithful', long serving ones had a great reputation of benevolence and concern for the well being of their employer.

The writer remembers:-

'Some of the best advice I ever received was to get good domestic staff and, once they had proved themselves, keep them. After beginning with long spells in the bush with second-rate cooks I eventually took on a man recommended to me who had 'retired' after service with the Army in Burma in World War II and with other expatriates. His name was Mohammadu Bauchi (Photo.132), and he was without

doubt the most loyal and devoted employee I ever had in Nigeria, and would often be at Kano Airport, unsummoned, to await my return from leave. He stayed with me for 15 years and was with me when the Northern Nigerian Survey came to an end in 1968 and I was posted to the NE State to work in his hometown, Bauchi. Age eventually began to get the better of him and, when my wife joined me, I purchased a house for him in the town and gave him a retirement income. His loyalty was such, however, that in spite of his deteriorating health, he just did not wish to sit down and do nothing, but would turn up at our house willing to work, and even followed us to Maiduguri for my final posting in Nigeria in 1976. I never ceased to be amazed at the ability of Mohammadu to quickly turn a meal for one into a meal for several when unexpected guests arrived. The arrival of a visitor's car and the off-loading of luggage was an automatic signal for him to start preparing without being prompted.'

Those arriving to work in station, rather than in bush, had better opportunities to 'shop around' a bit for suitable domestic employees. They were the Nigerians that many expatriates, especially non-working wives, would come to know and remember best, to whom they were often very patronising, but with whom good relationships were usually established. Many of them were not without their faults, but they performed their thankless tasks of cleaning, polishing, washing and ironing religiously and often under quite trying conditions, struggling with English in households where little Hausa was spoken. A cook might do his best to produce a meal at a pre-arranged time, and the steward would await the request to 'pass chop', and both might be kept waiting unreasonably or unexpectedly, but they had a remarkable ability to produce a meal which was not spoiled by quite long delays. Some domestics were undoubtedly lazy and incompetent, but clever enough to take advantage of their position of being close to the personal needs of those new to Nigeria. Tales of domestic mishaps and misunderstandings are legion and were the subject of endless anecdotes. Domestic staff were well practised in the art of recycling. Most of the waste from a European household seemed to have a market value. Nothing was ever wasted. Empty jars, bottles, tins, and old clothing, tyres and paper were all put to secondary use. Little milk tins became small oil lamps, cigarette tins became measures for salt, food tins became cups, and bottles for measures of cooking oil, and four-gallon kerosene tins were perhaps most prized of all for a great range of uses.

Jean Burnside, who was a Town Planner before marrying Clifford Burnside, remembers her domestic staff:-

'I returned to Kaduna in July 1963 but thereafter led a very different life looking after our two daughters until we left Nigeria in January 1966. I had, of course, the big advantage of having three Nigerian domestic staff to help in this early stage of bringing up a family. Cliff's three boys Momo, Usuman and Sale had stayed on after our marriage which, of course, did not always happen when the master was no longer a bachelor. Momo sometimes accompanied me when I had to go on tour as when I went to Sokoto. He reported that I drove very fast along corrugated roads, which he considered to be a characteristic to be encouraged. Momo did leave during our last tour in Kaduna and Usuman took his place as cook, with Sale as steward and one of Sale's young brothers, Ibrahim, recruited as garden boy. Usuman and Sale used to take turns at baby sitting, with Sale taking his responsibilities very seriously coming to tell me if one of the girls made a single sound (we were usually at a bungalow within walking distance). Ibrahim used to come with us when we played tennis before breakfast on a Sunday, looking after Susie and Sarah (in a push chair) while we played. We were very sorry to say goodbye to the boys when we left for good and we corresponded with them for several years after......'

Junior Surveying Staff

The majority of new arrivals were field surveyors, often with limited experience, who would spend their first few tours of duty carrying out field surveys, sometimes in quite remote places. They were often thrown into their first job at the deep end and depended to a considerable degree in the early days upon their junior field assistants, their chainmen (commonly referred to as headmen), their messengers, their labourers and their carriers. Most labourers and many chainmen spoke very little English but practically all expatriate surveyors quickly learned enough Hausa to not only make them understand instructions but to engage in a certain amount of good humoured discourse. One Chainman was convinced that the work of surveyors was mentioned in the Old Testament and was greatly encouraged in his work on bush clearance by the words of Isaiah ch.40 v.3 :-

> "The voice of him (the surveyor) that crieth in the wilderness, Prepare ye
> the way of the Lord, make straight (on the map) in the desert a highway for our God.
> Every valley shall be exalted, and every mountain and hill shall be made low: and
> the crooked shall be made straight, and the rough places plain'

The end result was usually an excellent working relationship, good dependability and that team spirit so essential for much field survey, especially under trying conditions. These tough men carried the equipment and soon learned survey routines, even if they were largely unaware of the reasons for their actions. They aligned ranging rods, set markers and pegs, built beacons and cairns, operated heliographs (*Photos. 134 and 136),* handled tapes and chains and were amazingly vigilant with the instrument umbrella, even when they had to stand for hours in the hot sunshine *(Photo.138).* Some acquired a reputation for inattention, particularly as they tired, a reputation seldom deserved, and some could not accept that, in spite of being the person in charge, the surveyor was not the object to be sheltered from the sun, but his instrument was. Most labourers *(Photo.137)* were assiduous workers, they cleared the surveyors sight lines, felled trees and sometimes mischievously cut growing crops, taunting the defenceless farmer that they were working under the instruction of the surveyor. This practice could however be stamped out by judicious withholding of wages and using the money to compensate the aggrieved farmer, an action which invariably sparked off a lot of leg-pulling and hilarity from the rest of the party.

The marked tribal loyalties of Hausamen were often transferred to the surveyor and they became good employees and advisers. They took pride in his achievements and worked well in a team. They were generally reliable, seldom let their employer down and up to a point seemed to enjoy hard, uncomfortable work, especially with the camaraderie of others. A certain amount of bribery and coercion were natural to him and since everyone in the country expected this sort of thing they did not take exception to it on a limited scale. They had a good sense of humour and a gift for mimicry, especially when making a point about a senior. At the same time they were quite formal in their behaviour and readily accorded the respect which was due to those of a higher rank than themselves or those in public office.

Chainmen were respected by the labourers and might find ways of doing things quite differently to an expatriate; perhaps more harshly, but effectively. They might show very little initiative, and with no great love of hard work, but they were undoubtedly loyal and accepted commands with a resignation typical of Northern people. Unlike labourers, chainmen were usually literate, up to a point, and could be relied upon to write down and remember a few words or figures. One Chainman's inventory of basic equipment included "amburelah, kut-las, aks, pohl, lebbel and taip", accompanied by an interesting drawing of each.

Roughing it under difficult conditions in the bush, most of the carriers, labourers and chainmen showed a degree of tolerance of expatriates' ways, good humour and forbearance that one would seldom come across in Europe. Confronted almost daily by ideas and instructions they did not understand, failing to comprehend why Europeans did so much running around in the hot sun, they invariably coped very well and very cheerfully to boot. Certainly they never seemed to worry unduly, after all, whatever happened was the will of Allah. Certainly they complained if they felt an injustice had been done, but generally, by offering the least resistance, they adopted a natural survival technique which made their lives bearable, if somewhat unfulfilling to European eyes.

Chainmen and Messengers were fundamental to the organisation and it was not uncommon for a surveyor, once he was aware of his deficiencies and idiosyncrasies, to become very dependent upon and closely attached to one of them for a long period. Most who served in Northern Nigeria can remember the names and personalities of those to whom they became attached. They were an ongoing presence whilst many around them came and went. Some had seen long service, sometimes with the

Army, had good memories, and were an asset to the man in the bush trying to find his way around, and to the man in the office wanting to find something, or wanting to know where to buy something in the town. They seemed to know everyone, could spot a bargain or a fraud, were often multi-lingual, and were invariably utterly loyal and reliable and more often than not had a good sense of humour. They wore the Survey badge of office on their uniforms; bold brass badges on which the surveyor's triangle merged with the Northern Star, ringed with the title NORTHERN NIGERIAN SURVEY and surmounted by a crown. The crown was officially deleted after Independence but Chainmen did not feel disposed to remove it from their badges. They also wore miniature versions of this badge on their Australian-style, wide brimmed khaki felt hats. They were guides, companions, personal assistants, mentors and friends. They were not paid high salaries, but might be rewarded by the surveyor for the personal help they gave.

John Street recalls:-

'In five years of bush work I never decided on a camp site. My headman, Audu Gora, who had visited Europe during the war, explained that it was his job and that he was liable for capital punishment if I was killed through his negligence. In those five years I never felt threatened by anyone, experienced incredible help from many local people, and our own people, and never lost any of my personal belongings'.

The writer also remembers some of the headmen with whom he worked:-

'I well remember how wise and useful Audu Gora was for me in my early days in the bush; I remember the alert and astute Saidu Hadejia who travelled with me for thousands of miles; the quiet and good-natured Dogon Marwa, one of the best heliomen we ever had; Tukur Zaria with a prodigious memory for Minesfield beacons; Bello Zabarma, not very bright but would walk 40 miles a day carrying messages, mail and money; the enthusiastic and intelligent young labourer Adeka Katsina Ala whom I promoted to Chainman as soon as he was mature enough to control the older labourers in my party; and Pantami Gombe, my devoted Messenger and companion on many a long and hot journey.'

In some towns, parties of prisoners could often be seen working along the roads and in the residential areas on light manual tasks, like grass cutting. Although potentially useful for some manual work to assist surveyors on special jobs, they were difficult to employ, worked at only one, very slow, pace and were governed by a rather different set of rules. They could sometimes be used for clearance of layout sites if they were within walking distance of the prison. They were always accompanied by a prison warder who, though technically in charge, would often relax or doze off in the shade while the men worked, delegating his responsibilities to the Survey Chainman. There was very little fear of them running away because life in prison was very often more comfortable than life outside and in any case there was little stigma attached to being locked up. If released from prison early, it was not unknown for them to petition to be allowed to return, to enjoy a life where they did not have to find their own food, shelter and clothing, where they did not have to repay debts, and where they were in part at least absolved from the responsibility of having to work to support their families. When, for example, there was wholesale release of prisoners to provide temporary safe accommodation for the harassed Ibos during Kaduna's disturbances in 1966, the prisoners voiced their great displeasure and pressed to be allowed to return as soon as possible. By being locked up they were deprived of very little, even women. The temporary services of women from the town could be obtained by the payment of bribes to the warders, and it was not unknown for leave of absence to be bought in the same way, a welcome and popular source of additional income for prison staff.

Junior office staff like draughtsmen, clerks, storemen, computers and records keepers were sometimes quite remarkable people, often the first in their line ever to move away from a traditional way of life to take up occupations they could never of dreamt of. At home, especially when they went on leave to their hometowns and villages, some stepped back into a totally different world, only a few steps removed from the much simpler existence of their peasant forbears. In one generation some had moved from a rural existence into acceptance of alien technical and educational values, to operate the newest surveying equipment and adopt the disciplined principles of surveying. Their grasp of a particular subject and their abilities could however sometimes hinder their own progress because, content to carry out ordinary tasks in a specialised field with limited prospects of advancement, they might miss the opportunity of progress and promotion available to their contemporaries in other occupations.

Meeting Local People

For the newly arrived expatriate there was a lot to learn about the habits, the spectacle, the customs and the languages of the local people with whom they would inevitably very quickly come into contact as their work commenced. First of all there was the genuine welcome they inevitably received, starting with the polite formality of daily greetings. The European grunt of acknowledgement is no good to the Hausaman. In his courtesy he will devote many minutes to his greetings, even if he has nothing of substance to add to them. The etiquette of greeting was dependent upon the circumstances and the time of the day. One of the shortest exchanges of greetings in the morning, for instance, would be *"Sannu"* (hello) to which would be given the reply *"Sannu"* or *"Yauwa"*. This was followed by *"Lafiya ?*"*(are you well ?), with the reply *"Lafiya lau"* (I'm well, thank-you); *"Ina gajiya ?"* (are you tired ?), *"Ba gajiya"* (I'm not tired); *"Ina gida?"* (How is your family?), *"Lafiya"*; *"To madalla"* (fine). It was very common throughout the day to continue to exchange simple greetings such as *"Sannu maigida". (hello, sir), "Yauwa , Sannu Isa"* (hello Isa).

Then there was the clench-fisted salute; the hand held aloft holding no spear was a symbol of friendship, welcome and respect and so often went with the expression *"Ranka shi dade!"* - "May your life be prolonged"; and the sharing of stimulant kola nuts, in the same way that Europeans might share a drink.

Surveyors and the Hausa Language

The mobile nature of their work often afforded surveyors little chance to absorb more than a superficial knowledge of an area in which they worked and the language and culture of the local people. But in the course of their work they did spend a great deal of time out in the open, under green umbrellas, getting a visually inverted view of Nigeria through the telescopes of their instruments, but generally at eye level with it, thus gaining considerable local tactile knowledge of the country and the everyday life of its people. Most, but certainly not all, acquired a working knowledge of the Hausa language, enough to see them through their work, but few acquired the fluency necessary for an in-depth understanding of the rich cultures of the North. A reminder of some of the everyday words and expressions which many eventually learned is given as *Appendix VI*. Expatriates in other professions often lived a less mobile lifestyle and settled for a whole tour of duty or more in one area and got to know more about the people around them and learn something of languages other than Hausa.

Keith Sargeant comments:-

'Some departments required that expatriate officers should pass a test in an appropriate African language before the end of the probationary period of three years. This did not apply to the original Survey Department because, in those days, surveyors were likely to work in any part of the country. After regionalisation and the formation of the Northern Nigeria Survey there might have been some point in requiring a minimum standard of Hausa which was very widely spoken in the Northern Provinces. However this was not done nor, as far as I know, was it ever suggested. Nevertheless a few NNS surveyors did excel in languages and one (Peter Redwood) passed the higher test in Hausa (HSH). Most of the rest of us picked up sufficient basic Hausa to enable us to communicate with the survey gang.

Apart from the African surveyors who mostly spoke reasonably good English, the use of pidgin English was wide-spread. This took some time for a newcomer to understand. In my early days I remember sending a chainman to see if there was a survey mark on top of a nearby hill. On return his reply was, "Sah! I look um, I find um - I no see um." it took me a while to realise that this meant he had looked in order to find it but had been unsuccessful. A pidgin phrase I particularly liked was to describe something of excellence as "fine pass kerosene" - kerosene being -something very special in primitive areas.'

John Street remembers learning Hausa :-

'Young and single, and enjoying bush travel, I tried to forget my 'defeats' in languages like French and Spanish and, sensing the rules to be flexible, rollicked into Hausa.

As my teachers were primarily labourers from many tribes, my progress was erratic, and I was aided by a large dictionary. There was, however, an incentive in that I got into a town perhaps twice a year and, in Kaduna or Jos, you could take a Hausa exam - and if you passed you got more money (about £40 per annum, I think).

I did the first exam and thought it money for old rope. It was, I think, nearly two more years until my next opportunity - in Jos. I drove to a big house and was ushered into a handsome room with a bay window. A middle-aged man came in and put his arm round my shoulder and walked me to the window. "Tell me what you see" he said, in a rather precise way, in Hausa.

Well this was like meat and drink - all those evenings sitting outside the tent with nothing but trees, fields, ditches, animals, the sky and the bush; all those long discussions with the Chiefs, the Master of the Women, the children, the market, the horses, the hills and the mountains. I just started to talk and talk, and my examiner stood beside me and said nothing. After some apparently long time he said "STOP".

He turned, smiled, and said "You have certainly passed, but can I advise you that, should you be invited to dinner whilst in the station, please don't speak Hausa. You are clearly unaware that much you say is couched in the forms and images learnt from your labourers. I was fascinated by what you said about the ditch and trees, and will happily recommend your increase, but do be aware you swear a lot. Thank you, Mr Street".

Despite living very close to groups of local people, and hearing only Hausa for five years, I still believe it was enormously difficult to understand the labourers' conversations, with their 'childlike' immediacy and laughter, their toleration of pain when fingers were struck whilst setting markers, or limbs badly slashed when clearing bush and, sometimes, their frightening disregard for the hurt of others. Similarly, linguistically, the variations were so numerous, the names of a plant, a tree or a hill so varied, it was much like Britain must have been before the Normans when the spread of written communication demanded a standard method of 'proper' speech.'

David Ball recalls an incident in Kaduna:-

'Birnawa was a small Hausa village within easy walking distance of my house in Kaduna South. Being an increasingly popular commuter settlement it was showing signs of bursting at the seams and the Chief asked for a plan to control its expansion. Early one morning, therefore, armed with a tape, prismatic compass, ranging rods, labourers and Audu my cook-steward as interpreter, I set off along the path leading eastward from the end of Eaglesome Road through the tall grass and scattered trees - typical savannah parkland country - to the village less than a mile away. We heard drums in the distance. "They make war on us, Audu?" I asked. "No, sir!" said Audu with a chuckle. "Dey makee farm. Drum make um strong!" And, sure enough, we soon came upon a line of men, their brown bodies, stripped to the waist, glistening in the sun, wielding their adze-like short hoes to the rhythm of the drummers who stood in a line facing them. In this way, inch by inch, bush was transformed into arable land. At the entrance to the village, in the shade of a mango tree, we were greeted by the Chief and his Right-hand Man, not to mention most of the inhabitants who crowded round as though they were expecting something important. I exchanged greetings with the Chief, hoping I had got the words and the etiquette roughly right:

"Sannu maigida!"

"Sannu! Rankiadede!"
"Lafia!"
"Lafia lo!"
"Yauwa! Sannu!"
"Allahumdelahi!"

I am not sure, now, who said what, and what else, but that was the gist. The Chief then addressed me further but my Hausa was exhausted. I appealed to the Right-hand Man. "Please tell the Chief that I am sorry but I do not speak Hausa and I should be grateful if we may speak in English". I had intended to stay for one tour only and it seemed pointless to attempt to learn the language. The Right-hand Man affected surprise and displeasure. "The Chief does not speak English," he said. "How long has Master been in Nigeria?" Was it my imagination or were the assembled villagers beginning to giggle? There were certainly smiles on the faces of the Survey Department labourers. "Eighteen months," I said, wondering how I was going to get out of this one. "Kai!" said the Right-hand Man and lapsed into pidjin. "Eighteen months for Nigeria and no speak Hausa?" By now there were certainly signs of mirth among the audience. To gain time, I said: "You speak good English!" "Yessah!" he replied, all smiles and standing to attention. "Where did you learn it?" I asked, hoping it was not obvious that I was floundering. "In the army, sir. Sergeant Major. Burma campaign, North Africa campaign, Italian campaign, VJ parade in London." "Really!" I said, very impressed, and the glimmer of an escape route entered my mind. "How long were you in Italy?" I asked. "Eighteen months," he said (I am not making this up). I silently gave thanks. "Do you speak Italian?" I asked. "Ha!" he guffawed. "No, sir." "You mean to say," I demanded, "that you spent eighteen months in Italy and don't speak Italian?" He let out a shout of laughter and I swear he slapped his thigh as he said, with a huge grin: "We go speak English, sah!" Little by little the burden of the conversation spread among the assemblage and soon the people were falling about laughing and their Chief permitted himself a dignified smile. Honours were even and the day was saved.'

Jean Burnside remembers an embarrassing incident in Sokoto:-

'I went on tour to Sokoto and Birnin Kebbi when I stayed with the D.O. and his wife in Sokoto. The main job I had was in Birnin Kebbi sorting out an area of unplanned housing, a workshop area and a couple of petrol filling stations!! I had an audience with the Sultan of Sokoto while I was there which I remember as my most embarrassing experience ever. A member of the N.A. was supposed to be introducing me but did not turn up and I was ushered in without more than 2 or 3 words of Hausa in my vocabulary. I thought that the Sultan could not speak any English (I was told afterwards that he did!) and he made no effort to do so. I felt a complete and utter fool. It surprised me greatly that the Sultan was not wearing fine clothes. If anything he was a bit shabby and wore old carpet slippers. Again I learned afterwards that this was done out of politeness so as not to overawe his visitor.'

David Ball recalls meeting Dr.G.P.Bargery who compiled the first major authoritative Hausa/English dictionary :-

'On one memorable occasion in Kano, at a dinner party, I met Dr Bargery, a living legend of a missionary who had first come to Kano in 1900, four years before the British arrived, where he was given a house, in the city, by the Emir who used to go on tour with him, the Emir visiting his Moslem faithful while Bargery sought to make Christians out of pagans (presumably he left the Moslems alone, as was shortly to be required by the British laws of the Protectorate of Northern Nigeria). He later wrote the first Hausa-English dictionary which remained the standard dictionary for many years - even, I think, up to the time I was there fifty, years later - and translated the Bible into Hausa. Some twenty years before the time

of which I write he had retired from Nigeria and taught in London University for several years before deciding that he was not happy in England and returned to Kano. When I met him he must have been over 90.

I mentioned that I had recently been to Keffi and seen the plaque commemorating the death there of the British Resident in 1902. Dr Bargery said: "I was staying with Maloney the week before he was murdered. I remember warning him not to trust the Magaji and Maloney replied: 'I don't. But I need his men to get the telegraph line through. As soon as that's done I'll lock him up.'"

"The next day" continued Bargery, "I left for my mission station which was roughly where Kaduna is now. I had twelve donkeys to carry my loads, all of which I sold when I arrived, but" he added with a chuckle "I had to buy one of them back again to carry the cowry shells which I received in payment. However," he said "that's by the way. The next day a runner arrived with a message on a torn scrap of paper and some of it was missing. All I could read was: 'all I can spare. Do what you can.' I sent a reply: 'Message incomplete and not understood. Please repeat.' And a few days later came the full message: 'The Magaji has murdered the Resident and is escaping to the north, we think passing near your mission station. You must stop him. These two soldiers are all I can spare. Do what you can.' I must say," concluded Dr Bargery with a twinkling smile, "I was very glad not to have got the complete message the first time because the Magaji had an army with him."

Later, someone mentioned the burning of his house and his dictionary, nearly complete after - was it ten or twenty years of work? "What on earth did you do?" I asked. Bargery replied: "I found a school exercise book, wrote a large capital A on the cover, gave it to my mallam and said: "I want you to write in this book every Hausa word you can think of beginning with 'A'. We're starting again."

I feel greatly privileged to have met such a man.'

If the mastering of local languages was a problem for expatriates, the learning of English by the indigenous people of the North was also difficult and limited to those with some education. In the south of Nigeria the story was rather different. English had been taught at the schools and had been in widespread use for a long time, as witnessed by the following contribution from Keith Sargeant. It was written by a Survey student who was obviously convinced that surveying was a respectable and gentlemanly science. He called it 'A Day in the Life of a Surveyor'

'A surveyor is a complete man. He uses all the talents which God and nature have endowed to humanity. To him life is an unceasing utilisation of all these talents and in him all the lofty and graceful attributes of man do not stagnate. Intelligence, muscles, courage, dignity, discretion, vigour, affability, tolerance and all the other ennobling qualities are exercised, cultivated and nurtured by him. As he rises from his camp-bed in the early morning hours, he commences to employ these talents for the benefit of his many less active friends who are daily pent up in the office, and day-dreaming over the desk.

He must be up very early in the morning to execute the duties which he had planned out for himself the previous night. His chainman and his labourers, tall, sturdy men capable of the most daring enterprises stand waiting at the door of his tent. There is five mile trekking to be done before they can reach the site of their work. He gives instruction to the headman, all instruments are packed out and the labourers are on their way to their destination. They know too well the requirements of their work and no sluggishness or any spirit of insubordination can be observed in their comportment.

The surveyor dresses himself up in his smart and soldierly habiliment. He wears no cumbersome tail-coat or top hat or any showy finery. He does not belong to the "tip-top-collar-and-tie" profession and does not make any attempt to tie the cord to his neck. As he emerges from his tent, he is the darling of Hebe, "So buksom blithe and debonair". He sniffs the morning air, and starts for his destination in brisk and manly strides. As he goes, he stumbles in some thorns and brambles, he extricates himself and pays no heed to the pricks and stings they inflicted on him. After all, those are but the tiny bugs that bite the surveyor. What matters to him is his work. He has been in the field some time, and his clock has lost its accuracy. He has to observe the morning sun for Time and Azimuth. Bear with me, dear reader, if the meaning of Azimuth baffles you. It is a secret which only he and the illustrious members of his Profession can unravel.

He gets to his destination and finds his labourers all waiting for him, all arrangements preparatory for the work having been made; for even these labourers understand the humble intricacies of the profession.

He starts his observation, "shoots" several times to the sun - not with a cannon but with his theodolite. 0 let me write it in block letters

- THEODOLITE -

the "Universal instrument" with which he can perform wonderful operations and cause the lay man to stare with eyes and mouth agape. His observations are carefully booked down in a neat, orderly and legible fashion.

He is now on active duty. There are ranges of hills at distances of about forty miles away. These he starts to observe. On these hills there are heliostats twinkling beautifully and reflecting direct rays of the sun. O how beautiful, how thrilling it is to intersect these luminous signals with the wires of the telescope. With what a satisfaction does a surveyor vibrate his head to assure himself that parallax has been eliminated and that focus is perfect. These are the thrills of the profession which the day-dreaming philosopher will never experience. Systematically the surveyor "shoots" to all the hills and records his measurements. He forms a mental picture at once of the possibilities of his observations and is satisfied for he is not doing a mean job at all. He is putting down into record framework points which are indispensable for intelligent land administration. He is on an operation which will give his sceptical friends the feeling of security in their system of land tenure. He is saving his country from the implications of land disputes both internal and external, and is making preparation for the peace and comfort of posterity.

On realising the dignity of his profession, he ensures that all his observations are of a respectable quality and are done with all faithfulness. Nor is he absolutely devoid of aesthetic appreciation. He appreciates the beauty of the prospect all about him. He is on the top of a hill 2,000 feet above sea level, and his heart melts away in rapture for the profuseness of this exquisite beauty. He sees the loveliness of nature in its untainted freshness and inhales the sweet moving air in its purity. Little wonder if he returns to his home with the sprightly feeling of a vigorous mind, little wonder if he turns a poet or a philosopher, little wonder if he becomes appreciative of the higher purpose of creation.

He now returns to his tent, by another route, having known the direction of his tent, there is no possibility of his getting lost. He cuts through hedges, fords streams, scrambles under fences and arrives at last to his tent.

Now starts the intellectual part of his work. He starts his computations, calling into a harmonious alliance the most up-to-date principles of mathematics, physics, meteorology and astronomy. He is at once a soldier, a poet, a philosopher and an intellectual.'

It is said that one in every five people in Africa is a Nigerian. The population of the country was said to be in excess of 80 millions in 1968, by 1985 was claimed to have risen to 95.7 millions and to 105 millions by 1988, growing at a rate of 3%. By 1992 the population was said to have reached 120 millions and was increasing by 3%to 4% annually and by 2025 it could be the world's third most populous country after China and India. Travellers in the country, witnessing the vast emptiness of the bush, are hard pressed to believe these figures. However, it was often said, even at the time of the Northern Nigerian Survey, that it was dangerous to fire a gun at random in the bush for fear of injuring somebody and if you stopped your car in a remote place to 'use the toilet' the odds were, even in thick bush, you would have an audience by the time you pulled your trousers down !

The rural population produced 90% of the wealth of the country using little but hand hoes (the plough was virtually unknown). The most common staple foods and crops of the North were *dawa* (Guinea corn), *gero* (millet), *gyada* (groundnuts), cassava, cotton, tobacco and beans, and in the wetter areas *shinkafa* (rice), yams and sweet potatoes.

Surveyors worked with and on behalf of the many and varied people of Northern Nigeria and with time became aware of the complex interplay of their origins, religions, cultures and traditions. The Northern people were generally very cheerful, polite, friendly, welcoming and hospitable and, despite the inevitable frustrations and misunderstandings which huge cultural differences engendered, helped to make the lives of expatriates interesting, rewarding and memorable. With the exception of the mining industry on the Plateau, the North had no major European-led enterprises like farms, plantations and industries, and there was no settled European population. The few foreigners that were scattered across this vast and densely populated land were totally insignificant to the vast majority of the ordinary local people. When untouched by the outside world, these people retained a natural unassuming dignity and pride, but when a hint of western knowledge, education or training had been acquired, those qualities were often replaced by an outspoken, faintly ridiculous and disenchanting veneer of civilisation. An element of graft, common enough the world over, had always existed in Northern society, especially amongst the trading community, and a newcomer would soon come across an awful lot of charming rogues !

Unlike many other parts of Africa, particularly in the East and in the South, Nigeria knew no colour bar. There were inevitably traces of racism from both sides from time to time, but most surveyors developed an admiration and respect for the people they were there to serve and amongst whom they lived and worked in welcome harmony. With the team spirit which quickly developed in most working situations there was an easy-going relationship between European surveyors and their Nigerian counterparts, assistants, headmen, labourers. They came to admire the dignity and natural courtesy of the local people, appreciated the fact that Nigerians did not like being laughed at, but enjoyed the fact that, like the British, they enjoyed laughing at themselves. Northerners had a great confidence in themselves, they were quite self assured and complacent, but with a certain dignity and infectious courtesy. Although they could be difficult to influence in any essential way, strong and lasting bonds of friendship were often established. It was difficult for most expatriates to live amongst Nigerians and not like them. Equality was absolute and respected but, except at the clubs and in sport, there was not much genuine mixing, especially in the North with its long social, cultural and Islamic traditions. Europeans and Nigerians tended to lead different lives, had different values and interests, and lived life at a different tempo, but on the whole there was mutual recognition and respect without intrusion into one anothers' affairs. Some European women would, in the spare time they had, have liked to have established closer relationships with Nigerian women, but such contacts and influence might have been resented. It was notable that Northern Nigerians, however wealthy and whatever their standing, seldom entertained white people socially, and their wives would be conspicuous by their absence on such occasions. The western idea of romantic love and equality with the opposite sex was almost unknown, or at least was very unimportant.

Jean Burnside recalls:-

'I went to Zaria once to attend a conference on the need for industrialisation in Northern Nigeria. There were not many white faces there and the man from the University running it had difficulty in getting the delegates to come to the conclusions which he favoured. He wanted their final communiqué to read "Notwithstanding the fact that it will mean our wives going out to work in factories, we believe that the Northern Region should be industrialised". However, the delegates would not agree to the first clause being included.'

Those who were not of the Moslem faith could be very different, as witnessed by David Ball:-

'On a visit to Funtua, preparing a plan for an urban extension, I was making a rough survey of the edge of the existing town. Seeing me looking at what turned out to be his house, a large African politely asked what I was doing. I told him. He said he was afraid I was going to knock his house down, and he was about to spend a lot of money on a new roof. I reassured him on that point and he invited me in for a drink. It being almost lunch time I gratefully accepted and we sat in his living room and talked, or rather he talked. "You see," he said, pouring us each a gloriously cold Star Beer, "You can't be too careful. Being a Yoruba I have no representation on the Native Authority council and I am not party to what is discussed. I can no more go inside that council chamber than I can go inside a

Hausaman's house - in case I see his wives!" Several women, incidentally, had walked through the room as we talked. "Now," he said, "I am a Christian man, a Roman Catholic born and bred. Owing to circumstances I have four wives - but that is beside the point!" I enjoyed that beer.'

Almost everywhere in the North the ruling and nomadic Fulanis were encountered and it is these people who left the greatest impression upon those who worked there. The ruling classes of the Fulani were very clever people and were convinced they could easily get the better of the British. Even the ordinary Fulanis regarded themselves as a cut above the ordinary people of the North and adopted an easy, friendly familiarity with Europeans, letting it be known that they were in some way distantly related to them. From the nomadic encampments Fulani girls *(Photo 2)* would pass by on their way to market in elegant single file with their blue body wraps, toning head-dresses and scrubbed calabashes of milk and butter on their heads, casting sideways glances, always talking and giggling. The writer recalls:-

'In camp some of my labourers were buying milk from a group of young, attractive visiting Fulani girls and taunting them with offers of marriage. "I would not marry you in a thousand years, but I will marry your European master if he wishes !" was one of the replies.'

And Clifford Rayner remembers Fulanis from his time in Yola in 1960:-

'About 7 o'clock in the evening somebody came round and asked if I could help him. A small boy of some Fulani friends of his had been bitten by a snake and would I take him to the hospital for treatment (about 8 miles away). So I took him to hospital together with four of these Fulani cowmen. I stayed long enough to ensure that the boy got treatment and then came back. It was a strange sight us all in the ward. The Fulani looking really native with their leaning sticks, swords and knives draped about them. They were all very grateful and thanked me profusely but I asked them why they asked me - (there are plenty of Africans in town with cars). Oh they wouldn't help - only Europeans help each other!! '

The writer recalls:-

'During the Kano-Nguru Tellurometer traverse in September 1961 Frank Waudby-Smith and I were invited to a village called Medi by Hakamin Gagarawa, who was indebted to us for the repair of his motor car, to witness, as VIPs with seats in the midst of the gathering, the whole of a Fulani sheriya (beating ceremony). We took him and a large number of his followers along sandy tracks in my Dodge kit-car to witness this initiation of young men into manhood, and the dancing of the women which followed.'

Such ceremonies *(Photo. 139)* had become illegal because of the serious injuries, even deaths, which sometimes occurred, but they were still widely practised and certainly carried a reputation for valour and bravery in the eyes of young female admirers and perpetuated the tough reputation of the Fulanis amongst other tribes. These young men had spent their lives looking after the grazing herds of white hump-backed cattle, dressed only in goat skins, with large sticks and distinctive decorated hats made from woven grasses, and sometimes reed flutes which they played to their charges. While the women went daily to the markets and the villages to sell their milk *(Photo. 2)*, and the other products from their herds, the menfolk, especially the younger ones, would stay with the cattle, watching over them as they grazed. They would often adopt a characteristic posture, standing on one foot, propped up by a long staff, while the other foot was held flat against the opposite thigh - a habit of cattlemen right across Africa, like the Masai, to whom they are no doubt very distantly related.

In a land so dominated by men, it was often a refreshing delight to come across the women and the colour, elegance and vibrancy they provided . They joined the procession of other people moving to market, everyone carrying something, even tiny children, not long walking, but already capable of carrying, upright on their heads, a single empty bottle. These strikingly beautiful Fulani women walked gracefully and unhurriedly, almost regally, their colourful hand-woven wraps sweeping the ground. Moving efficiently, upright and in single file, often carrying children on their backs over remarkably long distances, one hand on a hip, they carried a large calabash of milk, *madara* (a thick curdled milk, like yoghurt) and butter on their heads. They moved with such balance and poise that they often left their full calabashes on their heads as they stooped to rest or to pick up something from the ground. Their hair was arranged in long black plaits and they wore their principal treasured possessions, large earrings and clusters of bangles. Apparently shy, though always ready to respond if provoked, invariably slender, barefooted and smiling, they were the graceful beauty of the North. Stopping by at a survey camp they would cheekily taunt the men but be ready to lower a calabash to the ground if there was any prospect of a sale.

Mysterious Work

Surveying had always been something of an obscure occupation, even to people in developed countries, so it should not have been at all surprising that many in Africa found it even more so, even those with quite high levels of education. A surveyor brought nothing but a strange collection of equipment to the work site. Little tangible or visible, except perhaps cut lines and boundaries, township layouts, and some authoritative-looking concrete markers on the ground, appeared to result from his visit. Planners and Lands Officers on the other hand had a productive image and made decisions which often had discernible local physical and financial impact, while the work of other professionals like agricultural officers, foresters, veterinary officers, engineers, teachers and administrators was usually welcome and obvious for all to see. Surveyors might make a mess, cut down trees and crops, erect strange constructions on remote hilltops *(Photo.140),* in broad daylight cause bright stars to shine from distant mountains, dig holes in the ground, fill them with concrete and mark them with incomprehensible numbers, and go away, quite content, with no more than a few pages of meaningless numbers written into a small book, seldom returning, unless it was to repeat the operation. To some they appeared as missionaries, watching effigies of their gods on the hilltops, observing to the sun and the stars, always searching for something but never finding it, while to others they were money makers, the creators of new, straight paths through the bush, taxmen, or even slave raiders. Sometimes the gods would be angry and destroy the hilltop idols with lightning but the surveyors would return and build them up again.

Once in a while local people might get the opportunity to have a look through the surveyor's telescope and see the whole world had been turned upside down ! So that was it ! Upside down the earth's secrets would drop down and the hidden sources of minerals, water and perhaps money would be revealed ! And surveyors could also turn people upside down. Did the money fall from their pockets and was it collected by the theodolite ? After working at a hilltop near Zangwan Katab in 1957 the writer returned to his camp and paid his labourers their weekly wages. Local people had observed the entire proceedings - turning the world upside down from the local hilltop, the theodolite apparently connected to the ground marker by a suspended plumbob, and numbers being written into a book. Later back at camp numbers were read from a similar book and money handed to the men. The local people put two and two together and, when the survey party moved on the next day, they climbed the hill and dug up the ground marker seeking money for themselves !

TRAVELLING

Mobility

For many, service in Northern Nigeria meant a comparatively easy life spent with all the facilities of Kaduna or Jos, and little else except perhaps brief excursions to other towns with reasonable facilities, but it was common for surveyors, and in particular the bachelors, to work in the bush, and to move around a lot from station to station and from one small place to another. Some places would be regarded as 'punishment' postings, perhaps compensated by a posting to a much more amenable station at another time. One of the more pleasant aspects of being on the move was the frequency with which it was possible to stumble across people one had met before, sometimes in quite unusual circumstances and in remote places.

The writer recalls:-

> 'On my first tour in 1957-58 I stayed in 79 different places; 33 on my second tour; 40 on my third and 43 on my fourth. Most of this time was spent in the bush, but not always on foot. The number of different 'overnights' and changes of station declined on later tours as my responsibilities became more of a supervisory and administrative nature but, even so, in a 20 years period covering 11 tours of duty I stayed in 372 different places !'

A small number of surveyors spread thinly over a vast country implied a need to be constantly on the move over long distances, whether from station to station, from survey to survey or from base to work. In the very early days of surveying in Nigeria, before roads were built, the only means of carrying survey kit was on four legs or two, using donkeys, mules, oxen, horses, camels or human carriers. Wheeled transport was not extensively used until prepared surfaces were made and bridges and culverts built. Some bullock carts were brought in from India at about the turn of the century but were never successfully employed. In the open dry savannah country of the north the preferred method of travel was on horseback, though camels, cumbersome as they are, were occasionally used. In rough, hilly and rocky country, and in the thick bush and forests of the southern parts of the region where tsetse flies were endemic and the crossing of wide, deep rivers could only be achieved by boats and canoes, horses were almost a handicap and a great deal of moving about was done on foot. Bicycles were useful and, unlike horses, could be ferried across rivers in canoes.

Rail travel
(Map 38)

Before the introduction of motor vehicles, the Nigerian interior was being opened up by the development of railways; Kaduna was not accessible by road until 1927. A single track main line was constructed running from Lagos to Ibadan, Ilorin, the Jebba Bridge across the River Niger, Minna and Kaduna. From Kaduna a branch went on to Kafanchan and terminated at Jos. Another branch went from Kaduna to Zaria, Funtua and Kano with an extension to Nguru in the far north-western corner of Bornu Province. From Funtua a branch line went to Gusau and terminated at Kaura Namoda. Another main line came up from Port Harcourt on the coast and linked Enugu with Makurdi, where it crossed the River Benue, and joined the line from Kaduna at Kafanchan. This network was operational by the early 1930s and, before the second world war, another branch was planned to run from Lafia on the Makurdi-Kafanchan section, to Bornu. While engaged on mapping work Keith Sargeant recalls stumbling upon this proposed alignment in the form of a substantial concrete bridge spanning a raging torrent miles away from the nearest motor road. That bridge was destined never to carry a train. When finally completed in 1963 the branch started from Kuru, just south of Jos, went on to Bauchi, and Gombe and terminated at Maiduguri. A link from there across the Sudan to Khartoum was envisaged, but never materialised for want of political will and funding.

All major journeys in the early days were made by train, indeed much use was made of the railway for moving surveyors and their parties until the early 1960s. Trains moved at a sedate pace, were not entirely reliable, and arrival times a little unpredictable. Incidents, breakdowns and delays were common. On one occasion part of a train was backed into a siding at Minna and a section of connecting track removed to effect repairs. These repairs where not completed when it was time for the rest of the train to continue its journey and the wagons and their contents were left stranded with no prospect of recovery for some weeks.

Compared with other means of travel over long distances it was, however, a fairly comfortable way of getting around and, until just after the war all routes carried trains with couchettes and a good dining car. Most new arrivals in Lagos made their initial journey upcountry from Lagos to either Kaduna or Jos on one of the 'Limited' trains.

'Local' trains *(Photo.141)* lacked the facilities of the 'Limited' services and were a lot less comfortable. The writer recalls:-

> *'On a long bush job which involved trekking across country it would be common for the surveyor and his party to travel by train or lorry to the starting point, complete the work on foot, and then be picked up again some weeks or months later. In April 1959, I left Jos to work on the P Chain Primary trig, travelling as far as Udei, with my party and all my kit and supplies, on the local Enugu-bound train. The journey was quite dramatic. The arrival of a train in many small places was something of a festive occasion, platforms along the way were a hive of frenetic activity, with crowds of people, animals, confusion, buying and selling, shouting and laughter. The train was very hot, crowded, slow and liable to stop and break down almost anywhere. There was no food, no bedding, no soap, little water and unusable toilets (hasty excursions into the bush were necessary during the numerous unscheduled halts along the way). Eight months later, at the end of the work, I returned on the same local train from Oturkpo to Jos. The 240 mile journey took 21 hours.'*

Until about 1958 some of the drivers of the steam locomotives on the railway were Europeans, their skills with the controls apparently being of great importance on the steep gradients on the lines connecting with Kafanchan and the Jos Plateau. One of their great challenges was to start a fully laden train from Jos station and go straight into a very long steep climb for about 5 miles. No two locomotives could cope with this in the same way and much personal knowledge of each engine's idiosyncrasies was needed. The old hands were quite nonchalant about it, but time and again under inexperienced control, engines would run out of power on the embankment which overlooked the Jos Survey offices. But the day had to come when the old drivers were retired and Nigerian drivers took over. Skilled as they were, some lacked the experience and the 'touch' required to manage the ageing locomotives. Just before he left, one of the retiring men sat at the Anglo-Jos Club and watched as a passenger train failed time after time to make the gradient outside, constantly reversing back down the line to try again . Finally the old driver could take it no longer. He finished his beer, said to one of his friends "Meet me at Bukuru", drove down to the station and, for one last, glorious time, took over the controls of the locomotive. Less than half an hour later there was a great roar, clouds of black smoke and a long blast on the whistle as the train came steaming by on full power, with a triumphant wave from the driver. That man was to be envied, he retired on a high ! Climbing that gradient was no longer a problem when more powerful but impersonal diesel locomotives replaced the steam.

On the rivers

The very earliest penetration into Nigeria's interior, and access to the North, was along the major rivers and the Inland Waterways Department operated a service, principally along the Benue and the Niger south of its confluence, using steamers towing barges of freight *(Photos. 142 and 143)*. Limited passenger services were available, with accommodation on board, but were little used by surveyors. Long journeys by river were uncommon after the advent of rail and road travel but the surveyor would often find need to cross swollen streams and rivers in the course of his work and local canoes propelled by poles or paddles were used on many a precarious crossing *(Photo.180)*.

Work in the vicinity of major riverside towns like Makurdi and Lokoja could sometimes be aided by the use of smaller Inland Waterways boats. The writer remembers:-

> *'On a control survey for the mapping of the Jakura Limestone and Agbaja Ironstone area, which took me to both sides of the broad unbridged Niger near Lokoja in 196,1 I had the use of a small motor launch and boatman from the Inland Waterways Department. Here, uncharted hidden sandbanks, which moved from season to season after the floods, could make boating by the inexperienced a hazardous experience. At nightfall, with not a light in sight on either bank of the wide river, and well out of visible range of aid, our motorboat struck a submerged bank at speed and came to rest on its side in a few inches of fast moving water, surrounded by a great expanse of swirling dark brown water of varying and unknown depth. We jumped overboard and pushed the heavy boat with the current, but with great difficulty, for what seemed like half an hour, until at last it floated free. Not being much of a swimmer it was not the most pleasant of experiences standing in the middle of the Niger in darkness, so at all times I maintained a very strong grip, ready to drag myself aboard the moment it floated free. The boatman restarted the engine, and we twice more went aground, this time at low speed, and I shall never really know how he managed to find his way upstream, in the darkness, to Lokoja.'*

Travelling by road
(Map 39)

Perhaps the greatest hazard faced by all in Nigeria was that of travelling by road, yet, because of the nature of their work, surveyors did it a great deal. Early roads had set out to follow the old caravan routes or were built with the aid of local people who knew the directions from place to place and would go out and light fires to guide the construction towards the distant columns of smoke. As mentioned above Kaduna was not accessible by road until 1927 and it was not until 1930 that the road from Kaduna to Zaria was open and the Jos road construction was under way.

In his book *Into Africa (And Out)* David Ball describes the roads in Northern Nigeria:-

> *'Laterite, it is worth explaining, is a priceless gift of a road (and house) building material. Occurring throughout most of Nigeria - probably most of sub-Saharan Africa - it is a reddish clay formed by the weathering, over the millennia, of the continental "base complex" igneous rock. It makes rock-hard sun-dried bricks and, rolled, a good road surface. Roads are simply cut in the laterite through the bush by graders because in most places it is there at the surface and for many feet below. You " grade" a gently cambered road surface about fifty feet wide running into an open storm drain on either side, roll it and there's your road. In Northern Nigeria in the late fifties, of which I write, only a few of the most important trunk roads and urban roads had a nine-foot strip of tar in the centre. Approaching vehicles pulled over, without slowing down, onto the laterite "hard shoulder". Most roads outside towns, including the main north-south Kaduna-Lagos road (Photo.145), were not tarred. Laterite roads become corrugated and no one, at that time. knew quite why. I once read a scientific article about it. The corrugations, of fairly constant wavelength (some 8 inches(200 mm) between crests) and depth (about one inch - these are my field recollections so to speak), ran right across the road at right angles to the traffic flow and were made in the dry season when the laterite was hard but with a dusty surface. It was thought that they were produced at a pretty fundamental - if not molecular - level by shock waves arising from the oncoming wheels. In the rainy season these roads inevitably became rutted and had to be constantly re-graded and therefore constantly argued about in terms of the relative cost of tarring and re-grading. In the dry season, on the more remote roads of the North you were aware of following another vehicle, usually a "mammy wagon" perhaps a quarter of an hour before catching up with it by the dust hanging in the air*

above the road (Photo.148).

Incidents were frequent and few who worked for any time in the territory escaped without an accident of some kind. Jean Burnside recalls:-

> *'I visited Zaria quite a number of times - it was an easy journey from Kaduna with a tarred road the whole way. However, in the rainy season there were quite a number of potholes. I was driving back the last time when I was 7 or 8 months pregnant and picked up a Nigerian bus driver who had broken down; to take him into Kaduna to fetch a spare part. I was amused when he said to me "Madam should not be driving on this road". I could not imagine anyone in UK coming out with this remark. He was, of course, quite right............'*

An incident with which some surveyors can identify, through having similar though perhaps less serious consequences, comes from no less a source than the former British Prime Minister, John Major. As a young man he took up a post with the Standard Bank of West Africa in early 1966 and was posted to Jos. His recollections of the plateau were as pleasant as most others who visited the place and recalls "the biggest, tallest skies I've ever seen". The motor accident which would take him out of Africa happened in May 1967 when he was travelling back at night with a friend, Richard Cockeram, from a visit to the cinema at Bukuru. Somehow they drove into a ravine and he was thrown through the windscreen, suffering multiple fractures to his left leg and losing the kneecap. After a period in a mission hospital he was flown back to England. His recovery was never complete, he is discreetly handicapped, and walking further than a mile is too much for him.

In the course of time, the car had taken over from travelling on foot or by horse *(Photo.176)* but with roads so few and far between, the distance from the roadhead to the scene of work could be great and it could be argued that it was too wasteful of time to attempt to use a vehicle at all. As late as the 1940s, Hunter deplored the practice of spending more time travelling than surveying, though it became obvious from his wife Nora's diary that he was frequently guilty of this himself. Private transport was not common in the early days and the number of official vehicles was very limited *(Photo.147).* Curbs on spending for departmental transport and fuel made it necessary sometimes to beg vehicles from other departments, or the local authority, or hire one from local sources.

The writer recalls:-

> *'When I first arrived in Jos by train I was met at the station by a notorious driver called Ishola driving a very old Survey Ford kit-car and I wonder to this day whether it was the same Ford spoken of by David Anderson in his pre-war book Surveyor's Trek when he said ".....impossible to say from what period of prehistory it dated. It was better at going than standing still. It would not stay in gear when the engine wasn't running and always had to be jacked up. The cracked driving mirror was spending a purposeless old age at the end of a long iron rod. In its time it had reflected 200,000 miles of dusty by-roads. Now too cracked and tremulous to reflect anything except images of the past".'*

Many of the drivers of Survey Department vehicles were, if not closely controlled, tempted to take personal advantage of their authority to drive official load-carrying vehicles. Many Nigerians were, given the chance, great traders and travellers and they forever faced the problem of moving produce and goods to the markets. Almost without exception, drivers regarded it as a perk of their jobs that when running empty and not under the direct supervision of a senior officer, they would use their vehicle as if it were their own personal business property. They would pick up great loads and passengers willy-nilly, sometimes diverting hundreds of miles to illegitimate destinations with paying passengers and cargoes, using Government fuel, and explaining their failure to arrive on time with feigned breakdowns and bad road conditions. The writer recalls:-

> *'In 1964, when I was running the Survey Training Course at Kagarko a brand-new Bedford one-tonner, allocated for the use of the 12 trainees in my group,*

failed to return after being sent to Keffi for fuel supplies. On my way back from Kaduna, travelling in precisely the opposite direction I came across the driver parked at a roadside market, the new vehicle loaded and the springs and tyres flattened with 4 one-hundredweight sacks of gari, an assortment of mats, boxes, bags and trussed hens, a dozen steel railway sleepers weighing over ½ cwt each, 12 fare-paying passengers, several women, 2 children, 2 survey labourers, one of our survey assistants who was not supposed to be in that area at all, and 3 full 44-gallon drums of petrol (his only legitimate cargo !) - all this on a very rough laterite road.'

They were always required to maintain a logbook, each journey approved by the surveyor in charge, but it was uncanny how often an alleged broken odometer cable would go unreported for months at a time ! Details of the vehicle and its accessories were written in the front of the book and the following is an extract from one of these books with an inventory of the tools carried:-

Fulaya	-Pliers
Gilis Gom	-Grease gun
Pompo	-Pump
Jank	-Jack
Handul waini	-Winding (Starting) handle
Hanun jank	-Jack handle
Fula geje	-Feeler gauge
Fuluk sumhana	-Plug spanner
Wil sumhana	-Wheel spanner
Sibtin sumhana	-Shifting spanner
Sukul dileba	-Screw driver
Sifeya taya	-Spare tyre

When moving survey parties drivers were content to leave the loading of their vehicles to labourers and very soon loads would be piled up in a teetering, swaying heap on the back of the lorry, and when all was in place, the men would climb on top of the load. Witnessing the random loading of a lorry in this way the writer ordered it to be unloaded and personally supervised its reloading. The secure load then only took about half the space and the labourers smiled in amazement and said *"Kai, dubaran turawa !"* "Ah, the logic of Europeans !".

Official transport remained scarce right through the time of the Northern Nigerian Survey and parties might, to save a great deal of toil and sweat, occasionally make use of privately owned lorries. Many of them were owned by female-owned transport and trading businesses from the south of Nigeria, hence their name 'mammy wagons'. Wooden bodywork was built upon the chassis of powerful Mercedes and other diesels and each bore above its cab a brightly painted name or logo such as "Jesus Lives", "Son of Onitsha", "Trust in God", "Benin Boy" and "God Help Us", designed to bring good luck and to encourage business. Each lorry had an unavoidably dirty *karen mota* (dog of the motor), or motor boy whose job it was, in the absence of any form of rear view by the driver, to ride at the rear of the lorry, in choking clouds of dust *(Photo.148)*, and pull a long string attached to a bicycle bell mounted beside the driver's ear, or to throw forward a piece of wood to hit the roof of the cab or the bonnet, to warn him that another vehicle wished to overtake. Not wishing to suffer the dust from another vehicle himself this could spur the driver on to greater speeds in defiance, or result in a dangerous manoeuvre which allowed the following vehicle to overtake, perhaps with only feet to spare before a narrow bridge or road hazard appeared. The other important task of the *karen mota* was to be alert and ready with a large block of wood to wedge behind the rear wheels should the vehicle have to stop on a slope, because loads were invariably so excessive that the handbrake was ineffective. Panic would set in if the lorry started moving backwards, with great shouts of *"Sa weyji ! Sa weyji !!"* from the driver and passengers. He also had to assist when it came to roadside repairs and wheel changing, a dangerous and unenviable task. Innovation and resourcefulness were their watchwords; the rubber sole of a shoe or a piece of old tyre slipped between the inner tube and tyre could make tyres temporarily useful; branches of trees could provide temporary replacements for broken springs.

Standards of driving were appalling and the rough roads took a great toll on the vehicles. Very few roads had a tarmac surface. In 1956 there were very few tarred roads outside of the towns. Funtua to Zaria, Jos to Bukuru, Jos to Bauchi, Kaduna to mile 14 and a few miles in the middle of bush on the way to Jos from mile 14, were the only stretches of tarred road in the North at the time. Laterite roads could turn into impassable morasses in the wet season *(Photos. 153-158)* and barriers were lowered to protect them; and rough, dusty and corrugated in the dry season when they needed grading at frequent intervals. In both wet and dry seasons vehicles had to be robust enough to withstand harsh conditions. *(Photos. 163 and 164).* Taken at low speed, corrugations were extremely uncomfortable and guaranteed to shake the car to pieces. It was better to travel fast, and preferably on the wrong side of the road, and it was not unknown to meet another vehicle approaching from the opposite direction doing the same thing and neither driver bothering to 'pull over' and pass on the correct side !

Wrecks of vehicles, witnesses to an unending carnage, were scattered along the roadside, often stripped of all re-useable parts, left forever to rust in gullies and stream beds, slowly disappearing under a thick layer of laterite dust from the passing traffic *(Photos.149-152).* Journeys could often be measured in wrecks and punctures rather than in miles (an average of one wreck per eight miles could be counted on a journey from Lagos to Kaduna). The most dangerous places were the narrow wooden bridges *(Photo.146);* often with damaged or missing timbers, protruding nails, and missing guard rails; and wide enough for only one vehicle. As heavily laden and fast moving lorries, poorly maintained and with threadbare tyres, approached from each direction it was not unknown for neither to give way. More commonly they were driven at a frantic speed as if life depended upon it and so erratically that the approach would be misjudged with disastrous consequences. Drivers, hanging half out of little wooden doors held on with ordinary cupboard hinges, would swoop down in neutral or top gear towards the bridge, fighting with the steering, breathing a sigh of relief as the great weight gave the bridge an enormous pounding, then rush at the hill on the other side. The newer, wider concrete bridges were an improvement but not one was left long without broken guard rails.

The answer to survey party mobility had come after the war when surveyors were required to purchase and maintain their own private vehicles; which had to be of the load-carrying 'kit-car' or pick-up variety; in return for monthly basic and duty mileage allowances *(Photo.159).* This was certainly an inducement to travel light with few men and little equipment, and a bit of a challenge if the full range of camping gear was carried as well *(Photo.160).* Misfortunes, mechanical and otherwise, were apt to have a direct impact on the bank balance and it was sad indeed to see a tyre being torn to shreds by huge nails protruding from the plank bridges which were a feature of nearly all roads in the 1950s, and it was with a degree of trepidation that one drove the precious vehicle on to primitive ferries *(Photo.144)* made sometimes from little more than a few planks lashed to forty-four gallon oil drums. Though the devices seemed to work well enough it was considered wise not to stay inside during the somewhat precarious crossing.

Some people were exposed to the hazards of travelling by road immediately upon arrival in the country. Anyone arriving by sea in the days of Nigeria Surveys was, if he could drive, required to purchase a kit-car or had, without option, one purchased for him. He was then required to load all his kit and leave Lagos in great trepidation to fall off the edge of the map as he headed northwards. Nobody seemed to know if there were any roads north of Ilorin or, if they did, what condition they were likely to be in !

Trevor Brokenshire gives the following account of his early experiences:-

> *'Don Jones, Derek Woolhouse and I, all newly appointed surveyors, arrived in Lagos on 21st November 1951, having been on the maiden voyage of the M.V.Aureol. I had successfully completed a year's Land Surveying Course at University College, London; and had passed the Intermediate examination in Land Surveying of the Royal Institution of Chartered Surveyors.*
>
> *On 22nd November the three new boys were taken to a Lagos garage to take delivery of our Studebaker 'kit-cars'. Kit-cars were in short supply, and the Studebaker was a good looking vehicle. I suppose it was fate that decreed that I should be the 'tail-end Charlie' of the convoy of very desirable Studebakers that set off from the garage and that a policeman, an Englishman, in his car, should happen to have seen us leave the garage in what, surely, he must have assumed was a daring 'heist'. After following us for a short while he must have decided that he couldn't stop three desperate men, so he passed me and signalled me to pull over; I was, of course, a law abiding citizen, and, seeing his uniform, did so.*

Getting out of his car, he <u>proceeded</u>, as is a policeman's wont, to my car and, in time-honoured words, asked to see my driving licence. Looking back almost 50 years later, I can't remember being particularly bothered to admit that I didn't have a licence; I was more worried that I had perhaps made some driving error. I had learned to drive 3 years earlier on a 5 ton truck (double de-clutching et al) in the desert in the Trucial Coast (now part of the United Arab Emirates) and I had not had enough money in England to buy a car in which to take a driving test. My captor assured me that there had been nothing wrong with my driving, but there were no kind words like "Be on your way", no mild slap on the wrist, no "Make sure you have a licence before I see you again" and I was charged with driving without a licence.

Luckily, someone, somewhere, in the Lagos Survey Department must have had considerable influence or very good friends. I was in Court next day before, I think, a Nigerian magistrate. He was almost apologetic, saying that he thought it a poor show that this should be my introduction to Nigeria. I was given a discharge (was it unconditional or absolute ?) and told not to do it again. The next day our convoy of three took off for Jos, via Kaduna, but complete with licensed Nigerian drivers (I think Don Jones might have been in the same position as I). The trip up-country must have been very uneventful, since I can't recall any of it. I would guess that we arrived In Jos about 28th November. I passed the driving test in Jos on 30th November (and still have the licence).

The last days of November in Jos were hectic, preparing for an immediate posting to 'bush'. I was to provide photo-control on or close to existing roads and tracks in an area to the south of Jos; from Panyam, through Pankshin, and off the Plateau to Shendam and as far south as I could get.

Not many weeks later the Studebaker saga took a different turn. Both front and back springs of the kit-car were of the 'leaf' variety, and after driving the fully-laden vehicle over an atrocious bush track, we fell into a particularly deep hole (or hit a spare bit of rock, I can't remember which) and the main leaf on the front off-side broke, causing quite a sag !

We carried very substantial loads about with us in bush; could it be that the straw which broke the camel's back were my survey books ? Chambers' Seven-Figure Mathematical Tables (Logarithms of numbers 1 to 10,800, Trigonometrical, Nautical and other tables), 1947 reprint; Shortrede's Logarithms of Sines and Tangents for every second ("Revised Edition", undated), Close and Winterbottom's "Text Book of Topographical and Geographical Surveying", 1925 edition; David Clarke's "Plane and Geodetic Surveying for Engineers", volume 1, Fourth Edition, reprint 1949: Volume 2, third Edition, reprinted 1948, and a Star Almanac; together they weighed 10½ lbs.

We were in the middle of nowhere but luckily most of the survey gang were not far away, a messenger was sent to them, and they turned up in force; plus some local inhabitants, who, in circumstances like this, just materialise out of the bush. We unloaded the kit-car, surveyed the damage, and decided on a solution to the problem. This involved selecting a suitable small tree, felling it, cutting it to a length to extend beyond the leaf-spring supports, lifting the kit-car by brute force and a tree 'lever', fitting the timber under the broken spring, lashing it securely in place and lowering the kit-car on to it. Taking only the barest of necessities I set off to drive what I would guess to be the 60 or 70 miles to the garage at Jos. The drive, at slow speed, was accomplished successfully; although at some cost, both of the front tyres were worn down to the canvas because of their misalignment, and required replacement. Surprisingly there was a spare leaf-spring in stock, and, as far as I can recall, no-one seemed to think that I had done anything out of the ordinary.

Some weeks later, by which time we were even further from Jos I drove, I am sure carefully, along a track down into a steep-sided dry gully (we often had to make up bridges and culverts). Without warning there was an unusual noise in the engine region and I had no choice but to stop. On inspection I found that one of the engine supports had sheared off, with the engine being held more or less in place by its remaining supports - if the fan had fallen forward into the radiator even I wouldn't have had a solution for that ! Again a tree to the rescue; my labourers chopped it to a length to rest over the springs; fashioned the middle to the rounded shape of the sump; and when, somehow (how did we do it ?) we got the timber under the engine, it was lashed in place. My clearance was now just about zero but I got the kit-car back to Jos and again, repairs were done without undue delay.

The next event was not quite so serious. By the end of 1953 the engine was using so much oil that one of the essential items to be taken to bush was a gallon tin of engine oil; there <u>was</u> improvement in the apparent 'miles per gallon' of petrol. Oil consumption got so bad that with my help as 'assistant', Sid Williams, the Holman's air compressor rep. in Jos, and a fellow Cornishman, either put in cylinder liners or put in oversize pistons (I can't remember which) and the oil problem was solved.

Last but not least, I was despatched by Keith Hunter, from Kaduna, for some now unknown reason, to Sokoto, for a job which was to take just a few days. Joan, my wife, accompanied me, and we were well on the way to Sokoto when we encountered a particularly bad stretch of corrugated dirt road. The secret of driving on such a road is to find just the right speed to minimise the effect of corrugations, but, in this case that seemed to be impossible, at whatever speed we chose, we shook. After a short while the vibrations proved to be more than the Studebaker could stand; almost all of the exhaust system dropped off. I stopped to gather up the pieces, just in case something could be used again, but the rest of the journey was to the accompaniment of a loud-throated roar and a substantial loss of power. We had to stay in Sokoto for two days longer than we had planned, waiting for a complete exhaust system to be brought up by 'mammy-wagon' from Kaduna. Our only recollection of our stay is that we heard lions roaring and that on the way back to Kaduna, after a very late start, waiting for work on the kit-car to be finished, and driving in the dark, I was quite convinced from time to time, although perfectly sober, that I was seeing straying donkeys in the headlights and needed to slow down quickly. Is a surveyor's best friend his Studebaker ? (Photo.162) I sold it at the end of that tour.

In the course of time, motor agencies became established in the North and it was considered preferable for newly appointed officers to travel up-country by train and arrange purchase of a vehicle of their choice upon arrival at their base station. Officers were granted an advance with which to purchase the vehicle and this advance had to be repaid by monthly instalments from salary. Monthly basic and mileage allowances were paid to defray running costs, and there was a great inducement for those who had never before been involved in the purchase of such an expensive item, to save on costs by doing as much 'D.I.Y' servicing as possible. Being the owner of a vehicle used on government duty was certainly an inducement to look after the vehicle well and not allow other passengers to abuse it. Most pick-up trucks at the time were from America and had large engines, but fuel was not expensive and a consumption of a little over 20 mpg seemed normal. As time went on, however, smaller pick-ups from Europe became more popular, perhaps the first of them being the Standard Vanguard, and then the Peugeot (available in any colour so long as it was grey !). The construction of a protective frame and canopy over the cargo area was one of the first things done to a new pick-up, stamping a measure of individuality on each vehicle. These vehicles stood up to a great deal of punishment (Photo.161) but the quality of the design and construction at the time, combined with the conditions under which they were operated inevitably resulted in numerous mishaps and breakdowns. The writer remembers that, soon after bringing his Dodge kit-car into regular use:-

'The brakes failed about 150 miles from Jos on a very hilly road with lots of dangerous bridges and narrow culverts, but I somehow managed to get the vehicle back to the agents, where it was found that the master cylinder and all the wheel cylinder rubbers had perished through lack of use over the previous six months.

When I collected the car I had the unpleasant experience of having the steering wheel come off in my hands as I rounded a bend near the house at which I was staying. My car mounted an earth embankment, narrowly missing a startled European nursing sister driving her car in the opposite direction. She assumed I was drunk until I passed the steering wheel through the window and waved it at her. I think she still had her doubts'.

Elsewhere it is mentioned that Departmental policy, imposed by Hunter, was to issue a Wild T2 theodolite to every surveyor engaged on work which called for it and to make him personally responsible for its safety and routine maintenance at all times, whether he was in Nigeria or abroad on leave. Names would therefore be painted on the protective covers of the instruments, and sometimes on the instruments themselves. Security and safety of the instrument was paramount on journeys and the rule was that it should always travel in the cab of the vehicle, rather than with the kit in the back. This was to be done even if it meant passengers (including one's wife) sitting on the open back of the vehicle with the luggage ! The pyramidal box in which the cased instrument was normally stored and carried to the field was too large and sharp cornered to fit conveniently into the cab of most vehicles without sacrificing and ruining a passenger seat. The American pick-ups had a broad bench seat, which would take a driver and two passengers with comparative ease, so the instrument in its protective inner case, was strapped in place beside them. The European cars which came later were much smaller, with room for only one passenger. The problem of the instrument was, however, overcome in various ways and the rules were bent, but never, so far as can be recalled, to the detriment of a theodolite.

Perhaps it was a sign of the times to come, but in 1962 there was no longer outright insistence upon the purchase of kit-cars, although it was still very advantageous for many to do so, and the writer recalls:-

'I was permitted to purchase a saloon car to replace my well-worn Dodge pick-up, which I sold to a ground-nut trader in Kaura Namoda for the heavy work of moving sacks of nuts to the marketing area at Gusau. He paid me in shillings, which he had kept in earthen pots buried under the floor of his house. I had to wait while his assistants dug up and then counted the stacks of damp green coins. The bank in Gusau wanted to know where I had obtained such a pile of old and corroded coinage.'

WORKING IN THE BUSH

In at the deep end

Cadastral and township work was the bread and butter of surveying, but by far the most memorable experiences and human contacts were made on framework, boundary and mapping control work in the bush. Newcomers, especially the younger and single ones, could almost certainly expect to cut their teeth on bushwork at a very early stage.

When appointed just before the war, Keith Sargeant's first job was on topographic work:-

"A rail journey brought me (and my two boys) to Funtua in Katsina province where Wiggins (officer in charge) and the other members of the Topo Survey group were centred. Each surveyor was responsible for mapping a quarter of a 1/125,000 sheet, an area about 30 miles square, using several trig points fixed by an earlier surveyor. This was old fashioned topo survey (before the days of air survey) using a plane table to obtain additional fixed points by resection or intersection, sketching in the form lines and obtaining heights by barometer. Compass traverses were run, usually by junior African surveyors, where the topography was too flat for plane-tabling. It would usually take six to eight weeks to complete a quarter-sheet during which time the surveyor might not see another white face, except for the occasional visits by the O/C topo.

I well remember my first day's bush work when Wiggins accompanied me on an eight mile compass traverse (16 miles there and back). In those days I kept a personal diary and the entry for that day says it all:

"Called at 5.45am by Joe (steward boy); leave with Wiggins, Jatto (Headman) and survey gang to do compass traverse to Kogo. Take barometer heights. Get very thirsty! Return finally at 3.00pm in near state of collapse. Try to climb neighbouring hill to close barometer heights, but start vomiting so give it up and let Wiggins do it. Broken blisters on little toes. Think what a ruddy fool I was to believe I'd like to be a surveyor. After six glasses of lime juice feel better. Better still after five cups of tea. Not such a bad life but has its bad patches ..... Plot compass traverse after tea. Bed at 9.00pm."

However it did not take long to become fit enough to cope with much longer treks. This was towards the end of the dry season when one learnt the true value of eye-brows - to keep the sweat out of one's eyes.'

Newly arrived officers quickly taught themselves to be self-sufficient, to accept responsibility and how not to take everyday aspects of life for granted. They rapidly acquired an enhanced appreciation of the comfortable homeland they had left behind, and an understanding and respect for cultures so different from their own. They had good reason, perhaps, to ask themselves whether they should have been there at all, especially when things did not go right. It could be a lonely existence, because they often had little in common with, and could not at first communicate well with, those who depended upon them and upon whom they depended. It goes almost without saying that bush life called for physical endurance, mental fitness and commitment to see the task through. Logistics were fundamental to efficient work, travel and survival in remote areas. There were many hot and wet miles to walk, high and rough hills to climb and some serious planning and surveying to be done along the way, taking in unaccustomed sights and alone with, until they came to know them, unpredictable people whose lifestyles and thoughts differed. It was important to be able to cope with loneliness and difficulties single handed.

Preparations for bush

Plenty of advice was essential when preparing and packing for the first job in bush, but sometimes not enough was given, or insufficient heed was taken of the experience of others. It was important that nothing should be forgotten. Lists were vital because of the variety of things to be carried in boxed headloads, (or 'loads' as they were generally referred to) - survey and drawing equipment log. tables, star almanac, Brunsviga or Facit calculating machine (if the office could spare one), tools, materials, official forms and vouchers, money, medical supplies, tent, camping equipment, clothing, food, and a few personal items to make life tolerable. Vulnerable food like sugar, flour and salt needed to be packed in tins and jars. Food supplies in bush could be very limited and supplies carried had to be carefully judged, and a pilfer factor built in if the cook was in the least bit untrustworthy. Tinned butter would sometimes be available but the tins were too big for one man and would soon run to oil and spoil once opened. Condensed 'Peak' milk could be carried in very small tins, one of them probably sufficient for two days. Alcohol had to be considered a luxury on long treks and beer was far too heavy to carry in quantity. It has been said that any fool can be uncomfortable in bush. Any very inexperienced man with little guidance can be uncomfortable too. It was into that second category that many fell when they first arrived in Northern Nigeria.

It was wise, in spite of financial and manpower restrictions, to take everything that could possibly be needed, plus one or two little luxuries, to maintain the highest possible standards of hygiene, and to take regular balanced meals if possible. It was a good idea to have something else rewarding and relaxing to do, to keep the brain well exercised, and to take a good supply of books.

The following is a list of the equipment and supplies carried by the writer during the observation of the P Chain of primary triangulation in 1959:-

Camp furniture, equipment and supplies

Ridge tent (with flysheet, verandah and groundsheet), cook's tent, bath, camp table, chair, cushion, bed, mosquito net, pillows, blankets, sheets, pillow cases, spare mosquito netting, 2 handbasins, Tilley lamp, spares, mantles, vapourisers, burner and methylated spirit, kerosene, fuel can, jug and funnel, 6v lantern, torch and batteries, insect spray and gun, DDT powder, toilet seat, toilet rolls, padlocks.

Kitchen

2 kerosene cans and steel mesh for oven, 2 buckets, 2 clean kerosene cans for water, water filter and spare candle, 2 whistling kettles, metal water jug,bottles for drinking water, Primus stove, 2 Thermos flasks, 3 saucepans, frying pan, mincer, tin and bottle openers, Pyrex dishes, meat and bread tins, cook's knives, carving knife and fork. large tins for flour, sugar, polythene food bags, Kilner jars, rolling pin, pastry board, miscellaneous cooking items, wire wool, dish cloths, glass cloths, table cloth, plates, cutlery, teapot, glasses, cups, saucers, pepper, salt pots, kitchen lamp, spare hurricane lamp, wicks and matches, iron, linen line and pegs.

Survey and drawing equipment

T3 theodolite, tripod and accessories, heliographs, umbrella, plane table and tripod, binoculars, prismatic compass and tripod, steel tape, textbooks and notes, trig. register, technical instructions and Survey Regulations, calculating machine, Chambers and Shortrede mathematical tables, maps in map case, mapping pens and paper.

Office equipment and supplies

Typewriter, paper, carbon paper, inks, pen, rubber, pencils, scales, rule, pencil sharpener, penknife, pins, clips, map measurer, elastic bands, string, punch, stapler, scissors, gum, Sellotape, sealing wax, crayons, official and personal envelopes, notepaper, notebooks, diary, work diary, voucher forms, telegram forms, labour record sheets, Customs Declaration forms, rail warrants, stamps, airletter forms, files, 2 specie boxes with chains and padlocks.

Tools
Spade, pick, sledge hammer, axes, matchets, nails, hammer, pliers, spanners, file, trowel, screws, drills, metal cutters, soldering outfit, spare wooden box, headpans.

Food supplies

Including reserves (generally canned) of:-
Meat, fish, vegetables, fruit, margarine, cooking fat, baking powder, salt, pepper, curry powder, yeast, cheese, milk, tea, cocoa, Nescafé, Ovaltine, jam or marmalade, pudding, soup, flour, rice, biscuits, squash, sugar.

Clothing

Shirts, shorts, trunks, socks, stockings, sweater, trousers, swimming trunks, handkerchiefs, nylon socks, 2 pairs shoes, Wellington boots, mosquito boots, boot polish and brush, sunglasses, hat, raincoat.

Medical

Labourers' medical supplies including bandages, cotton wool, aspirin, Paludrine and Mepacrine, Personal medical case, Dettol.

Personal

Shaving mirror, soap, brush, blades, towels, flannels, sponge, toothbrush, paste, scissors, needles, thread, buttons, insect repellant, camera, film, filters, tripod and other accessories, reading matter Hausa/English dictionary, radio, batteries, aerial, bicycle, pump, patches, solution, oil.

Early lessons

The first spell in bush alone was a personal test, with nobody else to make decisions and overcome problems. Many mistakes would be made and early lessons learned. The experienced survey party and headman, for whom he had responsibility, would be very conscious of a new man's inexperience and dependence and were not averse to taking advantage of the situation to make their lives easier. Patience, tact, humour and ingenuity were soon put to the test. The writer learned several lessons on his first task when he made incorrect assumptions, based on pure guesses, as to how long it would take to climb a major hill and complete a set of secondary trig observations:-

'When I arrived in Nigeria in 1957 I was posted to Jos and spent my first three weeks settling in and assisting on mining surveys. My first major task was reconnaissance for the Jema'a Secondary Triangulation from the Kagoro Hills in the north, south to Wamba, Akwanga and the Mada Hills, and from the Primary trigs along the edge of the Plateau west to Gudi and beyond. The first stage of this was to resolve the complication arising from the existence of two trig points on the Ningishi summit, a very high, rugged and forested outlier of the Plateau rising well over 1,000 feet from the plain (Illustration 47). In the records these had been known as N22 and N22A and there was uncertainty as to which was which, and one of them had been very poorly fixed in the past. N22 was to be retained and the other one was to be renumbered XK 657 (Photo.48) and form part of my secondary scheme. Leaving Jos I stayed the first night in the gatehouse of the chief's compound at Mayir on the main Wamba road and was kept awake all night by drumming, barking dogs and the rattle of the lbo-owned mammy wagons on the rutted gravel road about 50 feet away. I then moved into bush and set up my tented camp near the farming hamlet of Tari at the foot of the hill on 31st May and climbed the hill for the first time. I quickly learned that to succumb to the desire to ascend spectacular hills like this is to understand that some things are better viewed from afar ! The ascent took two hours and we had to cut our way through rough grass and pick a route through a great jumble of enormous boulders. There was a lot to do at the summit - clearing, trying to unearth the old markers, and preparing for beaconing - and hacking our way through a deep overgrown col to the second summit. It was obvious that more than one visit was required, but just how many I could never have imagined, because on the 1st June the weather turned foul, clouds descended and it rained incessantly like it can only do on the west-facing Plateau edge area. The next day we toiled to the summit again and by our third climb the day after I was beginning to regret very much not pitching my tent on the very summit, particularly in view of the fact that there were three leopards in the trees above us in the camp that evening. On 4th

June I was ready to start observations and heliomen had been sent to the surrounding hills on the Plateau edge. We climbed to the summit for the fourth time and waited in vain all day for the clouds to lift off those hills, and did the same on our fifth ascent two days later. Our sixth ascent, on 7th June was one of those days of incredible frustration - high clouds, good visibility, but incompetent heliomen whose signals did not appear. I sent off Audu Gora and a couple of others to find out what was preventing them from getting their signals through and two days later on my seventh ascent I managed to complete some of the required observations at one of the summits. The next day the clouds were down again and on my eighth climb I did a bit more. On the ninth ascent on 12th June it was again cloudy and I could do nothing, but nearly met my end when I encountered a spitting cobra. My tenth ascent on 14th June was perhaps the most miserable of all. It started fine but by the time we had reached the summit the rain was falling heavily and we just stood there all day getting wet. We climbed the hill for an eleventh time on 15th June and were again frustrated by cloud, and that evening a messenger came back from Jos saying the observations I had taken were probably enough to resolve the confusion of the two trigs and a further attempt at completing the Secondary trig observations would have to await the completion of the Jema'a scheme upon which I then embarked. Ningishi is a name deeply etched upon my memory, as is the wisdom of camping near the site of the work. No assumptions should ever be made about how easy a job will be.'

Supplies

The arrival of a large party could severely strain the resources of small villages where food and water was perhaps only sufficient for the local people. Supplies would have to be carried to such areas and the surveyor himself might be dependent entirely upon the provisions he had brought from town. It was important not to run out of things because small privations could have very detrimental effects. What is a minor inconvenience in town, quickly sorted out the following day, could be much more serious in the bush. Hunter, who had considerable experience of life in the bush, was generally very understanding of the surveyor's problems when in remote places because he had been let down himself on more than one occasion and felt compelled to write this circular letter when he felt their needs were being overlooked by those living a much more comfortable life in station:-

No.A15.4/222
Headquarters
Northern Nigerian. Survey,
Kaduna Junction.
8th August 1956.

Principal Surveyors
Senior Surveyors
Surveyors.

In the course of conversation with three European officers while I have been on tour the question was raised of the difficulty a man in bush now has in obtaining provisions and other stores. I at once asked why men in bush did not send to a survey office and ask the man in charge to do their shopping for them, but my question was met with some surprise and it was suggested that some senior officers would not be best pleased at such a request. Years ago to make such requests to headquarters offices or even to the local D.O. was the usual practice. If it is true that to do so now would cause displeasure to some people, I feel sure that it would be only to those who have not had the experience of being out in the bush at the mercy of an inefficient canteen to which it takes days or weeks to send a message.

2. So that there shall be no uncertainty in future the following instruction is now issued.

(a) Any surveyor working in bush and unable himself to reach a canteen at reasonably frequent intervals may send orders for food and other essentials to this headquarters, to the Jos Office, or to a Provincial Survey office. Such orders must be accompanied by cash or a cheque to cover the cost unless arrangements have been made to charge the cost to the officer's own account. Orders must be for essentials only and, except in emergency should not normally be sent more often than about once in three months.

(b) In future it will be the official duty of the Administrative Assistant at this office, of the Principal Surveyor at Jos, or of a Provincial Surveyor, to arrange without delay for the purchase of the goods ordered and personally to ensure (a) that they are so packed that they are unlikely to suffer damage and can be easily head loaded over rough country, (b) that they are promptly despatched by the best available route and if necessary by messenger

(c) that the needs of the man in bush are catered for as well and as completely as is possible.

3. Those officers in the department who have been to bush very little may feel that this duty is something of an imposition. They should ask themselves what they would feel if when alone, possibly miles from a road or means of communication, they were unable to get some essential commodity just as a result of the carelessness or foolishness of some inefficient canteen clerk. At one time canteens were ready to look after men in bush. Now few people but ourselves go to bush and the canteens no longer cater for the bushman. We must therefore look after the well being of our own men and it is the very least we can do to help our friends to the best of our ability, Only when every possible source of supply has been tapped should the reply "Sorry none" be sent.

(Sgd) K. H. HUNTER
Director of Surveys
KHH/PNC./

To maintain a balanced diet, of the kind one might enjoy at home or in station, was difficult on long jobs in remote places. The monthly messenger could perhaps bring a few vegetables, but acceptable fresh meat, other than chickens, could be difficult to obtain. There was inevitably a dependence upon canned meat and fish and there was a very limited range of vegetables available in the bush, although onions, corn, sweet potatoes and yams were available in season. Working in the vicinity of the big rivers had its compensations because fresh fish was sometimes available. *Giwa ruwa* (river elephant) or Nile Perch is a huge fish with abundant, succulent, sweet white flesh. Fried in batter with yam chips it was a delicious alternative to the real thing. Very little in the way of fresh fruit grew in the North, unless it had been planted near stations, although mangoes could often be obtained in season. Generally speaking, the farther south one went, the better the chances of obtaining a wider range of fruit. The Jos area, because of demands from its European population, was generally well served with a wide range of fruit and vegetables. Potatoes and even strawberries grew well on the Plateau.

Nigerian surveyors in the bush

Europeans usually had to go to a great deal of trouble to live comfortably and survive in the bush, and this no doubt was the secret to the success of their endeavours, but there can be no denying that a great deal of time and expense was spent pandering to these needs, effort which local surveyors did not have to make. In theory such work should have been a cakewalk to Nigerian surveyors, but because of their training and conditioning they often wrestled with Europeans ways, even though they were masters in their own world, finely tuned to their environment and capable of following time proven ways of survival. They could better understand the aspirations of their own people, their sensitivities and their limitations, and how to tailor their efforts for effective results. To Europeans the Nigerian way of doing things, could appear quite different and their control over subordinate staff, though effective, might sometimes seem harsh. A well trained, enthusiastic and capable Nigerian surveyor should always have been able to outperform and outlast a European in the bush, but so very often this was just not the case. One exception to this was Dauda Alayo. Not only was he well trained, intelligent and astute, and skilled in mathematical work and photogrammetry, but he was a most capable and vigorous Northern field surveyor. He had a no-fuss and uncluttered attitude to work in the bush; he travelled light, without a tent and all the usual camp paraphernalia, lodged in local villages, ate local food, spoke the local languages, had great stamina, could walk long distances. Departmental production could have doubled in such capable hands. Unfortunately people like him were very few and far between and the seniority which they deserved and quickly achieved soon left them in administrative positions where their performance was not necessarily so spectacular.

Isolation

A surveyor might be many days trek from a road, and perhaps very many more from one likely to be carrying traffic *(Photos.165 and 166)*. Out in the wilds, with no other natural English speakers, could leave him a bit short on conversation but it was certainly an opportunity to acquire some Hausa. But the isolation was not something that kept preying on his mind, although he was conscious of the fact that he was perhaps the first European ever to climb a particular hill, or the last that would ever be likely to do so, standing at a place where very few Nigerians had ever been. The writer recalls:-

> *'During what was only my second month in Nigeria I did not speak to a white man and, since I was not working with educated Nigerians, I had very little conversation in English; not that it mattered too much at that stage, I was far too busy finding my feet and my bearings in a totally new environment. When I was sufficiently close to a road during my third month I did get a two hour visit from Denis Willey and Doug Eva but then it was back into the bush. The following month, September, I actually saw a white woman, the first since May, but she was in a car which passed as we crossed a road and she did not stop.*
>
> *Two years later, on the P chain, I had another long period of isolation when from April to November I enjoyed a total of only 20 minutes conversation with Europeans. It was a rare pleasure to be able to share my camp for a short period with somebody with whom I could hold a conversation, relate my experiences, enjoy a drink, or even open a can of something special for dinner, and perhaps share the incongruity, in the surroundings, of a little classical music on the radio or on a portable gramophone. I started the P Chain observations alone but found it useful when a pleasant young Nigerian trainee surveyor called James Magnus Kyuka, who had for reasons I cannot recall, been sent out to join me for a month in the bush as 'punishment' for his misdemeanours. When a large number of readings have to be taken as quickly as possible, theodolite work can be carried out more efficiently if the observer does not have to take his eyes and hands away from the instrument. James' job was to sit beside the instrument and record my readings in the fieldbook (Photo.39) He had a good education, spoke English very well, and though not a Hausaman, helped to correct my spoken Hausa. In the evening he would come across from his tent and we spent many a pleasant hour in conversation. It transpired that one of his social interests was ballroom dancing, something he was missing rather sorely in the middle of the Doma Forest Reserve, so he was glued to my radio when I tuned to the BBC World Service on a Saturday evening to listen to his kind of music played by Victor Sylvester. I feel that he might, perhaps, have wanted me to dance with him outside my tent by the light of the Tilley Lamp, but I was relieved when all he asked for was to borrow my camp chair, with which he then waltzed passionately for the next three or four minutes. Not long after that he received instructions to return to Kaduna so my blushes were spared, but James springs to mind whenever Victor Sylvester is mentioned.*
>
> *From the time of my departure from Jos in April the next white woman I*

saw was on 1st November at Oturkpo. In fact I saw a surfeit of them. As I walked exhausted and ill with malaria into town after my long bush spell, two Catholic Sisters went by in a VW and did not look in my direction. Soon after two more appeared heading a church parade down the middle of the road, carrying two enormous bright Union Jacks and followed by about a hundred children singing "Onward Christian Soldiers" at the tops of their voices. I doffed my bush hat to the passing procession but neither of the women acknowledged me. Had I not been so exhausted I would have felt like turning around and going back to bush !

It was there that I saw the first tarmac road for seven months or more, and when I reached Jos five days later I drove my car for the first time for a year. Not for the first time, however, there was little elation upon my return to 'civilisation', and my stay at the Leave Camp was very much an anti-climax to what had been the experience of a lifetime and undoubtedly one of the highlights of my surveying career. The surveyor in the bush could live a solitary existence; always coming and going, it was difficult for him to become part of the community if he stayed away for long periods and was regarded, when he did appear, as something of a curiosity.'

Most tasks in the bush were undertaken by surveyors working alone and it was unusual to share a tented camp except on field training schemes involving the survey school, on aerial mapping control schemes where as many as three parties might be working in collaboration, and on Tellurometer traversing. Visitors to tented camps were therefore comparatively rare but John Pugh recalled an occasion when he was visited by a travelling District Officer:-

'Near Gboko I was camped on Mkar Hill. The local D.O. came up one day and stayed the night in my tent, bringing his own camp bed. His attendants sat around for most of two days, looking at the views and chatting. Before he went, the D.O. thanked me for allowing the intrusion, and said it had solved three difficult cases for him. Listening to his people, he had gathered useful information. "Look over there - that's where Mbuta lives. Awful lies he tells the D.O. but he looks like getting away with it", etc.. While in the Tiv country the locals used to gather around the tent, out of curiosity, and were always breaking into song. They are lovely singers. When work permitted., I would write down the songs, or at least the tunes, and could still sing some of them for you !'

Wives in the bush

The view persisted for a long time that surveying was best done by bachelors, who could spend a maximum amount of time on productive bushwork without the distraction of wife and family. The two problems for a married surveyor had been how to obtain permission for his wife to join him in Nigeria and how to persuade her to accompany him if his work took him to wild and distant places, or to quiet stations with a harsh climate where she might be the only resident white woman and where there was nothing to do and nowhere to go. For a surveyor going off to bush the emotional and psychological needs of a family left behind might be a major consideration, but in the years of the Northern Nigerian Survey, ten years or more after the relaxation of the rules, some wives did spend limited periods on trek in the bush. Their arrival created subtle obligations upon headquarters for a more settled and amenable posting as soon as possible.

And I would love you all the day,
Every night would kiss and play,
If with me you'd fondly stray
Over the hills and far away

John Gay 1720   The Beggar's Opera

For some brave, intelligent wives, who were likely to be undaunted by the surprises along the way, accompanying their husbands to the bush provided them with a better understanding of, or even involvement in, surveying work. It was an alternative to, or a break from, domestic life and a rare opportunity for outdoor living. Some wives did live in the bush for limited periods, but were seldom very far from roads and access to a car. The most arduous work, the long distance trekking involving months rather than weeks in the bush, the trig work, was still done by single men or, occasionally, by a man who had left his wife behind in Europe and the writer can think of no example of a Nigerian surveyor taking his wife to bush.

Paul Ward remembers that he was alone, out in the bush, on Bima Hill in Bauchi Province, when he decided he would ask Barbara if she would marry him. Later, she agreed to do so and, immediately accompanied him through inhospitable country at the hottest time of the year:-

> ' We'd just been married. Barbara (who was a dentist) resigned and pulled her last tooth out in Derby on the Friday, and the following Thursday was on the Nguru 'Flyer'. I'll bet we were the last survey gang to walk from the Survey Office to Kano Railway Station. As we got to Matsena, Barbara got off her horse (she became an excellent horsewoman) and said "I've had a miscarriage, but don't worry, I'm of strong peasant stock". I had the best booker in the world for my string of astro observations along the top end of Kano and Bornu.'

> And o'er the hills and far away
> Beyond their utmost purple rim,
> Beyond the night, across the day,
> Thro' all the world she followed him.

> Tennyson   The Day Dream

………………………………..

Janet Wimbush was a surveyor's wife who joined him on a brief excursion to bush in about 1953. The following account of her experiences was published in the Overseas Pensioner No.45 in April 1983.

"Who's Afraid"

> When you leave the Plateau Province in Nigeria by the road to the West, you come to the escarpment. You then drop three thousand feet and three thousand years.
> The Plateau is the tin-bearing district of Nigeria, and it is the only part of the country where Europeans have ever made settled homes. And very lovely and very sophisticated many of their homes are. The indigenous people of that part of Nigeria are the Birom tribe, known generally as the Pagans. Their standard of living must be something like that of Neolithic man.
> Thirty years ago, when my husband was stationed at Jos on the Plateau as a Government Surveyor, there was a district at the foot of the escarpment called the Marma country, which had for some years been closed to mining. There were two reasons for this. Some of the Pagans had been so hostile to Europeans that there had been violence and bloodshed. And sleeping sickness and yellow fever were rife. It was before the days of inoculation against yellow fever.
> The day came when the authorities decided that the hostility and the disease had both abated and that the district could be reopened to mining prospectors. Before that could happen survey beacons had to be erected. That was where we came in. My husband was despatched to do the job, which was to take about a month, and I went with him. I was rather excited at the thought of going to bush for the first time.

"We are going to the Marma country tomorrow" I said to the Nursing Sister, when I met her at the Club. "I hope you am taking a doctor with you", she replied facetiously.

On the appointed day, we set off in our Ford truck, with the cook, steward, and odd-job boy, and the inevitable sordid-looking paraphernalia of beds and baths, lamps and filters, tin trunks, and camp chairs. Our own luggage looked grim enough and the servants' loads crowned it. Among their bedding rolls and tin kettles there were always some muddy yams rolling about and a couple of squawking hens with their legs tied together. Behind our truck came the lorry carrying the survey gang. This consisted of a Headman, two chainmen and a dozen labourers. They were all Hausas, and their chief characteristics were cheerfulness and beautiful manners, I was very fond of them.

The name of the Headman was Mallam Dogo, which means literally the Tall Teacher. Anyone who could read and write was given the title of Mallam. He and I became great friends. He used to carry me on his back over the streams when we were on trek, and seemed to look on this as his privilege. But the really important member of the party was the dan sanda. The literal meaning of this title is the Man with the Stick. He was a policeman in the service of the Native Administration, and was lent to us to act as interpreter with the pagan tribes.

We drove on the first day to the bottom of the escarpment and went on till the road came to an end. From there the journey was to be done on foot, with carriers recruited locally, and our nights were to be spent in resthouses. The word resthouse is a misnomer. They were neither houses nor restful. They were circular mud huts with a thatch of palm leaves. Doors and windows were rectangular openings in the mud walls. They contained no furniture. But all the same a resthouse can look like home to you when your camp beds and chairs are erected and your books and crockery set out on camp tables. Each resthouse was on the outskirts of a pagan village. The way of life in these villages was primitive in the extreme. The men went naked. The women wore two bunches of leaves attached to a bit of leather around their waists, which waggled as they walked. They carried their babies on their backs in slings of monkey skin. By way of ornament they threaded short pieces of stick through their nostrils.

The Pagans ate what they could grow or kill and had little use for money. In order to earn the few shillings a year that were needed to pay their tax, the women would walk for days to the nearest township with bundles of firewood on their heads. The men carried long knives fashioned from any strips of iron they could lay hands on. Barrel hoops were a favourite material.

We had been moving on for several days and were three days' walk from any road when the cook reported that our tinned food was running out. He had taken for granted that the usual local food would be obtainable and he had miscalculated. The Marma country seemed to provide no food that could be faced by Europeans. Feeling that Cook was being defeatist, I told him in English to find some chickens and eggs. Cook told the Dan Sander in Hausa to find some chickens and eggs. The Dan Sander told the village head to find some chickens and eggs. (I never knew how the Dan Sander managed to communicate, for the language of the Pagans changed every few miles.)

The answer that came back was quite clear. "There are no chickens. There are no eggs." "Never mind" said my husband " I have heard guinea fowl squawking up on that hill, I will take the gun up there tomorrow morning."

Next morning at first light he had gone, taking some of the gang with him. Others had gone off to cut firewood. The cook was presumably out looking for chickens, The odd-job boy and I had the camp to ourselves. He was an engaging child of about twelve, called Audu. He put out my deck chair, put a table beside me, and made me some tea. I relaxed with a six-week old copy of the Daily Telegraph. It was deliciously cool and there was a faint and pleasant scent of wood smoke wafting from the village. I was at peace.

After a quarter of an hour, something caused me to put down my paper and look up. Fifty yards away stood silently in a straight line ten naked Pagan men. Each one had his eyes fixed on me. Each one had a leather thong round his waist into *which was stuck a long knife. None of them moved or made a sound.*

Very deliberately I picked up my paper again and disappeared behind it. Perhaps I had dozed off and dreamed it ? I would count twenty and look again. I counted twenty and looked again. They were still there.

I looked round for Audu. There was no sign of him. I looked at the resthouse with its open gaps for doors and windows. There was no sanctuary there. The bush round the resthouse had been cleared and we were in the middle of a large open space. It looked to me about the size of the Sahara desert. I could not run away. There was nowhere to run.

Not a flicker of expression appeared on the ten faces and the ten pairs of eyes never left me. After twenty minutes or so I found that I had torn the front page of my newspaper into small shreds. I folded the remainder of it neatly and told myself that my husband would be back any minute now. But then I heard the distant sound of his gun from the hill top. The hill top was at least half an hour's walk away. The sun was up now, but I was very cold. I found I was biting my nails (a habit of which I had been cured at the age of six). I folded my hands, shut my eyes, and sat rigid.

It was half-an-hour later that my husband got back, flushed with success, laden with guinea fowl, gossiping cheerfully with his Hausa men. He looked in astonishment at the row of pagans. They had relaxed now, and ceased to stare at me. They were talking to each other. They did not look like the same people at all.

"What do these chaps want?" asked my husband.

I forbore to say that I did not know whether their object had been rape or murder. "Perhaps" I said "we could start the process of asking them?"

"What do they want?" I said to Mallam Dogo in English.

"What do they want'?" said Mallam Dogo to the Dan Sander in Hausa.

"What do you want?' said the Dan Sander to the pagans in their own tongue.

The answer worked its way back to me. They wanted money for their tax. They had heard that we were moving on the next day. They wanted jobs as carriers. "Why did they stand so long and stare at me?" I asked.

And the answer came laboriously back. "They have not seen a white woman before. They were afraid."

Afraid? Of me?

....

Beatrice MacPhee, wife of the late Donald MacPhee, joined him on trek, living in a tent. She recalls the routine of moving from one camp to the next, clearly not too far from good food supplies............

"Moving House"

Moving house is, I believe, along with marriage, divorce and death-one of the most traumatic events in ones lifetime. I wouldn't know. I have never moved house. ..but, if moving tent is on the same scale as moving house, then I must be over-traumatised.

Now, moving house means leaving your house in situ and removing its contents. Sounds a doddle to me. Moving tent means moving the tent and contents, men, equipment, food, drink and anything else necessary to make one comfortable in bush. No Pickfords or Happy Movers to ease the load. Firstly and foremost you need a degree in organisation and management together with a strong survival wish, a good memory, strong legs, infinite patience and an enduring love for ones mate.

A typical tent-moving operation always started with finding carriers - forty or more, and so the chief of the village was approached with appropriate gifts, monetary and comestible. In return he provided carriers, men, women and sometimes children. That part of the exodus was my husband's domain. My contribution was purely domestic and woe betide me if I forgot the whisky. First of all the strongest of the carriers were allocated the Survey equipment. Fair enough, without them there would be no point in the exercise. The rest carried the tent, camp furniture, food and drink and, sometimes, though fortunately not too frequently, us. It was most important and necessary for survival for the tent and its appurtenances, the cook and his kitchen to go on ahead of the rest of us, by at least an hour. Then we lined up, and just as the sun rose over the hills and the dawn chorus of birds succeeded the sounds of cicadas and the alarmingly louder sounds of nocturnal prowlers we set off. My husband, leader of the expedition kept very close to the bearer of the theodolite. Me, I just kept going, eyes on the ground, watching for snakes who, like us, woke up at dawn. After about an hour when pangs of hunger told us it was breakfast time, the glorious smell of sizzling bacon and fragrant coffee wafted past our quivering nostrils and there, round the next bend was breakfast. The table was set with its paste jar of frangipani; cook was busy over his fire. Fresh grapefruit, bacon and eggs, rolls and marmalade with heavenly coffee appeared as if by magic. Breakfast never tasted so good.

But soon it was time to go. Cook and cookie-matey, kitchen and food boxes left first, while we watched the carriers file past: tent, double bed, loo seat, carpet, fridge, box of clothes, bedding, tin bath - all the trimmings of modern living. The carriers' personal loads consisted of a light woven mat wrapped round their meagre belongings. Civilisation has a lot to answer for. For lunch, a few hours later, we sat under a shady tree, ate sandwiches and drank tepid water. Finally, in the late afternoon we reached journey's end. My legs were feeling decidedly wobbly and we were both sticky with heat. But, heaven is a tent in the middle of nowhere and there it was as if it had always been there. Our bath was ready, and, for once it was good to be a woman as I had first "go". There was only room for one in the bath and only water for one, so master had to wait his turn, Refreshed, we sat in the glow of a Tilley lamp along with the ever present insect life, listening to the sounds and smells of chicken roasting in its kerosene oven, sipping the first Scotch of the day. And so to bed under the mosquito net under the stars.

Next day, at dawn, it all began again.

....

Jennifer Cooper, accompanying her Federal Surveys husband M.A.R. (Michael) Cooper, who was engaged on observations for the re-definition of the scale of the Nigerian primary triangulation, experienced a method of living and travelling in various parts of the North in 1963 which was never tried by the Northern Nigerian Survey - living in a caravan. She produced the following short item as a contribution to the 50th Anniversary Conference of the Geomatics Division of the RICS, held at the University of Nottingham on 10-12 September 1999.

"Domestic Arrangements"

After spending my first tour in Lagos it was exciting on returning from leave to hear that we would be going to bush. Mike was given the job of re-defining the scale of the Nigerian primary triangulation using the Tellurometer MRA 2 to measure the sides of triangles at each chain junction. The work coincided with the issue of caravans to surveyors working in bush and ours duly arrived - silver in colour with FEDERAL SURVEYS painted in black on the sides. Gone were the days of pitching tents at each stop - instead we would do it in style with a brand-new caravan complete with an air conditioner, mosquito-screened windows and doors, bench beds, a wardrobe, writing desk and bookcase and a kitchen area with a kerosene cooker and fridge, cupboards and worktop, a sink, shower unit and last but not least an Elsan-type loo. There was enough room between the two beds for a cot - we were taking our three month old baby with us ...... and our dog Bannister.

In order to run the air conditioner and lights we had a generator and that is where the snags began before we even left Lagos. The generator didn't work, so it had to be taken to the PWD to be fixed. The intended date of departure came and it was still in pieces - the person responsible for mending it sacked, having sold off some of the parts! Mike decided that we would have to go without it. Makurdi, on the River Benue in the Northern Region, was to be our first base and after battening everything down in the caravan we loaded the car with the cold-store carrier, water filters, baby bath, carry cot, pram wheels, dog and of course - Nicholas. We set off leading the procession. A Land Rover towed the caravan. The labourers and all the survey equipment followed behind in a lorry. Finding that we had to keep stopping to wait for them to catch up we decided to bring up the rear, keeping a fair distance behind so as not to get covered in clouds of dust once we had left the tarmac. We had to stop by the roadside to feed Nicholas and I soon got used to the sea of faces that would appear from seemingly nowhere. We felt like a travelling circus with performances daily at 10 am and 2 pm.

Our first overnight stop was at Akure where we parked in the grounds of the rest house. Opening up the caravan we found the contents of both the kitchen cupboard and book-case strewn all over the floor, the front off the air conditioner and the desk lid jammed. My job was to see to Nicholas while Mike unloaded all the necessary bits and pieces from the car and Land Rover. I had the daily job of boiling water for the filters and sterilising bottles and after that making sure that everything was secure before we moved off again. Another night's stop - this time in a school compound and then an early start the next day in order to get the ferry across the Niger from Asaba to Onitsha. We joined the queue of cars, mammy wagons, lorries and foot passengers and eventually drove on to the ferry, hemmed in on all sides - no sign of the caravan which was ahead. We crossed the Niger in the heat of the day and discovered that the caravan was still on the Asaba side of the river. Several hours later it finally arrived but with a broken tow-bar. The driver had not unhitched the caravan, so as he drove up the ramp onto the deck of the ferry, the caravan was still coming down the ramp on the shore. Of course the tow bar broke. We had to book into the catering rest house until it was mended. Mike somehow managed the next day to find a welder in the middle of Onitsha market.

Off again at last and another night parked in another school compound. By now the scenery was changing to more open countryside. A relatively uneventful last leg of the journey before we reached Makurdi where Mike's work would begin. The next nine months would take us to the edge of the Sahara beyond Sokoto before going to a house in Okene where Mike's teaching career began at the Federal Survey School. Sometimes we only stayed in a place for three or four days before moving on to the next chain junction. Mail followed us around the country. We mastered the art of packing and unpacking the caravan without further mishap though the rutted laterite roads began to take their toll and we once saw the caravan ahead detach itself from the Land Rover and roll slowly into a culvert. It was important to camp near a source of water and if possible under the shade of a tree. Our water usually came from the river and was brought as headloads in jerrycans or from the local village well when it was hauled up in goatskin buckets. Laundry changed from Persil white to river water brown. We had stocked up on Heinz baby food before leaving Lagos and used the local markets to buy fruit, vegetables and meat, usually goat or chicken although further north guinea fowl were plentiful. There was sometimes a small local store which sold tins of Peak milk, tinned butter and bacon and sacks of Golden Penny flour complete with weevils. And of course, Star beer. I remember two of their exotic names - "Honolulu" and "Starlight" stores.

We all suffered from boils and bites which easily became infected by the dust and at times we had to find a mission hospital to get antibiotics. The temperature inside the caravan sometimes soared to 120° during the day. We rigged up a battery fan to keep Nicholas cool. When the repaired generator eventually caught up with us, we discovered that the air-conditioner was not working! Too much shaking on the corrugated roads had wrecked it. A nice idea, but...

Bannister produced nine puppies to add to our menagerie of chickens and guinea fowl (which we kept in wicker baskets for our later consumption) and a goat the labourers had bought. Mike went up and down hills with the Tellurometers and I pushed Nicholas out for walks in his pram with an eye on the birds of prey flying overhead. Life was never dull. A Fulani arrived with his daughter - she had nearly severed a toe and I was expected to render first aid. My ministrations with Dettol and a bandage were rewarded the next day with several chickens. Our Spode dinner service survived the bush and we still use it today, nearly forty years on, but there is nothing quite like dining off a camp table in the moonlight on the edge of the Sahara to the strains of Victor Sylvester on the BBC Overseas Service.

....

Labourers and porters

In the towns, labour always seemed to be in plentiful supply and, when a party was being set up, the news would spread like a bush fire. Those who had worked with surveyors before and had a difficult time did not seem to be perturbed and would cheerfully apply again, moving in and out of work, and others of all shapes, sizes, appearance and health would be assessed for suitability by the senior headman. Hausamen seemed to be quite at home in the bush and were very tolerant of the incessant and apparently purposeless journeying of surveyors *(Photo.174).* The size of the party accompanying the surveyor would of course vary very much with the type of work and the equipment to be carried, the availability of motorised transport, and the length of time to be spent on the task. In the 1940s, for instance, the Hunters needed 60 or 70 carriers for their reconnaissance for triangulation in Sokoto. In the late 1950s about 30 permanent people plus locally hired temporary carriers were employed on the writer's P Chain triangulation observations where, throughout the work, it was not possible to use motor transport, and on the triangulation work in the remote hills of the Cameroons, John Street had an army of men numbering between 200 and 250.

If anyone was entitled to adopt, for a maxim, the Latin expression *solvitur ambulando* (problems are solved by walking) then it had to be the surveyor. It was very common for transport to be in short supply or roads to be non-existent in the survey area, especially on triangulation work. It might occasionally be possible to hire a local lorry to save a long trek along a road, but loads would take priority and the men might still have to walk if funds for a second trip were not available.

Regular carriers would have their favourite loads, for some were lighter or easier to manage than others, and there was *girma* (pride) attached to the carrying of certain items such as the cash box, the theodolite, and anything of a personal nature to the surveyor. The standard ridge pole tent, flysheet, groundsheet and rear bathroom attachment were usually divided into three or four headloads. The wooden poles were always heavy, but the heaviest item of all could be the flysheet when it was wet after rain. On the first day's march there would be a scramble for the lightest load, which a man would have to carry as well as his own bedding mat and possessions, but the headman would see to it that loads were exchanged during the day and alternatives given on subsequent days. Placed together before the march, the loads were a very untidy and assorted collection of wooden and metal boxes, fire-blackened tins, headpans (which found universal use and which were far more common than buckets), bundles of tools, tripods, lamps, bedrolls, perhaps a bag of cement, buckets, a few live chickens, camp table, folding chairs and an assortment of personal bundles which might contain almost anything. Each carrier would make his own pad of grass or old cloth to place on his head beneath the load. If he was carrying a heavy or unwieldy item, two others would hold it up at arms length and then lower it on to the carrier's head *(Photo.167).* Many carriers would prefer to walk barefoot, especially when the going was muddy and everywhere slippery from the falling rain *(Photos 168 and 169),* but under harder conditions they might wear rough sandals fashioned from the treads of discarded motor tyres.

Finance would put a limit on the number of labourers and carriers and, for parties making intermittent moves in fairly well populated areas, locally engaged temporary porters *(Photo.172)* might be engaged at approved local rates of pay, which were invariably less than the daily wages commanded by permanent labourers. Local people, especially the women in the 'pagan' villages, were not however always suitable as carriers. They had no desire or intention to trek onwards all day to distant hills, which they knew lay outside their own tribal district. There were points beyond which they could not be persuaded to go. In their entire lives some had never been beyond the markets in adjacent villages and nothing could persuade them to go into the unknown. There was a lingering fear of abduction for slaving which had still been a risk until a generation or so before. Reaching these territorial limits they would put down their headloads, seek payment for their efforts, and return the way they had come. Without a reserve of labour, this could mean an enforced additional overnight camp for the party and wasted time until replacement carriers could be found from one of the villages which lay ahead. This was where an accompanying representative of the District Head or Emir was extremely useful. Unlike a survey headman, he could use his authority to commission such carriers. A survey headman, spreading the news of an approaching white man and his large party, might cause panic and cause the villagers to hide in the bush. Not only did the representative command a certain amount of respect but his presence could curb the excesses of some of the party's more exuberant members. He would act as a guide and a source of local information and he would go on ahead to arrange feeding and sleeping for the carriers.

John Pugh started his surveying career in Nigeria in 1942, and remembers an incident involving the use of local carriers. At Kebbi in southern Sokoto Province he had to intervene between labourers in a *chacha* (gambling) argument. A consequence of the trouble was that, trekking en route to survey a mining lease at Sabon Birni Abershi and the river Gulbin Ka, he had an overnight stop at Ungushi where he was abandoned by his labourers:-

> '*At dawn no carriers remained - nor any male inhabitants and Ungushi was a settlement of considerable size. My new headman said "No problem" and collected 30 pregnant women, stood each in front of a 56lb load, and said "Sabon Birni - march !" They all screamed, and their husbands appeared from under huts or in the bush., and we set off with these substitutes. We still found abandoned loads after 16 miles (through ,waterless and uninhabited bush), but finally reached Sabon Birni at about 3.0 a.m. next morning. Total distance from Kebbi about 45 miles.*'

Harry Rentema recalls his work in the bush in 1953:-

> '*........I was engaged on reconnaissance of trig points in the Kaduna-Ririwai area and I got an Emir's representative added to my party, who was a great help getting things done with the sarkis. He chartered extra carriers for me. Sometimes these forced labourers dropped their loads half-way and tried to escape into the bush with the Emir's representative on their heels. If he could not catch them, the first innocent farmer who crossed our way was forced to take over. On a few occasions rumours of my presence went ahead of us and the village was deserted by the men and we chartered women.*
>
> *Pay-day always was a hectic time. They each had to pay each their debts to one another and also the women, with whom they had spent some time, were lining up. A lot of noise. I tried to introduce a saving system and weekly pay instead of monthly. to prevent the everlasting money palavers and l was surprised how much they could save sometimes from their small salaries.*'

To the old regular labouring hands the avoidance of hard work was a perfected art. Overnight in a village, or along the way, a labourer might negotiate an extremely low rate with a penniless local villager to carry his load for him. This might be a woman, young, not so young or old, some with babies strapped to their backs or pregnant. The labourer might carry nothing except a thin cane to emphasise his authority and chivvy the carrier along and sound warnings about what the surveyor would do if the load was dropped or was late arriving at the end of the journey. Another of their ploys was to move on ahead of the party and warn the people of a village along the way that a white man was coming and they should provide them with free food and drink quickly or they might incur the surveyor's displeasure when he arrived *(Photo. 170)*.

At the start of the job a new permanent survey gang seemed like a collection of untidy, unco-operative weak-looking men but, as soon as the work or the travelling got under way, the chaff was quickly sorted from the grain by the headman. No party was without its problems. There were rivalries, insults, malingering and disobedience, but a strong headman could shelter the surveyor from much of it, and, in the circumstances, dismissals were relatively rare. A sort of hierarchy was fairly quickly worked out amongst the men. Characters including jokers, laggards, and showmen appeared from what had seemed an amorphous group, but as a general rule the party became a unit; tough and hard working. On a long job, life stories were told, imaginations ran riot, there was a great deal of light hearted leg-pulling based on half truths and total fiction, and a great saga of personal inter-relationships was worked out. Showing off, and having a good laugh at the expense of one another, was part of the Hausaman's character. Each had special names for one another, invariably not very complimentary, and the cause of constant hilarity, and they adopted a Hausa nickname for the surveyor, a name which might stay with him for the remainder of his years in the country. Even quite small framed men seemed to be tough and wiry and on trek they often showed remarkable endurance and good temper. Daily walks of 15 miles and more, carrying loads of over 40 lbs, were quite common, and in blistering heat along rough paths or in areas where there no paths at all, through streams and on rocky hills *(Photo.171)*, their performance was remarkable. Sweat would pour from their foreheads, their clothes would be saturated, but they were always ready with a big smile when greeted. Long treks were a monotonous business and they moved along through the heat of the day in a steady, mindless sleepwalk.

Looking back, it is easy to realise what a slender thread of trust held parties together and it is wondered how easy it would be to do the same thing today. Some men moved much faster than others and over the distances to be covered the party could be strung out over many miles, and it was not difficult to lose the way and become separated. The surveyor was dependent upon every load carried, for the luxury of duplicates, spares and extra supplies could not be afforded. There was great dependence upon water carriers and the prospect of being stranded with a large number of items and no supplies if the men had deserted anywhere along the way stirs a sense of gratitude that these people were as reliable they were.

Keith Sargeant recalls:-

> *'A surveyor in bush was very dependent on the quality of his headman and his gang of survey labourers. Among others I well remember Jatto with his walking stick marching at the rear of a column of carriers when moving camp. I described him in my diary as having "an extraordinary walk - very bow-legged with knees as least a foot apart, stoops like a gorilla and has gorilla-like arms". He was a very good disciplinarian and most of the labourers were frightened of him. He was also good at persuading local village chiefs to produce additional carriers when required to augment the normal survey gang of some eight or ten men.*
>
> *Another very important member of a survey party was the messenger. His main function was to trek to the nearest Treasury, often over 100 miles distant, to collect money to pay the gang and any extra carriers and to cover the surveyor's own costs. In particular, I recall Hama Aji (a Fulani) who was completely trustworthy and, despite his slim build, well able to trek more than forty miles a day. Although a surveyor was required by regulations to keep the party's money in an iron box, the so-called cash-tank (chained to his bed at night), Hama Aji - and most other messengers - preferred to carry cash wrapped in a bundle on his head rather than in a more obvious container.'*

Each man was issued with a machete, which became his prized and cared for tool and which he obviously regarded as highly as the surveyor regarded his theodolite. These machetes would be constantly honed until they were as sharp as razors, and personalised in various ways with carefully bound handles. It was not unknown, of course, for these working tools to become weapons and sometimes used as a threat or in self defence in times of trouble, but such incidents were extremely rare. A gang of men arriving at a remote village each 'armed' with a machete could sometimes strike fear into local people who would rapidly disappear into the bush, especially if mischievously threatened with the arrival of a white man. Many villages had never seen a white man and it was a memorable event in the lives when he actually arrived *(Photos. 181 and 183)*, stood in the village square, and even stayed the night in a local house or camped nearby *(Photo.184)*. Being part of his team, labourers might be tempted to use their 'power' to obtain concessions with accommodation and food in the villages in which they stayed, threatening 'consequences' if they were not well treated. In the course of their surveying work when clearing sight lines, labourers would sometimes, out of sheer exuberance or cussedness, cut down plants or bushes which were valuable to the local people, sparking off problems and demands for compensation. Rates for compensation did not seem very generous but they were, nevertheless, sometimes better than the crops were worth, and certainly saved the task of marketing and selling, and there was an incentive therefore to exaggerate a little, even to the extent of claiming compensation for damage which was nowhere near a survey area.

In the villages at night the men might enjoy good food and a lot of good-natured banter, but of course there could be, and often was, some trouble. This could involve women, the wives of villagers, unwillingness or inability to pay for food they had eaten, and running up debts with gambling. Some would gamble their clothes away *(Photo.175)*, get into difficult debt, and seek advances of their pay. Sometimes a distinctive shirt would appear on several different backs before the month was out. Those in real trouble might abscond and never be heard of again. There were no policemen in the bush and they would have to be sent for in times of trouble, although village chiefs or elders, especially in Moslem areas, would mete out justice on minor matters. The writer recalls an incident in the Jema'a District when, unknown to him, his men had caused a fracas resulting in serious injuries to some local villagers. The village head reported the matter to the police who set out in pursuit of the mobile party, locating it and apprehending the guilty men a week or so later. In certain areas it was considered advisable that the party be accompanied by a local authority policeman *(Dandoka)* and that he also travelled with the party's messenger on his monthly journey to collect money from the treasury.

Officially, pay day came once a month, but this was far too infrequent for parties on the move and weekly payment was more common. Some labourers did not wish to take their full entitlement and the surveyor would organise a savings bank which would pay out a useful lump sum when the tour in the bush came to an end. Others could not wait and were in constant debt, and some form of compulsory saving had to be imposed upon them which caused hardship at the time, but for which they were extremely grateful later on. The evasion of local authority tax was a common preoccupation of mobile survey labourers who alleged 'no fixed abode', but sooner or later vigilant tax collectors were likely to catch up with them.

John Street recalls:-

'Pay day was not only about money. It was also a rudimentary court day for punishments and a day for administering medicine. More seriously, it was also forum to agree rough justice for the many wounds inflicted when labourers clashed with local people, generally over disputes about women.'

It was usually not a bad idea for some women, preferably wives without children, to accompany a large party as camp followers. They would certainly help to keep some of the men out of mischief, could cook and visit local markets for food while the men worked, and even provided credit for those whom they trusted. Some had quite an entrepreneurial spirit and came back off a trek much better off than many of the men.

Some daily paid men took on or drifted into special duties and became acknowledged 'experts' at it. There was the man who carried the specie box, heavy at the beginning of the month when it contained a large amount in copper coin, but getting lighter as the weeks went by, and giving him the opportunity to accompany the messenger into town when the month-end replenishment was needed. The writer recalls that before setting out on his first bush job he had to fill the box with jute cash-bags from the bank containing £90 in shillings and pence. In local markets the *anini*, one tenth of a penny, a very small coin with a hole through its centre, was still in use in the 1950s, but when roofing washers became six a penny in the markets and hardware stores the people found it cheaper to use *aninis* and got their washers from the bank ! Paper currency was of much too high a denomination and was unlikely to be acceptable in many of the country markets and villages along the way. The specie box was of heavy galvanised steel construction approximately 18"x 12"x 9", with a completely detachable overlapping lid held in place by a long steel bolt about 3/4" thick, which passed through holes at each end of the base and lid of the box. Through one end of the bolt was a hole to take a padlock and chain. The key to the padlock was always carried by the surveyor and at night the chain was wrapped around the legs and frame of the surveyor's camp bed.

John Street recalls:-

' We often had 50 or 60 men, with some 20 to 30 more casual labourers

from local areas, and paying such a lot weekly meant two cash boxes and two policemen with us much of the time. Each box had a chain and a clamp to fasten around the carrier's arm. This was all about security, but Audu Gora asked me to agree these clamps would not be used once we were in bush. He had lost a man, tied to his box, drowned in a river crossing at some time !'

No account of the people with whom we worked would be complete without mention of the night watchmen, or *maigadi*. They were generally elderly, loyal men, some of them retired from the army, or seasoned labourers, old headmen or messengers. The watchman would generally arrive at the house or camp just before dusk, greet all those present "*Barka da yamma*". "*Barka dai*", and arrange his bedding and prayer mat. If he had been trekking with the party all day, it was unreasonable to expect him to stay awake on guard throughout the night so he would often sleep the night away, assuming his presence would alone be enough to deter intruders, human and animal. Just before turning in one might sarcastically say "Goodnight mai gardi, sleep well, *sai da safe* (until the morning)". "*To, Allah ya kai mu.* Goodnight Sir". On wet nights it was not unusual to be woken up by his snoring as he lay under the flysheet of the tent. But often he would be awake, and it was comforting to see his face highlighted by the orange glow of his small camp fire. "*Maigadi*, what of the night ?" "All is well, Sir" would come the reassuring reply. "*Barka da dare*". "*Barka dai*". These men had few physical powers but they were not afraid to loose off a shower of arrows from their hunting bows if necessary. This was demonstrated to the writer one dark night near Zangwan Katab:-

> *'I awoke to what I thought was one of the watchman's hens moving around under the flysheet a foot or two from where I lay. Whatever it was then crawled under the side-flap of my tent and I felt its movement as it touched the frame of the bed six inches beneath me and rattled the chain of the cash box. Suddenly, without warning, my bed moved violently, turned on its side, and then almost upside down as I fell out, in total darkness, in a tangle of blankets, mosquito net and rods. I shouted for the watchman, but he was sound asleep, and I tried to find my torch which was lost in the confusion. The bed continued to move and was apparently being dragged, with me still tangled inside it, under the side of the tent. By now I could hear the cash box rattling violently and realised that this was no chicken, it was a thief doing his level best to purloin our money. But it was securely fastened to my bed and the bed-frame strong enough to withstand his efforts. My shouting woke the watchman, and the would-be thief made off, followed by a shower of arrows from my watchman's bow, but too late and very wide of the target I am sure. The culprit turned out to be one of a group of local people who had been around when I paid the men earlier in the day, had seen where the money came from, and watched as the cash box was put away. Had he been able to steal it he would have been disappointed with its contents. It was late in the month and it was virtually empty.'*

Then there was the man who carried the theodolite, charged with considerable responsibility, and never far from the eyes of the surveyor. To drop the instrument, which was always carried in its padded, pyramidal-shaped heavy case, was a cardinal sin and the regular carrier was rewarded with a special personal bonus from the surveyor if the instrument was safely carried throughout the duration of the work.

Some men received simple training as heliomen. Once adjudged competent and reliable they might be sent alone to distant points on faraway hills to align their mirrors throughout the day towards the surveyor's station, monotonous, lonely, difficult and sometimes dangerous work. In one area of the P Chain in the late 1950s there were a few lions and it had to be arranged for heliomen to be accompanied by an armed policeman, though how effective his ancient rifle would have been had there been trouble can only be guessed. Some triangulation points were 50 or 60 miles apart and between them lay difficult country over which travelling could be very slow. Communication with the main party was by a simple code of light signals using the heliograph with meanings such as "More light", "Less light", "Finish for the day", and "Move to the next station". Sometimes there was no response to such signals and it was very frustrating for the surveyor, who could see through the telescope of his theodolite, that the sun was shining at the helio station. Perhaps the helioman had dozed off in his boredom, or in the intense heat shimmer had misinterpreted a signal and moved off and trekked away before work was complete, climbing to the next point a day or two later and directing the light of the sun to trig points not yet occupied. Heliomen depended upon their eyesight alone and did not have the surveyor's advantage of a telescope. The logistics of operating and moving an observation party could be quite daunting in the absence of voice communication between the hills, until the advent of the Tellurometer which provided a microwave telephone link and sounded the death knell of traditional triangulation.

Then of course there was the umbrella man *(Photo.138),* who had to remember that his principal task was to keep the sun off the instrument, not himself, and to ensure that the surveyor's face was also shaded when the instrument was in use. As his attention wandered with the boredom of his task, it was advisable always for the surveyor to be very conscious of the threat which the sharp ends of the umbrella frame posed for eyes, spectacles and the back of the neck.

Trekking

John Pugh recalled:-

'I did three tours in my seven years in the Survey. In those days roads were few and we walked everywhere - my best effort was 63 miles in 36 hours in order to catch a weekly lorry and so save myself another 120 miles to the railway. On average in the bush I saw another white face about once per month, my longest spell being 4½ months during the triangulation work. I never felt lonely, though - my Northern labourers looked after me, I looked after them, they pulled my leg unmercifully and I pulled theirs. We were friends, in spite of the differences in race and culture. I taught them how to sign their names, and gave them an extra penny per day (when the standard wage was nine pence) if they could sign on pay day. I had read the Koran and kept the Ramadan fast (partially - I would still be having breakfast at first light, and would look forward to a pot of tea when back in camp in late afternoon) because if I felt exhausted by early afternoon I knew they would be feeling even worse, and so we would stop work for the day. It was an enjoyable life, and very good for developing character and personality. When I came back to London in 1956 I felt a generation older than academic colleagues only four or five years my junior.'

For the Moslems in the survey parties, the month of Ramadan meant difficult days. During the hours of darkness they might eat, drink and be more awake than they were during daylight hours. Unfortunately for them, as government employees, this was when they were expected to work. From sunrise to sunset they might not drink, eat, or even rinse the mouth. This was a really stern test in the harsh and dry climate of the North, especially for men engaged in physical work or trekking. Normality was resumed after the confirmed sighting of the new moon and the excitement of the feast of Id el Fitr which marked the end of Ramadan. It was a day of *salla* (prayer), feasting and enjoyment. Towards the end of Ramadan came mounting excitement and it was a good idea for a travelling survey party to be camped near a large village or town so the men could join the celebrations. Id el Kabir, another public holiday came two months later and Id el Maulud was the Prophet's birthday.

The writer recalls:-

'It was normal to get a very early start for a long trek, getting up before dawn, and completing the greater part of the journey before it became too hot and clean clothes began acquiring stains of sweat and dust. Breakfast could be taken along the route but I preferred to eat before setting off, it was less bother for my men. Early starts were much easier in the open country of the north where the skies were larger and the pre-dawn light much better, but the dense bush and broken country of the southern part of the Northern Region made trekking in the dark very hazardous. Some long treks were tedious, interminable slogs, through drab, monotonous scrubland, with little but discomfort to occupy the mind, shadows growing shorter until there were no shadows at all at about mid-day. As they paced away the miles there would be little talking amongst the men, most of them in a sort of walking

trance. I found that counting footsteps and guessing the distance to the next distant visible feature could become an obsession. To this day I still find myself doing it !

In forested country, in rough hills and in the tsetse fly areas, horses were not used and the surveyor might find it easier to use a bicycle, which would have to be carried over the difficult bits. In any case I was never very fond of horses which, even at the best of times, could have a perverse mind of their own, stank, and attracted flies by the thousand. On reasonable paths beaten hard and smooth by the feet of local people, cycling was preferable to walking, but in soft sand, loose rocks, deep mud, elephant grass and thorn bush it could be very hard going. The use of bicycles by a few members of the party may have saved some walking, but it did little to improve the overall speed of a survey party which was dependent upon the rate of progress of the porters.

100 miles of trekking in a week was quite common, and 20 to 30 miles a day was done frequently, and messengers were known to cover 40 miles in 10 hours.

Villages encountered along the way were used as resting points, the men sometimes buying something to eat if it was available, and taking a drink, though many would take neither. In pagan areas, rather than drink the tepid discoloured water proffered, some of the lapsed or non-Moslems in the party might be tempted by the strong village beer. Alcohol on empty stomachs was a recipe for trouble and a good headman would see that his regular men did not indulge.

Trekking with a very large party was quite a rare thing by the late 1950s since most of the major trig schemes had been completed. Subsequent work called for mobility and was based to a great extent on the use of vehicles. It was therefore an unusual sight to see a long single file of men with their assorted headloads making their way along winding paths. On trig reconnaissance in 1957 my route between hills crossed a little used road along which a European motorist happened to be passing. Amazed, he stopped, photographed us, and said he had read about such things being done in the past, but just could not imagine that people still lived and travelled that way. "

River crossings

During the wet season, swollen rivers and streams could present a serious obstacle to the progress of a party. John Pugh remembered:-

It poured all night. At dawn 30 or so carriers appeared (arranged overnight with the senior village elder) ready to move me the 45 or so miles to Zungagara, equipped with food, etc., for a 2-day walk. It had stopped raining. After about 6 miles we came to a river in flood, but there was a dugout canoe, so that one person and a load could be ferried across by a paddler. It took about three hours to get us all across. After another three miles or so, the same again - flooded river, dugout canoe. I recall that while waiting at this point the headman's wife went to light a cigarette, and was roundly reprimanded by her husband, as we were in Ramadan. A few more miles and a third river, about 50 yards wide, in spate, and with no canoe. We took the guy-ropes off the tents and tied them together to make a lifeline. I and half-a-dozen other swimmers laid the line across the river, tied at each end. There were tree-stumps in the river on which one could stand with head above water, and we put one person on each, myself on the first. The carriers, all Tiv, were in no way worried - each man walked in up to his neck, took, a deep breath and walked on while holding to the lifeline. At first base I grabbed him, lifted him above water-level, and after a minute or two he would take another deep breath and disappear en route to the next base. We got them all across. Then there was a complication. The headman, chainmen and spare signallers had their wives with them, all Fulani or Shuwa Arab, aged between about 17 and 26, who watched all this in horror. The headman told them all to strip, collected their garments in one bundle, and took it across the river, keeping it dry, before returning. The wives, looking like a Follies Bergères chorus, remained on the bank. He told his wife she had to set an example, walked her in up to her neck, made her take a deep breath, and holding her left hand while she slid her right hand along the lifeline, brought her to me at first base. I seized this naked young woman and tried to lift her to get her head above water. She clung fiercely to me but climbed steadily to get as high as possible. I was smothered by wet female flesh and had to struggle to get my face free so that I could breathe myself. Finally I managed to turn her in the right direction with hand on lifeline, patted her back and sent her off towards second base, only to be immediately smothered by lady No. 2 as she arrived. It is the only time in my life that I have had six very attractive young women, not one of them wearing a stitch, successively clinging to me in tight embrace ! I was not wearing a stitch either but had been standing in a very cold river for three hours, and all I wanted was to get these confounded women over to the other side !

After a few more miles we camped for the night, exhausted. The next day dawned fresh and lovely. One could see the mountains of the Cameroons 100 miles away, beautifully clear. We set off again, the carriers singing as usual, and I joined in with tunes I knew, to their delight. After about six miles we met a cross-path, with two Tiv walking down it. All the loads went down, for conversation, after which all my carriers came and asked for their pay. I said I would pay them at Zungagara, but they wanted it then. Why ? They had just been told of a song festival being held 20 miles away on the Benue, and just had to go to it. I said that they could not leave me in the middle of nowhere and expect to be paid. They invited me to go with them, as I could already sing some of their songs. When I said "No" to joining them or paying them, they said "Oh well, too bad, bye-bye" or words to that effect, and started away. I stopped their going and paid them all - they had a tough time the day before, and they departed with happy smiles and hand-waves, already starting to sing. I was left with about 25 miles to go. I went on with my personal camp kit, food and steward, instruments, headman and signallers, and left everything else with the remaining people and the tents. We reached Zungagara, borrowed some empty huts, and started work next morning, while locally-recruited carriers went back to retrieve the rest of the party and stores. It did not really seem unusual - by then I had learned to expect upsets to any programme.'

Keith Sargeant also remembers river crossings:-

'Much of a topographical surveyor's work was in remote undeveloped country with few motor roads. A motor vehicle was rarely of little use and the surveyor would accompany his gang of carriers on foot, by bicycle or by horse in tsetse free areas. In the dry season most of the rivers - even large ones would dry up and presented few problems. During the rainy season however, many rivers were in flood and the carriers had a precarious job wading rivers without losing their head-loads (Photos.178 and 179). Often the only way across large deep rivers was by a calabash raft or other kind of makeshift boat.'

Harry Rentema remembers his first triangulation work:-

'In May 1953 the rains started and I got another task: reconnaissance and observation of second order triangulation in the area between Kaduna and Kafanchan. It brought me to many hilltops with my plane table, building beacons, and later on with theodolite and helios. I rented a horse (Photo.177) and sometimes a bicycle.

Observing angles called for good organisation and good instructions for the heliomen with their helios on the surrounding hills. Also good contacts with the local chiefs were important.

It usually rained once or twice a day and in between there was sunshine. Observations were done in the morning or late afternoon. Sometimes we were surprised by heavy thunderstorms and little streams would become wild rivers. Once, returning from a reconnaissance, it was pouring and I had to leave my horse behind with some labourers. I swam across the river with my boots and raincoat on. Liman, my chainman could not swim but managed to get across. After one hour walking in the rain and pitch dark we met my steward with some villagers and a Tilley lamp, looking for us and guiding us back home to the dry tent. My steward looked after me very well.'

Crossing deep rivers, forested gullies and streams was always a problem. The cry of "*Hankali*" from the men ahead was a warning of difficult conditions being encountered. Away from motor roads there were no bridges, though in some places slippery logs might span narrow torrents. The beds of the streams were often very uneven and rocky and a different technique might be needed for each crossing. Large trees could sometimes be felled to create a temporary bridge. Headloads were sometimes unavoidably dropped into the water, and it was a good idea to ensure that perishable food items and vital papers were kept in tins and sealed. Plastic bags were not so common in those days and the tropical outfitters' airtight steel trunks were invaluable for irreplaceable items. When crossing deep, brown opaque floodwater it was advisable to attach long lines and floating markers to locate anything dropped into the water. This was especially important when the cash box contained three weeks' wages for the entire party, plus their savings. Where the route crossed expanses of *fadama,* or deeply flooded swamp, each footstep could release bubbles of evil smelling gas which had a habit of going up inside the legs of your shorts. Major rivers would have to be crossed using canoes *(Photo.180),* and if there was only one canoe available, and that at a point several miles along the river bank, it could take a day or more to move a party of sixty men from one side to the other, carrying perhaps one or two men and two loads on each journey. The canoes were usually narrow, unstable affairs, and it was a considerable act of faith and balancing which allowed the very large T3 theodolite box to travel precariously perched astride the sides of the boat. Those who have not worked outdoors during a tropical wet season can have little conception of the suddenness with which a stream can rise, and an important decision was on which side of a river to establish camp; choose the wrong side and you may not be able to cross in the morning to the work site, or continue the trek. What had been a shallow, fordable stream might became a foaming, muddy brown torrent, tearing at its banks and carrying away branches and whole trees.

Local people

The further you moved from 'civilisation' the more courteous and untouched the local people became and, in areas which had not been influenced by Islam, the surveyor was privileged to catch glimpses of a fast disappearing Africa, with ways of life that few others might ever witness, where science was totally unknown, where nature and the spirits were in control. Hills, crevices, dark places, strange rocks, caves and even trees were believed by some to harbour powerful deities and were avoided for fear of retribution. It was sometimes difficult to get survey labourers to venture near if they had been warned off by the local people. Life there was seemingly primitive and unregulated. These people were perhaps being 'spoiled' by the contact the surveyor was making, watching him doing things they would remember for a lifetime, eating food that came out of tins, carrying mysterious objects, seeing him set out to climb hills only the menfolk with their hunting dogs and 'dane' guns may have visited, creating lights like bright stars in daylight on faraway hills, and leaving strange marks and effigies on the summits of the hills. Extraordinary and unconventional situations would often have to be accepted, if you were wise, with a smile and without embarrassment. Villagers would gather around to watch every single movement around the survey camp and even visits to the *zana* matting enclosure around the latrine pit were cause for speculation and curiosity.

John Pugh related the following story about the Mada people:-

'The summit of the Mada Hills was also part of my chain, a junction point with an East-West chain. The first surveyor there was Campbell, in 1910, not long after the British moved into the north. As a reference point, he put a flag on a pole about 1,000 feet from the trig. station, which cost him his life. The Mada Hills were a refuge centre for tribes driven off the surrounding plains during the 19th Century jihad of the Fulani. Six armed Madas approached Campbell and asked him to remove the flag. He refused, so they stabbed him with their spears and removed the flag, while leaving the pole. That was when one learned that flags were symbols of devils ! The second surveyor there was my colleague Blanchflower (known as Snowdrop). Having been warned about flags, he used a single pole as a reference point. I understand that for his first three days he was observed by six scowling

Mada males, all armed with spears, who watched him attentively. Each day he took the theodolite out of its padded box, put it on the tripod over the trig. point, and spent the day observing before putting the instrument away at dusk. After three days the locals appeared beaming with friendship, and offering him a chicken (real wealth there !). He sent a messenger to the local District Officer at Wamba to say that all was well, but the message was not received, the messenger having apparently absconded in view of local hostility. Snowdrop was given friendly greetings by the locals, including one day when a party of 50 or so, in full war-paint, waved to him as they passed. During the day he heard gunfire and yells - this later appeared to be the D.O. trying to collect tax, but driven off with one policeman dead and others injured. In the evening the local party again passed by, carrying wounded and waving cheerfully. Snowdrop stopped them and attended to the wounded with bandages and antiseptics, for which he was given appreciative gestures. In due course, having finished his observations, he moved on towards Naraguta. When the dry season stopped work, he returned to Jos, and on the way stopped to speak to D.O. Wamba, saying, that he , personally, had found the Mada people most helpful and pleasant. "Oh", said the D.O. "I had forgotten you were there. I had trouble and was driven off with no tax collected. You must be the mad missionary". "Me, a missionary ?" "Yes. I heard of a mad white man living on top of the mountain who each morning took his god out of a comfortable bed, put him on an altar and spent the day with his head against the god while walking round and round him until dusk, when he put the god back to sleep ! The Madas believe that mad men are favoured by the spirits, and they take special care of them" . Snowdrop asked if there had been any sign of the missing messenger. "Oh yes. We found his head and his boots, but think they ate the rest of him ".

I was the third surveyor on the Madas. On my first day half-a-dozen types dressed in spears turned up to watch. I hastily built an altar, took my god out of his comfortable bed and put him on the tripod, and leaned my head against him. The locals beamed, tapped their heads, and went away happily - another nut case !'

The Mada Hills were the home of the Eggon people and also the scene of the murder by local people of a survey labourer working with Captain Buckingham in 1929. A full description of this incident is given in Niven's book *Nigerian Kaleidoscope*.

In 1961 Clifford Rayner was engaged on photo control work for the mapping of various small towns and remembers:-

'The rest houses in Bama, Gwoza and Dikwa were spacious and comfortable. Bama rest house had a kerosene fridge, as did Gwoza, which made for very comfortable living. Gwoza, a tiny village close to G 14 trig station, has a magnificent view down the western edge of the Cameroon foothills. G 14 was the last trig of the Cameroon range, standing about 3,000 feet out of the plain. The area was reputedly rife with hostile pagan natives in the hills and certainly in living memory there have been serious incidents with tax collectors! On climbing G 14 we approached the 'guardian village' with care and caution. After some time and much 'parlez' we agreed that the locals could carry our loads to the top of the hill and, after we had finished our work, bring them down again! My labourers did not object ! With only about 40 minutes work at the summit, to tie the Gwoza town control to G 14, we were considered to be rather crazed to expend such effort, at least seven hours climbing, to such little effect !'

In his novel, *Descent from the Hills*, Stanhope White paints a detailed, humane and enthralling picture of the life of these hill people and the impact upon them of the white man's world.

The villages

The arrival of a party at a small town or village called for a courtesy call on, or by, the local chief or village headman *(Photo.185)*. The meeting, within the limits of the surveyor's Hausa, or through an interpreter if it was in an area where one of the minor languages was spoken, involved the exchange of simple goods of goodwill such as a few eggs or a hen, or an exchange of greetings if the party was merely passing through. The chief might mark the occasion by dressing in richly coloured clothes, but more often in the smaller places his clothes would be well worn and dingy and he would be scarcely distinguishable from the other villagers, and would come in a small procession of elders to see for himself what a surveyor's tented camp looked like *(Photo.191)*. Such meetings involved little more than the exchange of pleasantries and traditional enquiries about health, household, work and crops. There was little that the surveyor could give the chief in return but, thinking in retrospect, much that he could have carried for such an occasion. A few well illustrated magazines were, for example, highly prized possessions in places where they were never seen. Instead, small sums in silver were usually handed over.

John Pugh related a story of his experience in the Sokoto bush in 1942:-

'At Sabon Birni.......... I was made to realise that I was the first white man seen there, or at least for many years. We walked in past a 3-year-old playing in the sand, who responded happily to greetings from my labourers. My "Sannu, yaro" was rewarded with screams. His mother, an attractive Fulani aged about 20, shot out of a hut, seized her child, looked around, took a look at me and went behind a wall and was sick. That put me in my place !'

Trevor Brokenshire recalls:-

'Whenever we moved into a new area it was the custom of the local 'sarki' or village headman to bring us a 'dash' of a chicken, pigeons, or once, as I recall, freshly killed meat. This time the 'dash' was most unusual, fresh lettuce and spring onions ! We were very surprised, but very pleased. It wasn't until some days later, having moved camp some 20 miles and next day happening to use a photo-point detail near a mission outpost and talking to the missionary, that I heard the story of the mysterious disappearance of salad stuff from the well-stocked vegetable garden!'

John Street recalls:-

'Travelling alone for long periods, and moving camp every two or three days, I rapidly got introduced to horse riding. Early in the evening, after the camp was placed, a long, white-robed trail of people would be seen approaching the site. It would be the chief with all his officials, and many children behind, coming to see the strangers. We would lay out mats and clean up the site and at twilight the party would begin. Audu Gora, my headman, would sit on my left; Bayero Jalingo, the cook, behind on my right; and thus we greeted them.
First came the long introductory exchanges, which scarcely varied. (When very tired and trekking, I used to repeat these twenty-minute exchanges in my head !) Next came gifts. Forewarned, the man in charge of horses would come and offer a horse, saddlery and a boy, to accompany us as long as we were in their territory.
Then, slowly, the talk moved to more complex things and despite (later) years of practice, I would lose the thread. Some stories cannot be told; but one evening, late into the exchange of food and 'welcomes', something very serious was said. Audu Gora turned to me "The chief would like to know why the Europeans send such an old man to suffer in the bush with such hard work, when he should be with his women and children". I was all of twenty-six, but had long since abandoned any attempt to shave, no longer had a mirror, and was out-of-doors some six or seven hours daily. My internal image was of someone who was incredibly fit, battle-hardened, and a survivor...........and these people were very sorry for me !'

Villages were often characterised by the barking of dogs, the clink of a blacksmith's hammer, the shortened 'cock-ER-do' of demented cockerels, the pounding of corn, the discordant braying of donkeys, the endless cooing of doves, and later on, when all was quiet, the dogs would bay to the moon throughout the night. When staying in the rest house at Dogon Dutse on the Plateau the writer was so disturbed by a single dog one night that in sheer exasperation he took out his rifle and fired a single shot into the night sky. He should have foreseen that this would cause pandemonium. The entire village woke up and set off the barking of twenty or more other dogs.

During the evening, particularly on special occasions, such as the arrival of a survey party, there would be enthusiastic drumming. From a distance, and with echoes off rocks, the sound was a jumble of noise, but near to, the complex rhythmic patterns of sound and timing were clever and intoxicating. Clifford Burnside recalls:-

> *'I well remember my first Saturday night in a native village. Usually after dark things get remarkably quiet, but this particular night there was a great commotion with frantic drumming and much singing and shouting. Being brought up on a Sanders of the River concept of Africa, I carefully crept out of my hut to see what was going on; an orgy of some sort perhaps? But no, I was sadly disappointed. It proved to be nothing more than about a couple of dozen people lying about (literally) in front of a great bonfire and managing to make a remarkable amount of noise.*
>
> *At a much later date and in another part of the country I did experience an evening event which I still recall as an interlude of pure magic. It was in Bauchi Province in quite a large village on the edge of the Yankari Game Reserve, across which I was hoping to set out a chain of secondary trig points. This particular evening the village seemed to go to sleep at about 7 pm as usual but by about 9 pm there was a large harvest moon low in the sky that produced a scene more in keeping with what one might associate with tropical Africa. No doubt because of the lightness of the evening, a deep sounding bass drum began to beat out a slow majestic rhythm in one part of the silent village. And then, in another part of the village, as if in response to this, a single wind instrument with the sound of something like a cor anglais picked up the theme and then between them they began a stately duet; the one responding to the other in turn. Sometimes there are times when one wishes one was not alone and that an event could be shared by at least someone else. This was an event of this nature and by no means the only one I experienced in my 12 years in Nigeria. But the moon drifted down behind the palm trees all too quickly. The music became slower and slower in its beat until finally, it just stopped and the silence was again complete. It had been a wonderful form of African tenebrae.'*

Survey work in the bush

Apart from travelling, living and surviving, the surveyor did, of course, have to carry out technical and administrative work under uncomfortable conditions. After walking long distances through forests, or across dry, featureless sandy plains, through swamps and streams, climbing rocky mountains, and perhaps camping on summits *(Photo.188)* sometimes for weeks on end, his job was to carry out precise instrumental observations or linear measurements, often under extreme climatic conditions, with burning sun, glare, haze, heat shimmer and the distraction of a thousand insects, and the mathematical work which followed. *Sai da hakuri a kan taru* (only by patience can one gather it all together). There was also the preparation and maintenance of drawings, maps and fieldsheets, the care and adjustment of instruments, forward planning of the work and the logistics of support parties who might be in other areas (bearing in mind that the use of portable radios was unheard of). Government bureaucracy created substantial paperwork for payment vouchers, work diaries, reports and general correspondence. Money always seemed to be short. Directives from HQ were easily composed but very difficult to implement in the bush. An office accountant might have great difficulty in allowing for the problems and financial implications of difficult communications, long distance trekking, rivers in flood, illness, time spent on bush clearance, strikes, and poor visibility. The usual instruction in an attempt to save money was to give the men a rest day instead of extra pay, the very last thing a tough man in the bush may want, and which might hinder the completion of a job.

Surveying with optical instruments and tapes required line-of-sight conditions and the principal occupation of most survey gangs when they were not on the move was in bush clearance and tree felling, indeed there were many villagers who thought this was the principal task of the surveyor, and certainly a survey party's efforts could provide a source of ready-felled firewood for local people for many months or years to come. There were no power saws to assist this task and the work was done using machetes and axes. To ease their work labourers went to considerable lengths to keep their tools as sharp as possible, but there was danger when many axes were being used in close proximity, especially if broken shafts had been replaced with local green wood. On a large felling job one man at rest would begin an encouraging or slightly derogatory and bawdy chant, using a tin or a headpan as an improvised drum, or perhaps a single stringed instrument called a *molo*, to encourage the others to keep time with an easy and rhythmic swing of their axes. David Anderson, in *Surveyors Trek*, mentioned this when his men were drilling holes in rock with hand drills and hammers "*A-hank-ali da ai ki HUM*", the stroke of the hammer coming on the *HUM* ("Care-ful-ly we're working *HUM*"), or "*Kawo maza ma-ga-ni*", ("Quickly, bring me *magani*"), *magani* being water, medicine or cure, either to slake the thirst, or cool down the rock drills and flush the rock flour from the drill holes. An awful lot of trees were felled, even in Forest Reserves, where the Survey Department had a legal dispensation to do so, but surveyors always had a conscience about it, it seemed such a terrible waste of resources and time, especially when lines were cut only to be abandoned because they did not achieve the required results. But cutting broad swathes of vegetation down to the ground was the only way to achieve the necessary sight lines on many triangulation schemes, and it was a blessing when this work was much reduced by the use of traversing methods and the erection of observation towers.

Camping

Apart from the work itself, perhaps the most memorable aspect of life in the bush was the camping. The care which went into the positioning of the tent could make all the different between a comfortable and an unpleasant camp. *In za ka huta, ka huta a babbar inuwa.* (If you have to rest, be sure to rest where there is plenty of shade). The best shade tree of all, if one could be found, was the *dorowa* or locust bean tree, with pleasant dappled shade from its delicate fern-like foliage. In the wet season the daytime breezes, pleasant as they were, could increase in strength towards evening and it was tempting to align the open end of the tent down-wind. But the breezes were invariably blowing towards the storm breeding area and it was from that direction that later in the day or at night the great tornado and rainstorm would approach, blowing under the flysheet and threatening to blow the tent away. So it was a good idea in the wet season for the tent to face the daytime breezes, erected on a slight slope, facing downhill, surrounded by deeply cut *lumba twos,* or drainage trenches, to carry away the storm-water, and anchored to substantial pegs or large boulders. It was very difficult to keep things like bedding and clothing dry, especially when they were being packed, for the days of polythene sheeting had not arrived. A temporary excursion in the rain is one thing, but to live in almost perpetual rain at the height of the wet season is quite another.

As a rule, a survey party would travel with only two tents, a large ridge pole tent for the surveyor and his books, equipment and supplies, and a smaller one for his cook. It was generally arranged to set up camp in the vicinity of a village where the headman and the rest of the party could find temporary, if very basic, accommodation *(Photos. 184 and 187)*. Sometimes there was no village within reasonable walking distance and the men would construct their own temporary shelters out of whatever materials they could find in the bush - branches of trees, large leaves and dry grass - but not, of course, very waterproof. Drenchings during the night were not uncommon and any spare shelter under the surveyor's or the cook's tent would soon be contested ! During a disastrous night of violent storms in the Kagoro Hills at Agorumgorum Pam the writer's gang were sheltering as the wind got up when a fire inside one of the shelters suddenly went out of control and spread to the rest of the temporary structures. The ensuing panic was to no avail and the rain which followed left the party wet, cold and miserable for the rest of the night

The cook's first task on arrival at a new camp was to establish his kitchen site, preferably under the shade of a tree, and receive or organise supplies of water and firewood. His oven was made from two empty four gallon kerosene tins from which the tops had been cut, laid on their sides and a fire prepared between them. Forming a bridge between them was a piece of XPM on which kettle and saucepans were placed *(Photos. 189 and 190)*. With this simple arrangement excellent meals were prepared, and good bread was made, but so often with a flavour of wood smoke. Most cooks could do very well under rough conditions and produce meals very quickly, even when it was raining and the firewood damp. Grass matting or a spare canvas groundsheet would be used to provide shelter for the kitchen in dusty, windy or wet conditions. Boiling a can of water and filling the water filter was an early task. The quality of locally available water varied greatly. Carried from streams or collected from the tent flysheet it could be very good in the wet season, but streams would stop flowing in the dry season and water might then come from stagnant pools or village wells. Filtering and boiling of water could be a multi-stage operation. First of all, though, it might have to be strained through a piece of cloth to remove detritus and any living creatures. Boiling would turn the water from greenish to brownish, and the filter would generally make it reasonably clean for storage in bottles. It would then be boiled for a second time, and sometimes put through a second, cleaner filter before being used for drinking purposes.

To inhabit a tent with a lot of things that need to be kept dry required a certain discipline and tidiness *(Photos. 191 and 192)*. There would be lots of irreconcilable things like clothing, food, cement, writing materials, soap, books, kerosene, matches, and shoes. One of the major changes which had started to come about to lighten the loads of the survey parties was the introduction of plastic, but some things had not been properly tested under tropical conditions. John Street found this a problem *".....within weeks of being in Africa things like my shaving brush had exploded, boxes had distorted, and my shaving mirror had collapsed........."* Mobile 'cupboards' were wooden beer boxes to which hinged lids had been attached, each with its identifying name, the tops of which could make a useful standing area for various items. It was always advisable to stand these boxes on stones to prevent overnight termite attack and, if the camp was of longer duration, they would be moved and inspected every day to ensure that these voracious insects, or other wildlife had not taken up unwelcome residence. The rear or closed end of the tent was usually used as a store and a bathroom. If sufficient water was available, it was heated in a four gallon kerosene tin on the fire and tipped, with an equal quantity of unheated water and a little drop of Dettol to sweeten it, and deal with the day's crop of blisters, sores and bites, into a galvanised bath. Certainly not a luxurious bath in which you could wallow, but it was possible to wriggle about and bathe yourself by instalments. Alan Wright was over six feet tall and could not get himself and his legs into the bath at the same time so he could sit in the bath with his legs over the side and his feet in a separate handbasin.

A small enclosure made with *zana* (grass matting), containing a wooden perch above a hole in the ground, served as the *bayan gida*. A 'long drop' arrangement was desirable but not always convenient and quick to arrange, so 'shallow drop' it had to be, with attendant risk of flooding during thunderstorms. But a luxury some enjoyed was a portable lavatory seat made from nicely varnished softwood which stood on four detachable wooden legs about two feet high. In wet weather on soft ground lingering over a good book while comfortably seated thereon could become hazardous if one or more of the legs gradually sank, almost unnoticed , into the soft ground.

The arrival of a European and his tented camp might be a once-in-a-lifetime event in some places. It was an event which may well have disturbed the routine of centuries for some villagers and children in particular would sit around the edges of the camp watching every movement and getting more excited when the radio was switched on and strange music was played. They would gradually become more bold when they realised there was no threat and they would edge ever nearer and have great fun until warned to get back by the headman, the cook or the watchman. The radio was the only contact the surveyor might have with the outside world, and a one-way contact at that, but its critical importance to his work lay in the fact that the BBC broadcast six time pips before the news, the last of those pips defining precise GMT, the signal for starting a stopwatch and rating a chronometer for timed astronomical observations.

Insects

At night, the Tilley lamp gave a bright and useful light *(Photo. 192),* but in open spaces it was a beacon for every flying and crawling insect, and the creatures which lived off them. Bush babies' huge eyes would reflect like the headlights of distant cars from the surrounding trees and bats emerged from their daytime resting places to wheel around and join in the fun. Each night, it seemed, there was a different and renewed range if insects. Each new place seemed to have its speciality; sausage flies, stick insects, stink bugs, earwigs, huge flying beetles, praying mantises, moths which squeaked, and a great confusion of others which came to a scorched end when they came into contact with the top of the lamp which was almost red hot. Their corpses littered the ground for yards around, but by morning, the ground would be clear except for a few inedible wing cases, methodically removed by the ants, scorpions and hunting spiders which tore around everywhere at about 10 miles per hour. There were so many insects in some places, both by day and night, that it was possible to become totally obsessed by them. Sometimes it was best to eat a meal sitting on the camp bed under the mosquito net as the Tilley lamp nearby toasted the crazy swirling mass of winged life and produced a range of unusual and unsavoury smells.

Some insects would arrive in vast plagues, like the green 'stink bugs' of Maiduguri, the earwigs of Kano Province, and the flying termites everywhere. The writer's tent was invaded one evening by an enormous swarm of these stink bugs, so called because to crush one underfoot created a powerful and sickening odour, and, unknown to him, lay athwart the path of an army of driver ants:-

> 'The ants caused me no real bother because they were intent on marching straight through the tent from one end to the other but, when they came across the great clusters of stink bugs, they immediately attacked and a huge battle took place around me as I cowered under my mosquito net. Every bug set up a high-pitched squeal and the battle went on for hours during the night. When I awoke the next morning the tent was completely clear of insects, not a bug nor an ant to be seen.

> When the winged termites left their nests during the rains a headpan or bucket of water placed close to the Tilley lamp would soon be filled. Rolled into balls and fried in palm oil they are said to taste like scampi or whitebait, though I confess their appearance never gave me the stomach to try them. I am told I missed a treat.'

Cantharides beetles were very unpleasant. They bred in a tall stalks of corn and would emerge in large numbers at harvest time, and were very common in the Kano area. It was natural enough to try to remove one if it touched the skin or happened to drop down the neck of your shirt, but once alarmed it would exude a powerful organic acid which brought up large painful blisters. Unless treated very carefully these blisters would burst, spreading more acid, creating yet more blisters over a larger area. Scorpions or *kunama* are much feared and, though extremely common, were not difficult to avoid. There was something very insidious about them. They are slow, furtive and quite often on the point of disappearing into dark places just as you catch sight of them, making you wonder how close to you they had been. The big black ones *(Photo.197)* which measured a good 8 inches (200 mm) across, were fairly common on the Jos Plateau and looked like crabs as they walked around hunting for other insects, tail uplifted ready for the deadly sideways strike. The smaller brown ones could be found under rocks during the day and posed a threat to the fingers of careless labourers picking up rocks to build cairns on survey stations.

Trevor Brokenshire recalls:-

> '..........we woke to find that a night-time animal had left a calling-card on the rush mat between our camp beds, and the evening and morning ritual of upturning mosquito boots and shoes to make sure that no scorpions had taken residence. Talking of scorpions reminds me of one of my labourers who was a *protector* of scorpions. These were often found under rocks which we intended to use to build cairns, and whenever this particular labourer was around he would pick up the scorpion, put it in his shirt pocket, and go off somewhere to hide it. 'Allah' allowed him to do this, he said. Only once did I have a labourer stung by a scorpion, he survived, but he wasn't too happy for quite some time. I also had a labourer who quite happily and successfully pursued snakes, even into water, and caught them. However, he was not a 'protector', and after taunting other members of the labour gang he would kill the snake by cracking it like a whip. Even *he* was not amused, when walking in front of me along a bush track a black mamba slid over his bare feet; I am quite convinced that he went *pale* at his narrow escape.'

When surveyors later started using instruments which required an electrical power supply, they needed portable generators for battery charging. While this gave the opportunity to use the same source for lighting, the noise of the generator brought an end to the night-time peace of the camp. The comforting hiss and glow of the Tilley lamp was replaced by a cooler, harsher light, which could not roast the encircling insects and a tent could become uninhabitable !

At night

When the evening meal was cleared away and the camp retired for the night, it was time for the nocturnal sounds of crickets, frogs, and various unexplained rustlings and cries, to take over and for the solitude and contemplation to begin. The utter silence of the night on remote hilltops, interrupted perhaps by the distant sound of a lorry toiling on a gradient fully 20 miles away, distinctly heard; a black velvet sky absolutely full and crowded with huge intensely bright silver stars; or a huge white moon casting deep shadows, turning the trees and the landscape to a mysterious green-silver, shining through the mosquito net and giving enough light by which to read.

It was a good time to retire to bed with a good book and immerse oneself in a different world, the mosquito net providing a cocoon against the night, the sighing of the wind in the branches of the trees, and the distant deep rumble of thunder. After a hard day the camp bed was the most comfortable place on earth and it was easy to sleep right through until the early morning kitchen noises began, waking still stiff and sore from the day before, with the prospect of another day's toil ahead. But it was more common to sleep lightly in lonely, strange places, the night could be restless, and unexplained noises from the bush could bring instant wakefulness.

It was also a good time to experience the sounds of village life, which had been enlivened by the arrival of the survey party in its midst, and a ready supply of local beer or lots of singing and shouting as the village drummers started up a rhythm which would become more complex and intense as the evening wore on, perhaps lasting until midnight and beyond, only to start again for a while at dawn as if the drummers, still intoxicated by their efforts of the night before, were unable to resist the temptation to start again.

Rest houses

There is a lot to be said for living in the privacy and comparative cleanliness of your own tent out in the bush, but there were many occasions when it was just too wet, too hot and too inconvenient to use one. On trek the alternative was to sleep out in the open, make an unroofed enclosure of straw matting or perhaps use a small village house or room provided by a local chief. Over the years travelling administrative officers, and occasionally other government officers or commercial people, had arranged for the building of small unfurnished rest houses a short distance outside places to which they would commonly travel and where they might have need to stay overnight. These rest houses overcame the need to travel with a tent or find a room in the village, and were occasionally very useful to surveyors. The majority of them were situated close to a motorable track *(Photo.196)*, but some of the older ones were in more remote places to which the district officer would probably have travelled by horse. Most were basic mud walled structures *(Photo.194)*, rectangular or round, the better ones having inner and outer walls, sometimes cement-plastered and whitewashed, the space between them serving as a living area and, if in an elevated position, sometimes a verandah giving pleasant views. The better places actually had glass windows and corrugated metal roofs, but the majority were thatched and generally had only gaps where doors should be and holes for windows and privacy was achieved by the use of grass matting. Thick mud walls and thatch were very good for keeping out the heat, but also good for keeping it in and needed high roofs to be reasonably cool.

At Wamba *(Photo.195)* in 1957 a low grass roof almost led to a disaster. There were three rest houses in a group, one of them occupied by Alan Wright, a surveyor. The writer had spent the evening with him, enjoying a good yarn and several whiskies, and then retired for the night in one of the other houses. As he undressed and climbed into bed Alan accidentally knocked over his hurricane lamp and set fire to his mosquito net which in turn sent flames leaping into the tinder dry thatch above. In seconds the entire roof was alight and Alan stood outside, his nakedness silhouetted by a huge and very spectacular orange blaze with a great column of sparks rising high into the warm night sky, saying "I say, old chap, I think I have a problem, you wouldn't have a spare bed by any chance, would you ?"

A *sarkin bariki* was responsible for the upkeep of a rest house and to supply visitors with an initial supply of water and firewood, for which a small fee was generally paid, but these duties tended to be neglected if visitors were very infrequent. It was not uncommon to arrive and find the place inhabited by bats, swallows, toads, and other creatures both domestic and wild, and a multitude of insects *(Photo.197)*, and to have been used at night as a pen for goats and chickens, the beaten earth floor thick with a cocktail of sickly-smelling excrement and debris from the disintegrating roof where termites were at work. Such rest houses were seldom completely free of leaks and a survey umbrella was often very useful indoors, erected over the dining table or the bed. Toilet facilities were primitive and might consist of nothing more than an earthenware pot in a room at the back, hence the name *biyan gida*, and a portable toilet seat was a luxury worth carrying. The better class of rest house might have a thunder-box and pail system. The *sarkin bariki*, keen to demonstrate that he did not neglect his duties, once removed the pail through the trapdoor in the outer wall as the writer sat there. He was treated to a cheery "Good morning, sah" as he removed the pail from beneath him !

It was common courtesy to make an advance request for the use of a rest house, but very often this was either unnecessary or inconvenient since visitors were very infrequent at the more remote places. Permission to use the Resident's well appointed rest house at Offa was given to the writer on condition that he kept the administrator supplied for the duration of the stay with excellent avocados that grew on a huge tree in the rest house compound. If, upon arrival, a house was found to be already occupied, the two officers were usually very glad of the company for an evening or so and sharing was very welcome. At Tayu rest house beside the Jos - Wamba road the writer had the good fortune to stumble upon a Danish road engineer who made him extremely welcome. Unlike the surveyor, the engineer had the luxury of being able to transport a kerosene refrigerator on his travels and to keep it well stocked with bacon, butter and Carlsberg beer, rare treats indeed for an itinerant surveyor !

When working on the Kaduna-Zaria block topographic mapping control in 1963, however, the writer set up his initial camp based on a well built rest house at Kajuru, just a few miles out of Kaduna.

> *'Convenient as it was for my work, it was a mistake, for at the weekends the 'townies' of Kaduna had already got into the habit of visiting the area for day trips. What was one moment a private survey camp with my possessions and equipment all around was, the next, a place of curiosity and adventure for a crowd of Swiss textile workers and their children, intent on staying the weekend, making a lot of noise, drinking and yodelling into the small hours. They were rude intruders who had not the slightest regard for the prior occupier of the place. I was living much too close to 'civilisation'.'*

Missionaries

Once in a while one might come across one of the scattered mission stations, which were always accessible by road. If the missionaries were at home they would invariably make the surveyor very welcome and shower him with hospitality and good home cooking, sometimes of the American kind. In spite of the generous portions of blueberry pie, there was something slightly depressing about these outposts, perhaps because of the lack of progress they could make in Moslem communities, but also because of their prejudices, their piety and their lack of interest in the outside world. The writer personally found it much more refreshing to call upon a Catholic mission station. There the Rev. Father would usually be a very outgoing and practical man, not afraid to call a spade a spade, and often ready to lead you straight to his refrigerator where he kept a couple of bottles of cold beer, or four, for the occasion such as this when an interesting stranger might call who was desperate to talk the night away and be ever grateful for a clean bed and eggs and bacon the next morning. Arnold Voshaar recalls his own gratitude to such a mission station:-

> *'The second time I became ill was from a malaria attack, although I used my paludrine tablets daily and my mosquito net every night. Carried on my Houndsfield bed we were lucky to reach, after a day's journey, two missionaries of*

the Fathers of Mill Hill. They treated me very well. At night I had to play canasta with them. In this game you had to "sacrifice yourself", in order to prevent somebody else winning. Early the next morning I had to attend Mass.'

Memories

It is fortunate that our minds have a habit of dimming and reducing unpleasant memories and enhancing the pleasant ones, but the two combine to form a lasting image of life in the bush with its colour, sounds, smells and experiences. We suppress the memories of sickness, of salty, sunburned skin, the treks when every part of the body was sore and aching, the persistent insects, the unbearable screech of nearby cicadas in the dorowa trees, the hours of hard work, the strenuous climbs, labour disputes, the frustrations and the struggles during the collapse of the tent in heavy rain. The memories which remain uppermost are a thousand trivialities; travelling into the unknown for the first time; the new experiences, new sights, things never previously envisaged or read about; and the sounds, the drone and buzz of a myriad of insects and frogs, the calls of unusual birds, braying donkeys, the rhythm of village drums and the pounding of the grain; the distant echo of thunder in the hills; the roar of rain on metal roofs; and the comforting steady hiss of the Tilley lamp.

Health

Bush was certainly no place for hypochondriacs, nor for those prone to worrying or depression. Being alone and unwell was most unpleasant, and it was vital to take precautions to keep as well as possible. The writer recalls the epidemic of Asian 'flu' which struck the whole of the country in 1957:-

'The 'flu' was probably transmitted to my party from a messenger who had visited Jos. The affliction arrived at the height of the rains when I was camped on the western edge of the Jos Plateau. In the draughty tent, in the almost unceasing rain, it was probably as cold as Nigeria ever gets and it was miserable lying on the camp bed covered with all the bedding and clothing I could muster, trying to fight the infection which had laid me low.'

The malarial prophylactic, Paludrine, was taken by most people assiduously but it became obvious that it was by no means an absolute protection, and needed the back-up of alternatives. This disease was not uncommon in the bush and the writer recalls:-

'There were fewer tortures worse than lying on a cramped camp bed during the hot days and nights under a mosquito net, in a tent, with a high temperature, with no respite from the airless atmosphere and the incessant buzz of insects and the scream of cicadas in the trees. While suffering a severe bout in Benue Province I used to reward my men with cash for every cicada they managed to kill in the trees around my camp, but they were on to a good thing because the wretched things could fly very well and very fast, and one soon seemed to fill the territory vacated by another.'

John Pugh recalls an affliction of a very different kind, one which perhaps only a surveyor could suffer:-

'For my triangulation work I was issued with a Wild Geodetic theodolite, a truly lovely thing with which to work. During the War it could not be sent to Switzerland for servicing, and had been sent to Johannesburg. It came back with a note to say that the filter in the telescope had been found broken and they had no spares. I discovered this only later. When I started the observations I developed severe headaches, and about the fourth day I had to stop at 3.0 p.m., swallow a number of aspirins and wrap a bandage round my head to shield my eyes. I could no

longer bear to bring the cross-wires on to the brilliant helios. I solved the problem by getting a labourer to hold a khaki handkerchief in front of the telescope, and observed through that, at least to stations within 40 miles. With no filter in the telescope I was, of course, bringing the cross-wires on to the sun, or rather the reflected sun. In the 1960s I had to have my eyes tested, and the consultant asked when my eyes had been burned, as the eyeball was scarred, and all became clear. It was not a deliberate action by my colleague (the officer in charge of stores) - simply that with no experience he did not appreciate the importance of a filter.'

Keeping the party in good spirits could be very difficult under trying conditions and there was always risk of sickness and injury. The surveyor had medical responsibilities, for which he was usually ill-trained, and with which his simple medical supplies could not always cope, but in the land of the blind the one eyed man is king, and his treatment was likely to be more effective than many of the local remedies and treatments which involved the use, for example, of dried leaves and cords made from the bark of trees in the place of bandages. Wounds and sores, which were obviously beyond his control, were cases for the nearest dispensary or hospital, which might involve the sufferer in some very long distance walking or travelling. A remarkable range of ills could be cured by colouring aspirin with drops of different coloured drawing ink or poster paint, and iodine and bandages were always in demand, partly because iodine hurt, and any medicine which hurt or tasted awful was reckoned to be strong and therefore very good, but also because a bandage, no matter how dirty it became on the second day, was a sure sign that the victim had suffered and was a determined worker in spite of his handicap. These men could generally bear a considerable amount of pain provided its source was visible. There was usually a daily first aid session, held after camp had been established. But supplies were basic and limited and consisted mostly of dressings, bandages, iodine, ointments, boracic acid, cough mixture (very popular), Epsom salts, Mepacrine (which possessed the property of turning even dark skins a yellowish colour), Paludrine and aspirin. Unless a careful hold was kept on the situation the entire gang would queue up for *magani* of some kind or another, some unscrupulous men feigning illness to obtain 'European' medicine which they could sell in the local villages at high prices.

Trevor Brokenshire relates his wife Joan's experiences *(Photo.193):-*

'In 1951, part of my 'stores' in bush consisted of basic medicines in large glass containers to 'treat' labourers for coughs and colds, upset stomachs and the like; Epsom Salts in vast quantity for constipation, aspirin for headaches, and some plasters and bandages. In 1953, Nora Hunter, knowing that Joan had been a doctor's dispenser, and when necessary, 'nurse' helper, in England, had insisted that we take a much extended range of liquids, powders, bandages, etc., and, once in bush, Joan held a 'surgery' for sick labourers and local inhabitants every morning. Her first day in bush was one she will never forget. As the first white woman in the area for many years (if ever ?) she was the object of much curiosity, and after I'd left for 'work' she was besieged in the rest house by a large group of local women. Despite our cook's protestations, the women came into the one-roomed rest house and proceeded to closely examine everything in sight; the camp beds, the bedding, the sewing machine and even what Joan was wearing. Having satisfied their curiosity they dispersed, without as far as we are aware, pilfering anything. That wasn't the end of the story, I was still not back when darkness fell and Joan had to endure a time on her own in a grass roofed mud hut with bush fires burning all around her. My labourers (Photo.173) said that the villagers were such bad people that they had intentionally fired the long grass in the area around the resthouse.

Her greatest success was to cure (apparently) a local 'schoolmaster' of a tapeworm by a massive dose of Epsom Salts and the inevitable consequence of an unprecedented clear-out, tape worm and all. That brought the schoolmaster back next day, with a present of a chicken. Her greatest test had resulted from a disaster in the market place in one of the villages near which we were camped. Large branches of a tree which had given shade for generations decided to fall upon the people sitting underneath, killing two and causing major and minor injuries to many others. Joan did the best she could with the survivors and we took one poor chap, with a broken leg and several wounds, lying in the back of the kit-car to a hospital many miles away. We were told later that he survived.'

Wildlife

No account of surveying in Africa would be complete without encounters with wildlife. In spite of its huge size Northern Nigeria was, by African standards, a fairly densely populated country and local people had long been hunters and gatherers, and in consequence the huge herds of wild game animals which are associated with Eastern and Southern Africa had long been in decline or disappeared in West Africa. The surveyor was as likely as anyone to come across examples of the few that remained. It was perhaps unwise to be reliant upon bush-meat as a regular food source. A noisy survey party was likely to scare away most creatures long before it was possible to see them and shooting in the early evening or morning, with the guidance of a local hunter, was probably the most likely source of something for the pot. Warthogs, and various forms of what might generally be called deer, were still quite common, though the writer carried a rifle for hundreds of miles and seldom had an opportunity to make good use of it. A shotgun would have been more use for the plentiful guinea fowl. Local hunters *(Photo.186)* were more successful with their poisoned arrows, dangerous old muskets, dane guns and hunting dogs, and a small duiker could be bought from them for about four shillings in 1959.

John Street recalls some of his experiences with wildlife, and living off the land:-

'When working for long periods in the more remote areas, such as the Mambilla Plateau, keeping large parties at altitude was impracticable and, having carried the equipment in, all spare labour had to retreat to somewhere where food was more plentiful and the nights warmer. Carrying a rifle became very useful, especially on the plateau and the forest areas below. With local hunters to scout for me, we would perhaps go to a 'hide' on the edge of a village. One of the scouts would return, lead us through a herd of semi-tame cattle, and there, grazing on a hillside, would be a beautiful animal of the deer species. With a good sporting rifle, with a telescopic sight, I could kill accurately over a long distance. This meant food for the survey team and happiness and co-operation from the local people.

We were asked to 'lie out' for rogue lions on Mambilla, but never saw one. Sitting, as I did for weeks on end, waiting for the right combination of helio-lights, could be terminally boring. On one or two of the hills I could look down into truly tropical or semi-tropical forest, and one day I had the glorious experience of being able to see a pair of lions resting, and apparently playing, in a forest clearing perhaps 1,000 feet below us and two miles away. This display lasted for some two hours and my men were thrilled with it.

We did get a number of 'bush cows' (buffaloes), which made excellent eating, but you had to ensure you killed; the response to wounding was extreme aggression.

I was often asked to wound or kill one of the indigenous bush pigs in Adamawa, as they wreck the agricultural areas, and one wounded animal will frighten away perhaps a hundred others in the surrounding gullies and ravines. Unfortunately, the pigs were very large and have very unpleasant meat which nobody would eat, unless they were starving.'

The writer recalls:-

'Elephants (giwa) were seldom seen, though they still existed in a few isolated areas and had been protected, together with other species in the Yankari Game Reserve in Bauchi Province.

Small herds of buffalo roamed along the Benue Valley south of the river near Akweti and could be seen from isolated hilltops.

The hippopotamus was not uncommon in the quieter parts of the big rivers, and crocodiles, though not uncommon, were seldom encountered.

Baboons were often seen on hilltops in many remote areas and would bark in annoyance when their territory was invaded by survey parties. One memorable incident was when my labourers picked up rocks to throw at them and the baboons mimicked this action without having any concept of aiming, their efforts resulting in total confusion with stones flying everywhere.

Monkeys were also fairly common in the more southern parts of the region, especially near villages where they would raid the farms as the crops ripened. Joe Onugha, one of the students on my Advanced Survey Field Course at Kagarko in the 1960s was a good shot and always seemed to have one of them available for his cooking pot in the camp.

Secretive hyenas (kura) roamed the country and could be heard in the hills at night. It was not unknown for them to move through a tented campsite and I was awoken one night with one of them pressing its nose against my mosquito net as I slept out under the stars.

Leopards(damisa) were sometimes seen, three of them in the trees above my very first camp on the flank of Ningishi Hill off the western edge of the Jos Plateau in 1957, and my cook was molested by one in the evening as he descended from the Kagoro Hills in the dark.

Heliomen, alone on remote hills near Agam in Benue Province, reported lions and protection was provided by an armed policeman; though I only saw one lion in my 20 years in Nigeria, and it was a dead one at that, loaded into the back of a Landrover. It was an old and sickly rogue male which had been shot by a game warden because it had been molesting a village in Bauchi Province.

Snakes were seen quite frequently, but they seldom posed a threat, and on my first ascent of Ningishi Hill, where I had seen the leopards, I had three encounters which I thought, though quite mistakenly, would be typical of the rest of my life in the bush. My men caught a huge, black, non-venomous snake soon after we started climbing, removed its head, and left it among rocks until our return later in the day. When we descended it had gone, having crawled away without its head. The men did however manage to find it and took it down to the village where it was cooked that evening. Being very new to Nigeria I was squeamish enough at the time to refuse to eat any of it, but I was reliably assured I was missing out on something good. Higher on the hill that morning I hauled myself over a rock shelf and came face to face and only inches from a Gaboon Viper, a beautifully coloured and very dangerous creature, which remained motionless as I backed away, and at the summit a small and very agile spitting cobra (gamsheka) released a spray of its venom in my direction as I approached the rocks in which it lived. On another summit, while carrying out trig observations I saw the largest python imaginable, many feet long, moving amongst rocks usually occupied by a colony of baboons. I alerted my men who immediately gave chase but were unable to kill it with their machetes. Injured, it slipped into a deep crevice, from which the men attempted to extricate it by dropping down bundles of burning grass, but the creature defied their attempts to catch it and it was still surviving on the summit when our work there came to an end. Python steaks are said to be very good, and that snake would have provided enough to feed an army.

Most of the dry bush seemed to contain very little birdlife except guinea fowl, bush fowl, and crowned cranes, but hawks would patrol in the vicinity of bush fires to catch escaping lizards, snakes and small rodents. Vultures would appear as if by magic to clear up any carrion, it seems they must have been able to smell it from 20 miles away. In the open farmland areas of the north, quelea birds, about the size of sparrows, would gather in their millions to strip farms bare of corn and millet. White cattle egrets would follow the herds of cattle wherever they went, gathering insects disturbed as they grazed, and helping to rid their hides and their ears of ticks and flying pests which bothered them perpetually. These birds, and hornbills, storks, whistling teal, pigeons, weaver birds, and a host of small coloured birds, seemed to be more attracted to areas where there was water, especially along the river courses of the far north.

Of all the wildlife, undeniably the greatest scourge were the insects. Flies and mosquitoes were troublesome enough but it was the countless millions of others whose activities continued day and night that made one so glad to eventually escape to Europe on leave'.

John Street tells the story of how he came face-to-face with a 'gorilla' during his reconnaissance for triangulation in the Burra-Ningi district of northern Bauchi Province:-

'Some three or four months into trekking, we were zigzagging between the numerous exfoliated granite domes which rise clear from the plain some 100 miles north-east of Jos. One of these, which I had seen through the theodolite about ten miles away, had a lovely rock summit, about 150 feet high. Our scout took us to the well forested foot of the hill and my headman, being a sensible man, took a look at it and decided that, since it had a pure rock summit and no obvious way up, it could not possibly be the hill we were looking for ! To me it looked like Eldorado or 'some real rock to climb'.

We compromised that I should climb it, if I insisted, with three of the younger, strong carriers. They simply slipped their sandals off and started to climb on some steep open slabs. I went for a crack and a more devious ascent. Some 70 feet up it got harder and I decided to traverse right round a ledge, only to come face to face with what I subsequently wrote in my report was a 'gorilla'. It was certainly big, smelly and very frightened. Trapped at the far end of my ledge "there was no where for it to go". The next moments were 'black fear' as it shot along the ledge, appeared nearly to envelope me and was gone - down into the trees. I climbed back down, a very frightened surveyor.

Subsequently a letter arrived (a four to six weeks turn around with Kaduna) from on high i.e., from Mr Hunter, the Director of Surveys. God knows who showed my report to him ! His letter was human, but pointed, saying that there are no 'gorillas' in this part of Africa; it was a baboon, and would I kindly stop taking foolish risks in bush ! He ended on a kindly note saying how he had enjoyed his own first years in the bush.'

....

'As a group, our team did much clearing of hill tops, removing trees and rock in large amounts, and developed considerable respect for scorpions and snakes.

On a hill on which we had been working for many hours, all work suddenly stopped and the labourers and Audu Gora came back to say there was a highly dangerous snake in a cave just below the summit. We were desperate to get on with the work, but this was serious. Their idea was that I should shoot it.

I found the snake asleep, placed myself with care, took a long time over preparation, and fired. The bullet shattered its head, but I had overlooked the fact that it was in a cave. The bullet hit the walls and came back out with enormous velocity, passing about two feet above my head. I vowed to do better in the future ! The labourers roared with laughter about it for the next week. I did not put this event in my monthly report !'

Frank Waudby-Smith and his wife Joyce were both Bristol graduates, he a physicist and she a geologist. Frank joined the Northern Nigerian Survey and, with Joyce, worked in the bush for a while. He has contributed this account of a wildlife encounter:-

"THE BRAVE SURVEYOR FACES HIS FIRST LION - ALONE"

It was the middle of my first wet season, in July 1955, and almost immediately after Joyce had arrived (without permission) from England. I had just spent a few valuable weeks in bush with Peter Redwood learning the basic lessons on how to survive, when I received instructions from Doug Eva to complete the beaconing and observation of the Minesfield secondary trig using the hills around Burra in Ningi District. John Street had done most of the reconnaissance. My first task would be to visit each of the hills he had chosen, complete a panorama showing the visible, distant hills to be included in the observations and erect a cement beacon on the summit. Later on, when all was finished, I was to return to the hills to do the precise observing.

To help me do this I had been given Momo Sokoto and Ibrahim Katsina as my Chainmen, both very experienced men who would see that I didn't get into too many difficulties. I had been given about twenty survey labourers to carry the valuable loads, like instruments and the cash-tank with the money in it. As we brought with us all our belongings, tents, tent-poles, camp-beds and so on, and each survey labourer had his own bedding roll, additional carriers would be hired, or more likely press-ganged, when needed, by an Emir's representative, who would also arrange with local village heads to get accommodation for the men, a tent-site and water and so on for us.

With Joyce and me were our cook, Ali Bima, and his help-mate, called a 'small boy", together with all the basic foods, cooking equipment, pots and pans, the water filter, dishes, cutlery and camp chairs, tin bath -everything that goes to make for comfort in bush. Our small group drove in my Dodge kit-car to a rendezvous with John Street at Yarde Gungume while the Chainmen and the main party travelled there on foot. John was to give me his records and let me have a messenger/guide to help us find the right hills.

It didn't quite work out as smoothly as that but we met John at his camp and next day set off for the hills. As the kit-car would be useless on bush roads in the rains we left it in a village, Tulu, at the end of a dirt road and spent the next week trekking north towards Burra and finding and beaconing two of John's hills on the way. The path to Burra was a dry-season track of 20 miles including two rivers which would have to be waded unless the rains held off. Finally, in Burra there was a bush rest-house, full of bats but open to the winds and with a grass roof, where Joyce and I could sleep while the survey party stayed in the village. We paid off the carriers and planned the next stages.

The next day we trekked to a small village about 5 miles north-west which, Momo Sokoto advised, was as near as we could get to the next hill on my list. It would save time not having to trek the additional distance from Burra to the hill and back. As there was no rest-house in this village we set up the tent under some trees where we could get shade for part of the day; about ten of the survey party were accommodated in the village, the rest going back to Burra. The following day Momo Sokoto and I and about ten survey labourers trekked to the hill and started our work. We were interrupted by heavy rain and could not complete the beaconing so we set out back to the village. It was a very hot afternoon and, as I was feeling very hot, when we came to a small river across the path, I waded through it right up to my neck and this cooled me down. I had never before done this, it is not a sensible thing to do in those rivers.

During that night I woke feeling terrible and covered in sweat. I didn't need our thermometer to tell me that I had a fever and in the morning I woke in a confused state and told Joyce that something was wrong. She took my temperature; it was over 104°. During the day I kept falling into a sort of unconsciousness in which I couldn't stop counting out loud, but Joyce told me later I could only reach to 20 then had to start again at one. When I was conscious she fed me with cornflakes and milk and gave me aspirin and I would fall "asleep" again for an hour.

Nothing in our handbook of tropical diseases seemed to match my symptoms and Joyce was very worried. She talked it over with Ali and Momo Sokoto and they decided that being in a tent which was mostly in the sun was not the best thing; even the bat-ridden rest house back in Burra would be cooler. The next day Momo Sokoto found a horse which they put me on and propped me up for the 5-mile journey. Our camp followed, a sorry sight.

After three days in Burra I began to feel better and eventually my temperature returned to normal. I sent a messenger to Denis Willey at Minesfield Survey HQ in Jos with a letter explaining my condition. The next day, with Momo Sokoto and a few men, we went back to the hill to finish the work. As I was still feeling weak I rode on the only bicycle in Burra. The work didn't take long and I rode off back down the track ahead of the men to get to the rest house before the sun *was too hot.*

     The first half mile or so along the path was through overhanging bush, out of the bright sun and in the shade. It bad been raining in the night so the ground was muddy in places. Then, just before I reached the cooling river that I had waded a week before, the shade stopped abruptly and I was in a dazzling bright space about 20 yards across. Suddenly, across the gap, I saw a large brownish animal shape with two eyes in it! Sheer panic set in, I was alone, and face-to-face with a lion! I assure you that you will know a lion when you face one, no detailed identification is necessary. Don't wait to get out the book on tropical animals, don't be brave - run! Without thinking I spun that bicycle around in the muddy path and pedalled back like mad until I reached Momo Sokoto and the labourers. "There's a lion down there," I yelled. Their reaction was unforgettable -they kept on walking, they knew a sick man when they saw one. After a minute or so someone said softly that there were often lions around here and, very politely so as not to give offence, he added that if I stayed with them the lions wouldn't bother me. So I did and we walked quietly on to the space where I told them I had seen the lion.

     On our side of the gap were the unmistakable marks of a bicycle being turned around very quickly indeed: on the other side, I was so pleased to see, were the equally unmistakable signs of a lion doing exactly the same, with his claws. Now their attitude changed. It seems that there was a lion around (and it had been as frightened of me as I was of him, though I find this hard to imagine). We all decided to get back to Burra as quickly as possible and together.

     Back at the rest house I told my story to Joyce. But, like the others, she had seen me in a deep fever, unable to count beyond twenty and having to be carried on a horse like a sack of potatoes so she never believed me. (And even when it was obvious from what Momo Sokoto and the others told her that there had been a lion on the path, she never, never, never acknowledged it to me - she knew me better than that.. . Two days later, on the trek back to Jos, I was frightened out of my wits by a domestic cow which strode into our path from behind a bush, being chased by a very small local boy with a stick - which only helped to prove her right.)

     Postscript::   *Within a couple of days I was covered in nasty yellow sores, an after-effect of para-typhoid. It took us five more days of walking and driving to reach the hospital in Jos, where I was rebuked by the matron for not getting there earlier. Two weeks after my illness had started, Joyce developed typhoid in the hospital.*

Trevor Brokenshire relates incidents involving elephants and other creatures:-

     'My daily work was, generally, uneventful, but I think it was in this part of bush that climbing up to the top of a relatively low hill we saw below us a herd of elephant; I believe a rare sight for Nigeria. As I recall, our main concern was what we should do if the herd decided to come our way; there were no trees of any size anywhere, and really nowhere we could go. Luckily, the herd decided to move away from us, but I still remember the 'rear guard' member showing off his (her ?) strength by sparring with one of the few trees in the lower land.'

....

     'Trees were our salvation some time later. We were moving through wooded country when, in the distance there was quite a commotion, with the noise growing louder every second. One or other of my labourers, or the headman, must have met this situation before because there was the urgent command "Get up into the trees, quick, quick". We hastily scrambled up, complete with the theodolite, tripod, survey poles, et al; and not a moment too soon; within seconds a stampeding herd of Fulani cattle, huge horns flashing, thundered underneath us.'

....

'I can recall that I climbed to the top of Ningishi Hill twice; and the mayhem caused by a colony of bees. Quite a lot of the area being contoured was savannah country, with quite a few small trees. One of the barometer 'traverses' led us too close to a tree which was the home of a hanging colony of bees, 'reena' was, I think, their Hausa name. Our presence near the tree could not be tolerated ! The bees chased members of my party in all directions, stinging each of us as we went. I suppose our numbers were our salvation, no one person was targeted. After re-grouping to the headman's whistle, we each counted stings; my hat and beard had protected me to some extent (I was called 'mai gaimu' in Jos, 'the bearded one', but not to my face by any of my labourers) and I considered myself lucky to have only five or six stings, but unlucky to learn that, in the panic, the barometers, in their padded boxes (padded for such an occasion ?) had been discarded in the flight. Keeping a wary eye upwards into each tree, the barometers were all recovered but we then had to go back to the last heighted point so that the barometers could be re-read and corrections applied to all readings at new points.

....

David Ball, the Town Planner, was no bushman, but his work sometimes took him to Provincial towns. He quotes from his personal memoirs:-

"WINGED MENACE"

'I spent my first night in Katsina in the catering rest house and I nearly resigned on the spot when I entered my chalet. Opening the door, I was hit between the eyes by a dragonfly with a five-inch wingspan, and fluttering around the bedroom was what I took, at first, to be a green bird but was, in fact, a praying mantis. Bugs of varied sizes and colours were crawling up the walls and over the floor. "Don't panic!" I told myself "You've got two more years of this!" I had already discovered in Kaduna the priceless value of a mosquito net, not only to keep out the mosquitoes but to protect one from other, larger, less dangerous but to me, far more frightening creatures. The net was even more of a godsend here in Katsina where the night, indoors, at the end of the dry season, seemed to be teeming with indescribable insect horrors. The mosquito net was my only, but very effective, refuge. Sooner or later, however, even the best nets developed the odd hole, un-noticed until one woke up in the middle of the night in agony, having been well and truly bitten by a lone mosquito which had miraculously found its way in. Then followed a well-rehearsed routine. Switch on the light, locate mosquito - quite easy to do as it sat, plump and black, on the inside of the net - swipe it with a rolled up newspaper kept beside the pillow for the purpose, producing a streak of my own blood, then, with rather more difficulty, locate the hole and mend it temporarily with a piece of pipe cleaner also kept for the purpose and go back to sleep".

....

"SHINAKEY GO FOR TREE"

"The next day I moved into what was to be my home for the next three weeks - 14, The Circle - which was a laterite road enclosing a barely recognisable but quite attractive nine-hole golf course in the GRA (Government Residential Area). Number 14 was an ancient mud house but British-built and therefore probably 40 years old rather than the 400 it looked. It had an 80-foot verandah with eight arches, two-foot-thick walls, a fifteen-foot-high vaulted ceiling in the living room and a flat roof on which one slept in a camp bed in the dry season. One afternoon I was sitting reading on the verandah when a shower of lumps of earth landed in front of me, apparently coming from behind the house and over the roof. I went to investigate and found a crowd of boys pointing excitedly up into a tree. I said to Audu my cook-steward who stood there with them: "What on earth's going on?" "Ah!" he said, "Shinakey go for tree. Dey try knock um down" With some difficulty, following his pointing finger, I at last saw the snake, a small one about three feet long and no thicker than the small branch along which it was lying some twenty-five feet from the ground. I considered the situation. Several branches of the tree were touching the roof of the house on which I slept. Clearly the snake must be removed. "I'm going to borrow the DO's gun," I said, having noticed David Roberts' .22 rifle when I had dinner with him and his wife two days before. But driving to his house on the other side of The Circle I wondered what I had let myself in for - probably a huge loss of face in front of the assembled multitude which, even worse, I discovered when I returned with the gun, had been joined in my absence by an English nurse who had stopped to see what was going on. I located the snake, house-high in the tree, and, not without some trepidation, took aim. I shot it through the head, first time, and it hung down, with blood dripping from its nose. The crowd cheered and Audu said: "Dissee goodoo work, Sir!" But my huge relief was not unmixed with revulsion and sympathy for the poor snake which might well have been harmless. Oddly, I cannot remember what happened to it or whether it was identified. David Roberts, the D.O., must have been out at the time, otherwise he would surely have come with me or taken matters in hand himself. This was, incidentally, one of only two snakes I saw in six years in Nigeria, although the place was said to be teeming with them and the Surveyor General had only recently run over a six-inch-thick boa on Eaglesome Road near his house in Kaduna South.'

Trevor Brokenshire says:-

'Kaduna South was known for having a lot of snakes. In out last bungalow, during our last tour, puff adders, on the mat outside the front door, were a common occurrence. We had two snakes in the bungalow, both of which I killed; one after a chase into the bathroom.'

Norman Herring and his wife Eva also had an experience with a snake in Kaduna South. Norman was a good surveyor and mathematician, but he was undoubtedly an eccentric. The writer first met him at the Jos office as he passed through to Kaduna on his way from his posting down on the Benue.

'He walked into my small office, wearing an Australian bush hat, pulled out a revolver, and shot two holes through the straw-board ceiling and the tin roof. Placing the smoking weapon on my desk, he extended his hand and introduced himself.

"What do you carry that thing for ?" I asked
"There are a lot of snakes about, you know"
"Get away. You've been watching too many cowboy films"

Norman was not a beer drinker, but he was addicted to tea. He had a very great dislike of mundane office work and, when he worked in the Kaduna Cadastral office, much preferred to take work home to his bungalow. In the evening he would spread files, field-sheets, computations and his Facit calculator across the carpet and, lying on the floor, work late into the cool of the night, while Eva kept him supplied with pots of tea on the floor beside him.

He was stretched out there one evening, working as usual, when he casually said to Eva, who was sitting in a chair, reading "I'll bet you five pounds you can't keep absolutely still, without saying a thing, or so much as blinking an eyelid, for the next five minutes, no matter what I do". "You're on", she said, and froze.

Norman got up, went to the kitchen, and brought back a broom, and calmly dragged out a cobra which was underneath her chair, not three inches from her bare ankles ! She won her bet. It was perhaps the one occasion when he didn't trust his aim with the gun.'

....

John Pugh related a story of the Sokoto bush in 1942:-

'I had to survey a lease across the Gulbin Ka, which at that season, February, was not flowing. Near the village was a pool about 200 yards long. We had been working in the sun all day (I recorded 153°F (67°C) for ten consecutive days but the humidity was only about 2%) and being hot and sweaty the pool looked irresistible, and I decided to have a swim and cool off. My headman, a Fulani, did the unthinkable, restraining me physically. He spoke abruptly to a labourer, who ran to the village, and shortly afterwards two old men appeared and sat on the river bank. My headman then said I could go in for my swim. I swam up and down the pool for about 20 minutes, after which, refreshed, I came out. Getting into shorts while still wet, I rotated through 180° to see a large crocodile snout 20 yards away.

Unreasonably, I remonstrated with my headman, who told me that the crocodile had taken the sariki's horse the previous week, but I was quite safe as the two elders had the magic to keep the croc away from me. Had I been a true scientist I would perhaps have tested this by diving back in ! I assumed that the horse had satisfied the creature's hunger for the time being. But it taught me something about rivers and their snags. Not enough, as I suffered for nine years with bilharzia, as a result of wading in rivers while doing mining surveys on alluvial sediments.'

In his personal memoirs Kenneth Toms recalls an incident with a snake on the Jos Plateau:-

'Once, I went with Malam Buka and my labouring gang to inspect a trig station which had been destroyed by lightning on a high granite hill south of Jos. On the way down I slipped on the wet grass and grabbed at one of the small stunted trees to regain my balance. Out of the tree shot a bright green snake about five feet in length. It wrapped itself around my Australian style slouch hat. My God, I thought, it had to be a green mamba, one of Africa's deadliest reptiles. I ripped off the hat and hurled it and the snake as far from me as I could. When the hat hit the ground, the green snake took off and my hat rolled like a hoop to the bottom of the hill. Rarely have I seen a group of people so convulsed with laughter. It seemed that the snake was of a harmless tree variety and the sight of the bature playing bowls with his hat was too much.'

Climate

Their outdoor life made surveyors more conscious of the climate and the weather than those who lived and worked with a roof over their heads and who perhaps enjoyed the luxury of fans and air conditioners.

Northern Nigeria lies in a belt of climatic conflict between the dry Sahara Desert conditions from the north and the humid air from the Gulf of Guinea from the south. The Harmattan *(Photos. 198 and 199)* is the principal feature of the dry season, a desiccating, dust laden, north-easterly wind, sometimes reaching gale force, blowing from the desert towards the sea and caused by the seasonal occurrence of a subtropical anticyclone over the Sahara. The wind dissolves the clouds and removes the traces of the previous wet season from the land. Generally it displays a regular diurnal rhythm with almost calm conditions under clear skies at night, but picking up during the day, raising dust, the sky turning a sort of milky white and scattering the sun's insolation and sometimes restricting visibility to the extent that vehicles need to turn on their headlights. In the early morning it is sometimes particularly chilly, especially in the more open country of the far north, and warm clothing is essential. Minimum temperatures can be as low as 37° F in the far north in January and frost has been recorded at least 4 times in Katsina during the past century. Temperatures could also fall very low on the high Jos Plateau and at the elevated Bukuru Survey Rest House in the dry season of 1957-58 a shallow metal tray of water left outside for the dog had a very thin coating of ice on it one morning. According to climatological research, the dust appears to come from an area south of the Tibesti Mountains in Chad and an area of wind convergence at 19° E 18° N near Largeau and further west near Bilma in areas of sandy erg. It is most prevalent from November to February but, as surveyors have discovered to their great inconvenience and discomfort, it may sometimes begin well before and continue for a long time after these two dates. Relative humidity can fall to less than 10% in the middle of the day, especially in the semi-arid parts of Sokoto, Kano, Katsina and Bornu, and temperatures are relatively low, especially at night, when blankets become very welcome in this tropical zone. Such low temperatures frequently result in low level inversions in which smoke from domestic and bush fires, which may spread widely and rapidly under these conditions, is trapped in an acrid layer close to the ground and the air smells of burning grass and scorched wood. The dusty wind can blow right across Nigeria, decreasing in effect southwards, but can still be noticeable out in the Gulf of Guinea where dust has been known to accumulate on the decks of ships. The cooler conditions encourage more people to light domestic fires and fires in thatched roofs, spreading fast in the strong wind, have been known to devastate whole villages and towns. The cooler, drier air is at first welcomed as a relief from the heat and humidity which comes at the end of the wet season, but the dust can carry germs and viruses responsible for respiratory infections in crowded communities. It was said to cure the ills of the wet season, and for that reason named the 'Medicine Wind', but the opposite was usually the case. Though a change from the dampness of the wet season at first, the increasing strength of the wind had a perverse effect and tended to make everyone irritable with its persistence. With a tropical sun high in the sky it feels both hot and cold at the same time, not unlike a fever. Bronchitis and catarrh are common and can lead to pneumonia, tuberculosis and pleurisy and even meningitis. The lips, eyes and skin can become cracked and infected. Animals are not immune from similar effects and contagious diseases can spread amongst the large herds of cattle.

The restless, thirsty wind scorched during the day and shrivelled things overnight. Paper became brittle, fieldbooks curled, leather shoes creaked and split, and shaving lather dried on the face. The wooden legs of tripods warped, their metal heads and feet would become loose, and for precise work tripods would have be kept damp by wrapping in wet sacking or immersed in water overnight. This was the season for short range survey work; traversing, levelling, photopointing, cadastral work and boundaries, or even a retreat to the office. Haze at night sometimes obscured all but the brightest stars near the zenith and the absence of cloud was no guarantee of clear nights suitable for field astronomy observations. Triangulation observing and reconnaissance were so fraught by delays that it was better not to attempt this work until the chances of longer clear spells began during the equivalent of the European spring between March and May.

The abating of the desert wind and the sun overhead meant rising temperatures, to which might be added a whiff of humidity as small clouds gave a hint of the increasing influence of the south. This was an uncomfortable time everywhere, but particularly so for the man living and working outdoors. Rocks began radiating heat and the sudden temperature drop at sunset no longer occurred. Temperatures out of the shade approached 140° F in the rocky land of Sokoto and the plains of Bornu. Like weather everywhere there was never an even cycle of change and unexpected breaks would sometimes occur during the dry season, perhaps around Christmas or as late as February, and an isolated rain shower or storm would interrupt the monotony of the desert-like conditions. The probability of such breaks increased further south or close to the Plateau. There might be false hopes that the Harmattan had ceased, but all too often it came back with a vengeance, stronger and more unpleasant than before.

From March or April onwards wisps of high altitude cirrus began to streak the southern sky, there would be a shift of the wind direction, and small cumulus clouds would appear as if from nowhere. As the season progressed they would daily become larger and eventually the first towering clouds would start to rise over the storm-breeding hills. Winds became more varied and turbulent and small whirlwinds would sweep across the parched land lifting dried debris high into the air. If a tent lay in the path of such a dust devil, chaos and indescribable mess would result, unless everything was quickly stowed away and tied down. The writer remembers:-

> *'I recall watching as a particularly strong whirlwind swept through a small village near Kafanchan, pulling loose grass from roofs and spinning a maelstrom of leaves, rubbish and very surprised hens 200 feet or more into the air. This was the first time in their short and squalid lives that these fowls had ever been obliged to use their woefully inadequate wings, which were totally ineffective as they shed feathers and spiralled upwards and away from their village pecking grounds. At considerable altitude, as they reached the edge of the moving spiral, the lifting force of the wind declined and, now almost bald, they started long, curving and rapidly accelerating descents, without airbrakes or gliding sense, accompanied by raucous 'squawkings', making preparations for what promised to be unpractised and rather high speed landings. Their high velocity flapping only served to increase their suicidal rate of descent, reaching speeds that hens had probably never previously experienced. For some there was the realisation that their earthbound egg laying days were over and they hit the ground as dusty bundles of bones and feathers. Others, perhaps more fortunate, ended up in trees and farmland a half a mile of more from home, to which they might never return. I don't know if it was coincidence or not but my cook served curried chicken for dinner that evening, and scrambled eggs for breakfast.'*

It could be a mistake to begin major triangulation observations too early for until May there was a risk of a temporary return of the northern conditions, or a combination of dust and valley humidity to produce very poor visibility. Clifford Rayner writes:-

> *'The 'astro' programme in Sokoto Province finished in early May and after a bit of a rest in Kaduna I was posted to the Benue river valley 'P Chain' for more primary triangulation observations. The Benue area centred on Lokoja was less bush than Adamawa so that was an additional comfort. Malcolm Anderson was on the other end of the chain and it was his first time on primary triangulation. With the experience of Adamawa behind me, progress here was much improved and I had few long stays on any hill. Malcolm for his pains was not so blessed. His record, which happened to be his first hill, was 10 weeks! He must have thought that he would never get out. He had even cleared enough of the hill for a football pitch and was about to organise a tournament. The problem being that firstly there were a lot of rays to observe and also that the hill was very low in the plain and half of the others were high in comparison. Either they were in cloud or he was, but rarely were both clear. In contrast I was on one hill at the time of a partial eclipse of the sun. Fortunately my heliomen stayed at their station, the temperature dropped about 20°F (11°C) and shimmer disappeared. I was able to undertake the complete observation programme at that station during the 2 hour period of the eclipse!'*

Then came *damana, mai ban samu*, the rainy season, the giver of possessions. Even before the onset of the rains the trees started sprouting fresh soft, lettuce-green leaves, and flowers like spring crocuses broke through the hard dry earth in the bush. The wet season was a total contrast to the Harmattan. Its beginning was marked by a rise in temperature, and a totally different feel to the atmosphere as humidity increased dramatically. To drink a glass of water meant breaking out into an immediate sweat, salty perspiration started getting into the eyes and, as the season progressed, prickly heat became a problem. The early morning was the most delightful time, but later in the day the heat could become intolerable, and with the sun overhead at noon, there were scarcely any shadows, and living in a tent could be almost unthinkable.

The wet season never began gently with light showers from scattered clouds, but always with a storm, and the first storms were usually the most violent ones, those most likely to cause damage. A hint that changes were afoot began when the wind came from a different direction during the day. As white cumulus moved towards distant hills and gathered into towering cumulo-nimbus there would come the first distant rumble of thunder. As often as not, even though the approach of the first storm gave the unaccustomed breath of cool moist air, it would be a false alarm and the reversing and strengthening winds as the storm approached created no more that violently turbulent air and the dirtiest of dust storms. For a week or two oppressive clouds added their weight to the blanket of dry season dust, visibility was no better and the sun might be hidden for long periods.

The surveyors' preoccupation with the sky increased as the season progressed and the threat of the first storm became ever more real. It was fascinating to sit outside the tent in the evening and watch the progress of a distant storm *(Photo. 201)*, constant lightning illuminating the clouds from within, silhouetting the bush and the trees and throwing distant hills into bold relief. As the threat of rain increased so it was necessary to take additional precautions when locating and establishing campsites and overnight accommodation.

Then, late one afternoon or early evening the first storm would arrive. With clearer skies it had been possible to watch the white clouds soaring to 30,000 feet or more to form giant anvil heads, their bases merging and darkening to blues, purples and deep, formidable greys, and gradually moving nearer. To this visual spectacular was added an audible one as lightning flashed and thunder rumbled within, and progressed into increasingly frequent ground strikes as the storm reached a peak of intensity. Such storms were as fierce as anywhere in the world and lightning was so frequent at times that it was possible to sit outside after dark with sufficient flickering illumination to read a book.

The breeze which had been blowing towards the storm centre all day abated, literally the lull before the storm, and the air was heavy, warm and oppressive. This was the time to secure the camp, slacken the guy ropes, tie the tent flaps and cover everything that might be blown away or soaked. From a distance came the hint of a sound in the treetops, increasing as the storm approached, the trees suddenly began swaying and bending in the great rush of wind, dust and airborne debris. Suddenly everything was in motion and there was a smell of wet dust in the air. A few big, dirty, lukewarm raindrops, the first for perhaps six months or more, drilled holes in the deep dust and thudded on the concrete-hard ground, and it was a joy for a while to stand out in the rain, feeling the unaccustomed, natural, drenching coolness.

But soon the rain was so heavy that to be out in it was cold and uncomfortable, and hailstones, ice on the ground in such a hot place, underlined the dramatic change which was taking place. It was time to take shelter from the violence all around, the shell-bursts of thunder directly overhead, the noisy turbulence of the clouds above, the roar of the wind, the rain, loose objects and branches, flashes of white light illuminating a chaotic scene now utterly unrecognisable. Overwhelmed by such irresistible force it was time to feel very small, impotent, apprehensive and alone.

But within half an hour or so the first storm would probably be all over. The wind would drop, bringing a sense of calm and tranquillity, the rain would cease and there would be a silent stillness broken only by distant echoes of thunder, the drip of water and the croaking of frogs. The dust had gone, or turned sticky on the few remaining dry surfaces inside the tent. Outside there was a transformation, with new smells of moist earth and decaying vegetation and evening wood smoke filtering slowly through sodden grass roofs of the village houses and lingering in lazy blue layers in the valleys. In the morning the day would start fresh and delightfully cool, the bush would look freshly washed, the colours enhanced, the soil darkened to a deep red, and suddenly there were vast panoramas of green plains and distant blue hills standing out sharply against the background of a clear blue sky.

The first rain brought relief and an optimism, but there might be a long period before the next storm, and even a return to dusty Harmattan conditions for a while, but eventually a second storm would pass through and, more with increasing frequency until they became virtually a daily occurrence, with some completely overcast days in July and August. An evening storm might be followed by many hours of light rain, pattering on the flysheet of the tent, and would only abate as the sun began to break up the cloud cover. Seldom would it rain all day, except perhaps in the higher areas like the Jos and Mambilla Plateaux during July and August when the weather would not be unlike the cyclonic rain to which we are accustomed in England, and the temperatures very similar. The further north one travelled in Northern Nigeria the less the southern climatic influence and in some years the northern borderlands received very little rain at all, but it was general for that area to receive about 32", while at Kaduna and Jos it was 54", and in the main river valleys 47". In localities around the Jos Plateau, especially on the west-facing escarpments there are places where these figures are very greatly exceeded.

Constant tropical heat was accepted and, except at times of extremes, almost disregarded, but cold conditions felt out of place in Nigeria and more memorable for their occasional occurrence. In the extreme north, the hottest months are generally sometime between October and May when the average maximum can be 96° F with a minimum of 65° F. Between June and September during the rains these figures are 91° F and 72° F respectively. For the same periods the figures for Kaduna and Jos are 88° F/65° F and 81° F/62° F and along the Niger and the Benue valleys 95° F/71° F and 89° F/73° F; stifling places where often there did not seem to be any air and it was sometimes difficult to tell you were breathing.

As the season progressed, even in the far north, dry stream beds became wide, fast running brown rivers carrying the accumulated dirt and debris of the dry season, dry leaves turned to rich smelling damp compost, fresh green shoots appeared almost overnight and the farmland around villages was the scene of strenuous digging and ploughing. An uncomfortable aspect of the surveyor's bush life was then having to establish a campsite on wet ground when it was already raining. The cool dampness would be trapped inside, the groundsheets wet, and scarcely anything at all dry except, with luck, the bed.

Perpetual dampness went hand in hand with an increase in the insect population, especially mosquitoes, the deterioration of stores, food supplies, equipment and, inevitably, health. Books and papers now became soft, damp and brown stained, and there was insufficient time during prolonged rainy periods for laundry to dry before the next trek began. At such times it was difficult to imagine that only a few weeks before there was delight when the first few drops of rain brought relief from the heat and dust of the previous months. Skies might be grey for long periods, the sun might seldom appear and everywhere was lush wet growth, mud and water. Bare earth and scanty, dried, yellow, brown and black fire-charred vegetation *(Photo.200)* was replaced by tall green grass, corn and millet growing eight or ten feet high, and plantations of healthy cassava and ground-nuts. On trek you might be held up by flooded rivers and extensive *fadamas* and there was certainly no guarantee that the end of the Harmattan would give clear observing opportunities. Moist haze, mists clinging to the hill summits and filling the valleys, and cloud meant restrictions on the use of heliographs, but overall the rains were a precious season for the surveyor, as for everyone else.

John Pugh recalled some of his own problems in the late 1940s :-

> *'Angles had to be measured to hundredths of a second of arc, each angle on ten different zeros, to helios at ranges up to 80 miles. Because of cloud, the helios went in and out of appearance, making life difficult. Each round had to be completed within four minutes. One would observe to A, then to B, C would be invisible, sight on to D, and A would have vanished. When it reappeared one would start again: sight to A, no B., no C, no D, no A.. A would remain invisible so one would start on B, sight to C, no D, no A, no B. And so on. One started observing at 6 a.m. and stopped at about 7 p.m., after which one juggled with angles obtained.*
>
> *One of my colleagues, Wookey, working on the Cameroons chain, sat on Utange summit for six weeks, without completing a single round. He sent a telegram to Lagos H.Q. and received a reply : "Waste no more time at Utange start at the north end". I came back from leave at that time, saw this, and said to Kuenen, then acting as Deputy Director : "Stop wasting time ? He has been sweating blood to get some results". Bill Kuenen, a charming and most civilised individual, was horrified, and sent an apologetic follow-up, to his credit. Wookey trekked 300 miles*

to Yola, and tried again at that end. After 72 days he still did not have a single completed round, and in view of the despairing tone of his monthly reports he was pulled out on medical advice. I could sympathise !'

Everyone who has spent some time in Nigeria will be able to tell stories of the remarkable electrical storms. The writer's first 'near miss' was in Bukuru:-

'My first appointment in 1957 was to Jos, but I didn't stay there very long. Enough time to familiarise myself with my surroundings, do a little surveying with Arnold Voshaar and Ian Gilfoyle on the Minesfield and to prepare for my first spell in the bush, a secondary triangulation reconnaissance to the west of the Plateau and to the south of the Kagoro Hills. For a short time I lived in the Mines Rest House at Bukuru which had, in earlier days, been used as a police office. Each of the rooms had been equipped with telephones which now lay dormant. Dormant until I received one of the great shocks of my life. No sooner had I arrived than a violent early wet season storm arrived. Nobody had warned me that Bukuru has one of the highest rates of lightning strikes in the world. A telegraph pole in the compound was suddenly struck and the wiring throughout the house was vaporised in a great sizzling blue/white flash and all the telephone bells rang simultaneously for the last time before lapsing into an eternal solidified silence. The shock sent swarms of huge brown cockroaches scuttling across the floors.

Long term prospects for triangulation pillars on the surrounding hilltops were very poor !'

....

'A few months later I had my second shock. I was camped just 100 feet or so under the summit of a small hill near Fadan Tsoho somewhere to the north of Kagoro where I had earlier in the day established a resected point. It happened to be RP 13 and I had no reason until that day to be superstitious about that number. I sat in my tent that evening watching a storm advancing towards us (Photo.201) along the line of hills of which the Fadan Tsoho point was the highest, lightning flashing to earth every 20 or 30 seconds, while my cook prepared dinner, watched by a lonely vulture perched on top of the beacon pole we had erected on the hilltop. That vulture was either a very intuitive or a very lucky bird, for less than five seconds after it decided to fly away the pole was struck by lightning and the rocks supporting it were scattered all over the hilltop, some of them passing close to my tent.'

From Keith Sargeant:-

'I recollect having to re-observe a trig point where some years before a surveyor had been killed by lightning during the night as he lay in his camp bed. I was told that the Treasury authority was not so much concerned about the death of a surveyor but by how much was in his cash tank (chained to his bed as required) which had fused into a solid mass. Needless to say, having heard this story in advance, I camped at the bottom of the hill and climbed up each day to observe.'

And from John Pugh:-

'After the end of the war I spent two years on geodetic triangulation - the Lafia-Ogoja chain. This was the most stimulating, intellectually, of my years in the Survey, as well as being the toughest physically. One camped on hilltops up to 7,000 feet, which could be exciting with tropical storms. Two of my predecessors were killed by lightning, and one of my signallers was hit but survived. He was sheltering in a rough bush hut on the Madas, at about 4,500 feet, and a flash blew him out of his shelter. He was unconscious for about ten minutes, so his signaller colleague reported, but came round to find an enormous scar across his side, which he did not feel at all (high-frequency cauterisation ?). If he had been six inches to his left it

would have gone right through him. He decided that Allah wished him a long life, proudly showing off his scar as evidence. I always tried to camp below the summit, but it was not always possible. On Dutsin Doma I was faced with a flat-top surrounded by steep scarps, and had no option but to camp on top. We had the usual thunderstorm, with the nearest strike about 50 yards away - flash., bang and smell arriving together - not my most pleasant experience !'

John Street also talks of the threat from storms on the hills:-

'The coming of the wet season was a period of great tension. From the Mambilla Plateau we could see the 'front' weeks before it arrived. The horizon would suggest a 1914-18 battle scene. As the weeks of waiting went on, it came closer, and we would forbid anyone to stay high on the hills at night and issue strict rules about not leaving heliographs and other equipment up high. We lost one complete set of helio equipment and had two cases of bad burning through non-observance of sensible rules. It was utterly forbidden to 'stick out' to the last moment just because we only needed one more set of readings.'

Welcome as the wet season had been when it arrived it was a palpable relief to the worker in the field when the wettest period was over. Over much of the Northern Region, September was a glorious month, perhaps the best month of the year. The rain was still there, but decreasing in frequency and intensity. The air was very clear, the land prolific and green, and the rising temperatures which preceded the return of the northern desert influences had not yet begun.

Pleasures

One of the greatest pleasures in lonely places was when the messenger arrived from headquarters bringing eagerly awaited mail and newspapers from home, giving the reassurance that familiar things were still going on back there.

Arnold Voshaar remembers his anxiety when, in 1955, he was on tour for two months without hearing a word from his fiancée Ria, in Holland. It was with a mixture of relief and, perhaps, slight concern, that he eventually received a brief telegram from Delft, reading *"Alles OK. Ria"*. Obviously, for a lonely man out in the wilds, the lady was disappointingly reticent with her endearments ! But later, she made amends. She wrote to him every week, her letters numbered consecutively, but some of them went astray because, assumed Arnold, they bore attractive Dutch postage stamps !

Any bad news might, however, be unduly dwelt upon. For a short while the reading of personal mail might take priority over everything else. The newspapers were invariably much out of date when they arrived by surface mail, and were assiduously read from front to back in strict chronological order, but the BBC World Service on the short-wave radio was a source of recent events and it did not seem to matter that much that the papers were weeks old.

There was also great pleasure in the peace and beauty which came in those places, with great landscapes all to oneself *(Photo.202)*, magnificent African panoramas which few men had ever seen, and distant blue hills to explore. The crowded, dirty cities, the vast populations and the rat race were on a different planet millions of miles away.

Days ended abruptly, with but a brief twilight, cloudy skies in the west turning into a kaleidoscope of changing colours as the zone of night-time blue moved rapidly from the east, soon yielding to a huge black, silent sky, completely filled with millions more stars than could ever be seen at home. The Milky Way was a bright glow; hills 20 miles away could be seen, and if there was a bright moon, moonlight rainbows could sometimes be seen during showers of rain. In high, remote places, the clear sky could evoke a feeling of the earth's motion through space, a feeling which would be accentuated greatly when the apparent movement of the stars was viewed through the telescope of the theodolite. There was time for quiet reflection. Such pleasures could be enhanced if they followed an arduous working day; a cool bath; a bottle of beer which had been cooled by wrapping it in wet sacking and swinging it from a branch of a tree; dinner under the stars; the flickering of the watchman's fire; and the companionable hiss of the Tilley lamp.

Surveyors were great observers of the landscape, very conscious of the hills, and ever watchful of the skies. Northern Nigerian sunsets, especially in the clear skies towards the end of the wet season around September, defy description and it is difficult to find better words than those used by Nora Hunter in her excellent diary (*Where My Caravan Has Rested*) of the time she spent in the Sokoto bush with Keith in 1946:-

> *'The atmosphere was startlingly clear and the western sky a riot of changing colour as the sun sank towards the horizon. To the north and east hung gigantic thunder clouds, their colours merging from shades of pale violet to deep and angry purple and black. Below, lay the town, its mud walls and grass roofs caught in a shaft of brilliant sunlight, softly golden against the darkly sinister curtain of threatening cloud. In the weird light trees appeared emerald green, in strong contrast to the stark blackness of those silhouetted against the peaceful western sky. A big storm filled the southern sky, black clouds were torn apart by jagged streaks of lightning and a curtain of rain swept across the countryside. The perfection of this fantastic display of Nature with its infinite range of colour and contrast of calm and storm, all depicted, as it were, on one immense canvas, reached its climax when the complete arc of a brilliant rainbow suddenly framed the sky and bush from north to south, throwing its weird reflections on to cloud and countryside. The intense beauty held us spellbound'*

....

Returning to town

When the last observation was taken, especially if it was at the end of one's first major bush scheme, there was a certain elation and a sense of achievement of not only a survey task completed but also the knowledge that you could stand on your own two feet in remote places and would not be apprehensive about returning to the bush. Fears of the unknown had been conquered, many lessons learned, and rather special pleasures enjoyed. In spite of frequent discomfort, solitude, the monotony of the long distance trek, the sunburn, the fatigue, and the constantly attentive insects, days in the bush are remembered for the companionship with the survey party, and with a sort of inner satisfaction and a longing to do it all again. Those dedicated to the life spent as little time as possible in headquarters, deploring the routine and the bureaucracy back in headquarters and the stuffiness of some of the senior expatriate echelons in government. Harry Rentema recalls, of 1953:-

> *'For Christmas I was invited to Kaduna but I preferred to stay in the bush and camped on a hill, near my trig point, cook and steward near me in a grass hut. I always had the sarki informed beforehand and they were always friendly and came with presents: chickens, eggs and onions.'*

The writer trekked 530 miles between May and October 1957, one of the wettest wet seasons for some decades, but the brief return to Jos to pick up details of his next job, and his car, were something of an anti-climax and he was soon off to bush again.

Arriving from the bush, physically and mentally strained, surveyors were sometimes objects of curiosity and pity and were welcomed at parties. The only glimpse, or reminder, that headquarters staff might receive of life in the wilds was to watch the unloading of a dusty or mud-spattered Survey lorry as it brought in the battered paraphernalia of a bush party - dirty tents, well used survey kit, axes, machetes, old kerosene tins, a load of firewood, some scraggy hens, wooden boxes, sleeping mats, petrol drums and a top load of excited and shouting labourers in ragged clothes. Enough to put off any white-shirted, tie-wearing survey trainee for life !

Returning to town with its refrigerators, big beds, rooms with ceilings and clean floors, and water coming from taps could be a strange experience. One of the items missed most of all in the bush was the refrigerator. The life and well being of many revolved around this domestic appliance and it was perhaps rather easy to forget the fact that electricity had only recently come to many places and the first oil refrigerators did not arrive in the country until 1935. When you have lived without it for some time the convenience of electricity seems a great luxury, but perhaps the greatest luxury of all is a supply of reasonably clean running water and a proper, deep bath to wash away the sweat of the day and the anticipation and the satisfying hiss as the top came off the first bottle of ice-cold Star beer.

Men in from the bush had become more appreciative of the amenities of station life, the canteens and shops, the availability of fresh fruit and vegetables, medical and dental services, gardens, flowers, trees, the absence of dust and flies, and the club with its cold beer and snooker table. It was also a pleasure to be able to go to the local cinema as an escape, almost regardless of which film was showing (including the early 'Bollywood' dramas !).   There the audience would sit under the cover of a corrugated iron roof, protected if it rained, but the outdoor screen, a large wall painted white, would glisten and reflect like a mirror when wet, the picture disappearing completely during lightning, and the soundtrack drowned out by the thunder. But on warm, dry evenings it was a pleasure to sit and watch a film under a deep blue starlit sky.

Habits acquired in the bush would be brought back to town. It was natural enough to use the outdoors for many ordinary things like sleeping and eating if the weather was kind, and using the bush as a toilet. There was an unconsciously developing desire to get out from under a roof, to become very conscious of the sky, every aspect of the weather and every sound in the bush. Inevitably the isolation and self sufficiency led to a measure of detachment, of being withdrawn, satisfied with ones own company and being very sensitive to any lack of understanding and sympathy for what you had endured to bring in those precious pages of figures back to headquarters. Returning to station Clifford Rayner found that wearing shoes was uncomfortable for he had been wearing 'daps' for the whole time in bush and his feet had spread somewhat. Even in such rough terrain plimsoll-type footwear was the norm, but he was rarely without a walking stick. This was usually cut from fairly young bamboo, the root being the handle. He also found that after months of squatting, using a conventional lavatory was uncomfortable. There was a similar contrast between a camp bed and a normal mattress bed !

Accustomed, however, as many were to the spartan existence, it could be difficult to prepare for bush again soon after returning from an enjoyable leave in Europe, unpacking all the well used and familiar items hurriedly thrown into boxes a few months before.

WORKING IN THE PROVINCES

Provincial Surveyors

The foregoing description of life in the bush must not leave the impression that surveyors spent all, or even the greater part, of their time there. On the contrary, most work was, particularly in the later years, based on Kaduna headquarters, the Minesfield office at Jos, and scattered Provincial stations. Some people were glad to escape the doubtful pleasures of the big towns and preferred the greater freedom of a Provincial posting. To be accompanied by his wife, in the days of the Northern Nigerian Survey, undoubtedly improved a surveyor's chances of a favourable posting, either to headquarters, or to a Provincial station, and one of the more comfortable ones at that. Couples seldom found themselves living for very long in 'punishment stations' like Yola, Maiduguri, Makurdi, Lokoja or Sokoto.

Houses allocated to Provincial staff were equipped with a few basic hard furnishings, but all other domestic needs had to be provided personally and carried from station to station at each change of posting. This was not a great problem for a bachelor accustomed to living out of boxes in the bush. His possessions, which would generally fit into the back of his 'kit car', would seldom stretch to such luxuries as a dinner service, a coffee pot, delicate glassware and good soft furnishings, and the contents of houses he occupied invariably had that certain spartan and well used look.

It was a formality and a courtesy, something of a hangover from the colonial past, that to confirm his arrival in a Provincial headquarters station a surveyor would sign the Resident's book. He might in return receive a call or, especially if he was accompanied by his wife, an invitation to meet the Resident and his wife socially, but it was less common for single surveyors to be accorded this 'privilege'.

In remote stations, wives could be isolated in their houses all day, with few neighbours, little domestic work to do and no shops or outside entertainment. Life for them could be difficult if they had no outside interests. But some of them revelled in the alternative lifestyle, and the freedom that domestic assistance could bring, with opportunities to become involved in work of some kind, to take an interest in the country, the people and the language, and to have the time for reading and writing. It could also be a challenge coping with insects, sickness, domestic staff and their ways, the extremes of the climate, unreliable services and water supply, and domestic issues like the fine tuning of kerosene refrigerators and the struggle with wood burning stoves. When her husband returned from the field or the office she would claim his full attention, making it unlikely that he would bring work home with him.

The position of 'Provincial Surveyor' was not a rank, but a title, and reflected the officer's responsibilities. He was given a considerable amount of autonomy to carry out survey work of virtually all kinds in his Province, and in any adjacent Provinces if they were unmanned, taking instructions from, and reporting to, Survey headquarters. Most of his time, usually with the assistance of junior technical staff, was devoted to cadastral surveys and setting out sites for Government use, for approved schemes of township extension and for commercial purposes, and taking responsibility for other survey parties sent to work in his area. Under instructions from the Topographic Section he might be asked to establish and maintain networks of various orders of township control points by triangulation, traversing and levelling, for limited area topographic surveys, and provide co-ordinated and levelled control for large scale aerial mapping. He was also occasionally required to become involved in the investigation and re-survey of disputed administrative boundaries and to work in close collaboration with officers of other government departments and with the Provincial Resident or his administrative officers. He would provide assistance with their surveying and mapping needs, and with non-survey activities such as election and census duties, pest control, 'boards of survey' for the write-off of redundant Government equipment, local planning and services, etc. Provincial Surveyors and touring surveyors played a part in many of the projects which came about in the 1950's when Colonial

Development and Welfare funds started providing the wherewithal for projects which had always been beyond the Region's capacity, especially in the principal towns where land acquisition was fundamental to development progress.

John Adshead, who had served as a Provincial Surveyor in Ilorin, said of the Provincial Surveyor in 1965:-

> '*He is usually only supported by a few survey and technical assistants who are of a low educational standard and of limited ability. They are, however, competent at using the survey equipment on which they have been trained, and are capable of carrying out a number of survey operations to the required standard. A survey assistant can in fact carry out most simple survey work to quite a fair standard, and a technical assistant is competent at simple levelling and simple detail survey - but, with a few exceptions, none of them are capable of completing a job of work without proper supervision and without detailed instruction on the ground, and, in the main, are quite incapable of doing any work which is at all complicated or which requires any initiative on their part.*
>
> *The Provincial Surveyor, therefore, has to provide the brains and the 'know how' for his 'instrument men', and must so organise his work that he makes the maximum use of his staff to get through far more work than he could on his own. He must therefore analyse each job carefully, split it into its essential survey tasks, supervise the carrying out of these tasks, do the complicated bits himself, compile the results and then present the work as an integrated whole as if it had been done by one man. His ability to integrate the work of the Provincial Survey Staff in this way is the criterion of the Provincial Surveyor - however competent a man may be himself, if he cannot organise his staff efficiently he will fail to produce the amount of work of the standard required of him.*
>
> *The second big problem that faces the Provincial Surveyor is the nature of the terrain in which he is frequently expected to work. In the dry season in Northern Nigeria, there is little problem in the farmed areas since the ground is usually relatively level and vegetation is all but non-existent - but in the rainy season it is quite a different matter. Corn can grow up to ten feet in height and except in very special cases may not be cut. This presents a terrific problem to the surveyor because although the corn stalks appear to be widely spaced when one walks through them, it is virtually impossible to see more than ten yards in any direction. Boundary surveys carried out by theodolite traversing can be managed by dint of tying corn-stalks out of line or by actually digging them up and transplanting them - but this is laborious, and wasteful of both time and money, and although I have had to do this sort of thing on more than one occasion, it is not to be recommended; it is just about impossible to carry out any other kind of survey under these conditions - for example a contour survey by ground methods of such an area could not be carried out in the rains without an enormous waste of time and effort; tacheometry or plane-tabling would be impossible. Even where there are no crops, the grass in the rainy season can grow to such a height that tacheometry and plane-tabling are impossible and even though it is permitted to cut grass it would be a marathon task clearing large areas in order to do an accurate contour survey. Grass can be burnt off when it is dry but this is frowned upon since there is no means of putting the fire out once it has started and there is always the danger that a village may be set on fire in the conflagration.*
>
> *Under the heading of difficult terrain must also be included the densely built-up part of the more urban native areas where the straight line and the right angle are almost unknown and where compounds merge one into another in a most irregular pattern. Each compound is surrounded by a high mud wall and visibility is virtually nil from any standpoint. Tacheometry, plane-tabling and simple chain and offset surveying can be carried out, but to produce an accurate survey of such by such methods is difficult and complicated and requires a great deal of intelligence - precisely the quality that is lacking in the normal Provincial Surveyor's staff.*
>
> *The immediate reaction of every Provincial Surveyor nowadays is to make use of aerial photographs with which Northern Nigeria is happily very well supplied*

- but here again, a problem arises. Although headquarters is equipped with Wild and Santoni photogrammetric plotting machines, and various types of lower grade equipment, these are in continual operation on the enormous task of mapping the North and cannot be spared for the sort of job with which a Provincial Surveyor is constantly being presented. All that the latter has at his disposal is a hand stereoscope and occasionally a Zeiss Aerotopograph Sketchmaster - he does, however, have access to virtually any photographs he requires.'

Among the tasks he undertook were a 1:25,000 scale flatland survey of 50 square miles with 5 feet contours, a 1:4,800 scale contoured survey of farmland designated for urban development, a 1:2,400 uncontoured survey of a township with irregular walled compounds, and made proposals for mapping native land holdings. On this work he employed aerial photographs, simple techniques and the assistance of only junior staff to provide effective topographic and cadastral solutions. At the time his techniques were not adopted by the Survey Department but the methods he described in his RICS Thesis in 1965 were perfectly valid for the situation which developed in Nigeria in later years when trained and fully equipped surveyors became much more scarce than in the days of the Northern Nigerian Survey.

Provincial Survey Offices

With the aim of reducing unending, expensive and time consuming travelling, it had long been the aim to set up Provincial Survey Offices throughout the North. Except for a very short period this ideal situation was never achieved and did not start to become a reality until well after World War II when finance and staff numbers permitted. Until then, surveys were undertaken by touring officers working out of Kaduna, Jos and Kano. Provincial Survey Offices were not necessarily purpose-built. More commonly, they consisted of a room or two within the Provincial Administrative Office, or small temporarily acquired and partly-renovated buildings loaned by other Departments or Native (Local) Authorities.

Before the establishment of the Northern Nigerian Survey, when the central Survey Department in Lagos had responsibility for the whole country, cadastral work for the Northern Provinces was administered from an office in Kaduna, a sub-office concentrating on Minesfield work at Jos, a small intermittently manned office for cadastral and training work at Kano and, for limited periods, small bases elsewhere.

There was never a Provincial Survey Office, as such, in Kaduna and the needs of the Kaduna Capital Territory and agricultural Zaria Province were met by Survey headquarters departments. By 1957, pressure of work had, however, led to the establishment of a District Survey Office at Kaduna Junction with specific responsibility for cadastral work and township control framework in the capital. One of the first officers in charge there was Peter Taylor who was District Surveyor in 1958-59.

The Jos office, with its responsibility for the Minesfield, also had cadastral responsibility for Plateau Province and surrounding areas, and for a while, in an experiment to decentralise work from Kaduna, became headquarters of what was known as the Eastern Survey Area of the Northern Nigerian Survey, with responsibility for work throughout the area accessible from Jos in Bornu, Adamawa, Sardauna, Bauchi, Plateau and Benue Provinces.

Kano Province

Kano, the principal city of the north, had long enjoyed a Survey presence. From the early days of British influence survey training had been provided through a local survey school and the graduates from this school were involved in systematic survey of local agricultural holdings. Kano Province had a greater settled peasant agricultural population than anywhere else in Africa at this latitude, hence the need for a local survey department. More than a million people lived within a day's walk of the city's markets. It was a great trading, agricultural, manufacturing and communications centre, its international airport being the place where so many visitors would gain their first impressions of

Northern Nigeria. It lay at a very important staging point on air routes from Europe, to Lagos, central and southern Africa and to Khartoum to the east and was an important starting point for the holy pilgrimage by air to Saudi Arabia.

It was far and away the largest place in the north, with an internal population of around 135,000 in the 1950s, living in rectangular, flat roofed buildings, in an ancient settlement encircled by decaying red mud walls and battlemented gateways, dominated by the Emir's Palace and an elegant white, green-domed mosque. Kano was rich, powerful and influential, the seat of Northern politics and the home of aristocratic religious leaders and wealthy merchants. The original settlers lived in the vicinity of Dalla Dutse where blacksmiths made use of the iron rich rock and a manufacturing tradition had lived on with its pottery and silver, brass, and copper craftwork. Modern industries, spilling out beyond the old walled city, included a great assortment of small industries including the manufacture of steel furniture and building components, concrete blocks, terrazo tiling, groundnut oil, canned foods (Crescent corned beef, jollof rice, groundnut and guinea fowl stews), soft drinks and mineral water, leather work, tanning, shoes, perfume, face powder, pomade, confectionery, washing soap, tyre re-treading, kapok processing, tarpaulin manufacture, weaving, dyeing, and printing. A famous feature of the Kano skyline after the harvest were the huge, tall pyramids of bulging sacks of groundnuts, awaiting transport by rail to the coast for export. Each pyramid, and at times there were hundreds of them, would completely fill the covered freight wagons of an entire train. This was the time of intense market activity. Dusty roads and paths converged upon the busy markets and the railhead. The city was characterised by its haze of dust, the smells of agricultural and animal industries, and the constant movement of overloaded lorries, donkeys, handcarts, bicycles, occasional camel trains, horsemen, throngs of white-robed people and its white humped cattle and scavenging goats.

Except at the height of the wet season, when about 34 inches (863 mm) of rain fell, it was a hot and dry place, with average daily highs of 92°F(33°C) and lows of 66°F(19°C), and stood in very flat country at 1,560 feet above sea level, exposed to the desiccating Harmattan. Erosion of the exposed light sandy soils by the action of the wind, and overgrazing by voracious goats, was a perpetual problem. The preservation of trees was encouraged but only those yielding a crop tended to survive and the wide spreading *chediya* or silk cotton tree was common in Kano Province. The city's government and commercial residential areas were well planted with shade trees and spectacular scarlet flame trees. Early Government officers lived in large, comfortable, thick-walled, cool, mud built houses, built in the local style; some of which were still in use during the days of the Northern Nigerian Survey.

The arrival of the railway, and its extension toward Nguru in the north-west of Bornu Province, gave impetus to the commercial development of Kano and led to an increasing amount of cadastral survey work during the 1930s. With post-war decentralisation of Survey, a Provincial Survey Office was opened and was busy in 1951. Many members of the Northern Nigerian Survey saw service there over the years including Henry Cotton in 1956, Clifford Rayner, Frank Waudby-Smith, Jorgen Jensen, Jimmy Dickson, Peter Redwood, A.Laurberg, and Joe Umunna. Stan Klepacki became Kano State's first Surveyor-General after the dissolution of 1968 and he was succeeded by Jack Ashton.

In his book *Nigerian Kaleidoscope* Rex Niven says that early in the British occupation of Kano something might have been done to cause desecration of the old Kano mosque. He suggests that surveyors may have removed any sanctity it might have enjoyed by using it as a trig point. This was not a well known fact, but the problems of extending control for survey work in such a congested old city make it quite plausible, if somewhat regrettable, but perhaps provided the Emir with a compelling argument for his desire for a new mosque in the city, a desire which was in the course of time satisfied by the Public Works Department. Survey work for cadastral and improvement purposes did sometimes involve climbing on to the flat roofs of houses *(Photo.74)* and other buildings and leaving markers which could also be taken as signal for a compensation claim if there was a notion that demolition for road improvements was imminent.

Katsina Province

The Provincial town of Katsina, with a population of about 56,000 in the 1950s, lay at a height of 1,700 feet above sea level and less than 100 miles north-west of Kano, near the Nigerian border. Being so far north, it received only 27 inches (685mm) of rain a year, and experienced average daily maximum temperatures of 88°F(31°C). In the dry season it could be a very bleak place, with little protection from the Harmattan. Average daily minimum temperatures throughout the year were about 65°F(18°C). Being so close, and on a well-trodden trans-Sahara route, its surveying needs were generally handled from the Provincial Survey office at Kano, but occasionally residential surveyors were based there. Alan Wilkie was engaged on map revision of the town as his first job in 1956 and Cliff Burnside worked there in 1960. Like many other places in Northern Nigeria it had no important industries. A description of the town and work and life there in the late 1950s appears in David Ball's book entitled *Into Africa (And Out) Northern Nigeria 1956-62. (Photos. 203 and 204).*

Benue Province

The first Provincial Survey office to be purpose-built was in 1950-51, at Makurdi in Benue Province on the River Benue, and was opened with Kevin O'Shaughnessy in charge. At the time, the town itself was quite small, with a population of only about 22,000 people and owed its earlier livelihood to boat-building, commercial traffic on the river and the railway which crossed the Benue at this point. It was never a very popular posting and was very different to the dry north. There were no mountains, no desert and, because of the tsetse fly and sleeping sickness, no horses. At an altitude of only 300 ft above sea level, with average temperature highs of about 91°F(33°C), lows of 71°F(22°C), and rainfall of about 52 inches (1,321 mm), it always seemed humid, lifeless and airless. Until at least 1957 the town had no electricity and houses needed tall windows to let in the welcome breezes. Despite this, and because of the work in its hinterland, the Survey office was manned for longer than many others and the Northern Nigerian Survey based a Provincial Surveyor there for some years. While Norman Herring was serving there in 1957-58 he was visited by Kenneth Toms from Jos who recalls:-

> *'Norman was from the NCO ranks of the Royal Artillery Corps. He had a reputation for brilliance in mathematics. He had obtained exceptional passes in both the topographic and geodetic professional land surveyors examinations of the Royal Institution of Chartered Surveyors. His previous colonial service had been in Fiji, where he had worked with Australian and New Zealand surveyors. Consequently we had much common ground for discussion. His original posting in Nigeria had been to Kaduna. For some reason or other, he had fallen into the Surveyor-General's bad books and had been transferred to Makurdi, then regarded as a remote bush station.'*

Cliff Burnside took over from Norman Herring followed, in 1958-59, by Ian Gilfoyle. During the 1960s Makurdi became the Field Headquarters for Federal Surveys' mapping control activities in that part of Nigeria. After 1968 the new Benue-Plateau State maintained a Survey office there, run for a while by Denis Willey, at one time Surveyor-General of the North. Makurdi became a State capital when Benue-Plateau was divided.

Niger Province

In 1951-52 another Provincial Survey office was opened, this time at Minna in Niger Province. Doug Eva, who was to become the Surveyor-General of the North in succession to Keith Hunter, served there between 1951 and 1953. Others who worked there were Peter Taylor, Thadeus Moszynski *(Photo.206)* (who had escaped from Poland to England in the face of the German invasion at the start of the second world war), and Dauda Alayo. Minna was an old *gwari* (Gbagyi) settlement, many times raided and devastated by the Kontagora Fulani and populated by people from nearly all the main tribal groups of Nigeria, and a few Europeans. It was significant as a railway town, standing at the junction of the 100 mile branch line to the small Niger river port of Baro. Working from this town the Provincial Surveyor also had responsibility for work in Bida, with its population of about 20,000 people, which was famous for its brass ornaments *(Photo.205)* and trivia like bowls, trays and grotesque but distinctive animals, and its glass beads made from locally 'recycled' materials including beer and medicine bottles. At about 400 ft above sea level and similar temperatures to Makurdi, but with a lower rainfall and a much more open aspect in savannah country, the climate was more bearable. About 90 miles to the east lay the small town of Abuja, where Michael Cardew established a pottery based on local traditions and materials. In the late 1970s Nigeria made a decision to re-locate its Federal Capital to a site near the geographical centre of the country in what used to be Niger Province.

An ambitious programme of planning and development was begun and in the 1990s Abuja became the new Federal Capital of Nigeria.

Bornu Province

By 1955 the Northern Nigerian Survey had opened a Provincial Survey Office in the Bornu capital, Maiduguri, seat of the Shehu of Bornu. The last expatriate Provincial Surveyor there was Alan Wilkie in 1959-60. About 55,000 people lived there at the time, the vast majority of them Kanuris, many of them not admitting to being able to understand or speak Hausa and favouring the use of their own language. It had little in the way of industry, just a little leather work, tanning and dyeing, but it was a trading and marketing centre of some importance, with road links to Fort Lamy (N'djamena) in the Chad Republic and dried fish supplies from Lake Chad *(Photo.208),* and was the terminus of the railway which was extended from the Jos plateau via Bauchi and Gombe. Its strategic position on the route to the Sudan and Egypt from the Guinea coast, a staging point for aircraft and military supplies heading for North Africa, had led to wartime expansion and the construction of a large airfield. Until then, communications to the rest of Nigeria were very poor and the road from the west through Potiskum and Damaturu was sandy and very difficult. Until this road was improved, in spite of the thin tree cover in this arid part of the north, Maiduguri depended upon a locally supplied charcoal-burning power station for its electricity supply.

A vast, flat, arid plain, half as big as England, sparsely inhabited, with no rivers and just a few seasonal streams, lay to the north-west and north, sloping imperceptibly eastwards toward Lake Chad. Around Nguru and Gashua in the north-west of the province a few broad sluggish streams moved seasonally towards the Yobe river through the Sahel country of the Niger Republic borderland. Under a blue sky, long after the wet season had come to an end, shallow floods might suddenly occur, underground water rising in an artesian-like manner, perhaps reaching a few feet deep in a few hours, with no discernible run-off, and remaining that way for some weeks *(Photo.209).* Campsites were therefore chosen with care !

The Chad basin, with its geology of subsurface clays, proved to be a great artesian basin holding water which had migrated underground from the high plateau land perhaps hundreds of miles away. Boreholes drilled at about 10 mile intervals supplied good fresh clean water for drinking and watering animals *(Photo.207)* and held out the prospect for local small scale irrigation. The fertile soils around the lake itself led, during the 1970's, to the construction of a very extensive and expensive experimental irrigation scheme for wheat production using water pumped from the lake.

Maiduguri stood at an altitude of about 1,150 ft above sea level and had been established along a sandy ridge only about 20 ft or so above the plain, on an old shoreline of the original and greater Lake Chad, now about 80 miles away. It was a bleak, bare place of temperature extremes, with average daytime highs throughout the year of 95°F(35°C) and lows of 66°F(19°C). It was fiercely hot in April and May when windows and doors were left wide open in the hope of catching whatever breeze there might be, but closed by breakfast time to retain the coolness of the night as long as possible. To avoid working during the heat of the day in the hotter stations like Maiduguri, it was common to open offices much earlier in the morning than at Kaduna or Jos. At the height of the Harmattan it was forbidding, windswept, and dusty grey with deceptive daytime heat, followed by rapid radiation and cold nights. Early British administrators actively encouraged the planting of delicate evergreen neem trees throughout Maiduguri and some of the smaller towns of the province. These shade trees, brought originally from India, grew well in the sandy soils and over a million saplings were locally propagated and planted to provide avenues of shade for roads, markets and gardens.

In 1968 Maiduguri was declared the capital of the new North-Eastern State following the earlier nomination of Bauchi. Acting very swiftly after the original announcement, the new North-Eastern State Survey Department had been quickly set up at Bauchi but then had to remain there for the next eight years, principally for want of office accommodation in the capital nearly 300 miles away. Maiduguri became the capital of the new State of Borno (the spelling was changed from Bornu to Borno) when it was declared in 1976 and superb new Italian-built, spacious air-conditioned offices, part of a huge purpose-built State Secretariat, were made available to Survey at the time - spacious because there were so few staff to fill them !

Ilorin Province

1955 also saw the establishment of a small Provincial Survey Office at Ilorin, run by Peter Taylor *(Photo.211),* by Jorgen Jensen in 1959, by John Adshead and, in 1969, by the Nigerian surveyor Bassey Ekanem. The town was without significant industry and did not have an electricity supply until after 1957. It lay on the railway at about 1,200 ft above sea level, the first major town in the North on the line coming up from Lagos. In the 1950s it had a population of about 44,000. Its Catering Rest House *(Photo.210)* was a popular staging-post for an overnight rest on the journey by road between Kaduna and Lagos. The climate was humid and uncomfortable with a longer wet season than most of the North, with rainfall averaging about 51 inches (1295 mm), average daily maximum temperatures of 90°F(32°C) and lows of 70°F(21°C). The important Bacita Sugar Scheme lay 56 miles to the north.

Kabba Province

The historic town of Lokoja, the Provincial capital of Kabba, had a population of about 15,000 in the 1950s. It had developed from its beginnings as a river trading base and early administrative post, but had no industries. Lokoja seldom had resident Survey staff and its needs were served from Ilorin, although A.Umoren was based there in 1959. It was another unpopular, hot, airless and humid riverside town lying just 200 ft above sea level along the narrow western bank of the great River Niger at its confluence with the Benue. One or both of them always seemed to be in flood, carrying vast amounts of water from the distant regions of the Cameroon highlands in the east and the equatorial lands of Guinea and Mali over 1,500 miles away to the west. Average daily highs were 90°F(32°C) and lows 73°F(23°C), and about 46 inches (1,168 mm) of rain fell each year. Green trees covered the steep slopes overshadowing the town up to the top of the red ironstone plateau of Patti (the Nupe word for a hill). In 1961 Lokoja town still had no electricity and after dark it was a town of small oil lamps. The old clubhouse stood on open, high ground where it would catch a few breezes and enjoyed the luxury of a small generator which provided enough power to cool the beer and to provide a bright light over the snooker table. With the shutters wide open, this hilltop light was an attraction to every insect from miles around and a thousand different varieties, of all shapes, sizes and aggression, orbited the light and fell into a writhing carpet on the snooker table and the floor. But the game was not disturbed by such obstacles. It became one of luck rather than judgement, rather like playing snooker on a gravel path, with some insects crawling over the stationary balls, and nearly half as big !

Bauchi Province

Bauchi, a province which had previously been served by minesfield and cadastral touring surveyors from Jos, had a small Provincial Survey office during the second half of the 1950s, and was run in turn by various surveyors including Peter Taylor (1957), Ian Gilfoyle and John Tozer (1959). At the time, the small quiet market town had a population of about 15,000 people and no industries. The arrival of the railway around 1961 had no dramatic affect, but did facilitate the movement of cattle and agricultural produce and, in the 1970s, gave a spur to the establishment of a meat canning plant. With its nearby Zaranda market, the Geji rock paintings, the annual traditional *sallah* parade at the Emir's palace, and the nearby Yankari Game Reserve, Bauchi was a fascinating and scenic day excursion from Jos.

At 2,000 ft above sea level, with average daily maximum/minimum temperatures of 90°F(32°C) / 65°F(18°C) and an annual rainfall of about 44 inches (1,118 mm), it had a very tolerable climate. The accessibility of Jos, just 80 miles to the west, made it one of the more popular Provincial stations, in spite of the fact that it had no electricity until the end of the 1950s. Water supply was a problem. Bauchi had no river and only a few seasonal streams. The River Gongola, a major tributary of the Benue was only 25 miles to the east but was never used as a source of water for the town.

Adamawa Province

By 1957, a small office, run by Peter Redwood, had been opened at Yola (another 'punishment' station) to serve Adamawa Province. Then a small town, with only about 9,000 inhabitants, it had no industries but had long been a trading post on the River Benue. At only 575 ft above sea level it suffered from the stifling climate of the Benue plain, with average daily maximum and minimum temperatures of 94°F (34°C) and 71°F (22°C) and an annual rainfall of 39 inches (1,521 mm). Beyond Yola lay the hill country along the Nigerian borderland with the Cameroon Republic, the spectacular pinnacles of the Mandara Mountains running northwards towards Mubi and the Alantika Mountains to the south-east. This hill country was the safe homeland of groups of different pagan peoples, but Adamawa province was dominated by the Fulani who here retained their language and culture more markedly than in many other parts of the north.

Clifford Rayner was posted to Yola in 1960 to provide photo control for the town, one of the twenty towns in the north then being mapped at a scale of 1:2,400:-

> *'Yola is about 500 miles from Kaduna and a good two days drive via Jos, Bauchi, Gombe and Numan. It really was the back of beyond, and at this time there was no Provincial Surveyor there. It consists of two settlements, Yola which is the original native Fulani and Hausa town situated on the banks of the river Benue and Jimeta about 5 miles down stream and on a hill overlooking the river where the British made their settlement. All other non-indigenous tribesmen were required to live there also. Strangely, Yola was the cooler of the two places. Accommodation was limited in Jimeta so I moved into a very modest quarter in Yola town and was the only European living there for about 10 weeks.'*

From Yola he wrote home as follows:-

> *'Well there's no news to tell of so I shall describe a typical day. Get up at about 5.35 a.m. - the alarm goes at 5.30! Breakfast at 5.45 and meet labourers and others at 6. 10. We usually get off to work and are ready to start by 6.30. Work until 12. 30pm. Come back to the house, I write letters, listen to the wireless, read, have something to eat if I am hungry, a general rest period in the heat of the day. Labour gang congregate again and we are in the field by 4. 00. - work until 5.30, come back (its dark at about 6.15pm), have dinner then a bath. Bring all my work up to date, listen to records and in bed by 9.00-9.30 pm. Occasionally somebody will drop in for coffee or tea but generally it's a pretty spartan existence. '*

Sokoto Province

Perhaps not so remote as Maiduguri, but certainly as hot, was the administrative headquarters of Sokoto in the far north-west of Northern Nigeria, a town of about 55,000 local people and 35 or so Europeans, where the local industries were weaving, dyeing, tanning, leather work and pottery. It was situated at about 500 ft above sea level on the seasonal river Sokoto, a tributary of the Niger. Shade temperatures were commonly 110°F(43°C) and the rocky ground made it more heat-retentive than Bornu. Average daily highs were 95°F(35°C) and lows 70°F(21°C), and an annual rainfall of only 29 inches (736 mm) meant that for much of the year it was dry and dusty. Just after the war, Sokoto was still a very backward place with very poor roads and little in prospect from the country's 10 year development plan, and was never connected to the Nigerian rail network. Up to 1957 there were no resident survey staff and work was undertaken by touring parties. A Provincial Survey office was opened later and was manned by Alan Wilkie in 1961 and, for a while, by Cliff Burnside, neither of whom were there long enough to be accepted as a *Ba Sakkwache*, a Man of *Sakkwato* (Sokoto), an honourable title accorded to those with close association and understanding of the local people and their customs and language. Sokoto gained much more prominence in the course of time with the development of large scale rice irrigation schemes in the Sokoto-Rima valleys and the construction of a cement factory which was to play an important role in Nigeria's future development.

120 miles or so to the south-east of Sokoto, on the road to Funtua and Zaria, lay the railway town of Gusau, a place which in 1936 had been second only to Kano in importance as a business and marketing centre This was a collecting point for the movement of agricultural produce by rail, particularly groundnuts and cotton, and was also a centre for cotton ginning, spinning, and weaving, and dyeing with locally grown indigo to produce blue cloth. This tradition later led to the local establishment of a textile factory.

****

By 1958, with staffing levels near their peak, all provinces had resident surveyors, but very soon, with the beginning of the expatriate exodus in 1959, numbers of staff posted to the provinces declined and within a year Provincial Survey offices were retained only at Kano, Ilorin and Sokoto. Thereafter, until the establishment of the new State Survey Departments in 1968 at Sokoto, Kano, Bauchi, Jos, Ilorin and Kaduna, cadastral surveying in the Provinces was done by touring Nigerian surveyors and assistants, while topographic mapping control surveys were carried out by parties working out of Kaduna headquarters.

LIFE AND WORK IN KADUNA

Amenities and lifestyle

While Provincial towns were sometimes uncomfortable, the northern capital, Kaduna, could certainly not be described as a tropical paradise. The altitude of about 2,000 ft made it a reasonable place to live, with sufficient rain (approximately 52 inches (1321 mm)) and a year-round water supply to make the place pleasantly green. Average daily maximum/minimum temperatures were 88°F(31°C) / 65°F(18°C). Dust, humidity, flies and mosquitoes, which would breed in any small pockets of water around houses and well watered gardens, and the pressure and routine of a six day working week, invariably in hot survey offices without air conditioning, meant that discomfort was not the preserve of the smaller stations. But with its amenities, cultural and educational facilities, the British Council, services, hospital, canteens (stores), religious and social life, it was undoubtedly one of the best postings for married officers, even those with young children, for whom schooling was available. St. Christopher's Anglican Church in Kaduna North and the Roman Catholic Church at Kakuri were the main centres of religious activity for expatriates. The climate and conditions favoured sporting and outdoor pursuits such as gardening but there was still a risk that wives might become bored if they did not become involved in work or an activity or interest of some kind other than daytime socialising with other wives. Good mental strength was a distinct advantage when grappling with the problems of others at coffee mornings and parties. A number of them were able to find employment, but few ever worked in the Northern Nigerian Survey. An exception was Barbara Adshead who has contributed the following:-

"An Honorary Chap"

I want to tell you how I came to join the Northern Nigerian Survey Department and became one of the "chaps". I had specialised in Land Surveying in my Geography degree at London University so I was able to assist John, my husband, with his work when we were in the bush in our first tour. It was an interesting and a companionable thing to do and saved me from the boredom which afflicted some wives in the bush. I had a friend who admitted to unpicking and re-sewing her dresses !

We carried out astro-fixes and photopointing in Bornu and a road traverse from Bida to Mokwa along with various other jobs. I sat under an umbrella and did the booking and later back at the tent or rest house did half the computations. A keen eye at Headquarters spotted the different handwriting, and enquiries were made. The result was that on arriving in Kaduna for our second tour in April 1956 I was offered the job of Senior Computer in the Topo Section (which later changed to the less grand title of Technical Officer Computing). Apparently when the Minister was approached about my employment he wanted to know why I could not continue to work for nothing in the Department if I had been working for nothing in the bush !

I do not remember a lot about the work I did except that I thoroughly enjoyed it. A small number of Nigerian computers and I had to re-compute, twice, the work which came in from the surveyors in the field and to check the material going off to the D.O.S. I learnt the hard way about the value of checking and re-checking because an error slipped through in some work going to the D.O.S. and I was left in no doubt that the Northern Nigerian Survey Department did not need to be let down in this way. We used Brunsviga calculating machines at first and later the less interesting looking Facit.

A note in one of my letters home says:-

"At the moment I am very busy in the office drawing up large plans of all the triangulation they have ever done in the last 30 years or so. The plans are 40 inches square and there will be 12 of them covering Northern Nigeria. They will take several months to do as I have to plot them and ink them in carefully. It is a change from computing."

Later I seem to remember gathering together all the information about trig points in a sort of directory.

There is little else in my letters about work - they are mostly about the house (the one on the corner of Eaglesome Road) and how we were furnishing it and doing the garden, sketches of dresses I had to make or bought and long accounts of the social round of drinks parties, dinner parties, the cinema and the club.

Everyone in the office, both European and African, was very charming and helpful to me and I never suffered any male chauvinism. I did however have to put up with a lot of good humoured ribbing - would Keith Hunter, the Director of Surveys, call me laddie or lassie, would I have to wear knee socks, would I receive one of his letters about dirty feet in open-toed sandals, and so on. The worst of all was when I passed my driving test: somehow my driving licence was intercepted before it got to my office. It had a very serious photo of me looking as though I had just escaped from a mental home. A letter was circulated in the float file saying that warning signs had to go up in the Junction and a yellow flag would be carried in front of me when I drove. Also that all mothers had to be warned of the presence of a madwoman.

Having been brought up in a hamlet in Yorkshire with only boys for company I was well used to being teased and so I did not mind and I felt it helped to make me a full member of the Department. Advantages flowed from being treated as a male. I was invited to official functions when wives were excluded because of the purdah which existed in the Ministers' quarters and I could attend the doctor's surgery before 9 am along with the men rather than wait until after breakfast and have to waste time among the milling crowds of multiple wives with hordes of children belonging to the senior Nigerians.

Kaduna South was a most attractive place in which to live and work. I particularly recall the walk down to the office in the cool of the morning when all the flowering trees were in blossom. There was a very pleasant and lively atmosphere among those who lived and worked there, engendered I think by the constant comings and goings on leave with the attendant hail and farewell parties and the holiday mood of those who came in from the bush for a few days.

Eventually the end of the tour came and we flew home to have our first child. I worked in the Department again towards the end of our time in Nigeria and I did many and varied jobs in between but nothing quite matched the interest and enjoyment of working as Senior Computer and as an honorary "chap".

....

Housing

Housing in Kaduna South varied from some of the original rather solid and gloomy railway buildings *(Photo.213)* to newly built and more airy and spacious bungalows *(Photo.214)*, but all had electricity and running water. As mentioned earlier, the Surveyor-General occupied an old but beautifully situated house *(Photo.212)* on the bank of the Kaduna River, a stream which changed dramatically from season to season *(Photos. 220 and 221)*. David Ball describes the accommodation into which he moved in 1956:-

'The bungalow (though it and all the others were always called houses) was of the standard "Kaduna" type designed a few years earlier in the Regional PWD (public works department) architect's office. A sixty-foot veranda running the length of the front of the building extended, in the centre, into a square covered patio outside the French windows which opened onto a sitting room with a dining annex off to the right at the front. All of the floors were of shiny terrazzo or imitation marble which I hadn't seen before, partially covered by carpets. At the rear of the room a short corridor gave access, left, to the second bedroom, the bathroom and the main bedroom equipped with two beds side by side under a wooden mosquito-net frame. All the rooms had wide casement windows in the front and the sitting room and main bedroom at the rear also, to give a through breeze if there was one. The problem of the second bedroom and the corridor in this respect was overcome by

means of frosted glass louvers in the dividing wall and windows on the other side of the corridor. It was quite a clever design. With no air conditioning, a through-draft was vital especially in early May when I arrived and the rainy season was overdue. All windows, behind their expanded metal "tief netting", were kept open day and night. When there was no breeze one had to rely on the ceiling fans to stay reasonably dry. At the height of the six-month dry season, however, around Christmas, when the dry, dusty Harmattan blew down from the Sahara the nights and early mornings were often cold and you put on a sweater to go to the office. The dining room was connected to the kitchen, with its wood stove and oven, by a covered way, and a short distance away, at the rear of the house but backing onto the road, was a row of three "boys' quarters" with a kitchen and ablution room at the end.

About half-way through my first tour an alternative house was designed: the Muslim type house, in recognition or anticipation of senior Northern Nigerians in government service. These had purdah-type accommodation for up to three wives'.

Windows were invariably protected by thief-proof mesh and grilles, but these did not provide protection from the determined burglar (*barau or' tiefman'*) and it was a comfort to have a reliable watchman or a good guard dog. Good guardians or not, dogs were often kept as pets and were a constant source of good company and conversation. Jack Ashton's 'Ponto' held a departmental record for the fastest time and the most direct route from his house to roll in a pile of manure (*taki*) as soon as he was released from having a bath, and Frank Waudby-Smith's 'Heinz' (descended from 57 varieties of other dogs) was left in a survey camp 80 miles from Kaduna while Frank paid a visit to town. At mile 40 on his return trip Frank met Heinz travelling very fast and determinedly down the centre of the road in the opposite direction - a dog who resented being left to guard the camp and had a definite preference, like his master, for town life.

Communications and development

Kaduna, which was established by the British as the administrative capital of the Northern Provinces near a fording point of the River Kaduna, was scarcely 40 years old when the Northern Nigerian Survey came into being, but by then the population had risen to over 46,000. Around 1915 it was linked to the south by the railway, though road connections had to wait much longer (1927), and until the 1950s had no industries other than those set up to serve the capital's needs like printing, furniture making and construction. Until 1957 the only road crossing the Kaduna river was a narrow single-track bridge shared with the railway. Motor vehicles had to straddle the rails and the one-way traffic was controlled by a flagman at each end waving a green or red flag. But a two-lane road bridge was then built alongside the railway crossing, and the journey from Kaduna South, where the Survey Department lay, to the main parts of Kaduna *(Photos. 222, 223, and 227)* on the northern side became less time consuming and less hazardous *(Photos. 218 and 219)*.

With regionalisation in the 1950s Kaduna Capital Territory was excised from the Zaria Emirate and placed under the direct control of the Regional Government. The town gradually diversified and heavier industries were introduced. The first of these was a textiles factory which employed experienced technicians from Lancashire and Switzerland and, as a result of technological collaboration and joint financing by the UK and Holland, a brewery producing 'Star' beer was opened in Kaduna South in 1964, giving employment to 300 people.

Survey Headquarters

Kaduna South was both a residential and a working area for surveyors, and their neighbours the Federal Geological Survey. A reminder of the former surveyors' presence may perhaps still be found to this day in the residential area where Jack Ashton was responsible for the trial construction of an Ordnance Survey type trig pillar *(Photo. 215)*. The remainder of government and commercial business and most of the social and sporting activities took place in Kaduna North. Survey Headquarters consisted of a group of rather randomly located buildings of various ages on a large uneven piece of ground including the Topographic, Cadastral and Town Planning Sections, offices for administration, photogrammetry, drawing, , lithography, computing, records keeping and stores. The opening of the offices at 7.30 in the morning by the messengers signalled a routine of opening windows, crossing a day off the coloured commercial picture calendar from Wiggins Teape, F.Steiner, UAC or Gottschalk, the winding of the clock, the perfunctory dusting, moving the rubber date stamp forward a day, and a lengthy round of greetings. Some office walls were enlivened by reference information; maps, staff lists, leave charts, survey party locations, progress charts and flight diagrams showing aerial photographic coverage. An hour's break was taken for breakfast at about 9.30 and work then went on until 2.30pm or 12.30 pm on Saturdays. These were the days before common use was made of internal telephones and intercoms and an atmosphere of relative calm, quiet orderliness would prevail. Messengers would sit outside office doors on their own chairs, perhaps dozing gently as the temperature rose and would be startled into action by a 'ping' from a desk bell to fetch and carry files from one office to another. The arrival or departure of a party from the bush would disturb the routine and create a round of excitement, greetings, revving engines and shouting. Elsewhere clerks would be busy with their books, filling out vouchers and forms in quadruplicate and rattling their typewriters. The routine of administration, form filling and minute writing in voluminous dusty files was far removed from the independent, practical and technical work of field surveying and those who could, sought refuge in technical work in the office. Meanwhile, just outside, on the paths which led to the bridge and to the markets of Kaduna North, there was a daily reminder that the real Africa lay quite nearby - small groups of Gbagyi (Gwari) women moved by with their enormous shoulder-borne loads of firewood *(Photo.217)*.

Supplies

The United Africa Company, which came into being in 1929 when the trading company of W.H.Lever was renamed, was still one of the largest trading companies in the days of the Northern Nigerian Survey and its Kingsway Stores at Kaduna *(Photos. 224 and 225)*, Jos and Kano were the main source of expatriate provisions. Local vegetable sellers would barter their produce on open-air stalls close to these shops. Other familiar names in Kaduna, long established all over the North as trading companies, were CFAO *(Compagnie Française de l'Afrique Occidentale)*, John Holt, PZ *(Patterson Zochonis)*, Gottschalk and GBO *(G.B.Ollivant)*, wholesale and retail stores or 'canteens', sources of such commodities as cement, soap, paint, enamelware, ironmongery, tools and cloth, and from which a few household goods and provisions were sometimes available.

Social life

Kaduna was memorable for its sporting and social life. There were opportunities for tennis, cricket, rugby, golf, and swimming (in a large pool originally built by the Army and later a modern one at the new Hamdala Hotel *(Photo.223)* built alongside the racecourse). Polo was played in Kaduna and elsewhere in the North, but there was only one player in the Survey Department for it was regarded as a game for those who were more or less permanently settled in a station or could afford the luxury of being able to keep horses. Tennis was much more common, and the Surveyor-General built a court in his garden, but local people would sometimes stop, totally mystified as to why Europeans should be bothering to run about getting so hot and tired without apparently achieving anything.

To many people in England, where rugby was invented, it remains a mysterious game, a wild scrimmage in the mud with a rather obscure set of rules. Imagine the confusion in the minds of people in a country where it was only relatively recently introduced, where soccer was the only game played at school, and where they could watch the senior officers of government and managers of commerce pushing one another around in the mud on Saturday afternoons in the wet season. Kaduna Rugby Club, with its small clubhouse and bar, was a great social institution which enjoyed considerable support from surveyors whether players or drinkers or both. Members could purchase the maroon club tie (bearing crocodiles rampant), threadbare examples of which appear to this day at Northern Nigerian Survey reunions. The club had a pitch in a corner of Kaduna Racecourse *(Photo.230)* and regular matches were played against visiting teams, mostly expatriates, and not many of them really very fit, from Zaria, Kano, Jos and Lagos. In the course of time the game was taken up enthusiastically by very fit and strong young men from the Nigeria Police and from the Nigerian Army and they were soon outrunning many of the unfit, flabby office-bound expatriates who played for the sheer hell of it. A well attended tournament took place every year in Kaduna and another in the English-type conditions of the Jos in the wet season. A sports reporter from the Nigerian newspaper the 'Times', obviously a little new to the rules and objectives of the game, is alleged to have published the following report:-

'More than exactly 1 / 500 spectators, mostly people, watched Kaduna Association Rugby Union trounce Jos Club last Saturday night.

The next day they played rugby and after a fierce start Capt. J. Howard, Q.O.N.R., (Howard Jay) led the scrum over the line where they scrimmed for some tense moments. Then Scottish full-back MacEye passed to Reynaud (Rayner) the standoffish half, who gave it to the half-scrum Vurley, who hurled it on to little Duncan (Duncan Little), another Scotchman inside forward. Duncan was not fast enough to score since his wind was broken immediately.

Dick's son (Dixon) the forward half was not backward in dropping his ball but it went over the crossed bar. He was carried off.

After half-way time Kaduna tried playing in the opposite direction. This proved successful because Thomas Eaver (Doug Eva), Kaduna, touched himself down on three points to the delight of the spectators.

Quenton perverted and increased their side by two. He then did 25 drops out and Kaduna never looked back.

The final score when the whistle rang was 3 to 13 for Zaria.'

Private lunch and dinner parties were perhaps the most common of social activities. Cooling large quantities of beer for big parties could be a strain on the ordinary, overworked domestic refrigerator but it was fortunate that in Kaduna South, at the railway station, large ice blocks could be bought and the bushman's galvanised bath would come into its own. The writer recalls the occasion when he filled two of them with a large number of beer bottles, packed them with crushed ice and loaded them on to the back of his 'kit car' for a fast 60 mile dash by road to a party being held at the tented Survey Camp at Kachia.

Little excuse was required to justify the throwing of a party and Ken Toms recalls a good example:-

'Jack Ashton was a divorcee, who was wont to complain about the high level of alimony he was required to pay out to his ex-wife, until such time as she should remarry. Suddenly we received an invitation to a weekend "Fred party" at Jack's house in Kaduna. It turned out that his "ex" had been wed in England to a gentleman named Fred. It was a great and boozy party in honour of the good Fred.

M.J. "Mickey" Miles was a gentle English intellectual who had joined the Colonial Survey Service in the Gold Coast some years before. Holder of an honours degree in physics from Bristol University, Mickey was streets ahead of most of us in technical matters. An affable bachelor, he and Ashton were a great comic duo in the Flannigan and Allan style. Years later, we heard the sad news that Mickey had succumbed to blackwater fever in Southern Africa.'

As well as the traditional West African curry, groundnut stew was a great favourite, particularly for lunch on Sunday . Chicken, or Guinea fowl, was added to a thick gravy of freshly crushed groundnuts and chicken stock, and hard boiled eggs, and served, as with curry, with rice and an assortment of side dishes including diced fruit, onion, coconut, tomato, croutons, peppers and stink fish. A large meal like this, accompanied by a few drinks, was a recipe for a very drowsy, lethargic afternoon, especially during the languorous heat of the hot season and the residential areas would become very quiet as everybody, including the domestic staff *(Photo.226),* retired for a siesta.

Kaduna town had hotels and lively bars *(Photos. 228 and 229)* and an open-air cinema catering largely for local needs and showing all-singing, all-dancing and all-fighting Indian films, but the films screened on Sunday evenings often appealed to a wider audience. For most expatriates, however, the main social centre was the Kaduna Club with a variety of activities including dances, snooker, parties and films. Like the Rugby Club it issued a tie, examples of which still exist, but dark blue with crocodiles couchant reflecting, perhaps, the less energetic disposition of its membership. In common with other clubs established by expatriates throughout the North it was primarily a place for drinking, talking and relaxing with friends and colleagues and something of an antidote to male loneliness, and to congregate there was a pleasurable ritual after the physical and mental exertions of the day *(Photo.231).* A great deal of enthusiastic and argumentative 'shop' was talked, though the arrival of a newcomer or somebody returning from bush or from home leave could add new dimensions to the usual range of banter and discussion. The first cold beer after a hot day is one of the greatest pleasures known to man, but there was a risk in some that too much of it could lead to alcoholism, especially those depressed by their surroundings or lacking acceptable company, who saw it as the panacea for their boredom and frustration.

The flavour of domestic and social life in Kaduna in 1963-64 is provided by Janet Rayner *(Photo.216)* :-

"A Young Wife's Tale"

'Cliff and I were married in February 1963 in London. Cliff had been allowed to come home on local leave, for three weeks, as long as he paid his fare and all other expenses! We were married ten days after he came home and ten days after that we arrived in Nigeria from the depths of a very cold English winter where we had snow from Boxing Day onwards and it was still on the ground. The heat struck me as we landed in Kano and it took some time for me to acclimatise, although once acclimatised I found that anything below 80° and I began to feel cold. I am still like that to this day! The following account is of some of the first year's impressions and experiences.

I was very nervous when we first arrived, mainly at the idea of meeting all Cliff's friends that he had known for a long time, and myself not knowing any of them. Although I had travelled fairly extensively, for those days, and I had lived and schooled in France for a short while, away from my family, I was still only twenty two and had no idea what to expect. However, everyone was very welcoming and it didn't take long to settle in. Indeed even some of the labourers came to greet me at the breakfast time of Cliff's first day back at work.

Cliff was looking after Jack Ashton's dog Ponto and that was an experience in itself. Fortunately he welcomed me, but it didn't take me long to learn to tie him to the window frames when anyone was visiting. He was with us until Jack came back from leave and by the end I was sorry to see him go. I think he was too, as he often used to come and visit us afterwards, and we either had to take him back or Jack would come and fetch him.

Cliff introduced me to the joys of shopping in Kingsway and the other various stores, and on reading my diary I did seem to go an awful lot. I can't make out whether it was because there was never everything that was wanted at any one time or it was a social event. A bit of both I suspect.

The social side was certainly much appreciated and busy with lots of coffee mornings, lunch time drinks, evening drinks, dinner parties, parties at the club and the rugby club and trips to the cinema. It makes me feel quite breathless now, but I could still be a lady who lunches given half a chance! A sure sign of age creeping on. Still when we had to make most of our own entertainment it was easy to get into the swing of things. Evenings when we didn't go out seemed to be spent mostly in playing scrabble and reading. Cliff used to win lot in the beginning but gradually the tide turned in my favour.

Cliff used to play tennis at 8 o'clock most Sunday mornings with Denis, Jake, Pat Davies and various others, but tennis was never my scene so I only sometimes used to wander down at about 9 o'clock to watch. However I did play badminton with the "geologicals" and always enjoyed that. We also often used to go swimming at the army pool and later on at the Hamdallah Hotel when that was open.

Our cook steward was Jattoh, a very kindly old man with a good sense of humour, but he could be exasperating at times. I have quite a fund of stories which illustrate the culture gap. On one occasion I had to go a pick Cliff up from the office at 2 o'clock and I had just put some water in to boil to cook some frozen peas, so I asked Jattoh to put the peas in when the water had come to the boil. He asked me " How many madam? I replied "The whole lot", and that is precisely what he did, box and all. I abandoned trying to pick out the soggy bits of grey cardboard and we went without vegetables!

He also suffered with gravitational ulcers and bush sores, and he would never clean them. They were exacerbated by the fact that he left them untreated and with his trouser legs constantly flapping against them. In the end I insisted that he only wore shorts and I dressed his legs twice a day and in time they cleared up. I often seemed to have a stream of "boys" and their families come for medical attention. On one occasion Jattoh's youngest boy Sam had fallen out of the mango tree and cut his forehead open. We took him down to the hospital but, seeing the treatment he was getting by some complete incompetent, I finished up stitching the wound myself. The poor child had concussion as well, but seemed to recover quite well in a couple of days. So no lasting harm was done. On another occasion, Ali the garden boy, brought his baby who had a dreadful eye infection. He had been taking him to the hospital but it was getting worse and not better. The child was filthy, so I bathed it and then cleaned his eyes with Optrex, and I'm glad to say that the infection cleared up like magic, although I had to insist that he brought the child to see me, every day, for some time so that I could see that an attempt was being made to keep him clean.

I began to acquire all sorts of new skills, dressmaking being one of them. Jattoh used to watch me and once told me that he liked my dresses. I must admit that once we came home that is one thing I abandoned. I've always hated sewing. We also did a lot of gardening, which was fairly new for both of us although we both had parents who were fanatic gardeners. Maybe that's why we had never done much before. Ali the garden boy was always slightly horrified by us doing the gardening but unfortunately if it was left to him, weeding meant pulling up everything in sight, flowers included.

Cooking is something that I had always done and enjoyed, and on looking through my diary I seem to have done inordinate amounts. Every day I seemed to cook cakes, pies, biscuits etc. mostly before breakfast, with dinner party stuff done after breakfast, before going on the coffee round. I seemed to have a lot of trouble with eggs and always kept plenty in as I often had bad ones. Although I used the old water trick when buying from traders, even though I never bought "floating" eggs, lots of them were still bad. Occasionally if I was using them the same day, I would crack them into bowls whilst the trader was there and only pay for the good ones.

Cliff took me out and about when he could, and we went on trips to Zaria, Kano and Jos. I was always very impressed with the houses in Zaria. On one occasion we were looking at the Emir's palace in Zaria and we got chatting to a very strange dour old man who turned out to be the court jester. I trust he was a little more amusing in his master's company. In Kano we occasionally went to watch the camel trains arrive and that was very interesting. I later read a long article in the National Geographic about the salt trains from Bilma, which meant so much more having seen them come into Kano.

Once the rugby season was in full swing we did a lot of visiting to play matches in various locations culminating in the North-South Tournament in Jos. A splendid time for everybody. In our first year we had a problem coming home, as the road was out at Rahama 40 miles down the road. We were fortunate as we had left late and met Denis coming back. We had to do the long route around Kafanchan, Zonkwa and Kachia and it took about seven or eight hours to get home. We did stop to see Assob Falls which were very picturesque. The road was bad much of the way and at the American Mission at Kafanchan they had put straw, leaves and grass down to try and make things a bit easier.

We always stayed with Dick Dunning whilst in Jos. Cliff and he had been good friends for some time and in fact Dick was Cliff's best man at our wedding. He was always fairly wild and I dread to think of some of the things that the two of them must have got up to in their time! We always had such a good time when we stayed in Jos.

Our home was gradually turning into something of a zoo. Initially we had Ponto and our cat. She produced two kittens, which Ponto never minded and in fact they used to snuggle up around his ear to sleep; or play with his tail; but he never ever "went" for them. After Ponto left we had Benji, Bill Macleod's dog, whilst he went on leave. During that time we also acquired Josie a Boxer/Setter mix pup. We had her for all the time that I was in Nigeria and I was very sad to see her go when we left. We felt that we couldn't bring her back with us as she had never ever been chained up and also felt the cold. Keeping her in quarantine for six months would have been much too cruel. Benji was a real character and soon taught Josie how a well trained dog should behave. Unfortunately he had one great character flaw, as Val Macleod used to say so succinctly "That dog is so phallic"! I often had to tie him up when there were several women in the room as he could be quite embarrassing. For all that he was a very good-natured animal, although he always hated Zaki, Stanley's pooch, and we could never understand why. Battle lines were drawn on each and every occasion that they met.

We used to take the dogs for a walk every evening and more often than not the cats used to come too. It was a very social occasion as we so often used to meet others such as Stan, Cliff Burnside, and Jack doing the same thing that it nearly always finished up with "drinks" somewhere, other than on the nights Cliff went to rugby practice, where there was plenty imbibed anyway.

Although I had always been pretty healthy at home, I began to have days where I felt very ill. It took me a few weeks to realise that it is was always after breakfast on the days when I took Paludrine so I stopped taking it and hey presto I felt fine again. I started to take Nivaquine, but for the whole of the last tour we were in Nigeria I didn't take anything at all. I only went down with malaria two years after we came home!

I began to look forward to the beginning of the rains and the first time we could see a storm coming we jumped in the car and drove out beyond Kakuri to stand in it and get wet, as we could see that it was not going to get to Kaduna South. People at home would have thought us mad. We always enjoyed the storms, even when we had a eucalyptus tree through the roof over the bathroom. Occasionally the storms stopped the film showing at the Rugby Club and the old Radar cinema. Mind you, films at the Radar were an experience in themselves as they didn't often get the reels in the right order, but when you couldn't hear them for the drumming of the rain on the roof it was just as well to give up and come home, or go to one of the various clubs, than try to sort out what was happening on the screen.

When our neighbours the Parkers got a television we used to go round and watch a local quiz show, the name of which escapes me now. It was always a programme that generated total hysteria to those of us watching. The questions were fairly innocuous but the answers were not. For example "How long is the Suez Canal" - answer - "Could it be 4 million miles"? "What is the capital of England" - answer - "Is it Madagascar"? If a contestant got the answer right the quiz master would say "Right, Fiiiive points! This expression has remained in the Rayner household until this day, and covers a multitude of situations. The star prize in the show was a refrigerator: donated by J.K.Chellarams and Sons Ltd. However in all the months that we watched the programme somehow nobody ever managed to win it! I wonder if it is still the star prize?

In the May, after Minne and Jannie de Vries had left, we moved into their old house. It needed some work doing on it, so we asked PWD to come and fix the fan, mend some lights, repair cracked window panes and put new locks on the doors and repair the loo waste pipe. What a saga that turned out to be. First of all they appeared without any tools, so left and went away. Then one man arrived a couple of days later, but his mate didn't turn up, so off he went. After that things did improve imperceptibly. On one day they mended 2 panes and two locks, that was the high point. They did manage to mend the loo pipe but in the process broke the toilet, so then we had to have a new pan. Having installed it there were leaks from a different place!. All in all it took from May 20th until July 26th for all the repairs to be effected, but eventually all was ship shape, although Cliff, in desperation, eventually finished off some of the repairs himself. By this time I was getting very phlegmatic about delays. It was no good getting irritated, so I learned to go with the flow. It was all very different from being back in England where I had had a job that was very pressurised and there were continuous deadlines that had to be met.

After a few months I decided that it was time I did a bit of work, and I managed to get a part- time job in the Pathology Lab. The work permit was taking some time to arrange but I started anyway, but even so it was September before I started work when the wheels had been set in motion in June. I was to work from 10.00 until 2.00 Monday to Friday. This would curtail my daytime social life, but I was looking forward to working again.

I had only been at work for three days when I had a car accident. I was waiting at the exit to come out on to the road, when a WAITR Land-Rover came swinging in through the exit, taking a short cut, and banged the front of my VW. What a palaver that turned out to be. We had to get the police involved, and I couldn't let Cliff know where I was. In the end he and Frank Waudby-Smith found me at the police station. They were thankful that nobody had been hurt. The Land-Rover driver tried to make out that I was on the wrong side of the culvert, but, when Cliff made a plan that meant that my car was only 2 feet wide, it rather blew his defence to bits ! The police decided that a fine had to be paid, but that the Land-Rover driver would have to pay 90% of it and I would pay 10% as I had been there! The car was taken to UTC to repair, and on the first night that we took it out after getting it back we discovered that the headlight had been put in the wrong way round, and so was pointing straight up to the heavens. How they ever managed it I shall never know. In any event we had to have another new light as the other was broken.

I started to have a lot of headaches and migraines after starting work and decided that it was probably because I was using a monocular microscope when scanning all the TB films. I did enjoy the work but there was sometimes not very much to do. I had to go over to the Native Hospital on several occasions and once was roped in to help with some operating. I have never seen a theatre like it. The instruments were in an open glass case; windows open, letting in the dust and flies, and on that particular occasion the key to the blood frig had been lost so there was no blood available in any case of emergency. I seem to remember that it was some time before the frig was broken into and by that time all the blood had gone off anyway.

I only worked until the end of October, as Cliff was going on tour to Bida and I wanted to go with him. My headaches immediately began to improve, so perhaps it was a blessing. However, I hadn't yet been paid, as my work permit had still not come through. In fact when I gave my notice in the Ministry, they said that I couldn't resign as my appointment had never been confirmed!. Several weeks after having left, my work permit came through, and then eventually a clerk arrived at the back door with my money in a little bag, so all was well in the end.

In November we went on tour down to Bida for a few days, so that Cliff could sort out some problems for Victor Agbu. I did enjoy my time in and around

Bida. I walked for miles with the dog through the bush, and was always amazed how often I came across folk, especially children, although there were no obvious signs of habitation anywhere. It seemed to be an African "thing'. I remember going up to Jos once when we stopped to help somebody who had gone off the road in the middle of nowhere. Within a very short time there were Africans around and the car was soon pulled back on to the road. I remember Cliff going at the car with a crowbar to prise the wheel arch away from the tyre so that the motorist could carry on to Gombe.

Cliff had started to draw a large scale map of all the places where he had stayed in Nigeria. He spent many weeks on it. and it makes interesting reading now. One day we will get it framed and hang it up. Perhaps writing this will spur us into action.

After the New Year we were going home on leave, and so we organised for the Beales to look after Josie for us. The cats went with the house, so there was no problem there. So ended my first tour and back to winter in the UK from whence I had left the year before. Another climate shock for me and one more difficult to cope with. I was really looking forward to coming back at the end of our leave, but that is entirely another story.'

LEAVE AND DEPARTURE

Local leave

Deeply involved in their work, as many expatriates were, the majority (but certainly not all of them) nevertheless looked forward to a period of leave away from Nigeria, especially if they had spent a lot of time in bush, or in the more enervating stations. But if leave was still a long way off, by way of relief under certain circumstances, short periods of local leave might also be taken. Such leave was a privilege, not a right, which could be granted at the discretion of a head of department for special personal reasons, for recuperation from an illness, or for a break after long periods under extreme conditions, working seven days a week.

Perhaps the most preferred destination was the cool Jos Plateau, but it was always a matter of personal choice. Some chose to go elsewhere; to the coast at Lagos; to the Sonkwala Mountains of Eastern Nigeria at Obudu; to Bamenda in the Southern Cameroon highlands; or to the Yankari Game Reserve and the delightful bathing spot of Wikki Warm Springs in Bauchi Province. It was also possible to visit Nigeria's surrounding French-speaking neighbours for the unaccustomed luxury of colonial French cuisine at Birnin N'konni, Maradi or Zinder in Niger, Fort Lamy in Chad or the sight of abundant game, including giraffes and elephants, at the Waza Game Park near Mora in Northern Cameroon.

Travelling home by sea

A tour of duty, lasting for something between 18 and 24 months, was followed by a period of home leave, travelling by sea, until air services from Kano provided a faster, more convenient, but abrupt transition to the grey skies of Europe. Until the Elder Dempster services were withdrawn, some people still preferred the more gentle changes of the coastal route, enjoying the start of home luxuries as the ship set sail from Apapa, wearing tropical clothes until, northwards, the wind acquired an edge and cleared the decks of the sun-lovers. The personalities of the passengers seemed to alter as the warm, salty smell of the oily, blue-green sea gave way to cooler and deepening blues and greys, and finally to the bleak reality of the Mersey.

Travelling by air

There was always something overwhelming, glamorous and reassuring about going to the international airport at Kano to watch the big aircraft come in and, as friends flew away northwards, a sense of flatness and, perhaps, a tinge of regret at having to walk back to the car park and return to hot houses and offices in the sun *(Photo.237)*. But, in due course, one's turn would come to climb aboard one of those big silver aircraft and step at once into a very different, cool and comfortingly clean and efficient world. Leave would seem to start while still stationary outside the Kano airport building. Then, with a roar from the engines and a final brief glimpse of the sprawl of the red city and the yellow desert below, the return to a familiar world was swiftly under way. The abrupt change was completed just a few hours later at the rather unromantic Heathrow Airport, a far from glamorous place in the 1950s. But then came the pleasures of arrival, meetings friends and family and, perhaps the simplest pleasure of all, drinking cool water from a tap !

The return to Kano after the delights and relaxation of leave could, at first, be a melancholy experience. Reminders of the discomforts in store came with the first glimpse of the parched land from the aircraft window, and suddenly the next leave seemed an eternity ahead. But despondency would last only as long as it took to hear the familiar Hausa greetings of welcome, to renew friendships, to resume responsibilities and return to an accustomed way of life.

Final departure

But the returning could not go on indefinitely. Sooner or later, final departure was inevitable *(Photos. 232 and 236)*. From the moment a surveyor took up his first appointment in Northern Nigeria he knew he would not be able to settle there for good, indeed many had no intention of staying for other than a short period. Some arrived with optimism and ambition, perhaps expecting greater things, and quickly came to the conclusion that their future lay elsewhere.

Having arrived in 1952, Harry Rentema left Nigeria in 1954, but later returned for a short spell:-

> *'I had a very instructive and interesting time which stimulated my warm feelings for Africa, where I spent the following 10 years. I went on to Tanganyika and Liberia, and I worked my last year in Africa in Northern Nigeria when it was independent. I was on an F.A.0. project along the Sokoto river and I lived with my wife and two daughters in Gusau. I heard that Paul Ward was Director of Surveys in Kaduna at that time but unfortunately I did not get chance to meet him.'*

Arnold Voshaar says of his own departure:-

> *'We had a lovely time in Nigeria. Our first daughter was born in the hospital at Jos. But the political rumours about what might happen when in 1960 Nigeria became independent, and the threatened outbreak of civil war in the Congo, led us to the decision, in 1957, to leave Nigeria and not to sign for another tour.*
>
> *We still have a feeling of nostalgia when speaking about Nigeria and the men and women we met and worked with.'*

When his wife and son flew back to England toward the end of his one and only tour in Nigeria in 1959, Kenneth Toms intended to stay on for a few more months in order to save some money:-

> *'The "old coasters" liked to point out that life in West Africa tended to pall after a relatively short period. I had thought that this was a ploy for the maintenance of short tours. It did not take long after the family had left, for me to revise that view. Life did become stressful, and I applied to go on leave without further ado'*

The traditional notion of a 'career for life' was passing. Many officers, Nigerian and expatriate, had no long term plans to stay in surveying, especially if confronted with unacceptable conditions, such as where they had to work, and if offered limited financial and career prospects. With so many opportunities opening in their newly independent country, it should be no surprise that many Nigerians also used surveying training and experience as a stepping stone to other more attractive and perhaps more lucrative careers. Surveying was never a popular career in the UK and there was no reason to assume it would be more so amongst Nigerians. Of the 23 Nigerians occupying senior and technical positions in 1959, only six were still in the department in 1967, which then numbered 11 expatriate and 45 Nigerian senior and technical staff. In the year before Nigeria became independent in 1960, there were 13 expatriates in Survey Headquarters in Kaduna South, four on the Jos Minesfield, four on tour in the bush and eight in Provincial stations. All but five of the expatriates left Nigeria between 1961 and 1966 *(Photos. 233-235)*.

Some expatriates, it has to be said, though normally uncomplaining, did not long enjoy the itinerant and celibate lifestyle. They discovered they could not tolerate the climate, did not enjoy working with the local people, found it difficult to live with cultures largely closed to them and, having given scant regard to other potential problems at the time of their appointment, came to fear sickness, privation, frustration and loneliness. Some were very sensitive to the fact that, all too often, Nigerians did not share their enthusiasm for surveying; they could not come to terms with people they would never really understand and who would never really understand them. Though most expatriates were capable, energetic, good tempered and proud of their work, they did not hesitate to say what they disliked about Northern Nigeria. For some of them, it was a place to be appreciated, and never forgotten, but not a place for which they were ever likely to feel deep affection or attachment. Their wives might have even greater difficulty and would add to the pressure to return home, even if it meant a change of profession for their husbands. Survey was fortunate, however, to have very few of the restless and discontented people sometimes encountered, those who complained of life at home, regarded themselves as martyrs, and who had nothing good to say about Northern Nigeria and the people with whom they worked.

With very few exceptions, Nigerian staff and leaders, from Chiefs and Ministers down, appreciating the contribution to development which expatriates had made in the past, and which they might continue to make, showed respect, goodwill, tolerance and friendship with those who continued to serve after independence. Many Northern Nigerians, who had grown up with the expatriate presence, could not believe what was about to happen and did not relish a sudden mass exodus. Special financial provisions were introduced that would make it attractive for experienced expatriates to stay on to see the region through its initial difficulties, rather than replace them entirely with new overseas people who did not know the country, whose loyalty and dedication might be questionable, and who might come and go much more quickly on short term contracts.

In spite of the inducements, with large question marks appearing over the future, many experienced people left just when the country was beginning to need Survey more than ever before. Amongst the longer serving officers there was a realisation that the North was not ready, and endless discussion, apprehension and anxious sympathy about what lay in store for Survey as independence approached.   A few had given the best years of their lives to the service, which had become an integral and indelible part of their lives, and they retired only when age and regulations decreed it was time to go.

Some of these very experienced people, like Keith Hunter and Keith Sargeant, made extremely valuable and immeasurable contributions to the development and progress of the Northern Nigerian Survey.   Keith Sargeant was not alone in his unease about delaying his departure because, like others (some of them much younger than him), considerations for his family were paramount and his specialist experience and accustomed position of authority mitigated against finding a meaningful and commensurate position at home. He recalls:-

> 'As the time of independence approached, expatriates in pensionable posts were given the opportunity to take early retirement with lump sum compensation. In the Northern region at that time most of the more senior African staff were southerners (largely Ibos and Yorubas) and it was felt they might take over before the less well educated Northerners could be trained for the more senior posts. For this reason, rather than let the Europeans go, the Northern Government tried to persuade many to carry on for a few more years.
>
> In my own case, I was then acting head of the department and, in an interview with the Minister, was told that I would probably be promoted to the substantive post if I stayed on.
>
> It was not an easy decision to make as I liked Nigeria and the Nigerians. I enjoyed the work and felt it would be difficult to obtain a suitable job in UK at the age of 42. On the other hand we had two children at boarding school in England and my wife and I both disliked the consequent disruption of family life. After a lot of thought I decided to retire - and fortunately was able to start a new career in the Home Civil Service.'

There were as many reasons for deciding to leave as there were serving officers.   Few surveyors, if any, had arrived with altruistic notions of public service. Their aims had been straightforward; to practise their chosen careers while earning a good living, in secure and responsible positions; to advance their careers in ways which might not be possible at home; to satisfy a curiosity for travel, adventure and life in wild places, and, into the bargain, to enjoy the rewards of long leave. The curiosity element was sometimes soon exhausted. One by one, other issues came to the fore; apprehension about the future and about security (in the light of the events in other newly-independent countries); financial considerations; limited career prospects; concern about the erosion of a hitherto acceptable lifestyle as friends and colleagues departed; reaction to perceived rising antipathy towards foreigners by some sections of the public and the press (riding the anti-imperialist bandwagon of the times); and the murmurs of political discontent and ethnic unrest in various parts of the country.

Final departure was not without sadness. The decision to leave often meant parting from a close circle of colleagues and the reluctant severing of ties with domestic staff with whom long lasting and trusting relationships had developed.

Jean Burnside wrote:-

'We were very sorry to leave Kaduna but so many of our friends were also leaving that it seemed time to go. As it turned out, we left 36 hours before the lbo military uprising which resulted in the killing of Alhaji Abubakar Tafawa Balewa and the Sardauna of Sokoto. It was very, very sad to hear about it on our first Sunday at home. It seemed quite unbelievable. I enjoyed the years in Nigeria very much and always regretted that I did not go out there earlier. It was the best time in my life especially as it was there that I met Cliff.'

Departures led to a need for additional short term assistance for the technical services, especially if it promised an improvement in indigenous training, capability and prospects. During the latter half of the 1960s and into the 1970s, experienced officers were gradually replaced by less experienced and differently motivated local staff and politically and commercially motivated individuals and organisations from overseas aiding nations, some of whom might have been unemployable in similar capacities in their home countries. American Peace Corps volunteers, for example, started appearing on the scene in the 1960s and, in view of the never-ending Survey staff deficiencies, were able to find useful practical, supervisory and map completion jobs, even though they were of little, if any, direct or lasting benefit to the training of Nigerian surveyors and assistants. Nigerians were not slow to sense the naiveté and inexperience of some of these young idealists and recognised the transparency of their political motivation. The local press referred to them as *'Piece Crops'*, alluding perhaps to their sometimes bizarre hairstyles, and expressed considerable scepticism about their usefulness to Nigerian culture and advancement. If the momentum of planned progress was to be maintained, funding had to be found for surveying, mapping and planning contract work placed with capable overseas commercial organisations.

Staying on

Those who stayed on continued to find satisfaction in the way of life, fulfilment in the achievements of the surveying profession, enthusiasm for the development programme and enjoyment in the relationships established with the local people and Nigerian and expatriate colleagues alike. Amongst those who had undergone the test of self sufficiency in the bush and remote stations were some who feared difficulty in finding an alternative occupation as rewarding and challenging. After long periods spent in the undeveloped tropics, a few of them thinking of returning to their homeland risked finding themselves no longer temperamentally suited to that sort of life. Nigeria was apt to linger in the blood for a long, long time. To stay on required a measure of tolerance, moral integrity, good humour, strength of will and endurance. Some found comfort and accord with local women, the sort of women who had, for one reason or another, found themselves excluded from their own families and communities. The absence of European women could mean a life of prolonged and unwanted loneliness and celibacy was regarded as unnatural by local people. Those without marital ties, or those with very enduring relationships who could see that their departure, with no Northerners to replace them, would be detrimental to the Department (for the North did not relish the prospect of even temporary domination by people from the southern parts of Nigeria and were as a rule glad that expatriates were prepared to stay on), came back for tour after tour. They were willing victims of a sort of magnetism with a lasting commitment and attachment to their adopted country, regardless of the privations, and would continue to return until living and working conditions became intolerable, a decade or more beyond the wind-up of the Northern Nigerian Survey. But one by one each were bid a final, reluctant, farewell *(Photo.238):-*

"Ku sauka lafiya. Sai wata rana. Ku dawo lafiya".

"To, Alla ya kai mu"

"Amin."

The reward

Whatever the reason for ultimate departure, those who served in Northern Nigeria were enriched by the experience and retained vivid and recurring memories of the land and its people and a compelling attachment to a place that could never be called home. Even as strangers, they were treated with polite respect and invariably made welcome, with a salute of friendship wherever they worked and travelled. Even after the passage of three or four decades it is possible to feel that attachment and to have it renewed at the annual Survey reunions, or by the delight shown by a Hausaman when he is unexpectedly greeted in his own language when he is abroad.

Nearly everything that is best in the African character is embodied in rural, not city life. If it were possible to return to the North, if only briefly, many notions might be shattered, but in the backwoods, on the hills and in the remote areas surveyors knew so well, the familiar greetings are still likely to be heard, the kindness will not have changed and there would still be a welcome.

PART 5

THE LAST OBSERVATION

PART 5

THE LAST OBSERVATION

Difficult times

Nigeria's day dawned fine and fair, a quiet and promising beginning, with little to indicate that the small white clouds and morning breezes, the beginnings of political and tribal discontent, were the precursors of a darkening sky, with distant thunder announcing the approach of a great storm. When the deluge came, it marked the end of a chapter of progress, development and ordered land administration and was followed by a quiet aftermath of repair, and preparation for the future. In Northern Nigeria, *damana*, the wet season, was *mai ban samu*, the giver of good things, and marked the end of the drought; there was hope that good could come of a man-made disaster.

This has inevitably been a story about disappointment. In the early 1960s there was great optimism that Northern Nigeria was going in the right direction. The old 'colonialism', if it ever existed there, was gone, its successor in other places, communism, was never a starter and nationalism was apparently safely contained within the envelope of federation but progress through free-market capitalism became hampered by selfish polititians and military regimes.

The military coups and the civil strife of 1966-67 brought an abrupt and almost catastrophic end to a unique period of survey progress but, throughout the troubled times, there remained a small and devoted band of expatriate and Nigerian surveyors who were willing to assist in times of crisis and who carried on with hope and optimism, after the dissolution of the Northern Region, to build fledgling departments in the newly formed States.

In the light of subsequent events, it is arguable that those efforts were wasted. More coups were to follow; the States themselves divided, and divided again. Some of the new administrations were enthusiastic about development and sought to maximise their land resources, but at the same time appeared to be unwilling or unable to vote sufficient finance, and permit recruitment, for the staffing and operation of efficient systems of survey and land administration.

From 1972, in the North-Eastern State, the writer remembers:-

> *'Termites were working on the roofing timbers of our old mud-walled buildings at Bauchi. For their protection, the legs of the wooden shelves in the records and map stores stood in small tins of engine oil. In spite of the nation's increasing oil revenues, and the approval of large grants for prestigious development schemes, pleas for better accommodation for the Survey Department were studiously ignored. When a thunderstorm came, a violent one which swept away the roof and exposed the valuable contents of the offices to the wind and the rain, local townsfolk made off with the remains of the roof, unhindered by local police, and were only restrained by the efforts of faithful Survey headmen. The urgency of the matter appeared of little concern to supposedly responsible Ministry officials, no extra funds were granted for repairs, and it was extremely difficult to convince them that irreplaceable records of many years of painstaking technical effort were at risk.'*

Challenges and threats

With huge demands for residential and commercial building land, workloads increased to levels unimaginable in the days of the Northern Nigerian Survey. With inadequate financial and manpower resourcing, the small Survey units were unable to handle this volume of work. Through the 1970s the demands for land continued to exert increasing pressure on Lands and Survey departments and malpractices, attempting to by-pass the cadastral process, began to increase. The systematic and reliable statutory cadastre, which provided more precise property boundary definition than the system which operated in the UK, started to deteriorate. More than ever before it was becoming necessary to work with, and not in spite of, local systems, attitudes and unethical practices, with a prejudice in their favour rather than against them, thereby letting slip some of the accepted high standards and professional ideals of earlier days.

For the heads of the Survey Departments, optimism gradually gave way to a feeling of increasing inadequacy and dissatisfaction, inducing, in some of them, an attitude of ruinous self pity and abandonment of hope of ultimate success. Proposals for radical reform of the cadastral system to utilise aerial photography for the rapid coverage of township extension areas met with silent opposition or obstruction from those who stood to gain from underhand procedures, or were deemed too radical to appeal to inexperienced and inflexible administrations.

The factors which led to the expatriate exodus of the 1960s were still at play. Those still in service needed more than a modest salary to persuade them to remain. They sought satisfaction from and recognition of their work, combined with a secure and settled life for, and with, their families. Their professional ethics demanded freedom from an environment of indifference, hostility and latent corruption and nepotism; they sought support for their suggestions of more modern and efficient surveying practices; and they did not take kindly to a rising tide of envy, resentment of their presence and implications of exploitation, when so much good intentioned effort was being made.

Since long before the wind-up of the Northern Nigerian Survey, there had been an awareness that the established prosaic business-like attitudes of expatriates surveyors, involving excessive zeal and ceaseless work, might have little lasting local appeal, and so it was proving to be. Sometimes, if Nigerians did not respond to the perceived urgency of the surveying programme, expatriates were too ready to take on the work themselves; but as time went on, it became more and more obvious that it was a mistake to impose alien ideas if there was no local response or enthusiasm. Some Northerners, although appreciative of those efforts, even if they didn't fully understand why the surveying was necessary, ascribed the expatriate approach to a force which they did not fully comprehend.

With willing collaboration, it was possible to make progress and not difficult to train local people, with no previous technological experience, to carry out surveying and planning work. The fundamental problem, in some places, was to contend with an inherent improvidence and disinclination to plan ahead and an apparent inability of many to learn from mistakes. Come what may, prosperity or otherwise lay firmly and undeniably in the hands of Allah.

20 years of neglect

It is regrettable to have to record that, as recently as 1994, prospects for Survey still looked bleak. Daniel Omoigui, an ex-Director of Federal Surveys, went on record to say that there were, at that time, no up-to-date cadastral maps of any town or city in the north, and even the mapping of the new Federal Capital, Abuja, had not kept pace with development.

At the time, 85% of the country had been mapped at 1:50,000 scale, two-thirds of this by UK and Canadian technical assistance, but was then mostly 20 years out of date. Nigeria had adopted a basic national mapping scale of 1:25,000 in 1980, but not much of this had been done. There was no involvement in mapping, even during the prosperous times of the oil boom. Neither the Governments nor the Military were apparently much interested in mapping unless it was linked to development projects.

He said that the land tenure and surveying systems still in operation had been established in more spacious days when the objective was primarily to serve the needs of colonial, and then independent, administration. A greater emphasis on customary rights, and attempts to bring them into the statutory system, had compounded the problems. As the system failed increasingly to work, the blame was placed on the original colonial systems, which were designed for different times and different circumstances.

Viable alternatives were needed, but Nigeria's attempts to find them had, by 1994, been unsuccessful. A 'Land Use Act' had been passed in 1979, but not effectively implemented. It depended, as did the system operated by the Northern Nigerian Survey over thirty years earlier, upon the provision of up to date large scale maps in all urban areas, but it also called for the development of a new and comprehensive cadastral system. No new maps and control had, however, been established, many surveys still had arbitrary local origins, and litigation was becoming increasingly common. A Land Reform Commission set up a workshop in 1991 to review the Act and submitted proposals in 1992. Up to the time of the departure of the President, General Babangida, in 1993, nothing more had been heard about it.

In 1994, with a population of over 90 million people, the country had less than 1,000 qualified surveyors. The universities were producing 50 graduate surveyors per annum, but many of them were unable to find jobs in the profession. Dan Omoigui held that problems of resource management in survey departments had nothing to do with political upheavals; rather, they were the result of inefficient and corrupt management, while the devaluation of the Nigerian currency had made it extremely difficult to purchase mapping instruments and survey equipment.

Opportunities

Long after the demise of the Northern Nigerian Survey, the launch of the rocket which placed the first GPS satellite into earth orbit heralded the decline of traditional methods of land surveying all over the world. As in other developing countries, the level and quality of Nigerian training and experience has been outpaced by the developments in surveying, mapping and computing systems taking place in the developed world. To reach the same advanced level, Nigeria now has the opportunity to omit some of the expensive intermediate stages of technical progress. Since Independence, the country has been passing through a turbulent adolescence with graft, nepotism, malevolence and a degree of incompetence adding to its problems, but it is hoped that, with maturity and prosperity, it will have the wisdom to revitalise and maintain effective systems of land record and administration, using the opportunities being offered by modern satellite-positioning and remote-sensing technology.

Legacy

Nigerian independence was achieved at a time when it was fashionable to condemn colonial powers for the treatment of their former territories. Some western nations, who should have known better, totally ignored many of the benefits which had been conferred by the pioneering administrations. There has been a fashionably distorted and ignorant view, even supported to some extent by programmes put out by the BBC (and gratuitously insulting the tough, resourceful, hard working officers who dedicated the best part of their lives to the colonial peoples) that the colonies existed only to be exploited economically. There is often disregard of the provision of schools, colleges, hospitals, health services, security, law and order, transport, communications, and the effort put into information gathering, planning and the development of technical and professional services.

It was hoped that the example we set would allow the intelligent people of the North to find their own way and that our good intentions would neither hinder their development nor, as in some parts of the world, encourage a dependency culture with a demeaning need for external charity, aid workers and volunteers. Teachers of surveying believed they were providing a good foundation for Nigerian self sufficiency in the profession.

The importance of surveying was recognised at Federal and Regional government levels, but on the whole, with the notable exception of work on district boundaries, and the rather unique surveying activities of the Kano N.A., it probably had little real influence on the everyday life of ordinary people, of the Local Authorities and of the traditional rulers of the North. To the uninformed, surveyors arrived apparently self-invited, carried out work only they could understand and left without producing tangible and beneficial results; their presence was not usually a matter of dramatic or lasting importance and the maps they produced seemed to serve little purpose. On the other hand the surveyors, Nigerians and expatriates alike, were never in doubt that they were making a valuable and essential contribution to the processes of orderly administration and development and would always continue to do so.

In spite of the gloomy outlook for the country in the 1970s, and regret for the tasks left undone, expatriates left with a feeling of pride and accomplishment at having facilitated the most productive and firmly based phase of cadastral, planning and mapping work that Nigeria had ever seen. Future surveyors and administrators would only have themselves to blame if they did not utilise the potential of the established system to keep up to date with the changing needs of the country and the way that advances in the surveying world could serve those needs. In a contrasting environment of long established and proud indigenous cultures, Northern Nigeria had inherited a well organised and equipped system of land record and administration, and the best regional mapping unit in West Africa, leaving it sufficiently well equipped, given the will, to make its way in the developing world. There can be no denying these benefits and, in the light of subsequent events, there is perhaps now less prejudiced condemnation of the efforts made by at least two generations of *Geographic Labourers,* most of them British, before and after the war, many of whom took up their posts when the process of preparation for independence was already very advanced. They took pride in their achievements, and the maps and plans which evidenced their efforts, and gained satisfaction from playing a valuable and often understated rôle in the development of the Region.

> *'.......the growing good of the world is partly dependent on unhistoric acts; and that things are not so ill with you and me as they might have been, is half owing to the number who lived faithfully a hidden life........'*

George Eliot's fanfare for the silent majority
in the closing lines of *Middlemarch.*

John McIlwaine, who in 1997 compiled a resource guide to the maps and mapping of Africa, said:-

> *"The transformation of the cartographic record of Africa during the last two or three decades of colonial rule, continuing into the first decade or so of the newly independent states of Africa, has now been recognised as the really significant period in the cartographic history of the continent. Uniquely detailed records of the landscapes of Africa were compiled in the course of that work, landscapes which are rapidly changing as populations increase exponentially in parts of the continent".*

Relationships

A sense of inter-dependence with colleagues who shared common aims, qualifications and ideals, and commitment to the specialism of surveying and mapping, aided by a generally agreeable social life, led to the emergence, over a long period of time, starting long before World War II, of a remarkable *esprit de corps* and comradeship amongst the expatriate and Nigerian staff. Surveying often required team effort and the support of others. Co-operating in the pursuit of compelling aims, incorporating a genuine respect for the challenging pioneering work of their forbears, was natural to the British, whose success in the world owed much to corporate functioning. The administrative survey offices at Kaduna and Jos, which had sympathy for, and a true understanding of, the conditions under which field staff were working, were strong unifying influences.

Although there were individuals who did not fit the general mould, there was, amongst the majority, a natural concern for the welfare of the Nigerians with whom they worked and an inclination to set an example of hard work, enthusiasm, control, even-handedness and honesty. No doubt many mistakes were made out of ignorance, accident or inflexibility when dealing with the individual needs of Nigerian peoples of vastly different cultural, tribal and religious backgrounds, but such mistakes were genuine and not made out of malice.

In turn, Europeans were generally held in high esteem because of their approach and their incorruptibility, characteristics not always so common amongst local people. Ties were strengthened by these amicable relationships, by the common use of the Hausa language and the background of Northern Nigeria as a unique cultural entity, and led to a commitment to a distinctive, sometimes rather short-lived, but very memorable period in the lives of many surveyors.

The spirit not only reinforced the establishment and working of the Northern Nigerian Survey, but saw it quite strongly through the expatriate exodus in the post-independence years, gave it resilience to survive the traumatic events of 1966, engendered an optimistic and constructive strategy when the North was divided, and has survived through to the present day in the minds of individuals and their annual reunions in the U.K. *(Photo.239)*.

Over the next decade or two, the ageing *Geographic Labourers* now attending these reunions will, in all probability, climb to that great trig. point in the sky to take their last observations. They will carry with them fond memories of Africa, and will with gratitude leave behind all their concerns about measurements, calculations, correction factors, adjustments, grids, and projections and, according to J.C.T.Willis, will at last be spared the unenviable task of attempting to portray the spheroidal, uneven and ever changing earth on flat sheets of paper:-

When the last observation is taken,
The theodolite stowed in its box,
And the surveyor is coffined-up also
And his soul at St.Peter's gate knocks;
Then this surveyor, not understanding
That of all earthly troubles he's rid,
Says to Peter "Come over and tell me
What projection you use and what grid ?"
And Peter will answer benignly,
"There's no need to fuss about that.
Projections and grids don't concern us,
Ain't you 'eard ? This is heaven - it's flat !"

....

In the light of what has happened in Nigeria over the past 40 years or so, critics of Britain's colonial past will argue that more harm than good was done by the expatriate presence and endeavour, but those who served Nigeria all those years ago, and their Nigerian contemporaries, know differently. They will recall their enthusiasm, dedication and accomplishments, and will be glad that something of the lives and times of the *Geographic Labourers of Arewa* is at last put on record. In the difficult times it has experienced, Nigeria has been in need of friends. It is hoped that this collection of memories reflects something of the ongoing friendship and concern felt by those whose life was enriched by service in Northern Nigeria.

....

APPENDICES

APPENDICES

APPENDIX I

CONTRIBUTORS

	Introduction	Land & People	Survey Departments	Framework	Topographic Mapping	Planning	Cadastral	Minesfield	Boundaries	Training	Destination Nigeria	Making a Start	Travelling	Bush	Provinces	Kaduna	Leave & Departure	Last Observation	Appendix VII
B.Adshead																			
J.D.Adishead							▓								▓				
M.F.Anderson	I	I	I	▓	I	I	I	I	I	I	I	I	I	I	I	I	I	I	I
J.Ashton				I									I	I	I	I			
B.A.Babb			I																
D.Ball			I	I	▓	I					▓	▓		▓	I	I			
V.T.Brokenshire		I		I	I			I	I		▓		I	I		I			
C.D.Burnside		I		▓	▓	▓					▓			▓					
J.Burnside														▓			▓		
J.Cooper					I														
P.A.Daley			I																
C.Emmott			I	I			▓				I						I		
O.Eva			I		I														
N.J.Field			▓																
E.Hunter			I																
M.Lees			I																
B.MacPhee														▓					
J.Pugh				I	▓		▓		▓	▓		▓		I					
C.Rayner				I	▓				I					I	I				I
J.Rayner				▓	▓											I I			
H.Rentema		I	I	▓	▓			I		I	I I	▓	I	I I		I	▓		
K.M.Sargeant				▓	▓			I		I	I I	▓	I	I I			▓		
J.Street					▓					▓									
B.Till										▓									
K.N.Toms								▓						▓	▓	▓	▓		
M.Vegby						▓													
A.Voshaar			I					I		▓	I I			▓		▓	▓		
J.P.W.Ward					▓									▓					
F.Waudby-Smith																			
J.Wimbush														▓					

Legend:

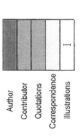

- Author
- Contributor
- Quotations
- Correspondence
- I Illustrations

APPENDIX II

CAREER SUMMARIES

Brief career details of those who have, directly and indirectly, helped to make the story possible.

B.M.(BARBARA) ADSHEAD BA(Hons) FRHS

Bar Convent Grammar School, York 1940-48
Bedford College, University of London 1948-51
Intermediate RICS (Part II RTPI) 1964

London CC Land Use Mapping 1949
Survey and mapping, medieval sites, Northamptonshire 1950-54

Senior Geography Mistress, Paston House, Cambridge 1951-54

Unpaid survey assistant, Kano and Bornu Provinces, astro-fixing and photopointing, 1954-55
Senior Computer/Technical Officer(Computing), Topographical Section, Kaduna 1956-57
Manager, Ilorin Catering Rest House, 1959
Manager, Atlas (Surveying and Cartographical Instruments and Supplies), Kaduna 1961
Teller, Bank of British West Africa, Zaria 1962
Technical Officer (Records), Cadastral and Town Planning Section, Kaduna 1963-64
Surveyor (i/c Records), Cadastral and Town Planning Section, Kaduna 1964-66

J.D.(JOHN) ADSHEAD   MBE MA (Cantab) MA (Nottingham) Dipl. Photogrammetry (UCL)
     Certificate in Education (Cantab) FRICS FRGS

Stockport Grammar School 1937-46
Royal Air Force 1946-48
St Catharine's College, Cambridge 1948-52
School of Military Survey, Officers' Long Survey Course No 11 1953-54
University College London 1959-60
University of Nottingham 1966-68

Senior Geography Master/Housemaster, Southwell Minster Grammar School 1952-53

Surveyor: Plateau - minesfield suveys; Kano and Bornu astro-fixing and photo- topographical traversing; Oi/c Topographical Mapping Section, Kaduna; Provincial Surveyor (topographical traversing), Niger Province 1954-55; District Surveyor, Kaduna Capital Territory: (township mapping and lay-outs); i/c School of Survey, Kaduna 1956-57
Provincial Surveyor, Kano (township mapping); Provincial Surveyor Ilorin & Kabba (township mapping and large scale contoured mapping of part of the Niger flood plain for sugar plantation development) 1958-59
Diploma Course in Photogrammetry, University College, London 1959-60
Senior Surveyor: Oi/c Cadastral Section, Kaduna; Oi/c School of Survey, Zaria 1960-62
Principal Surveyor: i/c Cadastral Section, Kaduna 1962-65
Assistant Surveyor-General: i/c Cadastral and Town Planning Section, Kaduna 1965-66
Retired from the Northern Nigerian Survey Service 1967

Joined the Planning Inspectorate of the Departments of the Environment and Transport and the Welsh Office as Inspector, in 1968; Senior Inspector 1971; Principal Inspector 1975; Assistant Chief 1977; Deputy Chief 1982-86.

M.F.(MALCOLM) ANDERSON   BSc FRICS FInstCES

City of Norwich School 1946-53; Bristol University 1953-56
School of Military Survey, Officers' Long Survey Course No.17 1956-57

Surveyor, Plateau and Benue, minesfield, secondary triangulation, cadastral and provincial boundary surveys 1957-58, Benue primary triangulation 1959, Kaduna Cadastral Section and township air mapping 1960, Lokoja-Agbaja, Offa, Kano-Nguru, Gusau, Bauchi and Jos control and mapping surveys 1961-62, Kaduna, Zaria, Kano and Sokoto Provinces topographic mapping 1963

i

Senior Surveyor, Topographic mapping Kaduna-Zaria and Kano blocks, Kano-Gusau
tellurometer traverse 1963-64; Survey School Zaria and Kaduna 1965
Principal Surveyor, i/c Survey School, Zaria, Kagarko and Kaduna 1965 - 66 and i/c
Topographic Mapping Section, Kaduna 1966
Assistant Surveyor-General, i/c Minesfield Division, Jos 1967-68
Surveyor-General, North-Eastern State 1968-76, Borno State 1976-77
Retired from Nigeria 1977

Chief Land Surveyor, Milton Keynes Development Corporation 1977-92

J.(JACK) ASHTON   FRICS

Rossall School 1936-44; Clare College, Cambridge 1944-45, 1952-53

Royal Engineers (Military Survey), 1946-53
Young Officers Survey Course No.9 1946
Officers Long Survey Course No.2 1948-49
Instructor, School of Military Survey 1949-51

Gold Coast Survey/Survey of Ghana 1953-57
Provincial Surveyor, Eastern Province 1954
Surveyor i/c Survey School 1954-57

Senior Surveyor, Survey School, Kaduna 1957-61
Principal Surveyor, Topographic Section, Kaduna 1961-65
Assistant Surveyor-General, Administration, Kaduna 1965-68
Map Production Officer, ICSA 1968-1970
Principal Surveyor, Kano State, 1970-77
Surveyor-General, Kano State, 1977- 1989
Retired from Nigeria 1989

D.R.(DAVID) BALL BA (Hons T&CP) MRTPI(Retd)

Bedford Modern School 1937-45; Royal Navy 1945-48; University of Durham (King's College
Newcastle) 1948-53

Bedforshire County Planning Department 1953-54
Kingston upon Hull Planning Department 1954-56

Town Planning Officer/Senior TPO, Kaduna 1956-60
Principal Town Planning Officer and head of Town Planning Division 1960-62. Plans for
towns, urban extensions, commercial and industrial areas, new towns, town planning
advice to central and local government, throughout Northern Nigeria

Essex County Planning Department: town centre surveys and plans 1963-65
Greater London Borough of Haringey Planning Dept: head of research and survey 1965-67
Department of the Environment (DOE) Building Research Station, Garston, Herts, Overseas
Division: Principal Planner. Physical development plans and reports for Botswana, Solomon
Islands, New Hebrides (later Vanuatu), Ellis Islands (later Tuvalu), St Helena, Ascension 1967-
74
DOE Airports Policy Division: Principal Planner. Preparation of Consultation Documents and
White Paper on the future development of the London airports and regional airports in Great
Britain 1974-78
DOE Planning Directorate International Division. Representing HMG on town planning and
related committees of OECD (Paris), UN Economic Commission for Europe (Geneva) and
Council of Europe (Strasbourg) (Chairman, Steering Committee on Urban Policies and the
Architectural Heritage 1988-90): preparation of reports and papers for committees, seminars and
conferences throughout Europe. 1978-90
DOE Eastern Regional Office, Bedford. Part-time principal planner (consultant)1990-92

V.T.(TREVOR) BROKENSHIRE BSc(Est Man) ACSM(Hons) FRICS

Truro School 1939-45; Camborne School of Mines 1945-48; University College, London Land
Survey Course 1950-51; Correspondence course for London University external degree 1963-66

Seismic exploration, Persian Gulf area 1948-50

Surveyor: Pankshin/Shendam topographic mapping control, Minesfield examination
section 1951-53; topographic mapping control, heighting and contouring (Zaria and
Plateau Provinces), Priority Sheet revision,   triangulation and survey administration
(Minesfield Division, Jos) 1953-56
Senior Surveyor: Ilorin/Sokoto boundary and Cadastral Section, Kaduna; 1957-58

Principal Surveyor: i/c Minesfield Division; Jos township control; Cadastral Section Kaduna; 1959-61
Acting Deputy Surveyor-General, Kaduna 1962
Retired from Nigeria 1962

Assistant, Site Survey Section, County Architect's Department, West Riding County Council 1963-65
Assistant, Surveyor's Department, Head Office, George Wimpey & Co. 1965-66
Assistant Surveyor, Properties Department, Unigate Ltd. 1966-68
Senior Lecturer, Estate Management Courses, West London College 1968-71
Principal Lecturer, Estate Management, Willesden College of Technology 1971-73
Area Surveyor, Unigate Properties Ltd. 1973-80
Deputy Chief Surveyor, Unigate Prperties Ltd. 1980-83
Chief Surveyor, Unigate Properties Ltd. 1983-85
Consultant: Valuation, Town Planning enquiries and appeals, checking title documents and problem solving, and compulsory purchase negotiations 1986-96

C.D.(CLIFFORD) BURNSIDE MBE BSc FRICS

Darlington Queen Elizabeth Grammar School 1940-45; University of Durham (King's College Newcastle) 1949-52 (BSc Maths & Physics)

School of Military Survey, Officers' Long Survey Course No. 11 1953-54

Surveyor, Minesfield 1954-1956. Provincial Surveyor Bauchi, Benue and Katsina Provinces
Senior Surveyor, Topographic Section, Kaduna. Astro control programme Sokoto Province 1958-1959
Principal Surveyor (Air Survey Officer), i/c Topographic Section, Kaduna 1964 - 1966
Retired from Nigeria January 1966

M.B.E. for contributions to surveying in Nigeria. New Year's Honours List 1966

North East London Polytechnic 1966 - 1986: Lecturer -Senior Lecturer - Principal Lecturer - Head of Department
Department of Photogrammetry, University College London: External examiner for MSc & PhD students 1976 - 1982; Consultant 1986 - 1999
Royal Institution of Chartered Surveyors: President (Land Surveying Division) 1988 - 1989; Examiner, Final Examination (Topographic Surveying) 1967 - 1987; RICS/SST Member/Chairman Technician Education Board 1968 - 1996
Photogrammetric Society: Awarded President's Medal for contributions to photogrammetry 1985; made Honorary Member of the Society 1987; Analogue Instrument Project (Photogrammetric Record, 14(82) - 15(90)
U.K. National Committee for Photogrammetry & Remote Sensing: Hon.Secretary 1967 - 1987

M.J.(JEAN) BURNSIDE (née CALLUM)   MA AMPTI

Roseberry Grammar School, Epsom 1938-46
University of Edinburgh 1946-50 (AM Geography)
UCL London 1950-54:
Diploma Course in Town Planning (part time) Town Planning Institute, elected Associate Member 1956.

London County Council (Architects Dept.) 1950-59:
Technical Asst. --Town Planning Officer.

Lagos Executive Development Board 1959-60: Planning Officer.
Ministry of Lands & Survey, Kaduna 1961-63: Planning Officer.
Married C D Burnside in Kaduna Dec. 1961.
Left Nigeria Jan 1966

1975-82: part-time teaching: Chelmer Inst. Of Higher Education; Chelmsford College of Further Education.
Birchanger Parish Council 1979-89: Parish Clerk.
Hatfield Heath Parish Council 1988-98: Parish Clerk.

J.A.(JENNIFER) COOPER (née WEBB)

Newbury County Girls' Grammar School 1948-54

Booth Anderson & Co., Chartered Accountants, Audit clerk 1954-1960

Married Michael Cooper, Federal Nigeria Survey Department, June 1960

Atlas Nigeria Ltd, Lagos. Sales Accounts 1960-1962
On tour with husband (Tellurometer measurements for scaling primary
triangulation) Lagos, Akure, Oturkpo, Makurdi, Gboko, Bukuru, Jos, Akwanga,
Pambegua, Kaduna, Kotorkoshi, Gundunga, Yelwa, Ilorin, Olokomeji, Oyo,
Okene 9 months in 1963
Federal Survey School Okene 1963-1964

St Albans, Hertfordshire 1964-present

C.(COLIN) EMMOTT BSc PhD FRICS

Burnley Grammar School 1947-49; Heaton Grammar School 1949-54; Durham University 1954-57

School of Military Survey, Officers' Long Survey Course No.20 1957-58

Surveyor/Senior Surveyor, Federal Surveys 1958-1967.
Ilorin Province; secondary triangulation, geodetic levelling, Kainji Dam pre-construction
survey, Nigeria/Dahomey boundary survey, fieldwork for 1:50,000 scale mapping
Sokoto/Jos; T4 primary triangulation observations
Zungeru/Minna/Abuja; fieldwork for 1:50,000 scale mapping
Sokoto; fieldwork for 1:50,000 scale mapping
Makurdi; Field headquarters administration and fieldwork for 1:50,000 scale mapping
Senior Surveyor/Cadastral Survey Officer, Northern Nigerian Survey, Kaduna 1967-68
Chief Surveyor, North-Central State, Kaduna 1968-69
Lecturer/Senior Lecturer, Ahmadu Bello University 1969- 1971
Retired from Nigeria 1971

Senior Lecturer/Principal Lecturer, Preston Polytechnic 1972-84
Head of Department/Vice Principal, Salford College of Technology 1984-92
Deputy Principal, University College Salford 1992-96
Pro Vice Chancellor, University of Salford 1996-98

N.J.(NEIL) FIELD BSc MPhil (Nottingham) PhD (Aston) FRICS

Hastings Grammar School 1945-53; Nottingham University 1953-56;

School of Military Survey Long Survey Course No 18 1956-57

Surveyor, cadastral surveys, Bamenda, Buea and Fyffes banana plantations, S.
Cameroons 1957-62.
Senior Surveyor, Federal Surveys, Nigeria, i/c Survey School, Okene; i/c various field
headquarters on topo mapping; Lagos HQ; 1962-66
Chief Surveyor, 1966-70.
Assistant Surveyor-General, Sokoto, North Western State, 1970-73.
Ahmadu Bello University, Zaria, Lecturer, 1973-75; Head of Surveying Department 1975-80; Professor of Surveying, 1980-91; visiting Professor 1993-95.

Honorary Research Fellow, University of Newcastle upon Tyne, 1991
Associate Lecturer, The Open University, East Grinstead, 1991-date; Assistant Staff Tutor 1995-date.
Visiting Lecturer, The City University, London, 1992-date.

B.(BEATRICE) MacPHEE MA Bcom

Arrived in Lagos in 1946 to join her husband, the late Donald MacPhee, who was serving as a
Surveyor.
After 40 years in Nigeria they retired to Penn in Buckinghamshire

C.(CLIFFORD) RAYNER   BSc ARICS(Resigned) FInstCES(Resigned)

Lord Wandsworth College, Long Sutton, Hants 1944-52; Bristol University 1952 -55;

School of Military Survey, Officers' Long Survey Course No.15   1955 -56;

Surveyor; cadastral surveys, primary triangulation observations (Adamawa and Benue), boundary surveys, topographic mapping control by astro-fixing 1956-60;
Senior Surveyor; i/c Kaduna computing office, township mapping control (Katsina and Adamawa) and Minesfield surveys, Jos 1960-65
Principal Surveyor; Cadastral Lands Office, Kaduna 1965 - 1966
Retired from Nigeria 1966;

Lecturer in Engineering Surveying, Nottingham Regional College of Technology   1966-74
Senior Lecturer in Engineering Surveying, Purdue University, Fort Wayne, Indiana, USA 1974-75
Senior Lecturer, Nottingham (Polytechnic) Trent University 1975-date(2001)

J.(JANET) RAYNER

Administrator (Retired), Department of General Practice, Nottingham Medical School, Nottingham University

H.W.(HARRY) RENTEMA

RHBS School Ter Apel 1939-44; Technical University of Delft 1945-52

Surveyor, Survey Department of Nigeria, minesfield surveys, secondary triangulation, aerial survey control 1952-54

Surveyor, MBEXCO, for columbite mining, Mbeya, Tanganyika 1955-58
Assistant at the Technical University, Delft 1958-59
Chief Surveyor, SENTAB, engineering surveys, Liberia 1958-63

Surveyor, FAO, irrigation studies, Sokoto River, Gusau, N.Nigeria 1963-64

Surveyor, GRONTMIJ Engineering, in Holland and Saudi Arabia 1964-85
Retired 1985

K.M.(KEITH) SARGEANT   MA(Cantab) FRICS FRGS

The Grammar School, Towcester   1928-35; St. Catharine's College, Cambridge 1935-38; Scholar 1938

Ordnance Survey training course 1938

Surveyor, topo survey Chafe and Gusau sheets, triangulation Sokoto province 1939
Censorship branch Lagos; Aerodrome Control Officer/Meteorologist, Maiduguri Minna and Kaduna airports 1940-43
Surveyor, inspection of primary trig points and determination of magnetic variation Bauchi-Yola chain, contour survey Maiduguri airport I943; i/c Oyo Survey School 1944-45; primary trig observing 1946; i/c Oyo Survey School 1946-48; road traversing Oyo province 1949; i/c Survey Assistants training centre Eke near Enugu 1949-50
Senior Surveyor, Provincial Surveyor Abeokuta 1950-51
Acting Assistant Director, West Nigeria 1951.
Acting Director, Kaduna 1952; i/c Minesfield District Jos 1952-54; Acting Deputy Director, Kaduna 1955; Kaduna Headquarters, including compilation of "Technical Instructions" 1956-57; Acting Deputy Director, Kaduna 1957; Chief Surveyor Kaduna 1957-58.
Acting Surveyor-General, Kaduna 1959-60
Retired from Nigeria 1960

Planning Inspectorate, Department of the Environment - conducting inquiries throughout England and Wales
Planning Inspector 1961-63; Senior Inspector 1963-71; Principal Inspector 1971-79.
Retired from Home Civil Service 1979.

J.(JOHN) STREET MA MRICS

Stockport School 1942-47; Leeds University 1948- 51;

School of Military Survey, Officers' Long Survey Course 1951 -52;

Surveyor, Secondary triangulation, primary triangulation, Benue, Bamenda and Cameroons Trustee Territory; Plateau minesfield; 1953 - 60;

Retired from Nigeria 1960;

After 1960; Senior management positions in product development, manufacture and marketing of calculators and computers, and computerised mapping in UK and USA.

Retired (early) in 1988, to write.

W.B.(BRIAN) TILL MBE BSc MRICS

Burnage High School, Manchester 1938-44; Manchester University 1944-47;
National Service 1947-49
ICI Dyestuffs Division Research Department 1949-52

School of Military Survey, Officers' Long Survey Course 1952-53;

Western Nigeria Survey 1953-65
> **Cadastral surveys; cadastral framework traverses**
> **i/c Survey School, Oyo 1958-61**
> **Survey administration (Assistant Surveyor-General) 1962-65**

Hunting Surveys Nigeria Ltd 1966-71
> **Trunk road location surveys; Warri-Escravos pipeline(Shell); Mobil Onshore Terminal Ibeno; coastal control Nigeria-Dahomey (Union Oil); GEC micro-wave telephone route survey;, mineral concession mapping (Sierra Leone)**

Head, Department of Topographic Science, Kaduna Polytechnic 1971-82
> **Developed ND and HND courses in surveying, photogrammetry and cartography; chaired Academic Planning Committee; organised survey camp training and revenue consultancy work**

Principal, School of Technology, Kano State Institute for Higher Education 1983-86
Senior Principal Lecturer, Department of Topographic Science, Kaduna Polytechnic 1986-90
> **Developed and taught Professional Diploma in Land surveying course (post-HND) and organised national seminars in surveying topics**

Retired from Nigeria 1990

K.N.(KENNETH) TOMS MBE BSurv BEcon MUS FRICS FISAust

Nundah Primary School 1933-40, Brisbane Grammar School 1941-44; University of Queensland 1947-51, 1967-72

Surveyor, Condominium of the New Hebrides 1952-54; Surveyor, Anglo –Iranian Oil Co 1954-56; Lecturer, College of Estate Management 1956-57

Surveyor, Plateau / Acting Senior Surveyor, Minesfield 1957-59

District Surveyor, Lands & Survey Department , British North Borneo 1959-65
Senior Lecturer, Queensland Institute of Technology 1967-72
Head, Department of Surveying, Tasmanian College of Advanced Education 1972-76
Head, Department of Surveying, Queensland Institute of Technology 1977-83
Professor and Head, Department of Surveying and Land Studies, Papua New Guinea University of Technology 1983-85
Manager, Cadastral Improvement Branch, Department Lands, South Australia 1985-88
Visiting Professor, Department of Survey Engineering, Chulalongkorn University, Thailand 1988-89.

M.V.(MOGENS) VEGBY (CHRISTENSEN) Landinspektør, Byplankonsulent.

Marselisborg Gymnasium 1948-1951
Stud. Geom. Den Kongelige Veterinær og Landbohøjskole 1951 - 1956

Surveyor, Kaduna township mapping 1957 - 58
Town Planning Officer, Kaduna 1958 - 1961
Retired from Nigeria 1961

Town Planning Officer, Ministry of Housing, Planning Section, Copenhagen 1961 - 1970
Private planning consultant 1971- 1996
Retired and Farmer 1996 - present

A.J.(ARNOLD) VOSHAAR   M.Sc (Geodesy and Land Information)

Erasmus College 1942-47; Delft University of Technology   1947-53

Surveyor, triangulation Bauchi and Sokoto Provinces 1954-55, Jos Minesfield and Kaduna Cadastral surveys 1956-58
Retired from Nigeria 1958

Surveyor; consolidation, land tenure, and construction; Netherlands 1958-60
Regional manager, Heidemij (Civil and rural engineering) 1960-1973
Director, KAFI (Land information and property valuation) 1973-1986
Management of ILIS (International Land Information Systems), Colombia, Indonesia and Surinam 1986-90
Retired 1990

J.P.W.(PAUL) WARD MA MRICS CBE

De Aston School, Market Rasen 1935-42; War Service 1942-48; University of Cambridge 1948-50;

School of Military Survey, Officers' Long Survey Course No.4 1950-51

Surveyor, Plateau minesfield 1951, Kaduna and Secondary Trig. Gombe-Biu-Tula-Kumbo 1952, Makurdi Igumale limestone traversing 1953, Bauchi-Gombe map revision 1954, Kano-Bornu astro 1955, Bauchi Provincial surveys 1956
Senior Surveyor, Plateau minesfield 1957-58
Principal Surveyor, Cadastral, and building work Kaduna 1959-61
Chief Surveyor, Kaduna, 1962-64
Surveyor-General, 1965-68
Surveyor-General, ICSA, 1969-70
Director, College of Environmental Studies, Kaduna Polytechnic 1971-72
Director, College of Science and Technology, Kaduna Polytechnic 1973-74
Principal, Kaduna Polytechnic, 1975-78
General Manager, Diyam Consultants (Land and Water Resource Technology), 1979-87
Retired from Nigeria 1987

F.W.(FRANCIS) WAUDBY-SMITH MBE BSc MEd ARICS(Resigned)

Wells Cathedral School, Wells, Somerset, 1936-43, SW Essex Technical College, 1943-45, Lieutenant Somerset Light Infantry, 1945-48, Bristol University 1948-52.
Married to Joyce Flook 1952, two children, Caroline and Peter, both born in Kaduna, Nigeria
School of Military Survey, Long Survey Course 1954-55

Surveyor; primary triangulation reconnaissance (Bauchi Province), Provincial Surveyor, Benue Province. Seconded to Federal Surveys for Geodetic Levelling of the Benue River, Provincial Surveyor Kano and Sokoto Provinces. Cadastral surveys, map revision, astro-photo pointing, tellurometer reconnaissance Kano - Nguru. 1955 - 1961
Senior Surveyor; Cadastral Lands Office, Kaduna, 1961 - 1965
Retired from Nigeria 1965 and emigrated to Canada.

Physics and Mathematics teacher and Principal, Ottawa Board of Education, 1965 - 1988.

The following have not made a direct contribution to the work, but their names appear in the text:-

J.F.(DERICK) BELL BSc FRICS

Gosforth Grammar School
BSc. Hons (Maths) University of Durham 1951
School of Military Survey
Directorate of Colonial Surveys Caribbean and Kenya
Northern Nigerian Survey 1958-62 (Topographic Survey Computing and Records)
Survey Production Centre Feltham 1964
Assistant Director Ordnance Survey Computer Services in the 1970s
RICS Land Survey Divisional President 1979-81
Manager, Cadastral Survey Operations, Ministry of Housing, Bahrain 1981
Retired 1994

D.C.(DOUGLAS) EVA

Attended School of Military Survey Course 1 at Warminster 1948
Jos Asst Surveyor 1948-50
His wife Olive in Nigeria 1951-60
Minna Asst Surveyor 1951-53 Kaduna 1953-61
Field Survey and Topo
Appointed Surveyor-General on the departure of Keith Hunter

I.(IAN) GILFOYLE

University of Bristol 1952-55
School of Military Survey at Newbury 1955
In bush Bauchi/Plateau boundary 1956
PS Bauchi and Adamawa 1956-57
PS Benue 1958-59
Involved with surveys to demarcate parts of the line of the track of the Bornu extension and to determine compensation to landholders from November 1959 to January 1960.
Survey School Kaduna 1960-61

K.J.(KEVIN) O'SHAUGHNESSY

Minesfield 1950
PS Makurdi and Enugu
Cameroons 1951-61
Kaduna Cadastral 1961, then PS Town Planning after departure of David Ball

P.J.(PETER) TAYLOR

Attended School of Military Survey Course 1 at Warminster 1948
1955-59
PS Ilorin and Bauchi
District Surveyor, Kaduna
Triangulation.   Cadastral.   Field completion.

J.W.(JOHN) TOZER

University of Bristol 1952-55
School of Military Survey Newbury 1955
First job, in 1956, was in Zaria Province on secondary trig.

A.E.(ALAN) WILKIE

University of Bristol 1952-55
School of Military Survey Newbury 1955
1956. In Katsina engaged in the revision of the town survey as his first job.

A.D. (DENIS) WILLEY

Attended School of Military Survey Course 1 at Warminster 1948
Kontagora bush. Groundnuts scheme 1949
Minesfield 1949-50 and 1951-53
Kaduna 1954. Lagos 1954
Jos (i/c Eastern Survey Area) 1956-58
ASG Kaduna 1960-65
Surveyor-General before leaving Nigeria in 1969

A.G. (ALAN) WRIGHT BSc

City of Norwich School 1945-53; Bristol University 1953-56
School of Military Survey, Officers' Long Survey Course No.17 1956-57
Surveyor, Plateau and Zaria, minesfield and cadastral surveys, Kaduna Cadastral Section 1957-58

APPENDIX III   COLLEAGUES

	APPOINTED	LEFT	LATER NIGERIAN SERVICE
SURVEYING			
ADEYEMO S.A.	1949	1963	
ADSHEAD J.D.	1954	1966	
AGBU V.	1956	1966	
AJE S.A.	1949	1968	North-Eastern State
AKA P.K.	1957	1968	
AKPAN M.A.	1949	1965	
ALABI A.K.	1966	1968	
ALAYO M.D.	1952	1968	Benue-Plateau State
ALERAIYE J.O	1962	1965	
ALIYU D.B.	1960	1968	
ANDERSON D.M.	1961	1963	
ANDERSON M.F.	1957	1968	North-Eastern State and Borno State
ARCHIBONG A.O.	1952	1966	
ASHTON J.	1957	1968	ICSA, Kano State and Katsina State
BABA KOLO M.	1953	1968	
BELL J.F.	1958	1962	
BROKENSHIRE V.T.	1951	1962	
BURNSIDE C.D.	1954	1966	
BUTER J.A.	1951	1968	
COTTON H.	1955	1959	
DARAMOLA J.A.	1957	1968	ICSA, Kaduna Poly. and Kwara State
de VREIS M.G.	1959	1964	
DICKSON J.W.	1956	1967	
DUROJAIYE C.K.	1961	1968	
EISINGA E.G.J.	1952	1958*	*Died on duty in southern Nigeria
EKANEM E.B.A.	1949	1966	
EKPENYONG E.U.	1949	1960	
EMMOTT C.	1967	1968	North-Central State and ABU
EMODI S.A.O.	1931	1957 ?	
EVA D.C.	1949	1961	
EVANS J.W.	1960	1968	Kano, North-Eastern and Borno States
EYAMBA E.E.J.	1949	1966	
FOLARANMI J.F.	1962	1968	
GILFOYLE I.	1956	1961	
HANSEN N.K.V.	1953	1959	
HERRING N.	1955	1960	
HUNTER K.H.	1928	1959	
IHEDIOHA R.O.	1949	1966	
ISHERWOOD H.	?	1951	Director of Surveys Gold Coast
JEGEDE S.O.	1949	1968	
JENSEN J.W.	1953	1965	
JONES D.R.	1951	?	
KARMA Y.S.	1966	1968	
KING C.	1950	1957?	
KLEPACKI S.	1962	1968	Kano State
KUSHO D.N.N.	1961	1968	North-Eastern State
KYUKA J.M.I.	1954	1968	Benue-Plateau State
LARSEN F.E.	1958	1962	
LAURBERG A.	1959	1966	
LEES A.(Fed. Surveys)	1947	1962	
MACPHEE D.M.	1946	?	Benue-Plateau State
MATHIASSEN I.W.	1955	1957	
MILES M.J.	1957	1960	

	APPOINTED	LEFT	LATER NIGERIAN SERVICE
MOSZYNSKI T.A.	1953	1961	
MOSS D.J.	1962	1968	
MUSA A.A.	1949	1968	North-Eastern and Bauchi States
NICKEL M.	1952	?	
OBENSON G.F.T.	1961	1965	
OCHEPA M.A.	1952	1968	
OFOEGBUNE I.U.	1941	1964	
OGUNMEKAN D.O.	1924	1962	
OJILE J.S.	1966	1968	
OKOLI F.C.	1949	1966	
ONUGBEDO J.O.	1959	1962	
ONUGHA J.I.	1952	1966	
ONIGBANJO M.A.	1948	1968	
ORAEKI G.I.	1946	1966*	* Died in service
O'SHAUGHNESSY K.J.	1950	1962	
PEAKE H.C.L.	1956	1958	
PRING R.W.	1948	1955	Nigerian College of Technology
RAYNER C.	1956	1966	
REDWOOD P.H.S.	1954	1965	
RENTEMA H.W.	1952	1954	FAO Sokoto-Gusau 1963-64
RICE A.N.	1953	?	
ROTIMI A.A.	1956	1968	
SALAMI J.J.	1963	1968	
SARGEANT K.M.	1939	1960	
STREET J.	1954	1960	
TAYLOR P.J.	1955	1959	
TENSE A.I.	1961	1964	
TERREL K.L.G.	1961	1963	
TOMS K.N.	1957	1959	
TOZER J.W.	1956	1962	
UFOEGBUNE I.U.	1941	1964	
UGBENYO M.	1965	1968	
UMOREN A.A.	1949	1960	
UMUNNA J.E.	1949	1966	
UPPERMAN P.M.	1954	1960	
USMAN BELLO	?	?	
VOSHAAR A.J.	1953	1958	
WAITE I.	1966	1968	North-Western State
WALKER R.D.	1960	1968	Kano, North-Eastern and Bauchi States
WARD J.P.W.	1951	1968	ICSA and Kaduna Polytechnic
WAUDBY-SMITH F.W.	1955	1965	
WEY F.T.M.	1926	1966	
WHILEY A.E.O.	1949	1968	North-Eastern and Borno States
WILKIE A.E.	1956	1962	
WILLEY A.D.	1949	1965	ABU and Benue-Plateau State
WILLIS J.D.	1966	1968	North-Western State
WIMBUSH M.D.	1928	1951	
WOODS F.J.	1954	1957	
WORLLEDGE J.A.G.	1950	?	
WRIGHT A.G.	1957	1958	

INSTRUCTING

BEALE G.N.D.	1962	1965
TUCK W.G.	1956	1957

	APPOINTED	LEFT	LATER NIGERIAN SERVICE
DRAWING AND MAPPING			
ABIGE Y.	1960	1968	
ADELEYE B.A.	1949	1968	North-Eastern State
ADIKWU M.O.	1957	1968	
ALABI J.A.	1953	1968	
ALABI J.S.	1960	1968	
ATIN O.E.	1930	1966	
ATTAT S.S.	1948	1966	
BARKO N.	1956	1968	
BARKO U.T.	1953	1968	
CHIKERE G.C.	1953	1966	
FAYOMI B.R.A.	1956	1968	
GWANI S.	1957	1968	North-Eastern and Bauchi States
INYANG A.A.	1949	1966	
ITSUOKO S.A.	1953	1968	
KANNO O.	1938	1966	
MAGBAGBEOLA A.A.	1931	1968	
NSUKABA F	1952	1966	
OBIANWU B.E.	1930	1966	
OBIKU D.P.O.	1944	1966	
OBOMANU D.J.I.	1936	1966	
OGWUJI E.I.	1958	1968	
OJO A.	1958	1968	
OJUKA M.D.	1950	1966	
OKEOYI J.Y.	1958	1968	
OKONO D.E.	1950	1966	
OKOROJI K.U.	1930	1966	
OLOYEDE G.O .	1950	1968	
OLLEY W.U.	1949	1966	
ONYILE B.	1951	1966	
OYEWUSI S.O.	1957	1968	
SHERRIF-DEAN S.A.	1949	1968	
WEST T.E.	1948	1966	
WILLIAMS B.	1953	1968	
WILLIAMS V.	1917	1966	
WILSON J.O.	1949	1968	
YOLA D.I.K.	1965	1968	North-Eastern and Gongola States
LITHOGRAPHY			
MAYOMI I.A.	1953	1968	
PARR G.S.	1961	1963	
STOPFORTH W.	1963	1968	ICSA and Kaduna Polytechnic
YELWA I.A.	1963	1968	
PLANNING			
AIMOLA C.O.	1960	1968	
AMEH P.I.	1966	1968	
ATTOE O.W.	1948	1965	
BALL D.R.	1956	1962	
BASHIR A.	1963	1968	North-Eastern State
BURNSIDE J.	1961	1966	
CHRISTENSEN M.V.	1957	1960	
ENE E.E.O.	1958	1963	
ROLLISON S.H.A.	1951	1958	

APPENDIX IV

STAFF RANKINGS

SENIOR STAFF

SURVEY	PHOTOGRAMMETRY AND MAPPING	TOWN PLANNING	VALUATION	LANDS	ADMINISTRATION
Surveyor General or Director of Surveys					
Assistant Surveyor General or Assistant Director of Surveys or Chief Surveyor					
Principal Surveyor	Map Production Officer or Air Survey Officer	Principal Town Planning Officer			
Senior Surveyor	Map Production Officer	Senior Town Planning Officer			Senior Accountant
Surveyor	Photogrammetrist	Town Planning Officer	Valuation Officer	Cadastral Lands Officer	Accountant

STAFF RANKINGS

TECHNICAL AND JUNIOR STAFF

SURVEY	CARTOGRAPHY	PHOTOGRAMMETRY	LITHOGRAPHY	TOWN PLANNING	VALUATION	LANDS
Principal Technical Officer (Survey)	Chief Draughtsman or Principal Technical Officer (Cartography)		Lithographic Instructor			Senior Executive Officer or Senior Deeds Registrar or Senior Assistant Lands Officer
Senior Assistant Surveyor or Senior Technical Officer (Survey)	Chief Draughtsman or Senior Technical Officer (Cartography)	Senior Technical Officer (Mapping)				Assistant Lands Officer Grade I or Technical Officer (Lands) or Deeds Registrar
Assistant Surveyor Grade I or Technical Officer (Survey) or Survey Instructor or Records Officer	Assistant Chief Draughtsman or Technical Officer (Cartography)	Technical Officer (Mapping)	Technical Officer (Lithography)	Assistant Town Planning Officer Grade I or Technical Officer (Town Planning)	Valuation Assistant Grade I	Assistant Lands Officer Grade II or Asstant Technical Officer (Lands)
Assistant Surveyor Grade II or Assistant Technical Officer (Computing) or Assistant Technical Officer (Survey) or Assistant Records Officer	Senior Survey Draughtsman Grade I or II or Assistant Technical Officer (Cartography)	Assistant Technical Officer (Mapping)		Assistant Technical Officer (Town Planning)	Valuation Assistant Grade II	
Survey Assistant Grade I						
Survey Assistant Grade II						
Technical Assistant						
Other posts:-						
Artisans (Carpenters and Masons)						
Drivers						
Storekeepers						
Chainmen						

APPENDIX V

O. C. S. 1
1956

COLONIAL OFFICE

APPOINTMENTS IN
HER MAJESTY'S
OVERSEA CIVIL SERVICE

Survey Appointments

1.   The work now being carried out by Colonial Survey Departments and the Directorate of Colonial Surveys is an essential part of the general scheme for the economic development of Colonial territories.

Colonial Survey Departments are for the most part concerned with cadastral and land registration work, while the Directorate of Colonial Surveys, under the control of a Director with his Headquarters in the United Kingdom, is responsible for geodetic and topographical survey work. The topographical surveys are for the most part done by air survey methods. Plotting from air photographs and drawing of the resulting maps are carried out by a staff of draughtsmen at the headquarters of the Directorate.

The present establishment of survey posts in Colonial Survey Departments and in the Directorate of Colonial Surveys is about 210. Generally speaking, the field work overseas is unsuitable for women. Women can, however, be appointed to the grade of Computer on the staff of the Directorate and in some Colonial Survey Departments.

Surveyors in Colonial Survey Departments are mainly engaged in work of a cadastral nature including the survey and layout of townships. Land laws affecting survey are learned on the spot. Officers may be called upon to execute topography, including the astronomical fixing of position, and to prepare and supervise the reproduction of maps. Subsidiary undertakings may include road location and reconnaissance surveys for water-supply, irrigation, river discharge, harbourage, and the like, with the necessary levelling. Special officers may be employed on geodetic survey, precise levelling, air survey or geodetic computation. A good deal of the year is spent in the field and a working knowledge of the local language is necessary. Close co-operation with Administrative and other departmental officers is essential.

Surveyors belonging to the Directorate are liable to undertake tours, of duty in any Colonial territory and may be employed on geodetic surveys or on topographical or other survey work. But they are unlikely to be employed on cadastral surveys. They may also from time to time be required for duty at Headquarters.

The conditions of service for junior Surveyors in Colonial Survey Departments and in the Directorate of Colonial Surveys, are not always suitable for married men. In any event they must be prepared to accept separation when on field duties.

2. Vacancies.

There are posts in the African territories, the Federation of Malaya, Sarawak, North Borneo, Hong Kong, Jamaica, Trinidad, British Honduras, Cyprus, Fiji and the Solomon Islands and in the Directorate. The majority of vacancies occur in the Directorate and Africa.

3. Selection Dates.

There is no annual selection; vacancies are filled as circumstances require. Completed forms of application may therefore be sent to the Director of Recruitment at any time of the year.

4. Age Limit.

The normal rule is that candidates should be under 30, but candidates over this age may sometimes be considered.

5. Qualifications.

The standard qualifications for appointment without further training are at present:-

Either (i)

(a) A degree (preferably with Honours) in Engineering or Mathematics or Physical Science or Geography, and

(b) The Intermediate Examination of the Royal Institution of Chartered Surveyors in the Land Surveying Section, or exemption therefrom, or such equivalent as may from time to time be accepted by the Secretary of State.

Or (ii) The full Professional Associateship of the Royal Institution of Chartered Surveyors in the Land Surveying Section.

Or (iii) A Licence to practice as a Surveyor in Canada, Australia, New Zealand or South Africa.

Subject to further training, candidates may also apply who possess any of the degrees specified in (i) (a) above but who have **not** passed or gained exemption from the Intermediate Examination of the Royal Institution of Chartered Surveyors in the Land Surveying Section.

N.B. As a temporary measure a limited number of candidates may be considered who lack the qualifications specified above but who, as a minimum qualification, have (A) *passed or gained exemption from the Intermediate Examination of the Royal Institution of Chartered Surveyors in the Land Surveying Section;*

and also

(B) *had some experience in surveying or work allied to surveying.*

Appropriate training for such candidates will be arranged according to the circumstances of individual cases.

6. **Salaries**.

(i) *Scale posts.*

Nigeria........	£750 to £1,560 rising by annual increments over 18 years.
Sierra Leone...	£742 to £1,562 rising by annual increments over 18 years.
East Africa.....	£816 to £1,620 rising by annual increments over 17 years.
Federation of Malaya.........	£870 to £2,044 rising by annual increments over 19 years.
Hong Kong....	£1,151 to £2,038 rising by annual increments over 14 years.

(ii) *Superscale posts.* Promotion from posts within the incremental scales to higher or superscale posts is not automatic but by selection based on qualifications, experience and merit. Promotion may be on transfer from one territory to another.

There is a number of senior posts for Chief Surveyors, Assistant Directors, Deputy Directors and Directors of Surveys. The salaries of these posts range from £1,750 a year to £2,130 a year in West Africa; from £1,740 to £2,600 a year in East Africa; from £2,128 a year to £2,660 a year in the Federation of Malaya. In Hong Kong the top salary is £2,456 a year. In other territories the salaries are lower.

NOTE.

The above figures include expatriation pay but exclude cost of living allowances, which are payable at present in East Africa, the Federation of Malaya and Hong Kong.

7. Training after Selection.

The standard of technical training for appointment to a Colonial Survey Department is that set for the Intermediate Examination of the Royal Institution of Chartered Surveyors in the Land Surveying Section. Candidates who have not reached this standard will therefore be required to do so before the end of their training.

Although promotion to higher posts is not, at present, conditional upon officers obtaining any further professional qualifications during their service, it will generally be in the interests of officers that they should, after taking up their appointments, work for and pass the Final Examination of the Royal Institution of Chartered Surveyors, and thus obtain the full professional qualification of A.R.I.C.S.

Post-selection training takes place, either at the School of Military Survey, where courses begin twice a year in April and October, or at University College, London, where there is one course a year beginning in October.

The standard course lasts twelve months but a shorter period of training may be sufficient in certain individual cases.

APPENDIX VI

HAUSA WORDS AND EXPRESSIONS

Some everyday words and expressions to remind readers of the language they may not have used for many years.

a kan	on top of	biri	monkey
a'aha	exclamation of dismay	birni	walled town
abinci	food	birnin Arewa	Capital of Northern Nigeria
aboki/abokai	friend/friends	buga	beat
acha	grass-like crop of the Plateau	buga waya	make a telephone call
adda	matchet	bushe	get dry
agogo	watch		
ah-ah	expression of surprise		
aiki/ayyuka	work/works	chiroma	a princely title
akawu	clerk	cigaba	continue
akwati	box	ci	eat
akwiya	goat	ciwo	illness, pain
alhamdulillahi	all's well		
Alkali	Native court judge under Muslim law	da sassafe	very early in the morning
Alla ya kai mu	may God see to it	dafa	cook
amin	may it be so	daidai	correct, exactly
anini	tenth of a penny	daji	bush
arewa	north	dama	to the right
arewa maso gabas	north-east	damuna, damana, damina	rainy season
arewa maso yamma	north-west	dan doka	N.A. policeman
arewa sak	due north	dan sanda	Government Policeman
arne	pagan	dan zamani	progressives
aro	borrowing	dari	coldness due to wind
arziki	riches	dattijo	wise man
asibiti	hospital	dawa	guinea corn
aure	marriage	dawo	forage
ayaba	banana	dawo	return
		dogo	tall, long
		doya	yams
ba dama	no chance, no bother	dutse	stone, rock, mountain
ba hankali	senseless, careless		
ba labari	without warning		
ba laifi	hat's all right	fada	fight, quarrel
ba Sakkwache	man of Sokoto (accepted by the people)	fadama	alluvial plain, swamp
		fadi	fall down
Bafaransi	Frenchman	fam	a pound (originally = two naira)
Bafilace	Fulani person		
bahago	left handed, unusual or awkward	fari	white
		farin ciki	kind hearted, happiness
Bahaushe	Hausa person	fili	open country, space
bakin daji	forest	firki	black cotton soil
banza	worthless	fitar	get rid of, dismiss
barawo	thief	fitila	lantern, lamp
bariki	rest house, camp, quarters	fito	guinea corn beer
barka	how are you ?	fitsari	urine
Bature	European person		
bayan	behind		
bayan gida	lavatory	gaba daya	all together
bazara	hot, muggy season before the rains	gabas	east
		gabas sak	due east
Beit-el-Mal	House of wealth (the N.A.Treasury)	gada	bridge
		gadon sarautar Musulmi	Muslim rulership

i

gajere	short		jahilci	ignorance
gani	see		jama'a	brothers
gara	termites		jangali	cattle tax
gari	flour		jatau	'red' man
gaskiya ne	it is the truth		ji	hear
gemu	beard		jirgi	train
gero	millet		jirgi ruwa	boat or canoe
gida	home, compound		jirgin kasa	railway train
gidan sauro	mosquito net		jirgin sama	aeroplane
gidan waya	telephone exchange		jiya	yesterday
giginya	palm tree			
gina	dig			
gindi	bottom		ka sauka lafiya	arrive safely
giwa	elephant		kai !	exclamation of astonishment
giwan ruwa	Nile (Niger) perch		kaji	hens
gona	farm		kaka	harvest season
gudu	run		kananzir	lamp oil, kerosene
gwada	measure		kare	finish
Gwamnati ta	The Northern Nigerian		karfe	metal, iron, o'clock
Arewa	Government		karfi	strength
gwangwan	tin (of food)		kasa	earth, land, country
gwauro	wifeless man, bachelor		kawo	bring
gyada	peanuts		kaya	load, outfit, belongings
			kayan aiki	tools of one's work
			kaza	hen
haba	come now ! don't be a fool !		keke	bicycle
	nonsense ! you're joking !		kobo	penny
hadari	storm		kofar	door, gate
hahraji	tax		kogi	river
haka	thus, so		kokari	praiseworthy
haka ne	that is so		kona	burn
hakuri	patience		kowa	everyone
hanga	see from a distance		ku tashi, mu tafi !	a command "Let's go,
hankali	intelligence, careful			everyone !"
hanya	road, path or route		kudi	money
hau	mount, climb		kudu	south
haushi	vexation, anger		kudu sak	due south
hayaki	smoke		kuka	baobab tree, cry
haye	mount, climb, cross over		kunama	scorpion
	(river)		kura	hyena
hula	hat		kusa	close to
hurumi	communal grazing area		kwabo	kobo (penny)
	outside town walls		kwai	eggs
huta	rest		kwalaba	bottle
huta lafiya	rest well		kwana	night time, a 24 hour day
hutu	resting, holiday		Kwara	River Niger
			kwarai	very much
i	yes			
i mana	yes indeed			
igiya	rope		labari	news
Ikko	Lagos		lafiya	health, well being, safety
ilmi	education, knowledge		lafiya lau	reply to a greeting
ina ine	Good morning, how are you ?		laifi	fault
ina ruwana	what do I care		lalace	spoil, idleness
ina wone	Good evening, how are you ?		lalachi	spoilt, lying, apathy, depravity
Ingila	England			and sloth
inuwa	shade		lamba two	roadside ditch
itace	tree, wood		Lamido	Fulani chief
iya	boat, canoe, ship		lebura	labourer

ii

leburori	labourers
likita	doctor
lissafi	adding up, arithmetic
littafi	book
lokaci	time
mace	wife, woman
maciji	snake
madafa	kitchen
madalla	splendid, fine
madara	fresh milk
madubin safyo	theodolite
magana	speech
magani	power, magic or medicine
magwaji	measuring rod
mahaukaci	madman
mahaukata	madmen
mai	oil, fat, grease, petrol
mai aiki	worker
mai gida	head of the house
mai ji dadi	the happy one
mai karfi	strong one (man if iron)
mai kyauta	generous person
mai magani	healer
mai taimakon Musulmi	he who helps Muslims
maigida	master of the house
Makama	High title in some emirates
Makaranta	school
malamanci	mixture of Hausa and English
manya-manya	important people
maraba	welcome
maza	quickly
mhm	greetings (in reply to greeting)
mota	lorry, automobile
mugu	bad, evil
mugunta	evil
mutu	die
mutum	man
na gode	thank you
nama	meat, wild animal
nasara	Christians
nesa	far away
raba	divide
rakumi	camel
rami	hole (in ground)
rana	sun, heat of sun, day
rani	dry season
ranka ya dade	long may you live
rashi	lack, without
rawa	dancing
riga	robe, gown
rijiya	well (water supply)
rubuta	write
ruwa	water, rain

ruwan sama	rain
ruwan sha	drinking water
sa	put, place, appoint
sa	bull
sabon gari	new town
sabulu	soap
safe	morning
sai	only, until
sai an jima	see you later
sai gobe	goodbye (until tomorrow)
sai ka dawo	until you return
sai wata rana	see you sometime
sak	exactly (direction)
salam alaikun	greetings called from outside compound
salamu alaikun	greetings (reply: alaika salamu)
salla	prayers
salla assuba	dawn prayer
salla babba	festival of the new Muslim year
sani	know
saniya	cow
sannu	greetings !
sannu da aiki	greetings in your work
sanyi	damp cold
Sardauna	Princely title meaning 'Leadership in War'
sarki	chief
sarkin bariki	caretaker
sata	steal
sauka	get down, arrive at
saya	buy
sayar	sell
sha	drink
shanu	cattle
shege	bastard
Shehu	religious leader
shekara	year
shida	six
shinkafe	rice
shiru	silence
shugabannin addini	leaders of religion
sifiri	zero
siminti	cement
sisi	sixpence (= 5 kobo)
sisin kobo	half a penny
so	like, want
sosai	well, correctly, exactly
sule	shilling
tabbata	to be sure
tafiya	travelling, going
taga	window, hole
taimaka	help
taimako	act of helping

takarda	piece of paper, note, ticket
takalmi	shoe
taki	manure
talakawa	ordinary people, peasantry
tambari	drum
tambaya	ask question
tande	skim or take something sweet or good quickly
taro	three pence (=2½ kobo)
tawada	ink
tebur	table, shovel
tesha	station
toh !	O.K.
toh, madala	that's fine
tsafi	fetish, idol
tsakani	between
tsakiya	centre, middle
tsawa	length
tsoho	old man
tuba	sorrow
tudu	hill
tukunya	cooking pot
turawa	white skinned people
turmi	pounding pot, made from wood
tusa	break wind
tuwo	guinea corn or millet mush
ungulu	vulture
uwa	mother
uwargida	mistress of the house
wahala	trouble
waje	outside
wake	beans
wando	trousers
wanke	wash
wasa	playing, dancing
wasika	letter
wawa	fool
waya	telephone
wayyo	alas (exclamation of despair)
Waziri	leading member of Emir's council
wuta	fire
wuya	difficulty
yadi	yard (measurement)
yaki	war
yaki da jahilchi	war against ignorance
yamma	west
yan iska	rootless, work-shy troublemakers
'yan tande	exploiters
yarinya	girl
yaro	boy
yaron sarki	chief's representative

yau	today
yauwa	splendid, that's fine
yawa	plenty
yi-shiru	be quiet !
zafi	heat
zagi	servant
zaki	lion, or a recognition of greatness
zalumchi	corruption
zaman arziki	peaceful well being
zana	woven grass mat
zawo	diarrhoea
zazzabi	fever
zuba	pour
zumunta	kinship

APPENDIX VII

THE DIRECTORATE OF OVERSEAS SURVEYS
IN NORTHERN NIGERIA

It is impossible to give an account of the work of the Northern Nigerian Survey without mentioning the huge contribution made to topographic mapping in Northern Nigeria after the Second World War through to 1976 by the **Directorate of Colonial Surveys** which, in 1958, changed its name to the **Directorate of Overseas Surveys**. *(See Map 41).*

Between the wars the British Government had, through its Colonial Survey and Geophysical Committee, been very conscious of the effects of retrenchment and inadequate training upon the conduct of geodetic and topographic surveys in its dependencies, and in 1943 Major General M.N.Macleod, who was Director-General of the Ordnance Survey, and Brigadier M.Hotine, who was Director of Military Survey, considered how their organisations could combine to address the issue.

A Colonial Planning Committee was set up under Lt.Col. G.J.Humphries, and proposals made for the establishment of a survey service, and the idea communicated to the administrations of colonial territories. It received a mixed reception, and strong opposition from Nigeria, because there was little specific funding provision attached to the proposals, and also because the then Commissioner of Lands and Director of Surveys in Lagos, Clouston, opposed the military domination of the proposed organisation, questioning its colonial survey experience. He resented the idea that it might attempt to control local geodetic and topographic work, records keeping, map production, and staff training, appointment and deployment. He felt that the imposition of a strong outside service might have an adverse effect upon the development of surveying in Nigeria and restrict local services to those of a cadastral nature.

But in 1945 the Colonial Development and Welfare Act was amended to make funding provision, the Secretary of State made numerous concessions to the flexibility with which the service would operate in Nigeria and the Directorate of Colonial Surveys came into being in March 1946 under the direction of Hotine, a position he held until 1961. Hotine visited Nigeria to resolve some of the differences of opinion about aerial photographic and mapping responsibilities, priorities, staffing matters and training. He had a great influence on triangulation and, following his wartime experience, saw the great potential of the application of aerial photography to topographic mapping.

Almost at once a photographic reconnaissance squadron of the RAF started work in West Africa and continued at intervals until 1953 when commercial operators took over. Photographic scale was usually 1:30,000 and was used to produce mapping at 1:125,000, or 1:50,000 in more developed areas, and 1:25,000 for special projects. 1:62,500 was also seen as a useful scale to some users.

The specification for this mapping was that it should be multi-coloured and contoured, but in many territories, including Northern Nigeria, there was such an urgent demand that preliminary monochrome mapping without contours was provided using simple and rapid graphical methods. The early maps were not gridded, showed settlements, communications, drainage and vegetation classes, but were produced without field completion and many settlements lacked names.

The following is a brief, but by no means complete, chronology of the DCS/DOS programme:-

- **1946.** Photo-Reconnaissance Squadrons of the RAF commenced aerial photography around a radar beacon at Funtua.
- **1947.** The Nigerian Survey Department started providing ground control to the DCS for the compilation of planimetric mapping.
- **1949.** 1:62,500 scale uncontoured maps of the Kontagora Groundnut Scheme were prepared by the DCS for printing in Lagos.

- **1951.** Aerial photography was carried out controlled by a ground radar beacon on Gubi Hill near Bauchi commencing in September. 130,000 square miles were photographed. 51 mapsheets in Northern Nigeria had so far been produced.
- **1952.** Ground control fieldwork was in progress for 30 sheets in the Shendam and Zamfara areas.
- **1953.** The first six sheets of the Shendam area were produced. Shettima Kashim, the Minister responsible for Surveys in the North, welcomed the contribution being made by the DCS.
- **1954.** Control for 13,000 sq. miles of mapping in Katsina and West Kano was sent to the DCS by the Northern Nigerian Survey.
- **1955.** Ten sheets north of Kano were in hand for publication. Hotine paid a visit to the Northern Region. The need was expressed to implement the full coloured and contoured specification for the mapping and for the local department to carry out field completion.
- **1956.** The DCS was awarded a contract for aerial photography of 15,000 square miles in Northern Nigeria, concentrating on the need for contoured mapping in the Jos Plateau and various project areas. A block of 24 uncontoured sheets at 1:50,000 was completed and another 10 sheets north of Kano. East of this a new block of 13 sheets was started with control again provided by the Northern Nigerian Survey.
- **1957.** 12,000 square miles of photography was flown. The specification for mapping east of Kano was changed to 1:50,000 and 49 sheets were compiled. Preliminary work on 48 sheets in the northern part of Bornu Province was carried out.
- **1958 - 59.** Work continued east of Kano and in northern Bornu. Contoured editions were prepared for eight sheets at 1:50,000 scale in the Jos area.
- **1959.** The British Treasury began to ask whether the DOS should continue, but the secondment of DOS staff for productive survey work got under way and Nigeria was one of the first countries to receive such assistance because of the sharp decline in expatriate staffing of local departments.
- **1960.** R.G.Moffet was providing height control for twelve 1:50,000 sheets north and east of Jos. Ground control was also being provided for mapping in the Lake Chad area. The allocation of Colonial Development and Welfare funds ceased with Nigerian independence but an agreement had been made that assistance could continue, provided 15% of the costs were met by the recipient. Martin Hotine from the Directorate attended the Pan-Nigerian Federal and Regional Survey Conference. In the period from 1957 the DOS compiled 25,300 square miles of mapping from ground control provided by the Northern Nigerian Survey.
- **1961.** B.B.Wigglesworth joined Moffat in the Jos area. Ground control was in progress for mapping in the Mambilla Plateau area. Tellurometers were being used for the first time by the DOS on Nigerian mapping control. In DOS headquarters at Tolworth, Hotine was succeeded by G.J.Humphries and W.D.C.Wiggins, both of whom had seen pre-war service with the Survey Department of Nigeria. The DOS became part of the Department of Technical Co-operation. J.A.C.Atkins took over from Wigglesworth. Work continued on Mambilla. The DOS received an urgent request to assist with 1:25,000 scale mapping of the Jakura limestone and Agbaja ironstone areas near Lokoja in connection with studies for an iron and steel industry along the Niger. M.F.Anderson of the Northern Nigerian Survey was seconded to join B.Murray and B.B.Wigglesworth *(Photo 23, located with Map 41)* on reconnaissance and Tellurometer traversing for this work. Work also continued on the Mambilla-Jalingo 1:50,000 mapping control.
- **1963.** Work continued in the Mambilla-Jalingo block and the DOS also produced 1:500,000 scale geophysical maps of the Lake Chad and Benue Valley areas.
- **1964.** The DOS joined the Ministry of Overseas Development and provided training in cartography and photogrammetry for technical officers from overseas governments. DOS personnel in Northern Nigeria were D.H.Franks, Corp.J.Smith, R.A.Bardua and H.Green. They were engaged on Mambilla, height control for the Ganye block and on the Yola-Bama block. *(Map 40 is an example of DOS 1:50,000 scale mapping).* Mapping of the Jos area continued and 19 sheets of Kaiama were also produced.
- **1965.** Plan control work continued in the Yola-Bama block and height control was in

ii

progress for Mambilla. 22 sheets of the Lake Chad block were printed.

- **1966.** The DOS photographed 6,000 square miles at 1:40,000 scale in the Jalingo-Mid Benue area. Fieldwork continued in the Mambilla, Yola-Bama and Ganye blocks and reconnaissance and ground control got under way in the Gombe block. H.Green was working from Yola with S.J.I.Adair. Four Technical Assistants were seconded from the Northern Nigerian Survey to work with them.
- **1967.** Some parts of the Mambilla block were completed.
- **1968.** D.E.Warren became the Director of the DOS. The DOS parties were concentrated in the north-eastern part of the Region and commenced work on a large Land Resources Project. Mapping work continued in Mambilla North, Yola-Bama and Gombe. Reconnaissance work and Tellurometer traversing was in progress in the Maiduguri area.
- **After 1968** work continued in this area, now part of the North-Eastern State of Nigeria. For some considerable time the DOS maintained a base on the Jos Plateau from which to service and operate its parties working in various parts of the North-Eastern State. Its staff included H.Green, J.Price, Macartney, Faulkner, M.Coulson, and J.Dean.
- The winding-up of the DOS was being discussed in Britain during the early **1970's** as moves were being made to increase the level of contract work.
- **1973.** DOS commitment was finally completed in northern Nigeria with observations on Zaranda and Buli Hills in the Bauchi area in August. *(Map 41 shows the total extent of the DOS contribution to Nigeria's topographic mapping programme).*

The eventual decision to close the DOS and incorporate it as a limited overseas service within the OS was seen as ultimate fulfilment of the ideas put forward by Macleod and Hotine in 1942.

MINING TITLES

A Guide to the Procedure for the Survey of Mining Titles

In 1966 the Ministry of Town and Country Planning, of which the Northern Nigerian Survey was a part, published a Handbook which contained an important section on Mining Titles. It was intended for use by the staff of the Ministry who had to deal with land matters and also by other persons, in and outside Government Service. Its contents were as follows:-

- Preface
- Introduction
- Definitions

Chapters

1	Administrative Reporting
2	Assignments
3	Compensation
4	Conditions imposed on Titles
5	Congested Areas
6	Delegation of Powers
7	Deposits
8	Fees
9	Forest Reserves-Mining within ...
10	Mining -A. General -B. Applications for
11	Mining Roads
12	Mining Statistics
13	Miscellaneous
14	Prospecting -A. General -B. Applications for
15	Refusals
16	Renewals
17	Rents
18	Surrenders .
19	Survey
20	Venerated Areas
21	Water Licences -A. General -B. Applications for
22	Withdrawals

Appendices (Lists of mining companies and operators)

Chapter 19 was of particular interest to surveyors and outlines the procedure at the Jos Survey Office.

CHAPTER 19

SURVEY

Survey of Mining Titles is carried out by the Principal Surveyor of the Survey Division stationed at Jos, under the Survey Law (Cap. 129 of the 1963 Laws) and the regulations made thereunder. There are three procedures-

(a) that following receipt of the original application;
(b) that following "Notification to Survey"; and
(c) that following "Exemption from Survey".

(a) Receipt of the original application

On receipt of his copy of an application from the Area Inspector the Principal Surveyor will register it and will cause it to be charted on the appropriate priority sheet in pencil, according to the applicant's sketch plan and to the tie shown thereon. The Principal Surveyor will then make a report on the application in accordance with what is laid down in the Minerals Act, and the Regulations made thereunder, and this report will include any overlap onto extant titles. The acreage is checked by planimeter against he applicant's figure and any discrepancy is included in the report. The Principal Surveyor then forwards his report to the Area Inspector, the Assistant Chief Inspector of Mines and the Provincial Secretary, together with his recommendation whether the application should be approved or refused from the survey aspect, stating his reasons.

If the applicant's sketch plan is in error, the Principal Surveyor will call for an amended sketch plan, upon receipt of which he will prepare his report.

In respect of an application for a mining right or exclusive prospecting licence, the Principal Surveyor will include in his report whether the application can be exempted from survey or not; he will also send a letter to the applicant asking if he wishes the applications to be exempted from survey, and will copy this letter to the Assistant Chief Inspector of Mines.

(b) Notification to Survey

On receipt of favourable reports from all concerned, the Assistant Chief Inspector of Mines will issue to the Principal Surveyor a "Notification to Survey". He will make mention therein of all areas such as villages, venerated areas and prior titles which are to be excluded in the survey.

A card index is kept by the Principal Surveyor of all "Notifications to Survey" received from the Assistant Chief Inspector of Mines and a small register is kept shewing the daily position of all areas for survey. When a survey field jacket is returned to the office on completion of survey, the fact is recorded in the register and the operations map is amended. This operations map will thus show if any survey is being overlooked.

The Assistant Chief Inspector of Mines will also keep a register of all "Notifications to Survey" and will furnish a quarterly list of outstanding surveys to the Principal Surveyor. The Principal Surveyor will compare it with his card index and will comment on any discrepancies. In this way there is an additional check that no areas awaiting survey are overlooked.

On receipt of the "Notification to Survey" the Principal Surveyor will prepare a field jacket containing all information relevant to the area to be surveyed. The application will be plotted on an operations map which shows when concentrations of mining titles in one area will warrant a survey party being moved to the area to undertake these surveys. This may take any time up to twelve months or more, as it is uneconomical to undertake single surveys in remote areas.

The Surveyor carries out the survey according to the Principal Surveyor's instructions. He will:-

- tie to trig. control;
- shew any water licence which affects the area;
- exclude any overlap onto an existing title;
- shew any village;
- shew any extant right of occupancy or mining title;
- shew any venerated area; and
- close any small gap between the area under application and any existing title.

The work submitted from the field is thoroughly scrutinised and checked and may be returned to the field for amendment. If the computation and plan pass the "X" section at this stage, they are passed on to the drawing office for preparation of the title deed plans and completion of a final report which includes a full description and the exact acreage of the area and the total cost of the survey. Five copies of these plans and the report are sent to the Assistant Chief Inspector of Mines.

The survey is also charted on the Priority Sheet in the Drawing Office. A copy of the title deed plan is then sent to the Revision Section where priority sheets are prepared for publication. The new title is plotted on the relevant priority sheet and in due course a new priority sheet will be provided, bringing it up to date since the previous printing; and it is then made available for sale to the general public.

If on preparation of the title deed plan the surveyed area is found to differ by 20 per cent from the plan of the area attached to the application, the Principal Surveyor should give details of such error, commenting on whether the discrepancy is due to any adjustment in the position of the beacons on survey, in which case a recommendation to overlook contravention of section 15(1) of the Minerals Act is made. Where such errors are marginal and are attributed solely to minor errors of computation, the Assistant Chief Inspector of Mines may query the applicant and request an explanation before putting his recommendation to the Permanent Secretary.

Where there has been surrender of part of a mining lease and the issue of a new title over the remaining area, or the grant of only part of a former lease on renewal, the Principal Surveyor will survey the area in the normal way. If any beacons are defaced or missing, he will issue instructions to replace them.

(c) Exemption from survey

Exemption from survey is only applicable to mining rights and exclusive prospecting licences. There is no exemption from survey for mining leases and water licences. Exemption both postpones and exempts; it is granted for a definite period and may be revoked.

The power to grant exemption from survey has been delegated to the Chief Inspector of Mines by paragraph (c) of Public Notice No. 61 of 1949. The Assistant Chief Inspector of Mines normally exercises this power on behalf of the Chief Inspector of Mines.

On receipt by the Area Inspector of an application for exemption, the Area Inspector informs the Principal Surveyor and the Assistant Chief Inspector of Mines. The former examines the plan and advises the Assistant Chief Inspector of Mines whether exemption is recommended or not. If exemption is approved the Principal Surveyor will prepare five copies of the title deed plan from the applicant's sketch plan, or from survey data, whichever fits the case more completely; and these will be sent to the Assistant Chief Inspector of Mines.

Where no formal application is made for "exemption from survey" the Principal Surveyor is nevertheless empowered to offer the applicant the option of accepting exemption, if conditions for exemption are fully satisfied. If this option is accepted, the title deed plan is then prepared as stated above.

APPENDIX IX

NORTH-EASTERN STATE SURVEY DEPARTMENT

In 1968, I was given the responsibility of setting up the new Department in the North-Eastern State at Bauchi which was, fortunately, no more than a fairly pleasant two hour drive from my last Northern Nigerian Survey posting at Jos along a very scenic, if slightly dangerous, road.

The following is the text of an article prepared for the Nigerian Institution of Surveyors, a body whose members were drawn largely from Licensed Surveyors in the private sector in the southern parts of Nigeria, who were entitled and encouraged, but always rather reluctant, to seek work in the north.

....

THE WORK OF THE NORTH-EASTERN STATE SURVEY DEPARTMENT

M.F.ANDERSON, B.Sc., A.R.I.C.S. Surveyor-General, N.E.State
BAUCHI December 1972

For many newcomers to the profession of land surveying, and for that matter for members of the profession outside government service, the activities of Government Survey Departments in Nigeria, particularly those in the dry north, are perhaps not well known. This short article is therefore intended to outline the aspects of land surveying and allied work carried out in the North-Eastern State, to identify some of the problems which are encountered and say how they are dealt with, and to give an indication of present thinking on future progress and methods.

First of all, it must be understood that the government surveyor in the North-Eastern State has more than just his own profession to occupy his working time, because he is bound into a system comprising the allied professions of the land dealing with planning, apportionment, alienation and valuation. Regrettably, these allied services are not well developed, suffer from acute shortages or complete absence of professionally qualified staff, and are, in consequence, inadequate and inefficient. The conscientious professional land surveyor unavoidably spends a considerable proportion of his time trying to 'put other people's houses in order'.

If he is not careful, he runs the risk of incurring the displeasure, or at least the misunderstanding, of an administration which, for various reasons, is sometimes unable to draw clear distinctions between the functions of the professions of the land. Consider, for instance, the relatively common inability, outside our own profession, to read and accurately interpret a topographic map; to appreciate the meaning of a representative fraction; to subdivide an angle; to interpret an aerial photograph; to know what is meant by 'control' and the need for it, and to have no feeling for the land surveyor's instinctively methodical and meticulous approach to work, and you will understand what I mean. The problems that this representative, but by no means complete, list of handicaps can create are often enough to make even the most enthusiastic surveyor think of quitting government service. I do not, however, set out to express wonder that a government land survey service exists at all, in these circumstances, but rather to outline what it is trying to do in spite of its handicaps.

Other problems are caused by the sheer size of the State. Most visitors are amazed at the enormous extent of Nigeria's largest State, taking up, as it does, 5 degrees of longitude and 7 degrees of latitude. It extends from the dry Sahel Savannah of the Sahara fringe and the shore of Lake Chad in the north to the cool wet Mambilla Plateau and the remote forests of southern Adamawa and Sardauna Provinces at the same latitude as Lagos in the south, and from the Cameroon border in the east almost as far west as the geographical centre of Nigeria. To cross the State takes about two days east to west and as many as four days north to south. In terms of work to be done, what it may lack in intense modern development it more than makes up for by virtue of its size, its large number of small but developing towns and the difficulties of communication over great distances in trying conditions. In many ways it presents, for land surveyors, the most outstanding and diversified challenge, and opportunity in the whole of Nigeria, particularly on account of the paucity of basic control and the vast areas yet to be covered with modern maps.

In an attempt to cope with its logistical problems, the State has been divided into six loosely-defined Survey Areas to be administered by Survey Offices at Bauchi, Gombe, Yola, Mubi and Potiskum, with headquarters in the State Capital, Maiduguri. The North-Eastern State Survey Department, or the Survey Division of the Ministry of Land and Survey as it is more correctly called, works from its temporary headquarters in Bauchi, pending the construction of new buildings in Maiduguri. Small offices have been set up at Yola and Maiduguri and it is anticipated that new buildings will be provided in all centres during the next major economic plan period. The Survey embraces a Town Planning service, as yet very small, which will, with the impetus now being added by overseas contract consultancy work on long-term development plans and gradual improvements in staffing, gradually expand into an independent Division of the Ministry controlled by professional Town Planners. At present it is engaged in small physical development plans and short-term proposals for townships, production of drawings for improvement schemes, acting in a supervisory capacity on Site Boards and in an advisory one on land apportionment and usage. As yet there is no Valuation Division, as such, but this will come in due course as the Land Division improves and expands. It is planned that each Survey Area office will have representatives of these four services working in close technical and administrative co-operation.

Cadastral Surveys

No matter what other work it may from time to time undertake, the Department is primarily a Cadastral survey unit, conducting surveys for the specific purpose of the grant of leases under statutory Rights of Occupancy and for the setting aside of land for government use. Its effectiveness in this role is very dependent upon the maintenance of support systems. Up-to-date topographic maps at 1:50,000 scale are required for Country Intelligence Master Plans. Desirably, these maps should be maintained by a revision system which records all country land applications and usage and which charts communications, settlement development and survey control information. Township Intelligence Master Plans are maintained at 1:2,400 (now changing to 1:2,500) scale, or 1:10,000 scale in urban peripheral zones. In an efficient system, cadastral priorities and charting would be supervised by a professional Lands Officer. In the North-East, for want of such staff, the work is largely done by surveyors and survey draughtsmen. The maintenance of fully referenced correspondence records is also part of cadastral recording and includes reports on all land applications and data obtained during field survey.

To facilitate the dispersal of land intelligence information, it is proposed to keep duplicate Master Charts on a stable transparent medium, for quick reproduction by diazoprinting. Cadastral field surveys, now mostly carried out by government surveyors, with increased participation by Licensed Surveyors planned, encouraged and commencing, involve residential, industrial and commercial layouts, individual Rights of Occupancy, and land being acquired for government use. The main problem here is the great volume of work, too much to be handled by government surveyors unless long delays are to be tolerated. **Locally based Licensed Surveyors, who are prepared to take cognisance of local prices and values, are likely to find steady and lucrative business in this field for many years to come.** Work will be passed to them by the Surveyor-General, who will receive it back completed, check it for compliance with issuing instructions, and prepare the title deed plan for attachment to the statutory documents. A Hewlett-Packard electronic desk computer, now being acquired, will assist in the checking of submitted work.

Consideration is being given to photogrammetric methods of cadastral survey in certain congested areas.

Township Control Surveys

As towns expand, and new ones like Dadin Kowa spring up, the surveyor must all the time be installing control networks based on local triangulation with breakdown traverses of various orders. This work is now considerably speeded up by the use of the Wild DI 10 Distomat and a Tellurometer 101 ties local networks to the national triangulation, where it exists. The ultimate aim is to establish a rigorously adjusted network of permanent control in every significant township in such a way that no point of detail is more than about 300 metres from a control point. Heighted control beacons provide a network of bench marks linked, where possible, to geodetic datum. Township control thereby provides a fixed framework for all cadastral surveys, datums for levelling, site development, and reference for new mapping and map revision.

Township Mapping

Initial mapping usually goes hand-in-hand with the establishment of a control network. Mapping of the major towns was first carried out by the former Northern Nigerian Survey, some ten or more years ago, at a scale of 1:2,400 with 5 ft contours. This mapping is now being superseded by the new metric 1 km x 1.5 km sheet series, with revised conventional signs, at 1:2,500 scale with 2 metre contours. At present, much of this work is put out to contract surveying by Licensed Surveyors. Aerial photography at 1:10,000 scale precedes photo-control and plotting. There is limited public demand for these maps at present and current procedure involves the production of 3-colour line maps in limited runs, and single colour combination transparencies which are used as cadastral and diazoprint production masters. A major task is the maintenance of these sheets by constant field revision. The Wild RDS Tacheometer has been found a very practical instrument for this work.

It is recognised that line maps, while having definite advantages for cadastral use, may not be the answer to mapping the large number of small towns in the State, a matter which now becomes more pressing as planning schemes, water supply, road improvements and electrification are introduced. More rapid means of production and revision are called for. Controlled or semi-controlled mosaics, or orthophotomaps, are now being considered the best solution, permitting fast production, omitting the fair drawing and lithographic stages, with periodic replacement based on pre-marked ground control. In many small towns, contouring is considered something of a luxury at present and a network of pre-marked ground control will provide height values if contour surveys are required later. For larger towns, a full 1:2,500 scale orthophoto sheet series will be established and can be replaced by line mapping if the need arises. Smaller towns, many of which are situated on very flat ground, can be covered by a single controlled photograph or overlap at 1:10,000 scale and enlarged after rectification. These 'photomaps' will have an overlay with a grid, map face information and place names. A constantly revised half tone transparency will be made for cheap local reproduction as the need arises.

Plans are being made for the establishment of photogrammetric and photo-lithographic units. The State may be able to undertake orthophoto processing within ten years or so.

Minesfield Surveys

A significant proportion of the tin bearing land of the central northern highlands falls within the western half of Bauchi Province. A Minesfield Cadastre is maintained on very similar lines to the system in use for other land applications. Intelligence Charts ,or 'Priority Sheets' as they are called, on a 1:50,000 scale topographic base, record the order of applications for prospecting, mining and land use in connection with mining activities, such as water storage and supply, mining settlements and land reclamation. These charts are maintained by on-going office revision, but the need for up-to-date replacement base maps is now being felt and, particularly in congested areas, re-mapping at 1:25,000 scale is suggested. On account of their short life and large size, Exclusive Prospecting Licences are not nowadays surveyed but are granted, with stipulated safeguards, on the basis of application plans and Priority Sheet inspection; hence the need for Priority Sheet maintenance. Mining Leases are surveyed like Rights of Occupancy, and to similar accuracies, but they are usually very considerably larger, are very irregular in shape and are often located in quite rough and remote country. A combination of traverse, triangulation and tachymetry is used in the survey of these leases and each is tied to National triangulation and adjoining rights. **There is a great deal of work outstanding on the Minesfield and**

the area is ripe for 'invasion' by Licensed Surveyors. Minesfield surveying is often hard work and the application of photo-surveying techniques by signalising lease corners is being considered. Particular methods based on common surveying techniques are employed for the survey of Water Licences and leats, Mining Rights and the field revision of Priority Streets.

Survey of Administrative Boundaries

Thousands of miles of international, inter-State and internal boundaries are in need of definition, demarcation, survey and description. The North-Eastern State Survey does not itself undertake international and inter-State boundary work but it is liable to be called in to assist on such exercises. It does, however, have to deal with internal District boundary issues. The aim is to have at least one survey party on this work at all times, but dealing only with those boundaries which are in active dispute. Later, the desirability of establishing a systematic boundary survey is to be considered. To save time and field effort, use will be made of aerial photography for measurement and description purposes, after the line has been beaconed and cleared to make it clearly identifiable on photographs. Present methods involve clearing a 5 metre strip of all vegetation, erecting large intervisible and very well made cairns or masonry pillars bearing metal enumeration plaques, leaving survey control nearby for future re-establishment of boundary markers when necessary, traversing, connecting to triangulation, photo-identifying, marking on topographic maps where they are available and preparing a written description supported by plans and ground photographic evidence. This work is time consuming but effective and electronic distance measurement speeds it considerably.

Topographic Mapping

In the North-Eastern State surveying by departmental staff for medium scales mapping is a thing of the past and they must now concentrate almost exclusively on cadastral surveys.

By far the greater part of the fieldwork for the half of the State which has been effectively mapped has been done by the Directorate of Overseas Surveys whose work still continues in the area north of Bauchi. More overseas technical assistance is expected in order to complete the mapping of the northern half of the State in a reasonably short period of time. In recent years Federal Surveys have started the fair drawing of D.O.S. compilations and the North-Eastern State has kept both organisations supplied with map face 'field completion' information. *(Map 42 is an index to State topographic mapsheets).* In the areas still to be mapped this is an enormous task, and will probably be beyond the means of the North-Eastern State Survey, but recruitment of suitable staff is now in hand and more is being planned.

From time to time the Department plays a role in the extension and maintenance of national triangulation, traverse and levelling control. Plans are now being made for the commencement of a programme of levelling along all roads in the State, to fill the wide voids between the lines of proposed geodetic levelling.

Other Surveys

Briefly, other work in which the Department has become involved in the field include ground and photo control for special farming, water supply and irrigation projects and detail and levelling surveys for industrial, commercial and military sites. Serious thought is being given to the need for a forest and grazing reserve surveying unit and surveys for the control of trade cattle along established routes throughout the State. It is felt that a highway survey unit involving aerial photographic techniques and ground surveys is also a desirable addition to the government survey service.

Other Services

Other services include the provision of survey support facilities such as standard bases, tape standardisation and the maintenance of a magnetic reference base; a photo and map library; a consultancy service for map and survey specifications for the public and private sectors; plan and document printing; an agency service for the survey and aerial photographic requirements of other government Ministries, especially on the large schemes now being undertaken by the Ministry of Natural Resources in the fields of agriculture, irrigation, forestry and livestock development.

A series of seven State maps at 1:1,000,000 scale is now at an advanced stage and will start appearing in 1973. It covers Development Areas, Administrative Boundaries, General Administration, Road Distances, Amenities and Tourist Attractions, Produce and Commodities, and a Physical Map. In another series, three sheets combine to make a large State Map at 1:500,000 scale. Other products include small handout maps, maps of townships and streets, maps for directories and catalogues, the Yankari Game Reserve, and a township series at 1:10,000 scale.

....

The North-Eastern State Survey is attempting to handle the ever increasing number of problems connected with the demand for land, as agriculture and grazing take more and more of the best each year and as towns expand. Small as it is, the Department is looking carefully at its responsibilities and the role it must play in assisting the orderly development of what has the potential to be the most important food producing area of Nigeria in the years to come.

APPENDIX X

ILLUSTRATIONS (Photographs and Diagrams)

Photographs by Malcolm Anderson unless acknowledged

Land and People

1. Kanuri women at Birniwa
2. Fulani milk sellers near Kano
3. Pagan village - Kenye near Kachia
4. The Emir of Bauchi
5. Horsemen at Bauchi
6. Ministers' houses at Kaduna
7. New States armorial bearings *(located with Map 15)*

Survey Departments

8. Group photograph at Kaduna Junction in 1950	Marion Lees
9. A Federal Surveyor and Sarkin Kaiama	Colin Emmott
10. Northern Nigerian Survey breast badge	
11. Harry Rentema	Harry Rentema
12. Evert Eisinga	Harry Rentema
13. Arnold Voshaar	Arnold Voshaar
14. Piet Upperman	
15. Jörgen Jensen	
16. Kjeld Hansen	
17. Survey Headquarters, Kaduna South in 1959	
18. Cadastral Block, Kaduna South 1962	
19. Survey display at the 1959 Exhibition	David Ball
20. Heliomen at the 1959 Exhibition	David Ball
21. Douglas Eva in the Topographic Drawing Office	Olive Eva
22. Tower at Survey Exhibition	
23. DOS party at Lokoja in 1961 *(located with Map 41)*	
24. The North-Eastern State Survey Headquarters	
25. Retiring junior staff in 1976	

Framework Surveys

26. Climbing Ludo Hill	
27. Bush clearing	Keith Sargeant
28. Jema'a trig reconnaissance point	
29. Gusau trig point	
30. Beacon designs	Northern Nigerian Survey
31. Trig point ground marker	Jack Ashton
32. Beaconing near Lokoja	
33. Beaconing by H.Rentema	Harry Rentema
34. Beaconing by Federal Surveys	Colin Emmott
35. Beacon on K2	Jack Ashton
36. Removing a rock obstruction on E 13	Clifford Rayner
37. Observing Primary triangulation	Keith Sargeant

38. Wild T 3 Geodetic Theodolite
39. Booking for Primary Trig observations
40. Observing shelter and camp on P 10 Nassarawa
41. Helioman on P IO
42(1). C Chain triangulation   Northern Nigerian Survey
42(2). C Chain country   Clifford Rayner
43(1). Wild T2 theodolite   Wild instruction booklet
43(2). Wild T2 theodolite   Wild instruction booklet
44. Observing Tertiary triangulation   Keith Sargeant
45. Minesfield Tertiary Trig Beacon design   Northern Nigerian Survey
46. Working with a Wild T2 theodolite   Trevor Brokenshire
47. Jema'a Triangulation Instructions
48. Beaconing Secondary Trig XK 657
49. Tellurometer MRA 2
50. Tellurometer at Dutsen Wai
51. Mills scaffolding reconnaissance tower
52. Internal view of a Mills tower
53. A reconnaissance tower
54. Tower being used by the DOS for observations
55. A Bilby Tower

Topographic Mapping

56. Survey Headman and a plane table   Keith Sargeant
57. Plane tabling on Rusu Hill in 1939   Keith Sargeant
58. Slotted template laydown   Clifford Burnside
59. Kaduna drawing office in 1960   Olive Eva
60. Kaduna drawing office in 1962
61. Santoni Stereomicrometer
62. Wild A8 plotter
63. Photo control diagram   Clifford Burnside
64, 65. Gusau photo control

Town Planning

66. Kano - Nguru railway straight
67. Hadejia Valley flooding
68. Mogens Vejby and the Emir of Zaria   Bente Vejby
69. John Adshead and David Ball

Cadastral Surveys

70. Cadastral control beacon
71. Cadastral beaconing at Gusau
72. Catenary traversing at Offa
73. Catenary traversing at Gusau
74. Densely-built compounds at Kano

Minesfield Surveys

75. Approaching Jos and the plateau
76. A rugged part of the plateau   Trevor Brokenshire
77. Birom villagers
78. Kafanchan Falls
79. Naraguta Street, Jos
80. Rex Cinema programme
81. 'Surveying' scene at a Roman Catholic mission station   Arnold Voshaar
82. 'Pagan' women   Arnold Voshaar

Boundary Surveys

Training

Destination Nigeria

Making a start

1. Kanuri women in the market at Birniwa near Nguru

2. Fulani milk sellers at a Survey camp near Kano

3. A 'pagan' village. Kenye, near Kachia

4. The Emir of Bauchi in 1958

5. Horsemen at the Bauchi sallah parade in 1958

6. The Ministers' houses at Kaduna. Scene of the assassination of the Premier in 1966.

8. The Kaduna Junction staff in 1950, marking the transfer of J.F.A.Lees to the
Minesfield Division at Jos.   Seated in the front line are Frank Wey (third from the left),
John Worlledge, 'Tishy' Isherwood, Alan Lees and Mike Wimbush

9. A Federal Surveyor, E.R.(Dick) Rogers, being entertained by Sarkin Kaiama

10. Northern Nigerian Survey badge.
Brass badges for the uniforms and caps of chainmen and messengers
were the inspiration of K.H.Hunter.

SOME CONTINENTAL SURVEYORS WHO WORKED IN THE NORTH

The Dutchmen

11. Harry Rentema
1952 - 1954

12. Evert Eisinga
1952 - 1958

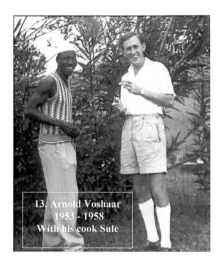

13. Arnold Voshaar
1953 - 1958
With his cook Sule

14. Piet Upperman 1954 - 1960
Photographed at Bukuru

The Danes

15. Jorgen Jensen
1953 - 1965
Photographed in
Ottawa in 1972

16. Kjeld Hansen
1953 - 1959
Here finishing his
last task, the
reconnaissance
for the 'P' chain
primary
triangulation

17. The front of Survey Headquarters in Kaduna South in 1959, with one of the old 'Railway' buildings

18. The 'Cadastral Block' at Kaduna South in 1962

19. At the 1959 Exhibition the Survey stand included murals and a model depicting surveying operations and aerial photography painted by J.W.(Jimmy) Dickson (Senior Surveyor) and P.H.S.(Peter) Redwood (Surveyor)

20. Dogon Marwa and Audu Gora (Chainmen) and A.A.(Alfred) Rotimi on the 'hill' at the exhibition, watching for a heliograph signal from the trig point on Kajuru Hill.

21. Douglas Eva (Surveyor-General) and O.Kanno (Chief Draughtsman) with visitors to the Topographic Drawing Office in 1960

22. Preparations for the Northern Nigerian Survey's Independence Exhibition at Kaduna South.

24. The offices of the North-Eastern State Survey Department were established in the buildings of the former Bauchi Middle School, within the Bauchi town walls. It was in this building that the first Prime Minister of the Nigerian Federation, Alhaji Sir Abubakar Tafawa Balewa, when still a young man, began his public career as a teacher.

25. A group of long-serving, former Northern Nigerian Survey junior staff, including Chainmen, messengers and a driver, who were compulsorily retired when the North-Eastern State was broken up into Bauchi, Borno and Gongola States in 1976. Eight years after the dissolution of the Northern Nigerian Survey, Barau Yola was still proudly wearing his Chainman's brass breast and cap badges.

26. A Wild theodolite in its padded transportation case being head-loaded to trig point B8 at the summit of Ludo Hill

27. Clearing sight lines during trig reconnaissance

28. A site is chosen, and a temporary cairn erected, for a new point in the Jema'a secondary triangulation near Akwanga, Plateau Province, in 1957

29. The trig point near Gusau, Sokoto Province, used as a reference point for the mapping of the town in 1962

BEACONING

Use was made of locally available materials

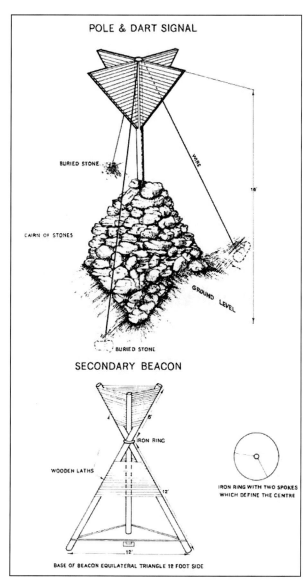

30. Guidelines for the design of opaque trig beacons were given in the Northern Nigerian Survey's "Technical Instructions for Field Parties"

31. The ground marker for the K2 trig point, set in rock

32. By M.Anderson near Lokoja in 1961

33. By H.Rentema in the 1950s

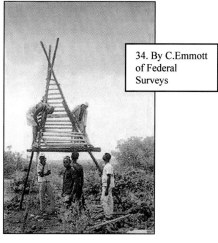

34. By C.Emmott of Federal Surveys

35. By J.Ashton on K2

36. At E 13 in 1957. Peter Redwood supervising the breaking-up of a massive granite block during the beaconing period and before the rains set in. After two weeks of endeavour all sight lines were open, much to the incredulity of Keith Hunter.

TRIANGULATION OBSERVATIONS

37. Keith Sargeant observing with a Wild T3 theodolite on Ambaka Hill in 1946.

For Primary observing, a shelter was constructed from locally cut wood and grass thatch, or canvas, to avoid the risk of dislevelment which could arise from exposure of the instrument and the tripod legs to the direct rays of the sun and the wind.

The shelter also provided comfortable working conditions for long periods, without the need for an umbrella.

For stability the feet of the tripod were cemented in place.

38. Wild T3 Geodetic Theodolite

39. A competent booker was invaluable during Primary trig observations. Here James Kyuka is recording observations taken by Malcolm Anderson at P16 in the Doma Forest Reserve in Benue Province in 1959.

40. The observing shelter and camp at the summit of P10 near Nassarawa

41. Chainman Tume Gboko sending heliograph messages from P10

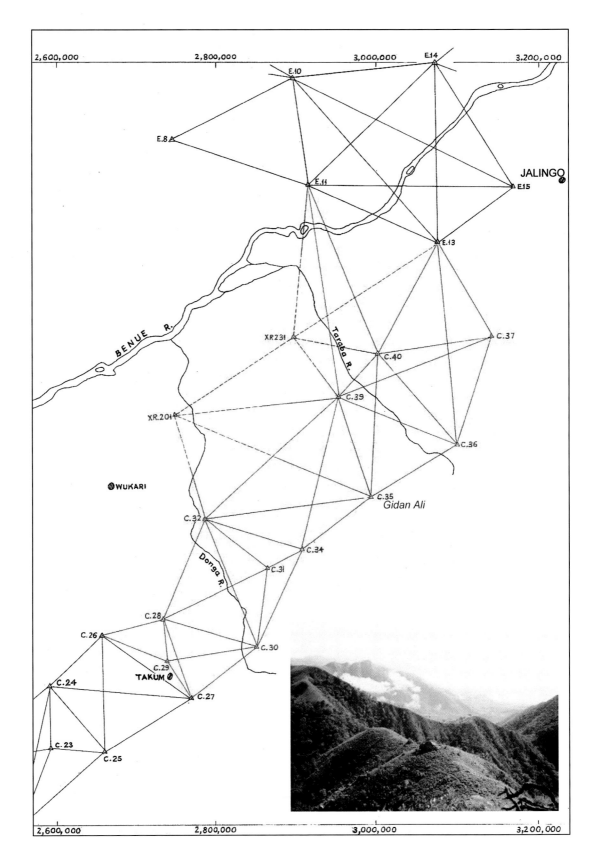

42 (1). C Chain Primary Triangulation in the Benue Valley 1959
From the Northern Nigerian Survey Annual Report 1956-57. Existing triangulation given in black and the new work in red.
42 (2). The view, taken by Clifford Rayner, is from C35 Gidan Ali; above the tree line and considerably cooler than the Benue plain. Visibility to low lying stations on the plain, e.g. E13 Jauromanu, was invariably poor due to persistent low morning cloud which did not burn off until mid day. Frequently, observing was limited to afternoon sessions.

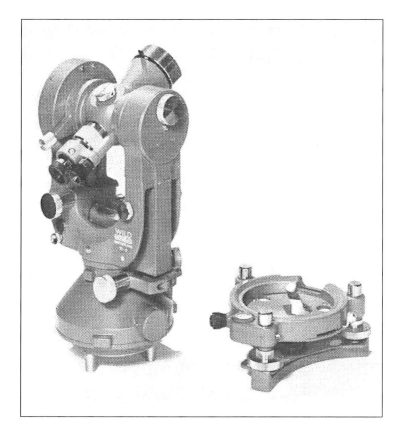

THE

WILD T2

Universal Theodolite

(1956 Model)

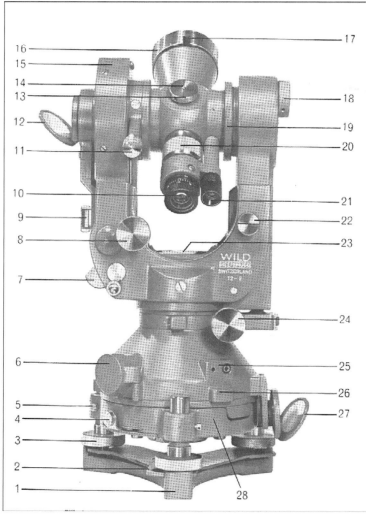

1   Base plate
2   Spring plate
3   Levelling screw
4   Spring lever of tribrach clamp
5   Tightening screw of levelling screw
6   Circle setting knob (under protecting cap)
7   Reflector for collimation level
8   Tangent screw for altitude
9   Level prism
10 Eyepiece for telescope
11 Clamping screw for vertical circle
12 Illuminating mirror for vertical circle
13 Illuminating mirror for diaphragm
14 Centre point and bead
15 Vertical circle casing
16 Objective lens
17 Front sight
18 Optical micrometer knob
19 Bearing ring for striding level
20 Ring for focusing telescope
21 Eyepiece for reading microscope
22 Inverter knob
23 Plate level
24 Tangent screw for azimuth
25 Electric light socket
26 Retaining stop
27 Illuminating mirror for horizontal circle
28 Tribrach

44.Keith Sargeant observing Tertiary triangulation in Katsina Province in 1939

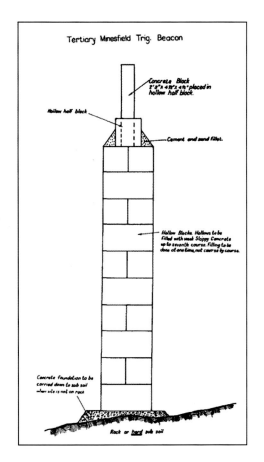

Tertiary Minesfield Trig. Beacon

45. The design for the distinctive Minesfield trig beacon, made from concrete blocks

46. Trevor Brokenshire working with a T2 theodolite in 1957

No. W1.9/

Headquarters,
Minesfield Division,
Northern Nigerian Survey,
Jos, 24th May, 1957.

M. F. Anderson Esq.,
Minesfield Division,
Northern Nigerian Survey,
J O S.

Triangulation – Jemaa Scheme
N22. Primary Triangulation Point.

Your first job which should be treated as separate from your secondary trig. reconnaissance is to clear up the ambiguous situation arising from the previous establishment of two N22's on the top of Ningishi Hill. (Immediately the Ningishi situation is tied up you will proceed on secondary – see my W1.9/6 of 24th May, 1957).

2. Copies of letters X5.2/60 dated 21st May, 1957 and X5.2/27 dated 20th July, 1954 are enclosed. You should move to Mayir Rest House by lorry on May 27th. The object is to :

    (1) Provide a final check on N22 by observing into as many of the following trigs as possible from the western summit. (Observations should be taken with on 3 lefts and 3 rights with your Tavistock):—

        N18, N23, N24, N25, N26, H14, H15, XK606(N20), XK655(N17).

Should cloud conditions or bad backgrounding cause trouble, observe as many as are necessary to give you a good resection. Beacon with a quadripod before you leave.

    (ii) Check the area round XK657 to see if witness beacons were emplaced. Only re-establish the cement if found. Otherwise erect a beacon on the point – or approximate point. (The cement can be re-emplaced and re-observed with the rest of your scheme later).

3. For personnel, stores, finance etc. see my W1.9/6 dated 24th May, 1957.

4. I shall visit you on May 30th, 1957.

Principal Surveyor.

JPWW/KOS/3.

47. The first job for a new surveyor. Instructions at the start of six months work in the bush

48. Beaconing the secondary trig point XK 657 in the clouds on the second Ningishi summit

TRAVERSING

During the 1960s the arrival of electromagnetic distance measuring instruments and the use of towers for reconnaissance and observations began to provide a solution to the problem of carrying control surveys into the flat country of the north.

49. An MRA 2 Tellurometer

50. At Dutsen Wai in Zaria Province in 1963, establishing framework control for the West Kano block of topographic maps

51. 'Home made' guyed towers constructed from Mills scaffolding were first used by Frank Waudby-Smith and Malcolm Anderson for the reconnaissance of a Tellurometer traverse from Kano to Nguru in 1961

52. An internal view of a Mills tower

53. The modular form of the scaffolding allowed transportation of a moderately sized reconnaissance tower in a surveyor's 'kit-car'. Pictured at Jogana in Kano Province.

54. Flanges were welded to each end of 10 feet lengths of 4 inch water pipe which were bolted together to form a vertical support for the instrument, inside the scaffolding tower, independent of the observer.

This inexpensive means of achieving sight lines above the trees was used successfully for second and third order control schemes until the demise of the Northern Nigerian Survey. The scaffolding and instrument support towers were later loaned to the Directorate of Overseas Surveys parties for mapping control work. This photograph was taken in the Yankari Game Reserve, east of Bauchi, in 1971.

55. Traditional survey Bilby Towers were used by the US 12th Parallel Survey Team in the 1970s. This one was photographed near Kari on the Bauchi - Potiskum road

PLANE TABLING FOR 1:125,000 SCALE MAPPING IN 1939

56. Keith Sargeant's Headman Jatto

57. At the summit of Rusu Hill in the south-eastern quarter of the Chafe sheet

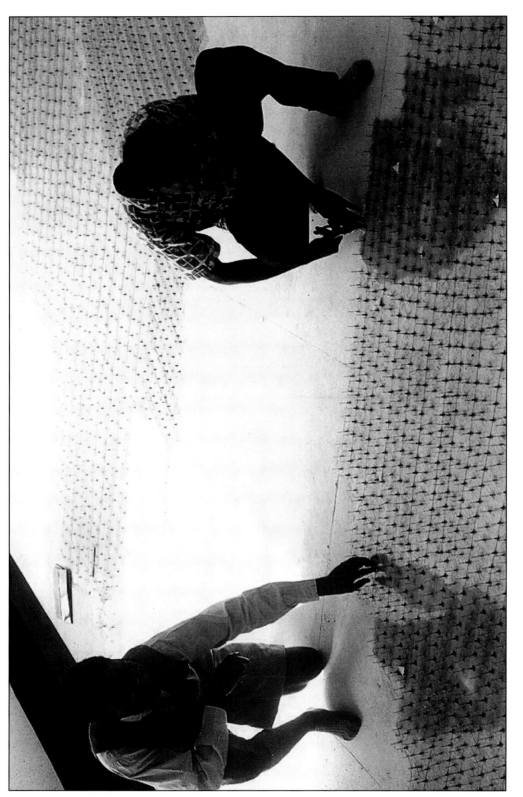

58. SLOTTED TEMPLATE LAYDOWN

The large laydown board in the air-conditioned building constructed at the Northern Nigerian Survey headquarters at Kaduna South. The assembled templates cover some hundreds of square miles of terrain and the curved flight lines of the RAF Lancaster aircraft (about Gubi Hill) can be seen quite clearly.

THE TOPOGRAPHIC MAPPING SECTION AT KADUNA SOUTH

59. The Drawing Office in 1960

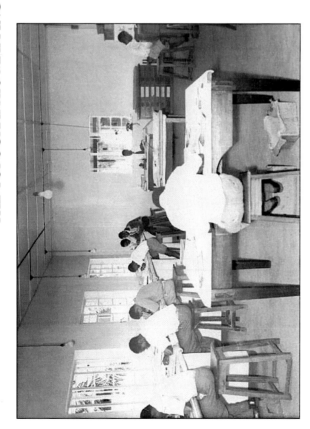

60. The Drawing Office in 1962

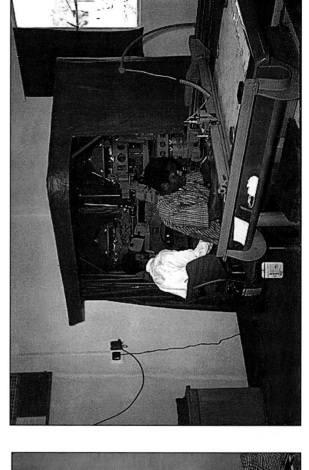

61. Plotting with a Santoni Stereomicrometer Mk.1 in 1962

62. Plotting with A Wild A8 in 1962

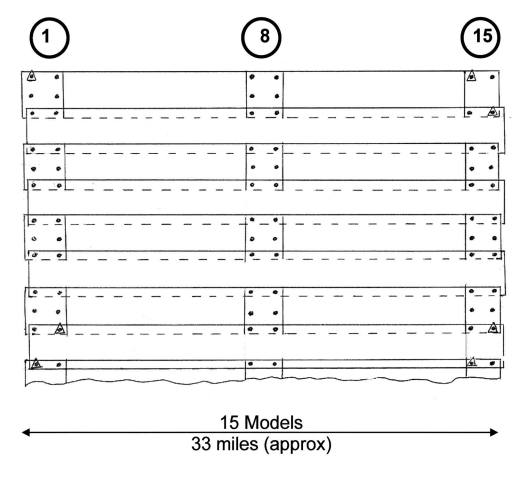

15 Models

← **33 miles (approx)** →

● Height   △ Plan

63. The distribution of plan and height control points
for a block of stereo models covering a standard mapsheet

64, 65. Two of the photopoints selected to control stereo models for the 1:2,400 scale mapping of Gusau in Sokoto Province in 1962.

These photographs were taken by the field surveyor as an aid to the resolution of any ambiguities which might arise at the mapping office during identification of the chosen points

66. Mogens Vejby remembers one of the longest railway straights in the world, on the Kano - Nguru line

67. The aftermath of storms in the Hadejia River valley.
The kind of flood encountered at Nguru

68. Mogens Vejby with the Emir of Zaria

69. John Adshead and David Ball at the Northern Nigerian Survey reunion at Malvern in October 2000

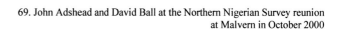

70. Primary cadastral control beacons were generally pre-cast concrete pillars about 2' 6" long and 9" square in section, with a 4" nail sunk to its head as the centre marker, and bearing a unique reference number.

71. Finding 'safe' and useable locations for control beacons was not always very easy in busy areas. Here a beacon is being positioned on railway land near the groundnut stacking area at Gusau, Sokoto Province in 1961.

72. Malcolm Anderson, catenary taping along a cleared line for the control survey of Offa, Ilorin

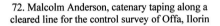

73. Catenary taping sometimes had to cover very rough ground. Here a traverse line is crossing the dry bed of the River Sokoto at Gusau.

74. A densely built town of high-walled compounds like Kano made traditional cadastral survey by ground methods very difficult.

75. The first glimpse of Jos and the plateau, on the approach from Kaduna

76. One of the more rugged parts of the Plateau, looking towards the primary N5 trig point

77. In a Birom hamlet in the Shere Hills

78. Waterfalls are common around the plateau edge. This one is at Kafanchan where the river flows over a basalt shelf

79. Naraguta Street in Jos in 1957; one of the town's main shopping streets, lined with 'canteens'.

80. A well-patronised venue on a Sunday evening

81. The staff at Roman Catholic Mission stations were genial, helpful and practical people.
Here Ria Voshaar looks a little bemused as 'adjustments' are made to Arnold Voshaar's T2 theodolite.

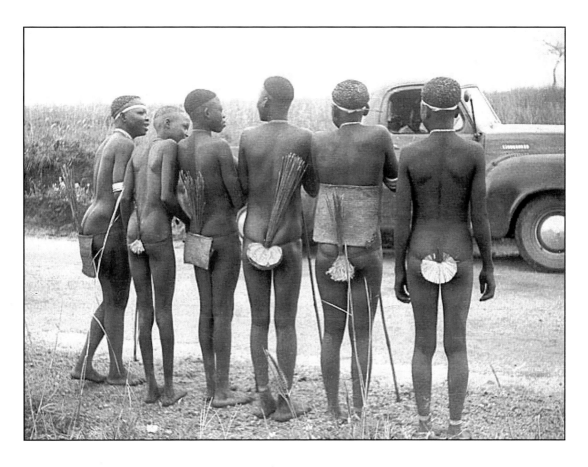

82. A group of pagan ladies, showing unusual interest in Arnold Voshaar's car or, perhaps, practising their kerb drill.(?)

ACCOMMODATION AT JOS

83. Jos Leave Camp. Basic lodging for travellers in the 1950s.

84. Jos Catering Rest House

85. The Hill Station

86. The Survey Rest House near Bukuru

87. The 'Doll's House', on the edge of the Jos golf course, home for surveyors for many years; here, in 1952, occupied by Trevor and Joan Brokenshire.

88. 'No.5 Bukuru Road'. The Principal Surveyor's house until 1968.

TIN MINING ON THE JOS PLATEAU

89. Hand-paddocking on a small scale mine.

90. Intensive hand-paddocking.

91. Large scale mining by the Associated Tin Mines of Nigeria.

92. An A.T.M.N. dragline.

93. A deep mining pit at Rayfield; the aftermath of dragline
working and used for water storage for sluicing operations.

94. The Makeri tin smelter at Jos.

SURVEYING ON THE JOS PLATEAU

95. The tertiary trig pillar near Barakin Ladi

96. The trig point at Kassa

97. Arnold Voshaar surveying a mining lease in 1957

98. Malcolm Anderson working on a mining survey close to the railway at Hoss

99. Survey labourers Adeka Katsina, Ibrahim Natawa, Jabo Yola and Adamu Wanke

100. Survey Assistant Joe Umunna and his team at Barakin Ladi

THE SURVEY OFFICE AT JOS

101. The staff of the Survey Office in 1952

102. 1957

103. M.J.Miles near the trig point marking the end of the
Primary trig baseline near the Survey Office in 1957

104, 105   The Survey Office in 1967

106. Witnesses from Nassarawa Eggon await the start of the Plateau - Benue Provincial boundary demarcation

107, 108. Trevor Brokenshire and Clifford Rayner used fire for the clearance of dry grass from the line of the Ilorin - Sokoto Provincial boundary in 1957.

109. At the Oyo Survey School in 1945.

Front row from left to right: Ogedegbi, Oluwole Coker (later Director of Federal Surveys), Keith Sargeant, Adedoyin and Godfrey Oraeki

110. The Royal Engineers' Officers' Long Survey Course No.17 at Newbury in 1956.

Standing, left, Malcolm Anderson; right John Bull (joined Federal Surveys); seated, right, Alan Wright.

111. The Survey School camp, established by Jack Ashton, at Kachia in 1960

112. The Survey School at Zaria in 1964

113. Staff and students at the Survey School at Zaria in 1964

114. The Survey School camp, established by Malcolm Anderson, at Kagarko, in 1964

115. The Advanced Survey Course during triangulation reconnaissance, on Kaharma Hill in 1964

116. A former Railway house on Keffi Road in Kaduna South, used for the Survey School in 1965

117. During practical training in 1965 the School's Advanced Course was engaged in productive work for the extension of the township control and large scale mapping of Kaduna.

Here R.O.Ihedioha is running a catenary traverse in a future development area.

118 - 121. Preparing for the journey. Elder Dempster luggage labels.

122. The mv Apapa, sister sip to the mv Accra.

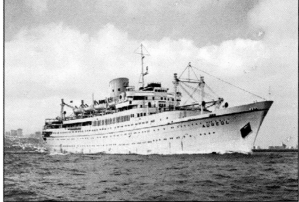

123. The last of the Elder Dempster ships, the mv Aureol

125. A model of the mv Aureol currently displayed in the Maritime Museum at the Royal Albert Dock, Liverpool

124. The shipboard day started with a comprehensive breakfast, as witnessed by Arnold Voshaar in 1954

126, 127. For travellers to Accra in 1939, the comforts of the First Class voyage came to an abrupt and undignified end with disembarkation by 'mammy chair' and surf-boat.

128. The 'North Mail' at Jebba in 1939

129. The River Niger from Jebba bridge in 1939

130. Climbing to the Jos Plateau

131. Improving air services led to a decline in sea travel. In 1958 Boeing Stratocruisers replaced the Argonauts on the BOAC service linking London with Kano and Lagos. The overnight flight from Kano to London took over ten hours, with stops at Tripoli and Rome.

132. Mohammadu Bauchi; Malcolm Anderson's devoted employee and mentor for over 15 years

133. Garba Bauchi; his 'Maigardi', with bow and poisoned arrows

134. Garba Yola; a helioman

LABOURERS AND CHAINMEN REMEMBERED BY HARRY RENTEMA

135. Liman Zakare; an excellent Chainman

136. "Old Umaru"; a helioman

137. Tukur Zaria with Malcolm Anderson's labour gang in Jema'a

138. Momo 'Mailema' taking care of Colin Emmott's T3

139. The *Sheriya*. Fulani youths at a 'beating ceremony'

140. A complete mystery to local people. What on earth could surveyors be doing at a place like this ?

TRAVELLING IN THE NORTH

141. The Enugu - Jos local train on the Jos Plateau. 1958.

142. A stern-wheeler on the Benue. 1959.

143. River transport on the Niger at Lokoja. 1961.

144. Crossing a major river by ferry in 1951.

145. The main laterite-surfaced road from Kaduna to Ilorin in 1957.

146. A plank bridge. A standard feature of many minor and major roads.

147. The Survey lorry. 1946.

148. A 'mammy wagon' on a dry season road.

149. Between Kachia and Zonkwa.

150. Between Gusau and Kaura Namoda.

THE HAZARDOUS ROADS OF THE NORTH

151,152. The Saminaka bridge on the Jos - Kaduna road collapsed in 1967 when struck by an overloaded lorry.
The diversion through the river caused a later accident.

MOTORING IN THE WET SEASON

153. Road closed *(Anrufe hanya)*. Even in the far north roads could become impassable in the wet season. This picture was taken at Zugachi, north-east of Kano in August 1961

154. Harry Rentema fording the Kogin Galma near Kudaru

155,156. Problems on the main road south of Jos.

157. The main Jos-Enugu road a few miles north of Wamba in 1958

158. Soft sand near Ringim, Kano Province

159. On first appointment surveyors were encouraged to purchase a 'kit-car' for personal and official use.

160. With a tent aboard a roadside camp could be established almost anywhere

161. These vehicles had to stand rough treatment.

162. Running repairs were often 'do-it-yourself affairs. Trevor Brokenshire 'gets out and gets under'.

163, 164. Office-based staff were more likely to purchase saloon cars.   Long journeys were seldom without incident.   The photograph on the left was taken after a wet season run along the Keffi - Kaduna road.   On the right, on the Bauchi - Ningi road, dense swarms of insects blocked the radiator, causing the engine to overheat, and left a thick coating on the windscreen.   On the return journey, at night, the second spare wheel proved useful when an encounter with a porcupine punctured front and rear tyres

165. For Clifford Rayner, working on triangulation in Adamawa in 1957, the view of 'home', the only natural clearing for miles, at C35, Gidan Ali. Camp was situated about an hour and a half climb from the plain and it was another half hour to the summit. There was plenty of wild life in the forest, including leopard. His *maigardi* spent most of the day collecting firewood and most of the night burning it ! He was glad to leave !

166. Six months without the attentions of a barber or a razor, and looking decidedly weary.
'Stress' was not in the colloquial vocabulary in those days !

167. Camp is struck, and the theodolite is lifted at the start of the day's trek.

168. Local porters carry some of the headloads

169. The difficult, steep descent of the edge
of the Jos Plateau

170. A pause for a well-earned rest at a wayside village

171. A trig party moving across the Kagoro Hills

172. Kadara porters in southern Zaria Province in 1963

173. Trevor Brokenshire's survey labourers in 1954

174. Malcolm Anderson's party, with James Kyuka at the centre, on the P Chain survey in 1959

175. Only 'bushmen' went around unclothed. A shirt, sometimes hired to others, would be worn by a government labourer as a status symbol.
Presumably, the umbrella was carried to keep it dry !

176, 177. In suitable country, locally hired horses saved much walking, but parties still progressed at the speed of the men with the headloads.

178, 179. Rivers in spate made crossings very hazardous

180. A trig party using canoes in Benue Province in 1959

181. Villagers at Ajojo in Benue stand watching as a survey party passes through

182. In the villages of the far north, children were always fascinated onlookers

183. The first glimpse of a white man for some people

184. Keith Sargeant's camp at Gobirawa village in 1939

185. Sarkin Ninkoro and his entourage greeting Harry Rentema, the first white man to visit the village since Keith Sargeant working on triangulation several years before.

186. Hunters bring in some bush-meat, a warthog

IN CAMP

187. Numwa Baba hill on the Jema'a triangulation

188. At P10 south of Nassarawa

189, 190. In camps that were occupied for some time the kitchen could be screened with *zana* matting

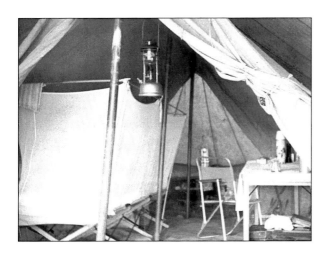

191, 192. The standard ridge-pole tent had an outer fly, a ground-sheet, an enclosed 'bathroom' at the rear and a 'verandah' at the front.

193. During the late 1940s and the 1950s surveyors working in the bush were sometimes accompanied by their wives. In 1954 Joan Brokenshire travelled with her husband Trevor.

REST HOUSES

194. Kujama Rest House, near Kaduna, had a circular inner room, earth floors, and gaps for windows and doors.

195. Wamba Rest House, with cement-plastered walls and floor and 'Crittall' window and doors frames with glass.

196. The rest house at Monguna Arna on the Jos Plateau. Just four mud walls and a pan roof. Usually a corral for goats.

197. A black scorpion, a common nocturnal visitor to a rest house verandah.

198. In the late afternoon during the Harmattan the sun became a pale disk in the dusty sky over a monochrome and inhospitable landscape

199. During the day the wind might reach gale force, raising dust from the dried land.

200. The aftermath of a dry season bush fire

201. The arrival of the rains was heralded by spectacular thunderstorms

202. The River Niger from the edge of the Agbaja Plateau, north of Lokoja.
The surveyor could have great landscapes all to himself, magnificent African panoramas, and distant blue hills to explore.

SOME
PROVINCIAL
SCENES

203. A group of children outside the eastern gate at Katsina

204. Off-duty stewards at Katsina Catering Rest House

205. A brass vendor at Bida

206. Thadeus Moszynski, for a while
Provincial Surveyor at Minna,
demonstrating the upside-down world
of surveying to a young girl.

207. An artesian water hole

209. Floods near Nguru, caused
by a rising water table

BORNU PROVINCE

208. Lake Chad, near Baga, in 1969

ILORIN PROVINCE

210. Ilorin Catering Rest House

211. Peter and Daphne Taylor with the staff of the Ilorin Provincial Survey Office

REMINDERS OF KADUNA IN THE 1950s AND THE 1960s

212. The Surveyor-General's house by the riverside in Kaduna South

213. The Survey Rest House, an old 'Railway' house, on Keffi Road

214. A 'Kaduna' type bungalow. On the right of the picture can be seen the Survey Department's 'practice' trig pillar.

215. Construction of the 'O.S.' type pillar in 1958.

216. Janet Rayner in Kaduna South in 1964, author of '"A Young Wife's Tale", which appears in the Kaduna section in Part 4.

217. A daily sight in Kaduna South as the Gbagyi (Gwari) wood- sellers passed through on their way to the market.

218. The Kaduna South road bridge under construction

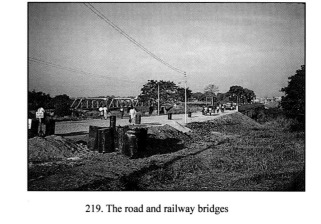

219. The road and railway bridges

220, 221. The Kaduna River from the same viewpoint in the contrasting dry and wet seasons

222. Lugard Hall

223. The Hamdala Hotel

224. Kingsway store, decorated for the Independence celebrations in 1960

225. Opportunists waiting at the butchery at the Kingsway store

226. Garba Kano, a Survey watchman, taking an afternoon nap.

227. A street scene in Kaduna Sabon Gari

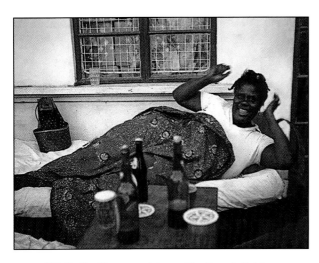

228. Paulina Okon, proprietress of the Queen's Hotel

229. Max Lock, the Planning Consultant, and Denis Willey 'off-duty' at the Queen's Hotel

230. Rugby at the Kaduna Racecourse ground

231. Surveyors and friends relaxing at the Kaduna Club

232. Farewell to Frank Woods at Kaduna South in 1957.
Those seated in the second row, from left to right, include D.Ball, J.D. Adshead, D.C. Eva, S.H.A.Rollison,
B. Adshead, F.Woods. V.Williams, K.M.Sargeant, Mrs Williams, W.G.Tuck, O.Kanno and M.V.Christensen.

233. Farewell to Derick Bell (Topographic Survey Computing and Records) at Kaduna South in 1963.
Those seated on the second row, from left to right, include G.N.D.Beale, O.Kanno, C.D.Burnside,
A.D.Willey, J.F.Bell, J.P.W.Ward, J.Ashton, A.A.Magbagbeola and S.Klepacki.

234. Farewell to Clifford Burnside at Kaduna South in 1966.
Those seated on the second row from left to right include W.Stopforth, S.Klepacki,
A.A.Magbagbeola, J.Ashton, C.D.Burnside, J.D.Adshead, O.Kanno and M.F.Anderson

235. Ben Obianwu speaks at the farewell gathering for John and Barbara Adshead and Clifford and Janet Rayner
at the UAC Club in Kaduna in September 1966

236. A Nigerian Airways
DC3 internal flight
leaving Kaduna for Kano.

237. A BOAC VC10 preparing to
leave Kano for London.

238. The writer's final farewell in April 1977, at the Works and Survey wing of the new Borno State Secretariat building in Maiduguri.
Those seated on the second row from left to right include S.Z.H.Jaffrey (Town Planner), J.W.Evans (Principal Surveyor), the Commissioner of
Works and Survey, M.F.Anderson, the Permanent Secretary, A.Tevendale (Chief Civil Engineer) and J.Oniye (Valuation Officer).

239. Some of the *Geographic Labourers* and their wives attending the reunion in October 2002, photographed during a visit to Audley End House near Saffron Walden.

APPENDIX XI

MAPS

Section		Source
Introduction		
M1	Index to maps of Nigeria	M.Anderson/NN Survey
M2	1 Kontagora - Sokoto area	M.Anderson/Federal Surveys
M3	2 Kaduna - Katsina area	,,
M4	3 Bauchi - Gashua area	,,
M5	4 Biu - Lake Chad area	,,
M6	5 Lagos - Ilorin area	,,
M7	6 Enugu - Minna area	,,
M8	7 Gboko - Jos area	,,
M9	8 Mambilla - Gombe area	,,
M10	9 Delta area	,,
Land and People		
M11	Nigeria in the mid 1950s	C.Burnside
M12	West Africa 1895	M.Anderson/G.W.Bacon & Co.
M13	Nigeria in the 1960s	M.Anderson/NN Survey
M14	The Provinces of Northern Nigeria	M.Anderson/Federal Surveys
M15	The new Northern States	,,
Survey Departments		
M16	Part of a 1902 War Office map	M.Anderson/Original
M17	An ancient map after Ptolemy	M.Anderson/NN Survey
M18	Part of a 1905 Stanford's map	M.Anderson/Original
M19	Part of a 1910 GSGS map	M.Anderson/Original
Framework Surveys		
M20	K Chain triangulation	H.Rentema/ Federal Surveys
M21	Triangulation reconnaissance diagram	,,
Topographic Mapping		
M22	Numbering of Nigerian mapsheets	M.Anderson/NN Survey
M23	An example of 1:500,000 scale mapping	K.Sargeant/Federal Surveys
M24	Chafe 1:125,000 sheet	,,
M25	Cover diagram of early aerial photography	O.Y.Balogun/BCS
M26	Part of 1:50,000 Naraguta sheet	C.Burnside/Federal Surveys
M27	Part of 1:100,000 Malumfashi sheet	,,
M28	Part of 1:4,800 Gusau mapping	M.Anderson/NN Survey
M29	Part of 1:2,400 Gusau mapping	,,
Minesfield Surveys		
M30	Jos Plateau index map	K.Sargeant/Federal Surveys
M31	Jos Plateau North-West	,,
M32	Jos Plateau North-East	,,
M33	Jos Plateau West	,,
M34	Jos Plateau East	,,
M35	Jos Plateau South-West	,,
M36	Jos Plateau South-East	,,
M37	Part of a Minesfield Priority Sheet	M.Anderson/NN Survey
Travelling		
M38	Nigeria. Topography and Railways	M.Anderson/Federal Surveys
M39	Part of 1:1,750,000 road map	M.Anderson/Federal Surveys
Appendix VII		
M40	Part of 1:50,000 Kam NW	C.Rayner/Federal Surveys
M41	DOS mapping coverage	O.Y.Balogun/BCS
Appendix IX		
M42	Index to medium scale mapping NE State	M.Anderson/NE State Surveys

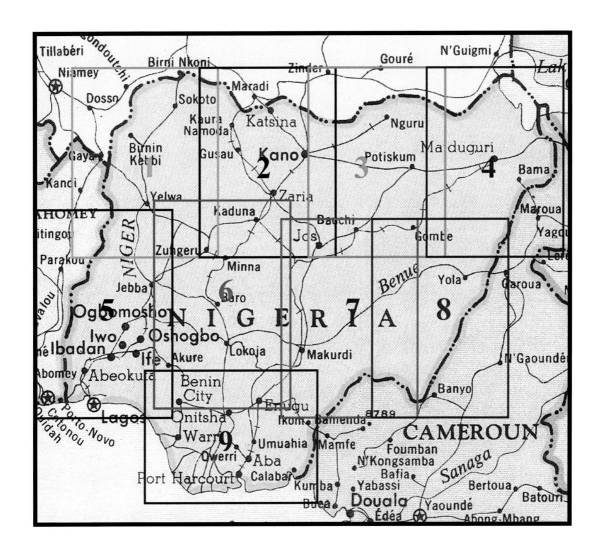

**M1. INDEX TO THE FOLLOWING 9 REDUCED-SCALE
EXTRACTS FROM THE 1972 FEDERAL SURVEYS'
1:1,585,000 SCALE ROAD MAP OF NIGERIA**

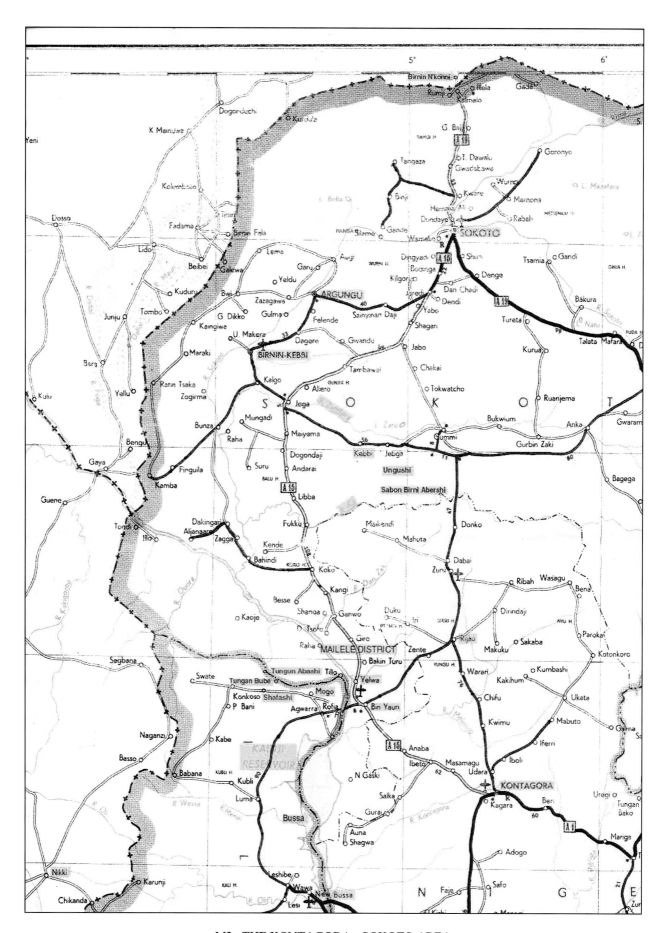

M2. THE KONTAGORA - SOKOTO AREA

Places highlighted in green are mentioned in the text.

1

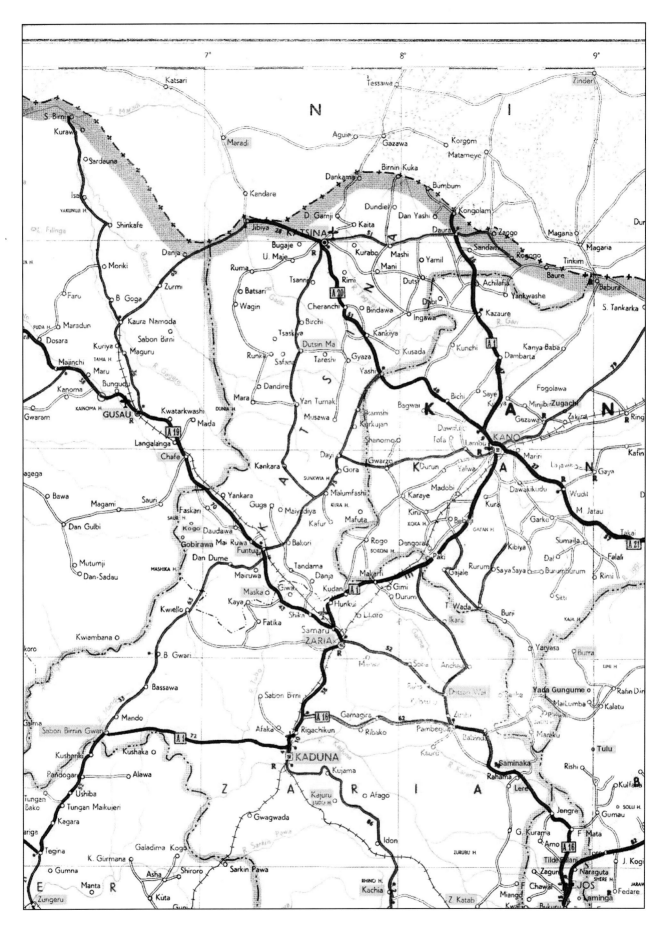

M3. THE KADUNA - KATSINA AREA

Places highlighted in green are mentioned in the text.

2

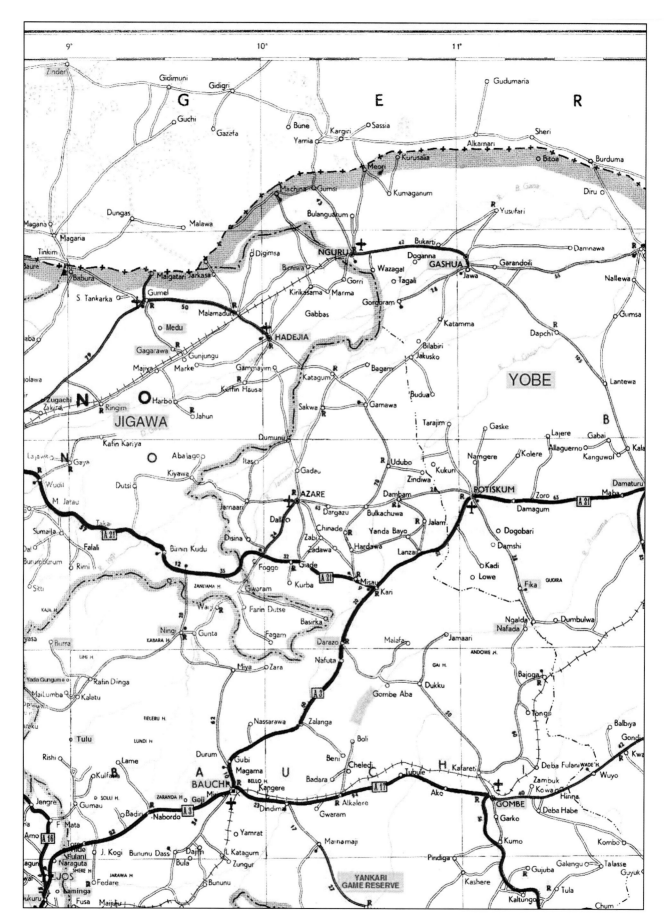

M4. THE BAUCHI - GASHUA AREA

Places highlighted in green are mentioned in the text.

3

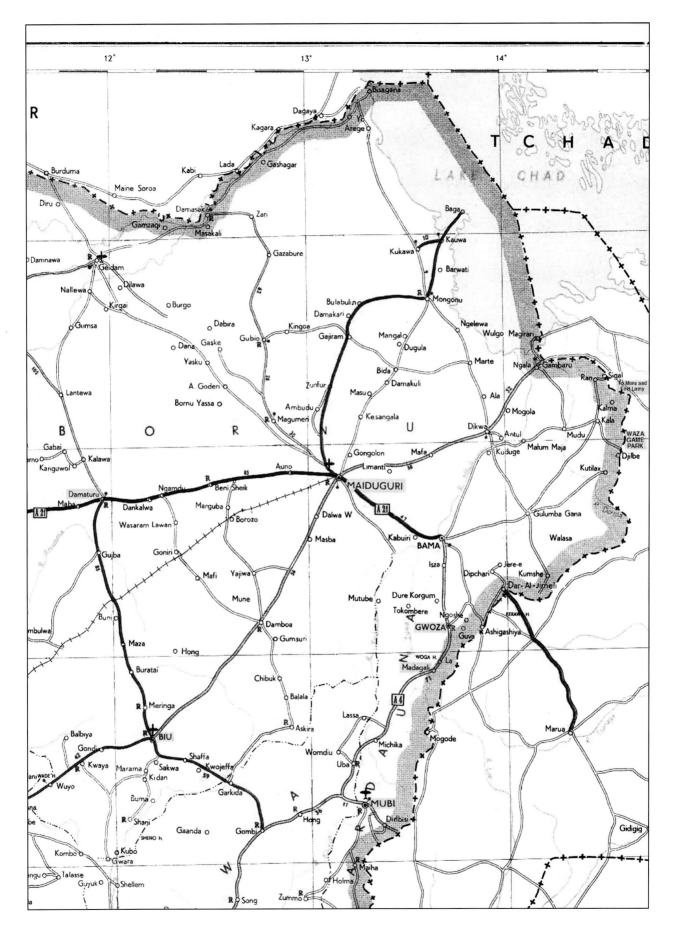

M5. THE BIU - LAKE CHAD AREA

Places highlighted in green are mentioned in the text.

4

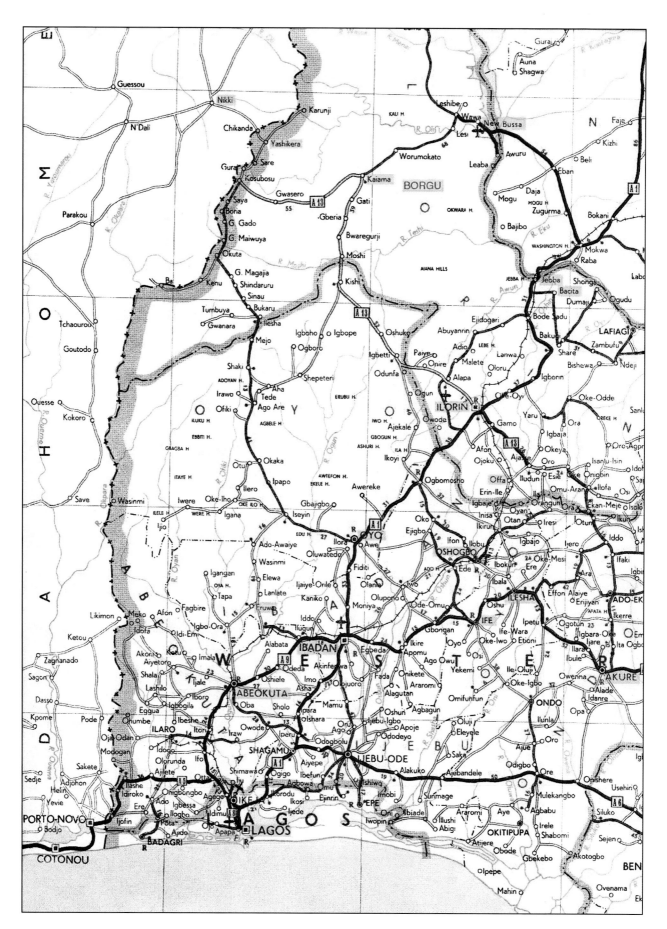

M6. THE LAGOS - ILORIN AREA

Places highlighted in green are mentioned in the text.

5

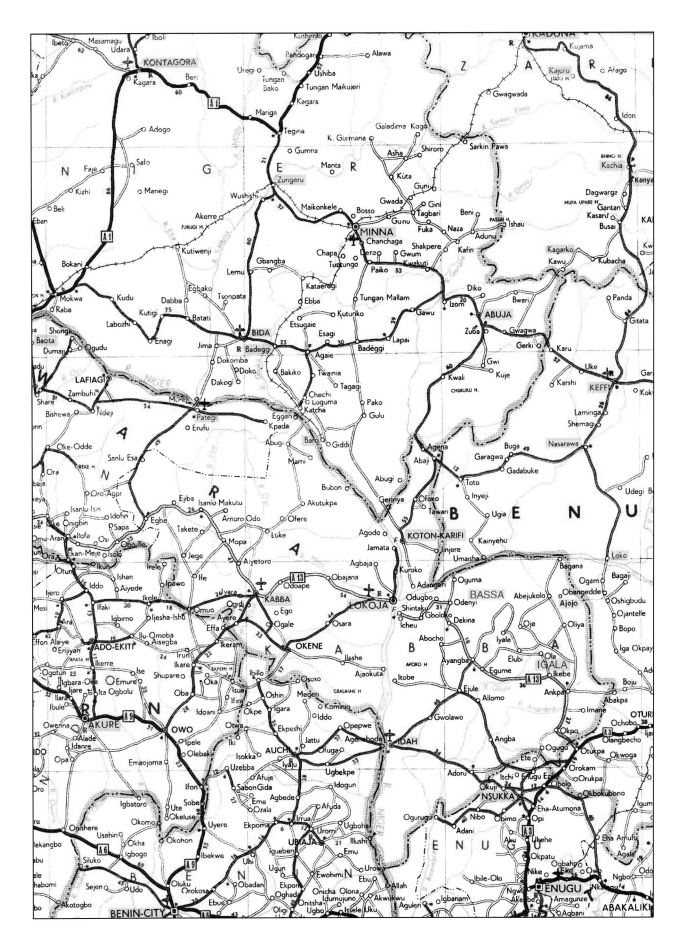

M7. THE ENUGU - MINNA AREA

Places highlighted in green are mentioned in the text.

6

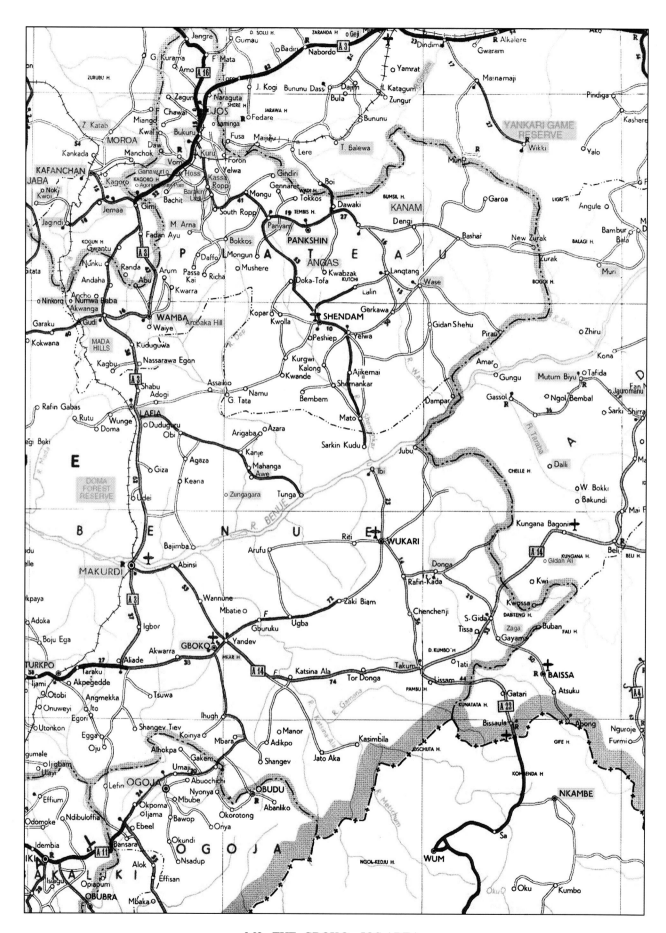

M8. THE GBOKO - JOS AREA

Places highlighted in green are mentioned in the text.

7

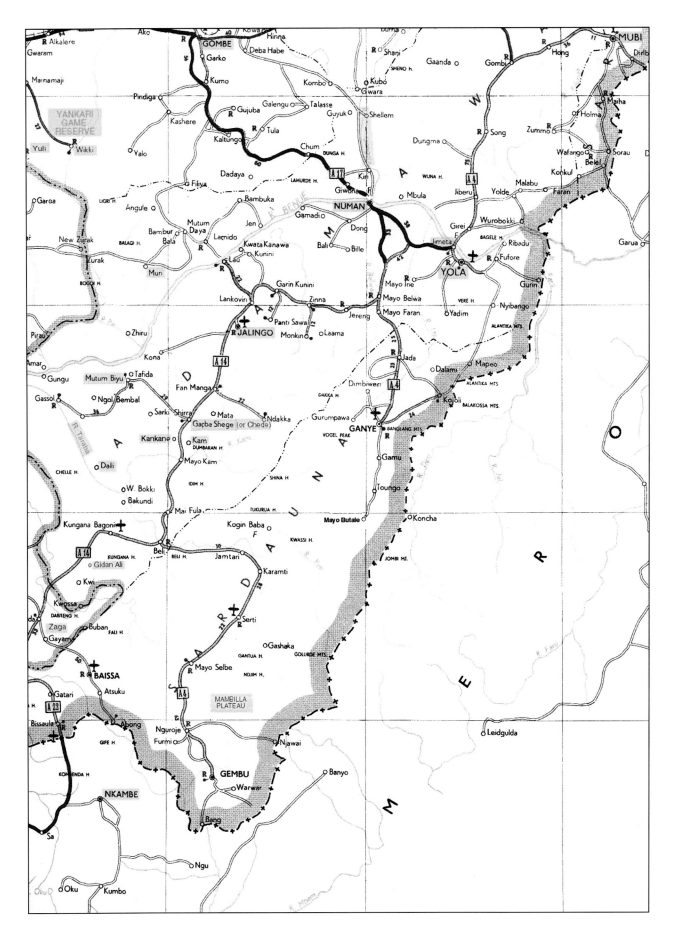

M9. THE MAMBILLA - GOMBE AREA

Places highlighted in green are mentioned in the text.

8

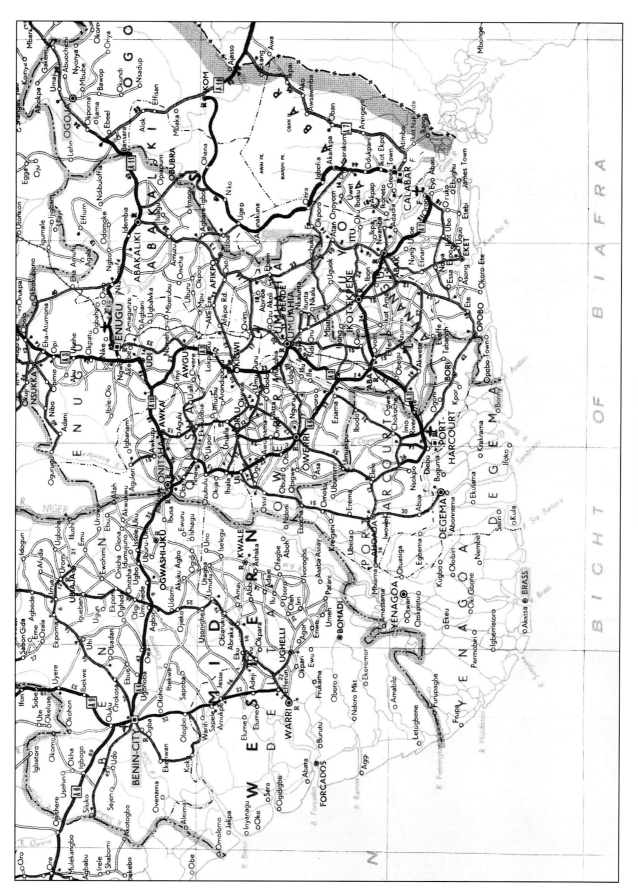

M10. THE DELTA AREA
Places highlighted in green are mentioned in the text.

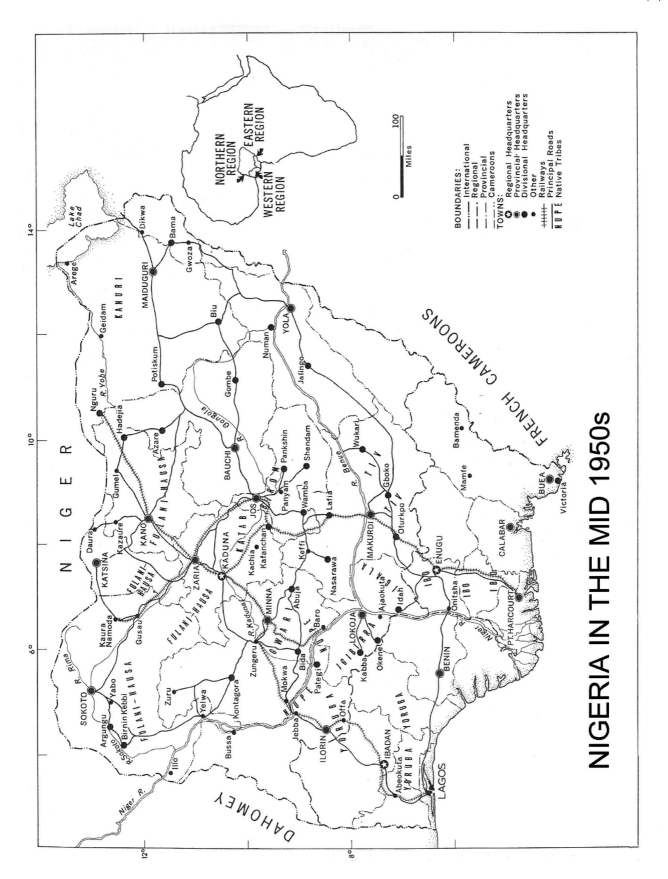

NIGERIA IN THE MID 1950s

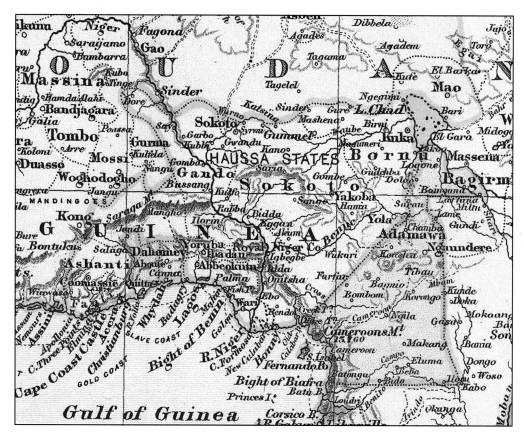

M12. Five years before the declaration of the Protectorates - from an atlas produced in London in 1895

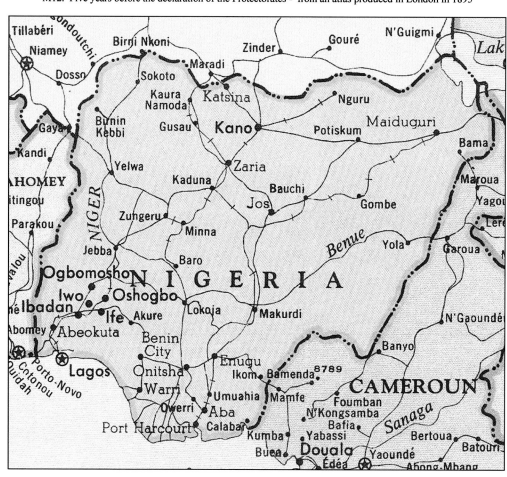

M13. Nigeria in the 1960s

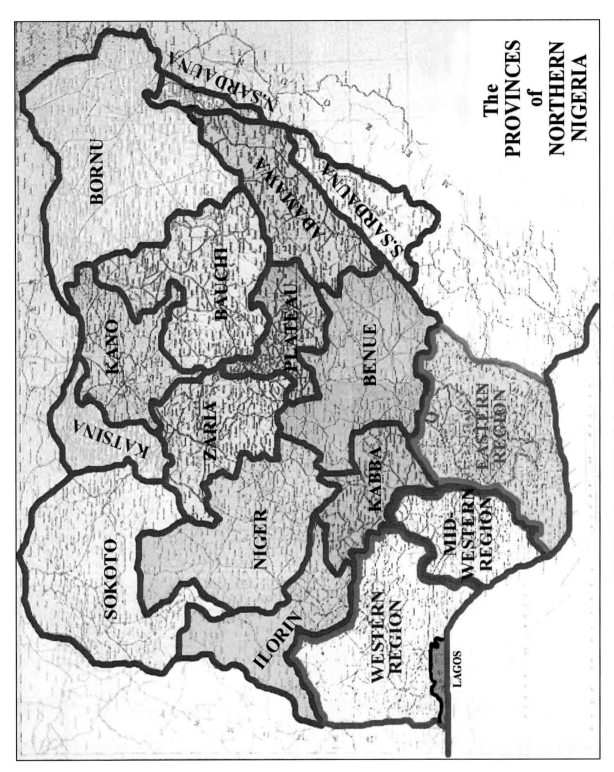

M14. The Provinces of the North before the 1968 declaration of the new internal States.

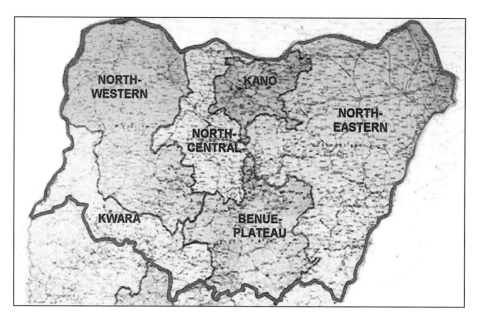

M15. In 1968 the Military Government abolished Nigeria's regional structure.
The north was divided into six new States, preserving the existing Provincial boundaries.

7. In 1968 the Interim Common Services Agency Survey Unit printed a
special Christmas card with the armorial bearings of the new Northern States.

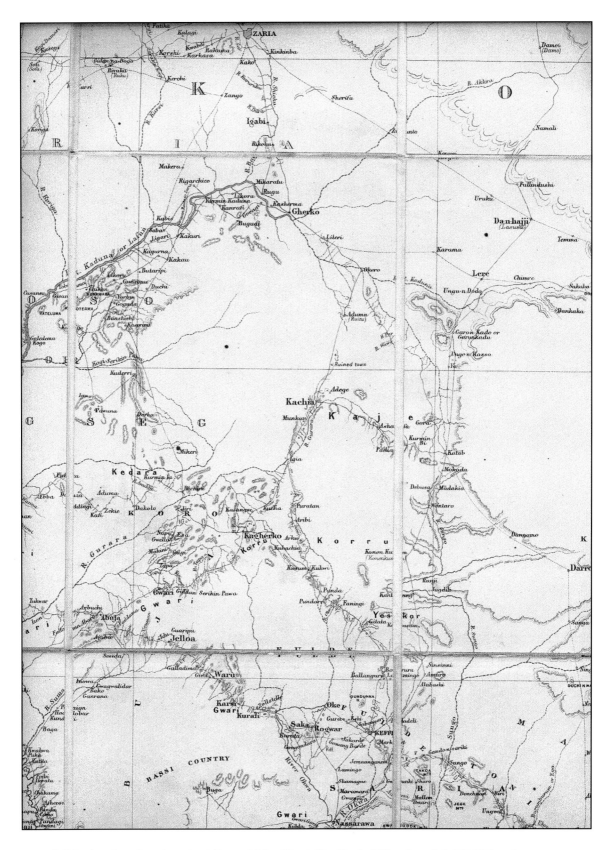

M16. A reduced-scale extract from Africa Sheet 62 - Central Nigeria   1:1,000,000 scale.

Reproduced and printed for the Intelligence Division of the War Office in 1902
by W & A.K.Johnston War Office and distributed by Edward Stanford, London

M17. An ancient map of Africa after Ptolemy (c.1500) was reproduced from one of the rare originals by the Lithographic Section of the Northern Nigerian Survey Department in 1966 as a training exercise in colour separation and four colour printing.

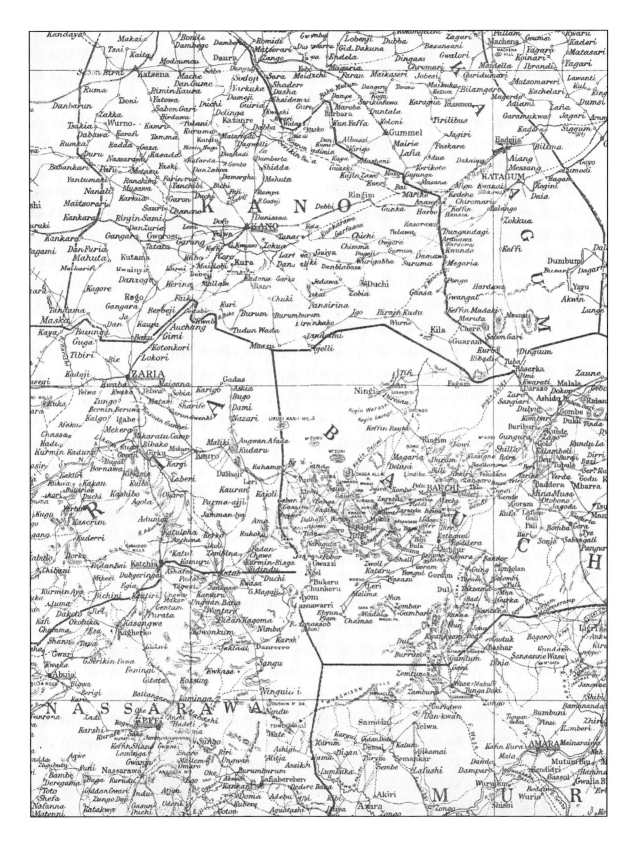

M18. A reduced-scale extract from a 1905 map published at 1:2,000,000 scale (or 1.014 inches to 32 miles)
by Stanford's Geographical Establishment, London
and reprinted as a lithographic training exercise by the Survey Department, Kaduna in 1969

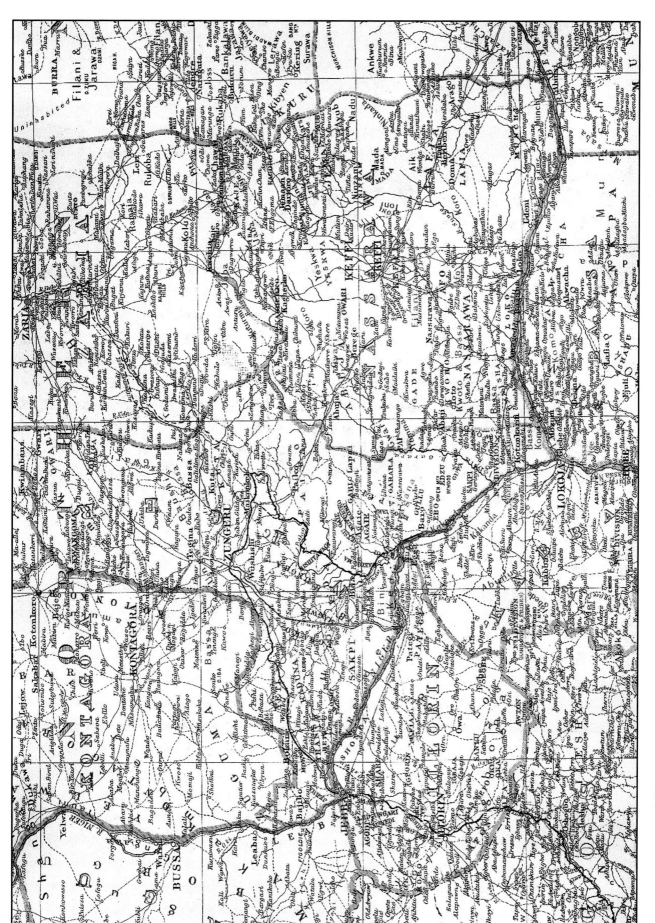

M19. A reduced-scale extract from the 1:2,000,000 scale "Northern and Southern Nigeria" map, compiled in the War Office from boundary commission surveys and material supplied by the Intelligence Officers of Northern and Southern Nigeria and published in 1910 by the Geographical Section of the General Staff.

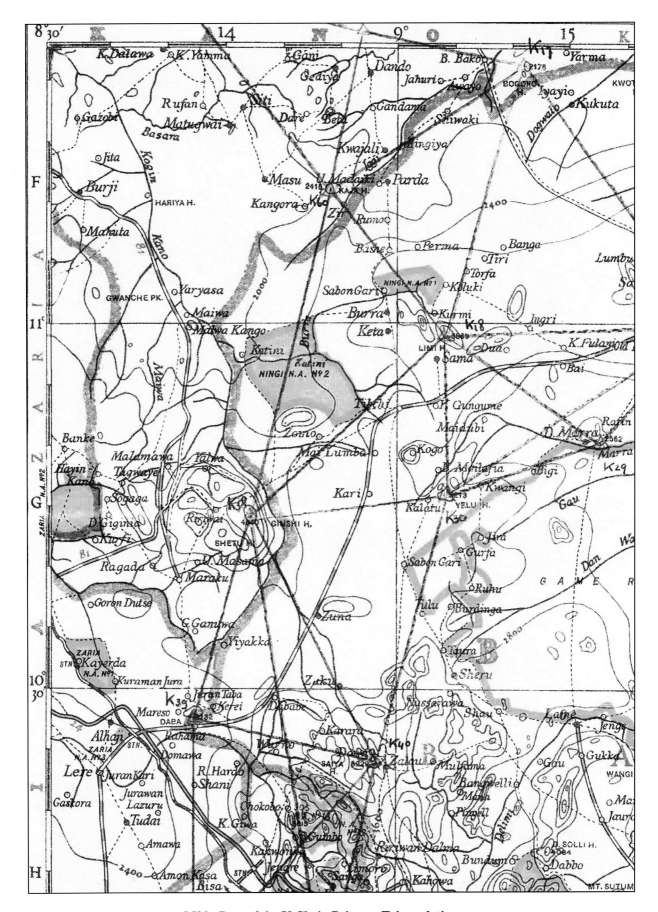

M20. Part of the K Chain Primary Triangulation

This reduced-scale extract from 1:500,000 scale mapsheet No.7 shows part of the K Chain triangulation covering an area at the junctions of the Provincial boundaries of Zaria, Kano, Bauchi and Plateau.

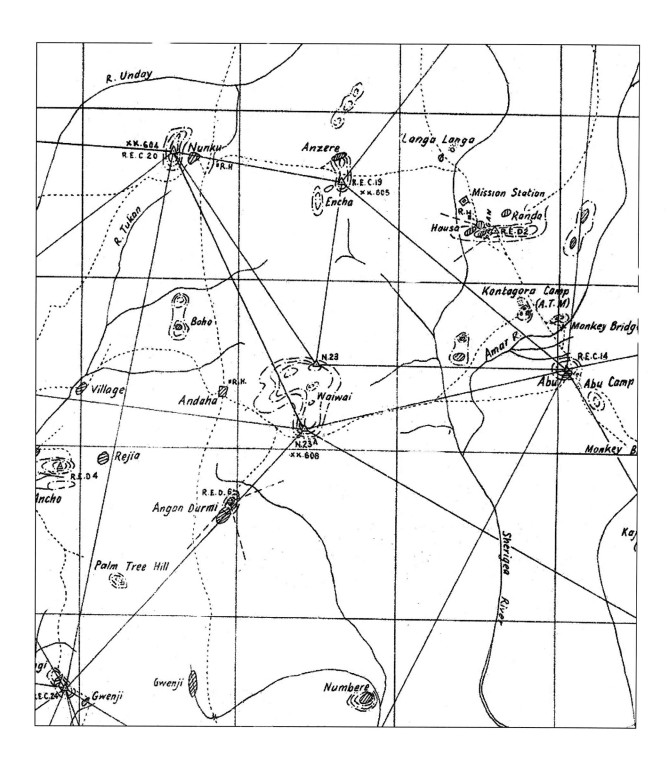

M21. An example of a triangulation reconnaissance diagram

This is a reduced-scale extract from a triangulation reconnaissance sketch map of the North and South Mada Districts
prepared by Lieut.F.G.Clark R.A. of 2nd Col.Surv.R.E. in 1928. It was drawn at a scale of 1:125,000.
The sides of the grid squares are 20,000 feet in length.
The diagram was handed to H.Rentema in 1953-54 as an example of the data required for his triangulation reconnaissance work.

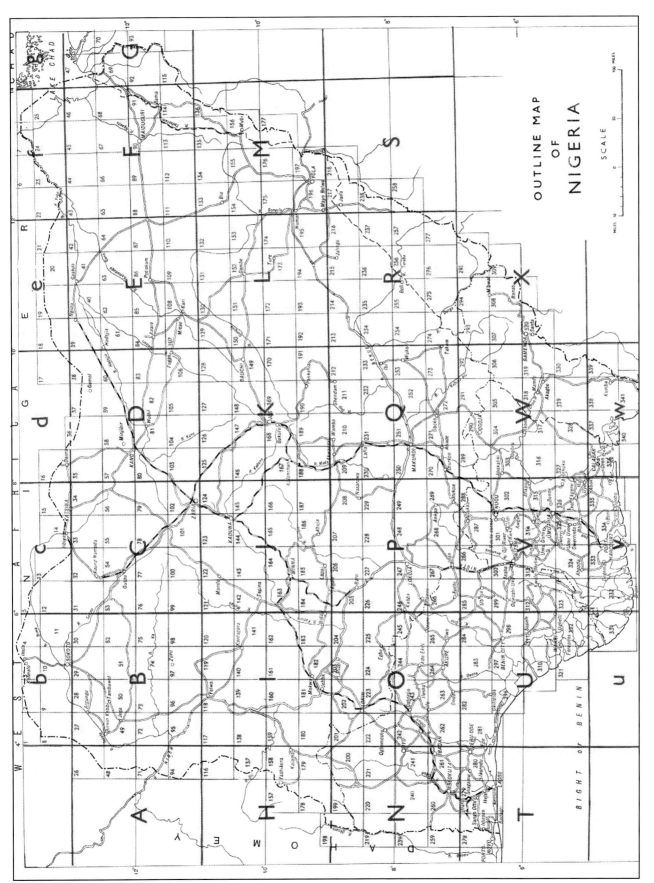

M22. Index to the numbering of standard 1:100,000 scale mapping.
Each numbered sheet was divided into quarter sheets at 1:50,000 scale.

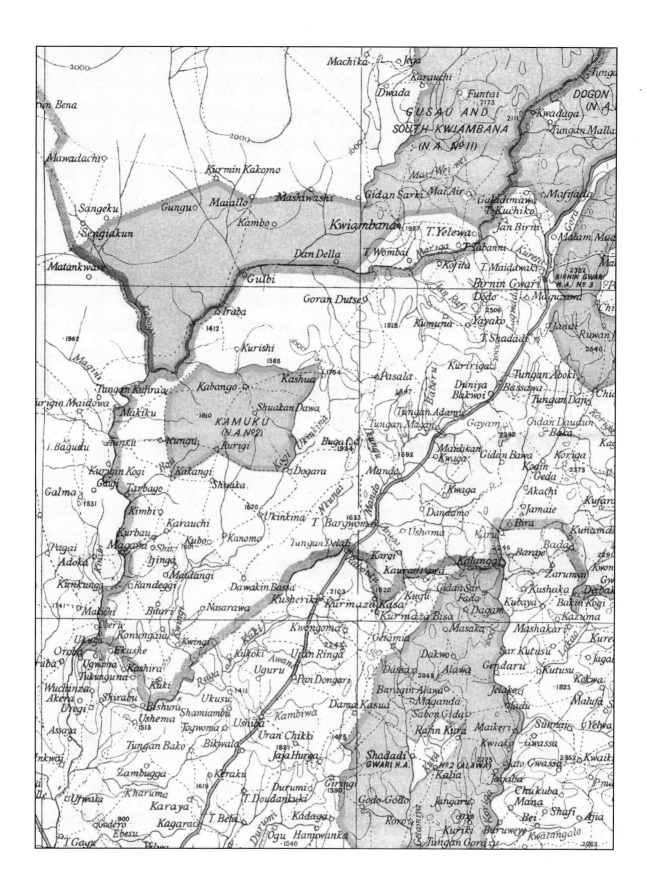

M23. Example of a 1:500,000 scale map

Maps of this kind formed a National series with a grid interval of ½° and form lines at 400 ft vertical intervals. This reduced scale extract is from Sheet 6 which was drawn and reproduced by the Land and Survey Department in Lagos in 1944 and reprinted in 1949. It covers the area at the junction of the boundaries of Sokoto, Niger and Zaria Provinces, and shows part of the Zungeru to Kano road about 60 miles west of Kaduna.

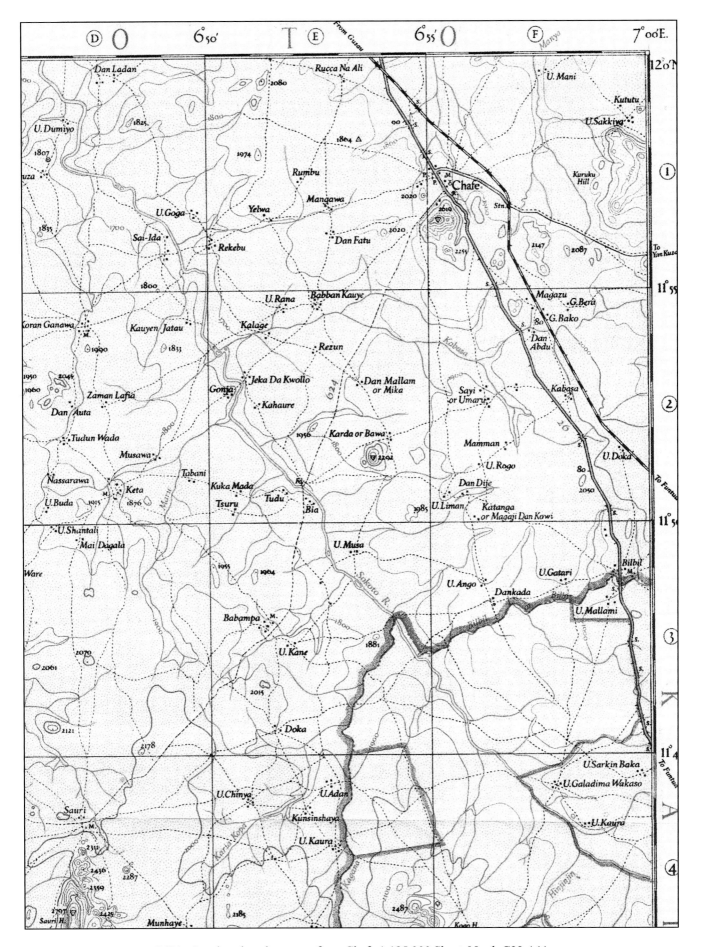

M24. A reduced-scale extract from Chafe 1:125,000 Sheet North C32 A11

This eastern part of the map was surveyed by Keith Sargeant as his first job in 1939.
The map was drawn and reproduced by the Land and Survey Department, Lagos in 1940 and reprinted in 1944 and 1949.
Transverse Mercator Projection.   Central Meridian 8° 30' E.   Sheet corners 6° 30' - 7° 00' E, 11° 30' - 12° 00' N
Altitudes above mean sea level at East Mole, Lagos.   Form lines at approximately 100 ft vertical intervals

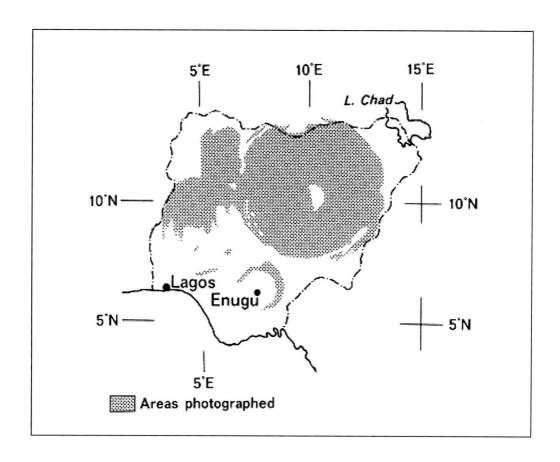

M25. Early aerial photography.

This diagram gives an indication of the areas flown between 1946 and 1956

(This illustration is reproduced with the kind permission of Professor Olayinka Y.Balogun
of the University of Lagos and was originally published in The Cartographic Journal
(British Cartographic Society), Volume 24 June 1987, in the article entitled 'The
Directorate of Overseas Surveys and Mapping in Nigeria)

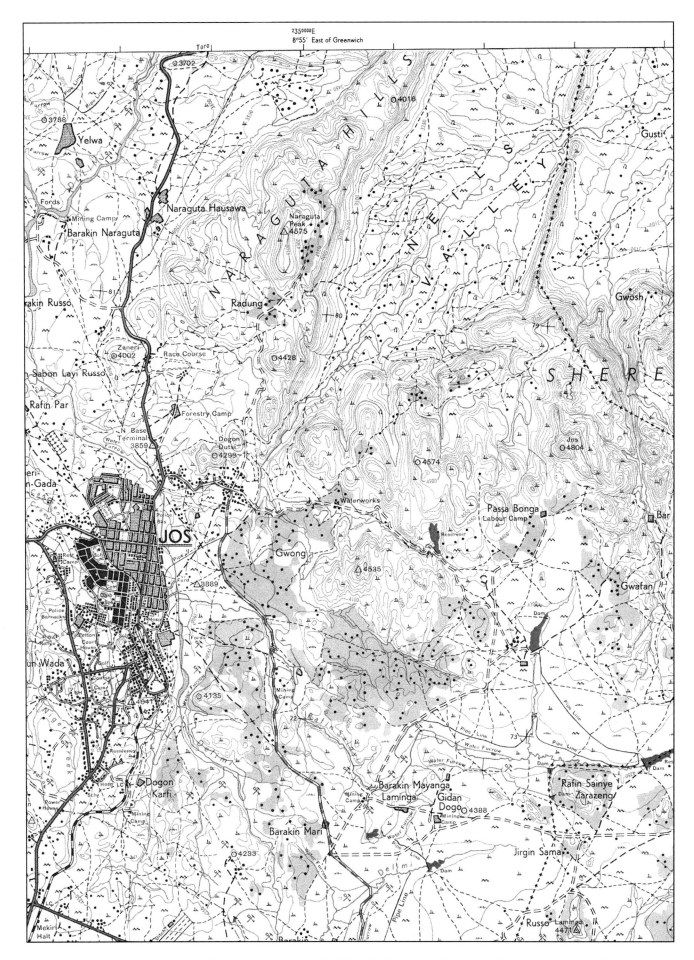

M26. A reduced-scale extract from the second edition 1:50,000 scale Naraguta Sheet 168NE, with contours at 50 ft vertical intervals. This map was produced by the Directorate of Overseas Surveys in 1959 from aerial photographs obtained by the Air Operating Company in October 1956. Control and additional information was provided by the Northern Nigerian Survey in 1958 and printing was done by the Ordnance Survey in the U.K.

Projection: Transverse Mercator   Spheroid: Clarke 1880   Grid: Nigeria Colony Mid Belt

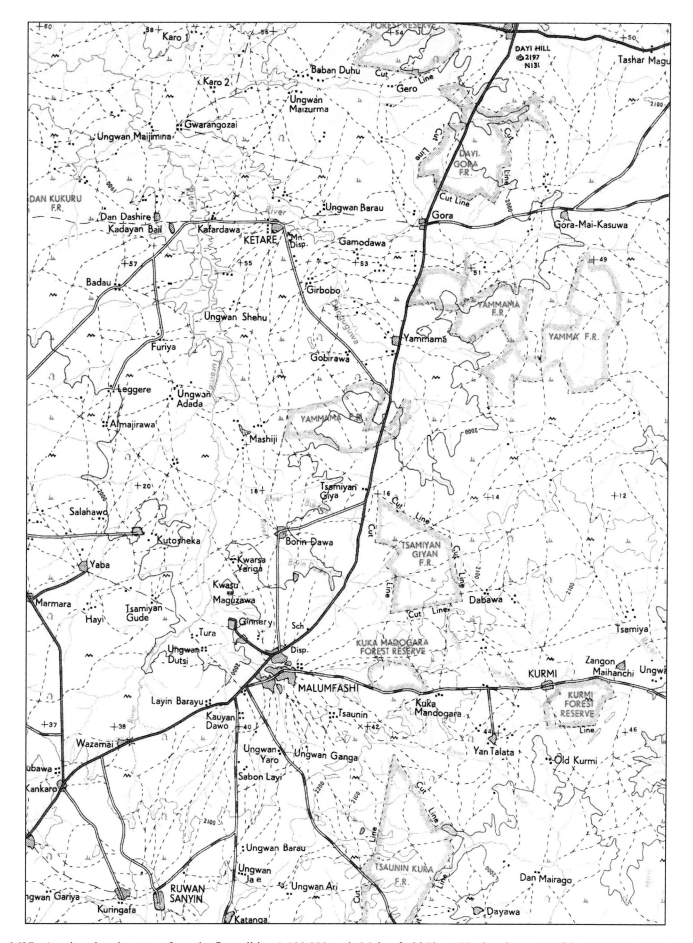

M27. A reduced scale extract from the first edition 1:100,000 scale Malumfashi Sheet 79, showing parts of the North-Central and Kano States with contours at 100 ft vertical intervals. This map was compiled, drawn and first printed by the Interim Common Services Survey Unit at Kaduna in 1969-70 from photographic reductions of 1:50,000 scale maps. Control and ground information was supplied by the Northern Nigerian Survey and the air photography obtained by Hunting Surveys Limited in December 1963.

Projection: Transverse Mercator   Spheroid: Clarke 1880   Grid: Nigeria Mid Belt

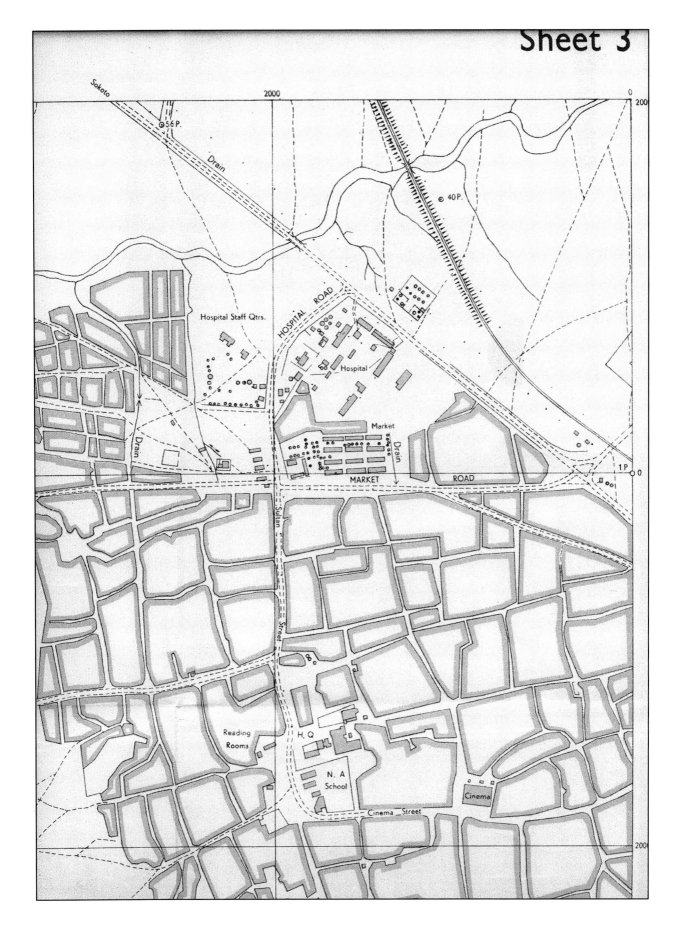

M28. GUSAU 1:4,800 SCALE UNCONTOURED MAPPING

An extract from Sheet 3 of the Gusau (Sokoto Province) township mapping, which was compiled and
drawn by the Nigerian Survey Department, Lagos from Departmental Air Photography taken in 1950.
Ground revision, recompilation and redrawing by the Northern Nigerian Survey in 1956.

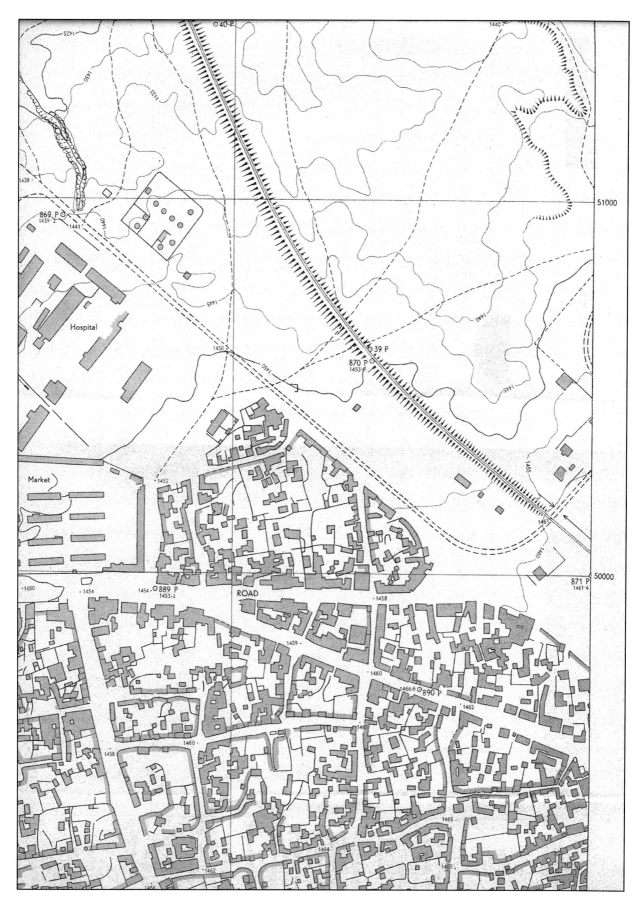

M29. GUSAU 1:2,400 SCALE CONTOURED MAPPING

An extract from Sheet 21 of the Gusau (Sokoto Province) township mapping, with contours at 5 ft vertical intervals.
Photogrammetric compilation by Fairey Air Surveys in 1962 using Air Photography taken by the
Air Operating Company in 1961and ground control by M.F.Anderson of the Northern Nigerian Survey in 1962.
Drawn, constructed, printed and published by the Northern Nigerian Survey in 1964.

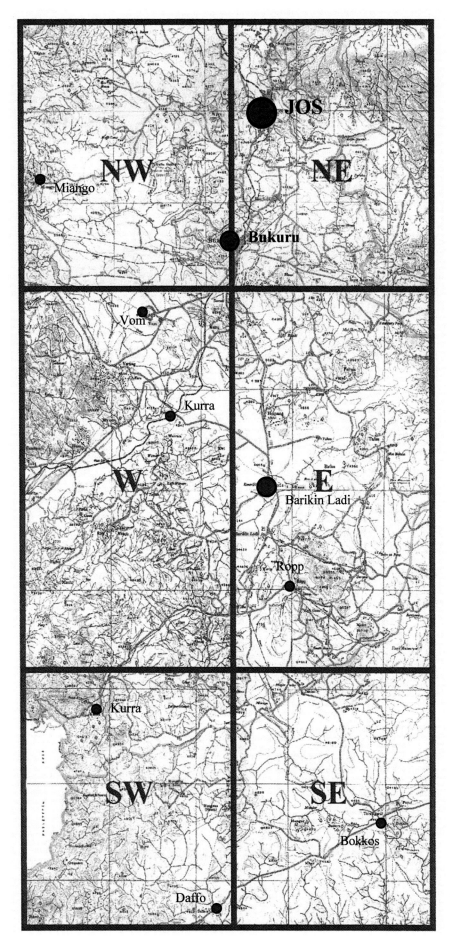

M30. THE JOS PLATEAU

The Minesfield 1:125,000 map, with form lines at 100 ft vertical intervals,
surveyed by plane tabling in 1930, and revised through to 1950, has been used in the following
six reduced-scale parts to locate the places familiar to tin miners and surveyors.

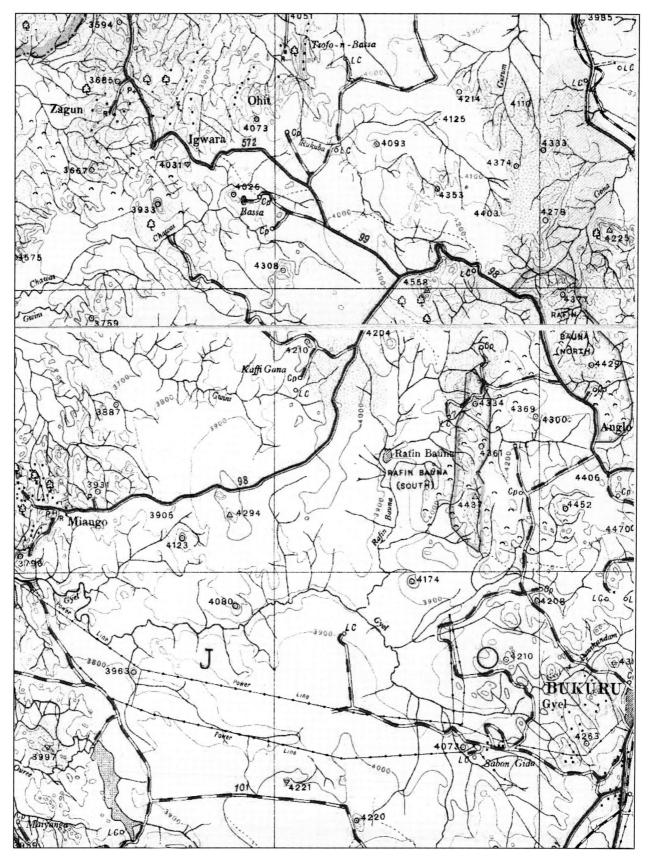

M31. NORTH-WEST PART OF THE JOS PLATEAU

Places highlighted in green are mentioned in the text

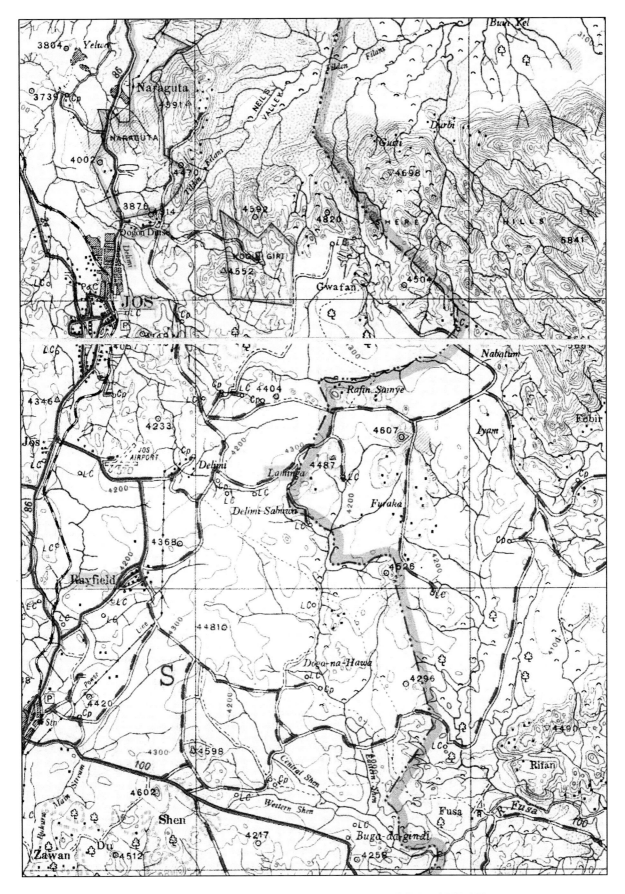

M32. NORTH-EAST PART OF THE JOS PLATEAU

Places highlighted in green are mentioned in the text

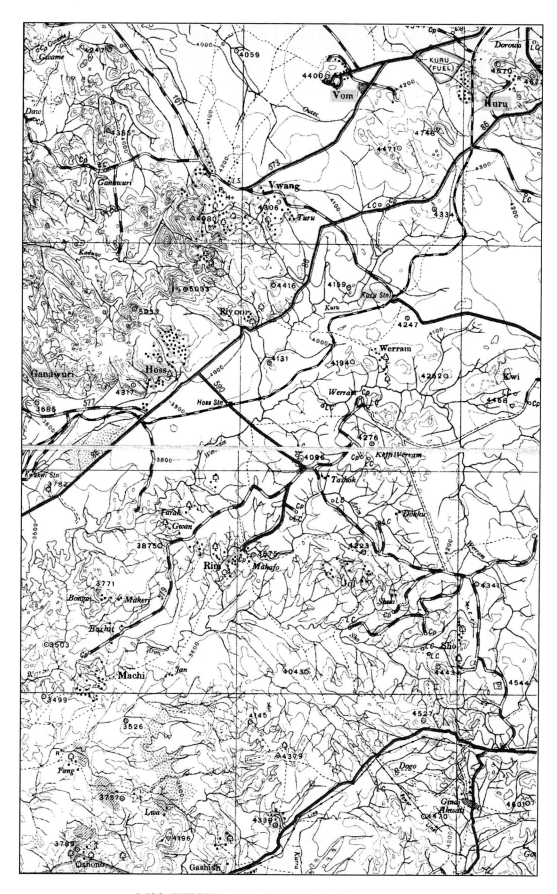

M33. WEST PART OF THE JOS PLATEAU

Places highlighted in green are mentioned in the text

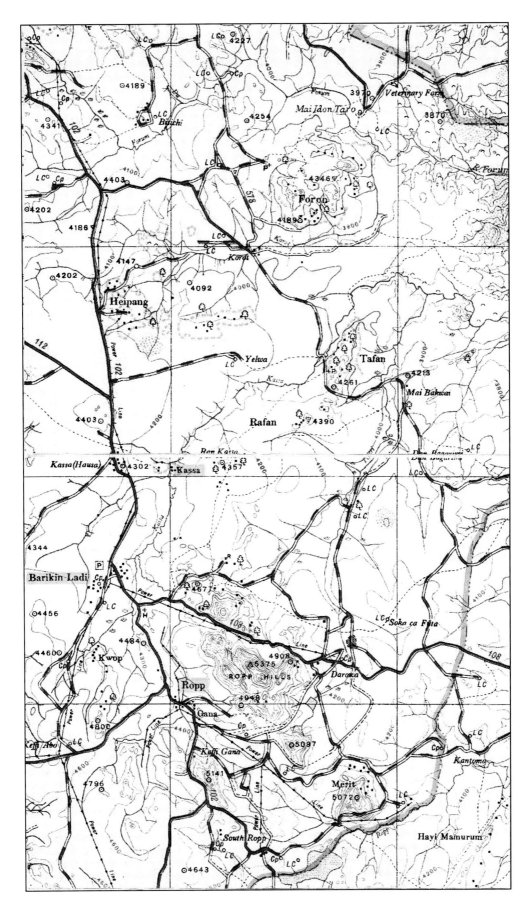

M34. EAST PART OF THE JOS PLATEAU

Places highlighted in green are mentioned in the text

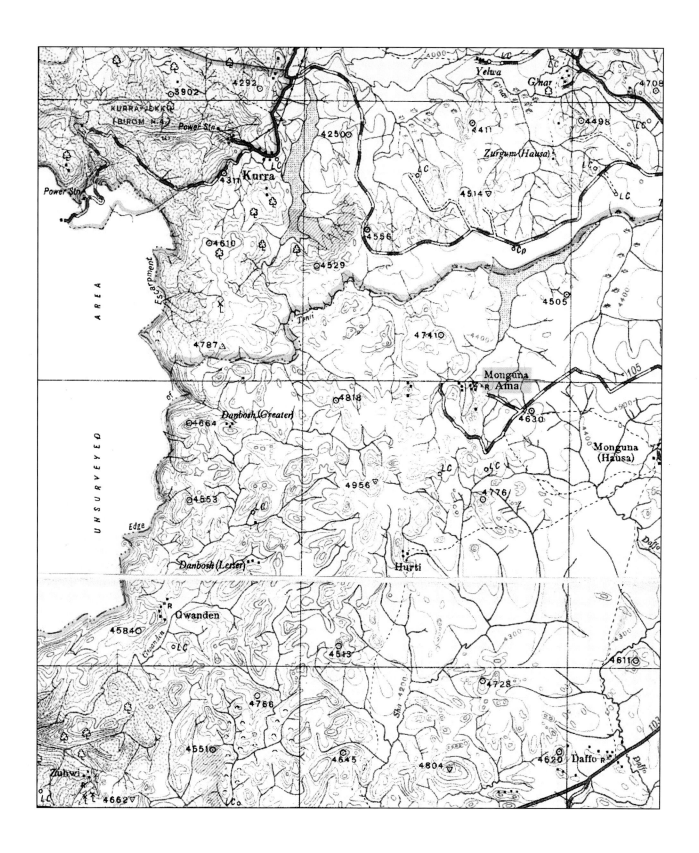

M35. SOUTH-WEST PART OF THE JOS PLATEAU

Places highlighted in green are mentioned in the text

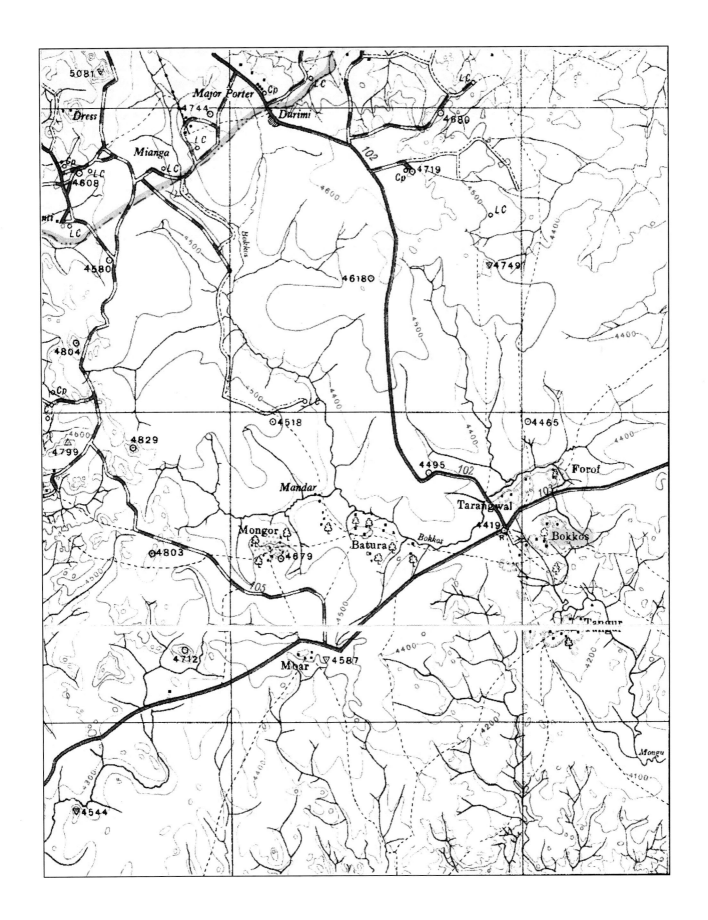

M36. SOUTH-EAST PART OF THE JOS PLATEAU

Places highlighted in green are mentioned in the text

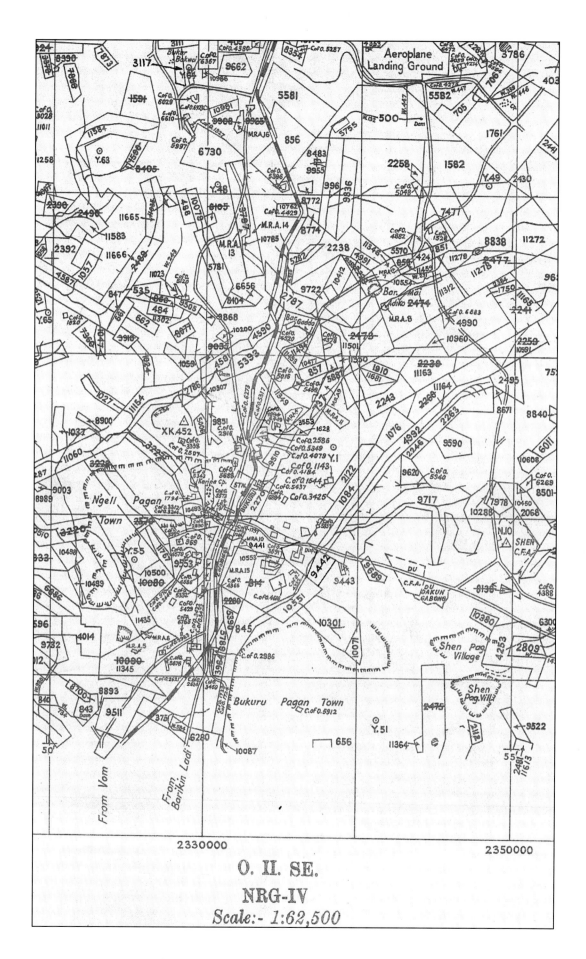

M37. A reduced-scale extract from a congested Priority Sheet illustrating
the problems created by intense mining activity in the Jos - Bukuru area.

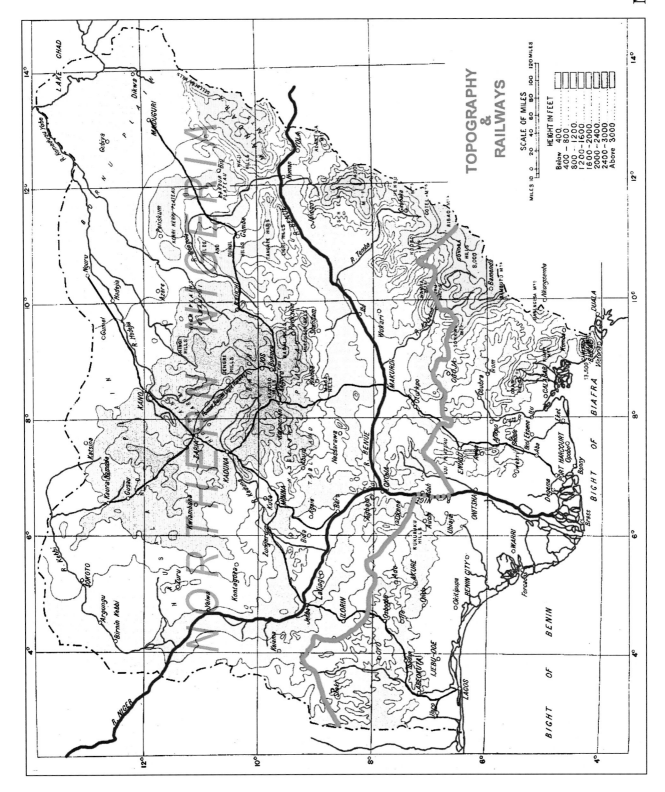

TOPOGRAPHY
&
RAILWAYS

SCALE OF MILES

MILES 10 0 20 40 60 80 100 120 MILES

HEIGHT IN FEET

Below 400 ....
400 – 800 ....
800 – 1200 ....
1200 – 1600 ....
1600 – 2000 ....
2000 – 2400 ....
2400 – 3000 ....
Above 3000 ....

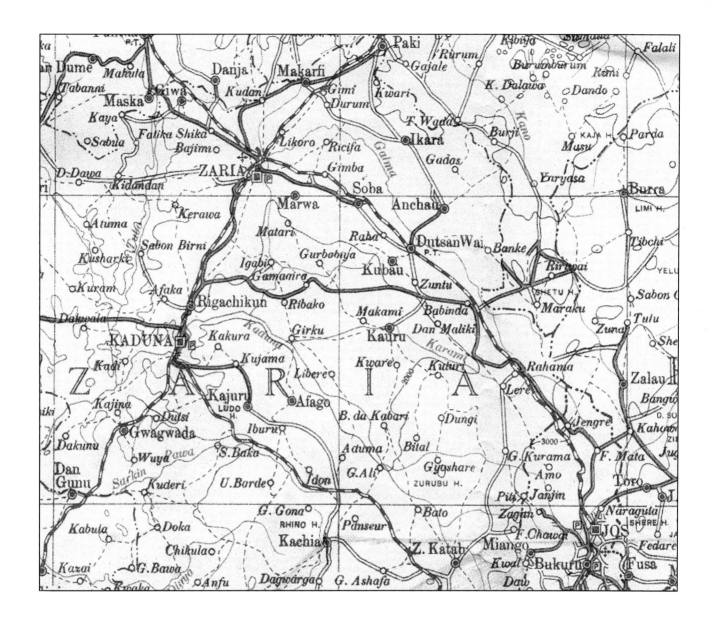

M39. Part of the 1955 edition of the Road Map of Nigeria, published by the Survey Department, Lagos
at a scale of 1:1,750,000 (or 1 inch to 27.62 miles).

This map, although periodically revised and reprinted, was not a dependable guide for the motorist.
It was an unreliable indicator of the quality, or even the continued existence,
of some roads, especially the minor ones.

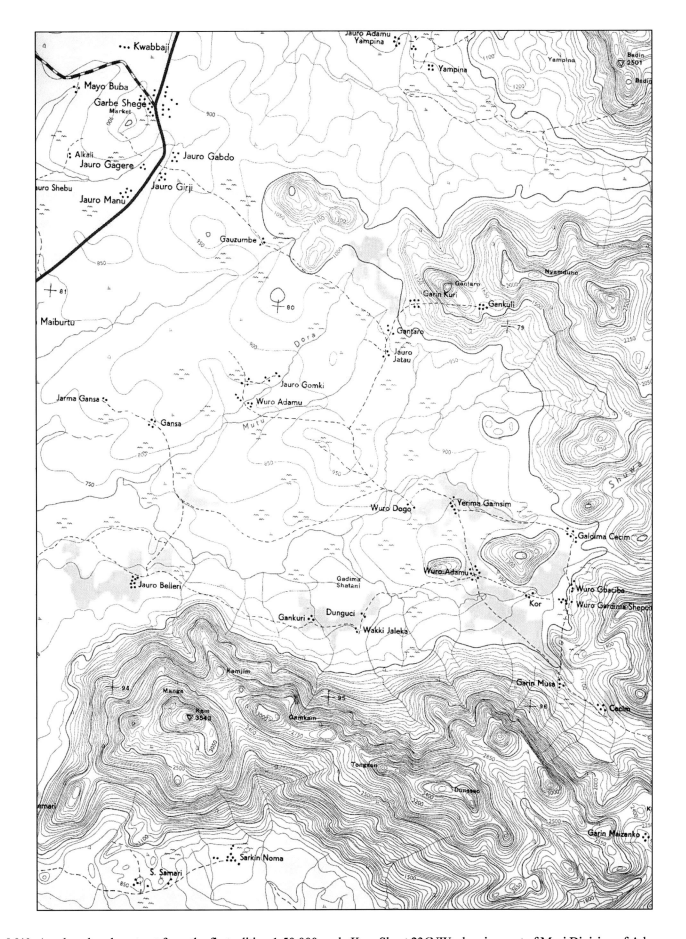

M40. A reduced scale extract from the first edition 1:50,000 scale Kam Sheet 236NW, showing part of Muri Division of Adamawa Province, with contours at 50 ft vertical intervals. This map was produced by the Directorate of Overseas Surveys and printed by the Ordnance Survey in 1965 under the Special Commonwealth African Assistance Plan from aerial photographs obtained by the Aircraft Operating Company (Aerial Surveys) Ltd. in 1957. Field survey data (partial control based on C Chain primary stations supplied by Federal Surveys), and field revision, was supplied by the Northern Nigerian Survey and the Directorate of Overseas Surveys.

Projection: Transverse Mercator   Spheroid: Clarke 1880   Grid: Nigeria East Belt

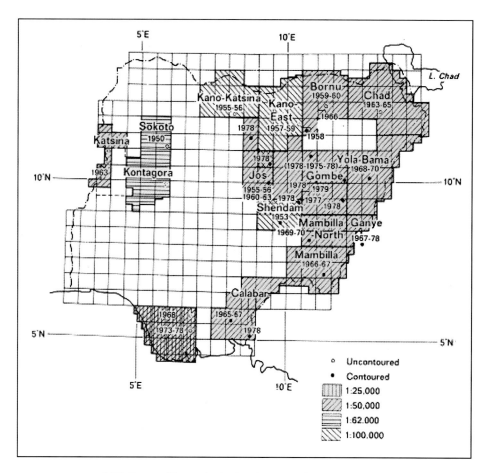

M41. Topographic mapping by the Directorate of Overseas Surveys

(This mapping illustration is reproduced with the kind permission of Professor Olayinka Y. Balogun of the University of Lagos and was originally published in The Cartographic Journal (British Cartographic Society), Volume 24 June 1987, in the article entitled 'The Directorate of Overseas Surveys and Mapping in Nigeria)

23. Wigglesworth, Murray and the author with the DOS party at Lokoja in 1961 during the survey of the Jakura Limestone and Agbaja Ironstone areas

NORTH-EASTERN STATE

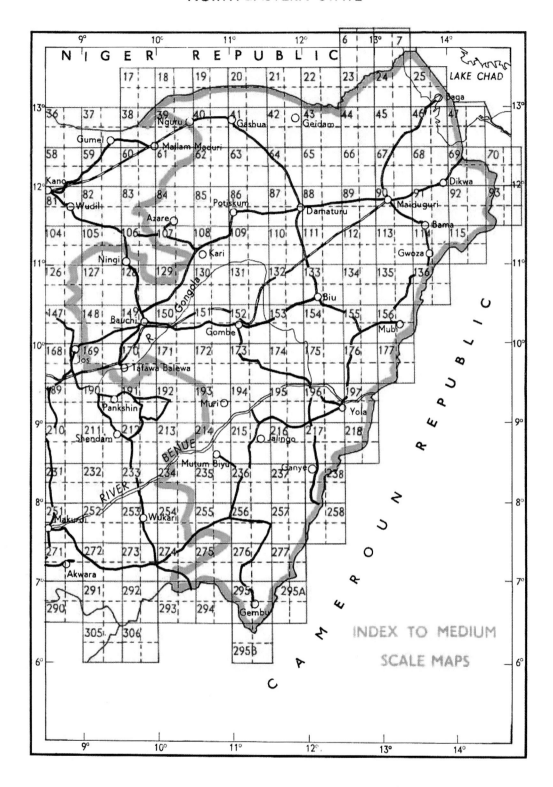

M42. Index to Medium Scale Mapping of the North-Eastern State

APPENDIX XII

ARCHIVES

Institution	Department
Afrika Studiecentrum, Leiden	Maps
British Empire & Commonwealth Museum	Press, Library, Image and Audio archives
British Library	Map Library (Catalogue of maps and plans covering Africa dated 1983
Cambridge University Library	Royal Commonwealth Society Records
Cambridge University Library	Official Publications Department
Cambridge University Library	Map Library
Department for International Development	Archives
Foreign & Commonwealth Office	Library
Library of Congress, Washington	Maps
Ordnance Survey	Maps and Aerial Photographic archives
Ordnance Survey	Book Library
Oxford University	Bodleian Library and Map Room
Oxford University	Rhodes House Library
Public Record Office, Kew	General Records and Map Room
University of London	Maps at the School of Oriental and African Studies

APPENDIX XIII

SOME SOURCES OF FURTHER INFORMATION

	TITLE	ARCHIVE REFERENCE
1	1:50,000 topographic mapping in Nigeria. Progress report Dec 1962 - Dec 1965	2nd UN Regional Carto. Conference for Africa. Tunis 1966
2	A century of colonial mapping in Nigeria 1861-1960. O.Y.Balogun	OSBL (R9691 528/(669))
3	Account of a D.O.'s wife in N.Nigeria 1951-60	RCSR.CUL (11c 99h HOL P68061)
4	Adjustment and strength analysis of the primary triangulation control network of Nigeria 1979: V.Ashkenazi & N.Field	OSBL (R6614 528.331/(669))
5	Aerial Survey in Nigeria. Application of new techniques.	Proceedings of UN Regional Carto. Conference for Africa. Nairobi 1963 1966
6	Blue Books (none produced after 1940)	PRO (CO465)
7	Breakdown of traditional land tenure in N.Nigeria 1969: C.M.McDowell	RCSR.CUL (4K P58426)
8	Collection of photos relating to service with No.2 Colonial Survey Section R.E. in Nigeria 1927-28. Also C.V. and memoirs of Nigerian Service. S.W.Joslin	OURHL (MSS Afr.s.1862)
9	Colonial Heritage Z.Nwosu	Surveying World Jul 1994
10	Control in N.E.Nigeria (RICS Thesis) M.F.Anderson 1966	OSBL (528.4 (669))
11	Diaries as Surveyor in Nigeria 1925-28. E.M.Lilley	OURHL (MSS Afr.s.2232 & Micr Afr. 649)
12	Directorate of Overseas Surveys and Mapping in Nigeria O.Y.Balogun Cartographic Journal June 1987	OSBL (R9583 354.88:528.4(669))
13	DOS Progress Reports	OSBL
14	Facts about the North F.O.Brice-Bennett R.I.S.Kano	RCSR.CUL (L43 151483) & OURHL
15	Federal Surveys Nigeria Annual Reports	OSBL& CUL
16	Fieldwork for 1:50,000 mapping in N.Nigeria (RICS Thesis) N.J.Field 1968	OSBL
17	Giant in the Sun R.W.Baxter	RCSR.CUL (435 141349)
18	Ground control for air mapping in Nigeria (RICS Thesis) C.Emmott 1967	OSBL (528.4(669))
19	Handbook of the Ministry of Town & Country Planning on Land, Mining titles and Administrative Boundaries	RCSR.CUL (435 151190)
20	Instructions for Examination Division. Survey Department 1934	OSBL (R23871 528.4/(669))
21	Kaduna 1917 1967 2017: A Survey and Plan of the Capital Territory for the Government of Northern Nigeria: Max Lock & Partners	ODA
22	Land Survey in Kano Emirate D.F.H.MacBride 1938	OSBL
23	Land surveying education in Nigeria M.B.Ebong	OSBL (R4180 341.222/(668.2:669))
24	Land Tenure: Nigeria's Answers A.Sanyaolu	L & MS Oct 1984
25	Map Production in Nigeria CSOC 1958	OSBL
26	Medical Effects on Land Surveyors D.Fraser	L &MS Jan 1987
27	Nigeria 1915-29. 15 vols with Staff List 1931	OURHL
28	Nigeria: A bleak prospect. D.Omoigui 1994	OSBL (R23662 528/(669))
29	Nigerian cadastre: a system under pressure. N.J.Field 1991	OSBL (R8656 528.44/(669))
30	Nigerian Government Gazettes 1914-1976 in 273 volumes	PRO (CO 658)
31	Northern Nigeria Gazettes 1900-1913 in 4 volumes	PRO (CO 586)

32	Northern Nigerian Survey Annual Reports	OSBL & CUL
33	Notebook 1914; personal pocket diaries as Surveyor. C.Evans (Gilbert E)	OURHL (MSS Afr.r.91)
34	Notes for the use of Departmental topographical survey parties. 1935. Nigeria Land and Survey Department	OSBL (R23875 528.42/(669))
35	Primary Trig and Traverse in Nigeria N.J.Field	Survey Review Jul 1977
36	Private collections 1869-1955 (6 pieces)	PRO (CO 959)
37	Procedure with regard to application for survey and demarcation of mining areas. Survey Department 1934	OSBL (R23874 528.481:622.1/(669))
38	Provincial Annual Reports 1951-1963	RCSR.CUL (L435)
39	Report on the Lake Chad Basin Survey DOS 1975	OSBL (Pamphlet No.32293)
40	Sources for Colonial Studies: Anne Thurston	PRO 1 (325.310216)
41	State of the surveys of British Africa in 1905-06. C.Arden-Close 1950	OSBL (R9020 528/(6)(091))
42	Survey and mapping in Nigeria, today and tomorrow. O.Adekoya	OSBL (R9522 528/(669))
43	Survey circulars in force 1932 (amended to 1936). Nigeria Survey Department	OSBL (R23877 528.3\.4/(669))
44	Survey Manual. Nigeria Survey Department 1935	OSBL (R23876 528.3\.4./(669))
45	Survey work by the Alexander-Gosling Expedition in Northern Nigeria 1904-05	Geog. Journal 1906
46	Surveying and mapping in Nigeria. O.Y.Balogun Surveying & Mapping 45 1985	OSBL (R10906 528:061.1/(669))
47	Surveying Nigeria. 1954	OSBL (R9054 528:061.1/(669))
48	The 12th Parallel Survey A.F.Mohsen 1974	OSBL (Pamphlets 29639, 31174 & 31505)
49	The Native Surveyor.(Nigerian surveyors under British administration) O.Y.Balogun 1988	OSBL (R10905 528.4/(669))
50	The Nigerian Cadastre N.J.Field	Survey Review Jan.1991
51	The story of N.Nigeria in its self-governing year 1959: R.W.Baxter	RCSR.CUL (435 152379)
52	Training of Nigerian surveyors in the colonial era O.Y.Balogun Surveying & Mapping 45 1985	OSBL (R10908 378:528/(669))
53	Triangulation 1927. Nigeria Survey Department	OSBL (R15843 528.41)
54	Tribute to the D.O.S. A.Macdonald	C.O.C.S. Cambridge Jul 1983
55	Use of air photographs in topo and cadastral surveys J.D.Adshead	(RICS Thesis) 1965

Abbreviations

CCSO	Cambridge Conference of Survey Officers
COCS	Conference of Commonwealth Surveyors
CUL	Cambridge University Library
ESR	Empire Survey Review
L&MS	Land and Minerals Surveyor (RICS)
ODA	Overseas Development Administration
OSBL	Ordnance Survey Book Library
OURHL	Oxford University Rhodes House Library
PRO	Public Records Office
RCSR	Royal Commonwealth Society Records

APPENDIX XIV

GENERAL BIBLIOGRAPHY

Ref.No.	AUTHOR	TITLE	PUBLISHER	DATE
1	ADEDIPE G.A.K.	A special list of records on land and survey	Held in the Nigerian National Archives. Ibadan	1963
2	ADEKOYA, O.	Survey and Mapping in Nigeria, Today and Tomorrow	CCSO Paper No.A6	1991
3	AJAEGBU, H.I.	Feasibility of automated cartography	Nigerian Geographical Journal	1972
4	ALLEN, Charles	Tales from the Dark Continent	Macdonald Futura	1979
5	ALLISON, Philip	Life in the White Man's Grave.	Viking. London	1988
6	ANDERSON, D.	A Pictorial Record of the British in West Africa	Faber & Faber	1940
7	ANDERSON, M.F.	Surveying the Coups	RICS Geomatics Division. Vol.1 of the proceedings of 'GEOMATICS 99'. Nottingham	1999
8	ANDERSON, R.G.	Palm Wine and Leopard's Whiskers	R.G.Anderson, Lake Hawea, New Zealand	1999
9	ATKINSON, M.C.	An African Life. Tales of a Colonial Officer	Radcliffe Press	1992
10	BAKER, Geoffrey L.	Trade Winds on the Niger.		
11	BALL,D	The Saga of the Royal Niger Company 1830-1971	Radcliffe Press	1996
12	BALOGUN, O.Y.	Into Africa (And Out) Northern Nigeria 1956 - 62	David Ball	2000
13	BALOGUN, O.Y.	Directing the State mapping programme: Surveyor-General or State Cartographer	7th Annual Conference of the Nigerian Cartographic Assn. Kaduna	1985
		Manpower problems and official mapping organisations in Nigeria	ITC Journal	1985
14	BALOGUN, O.Y.	Surveying and mapping in Nigeria.	Surveying & Mapping 45	1985
15	BALOGUN, O.Y.	Topographic mapping in Nigeria. Revision or new series.	12th Conference of ICA. Perth, Australia	1984
16	BAXTER, R.W.	Giant in the Sun		
17	BAXTER, R.W.	The Story of Northern Nigeria in its self-governing year		
18	BELL, Sir Gawain	An Imperial Twilight		1989
19	BRANDLER, J.L.	Out of Nigeria	Radcliffe Press	1993
20	BRITISH CARTOGRAPHIC SOCIETY	A Directory of U.K. map collections		
21	BURNS, Alan	Colonial Civil Servant	Allen & Unwin. London	1949
22	BURNSIDE, C.D.	A Few Back Sights	RICS Geomatics Division. Vol.1 of the proceedings of 'GEOMATICS 99'. Nottingham	1999
23	BURNSIDE, C.D.	Electro-Magnetic Distance Measurement 3rd Edition	BSP Professional Books	1991
24	BURNSIDE, C.D.	Mapping from Aerial Photographs. Second Edition	Collins Professional & Technical Books. London	1985

No.	Author	Title	Publisher	Year
25	BURNSIDE, C.D.	The Analogue Instrument Project of The Photogrammetric Society	The Photogrammetric Record	Oct. 1993 - Oct. 1997
26	BURNSIDE, C.D.	'Then and Now'. Photogrammetry: Radial Line Plotting	Surveying World	Sept/Oct 2000
27	CLARK, A.Trevor	A Right Honourable Gentleman: Abubakar from the Black Rock	Edward Arnold. London	1991
28	CLARK, A.Trevor	Was it Only Yesterday ? The Last Generation of Northern Nigeria's 'Turawa'	BECM Press. Bristol	2002
29	COKER, R.O.	Nigeria's participation in the 12th Parallel Survey	CCSO	1971
30	COOPER, J.	Domestic Arrangements	RICS Geomatics Division. Vol.1 of the proceedings of 'GEOMATICS 99'. Nottingham	1999
31	CORLSON, B.	African Tales	The Civil Engineering Surveyor	1985-1989
32	DALE, P.F.	Cadastral Surveys within the Commonwealth	HMSO. London	1976
33	DAVIDSON, Basil	The African Past		
34	de ST.JORRE, John	The Nigerian Civil War	Hodder & Stoughton	1972
35	DIRECTOR OF FEDERAL SURVEYS	A Gazetteer of Place Names. 2 volumes	Federal Surveys of Nigeria	1965
36	DIRECTOR OF FEDERAL SURVEYS	Catalogue of maps and plans. July 1959, revised in 1961, 1966, 1969 and 1971	Federal Surveys of Nigeria	1959
37	EBONG, M.A.	Report on the Nigerian geodetic levelling	Federal Surveys of Nigeria	1984
38	EMMOTT, C.	Borgu Boundary Blues	RICS Geomatics Division. Vol.1 of the proceedings of 'GEOMATICS 99'. Nottingham	1999
39	FALCONER	On horseback through Nigeria		1911
40	FIELD N.J.	Primary triangulation and traverse in Nigeria pre 1931, 1931-60 and post 1960	Survey Review No.185	1977
41	FROST, Richard	Enigmatic Proconsul: Sir Philip Mitchell	Radcliffe Press	
42	GAUNT, Mary	Alone in West Africa	Werner Laurie. London	1912
43	GILL, John M	Old Bill in the Bush	Pentland	1997
44	GRIFFITHS I.L.	Maps and mapping of Africa	London	1987
45	GUGGISBERG, Major F.G.	Handbook of the Southern Nigeria Survey and Text Book of Topographical Surveying in Tropical Africa	W. &.A.K Johnston. Edinburgh	1911
46	HARGREAVES J.D.	The End of Colonial Rule in West Africa	Macmillan. London	1979
47	HASTINGS, A.C.G.	Nigerian Days	John Lane. The Bodley Head Ltd.	
48	HAYWOOD,A.H.W. & CLARKE, F.A.S.	History of the West African Frontier Force	Gale & Polden. Aldershot	1964
49	HEUSSLER, Robert	The British in Northern Nigeria	Oxford University Press	1968
50	HODGKIN, Thomas Lionel	Nigerian Perspectives		
51	HOGBEN, S.J. & KIRK-GREENE, A.H.M.	The Emirates of Northern Nigeria		1966
52	HUNTER, E	Where my caravan has rested	Available at OURHL	
53	JAEKEL, Francis	The History of the Nigerian Railway	Spectrum Books, Ibadan	1997
54	KEAY, John	The Great Arc. Pioneering triangulation in India.	Harper Collins	2000

55	KERSLAKE, R.T.	Time and the Hour: Nigeria, East Africa and the Second World War	Radcliffe Press London	1993
56	KIRK-GREENE, A.H.M.	Barth's Travels in Nigeria		1971
57	KIRK-GREENE, A.H.M.	Crisis and Conflict in Nigeria (2 Vols)	I.B.Taurus	2000
58	KIRK-GREENE, A.H.M.	Glimpses of Empire	I.B.Taurus	1999
59	KIRK-GREENE, A.H.M.	On Crown Service (Contains a comprehensive bibliography for further Colonial Service reading)		
60	KIRK-GREENE, A.H.M.	West African verse	Overseas Pensioner No.72	Autumn 1996
61	KISCH, M.S.	Letters and Sketches from Northern Nigeria		1912
62	LEES, J.F.A.	Air Survey in Nigeria	Empire Survey Review No.10	1949
63	LEITH-ROSS, Sylvia	Stepping Stones: Memoirs of Colonial Nigeria 1907-1960	Peter Owen. London	1983
64	LLOYD, Christopher	The Search for the Niger	Collins	1973
65	LUGARD, F.D. and others	Colonial Reports - Annual 1901 - 1911	Colonial Office, London	
66	MACBRIDE, D.F.H.	Land and Survey in Kano Emirate	Journal of the Royal Africa Society No.37	1938
67	MACDONALD, A.	Mapping the World. A History of the Directorate of Overseas Surveys 1946-1985	HMSO. London	1996
68	MACINTOSH, Donald	Travels in the White Man's Grave	Neil Wilson Publishing	1998
69	MAIER, Karl	'This House has Fallen' - Nigeria in Crisis		
70	McCLINTOCK, N.C.	Kingdoms in the Sand and Sun. An African Path to Independence	Radcliffe Press London	1992
71	McGRATH, G.	Mapping for Development. The Contributions of the Directorate of Overseas Surveys	Cartographica. Vol.20. Nos 1 & 2.	1983
72	McILWAINE, John	Maps and Mapping of Africa: A Resource Guide. Item 2762 is the Northern Nigerian Survey catalogue of maps and plans dated November 1966, revised in 1968 and 1970	Hans Zell	1997
73	MEEHAN, MYRA	My Nigerian Journey	Pentland Press	1993
74	MEEHAN, Tony	Goodbye Maigida	Pentland Press	1991
75	METFORD, F.O.	Map Production in Nigeria	CCSO	1955
76	MILLAR (Miss)	Last train to Kano (Monograph)		
77	MORLEY, A.J	Development of Air Surveys in Nigeria	CCSO	1951
78	MORLEY, John	Colonial Postscript. Diary of a District Officer	Radcliffe Press	1992
79	MOSS,D.J.	Altimetric Heighting in N. Nigeria	RICS Thesis. Land Surveying Division	196?
80	MUFFETT, D.J.M.	Concerning Brave Captains	André Deutsch London	1964
81	NEWBURY, C.	British Policy towards West Africa 1786-1914 (2 Vols)		1968
82	NIGHTINGALE, Bruce	Seven Rivers to Cross		
83	NIVEN, Sir Rex	Nigerian Kaleidoscope: Memoirs of a Colonial Servant	Radcliffe Press / C.Hurst & Co. London	1983
84	OGUNLAMI, J.A.	Status and future of topographic mapping in Nigeria	Proceedings of Int. Archives of Photogrammetry & Remote Sensing 27	1988

	Author	Title	Publisher	Year
85	OYENEYE, G.A.	Use of the GPS for primary survey control in Nigeria	Survey Review 31	1991
86	PADEN, John N.	Ahmadu Bello. Sardauna of Sokoto	Hudahuda Publishing Co. Zaria	1986
87	PEARCE, R.D. (ed)	Enjoying the Empire. Letters of Robert Hepburn Wright	Radcliffe Press	1992
88	PERHAM, Dame Margery	Lugard. The Years of Authority.		
89	PERKINS, C	Topographic series mapping of Africa: a listing of the coverage held by some local collections	University of London	
90	ROBERTSON, Bridget M.	Angels in Africa. A Memoir of Nusing with the Colonial Service	Radcliffe Press	1991
91	ROYLE, Trevor	Winds of Change. The End of Empire in Africa	Murray	1996
92	RUSSELL, E	Bush Life in Nigeria. An account of the experiences of the wife of an Admin. Officer in Northern Nigeria 1935-1944: Sir Kenneth Maddocks		
93	SHARWOOD-SMITH, Joan	Diary of a Colonial Wife. An African Experience	Radcliffe Press	1978
94	SHARWOOD-SMITH, Sir B.E.	"But always as friends" Recollections of British Administration in the Cameroons and N.Nigeria 1921-57	Available at CUL (435L P58857) & FCOL. Allen and Unwin	1992
95	SMITH, Vic	Birds, Beasts and Bature	Pentland	1969
96	STAMERS-SMITH, H.A.	Aerial Photography in Nigeria	CCSO	1955
97	STAMERS-SMITH, H.A. & SONOLA, J.	Primary Triangulation of Nigeria	CCSO	1955
98	THOMAS. G.E.(ed)	Last of the Proconsuls: Letters of Sir James Robertson		
99	WATERHOUSE, G.G.	Some memoirs of Survey in Nigeria 50 years ago	R.E.Journal 76	1962
100	WHITE, Stanhope	Dan Bana. Memoirs of a Nigerian Official	Cassell	1966
101	WHITE, Stanhope	Descent from the Hills	John Murray	1963
102	WOOD, J.C.	Annual reviews of Survey in Nigeria 1930-39		
103	WOOD, J.C.	Survey Framework of Nigeria	ESR 3	1936
104	WOOD, J.C.	Surveys of towns and township layouts in Nigeria	ESR 1	1931
105	WOOD, J.C.	Triangulation of Nigeria 1912-14, 1923-26 & 1927-31	Conf.Empire Surveyors	1931
106	YEARWOOD, P.J.	From lines on maps to national boundaries: the case for Northern Nigeria and Cameroon	Available at OSBL	1994

APPENDIX XV

NORTHERN NIGERIAN SURVEY REUNIONS

	DATES	VENUE	HOSTS
1.	29th/30th October 1988	West Bridgford, Nottingham	Janet & Clifford Rayner
2.	14th/15th October 1989	Woughton, Milton Keynes	Monica & Malcolm Anderson Marcelle & John Evans
3.	13th/14th October 1990	Malvern	Shirley & John Tozer
4.	12th/13th October 1991	Birchanger/Hatfield Heath	Jean & Clifford Burnside
5.	10th/11th October 1992	Lincoln/Kettlethorpe	Barbara & Paul Ward
6.	9th/10th October 1993	Allostock/Knutsford	Alicia & Keith Sargeant
7.	1st/2nd October 1994	Castle Donington/W. Bridgford	Janet & Clifford Rayner
8.	14th/15th October 1995	Broughton, Milton Keynes	Monica & Malcolm Anderson
9.	12th/13th October 1996	Bath	Mary & Kevin O'Shaughnessy
10.	11th/12th October 1997	Marston/Scredington	Barbara & John Adshead
11.	10th/11th October 1998	Pulford/Chester	Betty & Ian Gilfoyle
12.	9th/10th October 1999	Bournemouth	Denis Willey
13.	6th-8th October 2000	Malvern	Shirley & John Tozer
14.	5th-7th October 2001	Marston/Scredington	Barbara & John Adshead
15.	12th-13th October 2002	Great Chesterford/Debden	Jean & Clifford Burnside
16.	3rd-5th October 2003	York	Monica & Malcolm Anderson
17.	8th-10th October 2004	Rossett, Wrexham	Betty & Ian Gilfoyle